Time Out

London
for Children

timeout.com

KidsOut

Edited and designed by
Time Out Guides Limited
Universal House
251 Tottenham Court Road
London W1T 7AB
Tel + 44 (0)20 7813 3000
Fax + 44 (0)20 7813 6001
Email guides@timeout.com
www.timeout.com

Editorial
Editor Ronnie Haydon
Deputy Editor Simon Coppock
Listings Checkers Jill Emeny, Monica Roche
Proofreader Tamsin Shelton
Indexer Jackie Brind

Editorial/Managing Director Peter Fiennes
Series Editor Sarah Guy
Deputy Series Editor Cath Phillips
Guides Co-ordinator Anna Norman

Design
Art Director Mandy Martin
Acting Art Director Scott Moore
Acting Art Editor Tracey Ridgewell
Acting Senior Designer Astrid Kogler
Designer Sam Lands
Junior Designer Oliver Knight
Digital Imaging Dan Conway
Ad Make-up Charlotte Blythe

Picture Desk
Picture Editor Jael Marschner
Deputy Picture Editor Kit Burnet
Picture Researcher Ivy Lahon
Picture Desk Assistant/Librarian Laura Lord

Advertising
Sales Director/Sponsorship Mark Phillips
Sales Manager Alison Gray
Advertising Sales Terina Rickit, Matthew Salandy, Jason Trotman
Copy Controller Oliver Guy
Advertising Assistant Lucy Butler

Marketing
Marketing Manager Mandy Martinez
Marketing Excecutives Sandie Tozer, Sammie Squire
Marketing Assistant Claire Hojem
Marketing Designer Sim Greenaway

Production
Guides Production Director Mark Lamond
Production Controller Samantha Furniss

Time Out Group
Chairman Tony Elliott
Managing Director Mike Hardwick
Group Financial Director Richard Waterlow
Group Commercial Director Lesley Gill
Group Marketing Director Christine Cort
Group General Manager Nichola Coulthard
Group Art Director John Oakey
Online Managing Director David Pepper
Group Production Director Steve Proctor
Group IT Director Simon Chappell
Group Circulation Director Jim Heinemann

Contributors
Introduction Ronnie Haydon. **The Story of London** Fiona Cumberpatch. **New London** David Littlefield. **Festivals & Events** Christi Daugherty, Jill Emeny, Ronnie Haydon. **Around Town** South Bank & Bankside Ronnie Haydon; The City Pendle Harte; Holborn & Clerkenwell Cyrus Shahrad; Bloomsbury & Fitzrovia Jessica Eveleigh; Marylebone Kathryn Miller; West End, Covent Garden & St Giles's, Westminster Cyrus Shahrad; Kensington & Chelsea Kathryn Miller; North London Sue Webster; East London Simon Coppock; South-east London Ronnie Haydon, Cyrus Shahrad; South-west London Nana Ocran; West London Kelley Knox. **Eating** Simon Coppock, Ronnie Haydon. **Shopping** Ronnie Haydon, Kelley Knox, Kathryn Miller, Nana Ocran, Sue Webster (It's in the post Cathy Limb). **Where to Stay** Ronnie Haydon. **Arts & Entertainment** Cyrus Shahrad. **Parties** Jill Emeny. **Sport & Leisure** Andrew Shields. **Days Out** Ronnie Haydon (additional features, The future's white Cyrus Shahrad). **Directory** Ronnie Haydon.

The editor would like to thank the following:
Ella and Arthur Delamare; Sophia Dibbs; Olivia and Ann Halliday; Sally Goldsworthy at Discover; Liam, Samuel, Benjamin, Emily and Marie Harris; Robert Hulse at the Brunel Engine House Museum; Jane, John, Bruce and Rick Jones; Finn Jordan; Brenda and N Bruce Jones; the Mayor's Press Office, Greater London Authority; John Styles; Teresa, Tony, Barney and Mary Trafford; Phoebe-Jane, Guy, Heather and Niall Weir.

Maps by JS Graphics john@jsgraphics.co.uk.
Illustrations The Story of London by Lucy Grant.
Cover photography and page 5 by Guy Hills; stylist: Marie-Clare Mawle at Michaeljon Management; makeup and hair: Joanna Bernacka at Fletchers; models: (from left to right) Ella Delamare, Sophia Dibbs and Arthur Delamare; clothes: Ella wears green top from Zara, fuschia trousers from Gap and shoes from Clarks; Sophia wears lilac trousers and red T-shirt from H&M, wrap top from French Connection, shoes from JONES the Bootmaker; Arthur wears red T-shirt from Zara, jeans from Gap and boots from Jones the Bootmaker.
Photography by Héloïse Bergman and Tricia de Courcy Ling, except: pages 10, 11 Heritage Images; pages 12, 15, 16 Hulton Getty; page 20 PA; page 21 Hayes Davidson and John Maclean; page 22 Keith Williams Architects; pages 42, 105 Natalie Pecht; page 47 Tate Photography; pages 49, 58, 69, 74, 97, 116, 130, 134, 138, 153 Mockford & Bonetti; pages 49, 55, 155, 177 Matt Carr; page 62 Amanda C Edwards; pages 66, 179, 275 Alys Tomlinson; pages 98, 230, 261 Jonathan Perugia; page 113 Hadley Kincade; pages 148, 149 Dominic Dibbs; page 165 Tristan Newkey Burden; page 242 Stephen Hepworth; page 265 Andrew Brackenbury; pages 266, 267 Janie Airey.
The following images were provided by the featured establishments/artists: pages 25, 26, 27, 31, 70, 76, 102, 115, 158, 208, 212, 222, 241, 251, 282, 284, 291.

Repro by Icon Reproduction, Crowne House, 56-58 Southwark Street, London SE1 1UN.
Printed and bound by Southernprint, Factory Road, Upton Industrial Estate, Poole, Dorset BH16 5SN.

ISBN 0 903 446 774
Distribution by Seymour Ltd (020 7396 8000)

THE GOLDEN HINDE

"I got to be a real Pirate on a real Pirate ship"

Sam, age 9

Contents

Introduction

It may have been born about two millennia ago and have the Roman wall to prove it, but London is a young city. Nearly a quarter of the population is under 18, a higher proportion than many other European cities – and a very large number to keep occupied during the school holidays. Fortunately, a city as vibrant and diverse as London has ample resources when it comes to providing for its young. Most of the city's visitor attractions, no matter how forbidding their exteriors, have sweet centres, programming whole series of events for children throughout the year. Some places – the Design Museum, for example – have such celebrated workshops for children they get booked up weeks ahead. At others, you feel you're missing out on the best stuff if you don't bring the kids. Some playgrounds won't let unaccompanied adults in at all. In this respect at least, London is one of the most child-friendly cities in Europe.

We could do better, though, was the message coming out of the Mayor's Children and Young People's Strategy, entitled *Making London Better for all Children and Young People*, published by the Greater London Authority in January 2004. Based on the United Nations Convention on the Rights of the Child, this was the result of a consultation with more than 1,000 kids across the capital. Their priorities – more places to play, safer parks, better sports facilities, more cycling provision and neighbourhoods designed around the needs of children – pretty much echo what any parent would wish for their children. What is gratifying, however, is seeing first-hand how London is adapting to these needs. Play strategies, refurbished parks, the promise of improvements to sports facilities with London having made the Olympics 2012 shortlist, free bus and weekend travel for kids – such innovations make this chaotic metropolis a more attractive proposition for families. After all, getting out and about, making the most of the city, is what life here is all about. As one child put it during the consultation, 'In small towns I guess you can get really bored, but in London there is always something to do.'

THE TIME OUT LONDON FOR CHILDREN GUIDE

This is the fourth edition of the *Time Out London for Children Guide*, produced by the people behind the successful listings magazines and travel guide series. It is written by resident experts to provide you with all the information you'll need to explore the city, whether you're a local or a first-time visitor.

THE LOWDOWN ON THE LISTINGS

Addresses, phone numbers, websites, transport information, opening times, admission prices and credit card details are included in the listings.

Details of facilities, services and events were all checked and correct as we went to press. Before you go out of your way, however, we'd advise you to phone and check opening times, ticket prices and other particulars. While every effort has been made to ensure the accuracy of the information contained in this guide, the publishers cannot accept any responsibility for any errors it may contain.

FAMILY-FRIENDLY INFORMATION

Having visited all the places with our children, we've added essential information for families. Where we think it's important, we've stated whether a building can accommodate pushchairs ('buggy access'), or if there's a place to change a nappy ('nappy-changing facilities'). We've also listed a spot nearby where you can eat your packed lunch ('nearest picnic place').

Attractions are required to provide reasonable facilities for disabled visitors, although it's always best to check accessibility before setting out.

Disabled visitors requiring information about getting around the city can call GLAD (Greater London Action on Disability) on 7346 5808 or check the website www.glad.org.uk.

PRICES AND PAYMENT

We have noted where venues accept the following credit cards: American Express (AmEx), Diners Club (DC), MasterCard (MC) and Visa (V).

THE LIE OF THE LAND

Map references are included for each venue that falls on our street maps (starting on p312), but we recommend that you follow the example of the locals and invest in a standard A-Z map of the city.

PHONE NUMBERS

The area code for London is 020. All phone numbers given in this guide take this code unless otherwise stated, so add 020 if calling from outside London; otherwise, simply dial the number as written. The international dialling code for the UK is 44.

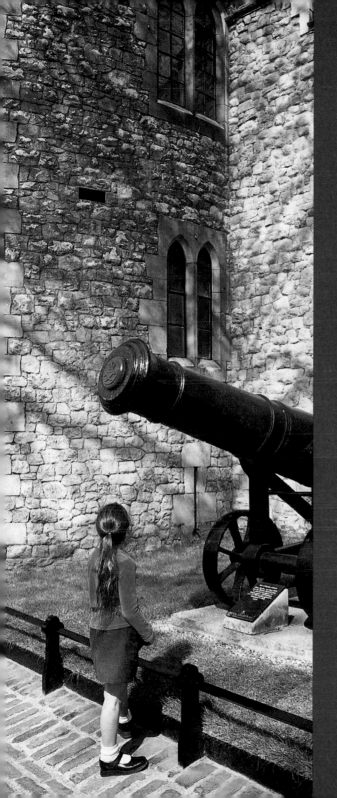

In Context

The Story of London

A rollercoaster ride of conflict, plague, pride – and progress.

London's story, as labrynthine as its streets, begins officially in AD 43 when Roman Emperor Claudius and his legions invaded. But were the Romans the first to settle on the banks of the Tamesis (their name for the Thames)? That's debatable. The Latin name Londinium could have its roots in any number of ancient origins. As historian Peter Ackroyd points out, raiding the old Celtic and Gaelic languages throws up various possibilities: Llyn-don, for example, means town (don) by the stream (llyn); 'lunnd' means marsh; 'Laindon', long hill; while the adjective 'londos' translates as fierce. Whoever was the first to stake their claim, we have the Romans to thank for our ancient city wall (built in AD 200), remnants of which survive in the City of London today. The first bridge across the Thames, which crossed at roughly the point of the present day London Bridge, was also a Roman achievement. It was built after the British outpost of the Empire was sacked by Boudicca, who led her armies against the soldiers who had seized her lands and raped her daughters. The settlement was almost destroyed, but the Romans rebuilt and surrounded their town with a defensive wall in an attempt to keep out native rebellions. Another 200 years passed with the Romans in charge, but with the eventual decline of the Empire, the last troops were withdrawn in 410 and London was left to Angles and Saxons.

PICKING UP THE PIECES

We don't know how much attention was paid to the scattered ruins of Roman London by the Saxon settlers, who crossed the North Sea to set up homes and farms in eastern and southern England during the fifth and sixth centuries. They certainly established a trading centre nearby. Lundenwic, 'wic' meaning marketplace, stood west of the Roman city, about where Covent Garden is today. What is now Trafalgar Square was the site of farm buildings. The Strand is so called because it used to be just that, a strand, or beach for grounding ships.

London's first bishop, Mellitus, was a missionary sent by the Pope who eventually converted the East Saxon King Sebert to Christianity. In 604 Mellitus founded a wooden cathedral, dedicated to St Paul, inside the old city walls. Although his people turned back to paganism after Sebert's death, later generations of Christians rebuilt St Paul's. In the ninth century another wave of invaders arrived: the Vikings. They crossed the North Sea to ransack London, forcing the king of the time, Alfred of Wessex, to reoccupy the old Roman town. The stone walls were still standing and could be defended by his soldiers. While Alfred reigned, churches were built and markets thrived in London, although Winchester was still the capital of England. As the Saxon city prospered, harassment from the Vikings continued until the 11th century when the English were forced to bow to a Danish king – Cnut (Canute), who reigned from 1016 to 1040. During this time London took over from Winchester as the capital. Edward the Confessor, an English king, gained the throne in 1042 and set to building Westminster Abbey. He died one week after his abbey was consecrated in December 1065.

Edward's death was a pivotal moment in history. Edward's cousin William, Duke of Normandy, swore that his kinsman had promised him the crown. But Edward's brother-in-law Harold was a solid favourite with the English people. Their armies tried to settle the mattter at Hastings. On 14 October 1066 William defeated Harold and marched to London. He was crowned in the abbey on Christmas Day.

MEDIEVAL MAYHEM

William knew he had to keep things sweet with the wealthy merchants in the City of London, so he gave them independent trading rights in return for taxes. The charter stating these terms is kept at the Guildhall. But the king was still bothered by the possibly rebellious population. So, 'against the fickleness of the vast and fierce population' he ordered strongholds to be built along the city wall. One of these is the White Tower, the tallest building in the Tower of London. Outside the perimeter the landscape was still pasture and woodland.

London became a hotbed of political struggle. Fighting for supremacy were three powerful bodies: the king and aristocracy; the Church; and the lord mayor and city guilds. In the early Middle Ages, the king made all the laws in the country, aided by lords and bishops. During the 14th and 15th centuries, the Palace of Westminster became the seat of law and government, and the king's meetings with the noblemen and clergy – called Parliaments – became increasingly important. As the number of advisors to the king grew, Parliament divided into two groups, the House of Lords (populated by nobles and members of the clergy chosen by the king) and the House of Commons (powerful people elected by rich merchants and landowners). Trade with Europe grew. Imports of spices, cloth, furs, precious metals and wine filled the wharves by London Bridge and people travelled from miles around to the markets, or 'cheaps' around Westcheap (now Cheapside). Foreign traders and craftsmen settled around the port of London. The population rocketed from about 18,000 in 1100 to more than 50,000 in the 1340s.

STINKY CITY

With the hordes came hygiene problems.Water was provided in the cisterns at Cheapside and elsewhere, but the supply, which came more or ess directly from the Thames, was limited and polluted. In the east, Houndsditch gained its name because people threw dead dogs into the boundary ditch.

At Smithfield, the meat market, butchers dumped animal guts willy-nilly. These filthy conditions became the ideal breeding ground for the greatest catastrophe of the Middle Ages; the Black Death of 1348 and 1349. The plague came to London from Europe, carried by rats on ships. During this period about 30 per cent of the population died of the disease. Although epidemic abated, it reoccurred in

The Great Fire of London. *See p14.*

Penury to paper-rounds

An advertisement for a chimney sweep in early Victorian times boasts of his 'small boys, and clean cloths, upon the most reasonable terms.' If ever there was a symbol of the utter grimness of child labour, it must be these unfortunate 'climbing boys', who were taken on as apprentices as young as four years old, to scale the twisting flues of London's blackened chimneys, their sore skins toughened up through vigorous rubbing with brine.

For centuries, children had no choice but to work, though not always in such brutal conditions. Until the 1840s, they didn't have to go to school, and very few did. In 1861, a government report showed that out of a population of 21 million, there were only 2.5 million children at elementary schools, and few stayed on beyond the age of ten.

Education cost money. Even church-run or charity schools for the poor charged at least a penny a week, and few working-class families could afford that. If they couldn't stay afloat financially, the grim workhouse beckoned. In *Oliver Twist*, Charles Dickens describes how poor people were given a choice 'of being starved by a gradual process in the home, or by a quick one out of it'.

The philanthropic Lord Shaftesbury formed the London Ragged School Union in 1844 and, over the next eight years, set up 200 free schools for the poor. William Locke, honorary secretary of the Union, explained: 'some friends and I, engaged in Sunday School teaching, found so many children excluded...in consequence of their filthy, dirty and ragged condition, that we were very anxious indeed to have another class of schools in London at that time'. The pupils were 'orphans, outcasts, street beggars, crossing sweepers, and little hawkers of things about the streets'. As well as reading, writing and scripture, boys were taught tailoring and shoe-making; girls learned to sew and knit.

In 1868, Dr Thomas Barnardo started a ragged school in Limehouse and, two years later, opened his first home for destitute boys in Stepney Causeway. Plenty slipped through the net, though; Henry Mayhew's research in 1850s and '60s London suggested that there were between 10,000 and 20,000 young street sellers, offering matches, firewood, fruit and buttons. Others held horses, cleaned the streets, sewed, hailed cabs and collected dog droppings to sell to tanneries.

Change for young workers finally came with the widespread introduction of compulsory education, mechanisation, which reduced the need for unskilled workers, and various ethical and political developments. Yet even in 1900 work was still considered a valuable part of a child's education.

It took the founding of the welfare state, and the relative prosperity of the 1950s to transform the lives of the young. It was around this time that the concept of the teenager arrived, along with wider opportunities in education and earning power.

Today, however, it seems that hard labour is still a reality for many teenage Londoners, albeit with a minimum wage and humane conditions. Now that students have tuition fees, repaying student loans and the cost of London living to worry about, they'll be grafting for years to come...

London on several occasions over the next three centuries, each time devastating the population.

With plague killing so many, London was left with a labour shortage, resulting in unrest among the overworked peasants. A poll tax – a charge of a shilling a head – was introduced, which prompted the poor to revolt. In 1381 thousands of them, led by Wat Tyler from Kent and Jack Straw from Essex, marched on London. In the rioting and looting that followed, the Savoy Palace on the Strand was destoyed, the Archbishop of Canterbury was murdered and hundreds of prisoners were set free. Eventually a 14-year-old King Richard II rode out to face the baying, angry mob at Smithfield, but the Lord Mayor William Walworth became angered by Tyler's belligerence and disrespect – so he stabbed him to death. This put a stop to the rioting, and the ringleaders were rounded up and hanged.

nick.co.uk

TRADING UP WITH TUDORS AND STUARTS

The city blossomed under the Tudors and Stuarts. Buoyed up by trade from newly discovered lands, it became one of the largest cities in Europe. Henry VII left his mark on London by commissioning the building of the Henry VII Chapel in Westminster Abbey, where he and his queen are buried. His successor was wife collector (and dispatcher) Henry VIII. His first marriage to Catherine of Aragon failed to produce an heir, so the king, in 1527, determined that the union should be annulled and defied the Catholic Church while doing so. Demanding to be recognised as Supreme Head of the Church of England, Henry ordered the execution of anyone who refused to comply (including his chancellor Sir Thomas More). So England began its transition to Protestantism. The subsequent dissolution of its monasteries changed the face of London: the land sold off was given over to streets. On a more positive note, Henry also founded the Royal Dockyards at Woolwich. The land he kept for hunting became the Royal Parks (Hyde, Regent's, Greenwich and Richmond). His daughter Queen Mary's five-year reign saw a brief Catholic revival. She was dubbed 'Bloody Mary' following her order that nearly 300 Protestants be burned at the stake in Smithfield.

Mary's half-sister Elizabeth I oversaw a huge upsurge in commerce: the Royal Exchange was founded by Sir Thomas Gresham in 1566 and London became Europe's leading commercial centre. With Drake, Raleigh and Hawkins sailing to America and beyond, new trading enterprises were developed. By 1600 there were 200,000 people living in London, 12,000 of whom were beggars. Conditions were overcrowded and rat-infested, so plague was a constant threat. London was a cultural centre, however, as well as a death trap. Two famous theatres, the Rose (1587) and the Globe (1599), were built on the south bank of the Thames, and the plays of William Shakespeare and Christopher Marlowe first performed. Earthier dramas took place on the street. Bankside was a 'naughty place' where people visited taverns and engaged in bear-baiting, cockfighting and brothel-visiting.

London was a violent place. Elizabeth's successor, the Stuart James I, narrowly escaped being blown up. The Gunpowder Plot was instigated by a group of Catholics led by Guy Fawkes, who planned to protest at their persecution by dynamiting the Palace of Westminster from the cellar. Unfortunately for Fawkes, one of his co-conspirators warned his brother-in-law not to attend Parliament on 5 November – prompting a thorough search and the foiling of the scheme. Four plotters were killed while resisting arrest, while the remainder of the gang were dragged through the streets and executed, their heads displayed on spikes.

Although James I escaped death, his son Charles I wasn't so lucky. When Charles threatened the City of London's tax-free status he stirred up trouble, which led to civil war: Charles and his Royalists were the losers. Charles was tried for treason and beheaded outside the Banqueting House in Whitehall in 1649. Once the Puritans, led by Oliver Cromwell, had declared Britain a Commonwealth, theatres and gambling dens were closed down.

The exiled Charles II was restored to the throne in 1660, and Londoners were relieved. But there was trouble ahead: the 1664-5 bubonic plague killed nearly 100,000 Londoners before a cold snap stopped it. At the height of the epidemic 10,000 people were dying each week. When plague was diagnosed in a house, the occupants were locked inside for 40 days, while watchmen outside ensured no one escaped. London reeked of death. And then, the following year, an oven in Farriner's bakery in Pudding Lane started a fire that lasted three days and destroyed four-fifths of the City. More than 13,000 houses were destroyed, along with 87 churches and 44 livery company halls. Rumours of a Popish plot abounded, and Frenchman Robert Hubert was forced to confess to starting the fire. He was later hanged. Today Christopher Wren's Monument (*see p51*) marks a spot near where the fire broke out. London was rebuilt in brick and stone. One of the busiest people at this time was Christopher Wren, who as well as completing his greatest work, the new St Paul's Cathedral, also oversaw the rebuilding of 51 city churches. The Royal Exchange was rebuilt in the City, but by this time many merchants conducted their business in coffee houses – one of which was later to become insurance giant Lloyd's of London.

GEORGIAN PEAKS – AND TROUGHS

With George, the great-grandson of James I, on the throne, the country had a German-speaking king. In Parliament, the Whig party, led by Sir Robert Walpole, was in power. Walpole was the first prime minister and was given 10 Downing Street as an official home. This address has been occupied by the serving prime minister ever since. It was at this time, too, that crossings over the river were built to increase accessibility. Westminster Bridge (built 1750) and Blackfriars Bridge (1763) joined London Bridge, which until then had been the only bridge to span the river. While the well-to-do enjoyed their Georgian homes, life for the poor was squalid. Living in slums, ruined by cheap and plentiful gin, it's little wonder people turned to street crime. Gangs emerged, who enjoyed near immunity from arrest. Thieves even set up their own market on Tower Hill. The infamous Gregory Gang, one of many that preyed on travellers, included notorious highwayman Dick Turpin.

Feasts to fast food

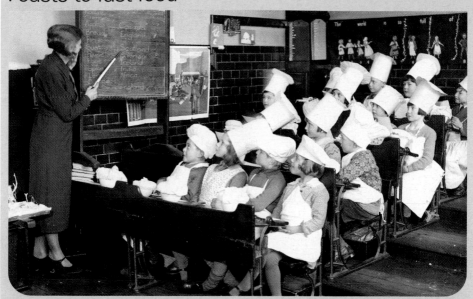

We may be turning rapidly into a fast-food nation, where a fifth of British families say they only eat together once a year on Christmas Day, but microwaves, ready meals, takeaways and imported foods have at least brought freedom – and variety. The nostalgic vision of families from yesteryear sharing nutritious home-cooked fare is misleading because the staple diet for ordinary people over the centuries was pretty grim.

In Tudor and Stuart times, it was chiefly bread and beer, with some cheese and bacon. Things hadn't changed much by the 1890s when businessman Charles Booth, in his survey of working class life in London wrote. 'a good deal of bread is eaten and tea drunk, especially by the women and children…' Not even the bread was home-baked by this time: in the grossly overcrowded living quarters of the urban masses, there were no ovens to cook it. Even the tea leaves were likely to have been recycled.

Good housekeeping, so prized by the Victorians, was nigh on impossible if you were a poor working-class woman, living on a tiny, uncertain income with many mouths to feed. Rickets, stunted growth and other diseases of malnutrition were rife.

This social problem was recognised by some. Mrs Beeton, the Nigella Lawson of her time, even offered a recipe for 'soup for the poor' at a cost of about 4d a gallon, in her bestselling 1861 Book of Household Management.

The rich were different. In medieval times, aristocrats demonstrated their superior status with vast feasts. Over time, quality was prized over

quantity. Table manners and fine tableware became fashionable, and by the 17th century the wealthy were using fine china and glass, on linen-covered tables.

Rich Victorians dined elaborately (children would eat separately, restricted to plain food, dispensed by nanny in the nursery). Yet there was also a parallel street food culture thriving in London.

According to Henry Mayhew's vivid chronicles, *London Labour and the London Poor* (1851–62), London's thoroughfares thronged with street sellers offering tea and coffee, apple fritters, watercress, plum duff, warm pies, fried fish, ginger beer, hot elder wine and 'rice milk' – like a liquid rice pudding flavoured with sugar and spice. 'The buyers are chiefly those who have a penny to spare, rather than those who have a penny to dine on,' wrote Mayhew.

Coffee, which had been brought to England in the 17th century, was now popular – and cheap – following a reduction on duty in 1824. The number of street vendors mushroomed, boosting their profits by adulterating the brew with ground chicory, even baked carrots. By the mid 19th century there were over 300 trading in London.

These stalls may have been the precursors of Starbucks and McDonald's. But there is one food phenomenon that's truly modern. The era of the kiddie meal, symbol of our child-centric culture, wouldn't dawn for over a century. Mrs Beeton, reliable barometer of domestic matters, does not even list 'party' or 'children' in her index. A sign of the times indeed.

Pigs' bladders to PlayStations

In the past, children have suffered hardship and abuse, but they have always found time for play. Pictures in medieval manuscripts depict a familiar range of kids' activities, from board games to wrestling. Archaeological evidence shows that there was a toy industry in England by at least 1300. Toy soldiers have been dug up in London from about this time. So, too, have child-sized kitchen sets, including pans, tripods and skillets strong enough to withstand the heat of a fire.

Of course, life could be nasty and brutish, and children's games sometimes reflected this. William FitzStephen, describing London life at the end of the 12th century, writes how 'every year, on the day called Shrove Tuesday, boys from the schools bring fighting cocks to their master, and the whole morning is given up to boyish sport, for they have a holiday in school that they may watch their cocks do battle.'

It wasn't all so bloody, though. Shrove Tuesday was also popular for football (played with a pig's bladder for a ball) and other outdoor pursuits.

Game-playing was just as important as it is now, with favourites such as 'cobnutte', (conkers), and 'cherry pit' or flicking fruit stones into a hole. In 1532 Sir Thomas More imagined an unruly boy bunking off school to play 'cherrystone, marrow bone, buckle-pit, spurn point or quoiting'. Animal shin bones were used as primitive ice skates.

Working-class youngsters in Victorian London spent their spare time out on the teeming streets, where free entertainment was plentiful. Organ grinders, acrobats and jugglers were often seen. Ginger beer fountains were popular during the summer months, for those with a penny to spare. One splendid mahogany and brass model was stationed in Petticoat Lane, by all accounts. Until 1868, children might indulge in a grisly pastime: watching the hangings outside Newgate Prison.

Wealthier children with more leisure time may have been taken to the zoo, museums, exhibitions and art galleries. From 1894, families could enjoy a ride on the revolving Great Wheel at Earl's Court.

Indoor games became increasingly popular. Among the many London toy shops was Hamleys Noah's Ark Toy Warehouse. In the Strand, a whole arcade, called Lowther's, was devoted to toys. One contemporary description reveals: 'shelves are piled up with boxes and in all of them, wrapped in tissue paper, are dolls. Baby dolls and dolls dressed as brides, some of wax, china or rag.'

As new forms of transport were developed, toy manufacturers were quick to reproduce them in miniature. At first, these model trains and cars had to be pushed or pulled along, but methods of powering them, including clockwork and friction, were soon invented.

But children's toys and the landscape of their leisure time probably underwent the greatest transformation during the 1950s when plastics became widely available. Their manufacture was automated, which was cheap and efficient. The advent of the silicon chip, in 1958, meant small toys could have electronic components, opening up a range of possibilities. By the mid 1970s, these chips were cheap enough to be used in toys and games, opening the floodgates for PlayStations, GameBoys and... well, you know the rest.

The writer Henry Fielding and his brother John established a volunteer force of 'thief takers' in 1751 to help the parish constables and watchmen catch these criminals. This force, originally known as the Bow Street Runners, eventually became the Metropolitan Police (established 1829).

If it hadn't been for the work of philanthropists, life for the poor in London would have been far worse. Attempts to alleviate their suffering included the founding of new hospitals. St Bartholomew's and St Thomas's, established by monks long before, were joined by Westminster, Guy's, St George's, London and the Middlesex Hospitals from 1720 to 1745. Sea captain Thomas Coram built his Foundling Hospital for abandoned children during this time (its entrance arcades remain at the top of Lamb's Conduit Street, in front of Coram's Fields park, *see p63*).

A TALE OF TWO CITIES

The rich had never had it so good when Victoria came to the throne in 1837. Progress was impressive: five more bridges spanned the Thames and the city's first railway line (London Bridge to Greenwich) had been laid. Yet this city, the administrative and financial capital of the British Empire, had a dark underbelly. Crammed into slums, the urban masses lead a miserable life. Down by the river Thames, it was malodorous. An elderly sewerage system meant that city dwellers' waste products flowed into the Thames. This resulted in filthy, disease-ridden water. Smallpox, typhus and cholera were everyday concerns. The summer of 1858 smelled bad: the 'Great Stink' meant that politicians in the Houses of Parliament could not work with their windows open. Nasty niffs continued until 1860, when Joseph Bazalgette's drainage system was completed.

Novelist Charles Dickens was one of many who wrote about London's problems. In 1872 an observer recalled 'the lanes which open off Oxford Street, stifling alleys thick with human effluvia, troops of pale children crouching on filthy staircases; the street benches at London Bridge where all night whole families huddle close, heads hanging, shaking with cold abject, miserable poverty'.

But as the years rolled by, improvements were made to ease the lot of Londoners. The new drainage system made a great difference, and some slum housing was replaced by social housing funded by philanthropists, such as George Peabody.

The new century started with a sparkle after Edward VII came to the throne in 1901. The Ritz Hotel on Piccadilly was opened; the Café Royal on Regent Street was deeply fashionable. Department stores, an American idea, made it across to England – the first to open was stately Selfridges, in 1909, followed two years later by Whiteley's in Bayswater.

LIFE IN A WAR ZONE

But the new gaiety wouldn't last. World War I saw the first bomb to be dropped on London. It came from a Zeppelin and landed near Guildhall. Terrifying nightly raids continued throughout the Great War, killing 650 people.

When it was finally over, and those soldiers who had survived were promised 'homes for heroes' on their return, political change was set in motion. Few homes materialised and the nation's mood was bleak. In 1924 David Lloyd George's Liberal Party was deposed in favour of a promised fresh start with the Labour Party, under Ramsay MacDonald. While the upper classes partied their way through the 'Roaring Twenties', the working classes were in the grip of mass unemployment. Dissatisfaction was expressed when all the workers downed tools to support the striking miners. The General Strike of 1926 lasted for nine days: the army distributed food and students drove buses. After the strike, unemployment continued to rise. The New York Stock Exchange crash of 1929 had a knock-on effect; the British economic situation was grim.

Nevertheless, the British, the London County Council worked to improve conditions for its people. As the city's population grew (8.7 million in 1939), so did its sprawl. Suburbia expanded, and with it the tube lines. The main entertainment for people was the radio, until 1936 at least, when the first television broadcast went out live from the British Broadcasting Corporation (BBC) at Alexandra Palace studios. On 3 September 1939 Britain declared war on Germany. Londoners began digging air raid shelters and sending children and pregnant women to the countryside. In fact, the air raids did not begin until almost a year later. In September 1940 600 German bombers devastated east London and the docks. The raids continued for 57 nights in a row. The Strand was hit, and so were the House of Commons, St Thomas's Hospital, Buckingham and Lambeth palaces and St Paul's Cathedral. Nearly 30,000 bombs were dropped on London alone; around 15,000 people were killed and 3,500,000 houses destroyed or damaged. People took refuge in the tube stations 79 stations became official shelters. They were safe unless the stations were hit. This happened at Marble Arch, Bank and Balham.

In 1944 a new type of bomb began flattening Londoners' homes – the fearsome V1 flying bomb, or doodlebug. These caused widespread destruction, as did their successor, the more powerful V2 rocket, 500 of which were dropped on east London. By the end of the war about a third of the great city and the East End was in ruins.

In the General Election that took place soon after VE Day, Churchill was defeated by the Labour Party under Clement Attlee. Swift changes went ahead to

Key events

c66 BC Ludgate built by King Lud (legendary).

AD 43 The Roman invasion. Londinium is founded.

61 Boudicca sacks the city.

122 Emperor Hadrian visits Londinium.

200 A rebuilt Londinium is protected by a city wall.

410 The last Roman troops leave Britain.

c600 Saxon London is built to the west.

604 The first St Paul's Cathedral is built.

841 First Viking raid.

c871 The Danes occupy London.

886 King Alfred retakes London.

1013 The Danes take London; King Cnut reigns.

1042 King Edward builds Westminster Abbey.

1066 William, Duke of Normandy, defeats Harold.

1067 Work begins on the Tower of London.

1099 First recorded flood in London.

1123 St Bartholomew's Hospital founded.

1197 Henry Fitzailwyn becomes the city's first mayor.

1240 First Parliament sits at Westminster.

1294 First recorded mention of Hammersmith.

1348-9 The Black Death ravages London.

1357 The first Sanitary Act passed in London.

1381 Wat Tyler leads the Peasants' Revolt.

1388 Tyburn, near Marble Arch, becomes the principal place of execution.

1397 Richard (Dick) Whittington becomes Lord Mayor.

1497 The first image of London published in a 'Chronycle of Englonde'.

1513 Henry VIII founds Woolwich Royal Dockyard.

1534 Henry VIII breaks from the Catholic Church.

1554 300 Protestant martyrs burned at Smithfield.

1571 The first permanent gallows set up at Tyburn.

1599 The Globe Theatre is built on Bankside.

1605 Guy Fawkes's Gunpowder Plot is discovered.

1635 London's first public postal service established.

1642 The Puritans defeat the Royalists at Turnham Green.

1649 Charles I is tried for treason and beheaded.

1664-5 The Great Plague kills thousands.

1666 The Great Fire destroys London.

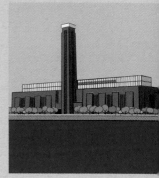

1675 Building starts on a new St Paul's.

1680 Downing Street built.

1686 The first May Fair takes place at Mayfair.

1694 The Bank of England opens at Cheapside.

1711 St Paul's is completed.

1742 Thomas Coram founds his orphanage.

1750 Westminster Bridge is built.

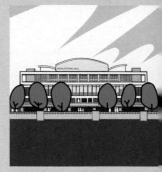

1769 Blackfriars Bridge opens.

1784 The first balloon flight over London.

1803 The first railway (horse-drawn) opens.

1820 Regent's Canal opens.

1824 National Gallery founded.

1827 Regent's Park Zoo opens.

1829 Metropolitan Police founded.

1833 The London Fire Brigade is established.

1835 Madame Tussaud's opens.

1843 Trafalgar Square is laid out.

1851 The Great Exhibition takes place.

1858 The Great Stink permeates London

1863 World's first underground railway opens.

1866 The Sanitation Act is passed.

1868 Last public execution in Newgate Prison.

1869 J Sainsbury grocery opens in Drury Lane.

1884 Greenwich Mean Time is established.

1888 Jack the Ripper preys on East End women.

1890 First electric underground railway opens.

1897 Motorised buses introduced.

1898 The first escalator installed in London, in Harrods.

1915-18 Zeppelins bomb London.

1916 Horse-drawn buses disappear.

1940-4 The Blitz devastates much of London.

1948 Olympic Games held in London.

1951 The Festival of Britain takes place.

1952 The last of the city's 'pea-soupers'.

1953 Queen Elizabeth II is crowned.

1966 England win the World Cup at Wembley.

1975 Work begins on the Thames Barrier.

1982 The last of London's docks close.

1986 The Greater London Council is abolished.

1990 Poll Tax protestors riot.

1992 Canary Wharf opens.

1997 A Labour government is elected; Britain mourns Princess Diana.

2000 Ken Livingstone elected Mayor.

2002 Queen Mother dies aged 101.

2003 London's biggest ever public demonstration – against the war on Iraq.

Lucy Grant

try to improve the life of the nation. The National Health Service was founded in 1948; public transport and communications services were overhauled. But for all these initiatives, life in the city seemed drab and austere. For Londoners facing a housing shortage there were ambitious initiatives. Some of the buildings whisked up – prefabricated bungalows – were supposed to be temporary, but many are still inhabited more than 50 years later. New high-rise estates were often put up in a shoddy fashion. Many have since been pulled down.

It was not all doom for Londoners, though. The city hosted the Olympic Games in 1948 and, in 1951, the Festival of Britain, which celebrated all that was great about British technology and design. It took place on derelict land on the south bank of the river, which eventually became the site of the South Bank Centre arts complex. During the 1950s Britain enjoyed a gradual return to relative prosperity. Families were inspired to move to gleaming new towns away from the filthy city, where air pollution was a problem. Clean Air Acts, the first in 1956 introduced as a result of the Great Smog four years earlier, finally ensured the reduction of noxious gas emissions. Inner London was facing a labour shortage. Workers from the country's former colonies, particularly the West Indies, were recruited for London Transport and in the hospitals. Many immigrants faced an unfriendly reception from indigenous Londoners: matters came to a head in the Notting Hill race riots of 1958. Some parts of London were more tolerant; Soho, with its jazz joints and clubs, for one. The 1960s saw London – fashion capital of the world – swing.

To find out where the gigs were, people bought a weekly guide to London called *Time Out*; the first issue came out in August 1968. People from around the world flocked to Abbey Road, NW8, because of the Beatles album of the same name. Hyde Park was the place to be in the summer of '69 when the Rolling Stones played for half a million fans.

In the 1970s the lights went out, often literally, on London's glamour. Inflation, unemployment, strikes, IRA bombs and an increasingly fractured Labour government all contributed to an air of gloom. The punk explosion made a few sparks fly, but that was shortlived. Margaret Thatcher came to power in 1979, and the 1980s are regarded as her decade. Her Conservative government made sweeping changes, and stood up for 'market forces'. This was the era of the yuppie (Young Urban Professionals), who cashed in on the Conservatives' monetarist policies and the arrival of the global economy. Meanwhile, the gap between yuppies and the less wealthy was only too apparent. It did not take long for the city's underdogs to snarl and riot, first in Brixton in 1981, and four years later in Tottenham.

Flowers for a dead princess outside Kensington Palace, September 1997.

One of the lasting legacies of the Thatcher era is the Docklands redevelopment. A scheme set up in 1981 to create a business centre in the docks to the east of the City, it was slow to take shape, but is now considered a success. Businesses and residents are continuing to move into buildings around the Isle of Dogs and the area exudes prosperity. But this is one prominent area of London with a split personality, because little of the wealth from the banks and businesses is filtering through to the community. In 1986 the Greater London Council, with its anti-Thatcher outlook (despite being Conservative back in the 1960s), was abolished and County Hall was sold to a Japanese corporation. But history has a way of turning on you – the GLC's former leader, 'Red' Ken Livingstone, bided his time and, in 2000, was voted mayor with authority over all the city. When a city's economy booms, however, a bust is often just around the corner, and that is what happened to London in the early 1990s. A slump in house prices saw the reign of the yuppies come to an end. The last straw for beleaguered Londoners was the introduction of a poll tax. Demonstrations led to riots in Trafalgar Square. It marked the loosening of Mrs Thatcher's grip, leading to her replacement by John Major in 1990. The recession continued; its effects only too evident in London. The numbers of rough sleepers rose as people lost their homes through unemployment and mortgage rate rises. The IRA stepped up its campaign against the mainland, bombing the City in 1992 (destroying the medieval church of St Ethelburga-the-Virgin) and Docklands in 1996. Many cheered up when Tony Blair's New Labour ousted the Tories in May 1997, but went into shock when, later that year, Princess Diana was killed. The gates of Kensington Palace were the focus for the nation's tears and bouquets.

TODAY AND TOMORROW

Fireworks for the new millenium weren't confined to the celebratory kind. Labour ill-advisedly continued with the Conservative-conceived Millennium Dome project. But the spectacular tent on the once-derelict Greenwich Pensinsula spectacularly failed to capture the zeitgeist and angry voices were raised about massive sums of money swallowed up by the enterprise. In 2004, after many false starts, the Dome is finally being transformed into a 20,000-seat sports and entertainment complex.

London has problems. Housing is both expensive and in short supply, leading some to campaign for a reintroduction of tower blocks. Transport is taking a long time to improve and, indeed, often seems to be getting much worse. Many campaigners against Ken Livingstone's £5 daily congestion charge hoped that the scheme would be delayed until the tube system was running properly, to no avail. But most seem to be paying the charge, and traffic levels have been significantly reduced, although controversy still surrounds the scheme, which Mayor Livingstone plans to extend still further. Terrorism threats continue to loom, taking their toll on tourism. But if history shows anything, it is that London (and Londoners) can weather any storm. Ever forward looking, imaginative building programmes continue, and the old city is keeping young and beautiful, because it still wants to be loved.

Will the **London Bridge Tower** really look like this?

New London

Giant-sized or designed for kids, London's new architecture hits the heights.

One can imagine the sense of disbelief among **National Gallery** staff in the summer of 2003. The Heritage Lottery Fund had already handed over a whopping £11.5 million to help towards the £21 million the gallery needed to hold on to Raphael's *The Madonna of the Pinks*; managers must have thought their application for a further £5.3 million to help remodel the building was a dead cert.

They were wrong. They didn't get the money. The moral maze surrounding this decision is not one for these pages (maybe the HLF just thought the National had been given enough), but it does characterise the way buildings are perceived and procured by, and for, Londoners. Now that the millennial rush is over, public building programmes have settled back into being efficient, value for money and often low-cost exercises. A couple of years ago, Londoners would have been forgiven for thinking that architecture was an activity designed to make their city a better place. This is, however, a by-product of architecture – its real end (in London, anyway) is to make money.

The amount of money being poured into office developments is staggering – as will be the impact these investments will make on the city's skyline over the next few years. Look at **Canary Wharf**; not so long ago this single, lonely obelisk marked the centre of a new office district. Then towers sprang up on either side of it, like bodyguards. Now, there's a forest of the things, none of them especially inspiring (decent shopping malls, though).

AIMING HIGH

In terms of high-rise buildings, we've barely begun. London Arena will disappear, most likely to make way for flats and a 430-foot-high (131-metre) office block. Further west, the former NatWest Tower (long vacated by the bank and now called **Tower 42**) will give up its status as the tallest building in the Square Mile. At 600 feet (183 metres), a shade taller than the **Swiss Re** 'gherkin', Tower 42 is not large by international standards – there are well over 100 buildings across the world that are bigger. But the move in London is generally upwards.

Nicholas Grimshaw & Partners, the architects behind Waterloo's Eurostar terminal and Cornwall's Eden Project, have received planning permission for what promises to be a stunning new tower near Aldgate tube station. This sleek, sharp-edged, 712-foot high (217-metre) structure will tower over its neighbours and provide a public restaurant on its 49th floor when complete in around 2007. Down the road, the Richard Rogers Partnership is planning a huge wedge of a building that is every bit as dramatic (and 23 feet or seven metres higher). Across the river, preparation will soon start on the mighty **London Bridge Tower** (*pictured*), a gigantic spike that will almost certainly dwarf everything else for years – 984 feet (300 metres) high, this 'Shard' will rank about 25th in the world.

After three years of argument, wrangling and hefty legal fees, there is no doubt that the quality of the design allowed this giant to make it through the

Keith Williams Architects' plan for the **Unicorn Theatre** (*see p23*).

planning process. Designed by the highly talented Italian Renzo Piano, the sheer scale of the thing inevitably got tangled up in a public enquiry, with property developer Sellar and Southwark Council fighting it out with English Heritage, which was concerned about spoiling views of St Paul's.

Nonetheless, deputy prime minister John Prescott, who has the final word on these things, is convinced of the overall quality of the proposal; so is Ken Livingstone, who likes the idea of tall buildings in London full stop. London Bridge Tower is just what a 'vibrant, populous and cutting-edge city like London needs', he says.

When complete (in around 2009), this £350-million beacon will rise 66 storeys. The bottom half is to be reserved for office use, with most of the rest being kitted out as apartments and hotels. A three-storey public gallery will be located halfway up, giving views comparable to those from the top of the London Eye. A further viewing platform will be located among the clouds on the 65th floor. The building will rise considerably higher than that, but, being largely ventilation vents, this last section will be unoccupied. Then it tapers away to nothing.

Towers are de rigueur. Barely a week goes by without the architectural press revealing plans for yet another one. Controversially, one is set to rise within 50 metres (160 feet) of the principal entrance to Tate Modern, a move that the gallery and local residents fought tooth and nail – and lost. Perhaps most audacious of all, architectural firm RHWL (which brought the Saatchi Gallery to County Hall) has sought planning consent for a curiously sculptural building on the doorstep of Waterloo station. This 120-metre-high (394-foot) tower could,

in fact, be a blessing: the proposal is to knock down the bland office blocks that line one side of York Road, expand the station with a new concourse and construct a curving, asymmetrical tower reminiscent of a block of melting ice. So keen are the architects to impress the Lambeth planning authorities that they brought in artist Christopher Le Brun to help define the form of this £240-million building. So far, people seem to like it – including local MP Kate Hoey.

'Everything gets better with this scheme. We wouldn't be ****ing things up by getting consent to do this,' says RHWL director Geoff Mann, who is acutely aware that most mega-projects south of the river have done precisely that. Mann hopes to start building in 2005, for completion late in 2007.

MONEY FOR ART'S SAKE
So, if office towers are where the serious money is going, what's happening to the rest? Some of it is being spent, of course, on the National Gallery. Building work was already far advanced as this book went to press and a grand new entrance, leading directly off Trafalgar Square without having to bother with flights of steps, should soon be ready. This represents the first phase of the scheme mentioned earlier – a £12-million job made possible thanks to £10 million from the Getty Foundation. This remodelling is good news for visitors to the National; with more than four million people visiting annually, its principal entrance can get crowded. A new East Wing entry point will ease the pressure elsewhere in the building, and provide what promises to be a stunning, light-filled space. There will also be a bigger and better café and shop, and more toilets and information facilities.

It is the second stage of the project that hit the buffers when the Heritage Lottery Fund refused to play ball. This stage involves restoring the main entrance to its Victorian grandeur and adding a low-level space to accommodate a micro-gallery and coffee bar. Actually, the HLF relented a few months later and awarded the National £900,000 to get on with the restoration work and fit the central hall with air-conditioning and better lighting. Part of the idea is to treat this entry hall as an exhibition space, so visitors will be confronted with paintings as soon as they walk in. If it lives up to its promise, it will be magnificent. The coffee bar and micro-gallery will have to wait for further funding, though.

Speaking of magnificent, opera fans are rushing to the newly restored **Coliseum**, home of the English National Opera, around the corner on St Martin's Lane. The wrappers have now come off this eagerly awaited, £40-million redevelopment and the results are first class. This century-old theatre is unrecognisable from what it was, and is much better off for it. As well as restoring the original colour schemes, new bars and ticketing facilities have been added, the number of toilets increased, and the amount of public space expanded by 40 per cent. Best of all is the new upper level public bar; encased under a curved glass roof, the bar offers superb views towards Trafalgar Square and **St Martin-in-the-Fields**.

SOCIAL SCENE

St Martin-in-the-Fields is, in fact, undertaking an ambitious building project of its own. When finished early in 2007, this £34-million programme will see the 1721 church restored to its original state, the surrounding grounds upgraded and a new entrance pavilion offering access to much-improved underground spaces. Burial vaults, condemned as unfit for the dead in the 1850s but now used to house a range of social care work, will be totally modernised. New rehearsal suites will be created for the church and visiting musicians.

'For many years we have laboured in Dickensian conditions to provide services to some of the most needy people in society,' said the Reverend Nicholas Holtam at the launch of the fund-raising programme in 2003. The National Gallery will be pleased to know that the HLF has granted St Martin's nearly £15 million for the work, designed by architect Eric Parry. With the north side of Trafalgar Square now pedestrianised, this corner of London is set to reach its potential as the proper heart of the city.

South London has gained its own new wide-open spaces. The More London development on the South Bank, between London Bridge and Tower Bridge, was boarded up for years, making the slab of valuable land alongside HMS *Belfast* seem like a

forgotten backwater. Not any more. The boards are now down and the entire development, of which the deformed egg of Norman Foster's **City Hall** is just one corner, is now an entirely new quarter of the city. In many ways, the grand corporate buildings that occupy this site are relatively nondescript – decent enough structures, but unlikely to set the pulse racing. What is clever about this regeneration project, though, is the way that the buildings have been configured to provide dramatic 'sightlines' clear through the site. Large channels slice between these buildings, providing glimpses of the Tower of London, Tower Bridge, the *Belfast* and so on. This is a commercial development with a very real sense of the importance of its site, genuinely trying to add to the amenities of the area. Shops and cafés are provided, as well as pieces of public art and landscaping. At last, this part of the South Bank is coming to life, replacing the wilderness that, until recently, seemed to isolate the Design Museum from the rest of the attractions along the river.

HIGH DRAMA

Some construction work continues, however, including what promises to be a neat new building for the **Unicorn Theatre**. Designed by Keith Williams Architects, a small but clever firm based in Covent Garden, this £12.6-million building is being designed as a series of interlocking boxes. Each box will contain a specific function: the largest box, probably to be clad in copper, marks the largest of the two auditoriums; a further box signposts the main stairway; a third box contains back-of-house facilities and rehearsal rooms. Intriguingly, the architects have not forgotten that the Unicorn caters specifically for kids – largely five- to 12-year-olds. Consequently, slots and windows will be cast into concrete balustrades at the eye level of a child, and seating is being designed as a series of steps with cushions – the idea is to create a sense of fun and informality. Before being finalised, plans were displayed in local schools for youngsters' approval. Originally scheduled for completion in summer 2004, funding delays pushed the opening date back; expect the theatre to open in autumn 2005.

Further west, plans are being hatched to re-erect the iconic 'Skylon' structure that signposted the site of the 1951 Festival of Britain. The **Royal Festival Hall** (which is currently the subject of a wide-ranging and on-going improvement plan) is the only surviving relic of the festival, which celebrated the centenary of the Great Exhibition and signalled a rise in optimism after the deprivations of the World War II. At the time, the RFH was surrounded by peculiar exhibition structures, including the UFO-like Dome of Discovery and the 91-metre-high (299-foot) Skylon. The Skylon was, effectively, a piece of sculpture, a slender spire that somehow managed to hold itself upright with the minimum of support (just three cables). After being in place for just 11 months, it was sold for scrap. Skylon II, if a planning application is successful, could appear on the South Bank some time in 2005.

DESIGNS ON THE FUTURE

By the end of 2004 families should also be enjoying the new architecture gallery in the **Victoria & Albert Museum**'s Henry Cole wing. Part of the £10-million 'Architecture for All' initiative set up jointly by the V&A and the **Royal Institute of British Architects** (RIBA), the new gallery will explore contemporary architectural issues through a 'cityscape' of models and exhibition towers. Each tower will tackle a different theme: 'Making', covering design and construction; 'People', about building form is shaped by society; 'Use', which examines planning and organisation; and 'Art', looking at the effect of aesthetics on people. The gallery is also to include a 'Hot Topics' area, for people to air their opinions about architectural issues, and a space for temporary displays.

As part of this project, RIBA plans to move its entire collection of 600,000 historical drawings over to the V&A, combining it with the museum's own drawing collection. At present the RIBA archive offers only limited access; the move will allow the public to get its hands on any drawing, free of charge, on demand. In fact, the V&A's archive already operates by these rules – according to curators, if your hands are clean you can see any drawing or print you like. And this includes kids.

The museum's most ambitious scheme is amazing. Designed by architect Daniel Libeskind (designer of the Ground Zero regeneration scheme in New York), the £80-million 'Spiral' building will provide a new entrance and exhibition spaces for the museum. Fund-raising for the extension, an asymmetrical structure that looks like a collapsing house of cards, is going slowly. It is hoped the building work can begin in 2005, reaching completion in 2008.

Libeskind has already finished another building on the Holloway Road. This new north London landmark is a post-graduate teaching centre for **London Metropolitan University**, so public access is limited. The metal-clad building is a curiosity. Libeskind is the same guy who designed the Jewish Museum in Berlin and the Imperial War Museum building in Manchester, both of which angular and asymmetrical buildings took their form (he said) from the inhuman and disorientating nature of the subjects they were dedicated to presenting. The trouble is, this university centre is made in much the same way, doing the rationale for his earlier buildings a disservice (unless it's a reflection

of the quality of LMU's teaching). This building is an eye-catching event on the way from Highbury Corner to Archway, but in terms of architectural merit it seems a triumph of style over substance.

Education buildings are, in fact, undergoing something of a renaissance in the capital. Everything from schools to college buildings are being renewed, rebuilt or constructed from scratch. Norman Foster (architect of the the Swiss Re tower and the **British Museum**'s Great Court) has even been brought in to design a new generation of **City Academies**. The fruits of his high-tech labours are now taking a bashing from kids in Bexley and Brent, and more are on their way.

Colleges, too, are investing in capital projects. Just up the road from Libeskind's wonky box, the **City & Islington College** has opened a new 'lifelong learning centre' on Finsbury Park's Blackstock Road. Designed by Wilkinson Eyre, the design practice that recently won the Stirling Prize for architecture two years running, this building is a stunning example of great community architecture. The way the new modernist building expands, and integrates with, the original Victorian school is exciting, intelligent and inspiring. The CIC is, in fact, commissioning a wave of new buildings – it has just opened a brand new sixth-form centre on Goswell Road that's so good student enrolments have risen by a fifth. All this is good news for London's youth: it's now possible for a child to do their GCSEs at a Foster-designed school, their A-levels at a Wilkinson Eyre college and move on to higher things in a Daniel Libeskind. Now *that's* education.

MONEY DOWN THE DRAIN?

It's a shame the same can't be said about the capital's sporting facilities. Everything will change should London win the 2012 Olympic Games (*see p258* **Olympic dreams**) – in which case, Stratford will get sports centres that will be the envy of the world – but the city's supply of high-quality sports buildings is currently very poor. Hackney tried to rectify this with its £30-million **Clissold Centre**, a building designed by Manchester-based Hodder Associates. Sadly, the project has gone spectacularly awry. Opened in 2003, the centre had closed by the end of the year after problems with leaky roofs, cracked walls and blocked pipes became embarrassing. The whole affair has exploded into a tremendous row, with no one prepared to take responsibility (not the council, not the contractor and certainly not the architect) for the building's shortcomings. As this book went to press, the Clissold was closed 'indefinitely' while legal teams tried to work out who should pay for repairs. This is a tragedy from which only one group of people will gain anything – the lawyers.

All dressed up for the **Mayor's Thames Festival**. *See p29*.

Festivals & Events

A Londoner's diary is always full.

There's always something going on in this city, whatever the season. The famous festivals, such as the **Notting Hill Carnival**, now 40 years old but far from middle-aged in outlook, are famous Europe wide and attract crowds accordingly (*see p27*). Perhaps more enjoyable for young families are the gentler park-based events, such as the **Country Fair** in Brockwell Park, and **Rotherhithe Festival** in Southwark Park (for both, *see p27*).

It's not only summertime that sees Londoners take to the streets with floats and banners. Parades take place for the **Mayor's Thames Festival** (*see p29*) in September, jumping dragons in the **Chinese New Year Festival**, which runs during the dog days of early February, and daft costumes galore when runners full of the joys of spring pound the streets in April's **London Marathon** (*see p32*).

In Autumn half-term come the fireworks – Guy Fawkes's plot is remembered on 5 November and the city skyline is ablaze with pyrotechnics. The Christmas holidays see festive lights a-twinkling and ice rinks a-glistening. Spring half-term has grand pancake races and May bank holidays see parties in Little Venice and Covent Garden. In fact, every school holiday there's something to celebrate in London, so here are some dates for your diary. Check *Time Out* magazine every week for details of more festivals and events.

Summer

Watch This Space
National Theatre, South Bank, SE1 9PX (7452 3400/ www.nationaltheatre.org.uk). Waterloo tube/rail.
Date 18 June-21 Aug 2004.
The National's summer festival of free events and activities outside in Theatre Square includes street dramatics, music and entertainment. There are performances six days a week from more than 75 acts, with alfresco gigs by contemporary musicians and sets from comics, acrobats and dancers. Waterloo Sunsets, on selected Saturday nights, involve spectacular music and theatre shows.

Wimbledon Lawn Tennis Championships
All England Lawn Tennis Club, PO Box 98, Church Road, Wimbledon, SW19 5AE (8944 1066/info 8946 2244). Southfields tube/Wimbledon tube/rail.
Date 21 June-4 July 2004; 20 June-1 July 2005.
The most famous tennis tournament in the world rarely disappoints, even when the weather's drippy, but making sure you get to enjoy your strawberries and cream courtside isn't all that easy. For Centre and Number One court seats, you'd have had to request an application form from the All England Lawn Tennis Club between August and November 2003. This form gives you access to the public ticket ballot; if you're one of the lucky ones, you'll be notified in late January. The only way to secure a ticket otherwise is to queue on the day of the match. Once in, you can wander the outside courts. In the afternoon, returned show-court tickets are available from the resale booth opposite Court One, so it may be worth hanging about to see stars in action.

> Axial Dance...

City of London Festival
Various venues in the City (7377 0540/www.colf.org).
Date 21 June-13 July 2004.
Now in its 42nd year, the festival sees music, theatre, literature and dance performances in some of the City's most beautiful and historic buildings; there are walks and art tours as well, and an extra bonus in 2004: free lunchtime events, ranging from music to theatre and dance, running from 1 June to 25 August. Check the website for a full programme.

Henley Royal Regatta
Henley Reach, Henley-on-Thames, Oxon RG9 2LY (01491 572153/www.hrr.co.uk). Henley-on-Thames rail. **Date** 30 June-4 July 2004.
It may be famously posh, but there's no obligation to don the striped blazer and boater if you fancy watching a bit of boating. Nearly 300 races are held over the five days, with crews coming from all over the world to row here. A fireworks display is usually held on one of the evenings – call to check – and while picnics are not allowed, catering facilities should keep the family's pecker up.

Greenwich & Docklands International Festival (GDIF)
Various venues near the Thames (8305 1818/ www.festival.org). **Date** 2-24 July 2004.
Greenwich & Docklands Festival has made a speciality of free outdoor spectacles and performances, ideal for families. At the Royal Naval College in Greenwich on 3-4 July, 'The Wisdom of Africa' will be a combination of theatre, circus and storytelling, with its climax the procession of the Kalabari goddess of destruction and creativity in her 25ft-high (8m) boat. 'Dancing City' (7-10 July) will use the architecture of Canary Wharf to stage a performance in a plastic bubble; a Bollywood-style Busby Berkeley routine, with fountains and stairs; and Spanish dance on a transparent stage, viewed from below. Then there are shows by the Vietnam National Puppetry Theatre (13-15 July), a Monsoon Mela (17 July) on Three Mills Green, and three floating alien heads in Walk the Plank's Supernova (23 July) on the Docklands Campus of the University of East London. The Mile End Park finale (24 July) promises huge inflatable birds will enact a version of 'The Conference of the Birds', along with music and shadow projections.

Coin Street Festival
Gabriel's Wharf, 56 Upper Ground, SE1 9PP (7401 3610/information 7401 2255/www.coinstreetfestival.org). Southwark tube/Blackfriars or Waterloo tube/rail. **Map** p320 N8. **Date** 3 July-22 Aug 2004.
A free cultural festival taking place in and around Gabriel's Wharf, Bernie Spain Gardens and the Oxo Tower Wharf, with food, craft stalls and free activities stretching along the riverside walkway. The programme is in development, but on 3 July two music stages, street theatre and workshops should be there to celebrate International Co-operative Day, while 25 July marks Coin Street's 20th anniversary with the annual fête: expect disco sounds from Lovetrain, talent and fashion shows, family workshops, storytelling and face-painting. Call or check the website for further details.

BBC Sir Henry Wood Promenade Concerts
Royal Albert Hall, Kensington Gore, SW7 2AP (box office 7589 8212/www.bbc.co.uk/proms). Knightsbridge or South Kensington tube/9, 10, 52 bus. **Map** p315 D9.
Date 16 July-11 Sept 2004.
If you choose carefully you should able to find something in the grown-up Proms programme that the sprogs will enjoy. Otherwise, put 24-25 July in your diary: it's the Blue Peter Prom, which has been so successful they're putting on an extra afternoon this year. Your chipper hosts are Simon Thomas and Liz Barker, and there'll be Chinese lion dancing and Japanese taiko drummers, as well as a thunderous organ rendition of *2001: A Space Odyssey* and some music from the Harry Potter films. After that you can sing 'Land of Hope and Glory' until your miniature Union Jack falls off its stick.

London Heathrow Youth Games
Crystal Palace National Sports Centre, Ledrington Road, SE19 2BB (8778 0131/www.youthgames.org.uk). Crystal Palace rail. **Date** 10-11 July 2004.
This mini-Olympics, now in its 27th year, sees 10,000 sporting hopefuls, all of them under 19, represent the 33 London boroughs in 24 different sports. The teams are selected locally, and activities include archery, fencing, canoeing, football, tennis, athletics and show jumping. Check the website for a programme. The Festival Village hosts DJs, street sports, graffiti art and dance demonstrations.

& Mirando Valse at **Greenwich & Docklands International Festival.**

Rotherhithe Festival

Southwark Park, SE16 2UA (7231 7845/www.timeand talents.org.uk). **Date** 11 July 2004.
Rotherhithe comes alive for families at this time, when the whole community, from Surrey Docks City Farm (*see p122*) to Decathlon (*see p199*), seems to get involved in putting on events and activities. There are usually bouncy castles, street performers, craft and food stalls, and music to enjoy.

Soho Festival

St Anne's Gardens & part of Wardour Street, W1 (7439 4303/www.thesohosociety.org.uk). Tottenham Court Road tube. **Map** p317 K6. **Date** 11 July 2004.
Food, crafts, book, face-painting stalls and various madcap competitions make up this bonkers event in Soho's calendar. Spectators can enjoy a tug-of-war between firemen and members of the Soho Society, or watch a spaghetti eating contest, for example. The traditional highlight is the waiters' and barworkers' race, but there is some question as to whether it will go ahead this year – check the website.

Swan Upping on the Thames

Various points along the Thames. **Date** 19 23 July 2004.
The Crown owns all unmarked mute swans in open water, and once a year the Queen's Swan Marker and the Swan Uppers of the Vinters' and Dyers' livery companies count, ring and check the health of the birds. Officials wear scarlet uniforms and ride in traditional Thames rowing skiffs. When a brood of cygnets is sighted, a signalling cry of 'All up!' is given and the boats move into position. On passing Windsor Castle, the rowers stand to attention with oars raised and salute the Queen. This archaic ceremony can be seen from the towpaths along the Thames, starting at Sunbury Lock.

Lambeth Country Show

Brockwell Park, SE24 0NG (7926 9000). Brixton tube/rail, then 2, 3, 68, 196 bus/Herne Hill rail. **Date** 17-18 July 2004.
This annual urban country show fills Brockwell Park with a mix of farmyard and domestic animal attractions (horse show, dog show, farm animals). Aside from meeting and greeting critters, kids can have fun on the bouncy castles and fairground rides, and there are also food and craft stalls, and a whole lot of music and dancing.

South East Marine Week

Various locations in south-east England (02380 613636/ www.southeastmarine.org.uk). **Date** 7-15 Aug 2004.
Marine Week comprises 50 free events in various places – all with the aim of introducing people to local marine life. Various conservation themed events take place throughout London. In the London Aquarium (*see p38*) there will be craft activities to mark the week, such as, 'Make a Turtle' and 'Colour the coasts of Britain', as well as a quiz to test your knowledge of British aquatic life. The Marine Madness Fun Day in Greenwich Peninsula Ecology Park (*see p124*) will offer the chance to try your hand at sand art, or making shark and jellyfish models as well as funky fish kites. You can test your knowledge in marine-themed quizzes. Call or check the website for information on what's happening in your area.

Notting Hill Carnival

Notting Hill, W10, W11 (7730 3010). Ladbroke Grove, Notting Hill or Westbourne Park tube. **Date** 29, 30 Aug 2004.
The carnival is celebrating its 40th anniversary this year. Family parade day, held from noon to 9pm on 30 August 2004, sees colourfully costumed dancers and performers from the many steel bands, Soca sound systems and floats, and an infectious carnival spirit.

Those wishing to avoid the crush would be wise to attend on children's day, as the sheer volume of beersoaked revellers on the Monday can be overwhelming. What's even safer is the dinky nursery and playgroups carnival, which happens in Kensington Memorial Park two weeks before the parent event. This scaled-down festival has a children's steel band competition; mini-floats, children's, mother's and buggy c ompetitions; and nursery fancy dress. Call the Parents and Children Carnival Association (8968 4840) for further infor- mation. Even better, why not buy a costume (from around £25) and enrol them with your nearest Masquerade or 'Mas' band through the carnival office? Clubs cater for various age groups, from babies to 16-year-olds, with the option of practising at meet-ups throughout the summer holidays or just turning up on the afternoon and falling into line with the others (smaller children will be given places on the floats). It's completely unchoreographed and quite possibly the most fun you'll have all year. Check the website (www.nhct.org.uk) for regular updates on all aspects of the carnival.

**Over 750 places to eat like
a prince and pay like a pauper**

Young Pavement Artists Competition

*Colonnade Walk, 123 Buckingham Palace Road, SW1W
9SH (7732 1651). Victoria tube/rail.* **Map** p318 H10.
Date 4 June 2005.
Part of what is now a huge national event (there were some
20,000 entrants in 2004, though it is still run by a single
family), this day out for lowdown scribblers celebrates its
20th anniversary in 2005. On the big day there is usually
entertainment laid on, in the form of music, magicians and
face painting. Children aged four to 18 compete, with their
work scrutinised by judges from Tate Britain and the Royal
Academy, and photographs of the best pieces are exhibited
the following month.

Derby Day

*Epsom Downs Racecourse, Epsom Downs, Surrey KT18
5LQ (01372 470047/www.epsomderby.co.uk). Epsom
Town Centre or Tattenham Corner rail then shuttle bus.*
Date 6-7 June 2005.
Oaks Day – the fillies version of the Derby and a classic in
its own right – is on 6 June; 7 June is the famous Derby Day.
Stands and spectator enclosures at this prestigious flat race
are open to all, from toffs in toppers in the grandstand, to
families picnicking on the hill in the middle of the course. The
race is the day's highlight, but a market, entertainers, jugglers
and funfair all add to the day's carnival atmosphere.

Trooping the Colour

*Horseguards Parade, Whitehall, SW1A 2AX (7414 2479
ext3). Westminster tube/Charing Cross tube/rail.*
Map p319 K8. **Date** early June 2005 (phone for date).
The Queen's official birthday is marked each year by this
colourful military parade that dates back to the early 18th
century. The ceremony is watched by members of the Royal
Family and invited guests; members of the public may
observe from vantage points at either side of the Mall,
beginning at 11am on Horseguards Parade. After the ceremony, the Queen rides in a carriage back to Buckingham
Palace at the head of her Guards, before taking the salute at
the palace from the balcony, when the Royal Air Force flies
past overhead and a 41-gun Royal Salute is fired in Green
Park. At 1pm there's a 62-gun Royal Salute at the Tower.

Autumn

Great River Race

*On the Thames, from Richmond, Surrey, to Island
Gardens, E14 (8398 9057).* **Date** 11 Sept 2004.
More than 250 boats compete in this 22-mile (35km) river
marathon, aiming to scoop the UK Traditional Boat
Championship. The race sets off from Ham House (*see p144*)
at 1.15pm and passes many historic landmarks on the way
to the finish at Island Gardens (*see p116*). This race not only
attracts fascinating entrants from all over the world, but
uniquely has crews of under-14s pitting themselves against
the adults. Would-be competitors should contact the organisers for further information. Look out for replica Viking long-
ships, Stone Age log boats and Chinese dragon boats.

Regent Street Festival

*Regent Street, W1 (info 7152 5853/www.regent
streetonline.com). Oxford Circus tube.* **Map** p318 J6.
Date 5 Sept 2004.
A record number of visitors – more than 190,000 – attended
this free festival last year: Colin Jackson fired the starting gun
at noon, and they were off! for eight hours of live music (rock,
pop, jazz, classical, the Tweenies), dancing displays and food

stalls. Regent Street will again be closed to traffic for the
whole day, so expect a similar range of activities to be laid
on this year as last: funfair, rides in a kids' train, toy demos
(Scalextric, Lego), a police exhibition area with dogs and
horses, and entertainers, storytelling, face-painters and
magicians on Hamleys (*see p206*) festival 'lawn'.

Mayor's Thames Festival

*On the Thames, between Hungerford Bridge &
Blackfriars Bridge (7928 8998/www.thamesfestival.org).*
Map p320 M-O7. **Date** 18, 19 Sept 2004.
A celebration of the river, with a wealth of activities taking
place over the weekend. Plans for this year include hundreds
of banners being hung from the Golden Jubilee Bridges,
flower sculptures and a floating stage for musicians, a
Children's Pleasure Garden at the London Eye (*see p37*),
which will be full of candlelit lanterns on poles, and the
illuminated Bajra Peacock Boat, as well as the usual stalls
and exhibitions. The highlight of the festival should be the
Night Carnival, with costumes, lights, music and dance, plus
an elaborate firework display in the middle of the river to
complete the spectacle. Check the website for current details.

CBBC Prom in the Park

*Hyde Park (booking/info line 0870 899 8001/
www.bbc.co.uk/proms). Hyde Park Corner tube.*
Map p313 F7. **Date** 12 Sept 2004.
This alfresco Sunday concert comprises the BBC Concert
Orchestra belting out Disney theme tunes. Rumours that
Mickey himself will conduct some of the numbers are, as yet,
unconfirmed, but you can rest assured there'll be dancin',
singin' and some great animation moments shown on giant
screens through the park.

City Harvest Festival

*Capel Manor Gardens, Bullsmoor Lane, Enfield, Middx
BN1 4RQ (8366 4442/www.capel.ac.uk). Turkey Street
rail (Mon-Sat only)/217, 310 bus.* **Date** 18 Sept 2004.
The urban farms we all love have a pleasant day out in the
leafy acres of Enfield for this agricultural extravaganza.
Events include a farm animal show and arena events,
milking and shearing demonstrations, vegetable and plant
sales, craft displays and stalls and children's activities.

London Open House

*Various venues throughout London (www.londonopen
house.org).* **Date** 18, 19 Sept 2004.
Now in its 12th year, this event is held to celebrate the wealth
of magnificent architecture across London. It's a wonderful
chance to gain free access to more than 500 buildings, many
of which are usually closed to the public, from private homes
to civic and industrial institutions, grand historical buildings
to pumping stations. Some local boroughs run architecture-
related workshops and activities for children. Check the
website for a full list of participating buildings in your area.

Horseman's Sunday

*Church of St John's Hyde Park, Hyde Park Crescent, W2
2QD (7262 1732/www.stjohn-hydepark.com). Edgware
Road or Lancaster Gate tube/Paddington tube/rail.* **Map**
p313 E6. **Date** 19 Sept 2004.
This ceremony dates back to 1969, when local riding stables
fearing closure held an open-air service to protest. Starting
at noon, a vicar on horseback rides out to bless and present
rosettes to a procession of horses and riders, and delivers a
short service with hymns and occasional guest speakers.
While there's little interaction between onlookers and the
horses, it's fun nonetheless to watch the equine pageant trip
through the lovely setting of Hyde Park.

Punch & Judy Festival

Covent Garden Piazza, WC2E 8RF (7836 9136/www. coventgardenmarket.co.uk). Covent Garden tube. **Map** p319 L7. **Date** 3 Oct 2004.

This festival celebrates the enduring appeal of the red-nosed patriarch, his long suffering wife, a crocodile and a baby, engaging in mischief and slapstick and providing shout-along fun for children of all ages. Performances take place around the market building and this year the organisers are looking for young performers to have a go at staging a show (call in advance for details) and to join the Punch and Judy Fellowship. Puppetry means prizes, and there's also puppet-related merchandise for sale. If one day's mischief isn't enough for you, there's a Christmas Pudding Race planned for 4 December 2004; check the website or phone for details nearer the date.

Pearly Kings & Queens Harvest Festival

St Martin-in-the-Fields, Trafalgar Square, WC2N 4JJ (7766 1100). Charing Cross tube/rail. **Map** p319 L7. **Date** 3 Oct 2004.

Arrive early for the 3pm Harvest Thanksgiving service to watch the arrival of London's pearly kings and queens, splendidly dressed in their 'flash boy' pearl button-covered suits. The pearly royalty has its origins in the hierarchy that evolved among Victorian costermongers. The vicar also wears a pearly stole during attendance, and St Martin's is decorated with fruit and harvest baskets. Should you wish to only observe the arrivals but not attend the hour-long service, the crypt downstairs houses a brass-rubbing centre and café (*see p82*), and there's a market in the church grounds.

Trafalgar Day Parade

Trafalgar Square, WC2 (7928 8978/www.sea-cadets.org). Charing Cross tube/rail. **Map** p319 K7. **Date** 24 Oct 2004.

This grand parade of uniformed sea cadets and marching bands commemorates the 197th anniversary of the Battle of Trafalgar. As the battle also saw the death of Admiral Lord Nelson, the parade ends with the laying of a wreath at the foot of Nelson's Column. Kids can board the Sea Cadets mobile display unit – a 1960s Routemaster bus converted into the control room of a Royal Navy submarine, where they can raise the periscope, stalk enemy ships with sonar contacts, and try out their skills on 'Dive! Dive! Dive!' action stations.

State Opening of Parliament

House of Lords, Palace of Westminster, SW1A 0PW (7219 4272/www.parliament.uk). Westminster tube. **Map** p319 L9. **Date** early/mid Nov 2004.

The opening of Parliament by the Queen is a colourful ceremony that has changed little since the 16th century. Large crowds watch her arrival and departure from the Palace of Westminster in the spectacular State Coach, attended by the Household Cavalry, and as she enters the House of Lords, a gun salute is fired. The actual Queen's Speech, delivered to the august Lords, can only be seen via a television link.

London to Brighton Veteran Car Run

Starting at Serpentine Road, Hyde Park, W2 (01280 841 062). Hyde Park Corner tube. **Map** p313 E8. **Date** 7 Nov 2004.

This annual commemoration of the Emancipation Run of 1896 is now more of a motoring spectacle than a race, although bronze medals are awarded to all who reach Brighton before 4.30pm. Some 400 beautifuly polished and generall buffed-up vintage cars take part, with the first and eldest (so presumably slowest) group leaving Hyde Park

Corner at 7.30am – so set your alarm clock if you want to catch the real classics. If you can't get there at such an ungodly hour, join the crowds lining the rest of the route, via Parliament Square and Westminster Bridge, then on through the streets of south London.

Bonfire Night

Date 5 Nov 2004.

Every year Britain celebrates the failure of the Gunpowder Plot of 1605, when Guy Fawkes attempted to blow up James I and his Parliament. A 'guy' is burnt on giant bonfires across the country and fireworks let off. Most public displays are held on the weekend nearest to 5 November; among the best in London are those at Primrose Hill, Alexandra Palace and Crystal Palace. It's best to phone your council or check the local press for specific details of individual firework displays (often free). It's also wise to check as near the date as possible: events have been known to be cancelled at the last minute, usually because of bad weather.

Lord Mayor's Show

Various streets in the City (7606 3030/www.lordmayors show.org). **Date** 13 Nov 2004.

This spectacle dates back to 1215, when King John signed a charter that granted the City the right to elect its own mayor. The parade has thousands of participants: military personnel, horses, floats, people in silly costumes, marching bands and the spectacular State Coach. Marked by an aircraft fly-past over the Royal Exchange, Mansion House and St Paul's Cathedral, the parade starts at 11am and proceeds to the Royal Courts of Justice on the Strand. There it pauses as the Lord Mayor takes his oath, then makes the return journey from Victoria Embankment to Mansion House. The order of procession is a closely guarded secret; check the website nearer the time, or pick up a programme on the day.

Remembrance Sunday Ceremony

Cenotaph, Whitehall, SW1. Westminster tube/Charing Cross tube/rail. **Map** p319 L8. **Date** 14 Nov 2004.

An annual ceremony during which the Queen, the Prime Minister and other dignitaries lay wreaths of poppies at the Cenotaph, Britain's national memorial to fallen heroes from both world wars. Two minutes' silence is observed in their honour at 11am. A short remembrance service, attended by hundreds of ex-servicemen, is led by the Bishop of London, followed by a march down Whitehall afterwards.

Discover Dogs

Earl's Court 2 (entrance on Lillie Road), SW5 9TA (7518 1012/www.the-kennel-club.org.uk). West Brompton tube. **Map** p314 A11. **Date** 13-14 Nov 2004.

In 2003 some 21,000 dog lovers attended this canine extravaganza. Far less formal than Crufts, here you can meet more than 180 dogs, discuss pedigrees with breeders, and gather info on all matters of the mutt. The Good Citizen Dog Scheme offers discipline and agility courses, and children can join the Young Kennel Club, which encourages interest in care and training, and organises competitions, classes and camps. You can also meet husky teams, watch police-dog agility demonstrations and witness silly (yet very watchable) doggy dances in Heelwork to Music displays.

Christmas Lights & Tree

Covent Garden *WC2 (7836 9136). Covent Garden tube.* **Map** p317 L6.
Oxford Street *W1 (7629 2738). Oxford Circus tube.* **Map** p316 G6.
Regent Street *W1 (7152 5853). Oxford Circus tube.* **Map** p316 J6.

May Fayre & Puppet Festival. *See p32.*

Bond Street *W1 (7821 5230). Oxford Circus tube.*
Map p316 H6.
Trafalgar Square *SW1 (7983 6586). Leicester Square tube.* **Map** p319 K7.
Date *All* mid Nov-early Dec 2004.

Each year since 1947 a giant fir tree has been given to this country by the Norwegian people in gratitude for Britain's role in liberating their country from the Nazis. Erected in Trafalgar Square, its lights are switched on while carols are sung. The main shopping streets boast impressive festive displays, particularly in the large department-store windows. The lights on Regent Street and Oxford Street are invariably switched on by some B-list celebrity. The lights on display at St Christopher's Place, Bond Street and Kensington High Street are often prettier than those on the main thoroughfares.

Winter

International Showjumping Championships

Olympia, Hammersmith Road, Kensington, W14 8UX (7370 8202/www.olympiashowjumping.com). Kensington (Olympia) tube/rail. **Date** 16-20 Dec 2004.
This annual jamboree for equestrian enthusiasts isn't just about the competitors – with more than 100 trade stands you can even get in some Christmas shopping. Events include everything from international riders' competitions to the Shetland Pony Grand National and dog agility contests. Olympia will also host a dressage competition in 2004: this comprises the Grand Prix (14 Dec) and Kür (15 Dec). For a complete timetable, check the website; tickets cost from £16 to £37, with some discounts available.

Frost Fair

Bankside Riverwalk, by Shakespeare's Globe, SE1 9DT (details from Tourism Unit, Southwark Council, 7525 1139). London Bridge tube/rail. **Date** mid Dec.
December 2003 saw the first modern frost fair on Bankside. It's a tradition started in the winter of 1564, when the Thames froze over and Londoners used the ice for their stalls and attractions. Sadly, no ice can be expected these days, but the food and wine stalls, children's shows and musical attractions set up on Bankside make for a good week's entertainment in the run-up to Christmas.

London International Boat Show

ExCeL, 1 Western Gateway, Royal Victoria Dock, E16 1XL (7069 5000/www.schroderslondonboatshow.com). Custom House DLR. **Date** 6-16 Jan 2005.
For 50 years this maritime convention has been showing off leisure boats to salty seadogs and weekend buccaneers. Now it takes place in this spacious Docklands exhibition centre there's a lot more scope for dockside exhibits and big boats.

London International Mime Festival

Various venues (7637 5661/www.mimefest.co.uk). **Date** 15-30 Jan 2005.
Surely the quietest festival the city has to offer, events include dance-theatre, circus, puppetry, animation and mechanical theatre performances, many of which are colourful and expressive, so eminently suitable for children. Venues range from the Royal Festival Hall and the Barbican to the Battersea Arts Centre and Croydon Clocktower.

Chinese New Year Festival

Around Gerrard Street, Chinatown, W1 (7439 3822/ www.chinatown-online.co.uk). Leicester Square or Piccadilly Circus tube. **Date** 9 Feb 2005. **Map** p401 K7.
Join the crowds following the Chinese 'dragons' through the streets. There are fireworks galore and the local restaurants prepare special banquets. Formalities begin around noon, with musicians and drummers accompanying lion dancers through the streets. The festivities spread into Leicester Square, with performances from Chinese acrobats and conjurers. Check the press for details of the 2005 festivities.

National Storytelling Week

Various theatres, bookshops, libraries, schools & pubs around London (contact Del Reid 8866 4232/www.sfs. org.uk). **Date** 29 Jan-5 Feb 2005.
The fifth annual storytelling week sees venues across the country hosting events for tellers and listeners. Details of the

2005 programme were unavailable as we went to press (check the website nearer the time), but last year there were classical and Irish myths at Jackson's Lane in Highgate, tales from India and around the world at the National Archives in Kew and the Museum of Childhood in Bethnal Green, and some swashbuckling stories of the adventures on the high seas on board the *Cutty Sark* in Greenwich.

Spring

Great Spitalfields Pancake Day Race

Spitalfields Market (entrance on Commercial Street or Brushfield Street), E1 6AA (7375 0441). Liverpool Street tube/rail. **Map** p321 R5. **Date** 11 Feb 2005.

Get a gaggle of friends together, pull on penguin suits (or dress up as a waddle of penguins if you prefer – there are prizes for the best-dressed team) and join these annual Spitalfields shenanigans. Held each Shrove Tuesday in aid of Save the Children, the race is for the prize of a shiny engraved frying pan – this alone is reason enough for entry. Tossing starts at 12.30pm (pancakes are provided, but bring your own lucky pan). It's quite a relaxed sort of affair, but would-be competitors should phone the organisers a few days in advance to avoid batter recriminations.

London Marathon

Greenwich to Westminster Bridge via the Isle of Dogs, Victoria Embankment & St James's Park (7902 0200/ www.london-marathon.co.uk). **Date** 16 Apr 2005 (phone to check).

Spectators can choose vantage points from Greenwich to the Mall to cheer the 35,000 competitors, both elite and novice, many of whom run the gruelling 26.2 miles in fancy dress for charities. There's also a wheelchair race and a mini-London Marathon for youngsters, as well as street entertainers and bands. If you think you're fit enough, runners' applications must be in by the October before the race.

London Harness Horse Parade

Battersea Park, Albert Bridge Road, SW11 (01737 646132). Battersea Park or Queenstown Road rail/97, 137 bus. **Date** 28 Mar 2005.

An enjoyable Easter Monday parade outing for animal lovers and families, with a fun fair, stalls and fast-food stands as extra draws. First held in 1886, this parade welcoming everything from splendidly groomed shire horses through to dinky Shetland ponies. Judging starts from 9.30am, with a grand parade of the winners around noon. Look out for the 'young whips' – carts driven by seven- to eight-year-olds. Spangly London pearly kings and queens chat to visitors.

Museums & Galleries Month

Various venues (7233 9796/www.may2005.org.uk). **Date** May 2005.

This is a national event, organised annually by the Campaign for Museums (www.campaignformuseums.org.uk) with support from museums and galleries across the country. Across London, over 250 venues will be running creative events and activities (classroom projects, open days) for all ages. This year saw the launch of the Discover London Trails, which links museums and galleries with other attractions in areas such as Wimbledon, Southwark, Greenwich and Rotherhithe as well as Covent Garden and Theatreland. To find out what's happening near you, check the website or phone the nearest museum (there are full listings for all London museums in **Around Town**; *see pp34-156*).

Flipping **Great Spitalfields Pancake Race**.

Canalway Cavalcade

Little Venice, W9 (British Waterways London 7286 6101). Warwick Avenue tube. **Date** 6-8 May 2005.

Organised by the Inland Waterways, this bank holiday boat rally sees the pool of Little Venice transformed with the assembly of more than 100 colourful narrowboats, all decked out in bunting and flowers. Events include all manner of craft, trade and food stalls; kids' activities (which may include canal-art painting and badge-making); music; and boat trips. The beautiful lantern-light boat procession is a must-see – pray for fine weather. Phone to confirm dates.

May Fayre & Puppet Festival

Garden of St Paul's, Covent Garden, Bedford Street, WC2E 9ED (7375 0441). Covent Garden or Leicester Square tube. **Map** p319 L7. **Date** 7 May 2005.

Commemorating the first sighting of Mr Punch in England by Samuel Pepys in 1662, (it took place on this very spot), this free day-long celebration of the art of puppetry makes for an unusually entertaining family outing. A grand brass band procession around Covent Garden is followed by a service held in St Paul's (*see p76*), with Mr Punch in the pulpit. Then there are Punch & Judy (and other puppet) shows, booths and stalls, as well as workshops at which children can either make puppets to take home or dress themselves up in hats and costumes. Bring a picnic to eat in the church gardens – all that joining in with the maypole dancing and juggling is hungry work.

Beating Retreat

Horseguards Parade, Whitehall, SW1A 2AX (7218 6645 ext 3). Westminster tube/Charing Cross tube/rail. **Map** p319 K8. **Date** late May-early June 2005.

An ineffably patriotic, smartly turned out musical ceremony with the Mounted Bands of the Household Cavalry and the Massed Bands of the Guards Division. The bandsmen beat a stirring and spectacular 'Retreat' on drums and pipes. Phone for tickets (for reserved tiered seating) to watch the hour-long march, which starts at 7pm.

Around Town

Introduction

You know it, the kids know it – this is the greatest city on earth.

Exploring a city as vast and complex as London is as much about unearthing hidden treasures as ticking off celebrity sights. In these **Around Town** pages we've included all types of attraction: the obscure and the obvious, the frivolous and the educational – just as long as they allow children through their portals. On the subject of looking and learning, we've given the best activities, courses, workshops and storytelling sessions for children in many of the places listed. With Transport for London's generous provison for children's travel – under-11s travel free on buses at all times, and all kids travel free with an adult family railcard holder at weekends – there's no excuse to confine yourself to one area. So hop on a bus and start exploring!

USEFUL INFORMATION

In every area we've covered, there's information on green spaces, playgrounds and shopping areas, wildlife sites and local landmarks. Suggestions on where to eat, featured as **Pit stops**, are also included for central London. Some restaurants and cafés listed in pit stop boxes are also reviewed in the **Eating** chapter (*see pp158-82*), but note that the review may refer to a different branch. In any case, it's always a good idea to ring to check that a listed place, whether it is a museum, gallery, restaurant or shop, is open before you visit, as some close at short notice.

If you want to extend your sightseeing options to more pricey places, such as **London Zoo** (*see p66*) and the **Tower of London** (*see p56*), a **London Pass** (0870 242 9988, www.londonpass.com) may be of interest. It gives you pre-paid access to more than 50 sights and attractions, and costs from £27 daily per adult without travel, or £32 with travel (for children the price is £18 without travel, £20 with).

If we have included the initials 'LP' before the admission price, it means your London Pass grants free admission. 'EH' means the sight is an English Heritage property, so members of that organisation and their kids get in free. 'NT' means National Trust members and their children get free admission.

Sights highlights

Feeding frenzy
Feed the sharks, piranhas and rays at the **London Aquarium** (*see p38*); watch the penguins get their fish in **London Zoo** (*see p66*), or the pelicans scoff theirs in **St James's Park** (*see p82*) between 2pm and 3pm each day.

All at sea
Shiver your timbers on board the **Golden Hinde** (*see p42*); young guns go for **HMS Belfast** (*see p42*); all aboard the **Cutty Sark** (*see p123*) for a ship-shape fundraising adventure.

We will remember them
Memories of past conflicts still resound at **Winston Churchill's Britain at War Experience** (*see p46*); doggedly at the **Cabinet War Rooms** (*see p79*), educationally at the **National Army Museum** (*see p87*), very loudly at **Firepower** (*see p127*) and movingly at the **Imperial War Museum** (*see p128*).

Is it art?
You can practise your strokes at **Tate Modern** (*see p45*) and **Courtauld Institute Gallery** (*see p57*), enjoy a magic carpet ride at the **National Gallery** (*see p81*) or get some Trolley action at **Tate Britain** (*see p82*).

Are you sitting comfortably?
Then they'll begin, with some Crow's Nest stories at the **National Maritime Museum** (*see p124*) or below stairs gossip at **Linley Sambourne House** (*see p149*); while the house is the story at **19 Princelet Street** (*see p106*).

Play up...
Get high with the **British Airways London Eye** (*see p37*), get certified at the **Monument** (*see p50*), live the **Tower Bridge Experience** (*see p55*) or take a kite up Parliament Hill on **Hampstead Heath** (*see p95*).

...play act...
Darling, you'll be wonderful this summer at **Shakespeare's Globe** (*see p45*), on a tour with the **Royal National Theatre** (*see p40*) or in improv at the **Theatre Museum** (*see p77*).

...and play the game
Everyone's for tennis at **Wimbledon Lawn Tennis Museum** (*see p141*); shove your way into the scrum at the **Museum of Rugby/Twickenham Stadium** (*see p143*); check out the world's unluckiest sparrow at **Lord's Cricket Ground & MCC Museum** (*see p94*).

See the sights

By balloon

Adventure Balloons *Winchfield Park, London Road, Hartley Wintney, Hampshire RG27 8HY (01252 844222/www.adventureballoons.co.uk).* **Flights** *London* May-Aug 5am Tue, Wed, Thur. **Fares** *London* £165 per person. **Credit** MC, V.
Balloon flights over London leave from either Vauxhall Bridge or Tower Hill, very early in the morning (this is the only time when the air space is clear). Flights must be booked well ahead and are dependent on the weather; tiny balloonists have to be at least eight years old and they pay full price for a trip. There's champagne or juice all round on landing.

By boat

City Cruises *7740 0400/www.citycruises.com*
The river's biggest pleasure cruise operator, whose fleet includes showboats and restaurant boats. City Cruises also organises sightseeing tours and sells Rail & River Rover tickets, which let you combine a cruise with unlimited DLR travel (£9; £4.50 children; *see also p114*).

By bus

Big Bus Company *48 Buckingham Palace Road, Westminster, SW1W 0RN (0800 169 1365/7233 9533/ www.bigbustours.com).* **Departures** every 10-15mins from Green Park, Victoria & Marble Arch. *Summer* 8.30am-6pm daily. *Winter* 8.30am-4.30pm daily. **Pick-up** Green Park (near the Ritz); Marble Arch (Speakers' Corner); Victoria (outside Thistle Victoria Hotel, 48 Buckingham Palace Road). **Fares** £17 (£15 if booked online); £8 5-15s; free under-5s. Tickets valid for 24hrs, interchangeable between routes. **Credit** AmEx, DC, MC, V.
Open-top buses that offer two-hour tours on three routes, with commentary (recorded on the Blue route, live on the Red and Green). Big Bus also runs cruises and walking tours.

Original London Sightseeing Tour *(8877 1722/ www.theoriginaltour.com).* **Departures** *Summer* 9am 6pm daily. *Winter* 9am-5pm daily. **Pick-up** Grosvenor Gardens; Marble Arch (Speakers' Corner); Baker Street tube (forecourt); Coventry Street; Embankment tube; Trafalgar Square. **Fares** £15; £10 5-15s; free under-5s. £1 discount if booked online. **Credit** MC, V.
Children on the Kids Club tours get entertaining commentary and an activity pack.

By duck

London Duck Tours *55 York Road, SE1 7NJ (7928 3132/www.londonducktours.co.uk).* **Tours** *Feb-Dec* daily (ring for departure times). **Fares** £16.50; £11 under-12s; £49 family ticket (2+2).
City of Westminster tours in a DUKW (a kind of amphibious vehicle that was developed during World War II) comprise a 75-minute road and river trip, starting at the London Eye and entering the Thames at Vauxhall.

By helicopter

Cabair Helicopters *Elstree Aerodrome, Borehamwood, Herts WD6 3AW (8953 4411/ www.cabairhelicopters.com).* Edgware tube/ Elstree rail. **Flights** from 9.45am-4pm Sun (over-7s only). **Fares** £129. **Credit** MC, V.
Memorable 'helitours' over London that take in all the sights.

By pedal power

London Pedicabs *(07866 628462/www.london pedicabs.com).* **Fares** from £2 per person.

Whitehall. *See p78.*

Pedicabs (where someone cycles you to your destination in a rickshaw-style bike) are based around Covent Garden, Soho and Leicester Square.

London Bicycle Tour Company *(7928 6838/ www.londonbicycle.com).* **Fares** £2.50 per hr; £14 per 24hrs; £40 per week.
In addition to bicycles, rickshaws are available (for up to three people); phone for more details.

By taxi

Black Taxi Tours of London *(7935 9363/ www.blacktaxitours.co.uk).* **Cost** £75.
A tailored two-hour tour for up to five people.

On foot

Original London Walks *(7624 3978, www.walks.com)* encompasses sorties on everything from the shadowy London of Sherlock Holmes to picturesque riverside pubs. There are walks to 'Jack the Ripper Haunts' at 7.30pm daily, and 'Jack the Ripper's London' is at 3pm on Saturdays; both depart from the Tower Hill tube exit and are suitable for kids aged 13 and above – younger children might enjoy the Ghost Tours. All tours cost £5.50 (£4.50 concessions). One great thing about **Cityside Walks** (8449 4736, www.cityside-walks.co.uk) is that under-12s go free (adults pay £5, or £4 for concessions). Cityside's most attractive walks to kids are 'Blessed, Cursed and Haunted' (meet outside Exit 1 of Blackfriars tube at 11.30am on Mondays), 'Meet the Romans' (outside Tower Hill tube at 11am on Fridays) and 'A City in Flames' (outside the Monument at 2.15pm on Fridays), all of which run from 1 March to 31 October.
Other walks companies worth noting include **Citisights** (8806 4325, www.chr.org.uk/walks.htm) and **Pied Piper Walks** (7435 4782). Good self-guided walks are listed in *Time Out London Walks* volumes 1 and 2 (£9.99 and £11.99).

With the specialists

Tour Guides *7495 5504/www.tourguides.co.uk*
Tailor-made tours with Blue Badge guides for individuals or groups, either on foot or by car, coach or boat.
Premium Tours *7278 5300/www.premiumtours.co.uk*
Private tours of specific sites and attractions in London and the south of England.

South Bank & Bankside

Art is just the start of the attractions down by the Thames.

Float on by the **South Bank**.

Half a millennium ago, **Southwark**, especially the marshy areas near the River Thames, was famed for its inns, theatres, bear-baiting and general seediness. These days it's still the most visited area of London, but with attractions that are far more wholesome. Families flock to the many galleries, museums and sights along the south bank of the river all year round, and on sunny weekends the promenade from Lambeth Bridge to Tower Bridge is busy with joggers, strollers, parents with buggies, children with bikes and skateboards and tourists clutching maps and cameras.

The area's modern incarnation as a family favourite began in the 1920s with the building of **County Hall**, now a mixed-use family entertainment centre. The Festival of Britain in 1951 led to the clearance of riverside warehouses and the construction of the Royal Festival Hall. The 1960s saw the emergence of the controversial **South Bank Centre**, while the **National Theatre** followed in the '70s. Later additions, such as **Tate Modern**, the **Design Museum** and the **London Eye**, continue to make the south bank what it was in Shakespeare's day – a place of entertainment.

A useful starting point for the first-time visitor is the Tourist Information Centre, which opened in March 2004 in the 'city of wine', Vinopolis (1 Bank End, SE1 9BU). Open 10am-6pm Tuesday to Saturday, it can be contacted on 7357 9168. It will remain here until at least March 2005, although the plan is to open a permanent tourist centre in the Millennium Bridge area. The site at Vinopolis has information on Bankside and Southwark accommodation, attractions and places of interest in the area. As well as information leaflets, the centre has a shop, a library area, toilet facilities and a coffee bar, and it will arrange attraction and travel ticketing and tours of this historic part of London.

The South Bank Marketing Group (7202 6900) can also help you find your way around with its excellent series of walking guides, entitled *Walk This Way*, which cover Riverside London, the South Bank, Bermondsey and areas north of the river accessed via the Golden Jubilee Bridge (usually still referred to as Hungerford Bridge by locals). Another good way to gauge the lie of the land is to hop on the RV1 bus, which links all the riverside attractions between Covent Garden and Tower Gateway.

The South Bank

If you're planning on seeing the delightful and tidily laid out **Museum of Garden History** to pay homage to the original Mr Greenfingers, John Tradescant, have a look at Lambeth Bridge, opposite St Mary's church. Its carved pineapple adornments are another, subtle, tribute to Mr Tradescant, whose plant-hunting habit brought the exotic fruit to England in the 16th century.

From here it's a short riverside walk east under Westminster Bridge to London's major tourist zone. Visitors have been drawn to the **British Airways London Eye** since the turn of the century, and once they've had their turn, a veritable thicket of banners announcing the **Saatchi** and **Dalí** galleries compete for attention. These galleries, together with noisy **Namco Station** and the **London Aquarium**, all attempt to fill up the huge spaces of County Hall, the former headquarters of the Greater London Council.

After paying admission for that little lot, some simpler, cheaper pleasures lie in wait in the form of the **Royal Festival Hall**, centrepiece of the South Bank Centre. There always seems to be some form of free entertainment going on in the foyer or ballroom here, especially at weekends when it seems like a vast, well-to-do crèche full of artistic yummy mummies and daddies who have brought the family along for a spot of cool jazz or half-term storytelling events and drum-banging. A weekend book market outside the **National Film Theatre** (*see p216*) attracts buskers and bargain hunters. Gabriel's Wharf, a little to the east, looks like a cutesy film set with its pastel-coloured crafty shops, friendly cafés with outdoor seating and carver Friedel Buecking's splendid wooden animals for children to play on.

BFI London IMAX Cinema

1 Charlie Chaplin Walk, SE1 8XR (7902 1234/ www.bfi.org.uk/imax). Waterloo tube/rail. **Open** 12.30-8pm Mon-Fri; 10.45am-8.45pm Sat, Sun. **Admission** £7.90; £4.95 4-15s; £6.50 concessions; add-on film £5.50 extra per adult or £3.95 extra per child; free under-4s. **Credit** AmEx, MC, V. **Map** p320 M8.
This drum-shaped 'image maximum' (IMAX) cinema, located within the roundabout at the southern end of Waterloo Bridge, contains the largest screen in the UK. The sheer size of the mechanics that make this system work is as impressive as the images you see on the screen: the projector is the size of a small house, while the visual and sound effects are enough to convince you that you're actually part of the action. The 480 seats are very steeply banked, so no one, not even a tot, has to look over anyone's head to see.

Most of the two- and three-dimensional films shown here are suitable for children or have a PG certificate, although *Matrix Revolutions* was a 15. *T-Rex: Back to the Cretaceous* continues to be a big hitter and *Bugs*, entomology writ large, is suitable for all ages. Details of changes to the programming should be available from June 2004.
Buggy access. Café. Nappy-changing facilities. Nearest picnic place: Jubilee Gardens.

British Airways London Eye

Riverside Building (next to County Hall), Westminster Bridge Road, SE1 7PB (booking line 0870 500 0600/ customer services 0870 990 8883/www.ba-londoneye.com). Westminster tube/Waterloo tube/rail. **Open** *End of Jan-Apr, Oct-Dec* 9.30am-8pm daily. *May, Sept* 9.30am-8pm Mon-Thur; 9.30am-9pm Fri-Sun. *June* 9.30am-9pm Mon-Thur; 9.30am-10pm Fri-Sun. *July, Aug* 9.30am-10pm daily. Closed 25 Dec, most of Jan. **Admission** £11.50; £9 concessions; £5.75 5-15s; free under-5s. **Credit** AmEx, DC, MC, V. **Map** p319 M8.
This giant wheel was originally intended to rotate over the Thames for five years, but it proved so popular that no one wants it to come down. It's now scheduled to keep spinning for another 20 years. The 450ft (137m) monster wheel, whose 32 glass capsules each hold 25 people, commands the best views over London. It attracts long queues in the summer, but it's worth the wait. A 'flight' (as a turn is called) takes half an hour, which gives you plenty of time to have an argument about which hill is which in south London, ogle at the Queen's back garden and follow the silver snake of the Thames. You can buy a guide to the landmarks for £2. Most people book in advance (although you take a gamble with the weather) but it is possible to turn up and queue for a same-day ticket. Night flights offer a more twinkly experience, with the bridges all lit up. The ticket office, found in the adjacent corner of County Hall, is well organised, and includes a shop and Costa Coffee outlet. You can take a buggy on board, and there is a baby carrier rental service.
Buggy access. Café. Nappy-changing facilities. Nearest picnic place: Jubilee Gardens. Shop.

Dalí Universe

County Hall (riverfront entrance), Riverside Building, Queen's Walk, SE1 7PB (7620 2720/ www.daliuniverse.com). Westminster tube/Waterloo tube/rail. **Open** 10am-5.30pm daily. Closed 25 Dec. **Tours** phone for details. **Admission** (LP) £8.50; £7 concessions; £5.50 8-16s; £3.50 4-7s; £1 under-4s; £23 family (2+2). **Credit** AmEx, DC, MC, V. **Map** p319 M8.
2004 is the centenary of Salvador Dalí's birth, so the curators at the County Hall Gallery have planned special events to mark it, including a summer programme, which was being finalised as we went to press (check the website for details).

The main exhibition, curated by long-term Dalí friend Benjamin Levi, leaves you in no doubt as to the Spanish artist's eccentricity. The wall-mounted quotes by, and (silent) videos and photographs of, Dalí give an insight into his life. There are sculptures, watercolours (including his flamboyant tarot cards), rare etchings and lithographs. Many of the works seem like artistic comedy: melting clocks, long-legged elephants, crutches, lobsters, ants and stretched buttocks casting long shadows over dream-like sunny plains.
Buggy access. Disabled access: lift. Nearest picnic place: Jubilee Gardens. Shop.

Florence Nightingale Museum

2 Lambeth Palace Road, SE1 7EW (7620 0374/ www.florence-nightingale.co.uk). Westminster tube/Waterloo tube/rail. **Open** 10am-5pm Mon-Fri; 10.30am-4.30pm Sat, Sun (last entry 1hr before closing). **Admission** (LP) £5.80; £4.20 5-18s, concessions; £13 family (2+2); free under-5s. **Credit** AmEx, MC, V. **Map** p319 M9.
This museum, tucked underneath the bulk of St Thomas's Hospital, is dedicated to the life and times of the pioneering nurse, and commemorates her birthday every 12 May. A permanent exhibition dedicated to the Lady of the Lamp marks

the 150th anniversary of Florence Nightingale's entry into the Crimea. Her nursing skills and campaigning zeal are honoured with a chronological tour through a remarkable life. Upon returning from the battlefields of Scutari she opened the Nightingale Nursing School here in St Thomas's. The rest of the space in the museum is given over to displays of mementos, clothing, furniture, books, letters and portraits dating from that period, as well as an audio-visual tribute. Free children's activities, such as art workshops, take place every other weekend; see the website or call for details.

The shop sells Florence Nightingale shopping bags, tea towels, teddy bears and stacks of books about nursing. *Buggy access. Nearest picnic place: benches by hospital entrance/Archbishop's Park. Shop. (In hospital: Café. Nappy-changing facilities. Restaurant.)*

Hayward Gallery

Belvedere Road, SE1 8XX (7960 5226/box office 7960 4242/www.hayward.org.uk). Embankment tube/Waterloo tube/rail. **Open** *During exhibitions* 11am-7pm Mon, Thur, Sat, Sun; 11am-8pm Tue, Wed; 11am-9pm Fri. **Admission** varies; phone for details. **Credit** AmEx, MC, V. **Map** p320 M8.

A new foyer extension and mirrored, elliptical glass pavilion (*Waterloo Sunset at the Hayward Gallery*) were completed in October 2003; the architects behind the scheme collaborated with American light artist Dan Graham. Inside the pavilion, casual visitors can watch cartoons on touch screens or just wander around the visually confusing space created by the curved, two-way mirrors. The neon tower on the gallery roof was commissioned by the Arts Council in 1970. Its yellow, red, green and blue tubes are controlled by changes in the direction and strength of the wind.

An exhibition of photography by Jacques Henri Lartigue (24 June to 5 Sept) will be complemented by a series of photography and portraiture workshops for children. Probably the most exciting exhibition for children this year, however, is provisionally titled 'Art of Illusion' (7 Oct 2004-2 Jan 2005). It will explore all manner of optical trickery, with a display of more than 1,000 objects, some dating back to the Renaissance, that includes magic lanterns, anamorphic images, flipbooks and kaleidoscopes. *Buggy access. Café. Disabled access: lift. Nappy-changing facilities. Nearest picnic place: Jubilee Gardens/riverside benches. Shop.*

London Aquarium

County Hall (riverfront entrance), Riverside Building, Westminster Bridge Road, SE1 7PB (7967 8000/ www.londonaquarium.co.uk). Westminster tube/Waterloo tube/rail. **Open** 10am-6pm daily (last entry 5pm). Phone for late opening during holidays. Closed 25 Dec. **Tours** (groups of 10 or more) phone for details. **Admission** (LP) £8.75; £6.50 concessions, disabled; £5.25 3-14s; £25 family (2+2); free under-3s. **Credit** MC, V. **Map** p319 M9.

Parents visiting with children hell-bent on spending as long as possible with the largest predatory fish in this darkened underwater world have to reconcile themselves to missing all the interesting information about the tidal River Thames in the mad rush to the shark tank. But the children are right, the biggest tanks are the most impressive. There's a vast one with shoals of silvery mackerel and hovering rays, and another containing the sharks, the stars of this show. The post-*Finding Nemo* generation are obsessive about the clown fish flitting about in the coral-reef section. There are touch pools, in which you can dabble your fingers to make rays and skates rise to the surface. The steamy South American rainforest area has mangrove swamps and paddling terrapins. The preponderance of visitors in buggies is testament to the aquarium's appeal for the under-fives, who stand mesmerised on the ledges by the tanks. Their enjoyment of the spectacle is unalloyed by adult guilt – is this cruel? Are the tanks too small? How short *is* a fish's memory?

In the end, however, the main deal is entertainment. You can watch sharks being fed on Tuesdays, Thursdays and Saturdays at 2.30pm; piranhas get theirs on Mondays, Wednesdays, Fridays and Sundays at 1pm. Divers descend into the Atlantic tank at noon on weekdays to feed the bottom dwellers (rays, skates, dogfish and conger eels). Talks takes place on the hour from 1pm to 4pm, on subjects including sharks and coral reefs. *Buggy access. Café. Disabled access: lift. Nappy-changing facilities. Nearest picnic place: Jubilee Gardens. Shop.*

London Fire Brigade Museum

94A Southwark Bridge Road, SE1 0EG (7587 2894/ www.london-fire.gov.uk). Borough tube/Southwark tube/rail/344 bus. **Tours** by appointment only 10.30am, 2pm Mon-Fri. Closed 25 Dec, bank hols. **Admission** £3; £2 7-14s, concessions; free under-7s, school groups. **Credit** MC, V. **Map** p320 O9.

Pit stops The South Bank

Good refuelling stops when you're at the **London Eye** or **Old County Hall** are **Azzuro** (1 Sutton Walk, SE1 7ND, 7620 1300), a cavernous pizza and pasta restaurant with a children's menu, and the lurid delights of the basic and inexpensive **Oriental Buffet** (County Hall, Westminster Bridge Road, SE1 7PB, no phone). With spring rolls for £1.60 and stir-fries from £3.50, the latter vies successfully with McDonald's for the attention of hungry tourists as they emerge from the **Aquarium**.

The **Royal Festival Hall** has a smart café restaurant, **Festival Square**, facing Waterloo Station, plus a large branch of **EAT** (7636 8309), looking over the river, that provides sandwiches, soups, salads and cakes. There are tables outside and plenty of room in the foyer for children to play.

The most splendid restaurant in the building, however, is the large-windowed **People's Palace** (*see p159*) on the third floor.

The **Film Café** (7960 3118) in the **IMAX** is good for sandwiches and snacks, while on Belvedere Road, just below the **Hayward Gallery** and its Starbucks, you'll find a **Pizza Express** (The White House, Belvedere Road, SE1 8YP, 7928 4091).

Gabriel's Wharf offers a couple of good options too. **Studio Six** (56 Upper Ground, SE1 9PP, 7928 6243) is a cocktail bar and American restaurant that lets kids share portions of steak or opt for just a bowl of chips; the **House of Crêpes** (56 Upper Ground, SE1 9PP, 7401 9816) does pancakes any which way. It is cramped inside, but in good weather there are the outside tables.

YOU'LL FIND HIM AT LONDON AQUARIUM

Have fun finding the real clown fish, not to mention several different species of sharks, including the Sand Tiger pictured. London Aquarium is full of surprises with over 350 unique underwater species to discover.

Located in County Hall and right next to the London Eye, London Aquarium is only a short walk from Waterloo Station and just over Westminster Bridge from Big Ben and the Houses of Parliament.

So don't plan time out in London without visiting London's only aquarium!
Open every day from 10am to 6pm.

For further details call **020 7967 8000**
or log on to www.londonaquarium.co.uk

LONDON
AQUARIUM

FLOOD YOUR SENSES

Raising the alarm at the **London Fire Brigade Museum**.

Visitors must book in advance for this museum about firefighting in London. Tours last roughly an hour and take in the appliance bay, where pumps dating back to 1708 stand in tribute to blazes past. Small children are given colouring pencils and encouraged to draw any of the 20 fire engines, ranging from a hand-pumped 1750s model to shiny red and brass vehicles from the early 20th century and today's streamlined marvels. Older kids can try on uniforms. Exhibits in the eight small rooms detail the history of firefighting since the Great Fire in 1666 and include uniforms, equipment and paintings, including those executed by firemen-artists recording their Blitz experiences. The museum also displays one of only three George Crosses to be awarded to firefighters.
Buggy access. Nappy-changing facilities. Nearest picnic place: Mint Street Park. Shop.

Museum of Garden History

Church of St Mary-at-Lambeth, Lambeth Palace Road, SE1 7LB (7401 8865/www.museumgardenhistory.org). Lambeth North or Westminster tube/C10, 3, 77, 344, 507 bus. **Open** *Feb-mid Dec* 10.30am-5pm daily. **Admission** free; suggested donation £3 (£2.50 concessions). **Credit** *Shop* (over £10) AmEx, MC, V. **Map** p310 L10.
Deconsecrated in 1972, St Mary's church became the world's first museum dedicated to gardening – a suitable function for a building that encompasses the tomb of the Tradescants, a pioneering family of gardeners and botanists. They brought the first pineapple to Britain. Captain William Bligh, of *Bounty* fame, is buried here, along with half a dozen Archbishops of Canterbury. The exhibits include giant seeds and gardening gear dating back centuries. Look out for the Pedlar's Window, a stained-glass window illustrating a man and his dog. History has it that an early 16th-century pedlar came into an acre of land (now the site of County Hall) and donated it to the church on condition that an image of him be preserved in glass. The current window is the fourth, made in 1956 after its predecessor was destroyed in 1941. Phone to check opening times before visiting, as the refurbished museum should be reopening from early January 2005.
Buggy access. Café. Nearest picnic place: Archbishop's Park. Shop.

Namco Station

County Hall (riverfront entrance), Westminster Bridge Road, SE1 7PB (7967 1066/www.namcostation.co.uk). Westminster tube/Waterloo tube/rail. **Open** 10am-midnight daily. Closed 25 Dec. **Admission** (LP) free; games prices vary. **Map** p319 M9.
This is one of those dark, noisy hideaways beloved of kids with spare pocket money. There are more than 200 types of video game to waste your 'Nams' on (the unit of currency used to feed them). Bumper cars, Techno Bowling and pool tables lurk downstairs (as do over-18s, who inhabit a bar tuned to the sports channel). This pleasure dome shares its entrance with McDonald's. Talk about teen paradise.
Bar. Buggy access. Disabled access: lift. Nappy-changing facilities. Nearest picnic place: Jubilee Gardens.

Royal National Theatre

South Bank, SE1 9PX (info 7452 3400/box office 7452 3000/www.nationaltheatre.org.uk). Waterloo tube/rail. **Open** 10am-11pm Mon-Sat. *Box office* 10am-8pm Mon-Sat. Closed 24, 25 Dec, Good Friday. **Tickets** *Olivier & Lyttelton* £10-£38. *Cottesloe* £10-£27. *Standby* £9, £18. *Backstage tours* £5; £4 concessions. **Credit** AmEx, DC, MC, V. **Map** p320 M8.
Sir Denys Lasdun's landmark concrete theatre complex may not look child-friendly, but it's accessible and full of bright ideas. There's a ground-floor terrace for refreshments, and free exhibitions and music are often to be found inside. The NT runs a wide range of education and activity programmes, from half-term events to school-based initiatives. Activities take place throughout the year (call 7452 3388 for details).
Backstage tours (not suitable for under-sevens) occur three times a day throughout the year, last an hour and may be booked at the information desk (£5, £4 under-18s). Tours take in the rehearsal rooms, workshops where costumes and props are made, dressing rooms and the stage, where the guide demonstrates some of the exciting items of stage machinery like the flying harnesses.
Café. Disabled access: lift. Nappy-changing facilities. Nearest picnic place: Bernie Spain Gardens. Restaurants. Shop.

Saatchi Gallery

County Hall (riverfront & Belvedere Road entrances), SE1 7PB (7823 2363/advance tickets 0870 116 0278/ www.saatchi-gallery.co.uk). Westminster tube/Waterloo tube/rail. **Open** 10am-8pm Mon-Thur, Sun; 10am-10pm Fri, Sat (group bookings by appointment). **Admission** £8.75; £6.75 concessions; £26 family (2+2); £5.25 pre-booked groups (over 10 people). **Credit** MC, V. **Map** p319 M9.

Here the work of Young British Artists (usually described as YBAs) is displayed in grand, wood-panelled Edwardian rooms that were once frequented by men in suits having meetings. Some trendy artists don't care for their work being displayed in such odd surroundings, but the public who come to see it enjoy the monumental architecture as much as the art. Advertising impresario Charles Saatchi's art collection includes notorious pieces by a young Damien Hirst (that shark remains, although Mr Hirst has taken some of the other famous pieces away), Tracey Emin (that mussed-up bed) and Marc Quinn (that creepy head made of blood). Such disturbing works are central to the permanent collection in the rotunda meeting room. Smaller spaces provide more intimate settings for individual pieces. Check the website for details of the current temporary show.

Buggy access. Nearest picnic place: Jubilee Gardens. Shop.

South Bank Centre

Belvedere Road, SE1 8XX (box office 0870 380 0400/poetry library 7921 0943/www.rfh.org.uk). Waterloo tube/rail. **Open** 11am-9pm daily (closes 8pm on non-performance evenings). Closed 25 Dec. **Admission** *Foyers* free. **Map** p319 M8.

The South Bank Centre is made up of the Royal Festival Hall, the Purcell Room and the Queen Elizabeth Hall. The RFH is the most accessible of the three, a 'people's palace' that frequently runs free lunchtime musical events. It's a pleasing place to hang out at weekends; there always seems to be something going on and the cafés are relaxed. *See also p213. Buggy access. Café. Disabled access: lifts. Nappy-changing facilities. Restaurant.*

Bankside

The area around London Bridge was the epicentre of bawdy Southwark in Shakespeare's day. Presiding over it were the Bishops of Winchester, who made a tidy income from fining the women of easy virtue who used to work round here. All that's left of the Palace of Winchester, home of successive bishops, is the rose window of the Great Hall on **Clink Street**.

The parish church during Shakespeare's time was St Saviour's, known since 1905 as **Southwark Cathedral**. It sits modestly away from the river, whereas the Millennium Bridge provides a pedestrian carriageway to the puffed-up competition across the water, namely St Paul's (*see p53*), from in front of **Tate Modern**. The wonkily ancient terrace of houses between Tate Modern and the Globe, is owned by Southwark Cathedral. Sir Christopher Wren stayed in one of them when building St Paul's.

Pit stops Bankside to Tower Bridge

If you get hungry while wandering the vast spaces of **Tate Modern**, you're in luck. The gallery's restaurant (on the second floor) is very good and has a £5.95 children's menu (7401 5014). You do often have to queue, though. A couple of pubs that welcome children during the day (you must keep kids away from the bar area, however) can be found either side of Blackfriars Bridge: **Doggett's** (1 Blackfriars Bridge, SE1 9UD, 7633 9081) has a children's menu listing tuna melt, pasta with sauce or fish and chips, and Youngs pub the **Founders' Arms** (52 Hopton Street, SE1 9JH, 7928 1899) is just fine for river views, fish and chips and roast dinners on Sunday. For great sandwiches, hot chocolate and pre-packed cakes, the Oxo Tower Wharf branch of **EAT** (Bargehouse Street, SE1 9PH, 7928 8179) is relaxed and friendly.

The smartest restaurant in the vicinity of the **Golden Hinde** is fish! (*see p158*), but for cakes and drinks you'll do well to try **Konditor & Cook** (*see p159*). **Southwark Cathedral Refectory** (Southwark Cathedral, Montague Close, SE1 9DA, 7407 5740) is a serene place for own-made cakes and daily specials, and there's a **Pizza Express** on Borough High Street (No.4, SE1 9QQ, 7407 2995). A cosy branch of **Starbucks** (Winchester Wharf, Clink Street, SE1 9DG, 7403 0951) will comfort you after you've experienced the grisly **Clink**.

There's a McDonald's on St Thomas's Street, as well as a Starbucks and a few sandwich bars. All of them handy for the **Old Operating Theatre**. Walking through London Bridge station to Tooley Street, you'll find **Auberge** (35 Tooley Street, SE1 2PJ, 7407 5267), a French brasserie with a children's menu (nuggets, bangers or fishfingers with chips, pizza, or pasta, together with a drink, for £3.50) but spectacularly slow service. Adult dishes include steaks, crevettes, moules, Toulouse sausage and tartiflette. It's well-placed to fortify you for the **Britain at War Experience**. Nearby, **London Dungeon** boasts the **Blood & Guts Café**, where £3.50 will buy a burger and chips. The rather ghosty **Hays Galleria** has sandwich bars and cafés, useful for visitors to **HMS Belfast**.

Anyone exploring the **Design Museum** is blessed by the welcome presence of cake supremos **Konditor & Cook** café and a rather too posh restaurant, but most families make a beeline for the **Pizza Express** (The Cardamon Building, 31 Shad Thames, SE1 2YR, 7403 8484). Well presented, posh brunches are available at weekends at the **Butler's Wharf Chop House** (Butler's Wharf Building, 36E Shad Thames, SE1 2YE, 7403 3403). Another Conran, **Cantina del Ponte** (*see p158*) has a children's menu of salads, pizzas, spaghetti and grilled chicken.

Bramah Museum of Tea & Coffee

40 Southwark Street, SE1 1UN (7403 5650/ www.bramahmuseum.co.uk). London Bridge tube/rail/381 bus. **Open** 10am-6pm daily. Closed 25, 26 Dec. **Admission** £4; £3.50 concessions; £3 under-14s; £10 family (2+4). **Credit** AmEx, MC, V. **Map** p310 P8.

A serene and refreshing tribute to the history of top hot beverages, this museum's displays are basic, but offer a wealth of information and forgotten tales of tea trade's power to influence the course of history. Take tea at any time in the café (you don't have to visit the museum) and enjoy a lovely cup, plus scones, muffins and cakes if you're peckish.

Buggy access. Café. Nearest picnic place: Southwark Cathedral Gardens. Shop.

Clink Prison Museum

1 Clink Street, SE1 9DG (7378 1558/www.clink.co.uk). London Bridge tube/rail. **Open** 10am-6pm Mon-Fri; 10am-8pm Sat, Sun. Closed 25 Dec. **Tours** hourly when available. **Admission** £4; £3 5-15s, concessions; £9 family (2+2); free under-5s. *Tours* £2. **Credit** DC, MC, V. **Map** p320 P8.

Signing a new lease in 2003 meant this prison museum can continue to hang its caged rotting corpse effigy outside for the next 15 years, which is good news for fans of the macabre, as the Clink was at one time threatened with extinction. The exhibition looks behind the bars of the hellish prison known as 'the Clink', which was owned by the Bishops of Winchester from the 12th to the 18th centuries. Thieves, prostitutes and debtors served their sentences within its walls. On display for the 'hands-on' experience are torture devices and the iron fetters whose clanking gave the prison its name. The museum does not take long to walk through, but several audio stories from inmates make you linger by the waxworks.

Buggy access. Nearest picnic place: Southwark Cathedral Gardens. Shop.

Golden Hinde

St Mary Overie Dock, Cathedral Street, SE1 9DE (0870 011 8700/shop 7407 7056/www.goldenhinde.co.uk). Monument tube/London Bridge tube/rail. **Open** daily, times vary; phone for details. Closed 25 Dec. **Admission** £3.50; £3 concessions; £2.50 5-16s; £10 family (2+3); free under-4s. **Credit** AmEx, MC, V. **Map** p321 P8.

This beautifully made replica of Sir Francis Drake's 16th-century flagship was built in 1973 to commemorate the admiral-pirate's 400th birthday, after which it sailed to San Francisco. The main gun deck can't be more than 3ft (0.9m) high. The present 'crew' are actors who dress up and shout a lot. Weekends see the ship swarming with pirate children, as the birthday party service (*see p250*) is as popular as ever. When it hasn't been taken over by cutlass-wielding youths, the five levels, recreated in minute detail, are fascinating to explore, but there can be no doubt that most of its income comes from its child-friendliness. 'Living History Experiences' are hugely popular with schools and groups, all of whom have to book ahead to live the Tudor life at sea. From May to September, families can book on 'Living History' overnighters (bring sleeping bags). These take place on a Friday and cost £34 per child or adult, costumes and entertainment provided.

Nearest picnic place: Southwark Cathedral Gardens/ riverside benches. Shop.

HMS Belfast

Morgan's Lane, Tooley Street, SE1 2JH (7940 6300/ www.iwm.org.uk). Tower Hill tube/London Bridge tube/rail. **Open** *Mar-Oct* 10am-6pm daily. *Nov-Feb* 10am-5pm daily. Last entry 45mins before closing. **Admission** (LP) £7; £5 concessions; free under-16s (must be accompanied by an adult). **Credit** MC, V. **Map** p321 R8.

The expectation of high adventure beckons children to this 11,500-ton World War II battlecruiser, now floating peace-

HMS Belfast.

Tales from... the Old Operating Theatre

Back in the early 19th century the result of merely breaking a leg could be a horrific amputation – that is, if you wanted to avoid a slow and painful death. If you were unlucky enough to have been brought to St Thomas's Hospital, near London Bridge, for emergency treatment, you were highly likely to end up enduring both.

This grim fact is explained to visitors during one of the most popular school-holiday events at the **Old Operating Theatre, Museum & Herb Garret** (*see below*). The Victorian Surgery demonstration, usually played to a fascinated – and slightly nauseated – capacity audience in the tiered seating surrounding the theatre floor, really brings home the horrors of early surgical practices.

The visitors take the role of students, packing out the theatre in 1822 to witness an operation. A volunteer is sought by one of the museum's curatorial staff, who is giving the talk in the guise of a surgeon. The victim... er, volunteer is asked to lie down on the original chipped and stained operating table, scene of hundreds of bleedings, cuppings, slicings and trepannings over the years, while the 'surgeon' dons a shockingly soiled apron, described with relish as 'stiff with blood and pus'. Old blood stains apparently used to reassure

patients, as it showed the surgeon had done this sort of thing before. Our patient, we learn, has been knocked down by a horse and carriage on busy Borough High Street and sustained an open fracture to the leg. This had become infected, necessitating a stay in hospital. This was the last thing any potential patients would have wanted in 1822, because so few people came out alive after the surgeon's ministrations. Cleaning their instruments or washing their hands, let alone their aprons, was not considered a priority by 19th-century surgeons. But holding down the patient was. This is pre-anaesthesia, after all. Once the speaker has shown everyone the tools of the amputator's trade – a tourniquet, the evil slicing knife, a bone saw and one stomach-turning little instrument for chipping off stubborn nubs of bone – she can take up the correct position and make the first incision. Her volunteer looks worried for an instant before she lets him go.

With the operation over, we medical students are free to wander round the museum and garret, blanching at speculums and vices, sniffing musty, ground herbal purgatives and poultices, and feverishly sending up a grateful prayer for 21st-century surgical procedures.

---

fully on the Thames between Tower Bridge and London Bridge. Guided tours take in all nine decks, from the bridge to the boiler room, visiting the galley, sick bay, dentist, NAAFI canteen, mess deck and the permanent exhibition entitled 'HMS *Belfast* in War and Peace'. Films, photos and quiz sheets enhance the experience. What kids really want to see are the guns that destroyed the German battleship *Scharnhorst* in 1943 and supported the D-Day landing a year later. There's usually a queue to climb into the port deck Bofors gun, which enthusiasts can swivel, elevate and aim.

The 'kip in a ship' experience is for groups of up to 50 children (schools and youth groups usually book these), who get to sleep in the original sailors' bunks for up to three days. Accompanying adults take the officers' cabins. School holidays bring a wealth of ship-based activities, often artistic, such as making your own medals for extreme bravery. Check the website for a calendar of events, but, as workshops are free, you could just drop in and see what's up. *Café. Nappy-changing facilities. Nearest picnic place: Potters Field. Shop.*

London Dungeon

28-34 Tooley Street, SE1 2SZ (7403 7221/ www.thedungeons.com). London Bridge tube/rail/35, 40, 133 bus. **Open** *Apr-mid July, 6 Sept-Oct* 10am-5.30pm daily. *Mid July-5 Sept* 10am-7.30pm daily. *Nov-Mar* 10am-5pm daily. Closed 25 Dec. **Admission** £12.95; £11.25 concessions; £9.95 5-15s; £2 reduction for wheelchair users, carers free; free under-5s. **Credit** AmEx, MC, V. **Map** p321 Q8.

Gluttons for punishment queue along Tooley Street in their hundreds for this world of torture, death and disease under the railway arches. Once inside, they file through a dry-ice fog past gravestones and hideously rotting corpses. Screeches and horror-movie soundtracks add to the experience. There

is plenty to offend. White-faced visitors experience nasty symptoms from the Great Plague exhibition: an actor-led medley of corpses, boils, projectile vomiting, worm-filled skulls and scuttling rats. Then there are the Wicked Women, the brutal lady leaders such as Boudicca, Anne Boleyn and Queen Elizabeth I. Telly's Anne Robinson gets a mention. Other hysterical revisions of horrible London history include the Great Fire and, revamped for 2004, the Traitor Boat Ride to Hell, in which visitors play the part of condemned prisoners (death sentence guaranteed). A 'seriously, folks' notice on the wall at the exit remarks that torture is still widespread in many parts of the world. More horrors await in the shop (severed fingers, bulgy eyeballs, fake blood). There's no lower age limit for access to all this, but those of a nervous disposition are advised to steer well clear. *Buggy access. Café. Nappy-changing facilities. Nearest picnic place: Hay's Galleria. Shop.*

Old Operating Theatre, Museum & Herb Garret

9A St Thomas's Street, SE1 9RY (7955 4791/ www.thegarret.org.uk). London Bridge tube/rail. **Open** 10.30am-5pm daily (last entry 4.45pm). Closed 15 Dec-5 Jan. **Admission** (LP) £4.25; £3.25 concessions; £2.50 6-16s; £11 family (2+4); free under-6s. **No credit cards**. **Map** p321 Q8.

Climb the spiral stairs in the ancient church of St Thomas to find a 300-year-old herb garret and Britain's only surviving 19th-century operating theatre. This was used between 1821 and 1862, before being boarded up and forgotten about until 1957. Displays of hideous instruments, bits of organs in formaldehyde and a scary child-size operating table are set out alongside bunches and jars of dried herbs in the atmospheric old room. An exhibition all about the Evelina Children's Hospital, formerly of Southwark Bridge Road,

Full throttle at **London Dungeon**. **See p43**.

demonstrates how pitifully long it took the adult world to decide that the health of children was worth worrying about. *See also p43* **Tales from… the Operating Theatre**. *Nearest picnic place: Southwark Cathedral Gardens. Shop.*

Shakespeare's Globe Exhibition

21 New Globe Walk, Bankside, SE1 9DT (7902 1500/ www.shakespeares-globe.org). Mansion House or Southwark tube/London Bridge tube/rail. **Open** *Oct-Apr* 10am-5pm daily. *May-Sept* Exhibition & Globe theatre tour 9am-noon daily; Exhibition & Rose theatre tour 12.30-5pm daily. **Admission** *Oct-Apr* £8; £6.50 concessions; £5.50 5-15s; £24 family (2+3); free under-5s. *Mid May late Sept* £8.50; £7 concessions; £6 5-16s; free under-5s. **Credit** AmEx, MC, V. **Map** p320 O7.

This is a reconstruction of the Bard's own theatre, the 'wooden O' referred to in *Henry V*, built only 100 yards from where the original stood. The project was masterminded and paid for by the actor Sam Wanamaker, who died before it was finished. Visitors can enjoy tours of the theatre all year round, although the historically authentic performances only run from May to September. This season is all star-cross'd lovers: *Romeo and Juliet*, *Much Ado About Nothing* and *Measure for Measure*. For more on education and workshops, *see p224*.

The remains of the Rose Theatre (56 Park Street, SE1 9AR, 7902 1500) lie around the corner in the basement of an office block. The Rose was where many of Shakespeare's early works were performed (he probably even acted in them). *Buggy access. Café. Nappy-changing facilities. Nearest picnic place: Southwark Cathedral Gardens. Restaurant. Shop.*

Southwark Cathedral

London Bridge, SE1 9DA (7367 6700/tours 7367 6734/ www.dswark.org/cathedral). London Bridge tube/rail. **Open** from 8am daily (closing times vary). *Restaurant* 10am-5pm daily. Closed 25 Dec, Good Friday. *Services*

8am, 8.15am, 12.30pm, 12.45pm, 5.30pm Mon-Fri; 9am, 9.15am, 4pm Sat; 8.45am, 9am, 11am, 3pm, 6.30pm Sun. *Shop* 10am-6pm Mon-Sat; 11am-5pm Sun. Closed Good Friday, Easter Sunday, 25 Dec. **Admission** (LP) *Audio tour* £2.50; £2 OAPs; £1.25 under-16s, students. **Credit** AmEx, MC, V. **Map** p321 P8.

This partly ancient building (once St Saviour's church, it has only been a cathedral since 1905) has an interactive museum, the Long View of London, a shop and a refectory. The church, which dates back to the 13th century, is a historian's treasure trove. As well as more recent memorials – including one for the 51 victims of the *Marchioness* riverboat tragedy – there are memorials to Shakespeare (whose brother Edmund is buried here), John Gower (arguably the first English poet) and John Harvard, benefactor of Harvard University. Children are drawn to the scary tomb in the chancel: it's topped by a stone carving of an emaciated body in a shroud. The windows contain images of Chaucer, who set off on pilgrimage to Canterbury from a pub in Borough High Street, and John Bunyan, who preached locally. *Buggy access. Disabled access: lifts. Nappy-changing facilities. Nearest picnic place: gardens. Restaurant. Shop.*

Tate Modern

Bankside, SE1 9TG (7887 8000/www.tate.org.uk). St Paul's tube/Blackfriars tube/rail. **Open** *Galleries* 10am-6pm Mon-Thur, Sun; 10am-10pm Fri, Sat. Last admission 45mins before closing. Closed 24-26 Dec. **Admission** free (charge for special exhibitions). **Map** p320 O7.

Visiting this former power station, with its awesome volumes of space, is an event in itself. The architects who converted it left relics of the building's industrial days – the original gantries and lifting gear in the vast Turbine Hall, where the Unilever Series of large-scale commissions are displayed, changing each year. The next artist commissioned for this series is Bruce Naumann, whose work will be unveiled on 28 October 2004 and remain on view until 28 March 2005.

Pieces bound to appeal to kids include Cornelia Parker's *Cold Dark Matter* (the contents from an exploded shed); Sam Taylor-Wood's *Still Life*, which uses time-lapse photography to show the putrefaction process in a bowl of fruit; and Mark Dion's *Thames Dig*, which comprises excavated objects from the banks of the Thames. All are on Level 3. (For details of activities, *see below* **Playtime at... Tate Modern**.) *Café. Disabled access: lifts. Nappy-changing facilities. Nearest picnic place: grounds. Restaurant. Shops.*

Winston Churchill's Britain at War Experience

64-6 Tooley Street, SE1 2TF (7403 3171/ www.britainatwar.co.uk). London Bridge tube/rail. **Open** *Apr-Sept* 10am-5.30pm daily. *Oct-Mar* 10am-4.30pm daily. Last entry 30mins before closing. Closed 24-26 Dec. **Admission** £8.50; £5.50 concessions; £4.50 5-16s; £18 family (2+2); free under-5s. **Credit** AmEx, MC, V. **Map** p321 Q8.

'The adventure of war torn London' is a testament to the austerity of life during the Blitz. Displays and set pieces take in a BBC broadcasting room, a pub and even a burning street, with battered, pyjama-clad legs poking out of the rubble – the whole effect is staged to make you feel the action happened just moments before and is rather chilling. Occasional workshops and displays take place during school holidays and, at any time, children can have a go at the Britain at War quiz sheets or try on a variety of wartime hats and uniforms in the dressing-up corner. *Buggy access. Nearest picnic place: Southwark Cathedral Gardens/William Curtis Park. Shop.*

Tower Bridge & Bermondsey

On the walk from London Bridge to Tower Bridge, you pass City Hall, the rented home of the current London government. The rotund glass structure

Playtime at... Tate Modern

A gallery as vast, diverse and, well, modern as **Tate Modern** (*see p45*), can be a bit daunting. Where should you start? The answer is in Studio C, on the third floor. This is where, on Sundays, families get stuck into the aptly named Start, a cleverly thought-out and impressively equipped art project aimed at children aged from five, but of interest to have-a-go artists of all ages. And, like the best things in life, it's free.

Kicking off in the bright pink and green studio with a friendly introduction to the fun from young Tate-modish men and women, Start has plenty to keep a child occupied. There are several activities to choose from. The double-sided puzzles are good fun: you try to piece them together while seated in front of a painting, then make links to other images found around the gallery using clues from line drawings.The final puzzle is working out why the gallery curators chose to arrange the works in the order they did. Those children who like playing

detective opt for the 'Tate Toolbox', which leads children to particular works of sculpture. The Toolbox is divided into many different drawers, some of which contain names of artists and others a series of clues in pictures, materials and writing. It's up to the player to decide how to match up all the elements in the toolbox using instructions and a map, but beware! there are a few red herrings. The third option, and our particular favourite, is called Picturing Landscape. It consists of a handsome art briefcase, containing oil pastels, stencils, graphite for sketching, and interesting colours and shapes to help you experiment with different artistic styles. A set of colour-coded cards and some instructions lead you around specific galleries as part of the exploration.

At first this may all seem rather complicated and arty-farty. When the assistant has issued you with the instructions and set you loose in the gallery, it seems pretty unlikely young children will stick to the detailed regime. Indeed, many children do start Start a little confused, but they soon become intrigued as they set to work feverishly sketching, then investigating the artists' techniques and visions of the material world. The activities take place mainly in the galleries called 'Landscape, Matter and the Environment' or 'Still Life'. With their instructions and sketchbooks in hand, adults and children can map the galleries and develop a more intimate relationship with the pieces their games lead them to. We can think of few better ways for a five-year-old to spend her Sunday morning than working on a view of St Paul's in the style of Matisse (*pictured*). Those artistic under-fives who want to join the fun are given their own activity books to draw, or scribble, in.

Start is just one of the ways that the education department at Tate Modern makes gallery-visiting fun, there are Tate Tales and Tate trails to get involved with, too; check the website for details.

leans away from the river to prevent it casting shade on the walkers below. There are regular exhibitions and a maquette of the proposed Nelson Mandela statue on the ground floor, a café on the lower ground floor and a pleasant outdoor amphitheatre for lunch breaks and sunbathing.

Just near Tower Bridge a noticeboard announces when the bridge will next open for tall ships to pass through (it does so about 500 times a year). The original steam-driven hydraulic machinery, designed by Horace Jones and John Wolfe Barry to lift the 'bascules' (the bits that go up), can be seen at the **Tower Bridge Exhibition**, although the lifting gear has been run by electricity since 1976.

Further east is the **Design Museum**. It's on Shad Thames, the main thoroughfare behind the wharves. Here, in days long gone, dockworkers unloaded tea, coffee and spices to be stored in warehouses (now expensive apartments and offices).

Up past the Design Museum, across Jamaica Road and down Tanner Street, is historic Bermondsey Street, site of Zandra Rhodes's **Fashion & Textile Museum**. Nearby, St Saviour's Dock was a place of execution for pirates. Once this part of Bermondsey was all slime-filled tidal ditches surrounding a nasty neighbourhood called Jacob's Island. Charles Dickens was so appalled by conditions here that he chose it as a place for the evil Bill Sykes to meet his end in *Oliver Twist*.

Design Museum

28 Shad Thames, SE1 2YD (7403 6933/ www.designmuseum.org). Tower Hill tube/London Bridge tube/rail/47, 100, 188 bus. **Open** 10am-5.45pm daily (last entry 5.15pm). **Admission** £6; £4 5-15s, concessions; £16 family (2+2); free under-5s. **Credit** AmEx, MC, V. **Map** p321 S9.

Once a warehouse, this elegant white building is now a fine container for exhibitions devoted to design in all its forms. Outside the main building, the Design Museum Tank is a little outdoor gallery of constantly changing installations by leading contemporary designers; it also offers a taster of exhibitions within the museum. The main space has oft-changing temporary shows. Upcoming exhibitions include 'The History of Modern Design in the Home' (until 5 Sept), which covers everything from the anglepoise lamp to the iPod, and the annual 'Designer of the Year' (Mar-June 2005), a celebration of the diversity of the UK's design talent.

Every child visiting the Design Museum is given a free Design Action Pack with observation and creativity exercises, including treasure trails of exhibits and a 'Spot the Building' game to identify the architectural landmarks that are visible from the riverfront terrace (among them Foster's 'Gherkin' and Rogers' Lloyd's Building). The Design Museum's acclaimed programme of children's creativity workshops – design-and-make sessions for six- to 12-year-olds – run on Saturdays and Sundays from 2pm to 5pm. The workshops, which are often run by leading designers (hat maker Philip Treacy and leather designer Bill Amberg were recent sell-out successes), are hugely popular so book well ahead; they're free with the admission price. During the summer holidays this year there are kite-making and -flying

The open spaces of **Tate Modern**. *See p45.*

activities (July) and mask-making workshops for the carnival season (Aug). September sees Move It! – animation workshops inspired by Saul Bass to complement an exhibition that runs until the end of the month – and, as part of the Campaign for Drawing's Big Draw 2004 initiative, October's Pencil Power – offering drawing activities for all the family. Marc Newson's wonderful model flying-machines are inspiration for November's workshops, and December is all about pop-up Christmas cards and decorations using a range of paper engineering techniques. Additional Kids' Creativity Workshops are run on Wednesdays during school holidays. *Buggy access. Café. Nappy-changing facilities. Nearest picnic place: Butler's Wharf riverside benches. Restaurant. Shop.*

Fashion & Textile Museum

83 Bermondsey Street, SE1 3XF (7403 0222/ www.ftmlondon.org). London Bridge tube/rail. **Open** 10am-4.45pm Tue-Sat; noon-4.45pm Sun. **Admission** £6; £4 concessions, 5 16s; £16 family (2+2); free under-5s. **Credit** MC, V. **Map** p321 Q8.

Just like the flamboyant fashion designer who dreamed it up, this pink and orange museum stands out like a beacon among the grey streets of south London. It's the first exhibition space in the UK dedicated to the global fashion industry. The grand foyer, with its jewel-inlaid floor, leads to a long gallery and exhibition hall. The core collection comprises 3,000 garments donated by Zandra Rhodes, along with her archive collection of paper designs and sketchbooks, silk screens, finished textiles, completed garments and show videos. Check the website for details of temporary exhibitions and of children's fashion-illustration courses (Mondays and school holidays). Museum staff aim to celebrate Children's Art Day (3 July) with some creative weekend workshops. *Buggy access. Disabled access: lift. Nearest picnic space: Bermondsey Playground/Leathermarket Gardens. Shop.*

The City

Money talks and tourists listen.

Tourists flock to the City, lured by dated images of bowler hats, pinstripe suits and essential Englishness. Londoners rarely visit unless they work in the area. While the Square Mile is bustling with business during the week, it becomes something of a ghost town at weekends when an unnatural and eerie calm descends on pristine swept streets. Visiting midweek, you'll be caught up in the bustle of commerce and probably feel very much the outsider in this self-contained financial world – but weekends offer a more chilled-out environment in which to take note of imposing architecture and historical sites. It's not the capital's best place for children by a long shot, but despite the grown-up atmosphere, there's a surprisingly wide choice of activities and attractions for kids.

Keep in mind that what is now known as 'the Square Mile' once encompassed the whole of London; the remains of Londinium's defences – impressively thick walls built by the Romans in AD 200 to keep out barbarians – can still be seen around Tower Hill and at London Wall. The **Tower of London**, a royal palace as well as being a fortress, vies with **St Paul's Cathedral** as the prime example of man-made magnificence hereabouts. On a smaller scale, the tiny, winding alleyways often lead to hidden surprises: a bomb site made into a garden, an ancient church lit by candles, or a row of higgledy-piggledy Tudor houses worthy of a chocolate box. In bad weather, the **Museum of London** is arguably the best free day out for families in the whole of London. In sunshine, outside trading hours, it's possible to cycle with quite young children around the City from one historic site to another, so sparse is the traffic.

Bank of England Museum

Entrance on Bartholomew Lane, EC2R 8AH (7601 5545/cinema bookings 7601 3951/www.bankofengland. co.uk). Bank tube/DLR. **Open** 10am-5pm Mon-Fri. Closed bank hols. **Admission** free; £1 audio guide. **Map** p321 Q6.

An awesome architectural monument, the Bank of England towers above pedestrians like the temple of Mammon it is. The banking hall brings to life the personal nature of banking in times gone by, with its bewigged mannequins in period costume and thick wooden counters. Part of this room is a gift shop, where fun souvenirs such as chocolate coins, mugs announcing 'I Love Money' and feather inkpens can be picked up. In the Rotunda, you can sit and watch a film about the bank's origins in 1694 – a predictable tale of monarchs in debt and modest burghers roped in to finance a war with France. But the story of the way paper money eventually replaced gold is fascinating, and there are enough interactive exhibits to keep children happy. Dummies move and speak as you pass; a hand-engraved printing plate for £50 notes can be examined with a magnifying glass for discrepancies; a touch-screen explains the origin of different features of British banknotes, and the replica dealing desk is fun for those who understand what it's all about. Children can fill out age-specific activity sheets (suitable for ages five to eight, nine to 12 and 13 to 16). Most popular of all is a glass case with a hole into which visitors insert a hand and try to lift the gold bar enclosed therein. Its value fluctuates daily (roughly £92,000 as we went to press), but its weight – 28lb (12.7kg) – constantly surprises young and old.
Buggy access. Disabled: lift, toilet. Nappy-changing facilities. Nearest picnic place: St Paul's Cathedral Garden. Shop.

Barbican Centre

Silk Street, EC2Y 8DS (7638 4141/box office 7638 8891/ www.barbican.org.uk). Barbican tube/Moorgate tube/rail. **Open** *Box office* 10am-8pm Mon-Sat; noon-8pm Sun. **Admission** free; phone for details of ticket prices for events. **Credit** AmEx, MC, V. **Map** p320 P5.

The architecture – labyrinthine walkways, blank tower blocks and an unappetising façade of discoloured concrete – may be off-putting, but the range of cultural offerings is vast. Familiarity may breed content: there are pockets of calm, even beauty, among them the inner courtyard with its summer fountains; the conservatory (open to the public on Sunday afternoons) with its exotic plants and lazy koi carp; the library, with its extensive children's section. And you can still see parts of the Roman walls on which the Barbican (originally a fortified watch tower) was built.

The Barbican Art Gallery reopened in April 2004, after a refurbishment, with a retrospective of Helen Chadwick's work and a show of modernist Mexican photography, both continuing until August 2004. Scheduled for later in 2004 is a show of post-1960s British independent graphic design. Check the website for details of family workshops.

The best kid-related reasons to visit are the Saturday morning Cinema Club, the Family Concerts given by the resident London Symphony Orchestra and the holiday activities. To join the Family News mailing list and find out more about LSO and Barbican projects for children, call 7382 2333 or email kcox@barbican.org.uk.
Bars. Buggy access. Cafés. Disabled access: lift, toilet. Nappy-changing facilities. Nearest picnic place: Barbican Lakeside Terrace. Restaurants. Shops.

Broadgate Arena

Broadgate Circle, EC2A 2BQ (7505 4068/ www.broadgateestates.co.uk). Liverpool Street tube/rail. **Open** *Mid Oct-mid Apr* noon-2.30pm, 3.30-6pm Mon-Thur; noon-2.30pm, 3.30-6pm, 7-10pm Fri; 11am-1pm, 2-4pm, 5-8.30pm Sat; 11am-1pm, 2-4pm, 5-7pm Sun. *From mid Apr* ring for details. **Admission** £7; £4 under-16s. **No credit cards. Map** p321 Q5.

The smallest and least expensive of London's three outdoor winter skating rinks (the other two are at Marble Arch and Somerset House, *see p259*) has a circular form, surrounded

Tales from... The Tower of London

If you can brave the queues and afford the hefty entrance fees, the **Tower of London** (*see p56*) has lots of tales to tell. Legends run rife at this royal fortress, many of which concern the notorious ravens that still inhabit the grounds. Tradition, as decreed by Charles II, says that if fewer than six remain, both Tower and monarchy will fall. Today seven ravens live next to the Wakefield Tower (an extra one for luck) and they are looked after by a Raven Master, who clips their wings to prevent them from escaping. Despite this, the birds can be quite unruly and have been known to seek sustenance outside the Tower grounds (they like to eat television aerials). They've even been spotted in nearby pubs. Ravens can live to a ripe old age, with some of the Tower's current flock in their late twenties. The birds are meat eaters and rumour has it that they used to have a taste for prisoners' eyeballs, so take note of the prominent signs warning that they may bite.

The Tower's many tales are regularly recounted by costumed guards and courtiers who roam the grounds holding forth and inviting questions from children. There's also an extensive programme of dramas devised to coincide with half-terms and holiday periods. Brutal tales of torture and bloodshed are always thrilling, and children delight in the story of the man who stole the Crown Jewels in 1671, enjoying the challenge of coming up with suitable punishments for him ('Throw him in the Thames!', 'Chop off his head!'). August 2004 brings 'Murder Mystery at the Bloody Tower', a month of interactive crime-solving events focusing on the Princes in the Tower, last seen in 1483. What could have become of them? Participants are invited to play detective – inspect the crime scene, interview suspects and hunt for clues – before casting their votes on the culprit's identity.

For October half-term there's 'Escape from the Tower' – an interactive escape trail that takes in the exploits of successful (and less successful) jailbreakers over the centuries. Stuntmen are on hand to recreate some of the more dangerous escape methods and children are encouraged to enact their own getaways by outwitting guards and employing props such as disguises, coins, knotted bedsheets and wine. Then, in December, it's back in time to 1098 to celebrate a Norman Christmas with King Henry I and his court, as they enjoy a slap-up feast in their new Thames-side tower.

by a sort of amphitheatre of offices and shops in Broadgate Circle. If you are prepared to support the kids in their first, clinging experience of the ice, skates available here range from child's size six. From April to October the rink is dismantled to make space for various corporate events, outdoor drama and music – call for details.
Buggy access. Disabled access: lift, ramp, toilet. Nearest picnic place: Finsbury Circus.

College of Arms

Queen Victoria Street, EC4V 4BT (7248 2762/ www.college-of-arms.gov.uk). Mansion House tube/Blackfriars tube/rail. **Open** 10am-4pm Mon-Fri. Closed bank hols. **Tours** by arrangement 6.30pm Mon-Fri; prices vary. **Admission** free. **Map** p320 O7.
This beautiful 17th-century house with heraldic gates in red, black and gold can be seen as you wander over the Thames across the Millennium footbridge that connects Tate Modern and the South Bank to St Paul's. The college occasionally holds temporary exhibitions, but the more serious business carried on here is the granting of arms by royal heralds to modern knights and the tracing of family lineages. You can get help with your own family tree by making an appointment, to which you should bring along as much genealogical information as possible; a fee is charged for the work according to how long it is expected to take.
Buggy access. Nearest picnic place: St Paul's Cathedral Garden. Shop.

Dr Johnson's House

17 Gough Square, off Fleet Street, EC4A 3DE (7353 3745/www.drjohnsonshouse.org). Chancery Lane or Temple tube/Blackfriars tube/rail. **Open** May-Sept 11am-5.30pm Mon-Sat. *Oct-Apr* 11am-5pm Mon-Sat. Closed 24-26 Dec, 1 Jan, bank hols. **Tours** by arrangement; groups of 10 or more only. **Admission** £4.50; £3.50 concessions; £1.50 under-18s; free under-10s; £10 family (2+unlimited children). *Tours* £3.50. *Evening tours* by appointment only. **No credit cards. Map** p320 N6.
Few tourists are aware of this immaculately restored Georgian house, once home to Samuel Johnson, the lexicographer famous for his love of the capital ('When a man is tired of London, he is tired of life'). The house can be found via a maze of alleyways off Fleet Street, while Gough Square is a pedestrianised backwater containing a statue of the good doctor's cat. Dr Johnson's house will appeal to young students of literature and lovers of old buildings; make sure you read the information sheets quoting Johnson's gossipy views and peruse the pictures of his friends – a motley lot of Christians, tarts and 'decayed tradesmen'. Highlights include a video, an 18th-century gout stool and a model of a toy workshop.
Buggy access. Nearest picnic place: Lincoln's Inn Fields/the Temple. Shop.

Guildhall

Corporation of London, PO Box 270, EC2P 2EJ (7606 3030/tours 7606 3030 ext 1463/ www.corpoflondon.gov.uk). Bank tube/DLR. **Open** May-Sept 10am-5pm daily. *Oct-Apr* 10am-5pm Mon-Sat. Last entry 4.30pm. Closed 25, 26 Dec, 1 Jan. **Tours** by arrangement; groups of 10 or more people only. **Admission** free. **Map** p320 P6.
The Guildhall survived both the Great Fire of London and the Blitz, making it the only structure (not counting the churches) in the City to date back to before 1666. Now it's the seat of local government and the Court of Common Council

Playtime at... the Museum of London

Where might you meet a 1920s cabaret singer, a Roman soldier, a Victorian street seller or a Tudor innkeeper? Or learn 19-century dances, silk weaving, Victorian knot techniques and Roman cooking skills? On weekends, there's no knowing who you might run into or what you might end up doing at the **Museum of London** (*see p53*). A special drama and storytelling programme runs alongside the museum's permanent and changing exhibitions, and every week colourful characters from London's past come alive to tell their stories. Glamorous cabaret singer Hilda Mae (originally from South Carolina but decamped to 1920s Regent's Park) will have you doing the Charleston while she gossips about nightclubs and reveals what she loves most about our city. Other characters include Abdul Miah, a fireman who describes working on the steam ship that brings tea from Calcutta; maidservant Martia Marina with the lowdown on serving in a wealthy Roman household; and nurse Mary Seacole, who tells of treating soldiers wounded in the Crimean War. Hear their stories, admire their costumes and ask questions about life in past times. Performances happen several times a day and have an impromptu feel, as actors casually appear in the exhibition space and interact with audiences.

As well as character performances, there's a programme of workshops inviting you to learn forgotten skills such as how to make your own soap, how to tie knots like the Victorians or how to decorate a Bronze Age sword. There are also object handling sessions (touch some everyday objects from different periods of history), tasting sessions (Roman food, anyone?), poetry sessions and opportunities to play musical instruments from around the world. Detailed monthly programmes are available from the museum or online.

Other playful attractions for children include a series of worksheets designed to be filled in as you tour the museum, with questions on the exhibits, wordgames and space to draw pictures. The ever-popular Victorian Walk recreates an aesthetically pleasing Victorian shopping street and a worksheet takes you on a guided tour, letting you into the mysteries of pawnbroking while you look for items on your assigned shopping list.

Programmes for summer 2004 include a season of Roman, medieval and Victorian games, where visitors are invited to try out old-fashioned board games and get involved in some sporting challenges. A series of Great Fire events are scheduled for Sundays and special activities take place throughout the school holidays.

It's a 311-step scamper to view a transformed cityscape from the top of **The Monument**.

meets at 1pm on various Thursdays each month in the 15th-century Great Hall (visitors are welcome; phone for dates).

You can visit the Hall when it is not being used for official business. It's a big, empty space with a vaulted ceiling and marble monuments, but there's little inside to inspire children other than two wooden statues of Gog and Magog on the West Gallery. These giants represent the mythical conflict between Britons and Trojan invaders; the result of this struggle was the founding of Albion's capital city, New Troy, on whose site London is said to stand. Visits to the Guildhall's enormous medieval crypt are allowed only in the context of group tours. Of more immediate appeal is a little room beyond the library devoted to a collection of watches, clocks and marine chronometers belonging to the Worshipful Company of Clockmakers. Arrive just before the hour for an enchanting sequence of chimes, tunes and strikes, or simply gaze in awe at the beautiful gold cases – often set with precious stones or enamelled – of watches whose innards are proudly exposed. The 700 exhibits include a silver skull watch said to have belonged to Mary Queen of Scots, the wristwatch worn by Edmund Hillary during his ascent of Mount Everest and tiny, quirky watch keys.
Buggy access. Disabled access: toilet.

Guildhall Art Gallery

Guildhall Yard, off Gresham Street, EC2P 2EJ (7332 3700/www.guildhall art-gallery.org.uk). Mansion House or St Paul's tube/Bank tube/DLR/Moorgate tube/rail/8, 25, 242 bus. **Open** 10am-5pm Mon-Sat (last entry 4.30pm); noon-4pm Sun (last entry 3.45pm). Closed 24-26 Dec, 1 Jan. **Admission** £2.50; £1 concessions; free under-16s. Free to all after 3.30pm daily, all day Fri. **Credit** (£5 minimum) MC, V. **Map** p320 P6.
This high-class but under-frequented gallery allows families ample crowd-free opportunities to see famous artworks as glowing originals. The collection – like its owners – now seems pretty conservative, but when the gallery opened in the 19th century its daring exhibitions of work by the Pre-Raphaelites earned it a certain glam notoriety. Start in the basement and you'll see works by Dante Gabriel Rossetti, Holman Hunt, Tissot and others, their lush photographic detail a feast for the eyes of any visitor enthralled by frocks, furs and fab complexions. A diptych by Millais (*First and*

Second Sermon) is just one of the paintings of children – this one illustrating the soporific effects of church attendance. Amen to that. Of the 250 works on display, highlights include a cluster of paintings of London dating from the 17th century to the present: pubs in Peckham, Chelsea pensioners and pre-war coppers all get a showing.

Even if the art leaves you cold, don't leave without popping down to the Roman amphitheatre, discovered in 1988 after 2,000 years of neglect and excavated over several years. Completed in 1998, the excavation secured a protective environment for the impressive remains, which have been open to the public ever since. Sections of stone wall are all that remain, but these have had an atmospheric makeover with eerie lighting, glowing mesh figures and a soundtrack evoking the thrills and spills of gladiatorial combat.

School groups visit free and teachers receive a pack in advance, detailing themes that accord with the National Curriculum. A small shop at the entrance has a selection of remarkably inexpensive prints and stationery.
Buggy access. Disabled access: lift, toilet. Nearest picnic place: grassy area by London Wall. Shop.

The Monument
Monument Street, EC3R 8AH (7626 2717). Monument tube. **Open** 9.30am-5pm daily. Closed 24-26 Dec, 1 Jan. **Admission** £2; £1 5 15s; free under-5s. **No credit cards. Map** p321 Q7.
Most children are only too eager to scamper up the spiral staircase, which numbers 311 steps, as you breathlessly try to explain the Monument's history as you trudge after them. At 202ft (65m), the column marks the exact distance to the bakery in Pudding Lane where the Great Fire of London broke out in 1666. It was built by Sir Christopher Wren and, despite the many skyscrapers being built nearby (the construction work and attendant cranes are best appreciated from the caged viewing platform at the top), still stands out thanks to the golden urn of flames on top. Children as young as two make it up the stairs independently, and two treats await them for their pains: from the top they can peer down the centre of the spiral and imagine they are inside an MC Escher painting, while at the bottom they're awarded a certificate to commemorate their climbing feat.
Nearest picnic place: riverside by London Bridge.

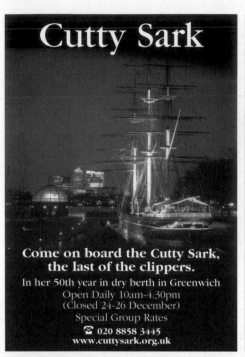

Museum of London

150 London Wall, EC2Y 5HN (7600 3699/24hr info 7600 0807/www.museumoflondon.org.uk). Barbican or St Paul's tube/Moorgate tube/rail. **Open** 10am-5.50pm Mon-Sat; noon-5.50pm Sun (last admission 5.30pm). Closed 24-26 Dec, 1 Jan. **Admission** free. **Credit** *Shop* AmEx, MC, V. **Map** p320 P5.

The Museum of London is one of the capital's best places for free indoor entertainment for children. Making so much history – from prehistoric times to the present – dynamic and appealing to visitors of all ages is no mean feat. Flint arrowheads and fragments of pottery usually rate high on the yawn scale, yet this museum's London Before London gallery takes off with an evocative soundtrack, lyrical text and clever mirror projections. Heathrow was once Caesar's Camp: look into the box and you can watch the roundhouses morph into jumbo jets. The Great Fire installation, an imaginative re-creation of the city in flames, has delighted and frightened children for decades and is still going strong. More recent times are covered in the World City gallery, where black and white photographs of royalty and commoners are enlivened by audio accounts of their lives. Antique model aeroplanes hang from the ceiling in this gallery; the Lord Mayor's red and gold state coach (still used annually in his Show) is parked by the computer terminals. The latter are wildly popular with young visitors. You can call up films of bourgeois bicyclists in Hampstead or a keeper taunting tiger cubs at the zoo. In good weather, the Barber Surgeons' Garden (partly enclosed by the ruined walls of the old Roman fort) is a lovely spot for a picnic; families can also eat packed lunches in the schools' room near the entrance.

Scheduled for 2004 is a major exhibition called 'The London Look', which opens in October and focuses on 200 years of fashion in the capital, from the street to the catwalk. Important London designers such as Alexander McQueen and Vivienne Westwood have pledged their support, and the show will inspire a season of family activities and events. And don't forget to visit the museum shop, which has an impressive library of London-related books (fiction and non-fiction) as well as classy nostalgic toys, period fancy-dress outfits and old-fashioned lollipops. *See also p50* **Playtime at... the Museum of London**.

Buggy access. Café. Nappy-changing facilities. Nearest picnic place: benches outside museum/grassy area by London Wall. Lifts. Shop.

Museum of Methodism & John Wesley's House

Wesley's Chapel, 49 City Road, EC1Y 1AU (7253 2262/ www.wesleyschapel.org.uk). Moorgate or Old Street tube/rail. **Open** 10am-4pm Mon-Sat, 12.30-1.45pm Sun. Closed 25 Dec-1 Jan, bank hols. **Tours** ad hoc arrangements on arrival. **Admission** free. *Tours* free. **Credit** MC, V. **Map** p321 Q4.

This lovely chapel, with its deep, gated courtyard ringed by Georgian buildings, is a haven from the thunderous traffic of City Road and known to Methodists worldwide as 'the Cathedral of World Methodism'. It was built by John Wesley in 1778 and his description of it – 'perfectly neat but not fine' – sums up its homely architecture.

Museum displays in the crypt allude to Methodism's beginnings. Hogarthian prints depict the iniquitous effects of poverty, alcoholism and moral degradation in 18th-century England. John Wesley experienced a moment of grace that persuaded him to devote his life to serving God and helping the poor, and his rigorous and methodical programme of prayer, fasting and so on led to him being dubbed a 'Methodist'. Evidence of this puritanical lifestyle is on show

in the preacher's house, which may be visited as part of the ad hoc tours given by stewards. This is naturally more lively than the museum and its missionary memorabilia; the house has been sympathetically restored and shows a kitchen with an open range and no running water, a bedroom with a tiny four-poster bed. There's also the study with its 'chamber horse' – if Wesley's foreign preaching tours did not offer enough equestrian exercise, this curious bouncing chair was supposed to simulate a good gallop.

Through the windows you can see Bunhill Fields, once set aside for victims of the Great Plague, but because it remained unconsecrated, became a dissenters' graveyard. Cross the road to wander through this secret garden, with its mossy graves tilted at odd angles and its memorials to nonconformists such as William Blake, Daniel Defoe, members of Oliver Cromwell's family and Susanna Wesley (mother of John and Charles). There's a large grassy area for picnics. *Buggy access. Disabled access: lift, toilet. Nappy-changing facilities. Nearest picnic place: enclosed courtyard at entrance; Barber Surgeons' Garden. Shop.*

Postman's Park

Between King Edward Street & Aldersgate Street, EC1R 4JR (7374 4127/www.cityoflondon.gov.uk). St Paul's tube. **Open** 8am-dusk daily. **Admission** free. **Map** p320 O6. Named for its proximity to a large sorting office (long since demolished), the City's most charming green space is prettily laid out with an old goldfish pond, lots of exotic shrubs and flagged paths. Its most famous feature is the Heroes' Wall, a canopy-covered expanse of ceramic plaques, inscribed in florid Victorian style, that pay tribute to ordinary people who died trying to save others. 'Frederick Alfred Croft, Inspector, aged 31,' begins one typical thumbnail drama. 'Saved a Lunatic Woman from Suicide at Woolwich Arsenal Station, But was Himself Run Over by the Train, Jan 11, 1878.' Many of the dead heroes were children who tried to rescue drowning companions, and so on; their fates draw gruesome morals for their modern peers. *Buggy access.*

St Bartholomew's Hospital Museum

West Smithfield, EC1A 7BE (7601 8152). Barbican or St Paul's tube. **Open** 10am-4pm Tue-Fri. Closed for Christmas, Easter, bank hols. **Tours** 2pm Fri. **Admission** free. *Tours* £5; £4 concessions; accompanied children free. **No credit cards. Map** p320 O6.

One of London's medieval hospitals, St Bartholomew's reminds modern students of medicine that theirs is a relatively modern science. St Bart's was built in 1123 by Rahere, a courtier of Henry VIII, after a near-death brush with malaria in Rome. The museum recalls the hospital's origins as a popular refuge for the chronically sick. Many sought miraculous cures, but more reliable (and easier to procure) remedies were rest, good diet and spiritual comfort. Leather 'lunatic restraints', a wooden head used by young would-be doctors to practise their head-drilling techniques (but also, apparently, as a football) and photographs documenting the slow progress of nurses from subordinate drudges to careerwomen make mildly edifying exhibits.

Don't miss the huge painting in grand historical style by William Hogarth, through the museum and up the stairs. Hogarth was born in Bartholomew's Close and offered his services free when he heard the hospital governors were about to commission a Venetian artist. His paintings of the Good Samaritan et al illustrate a fascinating range of skin and venereal diseases; quite a talking point, so have a suitable answer prepared for the youngsters if they're not ready for the whole truth.

Nearest picnic place: hospital grounds. Shop.

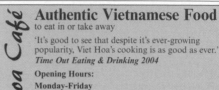

Tower Bridge is the tourists' pin-up.

St Paul's Cathedral

Ludgate Hill, EC4M 8AD (7236 4128/www.stpauls.co.uk).
St Paul's tube. **Open** 8.30am-4.30pm (last entry 4pm)
Mon-Sat; services only Sun, 25 Dec. *Galleries* 9.30am-4pm
Mon-Sat. Closed for special services, sometimes at short
notice. *Tours* 11am, 11.30am, 1.30pm, 2pm Mon-Sat.
Admission (LP) *Cathedral, crypt & gallery* £7; £3 6 16s;
£6 concessions; free under-6s. *Tours* £2.50; £1 6-16s; £2
concessions; free under 6s. *Audio guide* £3.50; £3
concessions. **Credit** MC, V. **Map** p320 O6.
This towering landmark on Ludgate Hill is bound to impress
children with its size and majesty, but its architectural details
may well leave them underwhelmed. To prevent little eyes
glazing over, you should try to book a tour, during which the
practised arts of enthusiastic old retainers will bring the place
alive with stories of royal christenings marriages and deaths.

The architect of St Paul's, Sir Christopher Wren, is buried
in the Crypt along with Nelson, Wellington and George
Frampton, whose statue stretches out a hand containing a
scaled-down replica of his Peter Pan sculpture in Kensington
Gardens. Holman Hunt's painting *The Light of the World* is
a highlight of the Middlesex Regiment Chapel, but climbing
up to the Whispering Gallery in the dome and testing the
acoustics has to be the most thrilling part of any visit.

Children too young to benefit from paying the entrance fee
can always take advantage of the cathedral's spacious café
in the Crypt. The shop, also in the Crypt, is full of tasteful
London souvenirs. To experience St Paul's as a place of worship, try Choral Evensong at 5pm daily, when the emphasis
is on heavenly singing (the boys' choir sings on Mondays).
*Buggy access. Café. Disabled lifts. Nearest picnic space:
garden. Restaurant. Shop.*

St Swithin's Garden

Oxford Court, off Cannon Street, EC4N 5AD (no phone).
Monument tube/Bank tube/DLR. **Open** 24hrs daily.
Admission free. **Map** p321 Q7.
This small but carefully tended walled garden (at the back
of Costa Coffee) is the burial place of Catrin Glendwr and two
of her children. Catrin was the daughter of Owain Glendwr,
the Welsh hero whose uprising ended bloodily in 1413. A
memorial sculpture is dedicated not only to her, but to the
suffering of all women and children in war. Benches and a
beautiful magnolia tree make this a pleasant place to sit.
Buggy access.

Tower Bridge Experience

Tower Bridge, SE1 2UP (7403 3761/
www.towerbridge.org.uk). Tower Hill tube/London Bridge
tube/rail. **Open** *Summer* 9am-6.30pm (last entry 5.30pm)
daily. *Winter* 9.30am-6pm (last entry 5pm), Closed 24-26
Dec, 1 Jan. **Admission** £5.50; £3 5-15s; £4.25
concessions; £14 family (2+2); free under-5s. **Credit**
AmEx, MC, V. **Map** p321 R8.
Seeing inside London's most famous bridge is a quite a thrill
for many visitors, depending on their age and enthusiasm for
engineering. A lift takes you up to the walkways over the
river, but the view is partially obscured by the glass
inserted into the original ironwork. A video acts out Victorian
opposition to the bridge's construction, and period
photographs show significant moments in its history, such
as the sandy 'beach' created below the bridge in 1934 to
entertain Londoners. Once at ground level again, the tour
continues in the south tower, where smartly liveried engines
slowly turn. Here there are talking animatronic coalmen and

Pit stops The City

The City is definitely not the most child-friendly part of town when it comes to restaurants. Many places cater exclusively for a weekday business clientele and you'll be hard pushed to find any high chairs or kiddie menus. In the area around the **Bank of England Museum** or the **Guildhall**, there's a spacious branch of child-friendly **Browns** (8 Old Jewry, EC2R 8DN, 7606 6677) or Japanese food at slick **Tokyo City** (46 Gresham Street, EC2V 7AY, 7726 0308); these are the best bets among posh restaurants for suits, and coffee chains.

Visitors to the **Museum of London** are better served. The museum's café is fine for family eating, with high chairs, a children's hot dish or little lunchbox full of goodies, and there are several indoor and outdoor picnic areas. Nearby **The Place Below** (see p160) is a favourite of ours, but the children's favourite is most definitely **Pizza Express** (125 London Wall, EC2Y 5AS, 7600 8880). That nice noodly **Wagamama** chain is represented on Ropemaker Street (No.1A, EC2V 0HR, 7588 2688). Over at Smithfield other options include **Carluccio's Caffè** (see p159 for gorgeous Italian grub, and trendy, usually buzzy **Smith's of Smithfield** (see p160).

The café in the crypt of **St Paul's Cathedral** can provide decent refreshments in a striking setting, while **Just the Bridge** (1 Paul's Walk, EC4V 3QH, 7236 0000) is a touristy favourite but OK for family meals; the waiting staff don't mind children sharing big portions.

Not far from the **Monument** is a branch of the **Gaucho Grill** (1 Bell Inn Yard, EC3V 0BL, 7626 5180), which offers reliable steaks and burgers and has high chairs for little ones.

Ice skaters from **Broadgate Arena** will be pleased to find the fast-food outlets in **Liverpool Street Station**; otherwise Bishopsgate offers a branch of **Chez Gerard** (No.64, EC2N 4AW, 7588 1200) where children are welcome, if not catered for in a kiddie menu sort of way. A perennial children's favourite is the **S&M Café** (48 Brushfield Street, E1 6AG, 7247 2252; see also p174), just outside the Square Mile but well worth the excursion for kiddie menus and some interesting variations on sausage and mash (vegetarian options available). Children's portions are no problem at either of the City branches of **Barcelona Tapas** (1A Bell Lane, E1 7LA, 7247 7014; 1 Beaufort House, St Botolph Street, EC3A 7DT, 7377 5111).

When you make your escape from the **Tower of London**, in most circumstances your best choices are the branches of chain restaurants, but you'll find **Auberge** (56 Mark Lane, EC3R 7NE, 7480 6789) is a happy combination of kiddie menu and proximity to the Tower. You'll enjoy its Belgian steak frites combos, but it is are closed at weekends. In fact, you need to be resourceful at round here on Saturdays and Sundays, for the quietness that makes the area pleasant to stroll in means there's no trade for caterers: most are closed. If you're making for Tower Hill and environs, take advantage of free Sunday parking in **Safeway's** on Thomas More Street (E1W 9YY, 7702 2863) and make use of its hot buffets. There's a conservatory to eat in.

If you're stuck for a place to eat, do what the workers do: buy a takeaway from one of the City sandwich bars and picnic. **Finsbury Circus Gardens** (Finsbury Circus, EC2M 7AB) is a reasonably big open space, near Moorgate tube, with a bowling green and bandstand, but it is hard to get a square foot of grass in a summer lunch hour. **Fortune Street Gardens** (Fortune Street, EC1Y) was refurbished in 2003 and is the City's largest park, with a brand new playground and lots of seating for parents. Barbican is its nearest tube station.

buttons to press – some of which start audio commentary on pumps and gaskets in eight different languages. More amusing is a wind-up seat demonstrating hydraulic power and a model that allows you to 'make the bridge go up'. This, after all, is what every visitor would like to see for real: it happens most often in summer (sometimes several times a day). To find out when the next opening will happen, call 7940 3984. *Buggy access. Disabled access: lift, toilet. Nearest picnic place: Potters Field/Tower of London Gardens. Shop.*

The Tower of London

Tower Hill, EC3N 4AB (info 0870 756 6060/booking line 0870 756 7070/www.hrp.org.uk). Tower Hill tube/ Fenchurch Street rail/15, 25, 42, 100 bus. **Open** *Mar-Oct* 9am-6pm Mon-Sat; 10am-6pm Sun (last entry 5pm). *Nov-Feb* 10am-5pm Mon, Sun; 9am-5pm Tue-Sat (last entry 4pm). Closed 24-26 Dec, 1 Jan. **Tours** *Beefeater tours* (outside only, weather permitting) every 30mins 9.25am-2.50pm daily. *Short talks* (40mins, by yeoman warder) 3 times daily. **Admission** (LP) £13.50; £10.50 concessions; £9 5-15s; family £37.50 (2+3); free under-5s. *Audio guide* £3. *Tours* free (advance tickets for short talks from kiosk outside Lanthorn Tower). **Credit** AmEx, MC, V. **Map** p321 R7.

Entrance fees at this picture-book castle may seem steep, but a day here for families turns out to be excellent value. This is because 'the Tower' is actually several towers, each with its own history and points of interest, and children are treated like royalty by well-informed and kindly staff. Most young visitors, if asked what impresses them most, will hesitate between the dazzling riches of the Crown Jewels and the tales of royal executions. A permanent exhibition of torture instruments – 'Torture at the Tower' – aims to nourish the healthy childish interest in violence and punishment, all the while keeping within the boundaries of good taste. Other attractions include the Norman loos in the White Tower, the monstrous suits of armour and the shocking display of weaponry. *See also p49* **Tales from... the Tower of London**. *Buggy access. Café. Nappy-changing facilities. Nearest picnic place: Trinity Square Memorial Gardens. Shop.*

Holborn & Clerkenwell

The Professionals: lawyers, medics and an architectural maverick.

Bar the enigmatic Code of the Playground, children don't have a lot of time for the law. That can change, however, during an afternoon's pottering among the brooding masonry of **Holborn**, which is to wannabe barristers what Savile Row once was to aspiring tailors. The labyrinthine Inns of Court at the Temple exude history: Shakespeare's *Twelfth Night* premièred in Middle Temple Hall, which is home to a table reputedly made from the hatch of Sir Francis Drake's ship, the *Golden Hinde*. Meanwhile, the Inner Temple Gardens (open 12.20-3pm Mon-Fri) make for a spectacular family picnic spot, with sweeping views across the Embankment.

To the north is an exhibition on Samuel Pepys in **Prince Henry's Room** and the church across the Strand from there, St Dunstan in the West (186A Fleet Street, EC4A 2HR, 7405 1929), is where the old goat (according to his own diary) tried to fondle a local girl during a sermon. St Dunstan's clock tower – still ticking away – was the first in London to acquire a minute hand. Two clockwork giants with enormous cudgels emerge from the tower at a quarter past every hour.

The wigs displayed in Chancery Lane's specialist judicial suppliers are good for a laugh (although that might cancel out any inclination towards a career in the law), but a little further west along the Strand the Royal Courts of Justice (7947 6000) are imposing. High-profile civil cases are heard here: public entry is permitted for children aged 14 and over.

Other churches of note sit closer to Aldwych: free lunchtime recitals (Wed-Fri) are still given at St Mary-le-Strand – despite the ungodly din caused by the encircling roundabout – and the restored **St Clement Danes** is home to a moving RAF memorial. The dubious **Roman Baths** are also within spitting distance, but by far the local focus of kids' attentions is **Somerset House**, with three separate galleries – the **Courtauld Institute**, the **Gilbert Collection** and the **Hermitage Rooms** – offering an entertaining and enlightening programme of children's activities and workshops courtesy of a new Learning Centre.

Away from the river to the north-east are Lincoln's Inn Fields. Kids still fired with legal ambition can wander over to Lincoln's Inn, the oldest and – with Palladian buildings and perfectly manicured gardens – most beautiful of the Inns of Court. But **Sir John Soane's Museum** will please everyone. Due to reopen in 2005, the Hunterian Museum of the Royal College of Surgeons will be a welcome addition to the area (phone 7869 6560 for details).

Keep walking and you'll arrive in **Clerkenwell**, which is dominated by new media offices and the gastropubs that fuel them. Still, there's the **Museum & Library of the Order of St John** for a rare insight into the development of medicine, as well as Hatton Garden's diamond dealers – providing a stark contrast to the diamond-in-the-rough stallholders of the market on parallel Leather Lane.

Courtauld Institute Gallery

Somerset House, Strand, WC2R 0RN (7848 2526/ education 7848 2922/www.courtauld.ac.uk). Covent Garden or Temple tube (closed Sun)/Charing Cross tube/rail. **Open** 10am-6pm daily (last entry 5.15pm); 10am-4pm 31 Dec; noon-6pm 1 Jan. Closed 24-26 Dec. **Tours** phone for details. **Admission** £5; £4 concessions; free under-18s, students, registered unwaged. Free to all 10am-2pm Mon (not bank hols). *Annual ticket £22.* **Credit** MC, V. **Map** p319 M7.

Among the exhibitions at Somerset House (*see p60*), the Courtauld offers a fabulous permanent collection. In residence is a huge corpus of Impressionist and post-Impressionist paintings, a range of work by Renaissance artists (including Michelangelo and Leonardo) and some Rembrandt. There are also an East Wing dedicated to contemporary creations by current students at the Courtauld Institute of Art and regular blockbuster temporary exhibitions. While this might all seem light years away from poster paint and double-sided sticky tape, the Courtauld's colourful programme of activities (*see p213*) brings everything to life for Young Masters. *Buggy access. Café. Lift. Shop.*

The Gilbert Collection

Somerset House, Strand, WC2R 1LA (7420 9400/ www.gilbert-collection.org.uk). Covent Garden or Temple tube (closed Sun)/Charing Cross tube/rail. **Open** 10am-6pm daily (last entry 5.15pm); 10am-4pm 31 Dec; noon-6pm 1 Jan. Closed 24-26 Dec. **Tours** phone for details. **Admission** £5; £4 concessions; free under 18s, students, registered unwaged. *Annual ticket £20.* **Credit** MC, V. **Map** p319 M7.

These extensive displays from the collection of the late Sir Arthur Gilbert, including jewel-encrusted curios, gleaming silverware and ornate Italian mosaics, are so resplendent families would do well to don sunglasses before entering. Hands-on activities designed to open up the collection to little ones include the design and creation of everything from mock jewellery to elaborate fabric shields, while 'Exploring Precious Stones' session let you ogle crystals through high-powered microscopes. Workshops take place every Saturday (daily during school holidays) and are tailored to illuminate current temporary exhibitions: a recent display of work by renowned children's illustrator Quentin Blake, for example, gave kids the opportunity to illustrate stories of their own. For upcoming events, phone the new Learning Centre on 7420 9406. *Buggy access. Café. Lift. Shop.*

The Hermitage Rooms

Somerset House, Strand, WC2R 1LA (info 7845 4630/ www.hermitagerooms.co.uk). Covent Garden or Temple tube (closed Sun)/Charing Cross tube/rail. **Open** 10am-6pm daily (last entry 5.15pm); 10am-4pm 31 Dec; noon-6pm 1 Jan. Closed 24-26 Dec. **Admission** £5; £4 concessions; free under-16s, students, registered unwaged. **Credit** MC, V. **Map** p319 M7.

The Hermitage Rooms are an ever-shifting window into one of the world's very greatest museums: the State Hermitage Museum in St Petersburg, Russia. The State Hermitage Museum is home to an unprecedented collection of paintings by Old Masters, Impressionist and post-Impressionist works, and Classical antiquities, among other items, and at any given time the Hermitage Rooms will have on show a selection of work highlighting a specific age or artist. Recent displays include 'Heaven on Earth: The Decorative Arts of the Arab World' (until 22 Aug 2004), as well as exhibitions of work by Peter Paul Rubens, Poussin and Picasso. A range of regular weekend and holiday workshops for children are themed according to the current exhibition: call the Learning Centre (7420 9406) for updated information.

Buggy access. Café. Shop.

Museum & Library of the Order of St John

St John's Gate, St John's Lane, EC1M 4DA (7324 4070/ www.sja.org.uk/history). Farringdon tube/rail/63, 55, 243 bus. **Open** 10am-5pm Mon-Fri; 10am-4pm Sat. Closed 24 Dec-2 Jan, bank hol weekends (phone to check). **Tours** 11am, 2.30pm Tue, Fri, Sat. **Admission** free; suggested donations for tours £5, £3.50 concessions. **Map** p320 O4.

These days the Order of St John is usually associated with those nice chaps at the side of sweaty stadium gigs, but it was founded by crusaders in 11th-century Jerusalem. The Order has been chasing disease and pestilence ever since, and this charming museum is an intriguing insight into the history not only of the knights, but also of the development of medicine. Exhibits are divided between a static collection of antiques (everything from holy relics to full suits of armour) and a brighter and more interactive room that showcases the Order's medical history. Here children can marvel at surgical models and tools of the trade (some of them satisfyingly gruesome), as well as a primitive wooden ambulance that's basically a wheelbarrow. The museum is beside the original St John's Gate, an evocative Tudor stone edifice, and if you

Sir John the Collector

It is said that, if Sir John himself were to march tomorrow through the front door of the **Sir John Soane's Museum** (*pictured, see also p60*), he'd find everything pretty much where he'd left it. This isn't because he was in life a tidy man. Indeed, following the death of his beloved wife Elizabeth in 1815, Soane began covering every available surface of their small home with curiosities from his vast collection, nailing broken pedestals to walls, hanging pictures and balancing sculptures in various corners until there was barely room to stroke a cat, let alone swing it.

While the immediate impression on entering the house is of overwhelming clutter, there is a meticulous method behind Soane's every madness. The Colonnade, for example, is laid out to resemble an arterial passage in a Greek temple, with shafts of natural light directed to illuminate the features of various jumbled busts and ancient friezes. In the Library Dining Room, Soane set up a playful combination of facing mirrors to suggest various non-existent adjoining rooms. Most alluring is the eerie Crypt, which can be viewed from the ground floor, with its Gothic statue fragments and leering gargoyles. Here Soane devised an entire myth, which surrounded a fictional monk (Padre Giovanni), whose ghost he insisted haunted the room.

This very fluidity of vision makes the place a perfect stage for young imaginations – filled with nooks and crannies, but small and homely enough to be seen in an hour. The staff, under the guidance of architect and education officer Jenny Monahan, offer a range of activities both in and out of term-time. School groups are led in a series of workshops tied closely into the national curriculum, with topics ranging from fascinating scientific explorations of light, shadow and reflection (suited to seven-to 11-year-olds) to the more challenging creation and testing of engineering crumple zones from cardboard (11- to 13-year-olds). Regular free Saturday workshops – most of them for kids aged seven to 11 – cover everything from building toy theatres to designing and decorating windows.

All of the activities relate to the science or aesthetics of architecture, and children are encouraged to develop designs of their own. The vision for this can be attributed to the master of the house: Soane dreamed that his two sons would follow in their father's footsteps, but it wasn't to be. So, before his death in 1837, Sir John made certain the house would be maintained and opened to the public, presumably hoping it might inspire children to pursue an architectural career. After everything he's given us, the least we can do is try to comply.

Somerset House. See p60.

take the grand tour you'll see the 12th-century crypt. There are activity trails for younger groups, but those whose idea of 'activity' is actually joining up can become (depending on their age) Little Badgers or Cadets – membership is free (you only pay for the uniform) and little lifesavers receive first aid training, with recognised exams at the end of it.
Shop.

Prince Henry's Room
17 Fleet Street, EC4Y 1AA (7936 2710). Temple tube (closed Sun)/11, 15, 23 bus. **Open** 11am-2pm Mon-Sat. Closed bank hol weekends. **Admission** free; donations appreciated. **Map** p320 N6.
This ornate, oak-panelled room is one of few in central London to have survived the Great Fire of 1666. The original Jacobean plaster ceiling is immaculately preserved, and is a popular subject for sketches by architecture students. Originally used by lawyers of Prince Henry, eldest son of King James I, the room was built in 1610 – the same year that the 14-year-old Henry became Prince of Wales. Four years later he died of typhoid, and it was his brother who succeeded to the throne as Charles I. The rest of the building – now an office – was once a tavern called the Prince's Arms, which happened to be a favoured haunt of diarist Samuel Pepys. So it is that the cases in Prince Henry's Room actually display a range of Pepys memorabilia, including original portraits, newspaper clippings and – of course – extracts from his famous chronicles of 17th-century life. Kids already predisposed towards this portion of history will enjoy it, but don't expect the place to inflame younger imaginations.
Shop.

Roman Baths
Strand Lane, WC2R 2NA (7447 6605). Temple tube (closed Sun). **Open** 1-5pm Wed. **Admission** free. **Map** p319 M7.
The search for Strand Lane will have you tearing up your map in frustration, but its inaccessibility is its own reward for it is as crumbling and atmospheric an alley as you could hope to find. The Baths – viewed through a grimy window – are less rewarding. The ruins have had a history both literary (a cameo in *David Copperfield*) and literal. At times, the two seem to merge: renowned collector William Weddell died

from 'a sudden internal chill' while taking a constitutional dip in 1792, yet a century later the facility's proprietor released a pamphlet claiming it to be 'the most pure and healthy bath in London'. Most recent scholars regard the Roman Baths as more modern reservoirs, built for the domestic offices of nearby Arundel House and then forgotten. In any case, don't bother to bring your swimwear and be aware that until Christmas there will be limited access to the baths due to extensive building work on the adjacent building. Access is through a covered pavement and is not suitable for buggies or wheelchairs.

St Clement Danes Church
Strand, WC2R 1DH (7242 8282). Temple tube (closed Sun)/4, 11, 15, 23, 341 bus. **Open** 9am-4pm daily. Closed bank hols. **Admission** free. **Map** p320 M6.
No longer believed to be the church namechecked in the popular nursery rhyme 'Oranges and Lemons', St Clement's nonetheless does have bells – they ring in an annual ceremony that involves children from the local primary school being presented with pickings from a veritable mountain of citrus fruits, as well as four times daily (9am, noon, 3pm, 6pm). They were almost eternally silenced when the church, rebuilt by Christopher Wren (a fourth incarnation since it was founded in the ninth century), was gutted by air raids in 1941. After the war, the Royal Air Force campaigned for its restoration, and on 19 October 1958 St Clement's was reconsecrated as the Central Church of the RAF. Spitfires may not get young pulses racing as they did 40 years ago, but a wealth of RAF commemoratives are on display for those who are interested. The statue of Arthur 'Bomber' Harris, the man behind the brutal raids on Dresden, may arouse mixed feelings.
Buggy access.

St Ethelreda's
14 Ely Place, EC1N 6RY (7405 1061). Chancery Lane or Farringdon tube. **Open** 8am-7pm daily; phone to check. Closed 26 Dec. **Admission** free; donations appreciated. **Map** p320 N5.
St Ethelreda's would be one of London's most charming churches… if only it were in London. Despite its postcode, Ely Place is, in fact, through a quirk of legal history, under the jurisdiction of Cambridgeshire. Much like the Vatican, it

is even subject to its own laws and precedents. Built by Bishop Luda of Ely in the 13th century, it's the oldest Catholic church in Britain, and serves as London's only standing example of Gothic architecture from that period. These days the upper church – rebuilt after damage caused by the Blitz – is used for services. Ely Place is where David Copperfield meets Agnes Wakefield in the Dickens novel, while the strawberries grown in the church gardens receive commendation in Shakespeare's *Richard III*. Strawberrie Fayre takes place here each year in June, with all proceeds going to charity. *Café.*

Sir John Soane's Museum

13 Lincoln's Inn Fields, WC2A 3BP (7405 2107/ education officer 7440 4247/www.soane.org). Holborn tube. **Open** 10am-5pm Tue-Sat; 6-9pm 1st Tue of mth. Closed bank hol weekends. **Tours** 2.30pm Sat. **Admission** free; donations appreciated. *Tours* £3; free concessions, under-16s. **Credit** *Shop* AmEx, MC, V. **Map** p317 M5.

The son of a bricklayer, John Soane was only able to indulge his passion for collecting artefacts after he married into money. But it was a passion he then indulged relentlessly and without prejudice. Far from confining himself to relics of a specific period, he filled his home with everything from an Ancient Egyptian sarcophagus to paintings by his near contemporary, renowned satirist Hogarth. The latter's *Rake's Progress* is on display in a room also containing several of Soane's own architectural plans, all nestled together in an elaborate and utterly charming series of folding doors and walls. It is such touches of ingenuity that elevate this museum from mere cabinet of (admittedly extraordinary) curiosities to something altogether more beguiling (*see p58* **Sir John the Collector**).

Nearest picnic place: Lincoln's Inn Fields. Shop.

Somerset House

Strand, WC2R 1LA (7845 4600/www.somerset-house.org.uk). Covent Garden or Temple tube (closed Sun)/Charing Cross tube/rail. **Open** 10am-6pm daily. *Courtyard & River Terrace* 10am-10pm daily (Apr-Sept only). Closed 25 Dec. **Tours** phone for details. **Admission** *Parts of South Building, Courtyard & River Terrace* free. *Exhibitions* varies; phone for details. **Credit** *Shop* MC, V. **Map** p319 M7.

One small step into the vast courtyard of Somerset House is one giant leap into the 18th century, with the elaborate stone edifices that surround the courtyard shutting out all but a whimper of traffic from the busy Strand. Erected on the site of a long-demolished Tudor palace, this grand exercise in neo-classical architecture – originally designed to house public offices – is now home to three of the UK's finest galleries: the Courtauld Institute Gallery, the Gilbert Collection (*see p57 for both*) and the Hermitage Rooms (*see p58*). Somerset House is a family destination in and of itself, most notably throughout December, when the courtyard is transformed into a jolly ice rink, which, vast crowds notwithstanding, is idyllic at Christmas time. Equally inspired is the big square fountain in the centre, which entertains everyone with waterjets that dance in formation every hour. On hot summer days, children love running down the brief corridors of water – even more so when the corridors collapse and everyone gets a bit of a soaking. The courtyard also plays stage for a varied programme of free family events during the summer holidays, including puppet shows, storytelling and creative workshops (the Family Free Time Festival runs from 23-6 July 2004). Throw in riverside views from the front of the building and a couple of colourful cafés, and you'll find your day has been pretty much planned for you.

Buggy access. Café. Lift. Nappy-changing facilities. Restaurant. Shop.

Pit stops Holborn and Clerkenwell

There are plenty of fast-food chains on the Strand, including a **West Cornwall Pasty Company** (79A Strand, WC2R 0DE, 7836 4800), as well as occasional family-friendly restaurants like **Smollensky's on the Strand** (*see p168*), with its weekend play areas and perky children's entertainers. It would be churlish, however, for anyone visiting the various galleries of **Somerset House** – or nearby **St Clement Danes**, for that matter – to look anywhere else for sustenance than the bright and airy **Gallery Café** (7848 2526) in the basement of the Courtauld.

Near **St Dunstan's** and **Prince Henry's Room** there are fewer places suited to families (although Inner Temple Gardens make a delightful picnic spot); those that there are tend to be chains in the mould of **McDonald's** (152 Fleet Street, EC4A 2DH, 7353 0543). For a more personable dining experience, there's a colourful children's menu at **Wagamama** (109 Fleet Street, EC4A 2AB, 7583 7889). The restaurant on **Lincoln's Inn Fields** was changing management as we went to press, but the area makes for idyllic picnics – right on the doorstep of the **Sir John Soane's Museum** – and there are plenty of sit-down alternatives a short walk away. Try **Fryer's Delight** (19 Theobald's Road, WC1X 8SL, 7405 4114), a fish and chip shop renowned across the city for its freshness and family value, or the **Bierodrome** (67 Kingsway, WC2B 6TD, 7242 7469), which lets two children eat free for every adult ordering from the main menu. There's also the time-honoured **Spaghetti House** (20 Sicilian Avenue, WC1A 2QD, 7405 5215), good for wholesome Italian food without the designer price tag, or a **Pizza Express** (99 High Holborn, WC1V 6LF, 7831 5305) just up the road.

You're never far from a good place to grub up in **Clerkenwell**. You don't have to go to all those swanky chop houses and gastropubs, either – there are some much better family options. Those marvelling at the ancient crypt of **St Ethelreda's** needn't look far: the on-site café does light lunches at a good price. Anyone after something a little more substantial can go to Farringdon Road and **Smith's of Smithfield** (*see p160*). There's also a rarely busy **Yo! Sushi** (95 Farringdon Road, EC1R 3BT, 7841 0785), as well as fantastic little **Strada** (8-10 Exmouth Market, EC1R 4YA, 7278 0800) for first-class pizzas and Italian classics (and free mineral water into the bargain). Both are only a short walk from the **Museum & Library of the Order of St John**.

Bloomsbury & Fitzrovia

Victorian poverty, Egyptian treasure – and everyone's favourite playground.

Once home to the literary elite and a centre for publishing and academia, Bloomsbury and Fitzrovia have provided capital stamping ground for the likes of Virginia Woolf, Dylan Thomas, Ford Madox Ford, George Bernard Shaw and George Orwell. They're also areas that are steeped in family history: Mary Ward developed the capital's first play centres here, reformer and key promoter of parks and play spaces Edwin Chadwick lived and worked in the area, while Marie Stopes based her pioneering birth-control clinic on Fitzrovia's Whitfield Street. The historical significance of this elegant Georgian neighbourhood – looked over by the looming tower of the University of London's Senate House, said to have been the inspiration behind the Ministry of Truth in Orwell's *1984* – might not immediately appeal for a day out with the kids. But take a look beyond the blue-plaque parade and you'll discover an area rich in childish treasures.

First up is London's famous park for children, the wonderful **Coram's Fields**, which alone provides sufficient reason to visit this area; **Russell Square**, another famous green space, offers kids the chance to splash around in the fountain in summer. After the tiny **Cartoon Art Trust Museum**, an inspiration for fledgling cartoonists, there is, of course, the **British Museum**. Its amazing hoard of antiquities has always been intriguing, but the addition of the spectacular Great Court, London's only covered public square, is an extra draw. The **British Library** is well known as the repository of the country's literary treasures, but in addition to being a research centre extraordinaire it houses fascinating exhibitions covering a dizzying range of topics. Nearby is the brand-new **Foundling Museum**, opening in the hospital partly funded by Handel, while further to the south the **Charles Dickens Museum** is in the house where the great author once lived. A visit there is entirely appropriate given the neighbourhood's impressive literary and less-than-impressive social history – this was once the setting for Hogarth's *Gin Lane*.

By April 2004 the estimable **Pollock's Toy Museum** (1 Scala Street, W1T 2HL, 7636 3452), a delightful slice of nostalgia whose exhibits evoked a pre-Game Boy era when wooden train sets and Snakes and Ladders were as fun as fun got, had failed to extend its lease. The website www.pollocksweb.co.uk will carry details of the campaign to reopen in a new location.

British Library

96 Euston Road, NW1 2DB (7412 7332/education 7412 7797/www.bl.uk). Euston or King's Cross tube/rail. **Open** 9.30am-6pm Mon, Wed-Fri; 9.30am-8pm Tue; 9.30am-5pm Sat; 11am-5pm Sun, bank hols. Closed 24-28 Dec, 1-3 Jan. **Admission** free; donations appreciated. **Map** p317 K3.

One of the greatest libraries in the world, the British Library has a staggering collection of 150 million items – growing all the time – spread over 625km (388 miles) of shelves in 112,000 sq m (1.2 million sq ft) of space. Each year the library receives a copy of everything that is published in the UK and Ireland, including maps, newspapers, mags, prints and drawings.

At the heart of the building is the King's Library, the library of George III, housed in a six-storey glass-walled tower. For the casual visitor, however, the John Ritblat Gallery displays the library's real treasures: the Magna Carta or Great Charter of 1215, Leonardo da Vinci's notebook, and Shakespeare's First Folio – the first collected edition of the Bard's plays. Children might prefer first editions of *The Jungle Book* by Kipling, *Alice's Adventures Underground* by Lewis Carroll or some of the Beatles' lyrics – handwritten. You can also listen to sound recordings of James Joyce and Bob Geldof. Other items of interest include the philatelic collection – the library has some 80,000 stamps from around the world.

The major exhibition for 2004 is 'The Silk Road: Trade, Travel, War and Faith' (until 12 Sept 2004), which brings together over 200 archaeological treasures from explorer Aurel Stein's adventures along the great Silk Road. Along with the earliest dated printed book in the world, the Diamond Sutra, the exhibition displays Central Asian manuscripts, paintings, objects and textiles left by these multicultural civilisations to lie buried for up to 2,000 years in tombs, tips and temples beneath the deserts of Eastern Central Asia. Other temporary exhibitions include displays on James Joyce (for Bloomsday in June), the Charge of the Light Brigade (Oct) and Oscar Wilde (end Nov 2004-Feb 2005) and Designer Bookbinders (Dec). For children, there are regular free demonstrations of bookbinding, printing and calligraphy. During holidays, the Education Office organises workshops, activities and storytelling sessions for children aged five to 11 and their families. To join the Education Department's free mailing list, write to the address above, call 7412 7797 or check the website.

Buggy access. Café. Disabled access: lift, toilet. Nappy-changing facilities. Nearest picnic place: St James' Gardens. Restaurant. Shop.

British Museum

Great Russell Street, WC1B 3DG (7636 1555/ textphone 7323 8920/www.thebritishmuseum.ac.uk). Holborn, Russell Square or Tottenham Court Road tube. **Open** *Galleries* 10am-5.30pm Mon-Wed, Sat, Sun; 10am-8.30pm Thur, Fri. *Great Court* 9am-6pm Mon-Wed, Sun; 9am-11pm Thur-Sat. Closed 24-26 Dec, 1 Jan. **Tours** *Highlights* 10.30am, 1pm, 3pm daily; phone to check. *EyeOpener* frequently; phone to check. **Admission** (LP) free; donations appreciated. *Temporary exhibitions* prices vary; phone for details. *Highlights tours* £8; £5 11-16s, concessions; free under-10s. *EyeOpener tours* free. **Credit** MC, V. **Map** p317 K5.

Hey, kid! Making friends at **Coram's Fields**. *See p65.*

Trying to see all the exhibits at the British Museum is a bit like trying to speed-read the *Encyclopaedia Britannica*: in both cases the best advice is simply not to attempt it. Embodying the Enlightenment concept that all of the arts and sciences are connected, the museum and its world-famous collections are best appreciated in bite-sized chunks.

Now into its 251st year, the museum is perhaps best known for its Ancient Egyptian artefacts – the Rosetta Stone, the monumental statues of the pharaohs and mummies in glass cases – and Ancient Greek treasures, including the Elgin Marbles. The Celts gallery contains the Lindow Man, killed in 300 BC and preserved in peat ever since.

The restored King's Library was built in the 1820s and its Grade I-listed interior is widely considered to be the finest neo-classical space in London. It now houses a splendid permanent exhibition, 'Enlightenment: Rethinking the World in the 18th Century', a 5,000-strong collection that examines that formative period of the museum's history.

Temporary exhibitions planned for 2004 include 'Portraits on Coins and Medals' (until 18 July), which looks at the whys and wherefores of printing images on money; more exciting is the 'Virtual Mummy' exhibit (1 July 2004-27 Mar 2005), precise details of which are being kept quiet, although displays are likely to explore the way in which experts uncover the secrets of Egyptian mummies using X-ray and other high-tech equipment; and finally 'Kingdoms of the Nile' (9 Sept 2004-9 Jan 2005), which will show treasures from the National Museum of the Sudan.

If the thought of making your own way round is all too overwhelming, the museum offers sampler tours of its top treasures (starting from the information desk) or EyeOpener tours, which concentrate on specific aspects of the collection, such as Africa, the Americas or Classical. They're not aimed specifically at children, but the volunteer guides are happy for families to dip in and out of them as they like. If you want to join one of the special family EyeOpeners, run twice daily during half-terms and irregularly through the school

holidays, book at the information desk on arrival. Museum trails in the Reading Room help families navigate their way through the galleries in a more independent way.

Lasting childhood memories are sure to be the result of a museum sleepover (*see p65* **Pyjama party**), available only to Young Friends of the British Museum (membership costs £17.50). Membership of the Young Friends also entitles kids to special activities aimed at all age groups, from handling sessions and behind the scenes visits with museum curators to lively discussion groups aimed at young teenagers ('Should the Elgin Marbles be returned to the Parthenon?' is a favourite topic). The treasures of the museum are also available for perusal in the souvenir guide (£6) or on the website. *Buggy access. Cafés. Disabled access: lift, toilet. Nappy-changing facilities. Nearest picnic place: Russell Square. Restaurant. Shops.*

Cartoon Art Trust Museum

7-13 The Brunswick Centre, Bernard Street, WC1N 1AF (7278 7172/www.cartoonarttrust.org.uk). Russell Square tube. **Open** 10am-5pm Tue-Sat. **Admission** free. **Map** p317 L4.

This small one-room museum, dedicated to collecting and preserving the best of British cartoons, caricatures, comics and animations, features a changing display of works from the Cartoon Art Trust's wide-ranging collection of humorous art. Heath Robinson, Steve Bell and Peter Brookes are among the many artists represented in the space. Exhibitions rotate every two months or so, although the calendar for 2004/5 remains unfixed. The museum is currently looking for larger premises, where it hopes to set up a permanent display documenting the history of British humorous art from the 18th century onwards, alongside temporary displays – check the website for the latest news. In the meantime, you're guaranteed to find something new to amuse on each visit. Perhaps the best thing, though, are the museum's workshops and events for young cartoonists (and their excitable guardians).

Children's cartoon workshops (£20/day) and animation workshops (£25/day) are run throughout the year. All the necessary materials are provided (young animators even get a video of their creations sent to them after the workshop) and the range of activities, usually based around popular characters and styles, such as the Bash Street Kids or manga, are aimed at all abilities. Age ranges vary according to the workshops, but the free drop-in family-fun days offer something for everyone, from toddlers to grandparents. The Cartoon Art Trust also runs the Young Cartoonist of the Year competition, awards for which are presented at the Cartoon Awards in October 2004.

Buggy access. Nearest picnic place: Coram's Fields/Russell Square. Shop.

Charles Dickens Museum

48 Doughty Street, WC1N 2LX (7405 2127/www.dickens museum.com). Chancery Lane or Russell Square tube/ King's Cross tube/rail. **Open** 10am-5pm Mon-Sat;

11am-5pm Sun. **Admission** £5; £4 concessions; £3 5-15s; £14 family (2+5); free under-5s. **Credit** AmEx, MC, V. **Map** p317 M4.

Charles Dickens had a miserable childhood. His family was sent to Marshalsea Prison for debt and, at 12, Charles was forced to leave school and work in a shoe-polish factory. So, when his career took off after the publication of *The Pickwick Papers* in 1836, Dickens fled his poverty-stricken past and moved to this, the poshest house he could afford. The good life agreed with Dickens: here he wrote *Oliver Twist* and *Nicholas Nickleby*, and entertained literary friends such as Wilkie Collins and William Thackeray.

But his three years at Doughty Street were marred by tragedy, namely the death of his 17-year-old sister-in-law Mary Hogarth, who collapsed suddenly in the house after a night at the theatre. Little Nell's heartrending death scene in *The Old Curiosity Shop* is thought to have originated in Mary's demise. Soon after this event, Dickens moved from Doughty Street to a new home near Regent's Park.

Around Town

Pit stops Bloomsbury and Fitzrovia

For juice or a cuppa and a snack, the **British Library** has a café on the upper ground floor; for a meal, there's a self-service restaurant on the first floor. Otherwise, picnic in the library's big courtyard. Just around the corner, **Terra Brasil** (36-8 Chalton Street, NW1 1JB, 7388 6554) offers what may be the only real culinary excitement in the area, with tasty, cheap Brazilian buffet eats. Alternatively, wander to Bloomsbury and **North Sea Fish Restaurant** (*see p160*), a convenient stopoff for a great British plate of fish and chips.

Visitors to the **British Museum** head in numbers to the **Court Café** (British Museum, Great Russell Street, WC1B 3DG, 7636 1555) for hot chocolate and yummy pastries in the Great Court. There is some good picnicking to be had in verdant Russell Square nearby, where you can get a simple plate of fairly priced nosh from the glass-fronted **Café in the Park** (no phone). Steps away from the British Museum's main entrance you'll find **Pizza Express** (30 Coptic Street, WC1A 1NS, 7636 3232) for scrummy pizzas; **Spaghetti House** (20 Sicilian Avenue, WC1A 2QD, 7405 5215), the local link in a chain that does good junior-sized pasta plates; and a couple of branches of **Wagamama** (4A Streatham Street, WC1A 1JB, 7323 9223; 14A Irving Street, WC2H 7AF, 7839 2323), serving oodles of noodles and healthy juices in a smoke-free atmosphere. A short walk away, toward Fitzrovia, is **Busaba Eathai** (22 Store Street, WC1E 7DF, 7299 7900), an atmospheric Thai restaurant where young culinary adventurers are welcome to take over one of the large communal tables. For a completely different feel, cross the road to **Lino's Café** (21A Store Street, WC1E 7DH, 7636 9133) for unfussy, unpretentious caff and Italian food – that'll be baked beans and sausages all round, please. There's a high fun factor at **Yo! Sushi** (myhotel, 11-13 Bayley Street, WC1B 3HD, 7636 0076), tucked off Bedford Square, which serves tasty morsels on colour-coded plates.

If you've been at the **Cartoon Art Trust** or **Foundling Museums**, grab a box of wholesome takeaway vegetarian food from friendly **Alara Wholefoods** (58-60 Marchmont Street, WC1N 1AB, 7837 1172) to eat inside the shop on the small trestle table, outside at the pavement tables or as a picnic in **Coram's Fields** or Russell Square. The **Coram's Fields Café** (7837 6138) also wins over many with its healthy on-site vegetarian food.

South, the **Charles Dickens Museum** is well placed for blossoming tales of Chinese food: they can tuck in at **Sheng's Tea House** (68 Millman Street, WC1N 3EF, 7405 3697). Hispanophiles get their dreams fulfilled round the corner at the swish Spanish tapas joint **Cigala** (54 Lamb's Conduit Street, WC1N 3LW, 7405 1717), while **Goodfellas** (50 Lamb's Conduit Street, WC1N 3LH, 7405 7088) does tasty sandwiches and American diner food at reasonable prices. **Fryer's Delight** (19 Theobald's Road, WC1X 8SL, 7405 4114) is unbeatable for fish and chips.

Egyptologists worn out by the **Petrie Museum** can picnic in Gordon Square, wander down to **Planet Organic** (7436 1929) at 22 Torrington Place, or head a little further and just around the corner to the much-loved **Table Café** in Habitat (196 Tottenham Court Road, W1T 7LG, 7631 3880, www.habitat.net). You're also close to Spanish delights at **Navarro's** (67 Charlotte Street, W1T 4PH, 7637 7713).

And don't let the odd location of **Apostrophe** (216 Tottenham Court Road, W1T 7PT, 7436 6688) put you off: it may be inside the 20/20 Opticians, but it serves great sandwiches and pretty cakes to eat in or take away. Goodge Street is lined with sandwich bars and even a **Tesco Metro** supermarket – ideal for a picnic in **Crabtree Fields**, tucked away on Colville Place. It's perfect in summer, as it offers plenty of shade and a small playground, but you'll want to avoid the lunchtime business crowd.

Strangely enough, Doughty Street is now the author's only surviving London residence; the opening of the Charles Dickens Museum on the premises made certain that it would be full of memorabilia and artefacts. Its passageways are decorated with paintings of famous Dickens characters, among them Little Nell, Uriah Heep and Little Dorrit. The rooms, meanwhile, are full of Dickens's personal effects: his lemon squeezer, a walking stick, his snuff box and more. Other displays include a fine array of his personal letters, original manuscripts and the desk on which Dickens wrote *Oliver Twist*. In the basement there's a short film covering Dickens's life in London, and children's handling sessions, in which kids can write with the same type of quill pen used by the author, are held in the Library most Tuesdays and Wednesdays (11am-3pm, phone ahead).

Special events include 'The Reading Tours' (until Jan 2005), a child-friendly series of interactive displays that look at Dickens's celebrity status on his renowned reading tours of the US and UK. 'The Bloomsberries' (date to be confirmed) will be a smaller exhibition commemorating other literary greats of the Bloomsbury area, including, naturally, Virginia Woolf alongside Dickens's friend Thackeray. During the festive season, there is, of course, 'Christmas for Dickens' (Dec) with readings from *A Christmas Carol* and other delights in a traditional Victorian yuletide setting.
Nearest picnic place: Coram's Fields/Russell Square. Shop.

Coram's Fields

93 Guilford Street, WC1N 1DN (7837 6138). Russell Square tube. **Open** *May-Aug* 9am-8pm daily. *Sept-Apr* 9am-4.30pm daily. Closed 25, 26 Dec. **Admission** free. **Map** p317 L4.
A visit to the neighbourhood would be incomplete without a stroll through one of London's most famous children's parks. Established back in 1936, these seven acres (3 ha) have become a city institution. Famous long before it became a park, the site dates back to 1747, the year retired sea captain Thomas Coram established the Foundling Hospital for abandoned children (site of the new Foundling Museum, *see p65*). After the orphanage was demolished in 1920s, developers were poised to swoop; happily, a campaign to turn the site into a children's park was successful.

Today it's a kids' oasis with lawns, sandpits, a paddling pool, an AstroTurf football pitch, a basketball court, a toddlers' gym, a wooden climbing tower, swings, a helter-skelter chute, an assault-course pulley and, most famously, a city farm, with sheep, goats, geese, ducks, rabbits, guinea pigs and an aviary – the under-fives can enjoy animal petting sessions. Throughout the year the ongoing wildlife garden project is where young green thumbs can try their hand at planting bulbs or take a close-up look at the worms busy at work, churning the soil. During the summer, bands and circus performers entertain picnicking families.

Parents love the park because it's safe. It's permanently staffed, and no adults are allowed in the park unaccompanied by children. What's more, bullying, swearing, disobedience and racism are forbidden. The park offers a range of sporting activities from football and basketball to aerobics and street dance, all free (call the office for a list). Then there's t'ai chi, drama and other activities – some free, some not. A youth centre has free IT courses for 13- to 19-year-olds, while the Connexions Personal Adviser offers informed, impartial advice. The healthy-eating, vegetarian café is now open year round and, to make life easier for parents, there are toilets and shower rooms with disabled facilities, a nursery, a drop-in playgroup, and after-school and holiday play centres.
Buggy access. Café. Disabled access: toilet. Nappy-changing facilities.

Foundling Museum

40 Brunswick Square, WC1N 1AZ (7841 3600/ www.foundlingmuseum.org.uk). Russell Square tube. **Open** 10am-6pm Tue-Sat; noon-6pm Sun. Closed 3 June, 7 Oct, 25, 26 Dec, Good Friday (25 Mar 2005). **Admission** £5; £3 concessions; free under-16s. **Credit** MC, V. **Map** p317 L4.
Due to open its doors on 15 June 2004, the Foundling Museum promises to be a fascinating collection, recalling the social history of the Foundling Hospital with an interactive, child-friendly permanent exhibition. The Hospital, established in 1739 and committed to the treatment of socially excluded children, claims to be the first public art gallery and a precursor to the Royal Academy of Arts. Inspired by William Hogarth, whose works were the first to 'ornament' hospital corridors here, other contemporaneous artists (including Gainsborough, Reynolds, Roubilliac, Rysbrack, Hudson, Ramsay and Wilson) donated their own creations. Such works of art will feature in the museum, alongside Coram's personal letters and memorabilia relating to Handel, who helped to found the hospital. There will be activity packs to guide children through the museum, and kids will be able to build fuzzy-felt versions of the collection's paintings, handle interesting artefacts and objects, and browse storybooks themed on the museum and its history, among many other things. Temporary, biannual exhibitions are also planned to run alongside the main exhibition; the first of these is 'The History of the Foundling Museum Project' (until Dec 2004).

The education programme, based around music and the arts, will be run in conjunction with local schools, while family fun days will feature such goings on as 'Forming Faces' (27 Aug, 10am-4pm), a series of 90-minute workshops during which children can make papier-mâché faces inspired by the museum collection. Call ahead or check the website (when it's up and running!) for details of other regular events.
Buggy access. Café. Disabled access: lift. Nappy-changing facilities. Shop.

Petrie Museum of Egyptian Archaeology

University College London, Malet Place, WC1E 6BT (7679 2884/www.petrie.ucl.ac.uk). Goodge Street tube/ 29, 73, 134 bus. **Open** 1-5pm Tue-Fri; 10am-1pm Sat. Closed 24 Dec-2 Jan, Easter hols. **Admission** free; donations appreciated. **Map** p317 K4.
If the British Museum has all the big Ancient Egyptian show-stoppers, the Petrie Museum of Archaeology contains the pieces that made up the minutiae of Egyptian life: make-up pots, grooming accessories, jewellery and, most famously, the world's oldest piece of clothing (a dress that was worn by a teenager in 2800 BC). Some of the collection might be rather heavy going for young children, but there are items that might just take their fancy: for instance, a collection of ancient toys, a rat trap and the coiffured head of a mummy, with eyelashes and -brows still intact. The dim surroundings give the place a wonderfully spooky, tomb-like atmosphere – pick up a free torch from reception and explore the dusty aisles like a true adventurer. In the summer holidays there are family backpacks with themed trails through the museum, and hieroglyphic writing workshops and play schemes, all based around the contents of the collections. Activities such as 'Animals in Egypt' let children handle animal specimens, including giant snake skins. To celebrate National Archaeology Day, the musuem holds a special weekend on 17 and 18 July, with family activities on the Saturday. Other events crop up regularly; call ahead to see what's on.
Buggy access. Café. Disabled access: lift. Nearest picnic place: Gordon Square.

Pyjama party

If you go down to the **British Museum** (*see p61*) on a Saturday night, you're in for a big surprise. That's if you time it right, of course. Four times a year the **Young Friends of the British Museum Sleepover** has 250 kids and adults queuing up with bed rolls and sleeping bags to spend a night among the Egyptian mummies.

Each Sleepover is based around a different theme: that means Egypt on 17 July 2004, while on 11 September it'll be the Orient. The Egyptian-themed Sleepovers are far and away the most popular, but tickets for each sell out within three weeks of the Young Friends' magazine *ReMUS* going out. The price, £27.50 per ticket, doesn't put anyone off either. 'I have mothers begging at the end of the phone,' says Young Friends events manager Rebecca Murdoch. 'They've promised their kids they can go for months and they're so disapointed when they can't get a ticket.'

Registration time is at 6.45pm and the games commence as soon as the formalities of a health and safety talk are over. The 250 participants are divided into five groups of 50 and then it's non-stop activity (bar a half-hour pit stop for refreshments) from 7.30pm until bedtime. Activities, which include craft, theatre and music workshops, handling sessions and storytelling, are all inspired by the evening's theme.

If it's Ancient Greece, for instance, expect re-enactments of Greek theatre, with pro actors in the lead and the children as the chorus. What's more, it's staged only a breath away from the Elgin Marbles of the Parthenon.

At each Sleepover there's always a curator-led educational activity too, which gives kids a real sense of gaining insider knowledge and provides the experts with a treasured opportunity to impart their wisdom to eager young ears. The event may

be aimed at children aged eight to 15, but that's not to say accompanying adults are any less enthusiastic than the littler people.

At midnight, it's time to snuggle up on... the cold, hard floor of the Egyptian sculpture galleries (Room 4). Yes, there's central heating in the museum, but the big, airy halls and stone floors don't exactly compare with the comfort of a cosy bed. There's no need to hold back on the bedding: you'd be well advised to bring as much as you want, or can carry – sleeping bags, duvets, roll mats, lilos, three pillows if you like, even a camp bed. Pyjamas probably aren't enough either, so wrap yourself and your kids up in tracksuits and hoodies for the night.

Not that you can expect much sleep. It can get pretty noisy when the lights go out. Torches provide an endless source of amusement for young boys, others are purely overexcited. And do any of the kids get frightened? 'No, they're not the problem,' says Murdoch, 'it's the parents that get more scared. One mother didn't realise that it was going to be dark.'

The most coveted camping spots include those next to Rameses' head, in the tiny apse beneath the Merymose stone mummy and beside the Rosetta Stone. Indeed, it's trophies like this that make the Sleepovers a must-attend event on the kids' social calendar. As Murdoch highlights, 'it feels like a very special, exclusive experience, doing such an intimate thing as sleeping in a world-famous museum. How many children get to go into school the next day and say "I slept next to the Rosetta Stone"?'

Should you want to bagsy one of the best places, then those in the know up the ante by contacting Murdoch in advance to ensure that they're put in the group allocated the sleeping space nearest to the artefacts of choice.

At 7am it's rise and shine for a breakfast of muffins, fruit, yoghurts, fruit juice, tea and coffee before the final activity at 8am, followed by a prize-giving ceremony. Awards are given for the most well-behaved kids and for those who excelled in activities, and everyone sings Happy Birthday for the lucky mites who've blagged a Sleepover for their party (if you're planning to do the same for your kids, then bear in mind that there must be at least one Young Friend to every four guests).

To talk of once-in-a-lifetime experiences may be a cliché, but a British Museum Sleepover really is just that. You could buy the 'I slept in the British Museum' T-shirt, but – come on – how many kids are ever going to forget such adventures? They'll be telling their grandchildren about it.
To find out more about becoming a Young Friend of the British Museum, contact Rebecca, YFBM, The British Museum, Great Russell Street, London, WC1B 3DG (7327 8605/7323 8566/www.the britishmuseum.ac.uk/friends).

Around Town

Marylebone

Wild animals and waxen celebs draw the crowds, a perfect park and priceless art inspire them.

It's official. This once rather quaint area between heaving Oxford Street and polluted Marylebone Road is now one of the most desirable 'urban villages' in the capital, if you believe the Sunday supplements. Marylebone Village (as it is termed by those who buy into the hype) is the chattering classes' favourite bit of London. It's full of modish shops, including organic butchers, grocers, cheesemakers, florists and fashionable purveyors of beauty products, as well as smart cafés and restaurants. Not bad for a part of town once considered a bit square; but then the local landowners, the Howard de Walden Estate, hand-picked incoming retailers and restaurateurs to ensure there was an interesting mix of new enterprises and established, top-grade names.

Shopping or just walking around with children in the area feels more relaxed than further south in the West End. Pedestrianised St Christopher's Place makes for particularly safe café pit stops with toddlers; and Paddington Park (entrance on Paddington Street) holds what must be the West End's only playground.

Some of the area's most enticing pleasures are free. These include the artistic treasures of the **Wallace Collection** on Manchester Square and **Regent's Park**, with its boating lake, playgrounds, cafés, gardens and open-air theatre. Of course, there's also **London Zoo**, which never fails to please; to make a visit even more of a treat, you can take a canal boat there from Camden Lock or Little Venice (the London Waterbus Company operates throughout the year; ring 7482 2550 for details). **Madame Tussaud's** is a laugh if you're out and about with starstruck older children.

The area north of the Marylebone Road is also designated Marylebone. It has its own Victorian railway station behind the Landmark hotel, and there's a lively market on Church Street that sells very cheap toys (as well as fruit and veg). These may prove a useful lure if your real reason for exploring is to visit the nearby antique shops.

London Central Mosque
146 Park Road, NW8 7RG (7724 3363/www.iccuk.org). Baker Street tube/13, 82, 133 bus. **Open** *9.30am-6pm daily.* **Admission** *free.*
Those venturing inside this mosque, whose golden dome can be seen from all over Regent's Park, will find the complex much bigger than the dome and minaret imply, if lacking the

Regent's Park. *See p69.*

awe-inspiring grandeur of Islamic masterpieces such as Istanbul's Blue Mosque. Modern offices around a large court-yard accommodate London's most important Islamic Cultural Centre; inside the reception are a bookshop selling Koranic texts, noticeboards advertising spiritual and charitable events and an old-fashioned booth offering information. Men and boys enter the prayer hall via doors on the ground floor; women and girls pass through the 'toilets & *wudhu*' (washing facilities) to head upstairs to a screened-off balcony. Inside the dome is a huge chandelier encircled by Arabic tiles; otherwise the hall is devoid of decoration or furniture. Visitors must remove their shoes; women should wear a headscarf. *Buggy access. Café. Disabled access: ramp, toilet. Nappy-changing facilities. Nearest picnic place: Regent's Park. Shop.*

London Zoo
Regent's Park, NW1 4RY (7722 3333/www.londonzoo. co.uk/www.zsl.org). Baker Street or Camden Town tube, then 274 or C2 bus. **Open** *8 Mar-26 Oct* 10am-5.30pm daily. *From 27 Oct* 10am-4pm daily. Closed 25 Dec. Check website for any changes. **Admission** £13; £11 concessions; £9.75 3-15s; £41 family ticket (2+2 or 1+3); free under-3s. **Credit** AmEx, MC, V. **Map** p316 G2.
London Zoo has always provided one of the city's best days out: with more than 600 species living here, there's certainly plenty to look at. Like Whipsnade (*see p282*), London Zoo is owned and run by ZSL (the Zoological Society of London), a worldwide conservation, scientific and educational charity.

Conservation goals are clearly stated around the zoo and informative talks given, often pointing out harmful practices that threaten wildlife. Each year new enclosures are built or existing enclosures improved.

On a sunny day encounters with the goats, sheep, pigs and chickens in the children's touch paddock are a delight, and youngsters of all ages enjoy the monkeys and the giraffes. If you're really lucky, you might catch a glimpse of the shy baby tapir, born in October 2003. Also popular are the otters and meerkats, whose habit of rising on their hind legs to peer at visitors seems the ultimate irony. New animal arrivals in June 2004 were the Komodo dragons, huge smelly lizards that are making the best of an Indonesian-style enclosure.

In rainy weather hang about in the reptile house with alligators, snakes and lizards or visit the aquarium, where the children can marvel at the brightly coloured tropical fish and the odd-looking shovelnose sturgeon. Make sure you don't miss the bats and slow lorises in Moonlit World. There's also B.U.G.S!, a brilliant biodiversity centre that teaches kids about conservation and protecting habitats. Exhibits are at child-height and there are regular animal encounters. In the B.U.G.S! activity den, children can (for 50p) make badges or brass rubbings to take home.

Follow the recommended route (which is painted green) or buy the official guidebook to ensure you don't miss anything important. The information kiosk near the entrance also has free activity trails; one for ages three to seven and another for the over-eights. At the entrance you'll be given a 'What's On Today' leaflet that lists the times and locations of special events such as storytelling, animal feeding or talks.

The shop is great for animal merchandise, but it's worth regulating the extra treats: paying for the merry-go-round (£1 per ride), bouncy castle (a whopping £1 for 5mins), snacks, automated rides and helium balloons at the exit will make this an expensive day.

Buggy access. Café. Disabled access: ramps, toilet. Nappy-changing facilities. Nearest picnic space: zoo grounds. Restaurant. Shop.

Madame Tussaud's/ The London Planetarium

Marylebone Road, NW1 5LR (0870 400 3000/www. madame-tussauds.co.uk). Baker Street tube/13, 27, 74, 113, 159 bus. **Open** 9.30am-5.30pm Mon-Fri; 9am-6pm Sat, Sun. Times vary during holiday periods. Closed 25 Dec. **Admission** (incl admission to London Planetarium, price depends on time of day) £10-£19.99; £8-£16.99 concessions; £5-£15.99 5-15s; £49 family (2+2 or 1+3); free under-5s. **Credit** AmEx, MC, V. **Map** p316 G4.

It's a Londoner's duty to sneer at Madame Tussaud's city of petrified celebrities, even if they've never been in. Inside, visitors stroll into a packed celebrity party entitled 'Blush'. Hosted by a waxen J-Lo, whose famous posterior comes in for a good deal of hands-on activity, the close-up encounters

Hands on: The Wallace Collection

Despite its imposing home and the hush of its galleries, the **Wallace Collection** (*see p70*) is a great place to take children. On your way in you can pick up themed children's trails ('Monsters' or 'Paws and Claws' for ages six and over, the 'French Revolution' for age ten and above, and the new 'Indian Arms and Armour' for over-sevens) to help them navigate the collection. Downstairs, in the Conservation Gallery, a regularly changing display explains how artworks are looked after by telling the story of a specific piece from the collection that has recently been cleaned and repaired. You can also find out how furniture and armour were made, or try on some armour yourself.

The Wallace Collection's Education Department, established in 1998, is one of London's best. It organises a wealth of activities in three broad categories: drop-in events, which are free and don't have to be prebooked; family workshops, which require booking, and adult lectures or workshops. Events and activities are based on quarterly themes; this summer it's 'Eagles and Empires' (June-Aug), then 18th-century France (Sept-Nov) and 'Fashion and Image' (from Dec).

For many children, the arms and armoury workshops and activities are the business. 'We have one of the finest private collections of armour in the UK,' explains David Edge, Curator of Arms and Armour. 'We take a really hands-on approach... Our family events might involve trying on a piece of armour, holding a sword, feeling the weight of a musket or comparing a cannonball with a bullet.' There are perhaps six or eight family

armoury events each year, mostly scheduled for school holidays. They usually comprise a storytelling session, illustrated with pictures, and some handling sessions. Numbers are kept down, so everyone gets a chance to grab the treasures.

Other activity days for families might encourage children to make collages or drawings inspired by pieces in the collection – say, *The Laughing Cavalier*. Workshops link up with other institutions, such as Wigmore Hall (*see p217*), to combine art and music activities, and there are activity days to coincide with historical anniversaries – Waterloo Day, for instance – or, to help children learn about different faiths, religious festivals. Drop-in events include an 18th-century day, held each February, which has art and dance activities, food tasting and talks. Look out too for Christmas events, a quiz and trail during Advent, and a Renaissance weekend in early December.

In 2004 the Wallace Collection will also form part of a country-wide Sikh trail. The trail, to be launched in July, will list items in British museums that are a significant part of Sikh heritage. Among several important pieces at the Wallace Collection is a sword that once belonged to Ranjit Singh. A drop-in event on 3 July will feature talks and hands-on events.

An indication of how good the Wallace Collection's workshops are, is that many of them are booked up a month in advance. Put your name on the free mailing list to ensure you get early notification of events; for details ring the Education Department (7563 9551) or see the website.

Pit stops Marylebone

For those needing a spot of lunch in the vicinity of **Madame Tussaud's** and the **Wallace Collection**, Blandford Street offers several options. **Fairuz** (*see p163*) does good Lebanese, **Giraffe** (*see p163*) has both a child-friendly menu and friendly staff, and there's super pizza and pasta at **La Spighetta** (No.43, W1U 7HF, 7486 7340). Also handy for the Wallace Collection are the excellent Italian **Caffè Caldesi** (118 Marylebone Lane, W1U 2QF, 7935 1144), **Tootsies** (35 James Street, W1M 5HX, 7486 1611; *see also p182*) for quality burgers and shakes and traditional fish and chip shop the **Golden Hind** (73 Marylebone Lane, W1U 2PN, 7486 3644). Even handier is the Wallace Collection's covered courtyard restaurant: **Café Bagatelle** makes an ideal venue for afternoon tea.

There are a couple of possibilities along the way to **Regent's Park** from Oxford Street: **RIBA Café** (*see p165*) has a safe outdoor roof terrace, while **Villandry** (170 Great Portland Street, W1W 5QB, 7631 3131) is a fancy delicatessen-cum-café. You might be better, though, eating within the park itself, with the **Boathouse Café** (7724 4069),

Honest Sausage (7224 3872) and **Queen Mary's Garden Café** (7935 5729) all open year round. Picnickers can get great sandwiches for Regent's or **Paddington Street Park** from **La Fromagerie** (2-4 Moxon Street, W1U 4EW, 7935 0341) or the excellent French chain **Paul** (115 Marylebone High Street, W1U 4SB, 7224 5615).

Within **London Zoo** the newly refurbished **Oasis Café** provides reasonably priced and healthy food. You can buy a kiddie lunchbox (a sandwich, a drink and a piece of fruit) for £3.50 and hot mains (around £6 for grown-ups or £2.95 for a child's portion). The zoo also has a fish and chips café and summer kiosks for ice-cream and hot dogs.

Other good places to eat around Marylebone include **La Galette** (*see p163*), for tasty Breton pancakes, and **Patisserie Valerie at Sagne** (105 Marylebone High Street, W1U 4RS, 7935 6240), for perfect confections. Vegetarians will want to check out the crypt café of **St Marylebone Church** (17 Marylebone Road, NW1 5LT, 7935 7315) or **Eat & Two Veg** (50 Marylebone High Street, W1U 5HN, 7258 8595).

with some of the celebrity guests (Geri, Hugh Grant, Tom Cruise or Chris Tarrant, for example) are vaguely unnerving. Many of the mannequins can be touched and prodded, and there's plenty of space for photo ops; if you forgot your camera, there are outlets inside where you can buy disposable ones. In a corner by the piano, topped by Kylie Minogue with her trademark bottom, you can pretend you're a Pop Idol contestant, as well as sitting on a stool between Ant and Dec or on the couch next to Simon Cowell for a photo.

Two interactive sporting attractions strive to appeal to modern audiences. Until September, visitors can 'Do the Jonny' – attempt to emulate the drop goal that won the Rugby World Cup. Keen footie fans get the Euro 2004 team trials. 'Première Night' allows you to enjoy close encounters with waxworks of Oprah Winfrey, Pierce Brosnan, Elizabeth Taylor, Marilyn Monroe, Charlie Chaplin and Elvis, while 'The World Stage' is dominated by Blair and Bush – although space is provided for more worthwhile figures, such as Charles Darwin and Isambard Kingdom Brunel. None of these is as popular as gawping at the breathing sleeping beauty (Louis XV's mistress, Madame du Barry) or donning a plastic tiara to be photographed with HM the Queen – the resulting low-grade snap is hardly value for money at £6.75.

Below stairs, you'll find the 'Chamber of Horrors', a little showcase of torture and gruesome death. For an extra £2, you can enter 'The Chamber Live' – winding dark alleys in which barely visible serial killers are played by actors paid to give you a funny turn. This is unsuitable for under-12s.

For most children the best part of Madame Tussaud's is the final themed ride: you hop into a London taxi for a whistlestop tour of significant events in London's history.

The exit is, naturally, through the shop, which sells the usual London memorabilia. Note also that ticket prices go up at peak times (such as school holidays) and that, if you're hungry, you're a captive consumer for the Costa Coffee concession – you can't leave the premises and return. Tussaud's doesn't permit entrance to baby buggies, but a £5 deposit secures use of a baby carrier – first-come, first-served.

Most visitors see the Planetarium as little more than an adjunct to the waxworks next door. But, due to reopen after refurbishment in June 2004, it is now offering a brand new star show called 'The Quest for Life'. Based on space missions of Voyager 1 and 2, the show carries the audience through a gravity-assisted escape from Earth's atmosphere and out into space, past Jupiter and beyond Saturn. Expect close encounters with the whole panoply of space pyrotechnics – nebulae, a black hole and exploding stars. A visit taking in Tussaud's and the Planetarium lasts around two hours.

Café. Disabled access: lift, toilet. Nappy-changing facilities. Nearest picnic place: Regent's Park. Shop.

Regent's Park

The Store Yard, Inner Circle, Regent's Park, NW1 4NR (7486 7905). Baker Street, Great Portland Street, Camden Town or Regent's Park tube. **Open** 5am-30mins before dusk daily. **Admission** free. **Map** p316 G3.

London Zoo. *See p66.*

This immaculately maintained park, once used as a hunting ground by Henry VIII, was landscaped in 1811 by the architect John Nash, Crown Architect and friend of the Prince Regent. Today the park is as much a joy for Londoners of all ages as it is for foreign visitors.

For children, there are four well-maintained playgrounds, each with a sandpit and children's toilets; one is close to the London Central Mosque (*see p66*) and the boating lake; there's another by Marylebone Road, north of Portland Place; the third is by the Camden Town entrance; and the last lies at the foot of Primrose Hill. The shallow boating lake is just lovely on a hot summer day, with rowing boats available for hire by the hour (£5.50 for adults, £3.50 for children), but there's also a small, circular lake for kids who want to mess about in pedalos. These cost £3 an hour and the youngsters must pass a height test to use them – they have to be big enough to reach the pedals.

The Regent's Park Wildlife Watch Group runs free activities for six- to ten-year-olds on the third Sunday of every month from 2pm to 4pm; for more details, call 7935 7430. If sport is more your thing, the park has tennis and netball courts, an athletics track, and football and hockey pitches; call 7486 7905 to find out about the range of coaching opportunities currently available. Regent's Park also boasts an alfresco performance season that runs from May to September. The Open Air Theatre (*see also p224*) is putting on Shakespeare's *Henry V* and *A Midsummer Night's Dream* for 2004, and free lunchtime and evening concerts on the bandstand by the boating lake are also planned.
Buggy access. Cafés. Nappy-changing facilities.

Sherlock Holmes Museum

221B Baker Street, NW1 6XE (7935 8866/www.sherlock-holmes.co.uk). Baker Street tube/74, 139, 189 bus. **Open** 9.30am-6pm daily (last entry 5.30pm). Closed 25 Dec. **Admission** £6; £4 6-16s; free under-6s. **Credit** AmEx, MC, V. **Map** p313 F4.

One of the more intriguing aspects of this little commercial museum is the fact that the fictional Victorian detective still receives letters from around the world from fans expressing their undying admiration and seeking help with contemporary crimes. A selection are on display in the front room on the second floor and in the first-floor letter rack.

The museum itself takes up four floors of a terraced house at 239 Baker Street (but labelled 221B, Holmes's fictional address). Set up as if Sir Arthur Conan Doyle's creation was actually in residence, it's a bit dull for little children as there's nothing much to play with. The room settings with their lit fires follow the descriptions in the stories closely enough to fascinate Holmes fans, but labelling is somewhat lacking – if you don't know what an opium pipe looks like, you'll be mystified by that exhibit, and if you're not up on Victorian criminals, you'll probably think the photos of them are of Holmes's relatives. The first and second floors have waxwork figures in murderous or cadaverous poses – these are labelled: 'The Blackmailer Charles Augustus Milverton and his surprise assailant' (woman shoots man with pistol) and so on. The children love 'em.

Collectors of cheesy Sherlockiana will be in their element here: the museum shop sells Holmes teddies, Holmes figurines and deerstalker hats (£20), while the associated Sherlock Holmes Memorabilia Company (across the road at 230 Baker Street) flogs videos, beer mats, magnifying glasses and pipes. It also has a small room full of photos and a set from Granada TV's version of the Sherlock Holmes adventures, which may be viewed in the presence of a shop assistant in cape and deerstalker (£2.50 per person).
Nearest picnic place: Regent's Park. Shop.

The Wallace Collection.

St James's Spanish Place

22 George Street, W1U 3QY (7935 0943/www.spanish place.hemscott.net). Baker Street or Bond Street tube. **Open** 7am-7.30pm daily. *Services* 7.15am, 12.30pm, 6pm Mon-Fri; 10am, 6pm Sat; 8.30am, 9.30am (Old Rite), 10.30am (Sung Latin), noon, 4pm, 7pm Sun. **Admission** free. **Map** p316 G5.

Locals sometimes call this Gothic edifice 'the Spanish church', although its associations with that country officially ceased in 1827. The first St James's was built in 1791, just after the repeal of laws banning Catholic worship; the present church opened opposite the original in 1890. A lot of continental Catholics live nearby, so it's well attended at Mass, and even weekday mornings see people sitting in quiet prayer or genuflecting at the altar. There's a palpable sense of peace, with the interior always bathed in a soft golden light, thanks to the ornate gilt decorations and many votive candles. The basement accommodates a Montessori nursery, and family events are held here; check the noticeboards for details. A repository, which is open after Masses over the weekend, sells crucifixes, cards and so on.
Nearest picnic place: Regent's Park. Shop.

Wallace Collection

Hertford House, Manchester Square, W1U 3BN (7935 0687/www.wallacecollection.org). Bond Street tube/2, 10, 12, 30, 74, 113 bus. **Open** 10am-5pm Mon-Sat; noon-5pm Sun. Closed 24-26 Dec, 1 Jan, Good Friday, 1 May. **Admission** free. **Credit** *Shop* MC, V. **Map** p316 G5.

Room after room of fabulous Louis XIV and XV furnishings, lush paintings by Fragonard, Canaletto, Frans Hals (*The Laughing Cavalier*) and Rembrandt (*Titus, the Artist's Son*), as well as gilded clocks, mirrors, snuff boxes, porcelain and armour. The collection was inherited by Richard Wallace from his father, the Marquis of Hertford, a great Francophile who had bought it for safe keeping from the ravages of the French Revolution. On her death in 1897, Wallace's wife bequeathed the collection to the nation on condition it be kept together, effectively confining it to Hertford House. There are visiting artworks in a special – separate – gallery. *See also p67* **Hands on: The Wallace Collection**.
Buggy access. Disabled access: lift, toilet. Nappy-changing facilities. Nearest picnic place: grounds. Restaurant. Shop.

West End

Where all lights are bright.

For most visitors, the glitzy West End is the beating heart of London; most Londoners see it as congested and on the verge of coronary collapse. Few, however, dispute its status as the capital's capital when it comes to the bright lights, big city energy that London is famous for. From the department stores to the garish neon and noise of the **Trocadero**, from the high culture of the **Royal Academy of Arts** to the bars and nightclubs, the West End is London's entertainment centre, irrespective of the kind of entertainment you seek.

The expansion of the 'West End' is as much the growth of a legend as of a district. The hub of activity is **Oxford Circus**, with the tube station a perpetually swarming hive of perplexed tourists. Don't hang around, unless you're looking for a flagship shopping experience (Nike Town and Top Shop tower overhead), but instead head down Regent Street to Hamleys toy shop (*see p206*). You'll also find the more cultured attractions of the **Handel House Museum** and the Royal Institute's **Faraday Museum** nearby.

For more conventional family mayhem, plunge into **Piccadilly Circus**. In its centre, the famous statue of Eros – the 'Angel of Christian Charity', but regularly mistaken for Cupid – is often home to impromptu musical performances, while on either side stand the Tower Records behemoth and the brain-scrambling **Trocadero**.

Adjoining Shaftesbury Avenue is dominated by some of London's most reputable theatres, while Soho – to the north – is home to some of its least reputable. It's still not really a place for younger children, peppered as it is with peepshows and adult cinemas, although it's nowhere near as seedy as it once was. Carnaby Street, on Soho's western edge, is always buzzing and, bang in the middle of Soho, there are bargains galore at Berwick Street Market. To the south, Chinatown is full of restaurants and a delightful place to briefly lose your bearings, but the place to lose your marbles is Leicester Square. Here prices for blockbuster cinema screenings beggar belief – throw in some overpriced popcorn, and you may well be walking home. Still, it is home to regular star-studded premières that ooze glitter from every gap in the paving stones – especially those that boast the handprints, Hollywood Boulevard style, of separated British starlets Jude Law and Sadie Frost. For a less extortionate cinematic engagement, try the **Prince Charles Cinema** (7 Leicester Place, WC2H 7BY, 7734 9127): cheap tickets and the singalong Sound of Music screenings (www.singalonga.co.uk) make it a favourite. For entertainment on an absolute shoestring, though, don't leave Leicester Square. It's the regular stamping ground for a wide range of mime artists and street performers, although it has to be said, the quality of their work is variable.

Pit stops West End

There are loads of places to eat around Leicester Square, but if you've splashed out on the big-screen first-run experience, you might want to ignore the bright lights and high prices and head into Soho for a cheaper and altogether more cheerful bite. If it's just a snack you're after, try the excellent cakes and pastries at **Amato** (*see p163*); if the kids need proper filling up, have pizza at smart but friendly **Spiga** (84-6 Wardour Street, W1F 0TA, 7734 3444). Or just wander into Chinatown: the restaurants are a bit hit and miss, but we've always been fond of the dim sum at family-friendly **Harbour City** (*see p164*).

If you can haul them away from the games in the **Trocadero**, **Yo! Sushi** (7434 2724) or **Ed's Easy Diner** (*see p163*) are good on-site options, although the **Rainforest Café** (*see p165*) offers the complete tropical dining experience.

There's nothing so theatrical at **St James' Church Piccadilly**, just an on-site **Caffè Nero** in a warm and pleasant glass annex that offers a reliable range of drinks and snacks. More elaborate and mostly Italian food can be found in the nearby **Quod Restaurant & Bar** (*see p165*), or well executed light noodly delights at the canteen-like **Miso** (66 Haymarket, SW1Y 4RF, 7930 4800). There's also **Planet Hollywood** (*see p164*) for those after a little less conversation, a little more action.

Equally loud is the **Hard Rock Café** (*see p164*), perfect for gung-ho urchins fed up with behaving themselves at **Apsley House** and ready to rock 'n' roll. Finally, you'll find dramatic flourishes at **Benihana** (*see p163*), which is roughly equidistant between the **Handel House Museum** and the **Royal Academy of Arts** or **Faraday Museum**.

THE
Miz Kids' Club

Spend an exciting 2½ hours on a Saturday morning
(and Wednesdays during school holidays)
enjoying the *Les Misérables* experience.
Take a behind the scenes tour,
try on the costumes,
take part in a drama workshop
and meet a cast member!

Suitable for children aged 8-15

**For details call 0870 850 9171
or email
education@camack.co.uk**

QUEEN'S THEATRE
0870 890 1110

Apsley House:
The Wellington Museum

149 Piccadilly, Hyde Park Corner, W1J 7NT (7499 5676/ www.english-heritage.org.uk). Hyde Park Corner tube. **Open** 10am-5pm Tue-Sun, most bank hol Mon. Closed 24-26 Dec, 1 Jan. **Admission** £4.50 (includes audio guide); £3 concessions; £2.30 under-18s. **Credit** MC, V. **Map** p318 G8.

The life of Arthur Wellesley, better known as the Duke of Wellington, was inextricably bound up with ceremony. As was his death: thousands turned out for the four-and-a-half hour parade of his funeral car through London to St Paul's Cathedral, where the 'Iron Duke' was entombed. Even Wellington's horse, Copenhagen, was buried with full military honours. A statue of both watches over Apsley House, the magnificent residence to which Wellington repaired after his victory over Napoleon at Waterloo. Wellington's descendants still live here, but ten rooms were recently restored to their original splendour and opened to the public.

The Waterloo Gallery was just one of many elaborate modifications made by the Duke on his arrival. It is 90ft (27m) long and houses his impressive art collection, which includes works by Caravaggio, Velázquez and Van Dyck.

War heroes nowadays tend to get a frostier reception than they once did, and the main exhibition might be a little formal for younger children, but recorded autoguides open the experience up to more historically minded kids and there is a comprehensive schools programme that includes tours led by costumed Victorian housekeepers. Best of all is the annual Waterloo Week in June, with family dressing-up and painting and craft workshops for all (phone for details). *Buggy access. Lift. Nearest picnic place: Hyde Park. Shop.*

Faraday Museum/Royal Institution

21 Albemarle Street, W1S 4BS (7409 2992/www. rigb.org). Green Park tube. **Open** 9am-5pm Mon-Fri. **Closed** 24-26 Dec, 1 Jan, bank hols. **Tours** by arrangement. **Admission** £1; 50p concessions. *Tours* £5. **Credit** *Shop* MC, V. **Map** p318 J7.

The Royal Institution runs a seasonal programme of school events, with classes for all ages, from 'cool science' and creepy-crawlies for infants to theoretical physics for A-level students. For families hoping to just drop in, a small on-site museum celebrates the life of Michael Faraday. Once a chemical assistant at the Institution, Faraday discovered electro-magnetic induction and created the first transformers and generators – on the same principles as inform the construction of modern power stations. The museum recreates one of Faraday's original laboratories, with a range of apparatus on display (including his first electric generator). The exhibition leans towards the scholarly, but it's nonetheless invaluable for those struggling with science projects. *Buggy access. Disabled access: toilet. Lift. Nearest picnic place: Berkeley Square/Green Park. Shop.*

Getting a Handel on London

It's barely been open two years, but the **Handel House Museum** (*see p74*) is already doing more to reveal the wonders of classical music to children than many institutions that pre-date the man himself. Rooms – including Handel's bedchamber and rehearsal studio – have been refurbished to match how they would have looked in Handel's day (he lived, worked and died here for 36 years in the first half of the 18th century), and there are numerous displays on his life and the London he inhabited.

London has changed significantly over the centuries – surrounding streets are now teeming with the flagship stores of fashion houses – but they're changes that the museum welcomes, and this is the key to its considerable success with younger audiences. In a city that too often sets the classics on a plane above popular music, this is one museum that embraces the relationship between past and present, allowing children to relate Handel's life to their own and his experiences of music to theirs. As an example of the staff's open-mindedness, a recent in-house exhibition of Jimi Hendrix photographs tied the composer in with his 20th-century rock legend neighbour. The compliment was repaid at a concert in May, which saw Acoustic Ladyland – a Hendrix covers band – take on work by Handel.

Nowhere is the museum's experimental edge better demonstrated than in its current programme of storytelling workshops. These often take as their inspiration pieces from Handel's Magic Opera series, renowned for its enchanting and family-friendly use of folklore and fable, and populated with fearsome gods, monsters and magicians aplenty. Each workshop is based around a simplified version of a tale, and given a musical voice when highlights of the opera it inspired is performed live by a singer and harpsichord player in Handel's own rehearsal room. Phone 7495 1685 for information – and book well in advance, as the room seats just 25 people.

Other intimate music recitals take place regularly on Thursdays at 6pm and 7pm (£5 adults, £2 children, including entry to the museum), mixing classical music with jazz, and family days are held on Saturdays throughout the school term. Staff up the ante on these fun-filled Saturdays, when Handel This! activity sheets – available throughout the week – are complemented by interactive Handel Bags. The former guide children around the museum with a series of amusing challenges, manage to work in pictures of contemporary pop icons (such as Christina Aguilera and Britney Spears (the Faustino Bordoni and Francesca Cuzzoni of our times, apparently); the latter are bursting with period-specific textures and smells – from lavender boxes to embossed wallpaper samples – that again get kids thinking about the London that Handel knew. An expanded programme of kids' activities runs throughout the school holidays. This included a Family Violin Day in March 2004, which offered young musicians an introduction to baroque music as part of National Violin Week (phone or check the website for a calendar of upcoming events).

Piccadilly Circus. See p71.

Handel House Museum

25 Brook Street (entrance at rear), W1K 4HB (7495 1685/www.handelhouse.org). Bond Street tube. **Open** 10am-6pm Tue, Wed, Fri, Sat; 10am-8pm Thur; noon-6pm Sun, bank hol Mon. Closed 24-26 Dec, 1 Jan, Good Friday, Easter Mon. **Admission** £4.50; £3.50 concessions; £2 5-16s; free under-5s. **Credit** MC, V. **Map** p318 H6.
Once the home of George Frideric Handel, this Mayfair house has been restored and opened as a museum devoted to the composer. Fans of Jimi Hendrix also flock here: during the '60s the rock star lived next door at No.23, the top floors of which (including Hendrix's flat) were incorporated into the museum. *See also p73* **Getting a Handel on London**.
Buggy access. Lifts. Nappy-changing facilities. Nearest picnic place: Hanover Square. Shop.

Royal Academy of Arts

Burlington House, Piccadilly, W1J 0BD (7300 8000/ www.royalacademy.org.uk). Green Park or Piccadilly Circus tube/9, 14, 19, 22, 38 bus. **Open** 10am-6pm Mon-Thur, Sat, Sun; 10am-10pm Fri. **Tours** times vary. **Admission** varies depending on exhibition; free under-8s. **Tours** free. **Credit** AmEx, MC, V. **Map** p318 J7.
The enduring appeal of the Royal Academy's annual Summer Exhibition (June-Aug) is its breadth. Work is submitted by members of the public alongside established artists, and all ages can enter pieces for consideration. There's nothing like a wander through the Academy – opened in 1768 as the nation's first art school – to get imaginations fired up. The 2004 Summer Exhibition is marked by a series of family-oriented activities, including two performances by the London Philharmonic Orchestra and weekly workshops. Both use pieces from the display as inspiration.
   Family events at the Royal Academy tie into exhibitions, some of which lend themselves more easily to kids' activities than others: papier-mâché death masks are less likely to make an appearance in activities related to the William Nicholson retrospective than at 2002's Aztec exhibition, for example. Still, there's always the Art Tray for kids and family tours to make light work of the gallery experience.
Buggy access. Café. Lift. Nappy-changing facilities. Nearest picnic place: Green Park/St James's Square. Restaurant. Shop.

St James' Church Piccadilly

197 Piccadilly, W1J 9LL (7734 4511/www.st-james-piccadilly.org). Piccadilly Circus tube/6, 9, 12, 19, 22 bus. **Open** 8am-7pm daily (phone for details of evening events). **Closed** 24-26 Dec, some bank hols (phone to check). **Map** p318 J7.
In otherwise staid and culturally serious Piccadilly, St James' is an oasis of colour and charm. This is especially true of its churchyard garden, which harbours a vibrant market offering antiques (Tue) or arts and crafts (Wed-Sat). The entire scene is shrouded in low trees, with weather-beaten statues, a glass-fronted Caffè Nero (with heated terrace) and even an old tin caravan (used as a Samaritans-style listening centre). Inside St James' is as vibrant as out: it has a well-founded reputation for indiscriminate openness.
   Sir Christopher Wren began the church in 1676 – it's believed to be one of his favourite works – and Haydn, Handel and Mendelssohn were all resident organists. William Blake was baptised here, although he died a pauper and was buried with other dissenters in Bunhill Fields (*see p51*).
Buggy access. Disabled: ramp. Café. Nearest picnic place: St James's Square/church gardens.

Trocadero

Coventry Street, W1D 7DH (7439 1791/www.troc.co.uk). Piccadilly Circus tube. **Open** 10am-midnight Mon-Thur, Sun; 10am-1am Fri, Sat. **Admission** free; individual attractions vary. **Credit** varies. **Map** p319 K7.
Hardly a paradigm of high culture, the Trocadero is a Neverland of neon lights and pseudo-space age stairwells, with crashing chart music punctuated by sirens and screams – as nauseating to adults as it is nirvana to kids. Funland batters the senses with arcade machines (everything from driving simulators to dated 'whack-a-mole' units), dodgems, a ghost train and (for over-18s) a pool hall. There's also ten-pin bowling, and a range of less immediately addictive activities for young children (bungee trampolines, claw grabbers and photo-sticker booths). There's also a multi-screen UGC cinema and a sports bar to which the oldies can retreat when they've had all the fun they can bear.
Buggy access. Cafés. Disabled access: toilet. Lift. Nappy-changing facilities. Nearest picnic place: Leicester Square/Trafalgar Square. Restaurants. Shops.

Covent Garden & St Giles's

Where the actors are outside and the buses indoors.

These days, **Covent Garden** is home to some of London's most fashionable residences – which is exactly what the Earl of Bedford had in mind when, in the 1630s, he commissioned master architect Inigo Jones to design a series of Palladian arcades based on the elegant central piazza in Livorno, Italy. A well-heeled clientele was quick to claim the area as its own but, as the riotous fruit and vegetable market expanded to dominate the main square over the next century, they headed west to more assured lodgings. Covent Garden soon became a hangout for poets and painters, a hotbed of intellectual activity. Then, as now, the area was to the stage what Leicester Square is to the screen, but it was only in 1973 – when the vegetable market moved south to Vauxhall – that the piazza was reclaimed by the cafés, bars and licensed street artists that today make it one of London's biggest tourist attractions.

The best performers book weeks in advance to act in front of the portico of **St Paul's Covent Garden** (see p76), but on any given day you'll find mime artists, actors and musicians scattered about the square; every summer there are open-air operatics courtesy of the **Royal Opera House** (see p76). The area's oldest theatre is the Theatre Royal Drury Lane (7494 5000); its largest is the Coliseum (7632 8300), home to the English National Opera and recently reopened after extensive renovations. For

an interactive look at the area's theatrical history, don't miss the **Theatre Museum** (see p77); for something completely different, try **London's Transport Museum** (see p76), whose collection of old buses and trains can make even the most docile children want to take over the driver's seat.

The rest of Covent Garden tends to be dominated by super-swanky shoe shops, although a homage to younger and more affordable fashion can be found in the alternative enclave of Neal's Yard. A lively clutter of co-operative cafés, herbalists and skate shops, the Yard is a testament to community sit-ins and hippie demonstrations that saved the area from corporate redevelopment in the 1970s, and remains blissfully unaltered.

St Giles's, meanwhile, is less renowned as a tourist attraction. The area's reputation is seedier than that of Covent Garden, with the latter's creative legacy substituted for one far more rooted in criminal activity. Once an Irish slum, when St Giles's was levelled to make way for New Oxford Street, only the church of St Giles-in-the-Fields (60 St Giles High Street, WC2H 8LG, 7240 2532) remained. Named after the patron saint of outcasts, the church originated as the chapel of a leper colony, founded in 1011; the first victims of the plague of 1665 were discovered in this same squalid neighbourhood. Nowadays, the churchyard gardens provide a

---

Pit stops Covent Garden

In **Neal's Yard**, open-minded parents are able to replenish their little ones with vegetarian dishes at the **World Food Café** (see p169) or fill up on home-made cakes and healthy snacks at the homely **Neal's Yard Bakery & Tearoom** (see p168). Those craving a ring-shaped snack will find help at the **Great American Bagel Factory** (18 Endell Street, WC2H 9BD, 7497 1115); for something more like a discus, try **Pizza Express** (9-12 Bow Street, WC2E 7AH, 7240 3443) or **Pizza Paradiso** (31 Catherine Street, WC2B 5JS, 7836 3609). **Spaghetti House** (24 Cranbourn Street, WC2H 7AB, 7836 8168) does a special pasta meal deal for kids, while for fish and chips the only place worth trying is the **Rock & Sole Plaice** (see p168), one of London's finest chippies.

Anyone visiting **London's Transport Museum** can grab drinks and snacks in the on-site café, but parents hoping to fill kids up properly might be

pleased to know there's a **TGI Friday's** (see p169) within spitting distance. Others might say spitting distance is close enough. More unusual (but no less hectic) is **Smollensky's on the Strand** (see p168), with play areas, live performers and some suitably sticky puddings all vying for kids' attention on weekends. Other places extending a warm, if less exuberant, welcome to children include **Maxwell's** (see p167) and **PJ's Grill** (see p168).

Inside the Covered Market you'll find the **Café Deli**, turning out irresistible chocolate waffles, and opposite St Paul's a **West Cornwall Pasty Company** (1 The Market, WC2E 8RA, 7836 8336). For kids who demand the finer things in life, **Browns** (see p167) is just around the corner, while more worldly wise children prefer **Café Pacifico** (see p167), for top-notch Spanish and Mexican, or **Belgo Centraal** (see p166), where kids' dishes are free if a paying adult eats with them.

Theatre Museum. See p77.

family-friendly spot, and there are lunchtime classical concerts here on Fridays at 1.10pm. **Phoenix Garden** is another welcome sanctuary from the surrounding chaos. Otherwise, a rich musical heritage makes Denmark Street – once known as 'Tin Pan Alley' – a draw for rock fanatics, with those who aren't buying or trying guitars heading to the intimate 12 Bar Club (22-3 Denmark Place, WC2H 8NL, 7916 6989, www.12barclub.com). It does a nice line in cheap lunches, but you'll most likely want to head back to Covent Garden if food's the main objective.

London's Transport Museum
Covent Garden Piazza, WC2E 7BB (7379 6344/www.lt museum.co.uk). Covent Garden tube. **Open** 10am-6pm Mon-Thur, Sat, Sun; 11am-6pm Fri (last entry 5.15pm). These times were uncertain as we went to press, so phone in advance. **Admission** (LP) £5.95; £4.50 concessions; free under-16s when accompanied by an adult. *Tours* free. **Credit** MC, V. **Map** p319 L7.
This well-managed museum charts the history of London transport from 19th-century carts to the present day, with plenty of actors and interactive displays to bring the journey to life, not to mention a resident poet (*see p77* **Playtime at... London's Transport Museum**). Kids love the shop, which is packed with colourful vehicular toys and souvenirs.
Buggy access. Café. Lift. Nappy-changing facilities. Nearest picnic place: picnic area in ground-floor museum gallery. Shop.

Phoenix Garden
21 Stacey Street (entrance on St Giles Passage), WC2H 8DG (7379 3187). Tottenham Court Road tube. **Open** dawn-dusk daily. **Admission** free. **Map** p317 K6.
This recently extended little public garden proves that all is not lost in the war against urban decay. Appropriately named, this Phoenix rose on the site of a great big car park, reclaimed and developed by the Covent Garden Open Spaces Association, which has campaigned for a local patch of greenery since the 1980s. The garden's collection of crooked pathways, charming wooden trellises and fragmented statues are an extremely pleasant surprise in one of London's least laid-back neighbourhoods. There's plenty of resident wildlife (including frogs, ladybirds and lacewings), as well as a couple of slides. None of this comes cheap: staff rely on volunteers and donations, so feel free to unburden your wallet – although seasoned gardeners might prefer to grab a spade and offer hands-on assistance. Tea and coffee are available from the shed; there are often plants on sale.
Buggy access. Kiosk.

Royal Opera House
Bow Street, WC2E 9DD (7240 1200/box office 7304 4000/www.royaloperahouse.org). Covent Garden tube. **Open** *Box office* 10am-8pm Mon-Sat. **Tours** 10.30am, 12.30pm, 2.30pm Mon-Sat. **Tickets** £8; £7 under-18s, concessions. **Credit** AmEx, DC, MC, V. **Map** p319 L6.
Kids with an interest in opera are few and far between. While language barriers and a lack of opera celebrities don't help matters, the lion's share of the blame must lie with divisions that are cultural in origin. Self-consciously 'civilised' and constantly flamboyant, opera isn't renowned for appealing to shorter attention spans. Still, the ROH is anything but stuffy: recently refurbished, its great glass ceilings make it a bright and beautiful break in Covent Garden's otherwise hectic agenda. The upstairs eaterie offers terraced seating with sweeping views of the city, and pint-sized performers will relish the guided tour, which affords kids a rare peek behind the scenes into dressing rooms and rehearsal halls – often in use. There's also an unpaid work-experience scheme that offers invaluable first-hand stage maintenance and administrative skills to over-16s. Families hoping to take in a show can attend pre-performance workshops explaining the nuances of this highly stylised medium, but there are several annual productions that are less likely to go over the heads of younger audiences: 2002's *Wind in the Willows* was a hit, and 2004 sees a further collaboration with the Unicorn children's theatre (*see p218*), whose opera *Clockwork* – for ages eight and over – is based on Philip Pullman's short story. *See also p219* **Sing it loud**.
Buggy access. Café. Lift. Nappy-changing facilities. Nearest picnic place: Covent Garden Piazza/St Paul's churchyard. Restaurant. Shop.

St Paul's Covent Garden
Bedford Street, WC2E 9ED (7836 5221/www.actors church.org). Covent Garden tube. **Open** 8.30am-5.30pm Mon-Fri; 9am-1pm Sun. *Sunday service* 11am. Closed 1 Jan, bank hols. **Admission** free; donations appreciated. **Map** p319 L6.
St Paul's is the last portion of Inigo Jones's original Palladian square still standing, and as such its peaceful interior continues to offer much-needed sanctuary from the carnival of tourists outside. That said, it's far from emotionally detached from the theatrical heritage of its surroundings: the consecrated 'Actors Church' has walls adorned with plaques commemorating the legends of screen and stage, including Charlie Chaplin, Noel Coward and Vivien Leigh. The church

has itself served as a backdrop for several cameos in the history of theatre: on 9 May 1662 diarist Samuel Pepys described being 'mighty pleased' after witnessing the first recorded Punch and Judy show here, a birthday marked by the annual May Fayre & Puppet Festival (*see p32*), and George Bernard Shaw set the opening to *Pygmalion* under the ornate portico. That same portico is most notable today as the site of performances by the finest street performers in town, wowing crowds on a daily basis throughout the year. We're not talking traffic cone trumpet-players, either: wannabes are first auditioned by Covent Garden Market, and even then performance slots are booked up weeks in advance. *Buggy access. Nearest picnic place: churchyard.*

Theatre Museum
Russell Street, WC2E 7PR (7943 4700/group bookings 7943 4806/www.theatremuseum.org). Covent Garden tube. **Open** 10am-6pm (last entry 5.30pm) Tue-Sun. Closed 24-26 Dec, 1 Jan. **Tours** noon, 2pm Tue-Sun. **Admission** free. **Credit** AmEx, MC, V. **Map** p319 L6.
This excellent museum weaves the colourful threads of Covent Garden's theatrical history into an enthrallingly vivid tapestry. Permanent displays include testaments to heroes of a bygone age (David Garrick, Edmund Kean, Eliza Vestris) as well as to the plays that cast them into the public eye.

There are regular make-up displays and costume workshops throughout the day, and storytelling sessions on the first Saturday of every month (2-2.30pm; also Wed and Fri in school holidays). Best of all is the comprehensive range of theatrical activities for kids, including the Stage Truck programme for three- to 12-year-olds (1.30-5pm Sat; also Thur in school holidays). For older kids, Your Shout workshops have proved excellent outlets for pent-up creativity. They take place over half-terms (3-4.30pm Wed), offering children a chance to design and act out a role under the tuition of a trained professional. A Kids Theatre Club (*pictured*), run by the Society of London Theatres, takes place 10am-noon every Saturday morning and costs £5; booking is essential, as places are limited.
Since May 2004, the museum's 2D>3D exhibition has examined the translation of performances from the script to the stage, hosting a number of pieces including the set-design for Handel's opera *Tamerlano*, costume designs for *A Midsummer Night's Dream* and the impressive giant spider designed by Abigail Hammond for a touring production of *The Hobbit*. Among the various workshops affiliated to the exhibition are a set-design competition (July 2004), the winning entrants to which will be displayed in the museum. *Buggy access. Nappy-changing facilities. Nearest picnic place: Covent Garden Piazza/St Paul's churchyard. Shop.*

Playtime at... London's Transport Museum

For many people, the only words inspired by London's buses are the four-letter variety. Not so for Abraham Gibson. As resident poet at **London's Transport Museum** (*see p76*) it's his job to find beauty in the capital's roads and rails, and he insists he doesn't have to look far: 'If there is a more beautiful sight than this big red carriage rolling through the cold, soft, black morning with all its lights on, I have yet to see it.' Right.

Between shifts as a Hackney Council caretaker, Abe spends a lot of his spare time on buses. When he started at the museum he regularly rose before dawn to spend the day riding the 73 in and out of town from his Tottenham home, listening intently to the snatches of conversation the rest of us ignore. The characters he conjures up from these researches are there to greet children at the museum, and when he speaks of them it's with a fondness many reserve for friends. 'There are no costume changes or elaborate props: when I shift from one character to another it's by simply altering my facial and vocal expressions. I'm starting to feel like I know some of them really well now.'

Among Abe's acquaintances are London's first black bus driver, Joe Clough, who almost 100 years ago steered a No.11 from Liverpool Street to Wormwood Scrubs, and Alfie, a jaunty Cockney. But the character closest to Abe's heart is Cedric, a Caribbean bus conductor working on the big red Routemasters of the 1950s, and engaging kids with tales selected from the hundreds he hears each day. As Cedric says, 'What is a journey without stories? We all have stories!'
After leading families on an imaginary train journey around London – stopping on the way to illuminate various people, places and points in time – Abe helps kids compose and perform their own poems in occasional creative workshops, the results of which are spliced together into a single narrative and posted on the museum's website.
Elsewhere at the museum, costumed actors bring transport history to life as they wander around the displays: a miner regales kids with claustrophobic tales of tube tunnel construction in 1906, while a female bus driver chats amiably about her World War II experiences. A variety of themed guided tours can be pre-booked, covering the museum itself, the Museum Depot in Acton Town (home to more than 370,000 objects, from classic carriages to antique ticket machines) or even train, tube and bus routes around the capital. Back in the museum, younger children can enjoy free family worksheets and maps, or hop aboard the Funbus and pretend to drive. There's also a year-round arts and crafts room that runs themed creative workshops in the school holidays. Activities are included in the price of admission: check the website for upcoming events.

Westminster

The Royals and Right Honourables may clamour for attention, but the art and architecture here demand it.

From the gilded, neo-Gothic façade of the Houses of Parliament and looming Westminster Abbey to Nelson, looking lost and forlorn atop his column, a library's worth of postcards, warehouses of T-shirts and an environmental catastrophe of plastic merchandise assures the world that this is the throbbing centre of London.

Architecturally, it is a stunning area to ponder. But the myriad pictures fail to do the place justice. What's worse, they barely describe half of what's worth seeing. The **Houses of Parliament** and **Big Ben** (a name that refers to the bell inside St Stephen's Tower), to be fair, you can hardly avoid, although you're unlikely to do more than wander around them getting a stiff neck. A visit inside **Westminster Abbey**, meanwhile, is a truly humbling experience, and worth every penny, and while **Buckingham Palace** has had its fair share of critics design-wise, kids never tire of the clockwork charms of the Changing of the Guard.

Yet there are plenty of other places that children will find engaging. Their thwarted desires to look out from behind the little hand of Parliament's famous clockface can be quelled, to a degree, by a trip to **Westminster Cathedral**, where a lift runs all the way up the Campanile Bell Tower to a four-sided viewing gallery at the top. Or they can find creative inspiration at **Tate Britain**, the **National Gallery** and the **National Portrait Gallery**, or try their hand at brass-rubbing in the atmospheric crypt of **St Martin-in-the-Fields**.

While tourists constantly fill the area's streets and spaces, lining up outside the Horse Guards Building on Whitehall to take snaps of each other alongside the mounted guards, there's always sanctuary to be found in **St James's Park** and the riverside **Victoria Tower Gardens**. The former faces the **Guards' Museum** on one side and the **Cabinet War Rooms** on another, while the latter is home to a small children's playground. It also offers a rare view of Parliament and tends to be relatively quiet. The intriguing **Jewel Tower** – the gardens of which make for a serene picnic spot – is a mere stone's throw away.

But even this 'grand' tour doesn't complete the picture. Westminster is an incredibly diverse place. From the peace of **Smith Square** to the child-friendly chippies and caffs of bustling **Strutton Ground** market, from the high-class car dealerships of Marsham Street to the heaving throngs of recently remodelled **Trafalgar Square**, Westminster is a place that defies being pigeonholed – despite all its pigeons (at least those not yet discouraged by their legally imposed restricted diet).

If one blanket statement can be made with confidence, it's that the area's political magnetism is weakening. The recent closure of longstanding government bookstore Politicos and the relative emptiness of once-thriving political hangouts such as Parliament's own Strangers Bar imply waning public interest in the machinations of professional politics. Not that the kids care: they'll be far too busy chasing pigeons.

Banqueting House

Whitehall, SW1A 2ER (7930 4179/www.hrp.org.uk). Westminster tube/Charing Cross tube/rail. **Open** 10am-5pm Mon-Sat (last entry 4.30pm). Sometimes closes at short notice; phone to check. Closed bank hols. **Admission** (LP) £4; £3 concessions; £2.60 5-15s; free under-5s. **Credit** MC, V. **Map** p319 L8.

The Banqueting House encompasses a history both glorious and gruesome. Designed by Inigo Jones for James I, the Hall was intended to be used for state and ceremonial occasions. Sure enough, its opening in 1622 was marked by a traditional Twelfth Night masque. But such jollities were a distant memory when, in 1649, James's son Charles I was found guilty of treason by Cromwell's revolutionary forces and beheaded outside the Banqueting House.

These rich historical associations pull in today's tourists (the Sealed Knot Civil War re-enactment society even plays out the execution one Sunday each January), although Jones's architecture is magnificent on its own: from the extravagant main hall to the cryptic undercroft (conceived as a drinking den for James I). Rubens's original ceilings are still in place, despite extensive fire damage in 1698 and removal for their own safety during World War II. Audio guides (included in the ticket price) bring the scene to life for children.

The Hall is also a venue for regular Monday lunchtime classical concerts throughout the year (£15): most are aimed at adults, but there's a lighter Christmas concert in December. *Nearest picnic place: St James's Park. Shop.*

Buckingham Palace & Royal Mews

SW1A 1AA (7321 2233/www.royal.gov.uk). Green Park or St James's Park tube/Victoria tube/rail. **Open** *State Rooms* early Aug-late Sept 9.30am-4.15pm daily. *Royal Mews* 1 Mar-31 July, 29 Sept-31 Oct 11am-4pm daily; 1 Aug-28 Sept 10am-5pm daily. Closed Fri during Mar & Jul, and last wk of Oct, during Ascot, state occasions, 25, 26 Dec. **Admission** (LP) £12.95; £11 concessions; £6.50 5-17s; £32.50 family (2+2); free under-5s. *Royal Mews* £5.50; £4.50 concessions; £3 5-17s; £14 family (2+2); free under-5s. *Queen's Gallery* £7.50; £6 OAPs, students; £4 children; £19 family (2+3); free under-5s. **Credit** AmEx, MC, V. **Map** p318 H9.

Playtime at... the National Gallery

The geographical prominence of the **National Gallery** (*see p81*) – looming over Trafalgar Square – makes it the first stop on many a tourist's must-see schedule, and the occasionally overwhelming holiday crowds combine with the sheer scale of the collection to intimidate many adults, let alone their children. Thankfully, the education department has made the National a genuinely family-friendly place – which is a relief, as its collection of European paintings is one of the finest in the world, including such masterpieces as Van Gogh's *Sunflowers* and da Vinci's *The Virgin of the Rocks*.

Members of staff endeavour to remain true to the spirit in which the gallery was founded in the early 19th century. The National's goal – then as now – is to create a free and accessible community resource, with activities designed to encourage the involvement of kids who wouldn't otherwise know a Manet from a Monet. There are listening posts offering headphone commentaries on more than 1,000 pieces from the collection, while a Micro Gallery allows children to personalise and print out their own themed tours from a number of computer terminals in the more modern

Sainsbury Wing. There are also child-oriented audio tours and paper trails (the bestial 'Monster Hunt', for example).

Best of all, though, are the laid-back children's workshops. In sharp contrast to the self-consciousness that comes with standing around being talked at, children will often be seen seated around pictures, being led in supervised but utterly informal discussions. The 'Magic Carpet' storytelling sessions are a case in point, and not to be missed: aimed at under-fives and run on weekdays during school holidays, the activity begins with a search for the rolled-up magic carpet itself. Provided the participants ensure their magical mat doesn't fly away, the carpet is carried to and set down in front of a certain picture: a member of staff then asks the children to shut their eyes and recounts a tale inspired by that picture, with the aim of creating in the children the sensation that they are a part of the work of art itself.

Similarly popular are 'Second Weekend' workshops, which fall (naturally) on the second weekend of every month. A different painting is featured each time, and for each one a different contemporary artist conceives a distinctive programme. In 2004 contributors included Matthew Burrows and Ansel Krut. A recent offering from the latter involved breaking down the geometric patterns that make up Uccello's *The Battle of San Romano*; Krut then used the concept of shifting shapes to motivate the children's own creative pieces. All materials are provided, and the sessions take place at 11.30am on Saturdays and Sundays (they are repeated at 2.30pm). The remaining three weekends of the month bring an array of lively staff talks, starting at 11.30am, which are constructed around paintings chosen specifically to appeal to all ages.

Children from across the globe crowd the gates of Buckingham Palace daily at 11.30am to coo at the 45-minute Changing of the Guard, a quintessentially English ceremony. The building itself is less lively: despite being the most famous palace on the planet, its construction was controversial. John Nash, originally commissioned to build it, was sacked in 1830 for careless and inconstant efforts. His replacement, Edward Blore, finished the job, but was dubbed 'Blore the Bore' for his formulaic design. More worrying for the Bore, he incurred the wrath of Queen Victoria, the palace's first royal resident, who deemed it 'a disgrace to the country'.

Certain rooms are open to the public during the brief period when the royals retire to the country each summer, and most of those are Nash's handiwork. Visitors who queue at the box office on Constitution Hill from 9am get to see 18 elaborately furnished State Apartments, including the Music Room, Ballroom and 42 acre (17ha) gardens.

The Queen's Gallery (7766 7301) situated on Buckingham Palace Road is a more permanent exhibition of parts of the royal collection. It opened in May 2002 and has displayed drawings by Leonardo da Vinci and a priceless selection of Fabergé eggs. Until January 2005 the gallery will showcase various artworks commissioned and influenced by George III and Queen Charlotte.

The fairytale gilded stagecoach created for George in 1761 (and used in the Golden Jubilee of 2002) is on display with many other coaches in the adjoining Royal Mews (open Mar-Aug; 7766 7302), working stables that offering an opportunity to chat to some of the best-dressed and well-mannered horses in the land.

Buggy access (Royal Mews). Disabled access: lift, toilet (Buckingham Palace). Nappy-changing facilities (Buckingham Palace). Nearest picnic place: Green Park. Shop.

Cabinet War Rooms

Clive Steps, King Charles Street, SW1A 2AQ (7930 6961/www.iwm.org.uk). Westminster tube/3, 12, 24, 53, 159 bus. **Open** *Oct-Mar* 10am-6pm daily. *Apr-Sept* 9.30am-6pm daily. Last entry 45mins before closing. Closed 24-26 Dec. **Admission** £7.50; £6.50 concessions; free under-16s. **Credit** MC, V. **Map** p319 K9.

Churchill's secret underground HQ in World War II, the Cabinet War Rooms resemble a time capsule, perfectly sealed against the intervening years. *See p81* **Opening up the Cabinet**. *Buggy access. Disabled access: lift, toilet. Nappy-changing facilities. Nearest picnic place: St James's Park. Shop.*

Guards' Museum

Wellington Barracks, Birdcage Walk, SW1E 6HQ (7414 3271). St James's Park tube. **Open** 10am-4pm daily (last entry 3.30pm). Closed 21 Dec-3 Jan. **Tours** by arrangement; phone for details. **Admission** (LP) £2; £1 concessions; free under-16s. **Credit** *Shop* MC, V. **Map** p318 J9.

Children will get the most out of this little museum as a follow-up to seeing the Changing of the Guard at nearby Buckingham Palace (*see p78*). Otherwise its static displays may seem a little dusty. The collection encompasses a chronological history of the five Guards divisions, with a huge number of original uniforms, accoutrements and weapons from throughout the ages. There are also displays dedicated to recounting (and occasionally reconstructing in miniature) decisive historical battles such as Waterloo, as well as both World Wars. New for 2004 is a room set up to resemble a tent in the Crimean War, with individual soldiers' possessions displayed above mock-up trunks. There's even a display of the first Gulf War, including helmets, a tin of Iraqi boot polish and, disturbingly, Allied instructions for the treatment of prisoners of war ('do not chat or show any other sign of kindness to PW').

It's not all gung-ho, however: other notable items at the museum include Florence Nightingale's cup and military tunics worn by a 16-year-old Queen Elizabeth. If the museum is quiet enough, staff happily let kids try on the 'one-size-fits-all' bearskin hats and regimental tunics they keep hidden behind the counter. There's also a charming range of military miniatures behind glass at the Guards Toy Soldier Centre and Shop – although mostly out of pocket-money range. *Buggy access. Disabled access: lift. Nearest picnic place: St James's Park. Shop.*

Houses of Parliament

Parliament Square, SW1A 0AA (Commons info 7219 4272/Lords info 7219 3107/tours 0870 966 3773/ www.parliament.uk). Westminster tube. **Open** (when in session) *House of Commons Visitors' Gallery* 2.30-10.30pm Mon; 11.30am-7.30pm Tue-Wed; 11.30am-6.30pm Thur; 9.30am-3pm Fri. Closed bank hols. *House of Lords Visitors' Gallery* from 2.30pm Mon-Wed; from 11.30am Thur; from 11am Fri. **Tours** summer recess only; phone for details. **Admission** *Public gallery* free. *Tours* £7; £5 concessions, 5-16s; £22 family (2+2); free under-5s. **Map** p319 L9.

This spectacular neo-Gothic edifice has overlooked generation after generation of political activists, not least among them being Brian Haw. The 54-year-old father of seven upped and left his Worcestershire home in June 2001 to begin a vigil in Parliament Square protesting sanctions (and later war) in Iraq. Across the road, the House looks on unmoved, as was the judge when Westminster City Council attempted to have Mr Haw forcibly ejected in 2002.

The Palace of Westminster became a permanent home for Parliament in 1532, when Henry VIII relocated to Whitehall. These days the only parts of the original palace still standing are Westminster Hall, where the Queen Mother's body lay in state before her funeral in 2002, and the Jewel Tower (*see above*); the rest was destroyed by fire in 1834. The extraordinary building we see today was rebuilt by Charles Barry and Augustus Pugin as a direct reaction to the more sedate and reserved character of its former incarnation.

Kids are usually satisfied by the mere proximity of the big old bell known as Big Ben. The various stories behind its name certainly make for more interesting listening than sessions of the Commons or Lords, but those sessions are open daily to families with children old enough to sign their name. The wait can stretch into hours. Prime Minister's Questions (every Wednesday) tends to be oversubscribed: it is easiest to get inside the Commons between 6pm and 10.30pm on Mondays, after 1.30pm on Tuesdays, Wednesdays and Thursdays, and at 9am on Fridays (phone to check opening times in advance). If possible, it's best to book tickets with your local MP, who can also arrange a tour of the building. *Buggy access. Café. Disabled access: lifts, toilets. Nearest picnic place: Victoria Tower Gardens. Shop.*

Jewel Tower

Abingdon Street, SW1P 3JY (7222 2219/www.english-heritage.org.uk). Westminster tube. **Open** *Apr-Oct* 10am-5pm daily. *Nov-Mar* 10am-4pm daily. Last entry 30mins before closing. Closed 24-26 Dec, 1 Jan. **Admission** (EH/LP) £2.20; £1.70 concessions; £1.10 5-16s; free under-5s. **Credit** MC, V. **Map** p319 L9.

One of the two parts of medieval Westminster Palace still standing, the fragmentary Jewel Tower or 'King's Privy Wardrobe' now serves as an intriguingly broken window into the distant past. Originally marking the south-western corner of the palace grounds, the tower was built in 1365 to house

Guards' Museum

Opening up the Cabinet

It may be stating the obvious to note the merciful distance between kids and the events of World War II, but the same is now true of their parents and even their grandparents. That fewer and fewer people can tell you where they were during Operation Overlord, the Allied invasion of Normandy in June 1944 that marked the beginning of the war's end, is now less because they're too young to remember and more because they weren't yet born.

2004 marked the 60th anniversary of D-Day, and is to be celebrated with due national pomp and circumstance. Nowhere was this more true than at the **Cabinet War Rooms** (see p79). From these halls – a subterranean maze of labyrinthine tunnels and secret rooms – Britain's military minds steered the war effort, and they've been immaculately maintained as a testament to those dark hours. The same maps chart progress on the same walls; the same steel beams – hurriedly put up to reinforce the building against bombs – still line the low ceilings. Fittingly, the occasion was marked here with a specially commissioned play and by expansion of the permanent collection with additional wartime memorabilia that includes a letter from King George VI urging Sir Winston to reconsider the attacks.

An even more lasting testament will be unveiled in January 2005, when the Cabinet War Rooms opens its new Churchill Museum, 40 years to the day since the death of a man recently voted in a BBC poll the greatest Briton ever to have lived. This museum will complement the War Rooms' existing exhibition: original copies of Churchill's speeches – written in his unique verse-like style – are already on display alongside the flag that was draped over his coffin and an invoice for the vast sums of government money blown on booze and fags while he was in office. Central to the new museum will be a cutting-edge digital archive set to contain thousands of Churchill-related records, documents and pieces of correspondence. Children will be able to access the information – liberally peppered with light-hearted animations and asides – simply by moving their hands over a vast interactive screen, designed to look like an electronic filing cabinet, with the material organised into chronological drawers that seem to 'slide' open to reveal their contents.

The new museum will treble the space available to the War Rooms, providing a lasting tribute to those long-dead few for the many thousands who come here to remember them.

the private treasures of Edward III. A moat (now filled) was channelled from the Thames – primarily to protect the royal loot, although it had the added advantage of bringing fresh fish to the kitchen door. Since being built the tower has served as both a repository for Parliamentary records and a Board of Trade testing centre for weights and measures, but these days English Heritage keeps it open to the public – winding staircases, unrestored ribbed vault and all.

A 'Parliament Past and Present' exhibition offers an insight into the development of today's parliamentary structure, but younger kids will probably be more interested in the ancient sword on display in the on-site shop. It dates back to around AD 800 and looks like something on loan from Middle Earth. The shop sells drinks and ice-creams, and the surrounding garden makes for a small but perfectly suitable picnic retreat. *Nearest picnic place: surrounding green. Shop.*

National Gallery

Trafalgar Square, WC2N 5DN (info line 7747 2885/ www.nationalgallery.org.uk). Leicester Square tube/ Charing Cross tube/rail/24, 29, 176 bus. **Open** 10am-6pm Mon, Tue, Thur-Sun; 10am-9pm Wed. *Micro Gallery* 10am-5.30pm Mon, Tue, Thur-Sun; 10am-8.30pm Wed. Closed 24-26 Dec, 1 Jan. **Tours** times vary; check info line. **Admission** (LP) free. *Temporary exhibitions* prices vary. *Tours* free. **Credit** *Shop* MC, V. **Map** p319 K7.
This national treasure has one of the finest collections of classic Western European paintings in the world, and it makes certain that its younger guests have a lot of fun discovering them (see *p79* **Playtime at... the National Gallery**). Upcoming temporary exhibitions include a survey of 19th-century Russian landscape art (until 12 Sept 2004) and retrospectives of Raphael (20 Oct 2004-16 Jan 2005) and Degas (10 Nov 2004-30 Jan 2005).

Buggy access. Café. Disabled access: lift. Nappy-changing facilities. Nearest picnic place: Leicester Square/Trafalgar Square. Restaurant. Shop.

National Portrait Gallery

2 St Martin's Place, WC2H 0HE (7306 0055/ www.npg.org.uk). Leicester Square tube/Charing Cross tube/rail/24, 29, 176 bus. **Open** 10am-6pm Mon-Wed, Sat, Sun; 10am-9pm Thur, Fri. Closed 24-26 Dec, 1 Jan, Good Friday. **Admission** free. *Temporary exhibitions* prices vary. *Audio guide* free (suggested donation £3). **Credit** AmEx, MC, V. **Map** p319 K7.
What makes the NPG so unique is its philosophy: the collections are concerned with history, not art, gathering together a pantheon of those who have contributed to creating British society. Thus a short wander around its halls will turn up faces as far removed as William Shakespeare and Benny Hill, captured in a variety of media (paintings, photographs, sculptures) by artists ranging from medieval illuminators to celebrity snappers like Mario Testino. The permanent collection is organised by period – the restored Regency galleries were reopened in 2003 – and there are regular temporary exhibitions, including (until August 2004) portraits by Bill Brandt and shots of Lucien Freud at work in his studio.

It's up to individual families to make head or tail (usually head) of the various displays, but to help them on their journey the gallery provides free family rucksacks, on a first-come, first-served basis. The rucksacks correspond to one of three galleries – Tudor, Victorian and 20th Century – and each is stuffed with activities (for three- to 12-year-olds) from jigsaws and dressing-up items to paper trails.

Buggy access. Café. Disabled access: lift, toilet. Nappy-changing facilities. Nearest picnic place: Leicester Square/Trafalgar Square. Restaurant. Shop.

St James's Park

SW1A 2JB (7930 1793/www.royalparks.org.uk). St James's Park tube/3, 11, 12, 24, 53, 211 bus. **Open** 5am-midnight daily. **Map** p319 K8.

As a Royal Park, St James's isn't exactly maintained with little ones in mind, but it's still a delightful spot for families to escape the crowds. Its immaculately manicured gardens may be no-go zones for bicycles, in-line skates and other wheeled instruments, but there's a good children's playground and plenty of space for an impromptu picnic. In 2004 the Inn The Park (*see p171*) restaurant opened its doors to a public of all ages. Best of all, however, is the range of feathered friends – gulls, swans, geese, pelicans – wandering over from their breeding grounds on Duck Island. You can watch the pelicans being fed between 2pm and 3pm each day. The park is bordered by the Guards' Museum (*see p80*), Cabinet War Rooms (*see p79*) and Buckingham Palace (*see p78*).

Disabled access: toilets. Nappy-changing facilities. Restaurant.

St Martin-in-the-Fields

Trafalgar Square, WC2N 4JJ (7766 1100/Brass Rubbing Centre 7930 9306/www.stmartin-in-the-fields.org). Leicester Square tube/Charing Cross tube/rail. **Open** *Church* 8am-6pm daily. *Brass Rubbing Centre* 10am-7pm Mon-Wed; 10am-10pm Thur-Sat; noon-7pm Sun. **Admission** free. *Brass Rubbing* (LP) £3-£15 (special rates for groups & families). *Evening concerts* (7.30pm Thur-Sat) £6-£18. **Credit** MC, V. **Map** p319 L7.

Believe it or not, St Martin offers more than a glorious porch for confused tourists to park on while checking their maps. For a start, the interior of the church is an unusually bright and cheering sanctuary of sculptures, paintings and potted plants, all presided over by an intricately carved baroque ceiling. It makes an inspired refuge from the mass of tourists outside, never more so than during one of the free lunchtime choral recitals or ticketed evening concerts (1pm and 7.30pm respectively; check the website for details).

What makes St Martin such fun for children, though, is its fantastic 18th-century crypt, home not only to hearty self-service fodder at the excellent Café in the Crypt (*see p169*), but

also to London's only Brass Rubbing Centre. Here kids can create their own lasting memento of medieval London, with knights and dragons among the images available. Rubbings – which take about an hour to complete – are supervised, and all materials provided. Major renovations of church and crypt are due to begin in 2005, and will take two years to complete. *Café. Disabled access: ramp to church, toilet. Nearest picnic place: Leicester Square/Trafalgar Square. Shop.*

Tate Britain

Millbank, SW1P 4RG (7887 8008/www.tate.org.uk). Pimlico tube/2, 3, C10, 77A, 88, 185 bus. **Open** 10am-5.50pm daily. Closed 24-26 Dec. **Tours** 11am, noon, 2pm, 3pm Mon-Fri; noon, 2.30pm Sat, Sun. **Admission** (LP) free. *Temporary exhibitions* prices vary. *Tours* free. **Credit** MC, V. **Map** p319 L7.

Since delegating responsibility for pickled sharks to Tate Modern, the 'old' Tate has been able to concentrate on expanding its collection of British fine art from 1500 to the present day, with a permanent collection that unites artists from Blake to Bacon in a grand riverside setting. This allows neighbouring galleries to focus on themes as diverse as 18th-century seascapes and visions of religious apocalypse, while still leaving several large halls free for staging regular temporary shows. Best of all is the Tate's ongoing effort to help younger audiences engage with and enjoy the art on display, with the Artspace studio, the Art Trolley (noon-5pm Sat, Sun) and, on the first Sunday of each month, Tate Tales. For more information, *see p215*.

Buggy access. Café. Disabled access: lift, ramps, toilet. Nappy-changing facilities. Nearest picnic place: lawns (either side of gallery)/Riverside Gardens (by Vauxhall Bridge). Restaurant. Shop.

Westminster Abbey

20 Dean's Yard, SW1P 3PA (7654 4834/www.westminster-abbey.org). St James's Park or Westminster tube/11, 12, 24, 88, 159, 211 bus. **Open** *Nave & royal chapels* 9.30am-4.45pm Mon, Tue, Thur, Fri (last entry 3.45pm); 9.30am-8pm Wed (last entry 7pm); 9.30am-2.45pm Sat

Pit stops Westminster

Anyone taking in the views from the Campanile Bell Tower of **Westminster Cathedral** will see the familiar clutter of child-friendly chains on nearby Victoria Street, including the ever-popular **Pizza Express** (85 Victoria Street, SW1H 0HW, 7222 5270). There's also a huge selection of delightful and devilish cakes in **Ponti's Café** (127 Victoria Street, SW1E 8RR, 7828 7242). **Jenny Lo's Tea House** (14 Eccleston Street, SW1, 7259 0399), just around the corner and but a short walk from **Buckingham Palace**, offers cheap and eminently cheering noodle and dumpling dishes.

A short wander from **Parliament**, the **Jewel Tower** and **Westminster Abbey** you'll find a colourful range of eateries on bustling Strutton Ground, including a **West Cornwall Pasty Company** (35 Strutton Ground, SW1P 2HY, 7233 3777) and excellent fish and chips at the **Laughing Halibut** (38 Strutton Ground, SW1P 2HR, 7799 2844).

No wandering at all is necessary from the **National Gallery**: the **Gallery Café** (7747 2885)

has high chairs and, on our last visit, free children's art books were being offered as part of a lunchtime meal deal. On the other side of **Trafalgar Square**, the **Café in the Crypt** (*see p169*) is the place to go for meals as filling as they are affordable – unheard of in this part of town. The **Texas Embassy Cantina** (*see p171*), roughly equidistant between the National Gallery and **Banqueting House**, wins kids over with a colourful menu of hearty Tex-Mex favourites.

Over in **St James's Park**, the new **Inn The Park** (*see p171*) is as forward-thinking as it looks, with plenty of kids' options and a timber terrace that's perfect for fair weather lingering after being cooped up in those **Cabinet War Rooms** or bitten by a moody goose. St James's Park is also the best bet for picnics (Inn the Park sells filled hampers for those who forgot their own), although **Victoria Tower Gardens** is usually quieter – and you're less likely to lose your prawn sandwich to marauding wildfowl.

Horse Guards parade. *See p78.*

(last entry 1.45pm). *Chapter House* 10am-4pm Mon-Sat. *Abbey Museum* 10.30am-4pm Mon-Sat. *College Garden* Apr-Sept 10am-6pm Tue-Thur; Oct-Mar 10am-4pm Tue-Thur. Last entry 1hr before closing. Closed 24, 25 Dec, Good Friday. **Tours** phone for details. **Admission** *Nave & royal chapels* £7.50; £5 11-15s, concessions; £15 family (2+2); free under-11s with paying adult. *Chapter House* free. *Abbey Museum* (EH/LP) free. (audio guide £2) **Credit** MC, V. **Map** p319 K9

As the backdrop for every coronation since 1066, Westminster Abbey has set the stage for more than its fair share of British royals. As the place where plenty of them are buried, it can also claim to have drawn many a final curtain. The abbey was consecrated in 1065, eight days before the death of Edward the Confessor. His body remains entombed in the abbey, although where exactly is unknown: it was removed from his elaborate shrine and reburied at an unmarked location during the Reformation. Elizabeth I is also interred here, as is Mary Queen of Scots. Poets' Corner is home to the graves of Dryden, Samuel Johnson, Browning and Tennyson, while several 20th-century martyrs (including Martin Luther King Jr) have been immortalised in 15th-century niches above the west door. Indeed, from the extraordinary nave – the highest roof in Britain at 101ft (31m) – to the seemingly endless sea of stained glass, Westminster Abbey is an inspired and inspiring place for all ages. Phone for details of free lunchtime concerts.

Buggy access. Café. Disabled access; toilets. Nearest picnic place: college gardens. Shop.

Westminster Cathedral

Victoria Street, SW1P 1QW (7798 9055/tours 7798 9064/www.westminstercathedral.org.uk). St James's Park tube/Victoria tube/rail/11, 24, 211, 507 bus. **Open** 7am-7pm Mon-Fri, Sun; 8am-7pm Sat. *Campanile* Apr-Nov 9.30am-12.30pm, 1-5pm daily; Dec-Mar 9.30am-12.30pm, 1-5pm Thur-Sun. **Tours** by arrangement; phone for details. **Admission** free (donations appreciated). *Campanile* £3; £1.50 concessions; £7 family (2+2). *Audio guide* £2.50; £1.50 concessions. **No credit cards.** **Map** p318 J10.

London's Catholic cathedral has relative newcomer status: the elaborate neo-Byzantine exterior (inspired by the Hagia Sophia in Istanbul) was completed at the beginning of the 20th century. Although the cavernous interior sparkles with coloured mosaics and marbled stone pillars – not to mention a cross the size of a semi-detached house hovering eerily above the altar – the high ceiling remains an ominous and unpainted black, casting a strange shadow over the many characters below who are crouched in prayer, crossing themselves with holy water or chatting quietly to the priest. Tourists are welcome (although they're respectfully asked not to break the reverie); the shop sells a neat little workbook that leads kids on an activity trail around the building, and the Cathedral Kitchen is on hand to provide half-time refreshments. If you have a head for heights, the 273ft (83m) Campanile Bell Tower is topped by a four-sided gallery with spectacular views across London, and there's a lift all the way to the top.

Buggy access. Café. Disabled access: ramp. Shop.

Kensington & Chelsea

Great museums, a top playground – and a whole lot of Albert.

Diana, Princess of Wales Memorial Playground.
See p85.

The Royal Borough of Kensington and Chelsea's historic connections with the gentry stretch back to the Domesday Book, but it wasn't until shortly after Queen Victoria's death that the borough was officially designated 'Royal', in recognition of the happy times the fierce queen had spent here as a flighty princess: she had been born in **Kensington Palace** in 1819. Also closely linked to Kensington Palace is a more contemporary (and arguably more famous) royal: Princess Diana. Today the enchanting **Diana, Princess of Wales Memorial Playground**, opened in Kensington Gardens in her honour, is a fitting tribute.

Yet it is Victoria's beloved husband, Albert, whom children should be taking warmly to their hearts. It is Albert who is credited with the huge, ambitious and successful Great Exhibition in 1851, profits from which went to build the area's famous museums.

Collectively dubbed 'Albertopolis', this august triumvirate – the **Science Museum**, the **Natural History Museum** and the **Victoria & Albert** – provide many excellent reasons to bring the kids.

The southern gates of **Hyde Park**, London's poshest park, lead to the streets of Knightsbridge, London's poshest shopping area and home to that most opulent of department stores, Harrods (see *p183*). From here, Sloane Street runs toward Chelsea, and the world-renowned Royal Court Theatre on Sloane Square. The King's Road, which runs through the square, was the height of trendiness from the heady days of Swingin' London in the '60s to the gobby days of the punks in the '70s. Now it's a big draw for parents, mostly because of the children's fashion shops (see *p195*). From the King's Road it's just a short walk south to Chelsea Royal Hospital, site of the hugely popular flower show, and of the **National Army Museum**.

Baden-Powell House
65-7 Queen's Gate, SW7 5JS (7584 7031/ www.scoutbase.org.uk). South Kensington tube. **Open** 7am-10pm daily. Closed 22 Dec-3 Jan. **Admission** free. **Map** p315 D10.
Opened in 1961 (and refurbished in 1997), Robert Baden-Powell's memorial hostel provides accommodation for about 300,000 people from 30 different countries each year, with family rooms for visitors with children. There's an exhibition about the Chief Scout's life on the ground floor, a life that included a stint as national hero after the seven-month defence of Mafeking – long before the woggle went global.
Buggy access. Café. Disabled access: toilet. Nappy-changing facilities. Nearest picnic place: Natural History Museum gardens. Shop.

Chelsea Physic Garden
66 Royal Hospital Road (entrance at Swan Walk), SW3 4HS (7352 5646/www.chelseaphysicgarden.co.uk). Sloane Square tube/11, 19, 22, 49, 137, 239 bus. **Open** *Apr-Oct* noon-5pm Wed; 2-6pm Sun. **Tours** 1.30pm, 3.30pm (check blackboard to confirm); phone for group tours. **Admission** £5; £3 5-16s, students; free under-5s. *Tours* free. **Credit** *Shop* MC, V. **Map** p315 F12.
Although the garden was set up in 1673, its key phase of development was under Sir Hans Sloane in the 18th century. A research and education centre, the garden's public opening hours are restricted – except during the Chelsea Flower Show (24-28 May 2005) and the Chelsea Festival (17-26 June 2005). Its beds contain healing herbs and rare trees, dye plants and medicinal vegetables; plants are also sold. Activities over Easter and during the summer holidays include nature studies and environmental art and calligraphy, dance and storytelling sessions. Activity days, for seven- to 11-year-olds, should be pre-booked and cost about £4 per child.
Buggy access. Café. Disabled access: ramp, toilet. Nappy-changing facilities. Shop.

Diana, Princess of Wales Memorial Playground

Near Black Lion Gate, Broad Walk, Kensington Gardens, W8 2UH (7298 2117/recorded info 7298 2141/ www.royalparks.gov.uk). Bayswater or Queensway tube/ 12, 148 bus. **Open** *Summer* 10am-8pm. *Winter* 10am-4pm (or 1hr before dusk, if earlier) daily. Closed 25 Dec. **Admission** free. All adults must be accompanied by a child. **Map** p312 C7.

Rangers see to it that this commemorative play area stays lovely. Unaccompanied adults aren't allowed in to spoil it, but they can view the gardens between 9.30am and 10am daily.

The focal point is a pirate ship in a sea of fine white sand. Children enjoy scaling the rigging to the crow's nest and adore the ship's wheel, cabins, pulleys and ropes. During the summer months the mermaids' fountain and rocky outcrops are fab for water play. Beyond these shipshape glories lies the teepee camp: a trio of wigwams, each large enough to hold a sizeable tribe. The tree-house encampment has walkways, ladders, slides and 'tree phones'. The area's connection with Peter Pan's creator JM Barrie, is remembered in images from the story etched into the glass in the Home Under the Ground (which also houses the toilets and playground office).

Many of the playground's attractions appeal to the senses: scented shrubs, whispering willows and bamboo are planted throughout, footfall chimes and touchy-feely sculpture engage young visitors. Much of the equipment has been designed for use by children with special needs.

From late July and throughout August a programme of free entertainment – perhaps visits by clowns or storytelling sessions – provides additional entertainment.

Buggy access. Café. Disabled access: toilet. Nappy-changing facilities. Nearest picnic place: Kensington Gardens.

Hyde Park

W2 2UH (7298 2100/www.royalparks.gov.uk). Hyde Park Corner, Knightsbridge, Lancaster Gate or Marble Arch tube/2, 8, 10, 12, 23, 38, 73, 94 bus. **Open** 5am-midnight daily. **Map** p313 E7.

The largest of London's Royal Parks (1.5 miles/2.5km long and about a mile/1.5km wide), Hyde Park was the first to be opened to the public. It's also the most potently symbolic of the Royal Parks, providing an end point for many protest marches and hosting Speakers' Corner, the world's oldest platform for public speaking. Members of the public exercise their right to free speech here every Sunday. The entertainment value is often rich for passers-by, but the kids may not yet have developed a taste for the campaigners, hobbyists and certifiable nutters you're likely to find. No matter: Hyde Park has plenty for active children to do. On South Carriage Drive there's a playground; the park's perimeter is popular with both in-line and roller skaters, as well as with bike and horse riders; and there are riding schools near Rotten Row, part of the wide riding track around Hyde Park. Every morning at 10.30am (9.30am on Sundays) you can watch the Household Cavalry emerge smartly from their barracks and ride across the park to Horse Guards Parade, prior to the Changing of the Guard.

As with other Royal Parks, Hyde Park's water feature provides another great attraction: the Serpentine has its complement of ducks, coots, swans and tufty-headed grebes, as well as rowing boats and pedalos (Mar to Oct) on what is London's oldest boating lake. To return to the subject of certifiable nutters, the Serpentine also has its own swimming club, whose members are so keen they've even been known to break the winter ice to indulge in their daily dip.

Buggy access. Cafés. Disabled: toilets. Nappy-changing facilities.

Pit stops Kensington and Chelsea

There are restaurants in all three major museums (Science, Natural History and V&A), but they're all a bit pricey and usually have long queues. It's better to aim for the cafés. In the **Science Museum**, the **Deep Blue Café** on the ground floor serves freshly made pizza, pasta and salad, and children's lunch-boxes are available from the **museum café** (zone 6). In the **Globe Café** at the **Natural History Museum** you can buy children's lunch boxes and snacks. All three museums have indoor picnic areas, where there's plenty of space to spread out and eat your sandwiches. Outside the museums, try the following: **Café Crêperie** (2 Exhibition Road, SW7 2HF, 7589 8947) for pancakes with a wide range of sweet or savoury fillings; **Green Fields Café** (13 Exhibition Road, SW7 2HE, 7584 1396) for a traditional French-style establishment with outdoor seating, sandwiches and cakes; or any of the Bute Street cafés, among them **Najma** (17 & 19 Bute Street, SW7 3EY, 7584 4434).

The café at the **National Army Museum** is quite basic, but there are loads of fabulous places to find a square meal along the **King's Road**. Try **Benihana** (No.77, SW3 4NX, 7376 7799; *see also p163*), home of stir-crazy chefs and frying fun; the

Big Easy (*see p171*), for children's Tex-Mex; brilliant burgers and shakes at **Ed's Easy Diner** (No.362, SW3 5UZ, 7352 1956; *see also p163*), or **Pizza Express** (No.152, SW3 4UT, 7351 5031). The newly opened **Gelateria Valerie** (9 Duke of York Square, SW3 4LY, 7730 7978) is a terrific ice-cream parlour – where some of the more exotic flavours include Nutella and Ferrero Rocher – that looks out on to the King's Road. Round the corner in pedestrianised Duke of York Square is its sister outlet, **Patisserie Valerie's Left Wing Café** (No.81, SW3 4LY, 7730 7094), and the square is also home to **Manicomio** (No.85, SW3 4LY, 7730 3366), a deli-cum-café with outside tables and safe toddling space for toddlers. When open, the **Chelsea Physic Garden** (*see p84*) does fine tea and cakes.

If you're in **Kensington**, **Giraffe** (7 Kensington High Street, W8 5NP, 7938 1221; *see also p163*) has fun, child-friendly food and **Patisserie Valerie** (27 Kensington Church Street, W8 4LL, 7937 9574) is ideal for an afternoon or mid-morning treat. **Wagamama** (26A Kensington High Street, W8 4PF, 7376 1717; *see also p163*) and **ASK** (222 Kensington High Street, W8 7RG, 7937 5540) are good fall-back options.

Kensington Gardens

W8 2UH (7298 2100/royalparks.gov.uk). Bayswater, High Street Kensington, Lancaster Gate or Queensway tube/9, 12, 28, 49, 148 bus. **Open** 6am-midnight daily. **Map** p312 C7.

On one side the gardens, which cover 260 acres (105 ha), meet Hyde Park at the Serpentine; on the opposite side is Kensington Palace (*see p87*). The best element, as far as children are concerned, is undoubtedly the pretty Diana, Princess of Wales Memorial Playground, with its pirate ship and jolly tipi encampment (*see p85*), but the gardens are perfect for picnics (if you haven't thought to pack one, the Diana Playground Café has a children's menu and outdoor seating)

and contain the Serpentine Gallery (*see p90*) and overblown Albert Memorial, complete with a thrice-life-size statue of Prince Albert, picked out in gold and seated under a 180ft/55m-high canopy and spire (for guided tours ring 7495 0916). Children like the Round Pond, home to eels and sticklebacks, where they can also watch ducks and geese. By Long Water there's a bronze statue of Peter Pan, built by Sir George Frampton in 1912 to honour Pan's creator, JM Barrie. The hundredth birthday of the boy who never grew up (although he's certainly old enough) is to be celebrated here on 17 July 2004 with the gardens transformed into a fantasy land thrumming with fairies, pirates and lost boys, and an extensive treasure hunt through the gardens.
Buggy access. Cafés. Disabled access: toilet.

Tales from... the National Army Museum

The **National Army Museum** (*see p87*) tells the story of 500 years of the British Army. No surprise, then, that many items on display are regimental memorabilia: ancient uniforms, helmets and caps, bits of kit... Highlights like Florence Nightingale's lamp and some deliciously bizarre exhibits – children love the frostbitten fingers of Major 'Bronco' Lane, conqueror of Mount Everest – only emphasised the fact that the museum should be a lot more broadly appealing.

'From the year 2000, we began trying to move away from a "lads and dads" visitor core,' explains Samantha Doty, the museum's education officer. 'We want to... explain that it was people like us, like them, who would have fought in those wars.' To this end, the museum is involved in living history events across Britain. These are acted out by specially trained performers, who dress up as soldiers from a particular period, then take up temporary residence on historical sites in tents, eating rations typical of that era. Andrew Robertshaw, who heads the events team of the museum, explains the idea behind such role-playng: 'Through living history, visitors can engage with the past in a very different way, by coming

directly face to face with it. At the museum encampment they can talk to characters from the past about their lives and experiences, see and handle original and replica kit and equipment, and try on uniforms. It brings history to life... '

Outdoor events this year, staged with the help of English Heritage, include a re-enactment of Elizabeth I's famous speech to the English Army at Tilbury Fort in Essex, preparing them to face the mighty Armada (28-29 Aug), and a reconstruction at Audley End in Cambridgeshire of the Battle of Naseby, a key confrontation in the English Civil War (4-5 Sept). At Chelsea Barracks in London, Operation London Soldier (25-26 Sept) will be a more general event: British soldiers from across the centuries – Agincourt, internecine struggles under the Tudors, the Napoleonic Wars, the Crimean, the First and Second World Wars – will be represented by costumed historical interpreters. For more details, call 7730 0717 ext 2228 or consult the museum's website.

The museum's monthly themed weekends have also gone a long way towards enhancing the museum's broad-spectrum appeal. One month they might cover the Royal Flying Corps in the First World War, on another they might be looking at infantry weapons or military dress. But the topic isn't necessarily the main attraction... it's the presentation. The National Army Museum uses historical interpreters who are either professionals or members of amateur re-enactment societies – and really bring the stories to life. 'Because they are historians and not actors, the interpreters are really knowledgeable and able to help people from a range of backgrounds... engage in history, making these events suitable for adults as well as children,' says Doty. The weekend events also offer art and craft workshops, keeping the children busy making paper aeroplanes, models of medieval catapults or hobbyhorses, all of which can be to taken home at the end of the day. The museum makes sure there's a range of things to do for all ages, so that little ones can participate in a simplified version of the activities the older siblings are getting stuck into.

Impressive dentistry at the
Natural History Museum.

Teeth: stab or s...

Kensington Palace

*W8 4PX (7937 9561/0870 751 7070/www.hrp.org.uk).
Bayswater, High Street Kensington or Queensway tube/
9, 10, 49, 52, 70 bus.* **Open** *Mar-Oct* 10am-6pm daily.
Nov-Feb 10am-5pm daily. Last entry 1hr before closing.
Closed 24-26 Dec. **Admission** (LP) including audio guide
£10.80; £8.20 5-15s; £7.70 concessions; £32 family (2+3);
free under-5s. **Credit** AmEx, MC, V. **Map** p312 B8.
William III and his wife Mary came to live in this Jacobean
mansion in 1689. Since then many royals have called it home.
The future Queen Victoria was born in the palace in 1819, it
has latterly been known as the last home of Princesses Diana
and Margaret, and the Duke and Duchess of Kent both have
apartments here. The palace is open for tours of the State
Apartments, including the ground-floor room where Queen
Victoria was baptised, the long King's Gallery (with its
Tintoretto nudes and Van Dyck portrait of Charles I) and, the
most popular part, the Royal Ceremonial Dress Collection,
which includes 14 lavish dresses worn by Princess Di.
*Buggy access. Café. Disabled access: toilet. Nappy-
changing facilities. Nearest picnic place: grounds.
Restaurant. Shop.*

National Army Museum

*Royal Hospital Road, SW3 4HT (7730 0717/
www.national-army-museum.ac.uk). Sloane Square tube/
11, 137, 239 bus.* **Open** 10am-5.30pm daily. Closed 24-26
Dec, 1 Jan, Good Friday, 1st bank hol May. **Admission**
free. **Map** p315 F12.
Established in 1971, the National Army Museum is tucked
away behind the bustling King's Road. No prizes for guess-
ing what's on offer: the whole history of the British Army
marching past in ceremonial uniform. Prime exhibits include
'The Road to Waterloo', a version of the famous battle starring some 75,000 toy soldiers, and the skeleton of Napoleon's
mount, Marengo. The 'Redcoats' gallery starts at Agincourt
in 1415 and ends with the redcoats in the American War of
Independence; 'The Nation in Arms' covers both World Wars,
with reconstructions of a Flanders trench and a D-Day landing craft. The splendid art gallery – displaying Reynolds and
Gainsborough, among others – is all very well for grown-ups,
but far more interesting to the youngsters will be trying out
the Challenger tank simulator in 'The Modern Army'.

In the Special Events gallery, a free exhibition called 'The
British Army and the Crimean War' (until 31 Mar 2005)
explains the impact made by people such as Florence
Nightingale. Soldiers from the past are brought to life by
actors on TV screens and children can try on replica uniforms
and try to solve a 3D puzzle or learn semaphore.

School and family groups are given trails to guide them
round the museum. There are also well-chosen special weekend events every month, usually involving costumed interpreters and craft activities (*see p86* **Tales from... the
National Army Museum**). Examples include 'Revolution!'
(3-4 July), which will focus on the history of the British Army
in America, and 'Culloden Field' (25-26 Sept), which will give
kids an insight into the last British rebellion and the Bonnie
Prince. In autumn, events will commemorate the 150th
anniversary of the Charge of the Light Brigade (23-24 Oct)
and the end of the First World War ('Remembrance', 13-14
Nov). 'Swinging Soldiers' (11-12 Dec) allows children to find
out how their grandparents and great-grandparents celebrated Christmas 1944. With some detail spared, we trust.
*Buggy access. Café. Disabled access: lift, ramps, toilet.
Nappy-changing facilities. Nearest picnic place: benches
outside museum/Chelsea Hospital grounds. Shop.*

Natural History Museum

*Cromwell Road, SW7 5BD (info 7942 5725/switchboard
7942 5000/www.nhm.ac.uk). South Kensington tube.*
Open 10am-5.50pm Mon-Sat; 11am-5.50pm Sun. Closed
24-26 Dec. **Tours** 11am-4pm daily, hourly (depending
on guide availability). **Admission** free; charges apply
for special exhibitions. *Tours* free. **Credit** *Shop* AmEx,
MC, V. **Map** p315 D10.
This is a vast museum, filled with some 68 million plants,
animals, fossils, rocks and minerals – a staggering amount
to see. Young folk zoom in on the dinosaurs but there's much
more to wonder at. As basic orientation, we deal here with
the museum's three main sections: the Life Galleries, the
Earth Galleries and the Darwin Centre.

From the front entrance on the Cromwell Road visitors
enter the spectacular main hall of the Life Galleries, with its
huge cast of a diplodocus skeleton. If you turn left, you'll find
yourself first in the Dinosaur gallery, with its animatronic
Tyrannosaurus Rex, and then in the human biology section

(gallery 22), which also has plenty of interactive exhibits for inquisitive children. From here, make your way to the blue whale (three buses long) via the stuffed mammals. Creepy Crawlies (gallery 33) has a colony of leafcutter ants and some robotic arthropods. To mug up on the earth's different environments and biological diversity, Ecology (gallery 32) is the place. Spare some time for the Bird gallery (gallery 40; there's a stuffed dodo there, and an egg from the elephant bird.

The Earth Galleries can be accessed directly from Exhibition Road. With fewer interactive elements, they're best suited to ten-year-olds and above, but the earthquake simulation is always a winner. You'll find it and the volcanoes upstairs, while downstairs exhibits trace the history of our planet from the Big Bang to the present.

The Darwin Centre, whose first stage of development was completed in 2002, allows visitors to go behind the scenes to see the 'type' specimens from which species were identified. Some of these, at two centuries old, were previously accessible only to researchers and sundry boffins. The Centre houses some 22 million specimens, with 450,000 stored in jars of alcohol – there's a mummified finger and whole monkeys in tanks. Twice-daily tours allow punters (children must be at least ten years old) to encounter the scientists who work here. For more details, check the museum website.

There are a wide variety school-holiday events and weekend workshops for families; check the website or ring 7942 5000 or 5011 to find out about current themes. Also themed – oceans, birds or mammals – are the Explorer Backpacks, available from the cloakroom in the Earth Galleries (free, but deposit required). Intended for under-sevens, these contain drawing materials and a trail of clues to help the kids find items in the museum. Investigate, a gallery primarily for seven- to 14-year-olds, is a hands-on area with hundreds of specimens that can be handled, measured and drawn. Museum staff help youngsters in their investigations.

Until 26 September 2004 'Hair', a special interactive exhibition for families, will focus on the barnet. The annual Wildlife Photographer of the Year show runs from October 2004 to spring 2005. The Festival of Fossils is on 1 July.

Outside, the Wildlife Garden (open Apr-Oct) provides a variety of British habitats for mammals, amphibians, insects and birds. Until October 2004 bronze animal sculptures by Tessa Campbell Fraser, share the plot. A popular mini-beast safari is among the regular tours (£1.50), which take place between April and July; check the website for availability. *Buggy access. Cafés. Disabled access: lift, toilet. Nappy-changing facilities. Nearest picnic place: indoor eating area/museum grounds. Restaurant. Shops.*

Around Town

Scient'rific

Most museums have learnt the valuable lesson that children having fun learn more than children being talked at, but the **Science Museum** (*see p90*) is a master of the dark art of tricking the little blighters into absorbing useful stuff in the guise of just mucking about. With play areas throughout targeted to particular age ranges or development stages, parents and teachers get to learn a thing or two as well: observing how a child interacts with new objects and friends, watching their reactions and seeing how they learn. Best of all, the six interactive galleries are all free.

For really little children, the galleries in the basement and on the ground floor are best, with specially trained Explainers available to answer questions while they look after and play with the kids. **The Garden** play area in the basement is a particular joy. Designed to help under-sixes discover basic principles of science, the Garden is divided into three areas: Water, Construction, and Sound and Light. Children always love water play, so the Water section's popularity is only to be expected, but the museum ensures plastic aprons are at the ready for games involving ripples and bubbles, building dams, and creating pressure pumps that turn a water wheel. In the Construction zone, play with pulleys teaches children to co-operate with new friends in loading and unloading a bucket full of beanbags, while the earthquake table, where youngsters build a tower that topples when the table shakes, helps them understand structure and balance. The Sound and Light area is perfect for toddlers, with soft floor mats, beguiling ceiling patterns and mirrors. Adults or Explainers help the kids dress up as a pink bunny or yellow duck, and get them to stage a puppet show.

There's also the **Pattern Pod**, on the ground floor in the Wellcome Wing, which introduces under-eights to patterns and repetition in the natural world. Although the area is relatively small, there's a lot of fun to had if you're accompanied by several young children at various stages of development: babies lie happily in their prams gazing up at the night-time patterns projected on to the ceiling, while their elder siblings get to make patterns on touch-screens, follow animal tracks on their hands and feet, or plant a seed in a projector to see a pattern 'grow' on the opposite wall.

If your particular gaggle covers a wide range of ages, you're best off in the **Launch Pad**. This is the museum's largest interactive gallery – be warned it's often heaving on rainy Sundays – and it's full of things to push, pull, listen to and look at, all the while encouraging the pushers and pullers to think about what's happening and why. The Launch Pad is aimed at fives and over, but there's plenty of play opportunities for younger ones as well, particularly if they're helped by big brothers and sisters or an energetic parent. They'll enjoy the shadow box, for example, where they 'catch' their shadow on a screen or play with the sound dishes, an intriguing way of demonstrating that sounds get fainter the further they travel.

A day at the high-energy Science Museum can mean an awful lot of playtime for the grown-up and weary. Adults get to take a deserved break in the **science show area**, where they can leave the entertaining entirely to experts: several times a day there's a 20-minute exploration of the concept of structure... or rather a great fun bubbles show. Heck, these Science Museum boffins – they're on to something, you know.

Oratory Catholic Church

Brompton Road, SW7 2RP (7808 0900). South Kensington tube/14, 74 bus. **Open** 6.30am-8pm daily; phone to check. **Admission** free; donations appreciated. **Map** p315 E10.

Also known as the Brompton Oratory, this is the second largest Catholic church in the city (Westminster Cathedral occupies top slot). It's full of extravagant marble and mosaics designed to strike awe into mortal hearts. Many of the internal decorations are much older than the building itself: Mazzuoli's late 17th-century statues of the apostles, for example, once stood in Siena Cathedral. If the kids are more bored than inspired, point out that the church was used by Russian spies as a dead letter box during the Cold War.

For those more interested in heavenly music than espionage, the Oratory's Junior Choir sings Mass at 10am each Sunday, and Schola, the boys' choir of the well-known London Oratory School over in Fulham, performs Mass on term-time Saturday evenings.

Buggy access. Disabled access: ramp. Shop.

Science Museum

Exhibition Road, SW7 2DD (7942 4454/booking/info line 0870 870 4868/www.sciencemuseum.org.uk). South Kensington tube. **Open** 10am-6pm daily. Closed 24-26 Dec. **Admission** free; charges apply for special exhibitions. **Credit** *IMAX cinema, shops* AmEx, MC, V. **Map** p315 D9.

The enduring popularity of the Science Museum is, in part, due to its vast collection of landmark inventions: these include Stephenson's Rocket, Arkwright's spinning machine, Whittle's turbojet engine, the Vickers Vimy aircraft in which Alcock and Brown crossed the Atlantic in 1919 and the Apollo 10 command module. The museum's other major draw is that it's great fun. The Wellcome Wing practically embodies the notion of learning while having fun (*see p89* **Scient'rific**). There's also the IMAX cinema (tickets are £7.50 for adults, £6 for under-16s), where you can catch eye-popping shows like *Space Station 3D*, filmed by astronauts and narrated by Tom Cruise.

The 'Science of Sport' exhibition (until 5 Sept 2004) is spread over two floors and filled with interactive displays for children and adults to test their capabilities in a variety of sports, including virtual volleyball, tennis and football. Video replays help you analyse your performance and thus learn how muscles function during exercise. You can also find out about the importance of diet.

'Science Night' sleepovers are held once a month (eight- to 11-year-olds, in groups of five or more), with an evening of hugely imaginative activities that might include creating slime or balloon powered buggies to take home, or seeing how objects can be frozen in nitrogen then shattered. They're extremely popular, naturally, so you might have to book as much as two months ahead (24hr information line 7942 4747). Then there are children's educational events and workshops every half-term and during school holidays – they can't be booked in advance, so turn up early on the day. To get advance details of these events, sign up for the email newsletter on the museum's website.

Buggy access. Cafés. Disabled access: lift, toilet. Nappy-changing facilities. Nearest picnic place: museum basement/Hyde Park. Restaurant. Shop.

Serpentine Gallery

Kensington Gardens (near Albert Memorial), W2 3XA (7402 6075/www.serpentinegallery.org). Lancaster Gate or South Kensington tube. **Open** 10am-6pm daily. Closed 25 Dec. **Admission** free. **Map** p313 D8.

It may be housed in a 1930s tearoom, but this lovely, light gallery is a coolly cutting-edge space for contemporary art. A new artist-led programme of family workshops on Saturday mornings will begin in autumn 2004. These are expected to be very popular, with bookings having been taken since May: call 7298 1520 for an application form. If you can't get a place, bribe the children with promises of cake down by the Serpentine afterwards (it's only a short walk) and just come for one of the exhibitions. Upcoming highlights include sculptures and drawings from conceptual and installation artist Gabriel Orozco (1 July-30 Aug 2004).

Buggy access. Nappy-changing facilities. Nearest picnic place: Hyde Park/Kensington Gardens. Shop.

Victoria & Albert Museum

Cromwell Road, SW7 2RL (7942 2000/www.vam.ac.uk). South Kensington tube. **Open** 10am-5.45pm Mon, Tue, Thur-Sun; 10am-10pm Wed. Closed 24-26 Dec. *Tours* daily; phone for details. **Admission** free; charges apply for special exhibitions. **Credit** *Shop* AmEx, MC, V. **Map** p315 E10.

Recently the V&A has shown an interest in trendy subjects with a series of well-publicised fashion retrospectives (the exhibition celebrating the extraordinary career of Viviennne Westwood runs until 11 Jul 2004). Perhaps this is to fend off any accusations that it's a rather dusty institution compared to its neighbours. Fashionable or not, it is a superb national repository of beautiful things. There are collections of costume, jewellery, textiles, metalwork, glass, furniture, photographs, drawings, paintings and sculpture from cultures across the world. From the Pirelli Garden you can properly admire the handsome red brick building, to be enhanced by Daniel Libeskind's 'Spiral' extension in 2007 (it is estimated).

Home-grown treasures are housed in the British Galleries, which opened in 2001 with a range of interactive exhibits for children. In the Victorian Discovery Area, for example, there are corsets and crinolines to try on; you can also try your hand at building a model Crystal Palace or a chair. The 18th-Century Discovery Area has children making domestic objects, and there is tapestry to weave and armour to be tried out in the Tudor and Stuart Discovery Area. The ground floor is where you'll find the World Galleries, which means sumptuous Chinese Imperial robes and huge Persian carpets.

Facilities for children include activity backpacks (available 10.30am-4.30pm Sat), which contain jigsaws, stories, construction games and objects linked to the collections. On Sundays (10.30am-5pm) children aged three to 12 should look out for the Activity Cart, which is crammed with art materials. Family trails (each keeping children occupied for around 45mins) are available daily; they consist of an activity sheet for the kids and an information sheet for adults. A wide range of activities are organised for school holidays and at weekends; for details, see the website or call 7942 2211.

The V&A's Photography gallery presents work from the museum's famous collection, with temporary shows including a centenary retrospective of 20th-century photographer Bill Brandt (until 25 July). The Vivienne Westwood exhibition shows off more than 150 examples of the British designer's clothing, from punk outfits to grand ball gowns and trademark corsets (until 11 July). But perhaps most impressive will be 'Encounters: the Meeting of Asia and Europe', exploring the art and culture of two continents over the past three centuries (23 Sept-5 Dec). A new architecture gallery and study centre is scheduled to open in autumn 2004.

Buggy access. Café. Disabled access: lift, toilets. Nappy-changing facilities. Nearest picnic place: Pirelli Garden (outdoors)/basement picnic room (indoors). Restaurant. Shop.

North London

Dead cool round Camden, dead posh in Islington, but the hills of north London are alive with the sound of happy families.

Camden Lock

Camden Town

Inevitably, teenagers will want to visit **Camden Lock**, despite all assurances that it is no longer the alternative, craft-oriented market of its '80s heyday. Brace yourself, then, for junky jewellery, leather, outlandish footwear, weird furniture and fashion that can err embarrassingly on the louche. You may also have problems trying to steer sulky ones past the greasy fast food stalls. Pizzas at Apertivo (30 Hawley Crescent, NW1 8NP, 7267 7755), next door to the MTV studios where teenagers like to hang about star-spotting, may be less offensive. When it all gets too much, smart weekend visitors leave the Camden crowds (in any case, the tube is exit only at busy times) to take refuge in Primrose Hill (*see p93*).

One way to escape the frantic atmosphere of Camden is on peaceful **Regent's Canal**, where traditional narrowboats offer a passenger service to Little Venice, a trip that could combine a visit to the excellent Puppet Barge (*see p218*). Boats plying a western course pass through London Zoo (*see p66*), and some allow you to break your journey there. The 45-minute one-way trip passes elegant terraces with gardens backing on to the canal, willow-fringed towpaths and converted warehouses.

Jewish Museum, Camden

129-31 Albert Street, NW1 7NB (7284 1997/www.jewish museum.org.uk). Camden Town tube. **Open** 10am-4pm Mon-Thur; 10am-5pm Sun. Closed public hols, inc Christmas Day, Jewish festivals. **Admission** (LP) £3.50; £2.50 OAPs; £1.50 5-16s, concessions; free under-5s; £8 family (2+2). **Credit** MC, V.

The history of the Jewish population of Britain, from medieval times up to the present day, is brought to life in this museum. Although it's undoubtedly of interest to students of history and world religion, it's neither too dry nor too academic for the young. Monthly activities for children (pre-booking essential) educate in a fun way with puppet shows, storytelling and family workshops. Permanent exhibits that draw crowds of youngsters include a sparkling, jewelled breastplate depicting the 12 tribes, a silver scroll case in the shape of a fish and a coconut shell kiddush cup. Temporary exhibitions can be fascinating: 2004-5 will see shows of children's drawings from Theresienstadt, one on the Jews of Gibraltar and one of bible stories done in tapestry.

Buggy access. Disabled access: lift. Nearest picnic place: Regent's Park. Shop.

Around Camden

The borough of Camden stretches south to Holborn (*see p57*), where the library at 32-38 Theobald's Road, WC1X 8PA (7974 6342) houses Camden's Local Studies and Archives Centre. No appointments are necessary and it's a lot more fun than the internet.

The hidden treasures of St Pancras

The industrial hinterland of King's Cross may not seem a very attractive proposition for a family outing, but children are easily entertained by its historic associations (many of them thrillingly gruesome). Adults can better appreciate the almost palpable atmosphere of excitement arising from the area's current regeneration. Go see it now, for the Covent Garden effect is not far off.

'Pancras' comes from Pancratius, a 14-year-old Roman boy put to death by the sword for failing to deny his Christian Lord and Master. He became patron saint of the young, as well as avenger of false oaths and perjury. The sixth-century **St Pancras Old Church** (St Pancras Road, NW1 1UL, 7387 4193; closed to the public except for daily 9am services) gave rise to a little community that flourished here until the 14th century, but constant flooding of the River Fleet (which now runs underground from Hampstead to Fleet Street) forced the parishioners to move north to what is now Kentish Town.

St Pancras continued to be sparsely populated until the late 18th century; Londoners used it as a rural retreat 'enjoying its country lanes and tea gardens'. But as the area was progressively taken over by the smoky, noisy railways, together with other noxious industries, it became less and less fashionable. It was worse further north; above Vale Royal on York Way was an area ironically named Belle Isle, a group of Victorian industrial buildings with tall chimneys dedicated to 'bone boiling, blood boiling, varnish making and the manufacture of artificial manure' – all derived, in part, from the old horses slaughtered on the premises. The current architecture – acre upon acre of '60s council flats – replaced damaged buildings hit by enemy bombers during World War II in their attempts to destroy the railway infrastructure.

Things could only get better. One gas holder remains (just behind Goods Way, but visible from a long way off), but this is now a listed building. It acts as a sort of beacon, guiding you to the entrance for the **Camley Street Natural Park** (*see p93*). This unexpected and delightful green space was created on the site of former coal drops, built in 1865-7. The drops have been removed, but cinephiles may remember a shot of them from the film *Alfie* (1966).

The churchyard of Old St Pancras, or **St Pancras Gardens**, was formerly St Giles Burial Ground. Sir John Soane, architect of the Bank of England, was buried here in 1837. His tomb has a canopy of Portland stone that seems strangely familiar in shape: it inspired Sir Gilbert Scott's red K2 telephone box. There is also a massive memorial to several dozen once notable people once buried here, whose graves were removed. It was commissioned by the millionaire philanthropist Angela Burdett-Coutts and is lovely to behold, with its plant mosaics, sundials and four beasts on guard (two were modelled on her own Collie dogs).

Lots of people of no interest at all suffered the fate of body snatching, body burning or simple reburial in this boneyard, simply to make room for others during the 1840s. Some 3,000 were buried here in six months during the cholera epidemic of 1849. The stench was appalling. Later, in 1874, the hapless Thomas Hardy, not then a novelist but living in London as a trainee architect, was deputised to oversee the exhumation of bodies from St Giles' in order to make way for the approach works of Midland Railway. He wrote a poem about the experience:

> We late lamented resting here
>   are mixed to human jam,
> And each to each exclaims in fear,
>   'I know not which I am!'

More eloquent, perhaps, is the Hardy Tree. Encircled by a hedge, it still grows in twisted, Gothic fashion from the centre of dozens of old headstones stacked up like mossy playing cards. It sends shivers down the spine.

East of Camden Town, there are two other as yet little-known destinations. The **Camley Street Natural Park** is tucked away in the industrial hinterland of King's Cross and, just across York Way, you'll find the **London Canal Museum**, which brings to life the history of the local waterways. King's Cross Station has become an unlikely tourist attraction in the wake of Harry Potter fever. Camera-wielding families come for the newly installed sign: 'Platform 9¾'. Children pose here, adopting a leaping stance as if they were about to enter the magical void famously used by the rookie wizard. (For more on this area's attractions, *see p92* **The hidden treasures of St Pancras**).

To the west of Camden Town, **Primrose Hill** has long been a chi-chi outpost of villagey smartness, but in recent years its reputation has been further enhanced by the numerous celebs who have opted to live – and bring up their kids – here. Separated from its brasher neighbour only by a railway footbridge, the high street (Regent's Park Road) is café heaven. Just off the main drag is Manna (4 Erskine Road, NW3 3AJ, 7722 8028), a spacious vegetarian place where the cooking is good enough for kids not to notice they're being asked to eat horrid green things. As well as attractive cafés, restaurants, pubs and shops alongside the park, Primrose Hill has some of the prettiest houses in north London, making it well worth an ogle, especially en route to nearby Regent's Park (*see p69*). Primrose Hill itself is a smallish park, with a nice play area that is secure for small children and has a big sandpit. The hill is ideal for flying kites and offers views over London Zoo and Regent's Park. As at many parks, there's a good local firework display on the weekend closest to Bonfire Night, but it can get horribly crowded, which means either a long walk for little legs or a long wait if you are able to dig in early.

If you're planning to eat afterwards, book well in advance, as nearby restaurants get packed out.

Back over the railway footbridge in **Chalk Farm** is the Roundhouse (7424 9991), a former train turning shed once celebrated as a rock concert hall. It's currently undergoing redevelopment into an exciting performance space, and reopens in 2005 as a centre for the arts, including music, theatre, dance, circus and digital media, as well as an outreach programme for children.

Camley Street Natural Park

12 Camley Street, NW1 0PW (7833 2311). King's Cross tube/rail. **Open** *May-Sept* 9am-5pm Mon-Thur; 11am-5pm Sat, Sun. *Oct-Apr* 9am-5pm Mon-Thur; 10am-4pm Sat, Sun. Closed 20 Dec-1 Jan. **Admission** free. **Map** p317 L2.

Despite assurances by the contractors building the Channel Tunnel link that works would be finished by 2004, road blocks continue to make visits to the London Wildlife Trust's flagship reserve something of a trek. This does have advantages, though: an area famously hostile to pedestrians can seem like a quiet backwater and anyone who does turn up is sure of a warm welcome and the ranger's undivided attention. The park itself is tiny by national standards, yet manages to combine woods, ponds, marshes and flower meadows. The visitors' centre is a rustic cabin stuffed with bird, bat and spider studies, arty insect sculptures and a wealth of information on urban flora and fauna. Eight-year-olds and over can join the Wildlife Watch and attend activities once a month; other children might like the bat walks, pond dipping and birdbox making in the holidays – book ahead to join in, but bear in mind these are not unaccompanied sessions. *Buggy access. Nappy-changing facilities.*

London Canal Museum

12-13 New Wharf Road, N1 9RT (7713 0836/www.canal museum.org.uk). King's Cross tube/rail. **Open** 10am-4.30pm Tue-Sun, bank hol Mon. Closed 24-26 Dec. **Admission** (LP) £3; £2 concessions, 8-16s; free under-8s. **Credit** MC, V. **Map** p317 M2.

Don't be put off by the odd elderly (do we mean grumpy and child-hating?) volunteer who tells you there is little here for children. In fact this small shrine to life on Britain's canals is perfect for youngsters of all ages. Apart from static panels of text relating the historic importance of these waterways, there is a real narrowboat to explore, complete with recorded domestic dialogue; a children's corner with canal-themed books and lots of pictures of Rosie and Jim to colour in; a life-size 'horse' in its stable; and videos intimating just how hard (and grimy) life afloat used to be.

An important personal element is available in the touch-screen display introducing visitors to the life and times of one Carlo Gatti. Gatti, sometime owner of the Victorian warehouse at 12 New Wharf Road, was an Italian-Swiss immigrant who rose from humble chestnut seller to wealthy ice-cream manufacturer, simply by importing ice blocks from the frozen lakes of Norway. The ice was stored in two deep, circular ice wells below the warehouse – throw in pennies to appreciate the drop. If boating leaves you cold, displays relating to the commercial history of ice-cream will fascinate.

The shop has some lovely, inexpensive artefacts with curious child appeal, from enamelware painted with 'castles and roses' to lace-and-ribbon plates. Craft sessions in the holidays often involve recreating such items – call for details. *Buggy access. Nappy-changing facilities. Nearest picnic place: museum terrace/canal towpath. Shop.*

St John's Wood

Not really north London except by virtue of its postcode, this upmarket residential area just west of Regent's Park is pleasant to stroll around but has few specific attractions for children apart from **Lord's Cricket Ground**. Among the pricey clothes shops is the useful children's shoe shop Instep (45 St John's Wood High Street, NW8 7NJ, 7722 7634) and a branch of Maison Blanc (37 St John's Wood High Street, NW8 7NJ, 7586 1982, www.maisonblanc.co.uk) to have tea in after a stroll around Regent's Park.

Further north is Abbey Road, home of the recording studios and immortalised on the cover of the Beatles album of the same name. Tourists

can often be seen risking life and limb on the zebra crossing to re-enact said cover. Have a giggle at their expense before sauntering to check out Oscar's Den (*see p249*) at No.127. This is one of the best party shops in town; it can provide everything from balloons to celebrity lookalikes.

Lord's Cricket Ground & MCC Museum

St John's Road, NW8 8QN (7432 1033/ www.lords.org). St John's Wood tube. **Open** *Tours* Oct-Mar noon, 2pm daily. Apr-Sept 10am, noon, 2pm daily. Closed 25, 26 Dec, 1 Jan, all major matches & preparation days; phone to check. **Admission** *Tours* £7; £5.50 concessions; £4.50 5-15s; free under-5s; £20 family (2+2). **Credit** MC, V.

Best known as the home of the celebrated Ashes urn, the Marylebone Cricket Club Museum is the world's oldest sporting museum. It includes, among paintings, photos and battered bats, eccentricities such as a reconstruction of the shot that killed a passing sparrow in 1936, together with the stuffed bird and the ball. The guided tour takes visitors into the Mound Stand (so-called because it's built on a burial mound from the Great Plague), the pavilion, the visitors' dressing room and the historic Long Room. (These last two may not be on view during refurbishment works in the winter of 2004-5. Phone to check.) Other displays include memorabilia and cricket kit used by some of the greatest players of all time – among them such luminaries as Victor Trumper, Don Bradman and WG Grace. There's also a useful range of cricket kit and equipment for both children and adults available for purchase.

Buggy access. Lifts. Nearest picnic place: St John's churchyard playground. Shop.

Hampstead & around

Like Highgate (*see p96*), **Hampstead** sits on a hill and was a place rich people went to live to escape the stench and disease of London in former times. It still has a villagey atmosphere, mainly due to narrow streets and graceful, period architecture. There is almost nowhere to park, so families often make a beeline for the heath car park on East Heath Road. From here, it's a 20-minute dawdle up to the village, perhaps pausing at the playground opposite 2 Willow Road (7435 6166). This modernist house was built by Ernö Goldfinger in 1939 and is now open on a tour-only basis, so there's no chance of dragging under-11s round it. But you get a very good view of many rooms while pushing a swing, and it's consoling to think that James Bond's creator, Ian Fleming, hated the architect so much he named a villain after him. Up in the village itself are legions of cafés (though none, perhaps, so atmospheric as Louis Patisserie at 32 Heath Street) and the pedestrian-only lanes make for peaceful shopping.

Hampstead has its many famous sons – witness **Keats House** and the Freud Museum (20 Maresfield Gardens, NW3 5SX, 7435 2002, www.freud.org.uk), home to a famous couch but strictly of interest to students of psychoanalysis. Burgh House (New End Square, NW3 1LT, 7431 0144, www.burghhouse.org.uk), a Queen Anne house

Camden Market. See p91.

Following a £4-million refurbishment programme, this intriguing venue dedicated to the visual arts reopened at the beginning of 2004. It now has three new galleries hosting exhibitions by international and British artists, a state of the art ceramics studio and a busy programme of courses for both adults and children. Typically, half-terms feature two-day courses in, say, clay and mixed media for £36 (£22 concessions). Four different term-time courses cater for young people in different age groups – call for details and inspiration. More casually, drop into the charming new café overlooking replanted gardens.
Buggy access. Café. Lifts. Nappy-changing facilities. Nearest picnic place: Arts Centre gardens. Shop.

Fenton House

3 Hampstead Grove, NW3 6RT (7435 3471/info 01494 755563/box office 01494 755572/www.national trust.org.uk). Hampstead tube/Hampstead Heath rail. **Open** *Mar* 2-5pm Sat, Sun. *Apr-Oct* 2-5pm Wed-Fri; 11am-5pm Sat, Sun, bank hols. Last entry 4.30pm. **Tours** phone for times. **Admission** (NT) £4.60; £2.30 5-17s; £11.50 family; free under-5s. **No credit cards**.
Another of Hampstead's covetable period dwellings, Fenton House is enjoyed by adults for its William and Mary architecture, its award-winning garden and its quirky Benton Fletcher collection of early keyboard instruments. Children enjoy it in a different way, for a summer stroll through the orchard, vegetable garden and lawns is always agreeable and the harpsichords, clavichords, virginals and spinets will probably be like no instrument they have ever seen before. There is also a porcelain collection that includes a 'curious grotesque teapot' and several poodles.

Apple Day in October is celebrated in the orchard, and older children may well be fascinated by the fortnightly summer concerts utilising instruments in the collection.
Baby slings for hire. Buggy access.

Hampstead Heath

NW5 1QR (7485 4491). Kentish Town tube/Gospel Oak or Hampstead Heath rail/214, C2, C11 bus. **Open** dawn-dusk daily.
This wonderful, undulating swathe of grass, woods and lakes is so apparently vast (almost 800 acres/320 ha) that it's possible to imagine yourself in several different places, all on the same day. Toil up Parliament Hill to fly a kite, watch other (often highly skilled) kite flyers, or simply rest awhile, gazing down over the city for miles and miles. Stay at the bottom of the hill to play tennis, bowls, boules; to feed the ducks on the first lake or admire the model boats (occasionally noisy) on the second. The heath is noticeably well maintained by the Corporation of London; in recent years, the various ponds, which are fed by an underground stream thought to be the old River Fleet, have been cleaned up. Bathing is segregated, and since the Ladies Bathing Pond is located in a secluded enclosure, entry is barred to all males and to girls under eight. Still, this makes for an enticing initiation ritual, bearing in mind that the pond water is always bracing, weedy and inhabited by ducks. Family bathing is probably best undertaken in the lido close to Gospel Oak station. The playground on that side of the heath is excellent, not least because it has a shallow paddling pool, open free in summer (note that costumes must be worn even by the tiniest children). Less well known is the adventure playground behind the athletics track, where leaping, bouncing and climbing from challenging, timber-framed playframes is the order of the day.

Though beautiful in winter, it is in the warmer months that the heath comes into its own as a source of entertainment for children. Clowns, bouncy castles, magicians, storytellers and puppeteers perform free of charge in different locations each

---

containing a small museum about the area's history, has a charming café and garden away from the weekend crowds. The natural pleasures of **Hampstead Heath** – running wild, cycling, gathering conkers and climbing trees – may be preferred to all of these, however. A good combination might be a walk through the Vale of Health (spot the blue plaque for DH Lawrence) to the top of Hampstead, then down the hill to the village for refreshment (there are several well-known chain restaurants here).

Several of the pubs between heath and village have been made over into sophisticated eateries and are no longer a good bet for fish and chips, but walking south on the heath to South End Green and the car park will bring you to Cucina (45A South End Road, NW3 2QB, 7435 7814). This is more café/deli-oriented than before, and staff members are friendly. On the same strip is Polly's (55 South End Road, NW3 2QB, 7794 8144), a nice place for tea. Alternatively, move on to the 'heath extension', or Golders Hill, where another Italian-oriented café (*see p172*), smooth, winding paths, a lovely playground, fallow deer and an aviary full of many pretty, exotic birds, await.

Camden Arts Centre

Arkwright Road, corner of Finchley Road, NW3 6DG (7472 5500/www.camdenartscentre.org). Finchley Road tube/Finchley Road & Frognal rail. **Open** 10am-6pm Mon, Tue, Thur-Sun; 10am-9pm Wed. Closed Mon & bank hols. **Admission** free. **Credit** *Shop* MC, V.

week (pick up a leaflet from the Parliament Hill information office). There are also tennis courses, learn-to-fish days, bat walks and themed nature trails. More accessible these days is a children's 'Secret Garden' and wildlife pond, near the tennis courts; call at the information centre to gain entry.
Buggy access. Cafés. Nappy-changing facilities.

Keats House

Keats Grove, NW3 2RR (7435 2062/www.cityof london.gov.uk/keats). Belsize Park or Hampstead tube/Hampstead Heath rail/24, 46, 168 bus. **Open** *Easter-Oct* noon-5pm Tue-Sun. *Nov-Easter* noon-4pm Tue-Sun. Closed 25, 26, 31 Dec. **Tours** 3pm Sat, Sun. **Admission** £3; £1.50 concessions; free under-16s. Weekend tours incl in admission price.

You need to be a real fan of Keats's poetry and the Romantics in general to appreciate the resonances in this house. It is, admittedly, on one of Hampstead's most beautiful streets, the white stucco Regency architecture set off by clouds of blossom in spring. Kindly Corporation of London attendants can provide line drawings of the house for baffled children to colour in while their parents tour august rooms once belonging to Keats's friend, Charles Brown. A chaise longue is set up in the position where Keats spent his days gazing out of the window after becoming ill in the 1820s, and the house is full of handsome pieces of antique furniture, portraits of the poet and his friends, and photocopied sheets of the poems. There's also a (new) tree in the garden near the spot where Keats is said to have sat writing 'Ode to a Nightingale'.
Buggy access (ground floor only). Nearest picnic place: house gardens. Shop.

Kentish Town City Farm

1 Cressfield Close, off Grafton Road, NW5 4BN (7916 5421). Chalk Farm or Kentish Town tube/Gospel Oak rail. **Open** 9.30am-5pm daily. Closed 25 Dec. **Admission** free; donations appreciated.

Completely hidden from view down a side road with a high, blank gate, this is a slice of the countryside in London. It's an absolute delight in almost any season, for it stretches way beyond the farmyard, where Aylesbury ducks bathe noisily, goats head-butt each other at the trough and a large white pig teeters about, like a fat old lady on stilettos. Horses, cows, chickens, cats and rabbits are other inhabitants, all of which seem to be busy reproducing. Several gardens (for locals, including Bangladeshi women growing coriander, mooli and curry plants; for pensioners in typical allotment style; and for visitors, featuring carnivorous plants and other curiosities), orchards and enclosures for sheep line the railway line.

A newly cleaned-out pond with dipping platform is full of frogs and a riding school is the scene of weekend pony rides (1.30pm Sat, Sun, weather permitting, £1). The railway arch forms an impromptu proscenium for children's drama, while a classroom is used for a plethora of inventive craft and play sessions. The after-school art club, cookery club and other classes are kept fairly quiet; everything here is free and very popular with locals. An energetic education officer, however, welcomes school visits from all boroughs and anyone can come to the Easter egg hunt, Apple Day (October) and so on.
Buggy access. Disabled access: ramp, toilet. Nappy-changing facilities. Nearest picnic place: on the farm.

Kenwood House/Iveagh Bequest

Kenwood House, Hampstead Lane, NW3 7JR (8348 1286/www.english-heritage.org.uk). Archway tube/ Golders Green tube, then 210 bus. **Open** *Apr-Oct* 10am-5pm Mon, Tue, Thur, Sat, Sun; 10.30am-5pm Wed, Fri. *Nov-Mar* 10am-4pm Mon, Tue, Thur, Sat, Sun; 10.30am-4pm Wed, Fri. Closed 24-26 Dec, 1 Jan. **Tours** by appointment only. **Admission** (EH) free; donations appreciated. *Tours* £3.50; £2.50 concessions; £1.50 under-16s. **Credit** MC, V.

Strike out across the verdant plains and wooded hillsides of Hampstead Heath from almost any direction and a path will lead you, willy-nilly, to Kenwood House. Hot chocolate and cream teas in winter or classy lemonade and ice-creams in summer persuade small feet that the trek is worthwhile, as the Brew House Café (*see p172*), set in the old kitchens, is the best catering venue for miles.

The house itself is a white stucco mansion, built in the classical style for the Earl of Mansfield by Robert Adam in 1767-9 and bequeathed to the nation in 1927. It houses the Iveagh Bequest, an impressive collection of paintings that includes works by Reynolds, Turner and Van Dyck, as well as a Rembrandt self-portrait tucked into a darkened corner of the Dining Room and a rare Vermeer (*The Guitar Player*). Hogarth, Guardi and a couple of classic flirtatious Bouchers round out the collection. There's also a vast library. Of special interest to children are the annual Easter egg hunt and the themed walks (for example, costumed actors got up as Lord and Lady Mansfield re-enact scenes from local history and take their audience to see the dairy buildings and other rarely seen parts of the house).

Volunteer group Heath Hands also has its office here – it too plans family events throughout the year, mostly to do with improving the look of the heath and the estate gardens. For details of forthcoming events here and around the heath, pick up a leaflet at the visitors' centre in the Kenwood House Estate Office. Left to their own devices, most youngsters will find ample amusement running through the spooky Ivy Arch, hiding in the vast rhododendron bushes or rolling down the grass slopes in front of the house.
Buggy access (limited in house). Café. Nappy-changing facilities. Shop.

Highgate & Archway

Like Hampstead (*see p94*), **Highgate** is a pretty, hilly village bursting with rummage-worthy shops, child-friendly pubs – and wealthy residents who greatly covet the sylvan backdrop. One of the main reasons to bring children here is **Highgate Wood**, one of the rare bits of surviving original woodland in the capital, which has a delightful setting, a well-designed play area and a pleasant café. Waterlow Park is also gorgeous, even more so once its extensive refurbishment is complete.

Next door, Highgate Cemetery (Swains Lane, N6 6PJ, 8340 1834, www.highgate-cemetery.org) is on the visiting list of many a tourist, much to the annoyance of the Friends of Highgate Cemetery, who prefer to play down the visitor pull of their historic patch. Kids are, in fact, discouraged from visiting the place unless they're coming to see the grave of a relative, but if you long to pay respects to Karl Marx, Mary Ann Evans (aka George Eliot), Max Wall or any of the other admired figures who now repose in the Eastern Cemetery, you can bring children to enjoy the peace and beauty of this delightful boneyard as long as they're well behaved.

Keats House. You can't miss it. *See p96.*

The Western Cemetery is out of bounds to casual visitors (adults and kids aged eight and over can pay £3 for a guided tour, which brings the departed to life and affords a chance to see the eerie catacombs). A little further down the hill from the tube station is Shepherd's Close, from where you can access the Parkland Walk (which runs to Finsbury Park). Hornsey Lane, on the other side of Highgate Hill, leads you to the Archway, a Victorian viaduct spanning what is now the A1 and offering views of the City and the East End. Jackson's Lane Community Centre (*see p223*), off Archway Road, puts on shows for children most Saturdays, and a popular, large-scale panto at Christmas.

Highgate Wood/Queen's Wood

Muswell Hill Road, N10 3JN (8444 6129). Highgate tube/43, 134, 263 bus. **Open** 7.30am-dusk daily.
These 70 acres (28ha) are some of the last remaining ancient woodlands in London, and are full of gently swaying oaks and hornbeams. The wood has been lovingly tended by the Corporation of London and its trusty team of woodsmen and -women since 1886, when the Lord Mayor declared the wood 'an open space for ever'. Carpeted with bluebells and wild flowers in spring and dappled with sunlight filtered by the trees, this corner of London really doesn't feel like London at all.

The wood is carefully managed: trees are coppiced in the traditional way, areas are fenced off to encourage new growth, boxes are provided for owls, bats and hedgehogs to nest in, and everything that moves is chronicled. The bird population has increased dramatically in recent years, both in types and numbers – 70 different species of bird have been spotted here, including nesting sparrowhawks and visiting rare golden orioles. Alongside the usual foxes and grey squirrels are five species of bat, more than 20 of butterfly, 100 of spider and a stunning 454 of beetle: expect much rustling in the undergrowth. You can pick up leaflets about the wildlife in the visitors' information hut beside the café, or join one of the bird identification walks or nature trails. There's always something going on: stories around the Story-Telling Tree in summer, Christmas tree recycling in January, beetle safaris and bat watch evenings. Some of the activities even result in

temporary 'wigwams' – little houses made of fallen timber merely propped together for anyone to play in.

The award-winning children's playground has been carefully planned to allow wheelchair-users and their more mobile friends to play together. The bridge and tower structure is accessible to buggies and wheelchairs, the swings are designed to be used by children who need more support, and there are braille noticeboards. For sporty types, there's a football and cricket field (in front of the café), and exercise equipment has recently been installed among the trees. The other big draw is the Oshobasho Café (*see p173*). On summer evenings there are concerts in the garden.

Highgate Wood even has its own newspaper, the *Treetop News*, with details of new sightings of birds and animals, puzzles and crosswords. It can be downloaded from the Corporation of London's website (www.cityoflondon.gov.uk) or picked up free in the visitors' centre.

Across Muswell Hill Road is Queen's Wood, which comes under local council management and is a wilder prospect – there are no resident staff and it can be quite deserted. Walkers can join the Parkland Walk footpath from here. *Buggy access. Café. Disabled access: toilet. Nappy-changing facilities.*

Lauderdale House

Waterlow Park, Highgate Hill, N6 5HC (8348 8716/ restaurant 8341 4807/www.lauderdale.org.uk). Archway tube/143, 210, 271, W5 bus. **Open** 11am-4pm Tue-Fri; 1.30-5pm Sat; noon-5pm Sun; phone to check weekend openings. *Restaurant* 10am-dusk Tue-Sun. Closed 24 Dec-mid Jan. **Admission** free. **No credit cards.**
The pretty, 16th-century Lauderdale House, once home of Nell Gwynne, is the centrepiece of Highgate's secluded park. A favoured venue for wedding receptions and other bashes, it's sometimes closed to the public. Saturdays, however, are sacrosanct, because that's when children come for their morning shows, usually aimed at the threes to eights. Ring for details of craft fairs, musical events, exhibitions by local artists and other events held in the arts centre (*see p223*). In the summer, weather permitting, the parkland surrounding the house hosts open-air shows. Whatever's on, it's lovely to sit on the terrace of the café and admire the view over a coffee and ice-cream or an Italian meal; book ahead if you fancy having Sunday lunch here. Fans of the house and park may join a free mailing list to be advised of upcoming events.

Highbury Fields. *See p100.*

Beautiful Waterlow Park, in which the house is set, has several lakes, a toddler's playground and grassy slopes that are great for picnicking. The Grade II-listed park, donated by Sir Sidney Waterlow as 'a garden for the gardenless', was awarded £1.2 million of Heritage Lottery money for improvement in 2003. Restoration of the 17th-century terrace garden is complete; work continues to convert the depot building into workshops, an activities room and toilets. *Buggy access (ground floor only). Café/restaurant. Nearest picnic place: Waterlow Park.*

Islington

'Merry' **Islington** was first famous as an idyllic village – Henry VIII owned houses for hunting in the area – but today is known as one of London's premier urban residential areas, a buzzy district characterised by its mix of graceful, listed Victorian and Georgian houses, trendy bars and shops, and flourishing arts centres. On a Friday night the streets are thronging with the after-work crowd, but there's also plenty here for those not yet of drinking age.

Islington has 11 theatres and is home to the Anna Scher Theatre School, where many *EastEnders* cast members learned their trade – would-be Walfordites can expect a five-year wait to join. The Little Angel Theatre (*see p218*) in Dagmar Passage is a celebrated, purpose-built puppet theatre. Every June the area hosts a two-week festival of music, theatre and art, and there are regular exhibitions at the Business Design Centre. Wednesdays and Saturdays see antiques markets in pedestrianised Camden Passage; many stalls have items of interest for older children, including classic toys.

Playground-loving kids rate **Highbury Fields**, where the equipment is challenging but extremely crowded on sunny days. Footie fans of the Gunner variety may like to tour **Arsenal Football Club** before it relocates for the 2006-7 season. Due north of Arsenal, the other big park in the area is Finsbury Park, for which the borough of Islington shares responsibility with the boroughs of Haringey and Hackney. It's a great sprawling green space that, until recently, had become very shabby and run down. Fortunately, there's help at hand in the shape of the Finsbury Park Partnership, set up to bid for a slice of the government's Single Regeneration Budget in 1999. The Finsbury Park area, which includes the huge railway and tube station, housing estates and commercial districts, was awarded £25 million. The park's regeneration is supposed to be complete by the time the project ends in 2006. There's no shortage of sporting facilities, notably the Michael Sobell Leisure Centre (*see p259*), with its climbing walls, trampolining, table tennis, squash and badminton. A star attraction for the under-threes is the Sobell Safari, an indoor playground on four floors, with tunnels, slides and ball ponds.

Nearby, on Green Lanes, the Castle Climbing Centre (*see p255*) is London's top climbing venue. You'll find it in a Grade II-listed Victorian folly (previously a water tower) modelled on Stirling Castle. Within the grounds, in a separate building, is another ball pond, relocated from Highbury.

Those who crave the scent of the countryside can commune with pigs at **Freightliners City Farm** or learn about green activities at the **Islington Ecology Centre**. Rural flavours – in a form trendy urban types can stomach (think ruby chard and brussels sprouts on the stick) – can be sampled every Sunday from 10am to 2pm at the Islington Farmers' Market (Essex Road, opposite Islington Green, N1, 7704 9659). Look out for happily picnicking families sampling their farmers' market goodies on the green. They're sensible: most eateries on Upper Street are expensive. The Turkish restaurants are better value than most and very friendly, with the two branches of Gallipoli (102 Upper Street, N1 1QN, 7359 0630; G II, 120 Upper Street, N1 1QP, 7359 1578) also serving hearty English breakfasts. The S&M Café (*see p174*) is another affordable option, as is Giraffe (29-31 Essex Road, N1 2SA, 7359 5999; *see also p163*).

Chapel Market (on the street of the same name) is a gloriously downmarket bargain bin of fruit and vegetables, linen, partyware, toys and not always durables, presided over by rowdy costers. It's still thriving, despite competition from the N1 Shopping Centre that links Liverpool Road with Upper Street. The centre is home to branches of reliable childrenswear chains, restaurants like Wagamama and Yo Sushi!, and an eight-screen cinema.

Arsenal Football Club

Arsenal Stadium, Avenell Road, N5 1BU (7704 4000/ box office 7704 4040/www.arsenal.com). Arsenal tube/ Finsbury Park tube/rail. **Open** 9.30am-5pm Mon-Fri, before & after all 1st-team home games. *World of Sport shop* 9.30am-6pm Mon-Sat. **Tours** 11am, 2pm Mon-Fri. **Admission** *Museum* £4; £2 under-16s. *Tours* £8; £4 concessions, under-16s. **Credit** *Shop* MC, V.
The bulldozers have dug in and work has begun on Arsenal's controversial new stadium at Ashburton Grove, but until it opens in 2006-7, Highbury is still, as it proudly claims at its entrance, 'the home of football'. So, if north London youngsters incline towards the red rather than the white, there is still time to visit this historic football ground. Tour guests may check out the pitch, changing rooms, trophy room, board room, press room and museum, which has memorabilia, information about the club's early days and a Gunner-glorifying video. The shop stocks replica kit (in all sizes) and souvenirs. *Nearest picnic place: Gillespie Park. Restaurant. Shop.*

Freightliners City Farm

Paradise Park, Sheringham Road, off Liverpool Road, N7 8PF (7609 0467/www.freightlinersfarm.org.uk). Caledonian Road or Holloway Road tube/Highbury & Islington tube/rail. **Open** *Summer* 10am-4.45pm Tue-Sun. *Winter* 10am-4pm Tue-Sun. Closed 25, 26 Dec, 1 Jan. **Admission** free; donations appreciated.

A stone's throw from Pentonville Prison, this city farm next to the playground in Paradise Park is a bucolic hint that all could be different in the world if only Nature were a universal inspiration. Forget run-of-the-mill establishments with their token livestock, Freightliners positively teems with birdlife, rabbits, cows, goats, cats, geese, pigs and so on. Labelling is not academic – instead of breed information, most plaques give pet names and imagined occupations in scenarios like 'The Village' (the doves and pigeons are the postmasters, natch). But the animals, many of them rare breeds, are nonetheless impressive. Giant Flemish rabbits are the biggest you will see anywhere; guineafowl run amok in other animals' pens; exotic cockerels with feathered feet squawk alarmingly in your path; bees fly lazily around their hives. You can buy hen and duck eggs of all hues, plus own-grown veg and plants when in season. Playschemes run in summer and are justifiably popular. And, at any time of year, there is an overwhelming scent of straw and manure – bliss. *Buggy access. Café. Nappy-changing facilities. Nearest picnic place: farm picnic area. Shop.*

Highbury Fields
Highbury Crescent, N5 1RR (7527 4971). Highbury & Islington tube/rail/19, 30, 43, 271 bus. **Open** *Park* 24hrs. *Playground* dawn-dusk daily.
Somewhat flat and featureless at first glance, Highbury Fields is Islington's largest outdoor space and repays careful exploration. Hidden behind Highbury Pool and a series of high bushes is an unusual playground that combines old-fashioned thrills (such as a circular train demanding passenger propulsion, Flintstone-style, and a long, alarmingly steep slide) with more recent additions, like the flying fox and giant, web-like climbing frames. The outdoor tennis courts have been refurbished and are used by the excellent Islington Tennis Centre (*see p265*), an all-levels club active all year. A stroll across Highbury Fields can take you from busy Upper Street past imposing period terraces to Highbury Barn, a small but trendy enclave boasting several excellent food shops, restaurants and cafés.
Buggy access. Café.

Islington Ecology Centre
191 Drayton Park, N5 1PH (7354 5162/www.islington. gov.uk). Arsenal tube. **Open** *Park* 8am-dusk Mon-Fri; 9am-dusk Sat; 10am-dusk Sun. *Centre drop-in sessions* 10am-noon Tue; 2-4pm Thur; for other times phone to check. **Admission** free; donations appreciated.
Imaginative redevelopment of former railway land led to the founding of Islington's largest nature reserve: Gillespie Park. It has woodland, meadows, wetland and ponds, and the Ecology Centre is its educational heart. Staff are endlessly enthusiastic and helpful on the subject of all natural things in the borough – in 2004 they were even running a photographic competition to challenge different age groups to capture Islington's wildlife on film. An events diary is published twice annually with events suitable for families and children, from moth evenings to junk modelling. Ring for details or a leaflet covering what's on.
Buggy access.

The Islington Museum
Islington Town Hall, Upper Street, N1 2UD (7527 2837). Highbury & Islington tube/rail. **Open** 11am-5pm Wed-Sat; 2-4pm Sun. **Admission** free.
The Islington Museum is housed in the former Assembly Hall, next to Islington Town Hall. It has two galleries: one houses a permanent collection illustrating, in an undeniably pedestrian way, the history of Islington. The other has temporary exhibitions that tend to be more fun. Until mid August

2004, for example, Clerkenwell's most famous clowning son, Grimaldi, will be featured, giving rise to clown-oriented children's activities throughout the summer. *Buggy access. Shop.*

Stoke Newington

North-east of Islington, **Stoke Newington** first became fashionable in the '80s when property prices in N1 became prohibitive, driving 'alternative' families into the next postcode along. Now the three-wheeled buggy brigade, long-term locals and Islington wannabes all co-exist more or less happily. 'Stokey' is a pleasantly bohemian, unpolished sort of area, with good independent shops and numerous places to eat and drink. The heart of the area is Stoke Newington Church Street, which hosts north London's best street festival every June. Stoke Newington is blessed with two fine green spaces: **Clissold Park**, where local families congregate, and the rambling old cemetery of **Abney Park**.

Dalston, which is Stoke Newington's down-at-heel neighbour, has the biggest street market for miles around, full of Afro-Caribbean, Greek and Turkish wares. Children love it; and you can buy them a T-shirt or pair of gloves for less than £1.

Abney Park Cemetery & Nature Reserve
Stoke Newington High Street, N16 0LN (7275 7557/ www.abney-park.org.uk). Stoke Newington rail/73 bus. **Open** dawn-dusk daily. Closed 25 Dec. **Admission** free.
At first glance another mossy, romantically decayed Victorian cemetery, Abney Park is actually a hub of conservation activity. An environmental classroom at the Stoke Newington High Street entrance is the scene of many free workshops for children and adults: the Abney Park Lion Cubs is aimed at two- to five-year-olds, while more sophisticated activities such as hedgehog- or squirrel-themed trails and crafts keep schoolchildren amused in the holidays. Most popular of all is the annual Easter egg hunt, but there are also guided walks with themes like family history (ring for dates) and woodwork for women. The visitors' centre doubles as a shop for guides to green London and other such environmentally aware literature.
Buggy access. Shop.

Clissold Park
Stoke Newington Church Street, N16 5HJ (7923 3660). Stoke Newington rail/73, 149, 329, 476 bus. **Open** *Park* 7.30am-dusk daily.
There is no tube station in Stoke Newington, but it is possible for energetic families to cycle to Clissold Park from Finsbury Park, utilising the parkland trails and the mercifully wide pavements along Green Lanes. The whole trip should take no more than 30 minutes – perhaps terminating at Clissold Park's café. The latter is set in a handsome, listed Georgian building, which is in need of some repair – the conjunction of past splendour and current decay sums up the area rather well. There is lots to discover on a pleasant amble around Clissold Park: enclosures of fallow deer, an aviary full of interesting, exotic birds, several ponds supporting various waterfowl, an outdoor stage for children to cavort on whenever it is not in use by bands, and tennis courts that carers

could use while kids are in the adjoining playground. The courts are home to the Hackney wing of the City Tennis Centre (*see p265*); ring for details of its programme – family tennis evenings, junior clubs and tournaments, and coaching are all available. The bowling green here appears run-down to the point of dereliction, but the playground is lovely, with modern equipment and lots of shady picnic tables. *Buggy access (in park, steps at café). Café.*

Crouch End & Muswell Hill

The twin postcodes of N8 (Crouch End) and N10 (Muswell Hill) have been on the up for some time – partly due to the fact that neither has a tube station, meaning that locals are inclined to shop locally so the retail scene can support many small independent stores. The former sits in a valley, while the latter sits on the hill, making each area distinct by topography. Architecturally, they are blessed with a wealth of Victorian and Edwardian housing (check out the scenery, pre-1890s building boom, at the Bruce Castle Museum – *see p104*), which in the past has not been expensive due to the lack of transport links. This, together with decent primary schools, has made these areas popular with young families, and many of the shops and cafés reflect that trend.

The area's best-known attraction has to be **Alexandra Park and Palace**, but there are plenty of other green spaces. Priory Park in Middle Lane is great for cycling, rollerskating and football, and has a paddling pool, formal gardens and tennis courts; its Rainbow Café is a shining example of what other park cafés could be like. Stationers Park, between Denton Road and Mayfield Road, has a good adventure playground, a pre-school children's play area and (free) tennis courts. Park Road Pools (*see p263*) has both indoor and outdoor swimming pools, though the latter gets packed out on summer weekends. Hidden tracts of greenery off Park Road allow ample space for the North Middlesex Sports Club, plus various other tennis and cricket clubs; these are the scene of various sport-related holiday playschemes and of after-school coaching.

There are so many family-oriented restaurants in Crouch End you'd stumble into one if you were blindfolded and spun round three times. Pizza Bella (4-6 Park Road, N8 8DD, 8342 8541) is a popular birthday party venue with saintly waiters to pick up the pieces, and Banners (*see p172*) is a massive favourite. All the Indian restaurants do buffet deals at lunchtime, but Satay Malaysia (10 Crouch End Hill, N8 8AA, 8340 3286) makes a nice change.

Alexandra Park & Palace
Alexandra Palace Way, N22 7AY (8365 2121/boating 8889 9089/www.alexandrapalace.com). Wood Green tube/Alexandra Palace rail/W3, 144, 184 bus. **Open** *Park* 24hrs daily. *Palace* times vary depending on exhibitions. **Admission** free.

Alexandra Park

Tales from... the Jewish Museum

In Japan, he would probably be a 'living treasure'. In Britain, **Leon Greenman**, 93, has an OBE and his business card reads 'Holocaust Educator'.

'I had everything: fleas, lice, scurvy. I was very weak towards the end of the war, but I always prayed to God that I would survive the concentration camps. I said to Him, if I can live and get out of here, then I will spend the rest of my life telling people the truth about what happened.'

Few of us fulfil the promises we make to a deity under extreme duress, but Leon Greenman, one of only a few thousand Jews to survive the Nazi genocide of 1939-45, in which six million died, has done just that. Every Sunday, he tells his story of imprisonment, beatings and starvation to visitors at the Jewish Museum in Finchley. He also tours the country speaking to schoolchildren (from around 13 years of age).

'There are not many nice things in what I'm going to tell you,' he warns. 'In fact most of them are bad.' His young audience seem quite composed. Of course they have been prepared by their history teachers for what follows, but there is still a palpable sense of privilege in listening to Greenman's personal story. He is so small and frail – his face perhaps naturally gaunt with age – yet for sheer moral strength there can be none to beat him.

The irony in Leon Greenman's story is that he was British. Born in the East End, he was only sent to Holland as a boy after his mother died and his father needed help bringing up his children. Having grown up with Dutch relatives, he married a Dutch girl, Else. They had a baby, Barney, and it was when Leon went to the British consulate in Rotterdam to register Barney's dual citizenship that he was first reassured about their fate in any impending war. All British subjects would be evacuated along with diplomatic staff, he was told. The Greenmans stayed. But by the time Holland was occupied and Leon had given his passport to Dutch friends for safekeeping, it was so dangerous to be associated with Jews in any way that his papers, mysteriously, could no longer be found.

The tragedy that followed is now all too well known. Leon Greenman and his family were taken from their home to Westerbork, a holding camp for Jews deported from the Netherlands. They managed to stay there for four and a half months, but all Greenman's complaints to officialdom about his British status fell on deaf ears. They were then sent in a group of 700 people by train (a journey of 36 hours, with no food or drink) to Auschwitz, where they were separated. Leon never saw his wife or child again, yet his belief that they were still alive somewhere in the camps kept him going, he says, through all the pain and hardship.

LEON GREENMAN
AUSCHWITZ
98288

In fact they were sent to the gas chambers within 20 minutes of arrival at Auschwitz. Of the 700 people deported that day, only two survived. A fellow inmate later told Greenman that only a quarter of an hour after the train left Westerbork, his name had been called on the camp's loudspeaker system. Documents had arrived in the post proving that he had British nationality and was entitled to internment with other British subjects.

Instead, Greenman spent the war doing hard labour, learning through kicks and blows how to maximise his chance of survival in the camps. He witnessed shootings, hangings, death by starvation and disease, and his descriptions of many of these events is graphic. His overwhelming message, however, is not one of bitterness or anger.

His mission, as he sees it, is to help prevent such things ever occurring again – a legitimate fear in the face of modern genocides in Rwanda, Bosnia and Romania. He explains that he still receives threats from the BNP and that they tried to kill him in 1994, claiming his story is all lies. They don't scare him, though. 'Always tell the truth,' he admonishes the children. 'You can't go wrong if you do that.'

Famously ill-starred, Ally Pally (as it is affectionately known) burnt down twice – once in 1863, just weeks after opening, and once in 1980 – only to rise like a phoenix on each occasion as a grandiloquent place of public entertainment. The only trouble is that, on closer inspection, the buildings are still in dire need of repair and the facilities badly run. Leaking roofs, mousetraps in the corridors, queues at reception and a distinctly downmarket café are all items on critics' agenda. But if you can overlook these things – or look ahead to the moment when a £3.6-million refurbishment project upgrades the children's curiously old-fashioned playground, dredges the lake, replants the trees in the park and so on – the palace on the hill and its environs have much to offer. Chief interest for kids is the ice-skating rink, along with (in summer) the boating lake and pitch-and-putt course. Walking around the park affords breathtaking views of London and good picnics. In bad weather, try the café in the garden centre. Firework night is the best night of the year, with plenty of room for spectators and pyrotechnics that may be seen for miles. *Buggy access. Nappy-changing facilities (ice rink). Nearest picnic place: picnic area by boating lake.*

Finchley

Finchley is one of those London outposts that have been waiting to 'come up' for several years now, but haven't yet managed it. Not that it isn't thoroughly affluent and well served by public transport (it has three tube stations). It just hasn't got the desirable status of other smart north London villages. Its saving graces are its cosmopolitan background (it has large Jewish and Japanese communities), air of general prosperity and peaceful, tree-lined streets.

Around Church End, Finchley Central, the true heart of what was once a village, you catch a whiff of Middle England and will hardly believe you're still in the capital. The attraction here is **Avenue House** and its beautifully landscaped gardens, which were given to the nation in 1918.

Victoria Park, just off Ballards Lane between Finchley Central and North Finchley, has a bowling green, playground and tennis courts; in July it also provides a venue for the Finchley Carnival.

For indoor entertainment, the Great North Leisure Park (Leisure Way, High Road, N12) – better known among the locals as Warner Village – is an ugly but useful US-style entertainment complex. The cinema, Finchley Warner Village (0870 240 6020), has a Saturday morning kids' club. There's also an extremely popular swimming pool – a good spot for children's parties – which has a vigorous wave machine and swirling currents for 'rough and tumble fun' (as all the signs say). Non-swimmers should take armbands. The Hollywood Bowl bowling alley (*see p265*) has a bar and burger restaurant; adjacent to it is an amusement arcade. A couple of rowdy games here, followed by pizza and pop next door at ASK (8446 0970), is a tried-and-tested children's party combination in these parts.

It doesn't have to be pizza and burger chains when it comes to eating out in Finchley, though. The area is well set up with excellent eating places. The coolest place to be seen with your kids is probably Rani (7 Long Lane, N3 2PR, 8349 4386), a brightly coloured Gujarati/East African vegetarian restaurant that does children's menus. Fish and chip lovers here are blessed with the renowned Two Brothers Fish Restaurant (297-303 Regent's Park Road, N3 1DP, 8346 0469).

In East Finchley, the Phoenix Cinema (8883 4080) has children's films on Saturdays. The Old Manor House, on East End Road, has been transformed into a cultural centre, which includes ritual baths, a school and the **Jewish Museum, Finchley**.

If you and your offspring decide to get away from it all, try the Dollis Valley Green Walk, which forms part of the London Loop that encircles the city and links green spaces from Moat Mount, near Mill Hill in the north, to Hampstead Garden Suburb in the south. Setting off with a map is advisable, as the way isn't very well signposted; for more details visit www.londonwalking.com.

Avenue House
15-17 East End Road, N3 3QE (8346 7812/www.avenue house.org.uk). Finchley Central tube/82, 125 bus. **Open** *Ink Museum 2-4pm Tue-Thur. Closed 25, 26 Dec.* **Admission** *free; donations appreciated.*
The Ink Museum, situated in one room of this lovely building, commemorates former Avenue House owner 'Inky' Stephens and his father Henry, inventor in 1837 of the blue-black ink that is used to this day on birth and marriage certificates. (Stephens' ink factory was once on the site of the Islington Ecology Centre, *see p100*) The rest of Avenue House is open to view only on certain days of the year – call for details – but some of the rooms can be hired out and it's a grand venue for children's parties. Otherwise the grounds are open free from 7am until dusk, and offer a pleasantly situated playground and buggy-accessible tree trail. An annual highlight is the Church End Festival (9 May), a public entertainment with bouncy castles, a fun train and other jolly diversions much enhanced by the setting. *Buggy access. Café (Mar-Sept). Disabled access: toilet. Nappy-changing facilities. Nearest picnic place: Avenue House grounds.*

Jewish Museum, Finchley
Sternberg Centre, 80 East End Road, N3 2SY (8349 1143/www.jewishmuseum.org.uk) Finchley Central tube/143 bus. **Open** 10.30am-5pm Mon-Thur; 10.30am-4.30pm Sun. Closed bank hols, Jewish hols, Sun in Aug. **Admission** (LP) £2; £1 concessions, 12-16s; free under-12s. **No credit cards**.
The more northerly branch of the informative Jewish Museum (*see p91*) focuses on Jewish social history. There's a reconstructed sewing workshop on the ground floor, which gives an idea of sweatshop life in the 19th century, and a display on the evolution of an East End family bagel business. Upstairs an exhibition traces the life of Leon Greenman, a British Jew who survived Auschwitz (*see p102* **Tales from... the Jewish Museum**). The Holocaust Exhibition may be considered too upsetting for young children, but staff leave it to the discretion of parents; the images are more

Around Town

likely to be understood by people of at least secondary school age. This branch also has a 12,000-strong photographic archive, augmented by 2,000 oral history tapes.

Buggy access. Café (lunchtimes Mon-Thur). Nearest picnic place: museum garden/Avenue House gardens. Shop.

Further north

Jump on a bus going up the dreary A10 towards Tottenham and you eventually pass White Hart Lane, the home of **Tottenham Hotspur Football Club**, a tour of which is much easier to get into than a match. Just down from here is **Bruce Castle**, an island of stateliness in run-down surroundings.

Further west, the North Circular (an escape route or a vehicle trap, depending on traffic) leads to Brent Cross Shopping Centre with its large range of chains and a handy crèche, thence to IKEA, home of the affordable flatpack. It's not just the home furnishings that attract people here: take the Edgware Road if you have a yen for Japanese goods. Oriental City (399 Edgware Road, NW9 0JJ, 8200 0009) is a mall with several good places to eat, including a big self-service buffet. The shops are fascinating, with wind-dried ducks, odd-looking veg and oriental toiletries, though it's the state-of-the-art amusement arcade that children love – it's a lot less seedy than its counterparts in central London.

Set sail in a westerly direction from Brent Cross to the peace and quiet of the Welsh Harp Reservoir (Cool Oak Lane, NW9 3BG, 8205 1240). This huge open space is not only a beauty spot, but has been recognised as a Site of Special Scientific Interest. The informative environmental centre is a good starting point for nature trips. The leafy waterside areas provide space for games pitches, tennis courts, playgrounds and picnics.

Further north, in Hendon proper, the extensively revamped **Royal Air Force Museum Hendon** is a lavish tribute to the history of flying machines and the magnificent men who piloted them.

Bruce Castle Museum

Lordship Lane, N17 8NU (8808 8772/www.haringey. gov.uk). Wood Green tube, then 123 or 243 bus/Seven Sisters tube/rail, then 123 or 243 bus/Bruce Grove rail. **Open** 1-5pm Wed-Sun. **Admission** free.

Forget dreary glass cases full of old Roman pots. This local museum, set in an unexpectedly beautiful 16th-century manor house and holding the entire collections of the borough of Haringey, is a lively place much appreciated for its weekend and holiday children's activities. Sunday afternoons (2-4pm) always see some craft session or other in progress; this means adults can peruse the photographs of local streets in Victorian times undisturbed (Muswell Hill as a muddy cart track; quaint shopfronts on North London high streets; rolling green pastures now filled with housing). The building itself was owned by successive generations of the Coleraine family and is said to be haunted by one of them still. More concrete is the lasting influence of Rowland Hill,

a progressive schoolmaster on this site and subsequently a postal reformer: his ideas led to the formation of the Penny Post. He is featured in a room devoted to local inventors, which has plenty of buttons to push and pull. Other displays, geared towards the war years, are popular with grandparents. The museum's archives may be visited by appointment; if you live in Haringey, there's every chance your own street will be featured in an historic photo that may be copied to take home. Outside, the 20 acres (8ha) of grounds make for good picnicking; there's a playground and a collection of antique postboxes.

Buggy access. Car park (in Church Lane, free). Disabled access: lift, toilet. Nappy-changing facilities. Shop.

Royal Air Force Museum Hendon

Grahame Park Way, NW9 5LL (8205 2266/www.raf museum.org). Colindale tube/Mill Hill Broadway rail/303 bus. **Open** 10am-6pm daily. Closed 24-26 Dec, 1 Jan. *Tours daily; times vary, phone for details.* **Admission** (LP) free. *Tours* free. **Credit** MC, V.

Even if – in theory – the flying machines of yesteryear leave you cold, the newly renovated RAF Museum makes a brilliant day out. A substantial lottery grant has resulted in an ultra-modern Milestones of Flight building, where the exhibits – Camel, Tempest, Gypsy Moth, Mosquito, Harrier and so on – are parked at ground level or hung in dogfight poses from the rafters. As you take a break in the café, helicopter blades jut out above your head, while a little further on miniature parachutists go up and down in a tube or drop off a wire into the hands of kids eager to learn about the laws of gravity. More interactive games are available in the Aeronauts gallery, many in the guise of pilot aptitude tests. This gallery is really one giant playground: who could resist guiding a beach ball through hoops on a stream of hot air, or trying out the controls in a Jet Provost cockpit? Only the flight simulator (over-8s only) carries an extra charge; everything else is gloriously free, so although a comprehensive tour is exhausting, you can come as often as you like. More low-key than the Milestones of Flight gallery are the atmospheric and dimly lit Battle of Britain building, and the restored Grahame-White Aircraft Factory, with its pleasing architecture and beautiful biplanes, their propellers all polished mahogany.

Activities for children and adults take place all year: workshops include hot-air balloon making, rocket science, and Search and Rescue role-playing. The workshops are always very popular, so book ahead. Quizzes, Pulsar Battlezone interactive laser games, face painting, aircraft displays and giant garden games are also on the cards. The fun-packed Summer Festival Weekend at the end of August is a must.

Buggy access. Café. Lift. Nappy-changing facilities. Nearest picnic place: on-site picnic area. Restaurant. Shop.

Tottenham Hotspur Football Club

Bill Nicholson Way, 748 High Road, N17 0AP (8365 5000/ticket office 0870 420 5000/www.spurs.co.uk). White Hart Lane rail. **Open** *Tours* 11am Mon-Fri; 11am, 1pm Sat. **Admission** *Tours* £7.50 adults; £4.50 under-16s, OAPs. **Credit** (only in advance) MC, V.

Tours of the pitchside, the tunnel, changing rooms, board rooms and press rooms take place regularly, but the Saturday ones tend to be booked up well in advance. Note that they cannot take place on a match day, nor the day before; indeed their regularity depends on a minimum number of customers, so don't turn up on spec. Tours last about an hour to an hour and a half, depending on how chatty the punters are. Finish in the megastore, where you can blow £50 on a shirt or 50p on a souvenir pencil.

Buggy access. Disabled access: toilet. Shop.

East London

As Cockney gives way to City slang, families get the best of both worlds.

North Woolwich Old Station
Museum. See p117.

Spitalfields & Whitechapel

The East End is rarely discussed these days without the term 'gentrification' tugging at the hem of its coat. Fair enough: in 2003 PRs even tried to give the area a new name – Eastside – in an attempt to unite it with Docklands, Greenwich and Lewisham. Still, new money has meant increasingly inviting family attractions, and the ease of access to **Spitalfields** from the rest of the city makes it a good starting point for an East End adventure.

You could head north from Aldgate East, past Tubby Isaacs' stall (purveyor of whelks and jellied eels since 1919) on Goulston Street or up Old Castle Street, to a former washhouse, now the Women's Library (7320 2222, www.thewomenslibrary.ac.uk) in 2002. It holds free exhibitions (9.30am-5.30pm Mon-Wed, Fri; 9.30am-8pm Thur; 10am-4pm Sat), workshops and drop-in family activities (11am-1pm, 2-4pm Thur, 22 July-19 Aug), not to mention the best collection of women's history in the country. The less studious will be interested in the café upstairs,

particularly those too fearful to have attempted Tubby's wares. Petticoat Lane Market, just north, usually has a handful of stalls, but on Sunday afternoons becomes far more hectic. A little further up Commercial Street is the terrific Spitalfields Market (*see p187*).

The market can also be reached by heading east from Liverpool Street Station. Brushfield Street will provide a great view of Nicholas Hawksmoor's awe-inspiring Christ Church (7247 7202). Built in 1714, it is due to reopen in July 2004 after restoration work. If the kids are too young to be spooked by sinister architecture but old enough to want to be spooked, remind them about Jack the Ripper: the Ten Bells, right next to the church, is where some of his unfortunate victims supped their last gin.

North of the market and church, atmospheric Folgate Street has **Dennis Severs' House**. Branching off elegant Fournier Street (which runs alongside the church towards Brick Lane) you'll find the minor jewel that is **19 Princelet Street**.

Brick Lane, now well established on the tourist map, was the focal point of a new immigrant community of Indians and Bangladeshis from the '50s to the '70s, hence its fame as curry central (try the lunchtime buffet at shiny Café Naz, 46-8 Brick Lane, E1 6RF, 7247 0234). Brick Lane Beigel Bake (159 Brick Lane, E1 6SB, 7729 0616) harks back to an earlier period of Jewish immigration.

Whitechapel's attractions include Whitechapel Bell Foundry (Nos.32-4 Whitechapel Road, E1 1DY, 7247 2599, www.whitechapelbellfoundry.co.uk; 10am, 2pm Sat). Tours of the foundry aren't available to under-14s and probably won't interest teenagers, but it's worth popping into the foyer for a peek at the huge frame of Big Ben, which was cast here in 1858. The **Royal London Hospital Museum**, has more macabre appeal. Nearby the New Tayyab (89 Fieldgate Street, E1 1JU, 7247 9543) serves curry as authentic as it gets.

Dennis Severs' House

18 Folgate Street, E1 6DX (7247 4013/www.dennissevers house.co.uk). Liverpool Street tube/rail. **Open** 2-5pm 1st & 3rd Sun of mth; noon-2pm Mon (following 1st & 3rd Sun of mth); Mon evenings (times vary). **Admission** £8 Sun; £5 noon-2pm Mon; £12 Mon evenings. No under-10s. **No credit cards. Map** p321 R5.

Only the Sir John Soane's Museum (*see p60*) can rival Dennis Severs' House for atmosphere, especially on the candlelit evenings. Bought in the late 1970s by Dennis Severs (who died in 1999), the building is now what its founder called a 'still-life drama'. Each of the ten rooms stages a period in the life of the house, making it appear that the various occupants from 1724 to 1914 might pop back at any moment: the hearth crackles, the wine glasses stand half-drunk, the smell of cooking lingers. Severs wouldn't let children in the place, feeling they couldn't muster the level of imaginative engagement his house demanded; staff now welcome 'young adults', but a reverential hush is the mode – no giggling when you see the chamber pot upstairs is full of wee.

Nearest picnic place: Broadgate Circus (Liverpool Street station). Shop.

19 Princelet Street

Spitalfields, E1 6QH (7247 5352/www.19princeletstreet. org.uk). Aldgate East tube/Liverpool Street tube/rail. **Open** see website, or by appointment. **Admission** free; donations appreciated. **Map** p321 S5.

This Grade II-listed building makes an unusual museum. First, there's the subject: immigration. Second, there's the opening hours: infrequent, so that the fragile building can be preserved. Third, there's the contents: 19 Princelet Street has been home to numerous immigrant groups over the last 100 years, so contains a hidden synagogue, but also was a home to Protestant Huguenots and a school for Bangladeshi women learning English. The trustees are seeking funds to open the property on a regular basis. *See also p107* **Tales from... 19 Princelet Street**.

Royal London Hospital
Archives & Museum

St Philip's Church, Newark Street, E1 2AA (7377 7608/ www.brlcf.org.uk). Whitechapel tube. **Open** 10am-4.30pm Mon-Fri. Closed 24 Dec-2 Jan, bank hols & adjacent days. **Admission** free.

This single-room museum covers the hospital's growth from 18th century voluntary institution to pioneering 20th-century hospital (the 1930s X-ray machine looks like it was created by mad inventor in a B-movie), and the development of nursing and childcare, with displays on such as Florence Nightingale. There's a replica of the hat former patient Joseph Merrick (the 'Elephant Man') wore to conceal his swollen head, a video screen showing quaint period films about the hospital, and a small case on forensics with fascinating material on Jack the Ripper, including his foul letters to the police. It's all a bit wordy for children, though: they'd be better visiting during the hospital open day in September.
Buggy access. Café (in hospital). Disabled access: lift, ramp. Nappy-changing facilities (in hospital). Shop.

Spitalfields City Farm

Weaver Street, off Pedley Street, E1 5HJ (7247 8762/ www.spitalfieldscityfarm.org). Whitechapel tube. **Open** 10.30am-5pm Tue-Sun. Closed 25 Dec. **Admission** free; donations appreciated.

This community farm was established in 1978 after local allotments were lost to property developers. It now has geese honking about, cows, donkeys, pigs, sheep and goats, and a cuddly small mammal section for mice and rabbits. Poultry, gardeners and all the livestock produce free-range eggs, seasonal vegetables and manure (in that order). Keen eight- to 13-year-olds can join the Young Farmers Club, which runs a playscheme (Sat; Tue-Sat in school hols); there's a parent and toddler group for under-fives (Sun; Tue, Sun in school hols). Children can also join the Mascot Scheme and learn how to show animals, and visitors often get to enjoy donkey rides (ring in advance to check). Local schools can book into the farm's egg incubation service, giving children the opportunity to watch hatchlings make their way into the world.
Buggy access. Café. Nappy-changing facilities. Shop.

Whitechapel Art Gallery

80-82 Whitechapel High Street, E1 7QX (7522 7888/ www.whitechapel.org). Aldgate East tube/15, 25, 253 bus. **Open** 11am-6pm Tue, Wed, Fri-Sun; 11am-9pm Thur. Closed 24-26 Dec, 1 Jan. **Tours** 2.30pm every other Sun (free). **Admission** free (1 paying show a year). **Map** p321 S6.

The Whitechapel has a strong education and community programme for children: when the gallery was founded in 1901, Reverend Canon Barnett insisted that every exhibition should have one. So while bringing excellent modern art shows to the East End, the gallery has ensured local schools benefit from a progressive programme of artist residencies, sometimes resulting in collaborative exhibitions. There are also exhibition-specific workshops. The swish refurbished café was redesigned by Turner Prize nominee Liam Gillick.
Buggy access. Café. Disabled access: lift, toilet. Nappy-changing facilities. Nearest picnic place: Altab Ali Park. Shop.

Shoreditch & Hoxton

In 1598 James Burbage founded London's first theatre in Shoreditch, and 19th-century Hoxton was famous for its music halls, but the area's current fame has much more to do with trendy advertising types that flocked here in the '90s. For families, the **Geffrye Museum** makes the place well worth diverting to, though a bite at Faulkner's (*see p176*) or Sông Quê (*see p177*) enhances the pleasure.

Tales from... 19 Princelet Street

In a small village in Russia, there lived a Jewish tailor. Each day the local children gathered outside his shop to taunt him: 'Jew! Jew! Jew!' Desperate, he hatched a plan. The following day, the tailor announced he would pay each of his taunters the sum of ten roubles for shouting at him. He did so, and of course they returned the next day to taunt him again. 'I'm afraid I don't have enough money to pay you ten roubles today,' he told them. 'You'll have to accept five.' Which they did. The third day, they came back again. 'Today I can only pay you one rouble,' said the tailor. 'But two days ago you paid us ten roubles', grumbled the children, 'and yesterday you paid us five. We're not going to call you Jew for just one rouble.' 'So don't,' the tailor replied. And they didn't.

This folk tale originated with the Yiddish theatre, which opened its first permanent home on Princelet Street (then Princes Street) in 1886, and it's just one of the many tales told at **19 Princelet Street** (*see p106*), a house that seems full of stories. Built in 1719, it was first home to a family of Huguenot silk weavers called the Ogiers, who had fled persecution in France – you can still see a big bobbin hanging above the door, marking it as a weaver's house. When they prospered and moved on, the tall house was divided into lodgings and workshops for less fortunate weavers, and the attic windows extended to let in more light for them to work by. Each new wave of immigration to the East

End brought new occupants to the house: the Irish first, and later Eastern European Jews. In 1869 the house became a synagogue, which was built out over what had been for the Ogiers a garden.

When families arrive these days, they are greeted at the door. Adults are given a description of the house's history to peruse while they queue (only restricted numbers are allowed into the house at any one time because of its decrepit state) and children get a quiz sheet as they go in, which helps guide them round the house. 'Suitcases and Sanctuary', the house's main exhibition, was made by artists in collaboration with nine- and ten-year-olds at six local schools. In each part the schoolchildren, themselves from all over the world – Bangladeshi, Irish, Bosnian, Somali – attempt to see the world through the eyes of previous immigrant groups. So they've written diary entries in the role of Huguenots fleeing persecution, acted out the plight of Irish families forced to leave their land by the potato famine or striking for fair pay on the docks (*pictured*), and they've designed posters that might attract West Indian migrants. On the way round the house you can read the diaries and poems, watch videos (including one that tells the tailor's story – with an ethnically diverse group of kids throwing the racist abuse). Children enthusiastically fill in luggage tags with details of what they'd pack if forced to leave their homes with but a single suitcase, and scribble down the details of the most recent migrant in their own family. In the main room explainers are on hand to tell you about the house or their own experiences of the working synagogue.

Upstairs, in the gallery where female worshippers used to gather, the temporary exhibition 'Leave to Remain' includes a very serious game. Margareta Kern's *Standard-Class Opinions* consists of photos of people in standard class train carriages, together with their comments about asylum seekers coming to Britain. The first half has photos with the comments already attached; in the second you're invited to attach comments to the appropriate photos – cause for much head-scratching and deliberation for the children, and a valuable lesson when they see how few they get right (we have no intention of putting on record how few we got right ourselves). The melancholy beauty of the gallery itself – dusty skylights in green, yellow and pink, creaky ancient floorboards, railings too fragile to bear any weight – only increases the exhibition's impact.

Teachers can book class visits by calling the staff at the house; the rest of us can visit for the scheduled openings, which during 2004 are noon-7pm 13-20 June, noon-5pm 11 July and 5 September, and 10am-7pm 18-19 September. Do check the website or phone in advance to confirm before you make the journey.

Museum of Childhood at Bethnal Green: where fun means fun.

Geffrye Museum

136 Kingsland Road, E2 8EA (7739 9893/www.geffrye-museum.org.uk). Liverpool Street tube/rail, then 149, 242 bus/Old Street tube/rail, then 243 bus. **Open** 10am-5pm Tue-Sat; noon-5pm Sun, bank hol Mon. Closed Good Fri, 24-26 Dec, 1 Jan. **Admission** free; donations appreciated. *Almshouse* £2; £1 concessions; free under-16s. Under-8s must be accompanied by an adult.

The Geffrye is gorgeous inside and out. It was built as almshouses in 1715, one of which has been restored to its 18th-century glory (check the website for public openings). In 1914 it was converted into a furniture and interior design museum. Now rooms represent different periods in history from the Elizabethan era to the present day. You can't actually enter them – all are open on the third side so you can see everything, without having to worry about precious objects slipping from grubby little fingers – but there are period chairs in several anterooms that can be rigorously tested for comfort. The second, newer half of the museum has rooms from the '30s, '60s and '90s, and temporary arts and crafts exhibitions downstairs. The airy restaurant is a pleasure year round, but there are plenty of other places for a sit-down if you can't afford tea and cakes for everyone.

An imaginative and extremely popular programme of school-holiday and weekend events for children reflect the changing exhibitions. Monthly Family Sundays combine music, storytelling and a craft activity, but this year it's the three weeks of garden events (27-30 July, 3-6 Aug, 10-13 Aug) that really catch the eye. Called 'Bugs and Blooms', these will help children create miniature gardens or insect sculptures, as well as exploring the museum's lovely gardens. Each Christmas the museum's 12 period rooms are evocatively decorated in appropriately themed festive style, tracing the development of modern Christmas and showing just how indebted to the Victorians we are for so many yuletide traditions. Activities are generally for six- to 15-year-olds, but there are summer workshops for threes and over (with carers). Phone or check the website for more details.

Buggy access. Disabled access: lift, toilet. Nappy-changing facilities. Nearest picnic place: museum grounds. Restaurant. Shop.

Bethnal Green

East of the Spitalfields cluster you'll find East End characters in much greater profusion. Bethnal Green, infamous in Victorian times as the 'poorest district in London', has more recently been known for its notorious gangsters (the Krays) and soap stars (Babs Windsor was born here). But if you're here to pay homage, look no further than the glorious **Museum of Childhood at Bethnal Green**. Just next door York Hall, 'arguably the most famous boxing venue in Europe', has been saved by a 15-year deal between Tower Hamlets council and Greenwich Leisure – good news for children who want to step into the ring… the inflatable kind for fun sessions in the swimming pool (*see p266*). If you can get everyone up and out in time on a Sunday, Columbia Road Flower Market (*see p184*) is another good reason to visit: Jones Dairy Café (*see p176*) is a great refuelling stop.

A daily programme of events includes staff-led dance, puppetry and arts and crafts sessions, as well as family fun days for over-twos. It's worth joining the free kids' club if you enjoy visiting the museum: it gives a 10% discount in the lovely little shop and free soft-play sessions for pre-schoolers. *Buggy access. Café. Disabled: lift, toilet. Nappy-changing facilities. Nearest picnic place: tables in front of museum. Shop.*

Hackney

The land that tubes forgot, Hackney has been the subject of plans for improved transport links for well over a decade. Currently serving only nine stations, the East London Line would be extended north through Hackney as far as Finsbury Park, as well as south to Wimbledon and West Croydon. With London bidding to host the Olympics in 2012 (*see p258* **Olympic dreams**), there is some hope that money will be found to make this project a reality. Until then, the combination of buses and overland trains will either seem like a conspiracy to run you out of I-Spy variants to play while waiting, or convince you that you never need to use the underground again (the feeling won't last).

In Hackney proper (centred on Mare Street rather than Hackney Road), the beautiful old Hackney Empire (*see p221*) finally reopened in January 2004 after painfully slow refurbishment. The handsome new look of the Empire is just one part of Hackney's plan to create a 'cultural quarter' around the Town Hall Square, most of which came to fruition back in 2002. Central to this scheme were **Hackney Museum**, housed with the Central Library in the Technology Learning Centre, and a large-scale local music venue, the Ocean (*see p232*).

For somewhere so definitively urban, there are a surprising number of green spaces hereabout – surprising, that is, until you learn that as late as the 19th century Hackney was almost entirely rural. Just by **Hackney City Farm**, Haggerston Park (Audrey Street, off Goldsmith Row, E2 8QH, 7739 6288) has pretty gardens; places for softball, BMX riding and ball games; as well as a playground that was being finished as we went to press. Cross Regent's Canal and you're on Broadway Market. The chi-chi shops and restaurants along this strip include Little Georgia (No.2, 7249 9070) for Eastern European meze and Holistic Health (*see p272*), specialists in tot aromatherapy. F Cooke (No.9, 7254 6458), a proper pie-and-mash shop, reminds the sleek incomers what they're missing, but those newbies are more interested in the Saturday farmers' market (www.broadwaymarket.co.uk). Try to time your visit to catch the opening times of the **Clowns International Gallery**, further to the north-west, or dive into London Fields (Westside, E8) for the sports and play facilities, or summertime pétanque

Museum of Childhood at Bethnal Green

Cambridge Heath Road, E2 9PA (8983 5200/recorded info 8980 2415/www.museumofchildhood. org.uk). Bethnal Green tube/rail. **Open** 10am-5.50pm Mon-Thur, Sat, Sun. Closed 24-26 Dec, 1 Jan. **Admission** free. Under-8s must be accompanied by an adult.

The Museum of Childhood was established in 1872, as part of the V&A (*see p90*), although it wasn't until the mid 1970s that it took its present title. It is now the UK's biggest collection of toys and childhood paraphernalia, containing some 6,000 games and toys, stretching over five centuries. Neat cabinets display board games, early electronic toys, puppets from all over the world and children's clothes from various periods. The several huge dolls' houses on the first floor draw a lingering crowd to eye the carefully constructed miniature furniture or admire the porcelain dolls and their tiny accessories. To celebrate Sindy's 40th birthday, the museum has an exhibition space devoted to the plastic icon (sadly, we know of no plans to release a version of the doll showing her age). There are also displays to accompany the Indian season, which will culminate in half-term activities involving kite-makers and toymakers.

The 'Good Times' play area, with its dressing-up box and pier-end wonky mirrors sitting happily alongside interactive computer stations, was part of the major refurbishments completed in 2003. Staff lead a daily programme of events at which they teach craft skills and puppetry to under-fives; there's also a soft play area that can grant you 40 minutes to chill out in the ground-floor café should you wish. A preferable plan during the summer is to bring a picnic to enjoy in the front garden, or perhaps in the attractive (and usually more peaceful) park next door.

at the Pub on the Park (19 Martello Street, E8 3PE, 7275 9586). Hackney Downs (Downs Park Road, E8) has tennis courts, basketball, a bowling green and a playground. The 300 acres (120 hectares) of Hackney Marsh – fine kite-flying country – are a muddy home for English Sunday League, American and Gaelic football, rugby and cricket. Springfield Park in Clapton looks over the River Lea to Walthamstow Marshes and Springfield Marina. All these parks can be contacted on 7923 3660.

Around Town

Clowns International Gallery

All Saints Centre, Haggerston Road, E8 4HT (office hours only 0870 128 4336/www.clowns-international. co.uk). Dalston Kingsland or London Fields rail, then 38, 149, 236, 243 bus. **Open** noon-5pm 1st Fri of mth; other times by appointment. **Admission** free; donations appreciated.
Run by volunteers and festooned with red, yellow and blue bunting, this gallery is the work of the world's oldest-established organisation for clowns. It traces the history of clowning from 16th-century commedia dell'arte to clown doctoring in present-day hospitals. The displays of props, costumes and photos includes a comedy car suspended from the roof and a case full of painted eggs, each showing a real clown's particular make-up. New items are constantly being donated: look out for newly acquired automata (a life-size clown blowing bubbles, another smaller one on a trapeze). For details of the Clown Social or other events, check the website; to arrange a workshop or school event, phone Matti Faint on the above number.
Free parking. Nearest picnic place: Stonebridge Common (opposite).

Hackney City Farm

1A Goldsmiths Row, E2 8QA (7729 6381/www.hackney cityfarm.co.uk). Cambridge Heath Road rail, then 26, 48, 55 bus. **Open** 10am-4.30pm Tue-Sun & bank hol Mon. Closed 25-26 Dec, 1 Jan. **Admission** free; donations appreciated.
This former brewery reaches its 20th anniversay as a city farm this year. It has a cobbled farmyard, with pigs, geese, chickens, sheep and cattle. If you visit in spring, there's a good chance you'll get to bottle-feed the lambs (phone to check, though). There are weekly pottery- and textile-making sessions, cycle workshops, and storytelling, circus skills and music and movement events, as well as popular playschemes in the summer holidays. Revive yourself in the fabulous new organic café, Frizzante (*see p176*), and stock up on fresh honey and eggs from the shop.
Buggy access. Café. Disabled access: ramp, toilet. Nappy-changing facilities. Nearest picnic place: farm gardens. Shop.

Hackney Museum

Technology & Learning Centre, 1 Reading Lane, off Mare Street, E8 1GQ (8356 3500/www.hackney.gov.uk/hackney museum). Hackney Central rail. **Open** 9.30am-5.30pm Tue, Wed, Fri; 9.30am-8pm Thur; 10am-5pm Sat. Closed bank hols. **Admission** free.
Hackney Museum's resources and hands-on activities were financed to the tune of £400,000 by the Heritage Lottery Fund, with the museum designed to help visitors explore 1,000 years of cultural interchange that have made Hackney what it is today. There's a full-size model Anglo Saxon boat to clamber on board (the original is sunk into the floor beside it), a coin-operated zoetrope, and you can time yourself

making matchboxes to see whether you would have survived working in a Victorian factory (in the 1860s you earned tuppence for 144 boxes). Touch screens let you trace family history or take a virtual tour of a Victorian house. There are also free Explorer Pads, full of activities, available at the entrance. Ring for details of exhibitions and the changing programme of drop-in events (family workshops are usually on the first Saturday of the month).
Buggy access. Café (in Ocean opposite). Nappy-changing facilities. Nearest picnic place: benches in square/London Fields. Shop.

Sutton House

2 & 4 Homerton High Street, E9 6JQ (8986 2264/ www.nationaltrust.org.uk). Bethnal Green tube, then 106 bus/Hackney Central rail. **Open** 1-5.30pm Fri, Sat; 11.30am-5.30pm Sun, bank hol Mon. *Gallery* 11.30am-5pm Wed-Sun. **Closed** *Gallery* 19 Dec-21 Jan. *Historic Rooms* 19 Dec-early Feb. **Admission** (NT) £2.20; 50p 5-16s; £4.90 family (2+2); free under-5s. Tours free after entry, phone for details. **Credit** MC, V.
This is the oldest brick house in east London, built around 1535 for Henry VIII's secretary of state Sir Ralph Sadleir. In the late 1980s this essentially Tudor house was used as a community centre, until a grand National Trust restoration project saved the building's original interiors, such as the decorated oak-panel rooms. As well as Jacobean paintings and Georgian and Victorian interiors, there's some squatters' graffiti – and don't forget to look in on the 16th-century garderobe. On Fridays through August 'Art in the Courtyard' lays on free crafts activities for kids (£2.20 for adults). Seasonal events include the spooky Hallowe'en House Tour (6pm, 7pm, 8pm 29 Oct) and Christmas carol singing (5.30pm 10 Dec). Free Discovery Days (11.30am-5pm last Sun of the month) include Tudor and Victorian dressing-up and cookery, as well as the popular Christmas Past and Christmas Presents. Light meals, cakes and drinks are served in the cosy Brick Place Café, and pretty courtyard. Prices may go up in 2005 – call ahead to check.
Café. Disabled access: toilet. Nappy-changing facilities. Nearest picnic place: St John's churchyard. Shop.

Mile End to West Ham

Mile End, a confusing sprawl of busy roads and housing developments, has two fine parks: **Victoria Park** is the grand older statesman, **Mile End Park** the upstart. The **Ragged School Museum** makes a visit to Mile End Park even more worthwhile, and – if you cross the canal and head more-or-less 'gherkin'-wards – you'll find **Stepping Stones Farm** next door to the Norman parish church of St Dunstan's, with its tranquil cemetery. Stepney Green's playground is on the other side of the farm.

Further east you'll find industrial heritage that's ancient even for these parts: grain was transported by boat from Hertfordshire and unloaded at **Three Mills** in Bow since the 11th century. Keep going and you'll reach an increasingly perky Stratford. The new bus station, Jubilee Line and recently completed tunnelling that connects Stratford to King's Cross (part of the Eurostar link) all make Stratford's future as the centre of ambitious regeneration plans for the whole of east London –

Playtime at... Discover

Venture as far east as the Jubilee Line will take you, cross to Stratford Broadway and then follow the signs and you'll discover **Discover** (*see p112*). Here a baby space monster by the name of Hootah does the meet and greet, with the help of some beaming humanoids called Story Builders, who invite you in to play.

This interactive play centre, which is all about making stories, has an interesting story of its own. It started life as just a sad bunch of disused council offices, before an independent charity took it over and spent £6 million transforming it into a play paradise – the first of its kind in the UK – for children aged from two to seven.

The idea for Discover came from the charitable grant-giving trust the Calouste Gulbenkian Foundation, dedicated to promoting the development of centres for family activity and learning in the UK, having studied the progress of the 'children's museum' movement, which began in North America in the late 1960s. With their play equipment and activities, such centres, now well established across the pond and in Europe, help children understand themselves, other people and the world around them by fostering curiosity and creativity.

There's certainly lots to do, both indoors and out. The Discover Garden (free) has a space rocket to climb in, slides and chunky wooden climbing frames, living willow tunnels for hide and seek, a wet-play area for fine weather, and picnic benches. It's a beautiful resource for local children in an otherwise bleak part of town. Inside the centre, Hootah is always hungry for new stories made up by his guests and ready to share tales; the friendly Story Builders are here to help make them. Visitors are given a special storybook bag in which to keep all the stories and treasures they make along the way.

The journey starts with the Lollipopter, which takes them through a whole series of story settings. Children, with a little help from their adults, take a dream ticket and write or draw the place they want to visit. Then it's all aboard to the fantasy world. Further in, there are opportunities to fly on a magic carpet, cross a rickety-rackety bridge across the sparkly river, get lost in curtains of plastic worms, hide in secret caves, dress up, and make puppets out of wooden spoons at the well-equipped art tables.

All these activities were dreamed up by the children, of all different ages, who acted as consultants during the five years it took to create Discover. The aim of this most ambitious learning-through-play experience is to promote the idea of shared story-making, enthusing children and their adults by encouraging imaginative play and self-expression, which in turn help people gain confidence and improve their quality of life. The methods and processes used in shared story building are based on sound educational theory, but as far as the children are concerned, it's all about having fun in a land of make-believe, full of monsters and magic, parties and princesses.

You could stay here all day. Many do, making full use of the refreshment area (tucked away in the corner of the foyer) for coffee, cold drinks and snacks, or bringing a picnic to share in the garden. There are regular weekend drop-in activities, such as 'Stories in a Bag', during which children and a Story Builder create a tale using a random selection of objects. Bookable events for half-terms and holidays may include mask-making and home-made puppet shows. Discover also does parties. The gratifyingly low fee (£6 per head) includes an hour on the Story Trail and an hour for tea in the bright Garden Room.

Going up at **Discover**...

not to mention that Olympic bid – seem just about credible. The centre is focused around the Broadway and a soulless shopping centre, but the **Theatre Royal Stratford East** (Gerry Raffles Square, E15 1BN, 8534 0310), which reopened in December 2001, is a delightful venue. The refurbishment added a café/bar and improved disabled access to the Grade II-listed auditorium. But you'll need to head to the other side of the bus station to find Stratford's only die-cast children's attraction: brand new **Discover**.

Beyond Stratford? **West Ham Park** is well kept, and the museum at **West Ham United Football Club** draws the Happy Hammers' many fans.

Discover

1 Bridge Terrace, E15 4BG (8536 5563/www.discover. org.uk). Stratford tube/rail/DLR. **Open** *Term-time* 10am-5pm Tue-Thur, Sat, Sun. *School hols* 10am-5pm daily. **Admission** *Garden* free. *Story Trail* £3; £2 concessions. Stratford may not seem the most likely place for a new children's attraction, but this interactive play centre has made the area well worth dropping in on: take those imaginations on an adventure. *See p111* **Playtime at... Discover**. *Buggy access. Disabled access: ramp, toilet. Nappy-changing facilities. Nearest picnic place: ground-floor area. Shop.*

Mile End Park

*Locksley Street, Stepney, E14 7EJ (7364 4147/ children's park 7093 2253). Mile End tube.***Open** 24hrs daily. **Admission** free.
Mile End Park is for many the quintessential modern urban park. Since 2002 its credentials as a destination for children have also been firmly established: the south end of the

park then gained a great playground (funded by HSBC to the tune of £2 million), with rope slide, scrambling wall and complicated climbing frame, as well as the normal swings and see-saw. There's also a fully staffed drop-in centre for 11 to 17s. A little to the north the go-kart track provides thrills and spills for the older children. Then there are placid strolls to be taken past the pretty fountain in the Terraced Gardens or over the landmark Green Bridge that spans Mile End Road, complete with trees growing above the passing traffic, into the northern section of the park. Here, thrill-seekers find Mile End Climbing Wall (*see p256*). There are also the tranquil ponds at the centre of the Arts Park and Ecological Park (pumped using power from a 30ft/9m tall wind turbine – the park has planning permission for another). Beside it all, the Regent's Canal supports birdlife, cyclists and local fishermen. There about 850 species of plants in the park, as well as various waterfowl and the first Jumping Spider found in the UK (the May 2004 Spider Safari is likely to be repeated).

The park has praiseworthy educational and community development aims, bringing sculptures into the park and holding temporary exhibitions (there's a children's art expo in July 2004) and volunteer-led activities; weekly fun continues in the Play Pavilion (including Stay and Play sessions between 12.30pm and 3pm daily). Improvements to the park this year include a new eco-friendly earth-sheltered building with toilets and a snacks kiosk, which should be open by June or July, and an adventure park for 11- to 17-year-olds. *Buggy access.*

Three Mills Island

Lea Rivers Trust, Three Mill Lane, E3 3DU (schools programmes 8981 0040/Lee Rivers Tidal Mill Trust 8980 4626/www.learriverstrust.co.uk). Bromley-by-Bow tube. **Open** *House Mill* June-Sept 2-4pm Sat, Sun. May, Oct 2-4pm Sun. *Funday Sundays* Mar-Dec 11am-4pm 1st Sun of mth. **Admission** *Mill tour* £2; free under-16s. **No credit cards.**

The House Mill, built in 1776, is the oldest and largest tidal mill left standing in Britain. It was used to grind the grain for gin distilling. Taken over in 1989 as part of a big restoration project by the Tidal Mills Trust, it now has a visitors' centre that provides a history of the area and maps for walkers. Green to their roots, the trustees are exploring using a water wheel to power the offices. Outside, Riverside Green and Three Mills Green are pleasant for picnicking and strolling, with the latter giving a good view of Bazalgette's wonderfully restored Victorian pumping station. You can wander along the network of the Bow Back rivers and enjoy the wildlife in this pocket of peace and quiet. Narrowboats sometimes moor along the river, especially during the annual boat rally (17-18 July) – there are usually boat tours for visitors.

The first Sunday of the month (Mar-Dec) is Funday Sunday, which includes a popular craft market. Children can take part in workshops: making recycled paper (July) or designing jewellery out of rubbish (Aug), making bird feeders (Sept) and bread (Oct). The Christmas Fayre (5 Dec) is always popular: 4,000 people came to the last one. All the activities are free and run on a first-come first-served basis.
Buggy access. Café. Disabled access: lift, toilet (in 24hr Tesco if House Mill is closed). Nearest picnic place: Riverside Green/Three Mills Green. Shop.

Ragged School Museum

46-50 Copperfield Road, E3 4RR (8980 6405/www. raggedschoolmuseum.org.uk). Mile End tube. **Open** 10am-5pm Wed, Thur; 2-5pm 1st Sun of mth. Closed 24 Dec-1 Jan. **Tours** by arrangement; phone for details. **Admission** free.
Ragged schools were charity schools that provided a basic education for orphaned, poor or down-and-out children. Established by Dr Barnardo in 1877, these converted warehouses were until their closure in 1908 London's largest ragged school. One typically sparse Victorian classroom has been recreated and school groups come from all over London

to don Victorian togs and sit in it. Their own teachers give the kids old-fashioned names such as Walter and Agatha and hand them over to a hatchet-faced 'schoolmistress' (a museum actress) – that'll teach 'em. Downstairs is Tower Hamlets: A Journey through Time (local history), with objects to handle, and a replica front room from 1900. Free family events take place in the school holidays, which either tie into the collections or the canal.
Buggy access (ground floor only). Disabled access: toilet. Nappy-changing facilities. Nearest picnic place: Mile End Park. Shop.

Stepping Stones Farm

Stepney Way (junction with Stepney High Street), E1 3DG (7790 8204). Stepney Green tube. **Open** *Apr-mid Oct* 9.30am-6pm Tue-Sun. *Mid Oct-Mar* 9.30am-dusk Tue-Sun. All public & bank hols.
Admission free; donations appreciated.
This 4.5-acre (2ha) community farm has been run by hard-working volunteers since 1979. The livestock is constantly changing – this spring saw a calf, kids and lambs added to the population. There are also pigs, chickens and donkeys, as well as rabbits, guinea pigs and ferrets. Young ones can let rip in the play area, where a sandpit and toy tractors await, keen gardeners can buy manure or stock up on jams and chutneys from the shop, and conscientious greens bring kitchen waste to the community composting bins. The activities room has arts and crafts materials. Annual events include an Easter egg hunt, the Winter Festival at Christmas and summer weekend activities; ring for details.
Buggy access. Café. Disabled access: toilet. Nappy-changing facilities. Shop.

Victoria Park

Old Ford Road, E3 5DS (8533 2057). Mile End tube/ Cambridge Heath or Hackney Wick rail/8, 26, 30, 55, 253, 277, S2 bus. **Open** 6am-dusk daily. Closed 25 Dec.

...and going down at **Victoria Park**

Victoria Park was opened in 1845 after demands for more public space were met by an extraordinarily generous £100,000 in donations. With its wide carriageways, smart lamp posts and wrought-iron gates, the Victoria was conceived as the Regent's Park of the East End (at 240 acres/97ha it is the largest area of formal parkland this side of town). The poverty-stricken locals may have been short of carriages to drive through the grand tree-lined drives, but they made good use of the park's two lakes instead… as baths. The Western Lake survived this ordeal and is now happily fished (you do need a licence to join in, but it is, at least, free), and the country's oldest Model Boat Club convenes around the lake near Crown Gate East every second Sunday. There are fallow deer on the east side of the park and tennis courts, a bowling green and football, hockey and cricket pitches (the hard-surface athletics track is still awaiting refurbishment after a fire years ago). There's also a One O'Clock Club and playgrounds. After a morning in the playground, stop off for refreshments at the Lakeside Pavilion Café (which reopened after refurbishments in May 2004) and watch the geese and ducks play under the fountain. The Royal Ballet's performance of *Onegin* will be broadcast live from the Royal Opera House to a giant screen here on 17 July 2004 (*see p219* **Sing it loud**).
Buggy access. Café. Disabled access: toilets.
Nappy-changing facilities.

West Ham Park
Upton Lane, E7 9PU (8472 3584/www.cityoflondon.
gov.uk). Stratford tube/rail/104, 238, 325 bus.
Open 7.30am-30mins before dusk daily.
Run by the Corporation of London, West Ham Park has quality facilities and a busy programme of events: this summer there are Punch and Judy performances, magic shows from Do-not the Talking Dog and Fred Rabbit, a bouncy castle (Tue, Thur) and Sunday jazz and brass or steel band concerts; check the local press for details of current events. There are nine tennis courts (an annual tennis clinic runs 10 May-7 June 2004), two cricket squares, two football pitches, a running track and a rounders area. The summer cricket clinic for under-16s is run by Essex Cricket Club (22-23 July 2004). The playground has a full-time attendant to look after the swings, roundabouts and climbing frames; the playground also still has its pre-war paddling pool. Recent improvements to the rose garden – including new Australian and New Zealand beds – should make it particularly lovely in July and August.
Buggy access. Disabled access: toilet.
Nappy-changing facilities.

West Ham United Football Club
Boleyn Ground, Green Street, E13 9AZ (8548 2748/
www.whufc.com). Upton Park tube. **Open** *Museum/*
shop 9.30am-4pm Mon-Sat. Closed 25 Dec. **Admission**
Museum £6; £4 concessions, 5-16s; free under-5s;
£15 family (2+2). *Tours* £10; £5 concessions, 5-16s.
Credit MC, V.
By the time you read this, West Ham may well have won through their play-offs and secured a renewed tenancy in the Premiership – relegation in 2003 was a bitter blow given the £35-million redevelopment of their home ground that preceded it. The museum tells the story of the club from its origins in 1895 as the Thames Iron Works FC through to the present. Those who aren't themselves fans of the claret and blue will make a bee-line for displays showing Bobby Moore's caps and medals. Book in advance if you're visiting the museum on a match day, or phone ahead for dates when a 90-minute tour of the ground can be combined with a visit to the museum.
Bars. Buggy access. Disabled access: toilet. Shop.

Docklands

The first attempt to regenerate London's derelict dockland foundered with the early 1990s recession. Since then, more businesses have moved in and towerblocks shot up around Canary Wharf Tower. The area's 18th- and 19th-century heyday as a dock, with boats coming from all over the Empire to unload precious cargos here, is long gone. But that past of piracy and hard labour is not forgotten: the area's history and dramatic architecture, old and new, are attracting growing numbers of visitors.

The best way to get around **Docklands** must be the Docklands Light Railway (DLR) network (7363 9700). With various extensions over the years (a new spur will add easy access to London City Airport and Thames Barrier Park, *see p117*), the DLR now reaches from Bank in the City to Beckton in the east, from Lewisham south of the Thames to Stratford in the north. The real beauty of the network is that much of it runs on raised tracks, making a journey a sightseeing pleasure. Pick quiet times (weekdays after 10am, say, and before 5pm) and the kids can sit in the front windows of the train and pretend to drive. Buy a day Travelcard and hop on and off, using the Jubilee and District Line tube connections to open up the nooks and crannies of east London.

The DLR has joined forces with City Cruises sightseeing boats to offer the **Rail & River Rover** ticket (£9 adult, £4.50 children, family (2+3) £25, under-fives free), which throws in boat travel with all the fun of the DLR. The boats offer warm seats inside or a breezier berth upstairs, plus a chirpy commentator to name bridges and riverside buildings. Disembark at Tower Pier to check out the marina of St Katharine's Docks, with its flash yachts, shops and restaurants. Then stroll the ten minutes past Tower Bridge (*see p55*) and the Tower of London (*see p56*) to the DLR station at Tower Gateway. Alternatively, stay on board until you reach Greenwich Pier (for Greenwich's numerous attractions, *see p123*), then take the DLR back under the river for sightseeing on the Isle of Dogs. Other stopoffs are at Westminster and Waterloo; if you want to dock at Canary Wharf itself, there's a separate fast commuter service.

The westernmost point to fall under the Docklands banner is **Wapping**. Until well into the 19th century, convicted pirates were brought at low tide to Execution Dock (at Wapping New Stairs), hanged and left in chains until three tides had washed over them; a rather new-looking noose dangles by the recently reopened riverside balcony of the 16th-century Prospect of Whitby pub (57 Wapping Wall, E1W 3SH, 7481 1095). There's also a pirate ship (that you can't board, sadly) by the deserted Tobacco Docks shopping mall to the

A pause for thought on
Canary Wharf's sculpture trail

west. You can take in one of the rather grown-up art shows or quality nosh in the converted Victorian pumping station now called Wapping Project (Wapping Wall, E1W 3ST, 7680 2080). Children are welcome, but the bare aesthetic may not appeal; better options for kids are Pizza Express (78 Wapping Lane, E1W 2RT, 7481 8436) or Smollensky's (Hermitage Wharf, 22 Wapping High Street, E1W 1NJ, 7680 1818), which doesn't run to the child-centred joys of the Strand branch, but will do half portions.

Between Wapping and the Isle of Dogs is **Limehouse**, so-called because medieval lime kilns once stood here. A century ago this was a bustling commercial port; now it's a marina with posh yachts and jolly narrow boats, surrounded by luxury flats. The white church north-east of the basin, St Anne's Limehouse, was designed by Hawksmoor between 1712 and 1724. It has the second-highest (after Big Ben's) clock tower in Britain, and a man-size pyramid in the north-west corner of the churchyard.

The most visitor-friendly of all Docklands areas, however, is the **Isle of Dogs** – not a sentence many would have uttered during the area's long years of post-war neglect, nor during the divisive redevelopments of the '80s. It's only an island because the stretch of water that makes up West India Docks cuts the peninsula off from the mainland, and the origin of the name is routinely

disputed: perhaps it's named after the royal hunting kennels that were once here, perhaps 'dog' is a corruption of 'dyke' (many were built here by Flemish engineers in the 19th century). You can explore such debates and the rest of Docklands' 2,000-year history at the **Museum in Docklands**.

Docklands' present-day splendour can't fail to impress. There's the great glass-and-steel structure of Canary Wharf's Jubilee line station, designed by Lord Foster, and there's that tower: the impact of Cesar Pelli's 800-foot-high (244-metre) monster, more properly known as **One Canada Square**, may have been diminished by the duller buildings that now surround it, but it's still a stunner – the tables outside Carluccio's Caffè (Nash Court, E14 5AJ, 7719 1749) are a good place to sit at its feet and ponder the enormity of modern commerce. The kids might enjoy locating the artworks on Canary Wharf's public sculpture trail (click on the 'Lifestyle' link on www.canarywharf.com or contact 7418 2000 for a map): they include bits of floor or wall or light, as well as more impressive pieces like Pierre Vivant's *Traffic Light Tree*, Ron Arad's futuristic *Big Blue* or Giles Penny's *Two Men on a Bench*. The fountain in Cabot Square is lovely, and has some benches, but the Japanese Garden beside the Foster's station is the best place to picnic. There are useful shop chains in the mall (Gap Kids, HMV, Maxwell & Kennedy), with the branches smaller than their West End daddies but blissfully low on crowds. You can also enjoy riverside walks, commuter boat rides or treat yourself to posh dim sum at Royal China (*see p176*).

A southbound DLR ride takes you to **Mudchute**. Once just a dump of spoil and silt left over from the construction of Millwall Dock, the Mudchute began to support a thriving habitat. In the '70s locals fought property developers to ensure it became a park. **Mudchute City Farm** is one excellent result.

You can also get off the DLR at **Island Gardens**. The gardens are on the other side of a main road from the station, but worth the trouble for views of Greenwich over the Thames and the entrance to the spooky Victorian foot tunnel. This is free and has attendant-operated lifts (7am-7pm Mon-Sat, 10am-5.30pm Sun) large enough for a platoon of buggies – but it's quite a walk through to the *Cutty Sark* (*see p123*) on the other side. But the echoes keep children happily shouting and whistling all the way.

Mudchute City Farm

Pier Street, Isle of Dogs, E14 3HP (7515 5901/www.mud chute.org). Crossharbour/Island Gardens DLR. **Open** 9am-4pm daily. Closed 25 Dec-1 Jan. **Admission** free; donations appreciated.

Ducks, chickens, goats, pigs and llamas, plus a small flock of sheep and some cattle all live here; depending on the time of year, you can help the farmers bottle-feed lambs or shear sheep, as well as milking goats or collecting eggs (phone in advance to find out what's happening). Local kids can join the pony club (*see p262*) or the Young Farmers Club, and everyone, wherever they live, can enjoy summer arts and crafts workshops and playschemes. There's a small aviary and petting corner for bunny-hugging, a volunteer-run café (usually open mid morning to early afternoon) and, during school hols, a shop for souvenirs and riding accessories. A new 64-place nursery opened in 2004, along with a garden centre. *Buggy access. Café. Disabled access: toilet. Nappy-changing facilities. Shop.*

Museum in Docklands

No.1 Warehouse, West India Quay, Hertsmere Road, E14 4AL (0870 444 3857/recorded info 0870 444 3856/ www.museumindocklands.org.uk). Canary Wharf tube/ West India Quay DLR. **Open** 10am-6pm Mon, Tue, Thur-Sun; 10am-8pm Wed. **Admission** (annual ticket, allows for multiple visits) £5; £3 concessions; free under-16s. Free entry 6-8pm Wed. **Credit** MC, V.

This £15-million museum is just across the dock from Canary Wharf – you can cross from Cabot Square on the permanent floating bridge. Housed in a Grade I-listed Georgian warehouse, it shares its collection with the Museum of London (*see p53*). Divided into five floors and 12 galleries, displays range from a 4,000-year-old timber figure found in Dagenham to a discussion of the economic effects of containerisation. First, Tony Robinson enthusiastically narrates the city's Roman history on a series of touch screens. Then you pass impressive models of London Bridge, narwhal tusks in the section on whaling, a dangling gibbet cage for exclusive use by captured pirates, a reconstructed quay and smelly Wapping slum, as well as harpoons, cutlasses, blunderbusses, rattles, and rowing skiffs and pilot boats (on an easy-to-miss mezzanine below the second floor). The Docklands at War gallery is as moving as it is vivid, but the more recent history is unlikely to grab young 'uns. They will like the Mudlarks Gallery,

The Pavilion of Remembrance at **Thames Barrier Park**. *See p117.*

though. It gives under-12s the chance to weigh shipping loads or search for buried treasure, and under-fives can enjoy the soft play area. (You sometimes have to wait a little, as places in the gallery are limited.)

Notable events run by the museum include dramatic narratives from costumed actors playing, for example, a Lascar (Indian) sailor or an Irish pub landlady, festival events celebrating New Year, Eid or Channukah with storytelling, puppets and workshops, and holiday and half-term drop-in craft and handling events; check the website for details of forthcoming activities or to join the mailing list. *Buggy access. Café. Disabled: lift, toilet. Nappy-changing facilities. Nearest picnic place: quayside benches, refectory. Restaurant. Shop.*

East of Docklands

The DLR splits after Westferry station: one branch goes south to Island Gardens (*see above*) and Lewisham, the other east via Poplar to Beckton. The route towards Beckton gives a fine view of the Dome across the river. Active families heading for **Thames Barrier Park** can take a half-hour walk from Custom House DLR. It takes you over the pointy footbridge high above Royal Victoria Dock (there are lifts at each end, though they're not always working), but you'll have to negotiate the frankly unpleasant North Woolwich Road – there are wide pavements, at least.

Over Connaught Bridge on the north side of Royal Albert Docks is the London Regatta Centre (Dockside Road, E16 2QD, 7511 2211; open daily). Sit and watch rowers puff and pant or follow the planes landing at London City Airport from the Regatta Centre's restaurant and bar. A footbridge over Royal Albert Way takes you into Beckton District Park (Stansfeld Road, E6 5LT, 8430 2000), which has a wild flower meadow and woodland walk, plus a good-sized lake at the northern end. There are play areas, cricket and football facilities, a trim trail and a summer snack kiosk.

To the south, **North Woolwich Old Station Museum** is next to the North Woolwich Silverlink station. The tidy Royal Victoria Gardens are next door; the café opens in summer. There's a foot tunnel for anyone who wants to walk to the south bank; otherwise the Woolwich ferry will take you over the river to enjoy a bit of Firepower (*see p127*).

Eastbound, **Beckton** is the last DLR stop. The 'Beckton Alp' – a dry ski slope built on a huge pile of rubbish – is closed, but there are rumours of a new 'snow dome'. Lovers of flora and fauna are well served, though, with Docklands Equestrian Centre (2 Claps Gate Lane, E6 7JF, 7511 3917), the little **East Ham Nature Reserve** and **Newham City Farm**.

East Ham Nature Reserve
Norman Road, E6 4HN (8470 4525). East Ham tube/ Beckton DLR. **Open** *Nov-Feb* 10am-5pm Tue-Fri; 1-4pm Sat, Sun. Closed bank hols. **Admission** free.
Pick up a nature trail round the nearly nine acres (4ha) of this Norman churchyard, or visit the natural and local history museum. Current displays include a Victorian schoolroom to terrify the kids, a Victorian kitchen to terrify the mums, and cases of stuffed animals, stag beetles and butterflies to fascinate everyone. As with all volunteer-run attractions, it's best to ring before you set out to make sure it's open.
Buggy access. Disabled access: toilet. Nappy-changing facilities. Shop.

Newham City Farm
Stansfeld Road, E16 3RD (7474 4960/recorded info 7476 1170). Royal Albert DLR/262, 300, 376 bus. **Open** *Mid Oct-mid Feb* 10am-4pm Thur-Sun. *Mid Feb-mid Oct* 10am-5pm Thur-Sun, bank hols. Closed 25 Dec, 1 Jan. **Admission** free; donations appreciated.
Unsure about its funding as we went to press, the farm is short-staffed, which means it's currently closed Monday to Wednesday (ring ahead to check if this is still the case). Nonetheless, it was recently amalgamated with a little zoo, which means the farmyard beasts (horses, cows, pigs, sheep and ducks) and cuddly little animals (rabbits and guinea pigs) have been joined by a collection of exotic finches, pheasants, a kookaburra and birds of prey (including a buzzard). The farm's visitor centre welcomes families and school groups and there are ample picnic areas.
Buggy access.

North Woolwich Old Station Museum
Pier Road, E16 2JJ (7474 7244). North Woolwich rail/ 101, 473, 474 bus. **Open** *Jan-Nov* 1-5pm Sat, Sun. *School holidays* 1-5pm daily. *Miniature railway* Apr-Oct 1st & 2nd Sun of mth. **Admission** free. Rides £1.

The Old Station Museum contains carefully preserved old engines, ticket machines, timetables, signs and other relics from the bygone age of steam travel. There's a preserved ticket office and plenty of models and info, but the children will probably want to head out to the back and poke around the pair of trains on display: Coffee Pot (a Victorian commuter train from the 1890s) and Pickett (from the 1940s). They can climb all over Dudley the Diesel, who will sometimes even be able to take them for a spin (pretty much just along the platform and back). There's outside play equipment, and a Brio layout indoors, plus a computer with a Thomas the Tank Engine programme and the Hornby Virtual Railway. The small shop sells souvenirs and snacks, and, during school holidays, Wednesday afternoon art and crafts sessions keep small people amused – the nicely worked-out programme aims at getting them to make something they can take home: a model train station, tin can pencil pots or a Victorian-style trinket box. For Museums & Galleries Month (*see p32*), they'll be making a big 'Trains, Boats and Planes' mural that should remain on display for the rest of the year.
Buggy access. Disabled access. Kiosk. Nappy-changing facilities. Shop.

Thames Barrier Park
Barrier Point Road, off North Woolwich Road, E16 2HP (7511 4111/www.thamesbarrierpark.org.uk). Canning Town tube/DLR, then 474 bus/Stratford tube, then 69 bus. **Open** dawn-dusk daily. **Admission** free.
Right on the river by the space-age Thames Barrier (the Barrier's visitor centre is actually on the south side, *see p127*), this crisp, new park centres on a concrete and granite channel the size of a small motorway. Called the Green Dock, it is filled with hedges and fragrant honeysuckle, and leads directly to the riverfront and a 'Pavilion of Remembrance' commemorating those who lost their lives in the Blitz. The flat lawns are beautifully manicured, perfect for picnics and games (though a little exposed until the young trees grow a little more foliage). There's a playground, too, and plenty of ducks, geese, swans and wading birds picking around the gleaming mudflats. The tea pavilion is now open (officially 10am-4pm Mon-Fri, but often as long as the park remains open) and you can use the toilets at any time (don't worry if they look shut: the doors open automatically). While work continues on the new DLR station (due for completion in November 2005), the park entrance and temporary car park are on the north-east corner. Until it's complete, look on the bright side: the poor transport links mean you'll have the place practically to yourselves.
Buggy access. Café. Disabled access: toilet. Free parking. Nappy-changing facilities.

Walthamstow & Wanstead

Walthamstow has something of a split personality. Five minutes' walk east of Walthamstow Central (the last stop north on the Victoria line) you'll find yourself in quaint and charming Walthamstow Village. Around St Mary's Church there's a village ambience and some grisly history: Vinegar Alley was once a trench full of the stuff, intended to prevent pestilence spreading from the mass graves of Black Death victims in the churchyard. The half-timbered Ancient House opposite pre-dates the Plague, although the current incarnation is a painstaking 1934 restoration designed to look authentically saggy. Pamphlets recounting such historical gems are available at the **Vestry House Museum** just down the road, but the churchyard is pleasantly shaggy enough to happily explore with or without the detail. Orford Road boasts the Village Kitchen (No.41, E17 9NJ, 8509 2144) for reasonably priced lunches (Fri-Sun) and more formal evening meals, otherwise the Village pub (No.31, 8521 9982) has a patio and giant Connect 4.

The rest of Walthamstow is as busy as the Village is quiet, especially the famous street market. Muttering and fussing in the best east London style, its 450 stalls run the length of Walthamstow High Street, and lays reasonable claim to being the longest daily street market in Europe. L Manze (No.76, E17 7LD, 8520 2855) will do you proud with pie and mash if you're in geezer mood. Heading north, you'll find **Lloyd Park**, on Forest Road. The **William Morris Gallery** stands proud at the southern entrance, near a scented garden for the visually impaired, an aviary of budgies and cockatiels, and a strangely black-looking lake. At the far end is a children's play area and skate park, the Café Horizon and Changing Rooms Galleries (8496 4563, www.lbwf.gov.uk/crg). Open from late May through October (11am-5pm daily), it hosts contemporary arts and crafts exhibitions, as well as providing studio space for local artists and children's workshops. Across the North Circular Road the art deco façade of Walthamstow Stadium is well worth a look, and the Stowaway Grill within perfect for dogs' dinners (*see also p273*). The Walthamstow Marshes are at the end of Coppermill Lane (you might prefer to cycle or drive there: it's a good 15-minute walk from St James Street rail station). Ideal for picnics and walks by the River Lea, the marshes are where doughty Sir Edwin Alliot Verdon Roe made the first all-British powered flight in July 1909 – a plaque on the railway arches commemorates the feat.

East of Walthamstow, **Wanstead** is another urban village – as local homeowners are proud to point out. There's a Grade I-listed church from 1790, again called St Mary's, but the attraction for visitors, especially those with kids, is Wanstead's greenery: Wanstead Flats and especially **Wanstead Park**, the southern tip of glorious Epping Forest (*see p119*).

Wanstead Park
Warren Road, E11 (8508 0028). Wanstead tube. **Open** dawn-dusk daily. **Admission** free.
Nowadays, Wanstead Park is managed by the Corporation of London as part of Epping Forest. Its most appealing aspects are the several water features (the Ornamental Water and the three ponds – Perch, Heronry and Shoulder of Mutton) and the associated wildlife. At the fenced-off end of the Ornamental Water is a ruined grotto, built in the early 1760s with a boat house below and domed, shell-encrusted

chamber above. The other important ruin in the park is the Temple, once a fancy summerhouse, which has the park toilets to one side. Both structures (the grotto and Temple, that is) are Grade II-listed, but the children will get far more excited by the ball-throwing and kite-flying possibilities on the grassy area between the Temple and the tea stall. The Wren Conservation and Wildlife Group website (www.wrengroup.fsnet.co.uk) provides a comprehensive history, map and guide to the plants and birds here, and there is a programme of activities that includes family walks (book on the above number) and drop-in arts and craft sessions – hat-making, perhaps, or cardboard sculpture.
Buggy access. Café. Disabled access. Free parking.

Vestry House Museum
Vestry Road, E17 6HZ (8509 1917/www.lbwf.gov.uk). Walthamstow Central tube/rail. **Open** 10am-1pm, 2-5.30pm Mon-Fri; 10am-1pm, 2-5pm Sat. Closed 25, 26 Dec, 1 Jan, bank hols. **Tours** groups only, by prior arrangement. **Admission** free.
This museum includes one of the original police cells (the building was a prison from 1840 to 1870), a gallery of toys and games, and a car built by local engineer Frederick Bremer in 1892-4 (it was one of the first cars built in Britain – certainly the first in London). A Lottery-funded refurbishment in 2002 created a gallery for the Bremer car, relandscaped the garden and opened the ground floor to the public. The Vestry House museum also holds archive material on Alfred Hitchcock, who was born in Leytonstone. As we went to press, the Vestry House's programme of children's activities was temporarily at a halt until new curatorial staff could be appointed (phone or consult the website for up-to-date info), but you'll find a play table with drawing materials upstairs.
Buggy access (downstairs only). Disabled access: toilets (downstairs only). Nappy-changing facilities. Nearest picnic place: museum garden. Shop.

William Morris Gallery
Lloyd Park, Forest Road, E17 4PP (8527 3782/ www.lbwf.gov.uk/wmg). Blackhorse Road tube, then 123 bus. **Open** 10am-1pm, 2-5pm Tue-Sat; 1st Sun of mth. Closed 25, 26 Dec, 1 Jan, bank hols. **Tours** phone for details. **Admission** free.
This was the childhood home of the famous designer and socialist, who was born in Walthamstow in 1834. The gallery seems rather muted, with the lighting kept low to protect exhibits, although the family quiz trail encourages younger children to examine the beautiful designs. *Objets* cover everything from Morris's medieval-style helmet and sword (costume for a Pre-Raphaelite mural) to an edition of Chaucer to the distinctive wallpapers, while the great man's biography is filled out with more mundane items: his coffee cup or the satchel in which he transported his political tracts. Major refurbishments added a display of Century Guild furniture, plus some new stained glass. Occasional holiday activities might include china-painting (once fired, the mug, tile or bowl can be taken home); check the website for details.
Buggy access. Disabled access: ramp. Nearest picnic place: Lloyd Park. Shop.

Lee Valley Regional Park

Starting in Hackney (*see p109*) and heading north-east all the way into Hertfordshire, Lee Valley Regional Park is a network of lakes, waterways, parks and countryside areas that covers a vast area on either side of the River Lee. There's plenty to do, though a gentle guided walk is a good way to set about it. The park's ideal for picnics, walking or fishing, it's well signposted and open year round.

It's a twitcher's paradise – more than 200 bird species have been seen here, despite its proximity to London, and the **Middlesex Filter Beds** on the Hackney side of Lee Valley are now a dedicated marshland bird reserve. Other attractions include the Lee Valley Riding Centre (*see p262*) and Lee Valley Cycle Circuit (*see p256*), next to the M11 extension. The Lee Valley Boat Centre (Old Nazeing Road, Broxbourne, Herts EN10 6LX, 01992 462085) is the place to hire a boat or book a narrowboat holiday.

The small town of **Waltham Abbey** is a good point of access. It has plenty of little cafés and shops and an Augustinian abbey to visit: founded in 1060 by King Harold, it is reputed to be where he was buried too. Once one of the largest in the country, the abbey had its own farm, fishponds and brewery; only the gateway, a few walls and a stone bridge remain, but the gardens contain a variety of public artworks and there's a 'Sensory Trail' highlighting the natural history of the area. Also in Waltham Abbey, Lee Valley Park Information Centre (Stubbins Hall Lane, Crooked Mile, Essex EN9 2EG, 01992 702200, www.leevalleypark.org.uk, open 10am-4.30pm daily) has literature about the various activities available to visitors, including messing about on the reservoirs in boats and canoes. Fishing permits can be obtained here, and there are maps of cycle routes and information about scenic riverside pubs. The centre also has nappy-changing facilities, a café and a shop. The **Royal Gunpowder Mills**, and Epping Forest is but a ten-minute drive.

Lee Valley Park Farms

Stubbins Hall Lane, Crooked Mile, Waltham Abbey, Essex EN9 2EG (01992 892781). Broxbourne or Waltham Cross rail. **Open** 10am-4.30pm Mon-Fri, 10am-5.30pm or dusk if earlier Sat, Sun. **Admission** £4; £3.50 concessions; £3 3-16s; £16 family (2+3). **Credit** MC, V.
Hayes Hill Farm is a rare breeds centre, with a Tudor barn, a restored gypsy caravan and plenty of space in which to play. Visitors can watch the milking of cows (from 2.30pm daily). There are guided tours for school parties.
Buggy access. Café. Disabled access. Nappy-changing facilities. Shop.

Royal Gunpowder Mills

Beaulieu Drive, Waltham Abbey, Essex EN9 1JY (01992 707370/www.royalgunpowdermills.com). Waltham Cross rail, then 213, 250, 251 bus. **Open** 24 Apr-26 Sept 2004 11am-5pm Sat, Sun (last entry 3pm), bank hols, daily for school groups. **Admission** £5.50; £4.50 concessions; £2.50 5-16s; £16 family (2+3); free under-5s.
The Royal Gunpowder Mills were involved in the making of explosives for more than 300 years: first gunpowder production, which relied on water supplied from the nearby River Lee, began in the 1660s; later the site began to manufacture guncotton, nitro-glycerine, cordite paste and the highly explosive tetryl; after World War II the mills were a research centre for non-nuclear explosives and propellants.

Few of the buildings have been renovated, in a deliberate attempt to convey their long and complex past. It's a good idea to start at the visitors' centre, which runs an introductory film full of bangs and flashes, as well as an informative hands-on exhibition that concentrates on the human story behind gunpowder. Much effort has been taken over the educational programme too. On a warm summer's day, rugs are set out on the central grassy area and activity packs suitable for all ages handed out. Special events include an art weekend, military re-enactments, craft fairs and sports days. It's a big site, so wear comfy shoes.
Buggy access. Café. Nappy-changing facilities. Nearest picnic place: on-site. Shop.

Epping Forest

Epping Forest (www.cityoflondon.gov.uk/openspaces) is a gift for walkers, riders and cyclists; 6,000 acres (2,430ha) is left of massive ancient forest – that's still plenty in which to lose sight of the city. It's the biggest public space in London – 12 miles long and 22 miles across (19 by 35 kilometres) – saved from development by the Corporation of London in 1878. Commoners still have grazing rights and, each summer, English Longhorn cattle can still be seen chewing the cud. The forest contains two listed buildings – the restored **Queen Elizabeth's Hunting Lodge** in Chingford (Rangers Road, E4 7QH, 8529 6681; under-16s must be accompanied by adults) and the Temple in Wanstead Park (*see p118*), as well as two Iron Age earthworks.

If you're coming to the forest by public transport, Chingford railway station gives access to Queen Elizabeth's Hunting Lodge and some lovely strolls. There are also caffs in Chingford and a couple of cheery, child-friendly pubs. Loughton and Theydon Bois (Central Line) are the forest's nearest tube stops, though it's a two-mile (three-kilometre) uphill walk from both a struggle with small children. The best advice is to get a map and plan your route in advance – or to use a car. At High Beech car park there's a tea hut as well as the **Epping Forest Information Centre** (High Beech, Loughton, Essex IG10 4AF, 8508 0028, www.eppingforest.co.uk, open Apr-Oct 10am-5pm Mon-Sat, 11am-5pm Sun; Nov-Mar 11am-3pm Mon-Fri, 10am-4pm Sat, 11am-4pm Sun), with children's area, disabled toilet and shop.

The forest is an important conservation centre, home to woodpeckers, nightingales, treecreepers and nuthatches, plus waterfowl like great crested grebes, goosanders and wigeons. There are also 650 species of flower and more than 1,000 types of fungus. For a real back-to-nature feeling, between May and September you can pitch a tent at the Debden House campsite (Debden Green, Loughton, Essex IG10 2BA, 8508 3008; £4.50/night, £2.50/night children). Riders have miles of trekking space; there are several stables in the vicinity (contact the Epping Forest Information Centre).

South-east London

Maritime pride, bosky parks and an unpleasant Elephant.

Rotherhithe

Down river from the stews of the South Bank, Rotherhithe (from *Redriffe*, meaning 'mariner's haven') was once where ships were built and broken. It was from here that the Pilgrim Fathers set sail in the *Mayflower* in 1620. Among the old wharves and warehouses are a couple of legendary seafarers' pubs: the **Mayflower** (117 Rotherhithe Street, SE16 4NF, 7237 4088) and the 17th-century **Angel** (101 Bermondsey Wall East, SE16 4NB, 7237 3608), with smuggler's trapdoor. Just along from the Angel on Bermondsey Wall East a small patch of grass has the scant remains of King Edward III's palace.

The St Marychurch Conservation Area is the most antiquated bit of the neighbourhood. St Mary's Rotherhithe (St Marychurch Street, SE16 4JE, 7231 2465) was built by local sailors in 1715. Nearby, housed in a former mortuary, is the Time & Talents Association (7231 7845). Still running numerous arts and social programmes (including drama courses for children), the association was set up by local women in 1887 to help poverty-stricken local families. The **Brunel Engine House & Tunnel Exhibition** celebrates a different aspect of the 19th century: the masterful engineering that created the Thames Tunnel, the world's first underwater tunnel.

Not far from the conservation area, toward the fume-filled Rotherhithe Tunnel, is St Olav's Square, home to the Norwegian Church and Seamen's Mission (7740 3900). Along with the Swedish and Finnish churches nearby, this centre is a reminder of the area's salty Scandinavian links, which date all the way back to those early Norse sailors, the Vikings. Come mid November, it's the scene of a gloriously atmospheric two-day Norwegian Christmas bazaar, celebrating the food, crafts and traditions of the country.

Rotherhithe's green spaces include Lavender Pond and Nature Park (Lavender Road, SE16 5DZ, 7231 2976), one of the oldest urban nature reserves in England. It was created from an old dock inlet in 1981 and now supports newts, frogs, dragonflies, herons and tufted ducks. The refurbished Pumphouse here is used as a river museum for school groups. Other ecology parks, tirelessly promoted by the Trust for Urban Ecology and its volunteers, include Russia Dock Woodland and Stave Hill Ecological Park, both havens for wildlife. Across Salter Road, back by the river, lies **Surrey Docks Farm**. But the most immaculate green space is **Southwark Park**. Every summer it hosts music, crafts, food and fun in the form of Rotherhithe Festival (11-17 July 2004). Nearby, the Seven Islands Leisure Centre (100 Lower Road, SE16 2TU, 7237 3296, www.fusion-lifestyle.com) has a good pool with children's swimming programmes.

Crossing Lower Road from the park brings you to Canada Water, the Surrey Quays Shopping Centre and attendant leisure activities: a cinema, Arbuckles burger restaurant (Mast Leisure Park, Surrey Quays Road, SE16 2XU, 7232 1901), the biggest sports store in Europe (Decathlon, *see p199*) and a Hollywood Bowl. You'll also find the Surrey Docks Watersports Centre (Rope Street, SE16 7SX, 7237 5555; *see also p272*), which runs sailing and canoeing courses for eights and over in school holidays and at half-term.

Brunel Engine House & Tunnel Exhibition

Brunel Engine House, Railway Avenue, SE16 4LF (7231 3840/www.brunelenginehouse.org.uk). Rotherhithe tube. **Open** 1-5pm Sat, Sun; tours by appointment only. **Admission** £2; £1 concessions; £5 family (2+2); free under-5s. **No credit cards**.

The story of the Eighth Wonder of the World, which is what the Victorians called the first underwater tunnel in the world, is told in this little museum, housed in the original engine house. The Thames Tunnel was designed by Marc Isambard Brunel with the help of his more famous son, Isambard Kingdom Brunel – the only time they worked together. The main thrust of the exhibition is the construction of the tunnel, completed in 1843, and now used for the East London tube line. It also provides a good general Victorian history lesson: the museum welcomes school groups and has information packs for Key Stages 2 and 4.

During the week of the Rotherhithe Festival (11-17 July 2004), admission is free and museum volunteers run activities and entertainment for children. The museum possesses a giant Brunel model, which comes out wearing an unfeasibly large and steaming topper for special parades, such as the Bermondsey Carnival (17 July) and the Thames Festival (18-19 Sept). The main event for children in the local community, however, is the summer playscheme (26 July-6 Aug). They get to work with artists in residence on environmental projects, which this year means they'll be helping a sculptor create ornamental ironwork for the new Brunel Gardens and picnic area outside the museum.

Buggy access/storage. Nearest picnic place: museum gardens & riverbank. Shop.

Southwark Park

Gomm Road, SE16 2UA (park rangers 7232 2091/art gallery 7237 1230). Canada Water tube. **Open** *Park* 8am-1hr before dusk daily. *Gallery* (during exhibitions) noon-6pm Wed-Sun in summer, 11am-4pm Wed-Sun in winter; phone ahead to check. **Admission** free.

Larks in **Greenwich Park**.
See p124.

All hands on deck

The venerable **Cutty Sark** (*see p123*), the only Grade I-listed ship in the world, needs all the shipmates she can get these days. Having withstood gales, storms and heavy seas around Cape Horn in her glory days, she's now in danger of being wrecked by London's miserable weather.

Sat in dry dock at Greenwich for 50 years, the *Cutty Sark* is one of London's great landmarks, visited by thousands of tourists every year. Her roof is leaking, however, and the salt water that has soaked into her timbers is accelerating the corrosion. What's worse are the bugs: dormant bacteria could eat away at the ship if they're reawoken by the radical new procedure being considered to stop the rot.

The Cutty Sark Trust, which has looked after the ship since 1953, has been liaising with maritime conservation experts, scientists, historians, interpretation and visitor-attraction experts to devise a conservation strategy. A daring rescue package planned for the ship involves a method called electrolysis, during which the ship's hull and dry dock are filled with water, and chemicals put in the water inside to kill off the bacteria. Then the ship's iron frame is connected to one side of a power source, with metal mesh mats in the water as the other terminal, and an electric current is passed between them for perhaps a year or more. This should draw out the chlorides in the iron and the wood, thus stopping the corrosion. The trouble is, this electrolysis business has never been done on an ancient ship made of wood and iron before. If the experiment goes wrong, there's a possibility that the wood could be turned into mush.

Nonetheless, something – however risky – has to be done. The alternative is letting the *Cutty Sark* rot to pieces. She's safe for visitors to board until 2006, but after that a lengthy conservation programme will – pending Heritage Lottery Funding (HLF) – commence. While it's at it, the Cutty Sark Trust want to improve visitor access and is talking to architectural experts about how best to manage the renewed interiors of the ship.

All this means that between 2006 and 2009 visitors to the ship will get to learn about a live maritime conservation project, even though access to the ship will necessarily sometimes be limited. It also means that the Trust has to raise more than £12 million; it is anticipated that even if the HLF bid is successful, the Trust will have to find a minimum of £4 million matched funding – a major hurdle for the very small crew who are currently navigating their way through the fundraising seas.

The fastest tea clipper that ever sailed, the history and significance of the *Cutty Sark* are celebrated lovingly on board. It's a fascinating glimpse of life at sea, from the primitive loos with their salt-water pumps to the crews' cabins and the rather more salubrious chambers inhabited by the officers (ceiling leaks notwithstanding). A polished dining table, cut-glass decanters and cosy fireplace show that a seafarer's life was not all hard tack and watery rum.

Weekends and school holidays see a range of on-board activities for children, and they're all included in the admission charge (*see p123*). 'Tying Up Loose Ends' is all about ropework and a salty old sea dog and general knot expert who has some chilling tales to tell about life at sea. Another popular attraction is dapper Captain Wait, an avuncular officer who knows his blocks from his tackles and can demonstrate the mechanical advantages of a double luff. Groups of children sporting captains' hats follow him up on deck to splice mainbraces, check the mizzens and get their ports confused with their starboards. With storytelling in Nanny's Nook, arts and crafts in the figurehead collection down below, singing of sea shanties and treasure hunting during the school holidays, it's always worth checking the *Cutty Sark* website to see what's on before you visit. But do visit – and dig deep for the fundraising appeal. If everyone heaves to and lends a hand, the world's last surviving tea clipper – national treasure and pride of the Merchant Navy – will rule the waves, or at least Cutty Sark Gardens, once more.

This well-tended green acreage constitutes London's oldest municipal park, but for many years it was a bit of an embarrassment, falling into neglect and becoming a target for vandals. All that has changed now. Southwark Park was restored with the help of £2.75m lottery grant, and now the Victorian park is one of south London's prettiest. The busy park rangers (on site seven days a week) are doing their best to keep it looking gorgeous. The loveliest bit is the boating lake (fully operational in summer), where kids can feed the ducks and swans, but the whole place is pleasing. There's a bird-filled wildlife garden, a soothing place to rest awhile, an ornate old-fashioned bandstand, tennis courts, a bright new playground, playing fields and an information centre. There's also a curious little gallery smack in the middle of the park. Its shows include the annual Open Exhibition (19 Nov-14 Dec), which always features children's work.
Buggy access. Nappy-changing facilities (in gallery).

Surrey Docks Farm

Rotherhithe Street, SE16 5EY (7231 1010). Canada Water or Surrey Quays tube. **Open** 10am-1pm, 2-5pm Tue-Thur, Sat, Sun. **Admission** free (except for school parties & playschemes, phone for details); donations appreciated.

This riverside organic farm was opened in the early 1970s in an attempt to bring a bit of nature to a depressed neighbourhood. Currently its residents include a herd of milking goats, sheep, cows, pigs, poultry, donkeys and bees. There's a classroom in the shape of an enchanted forest, a dairy and a forge where a blacksmith holds evening classes. The duck pond and a herb and vegetable garden offer further bucolic delights. Children enjoy clambering over the animal sculptures. Call about holiday playschemes and workshops.
Buggy access. Café. Shop.

Deptford & Greenwich

The mucky strands and abandoned wharves of grubby old **Deptford** constitute Lewisham borough's share of valuable riverside land. It's all ripe for redevelopment, but the move to build smart Thameside homes in one area – Convoys Wharf – is being hotly opposed by environmental campaigners.

Ecology is already king if you take a walk on Deptford's Creekside. The Creekside Centre (14 Creekside, SE8 4SA, 8692 9922, http://home.bt connect.com/creekside) is open to school and youth groups, running regular weekend activities for families (see the website for details and to sign up for the mailing list). Also here, the iridescent Laban, an award-winning design by Herzog and de Meuron, brings Deptford right up to date. Visitors are allowed into the reception area, café and grounds of this dance centre, but if you want a closer look you have to sign up for classes (*see p228*) or book yourself on a £5 tour.

Away from the riverside newbuilds, Deptford is a fascinating neighbourhood. Still quite traditional in outlook (think pie and mash shops and street markets), Deptford is increasingly trendy: witness its smart cafés and galleries. There's also St Nicholas on Deptford Green; known as the sailors' church, it dates to 1697 and has timber-shivering skulls and crossbones carved on the gate piers.

Historic maritime **Greenwich**, a worthy UNESCO World Heritage Site, is much more accommodating to visitors than its westerly neighbour. Then again, it has enjoyed centuries of public adulation, thanks to its royal associations. Henry VIII loved this part of the world so much that he built a palace here. Since his time, Greenwich has been in and out of fashion: William and Mary chose not to live in the palace, turning it into the seamen's hospital now known as the **Old Royal Naval College**. For a good overview of Greenwich delights, visit the Tourist Information Centre: it can be found within the Greenwich Gateway Visitor Centre here.

The best way to arrive in Greenwich is, like King Henry, by boat. Thames Cruises (7930 3373, www.thamescruises.com), Catamaran Cruises (7987 1185) or City Cruises (7930 9033, www.city cruises.com) all float by Greenwich Pier, just by the tea clipper, the **Cutty Sark**. From the riverside it's a heart-pumping ten-minute walk up the steep slopes of gorgeous **Greenwich Park** to the **Royal Observatory** and **Planetarium**. For little and elderly legs that can't handle the journey, a shuttle bus runs from Greenwich Pier to the **National Maritime Museum** and onwards up to the top of the hill every 15 minutes or so. Tickets last all day and cost £1.50 for adults, 50p for children and nothing for under-fives. The Docklands Light Railway (DLR) offers the Rail & River Rover (details on 7363 9700 or www.dlr.co.uk), a family pass that is also valid on some cruise boats.

If you're visiting at the weekend, take a turn round Greenwich Market (*see p187*), before you head parkward. Even when there's no market, there are fascinating shops to ponder in the area. Compendia Traditional Games (*see p205*) is a must-stop for children. Just across the road, the maritime extravaganza, Nauticalia (25 Nelson Road, SE10 9JB, 8858 1066) has everything shipshape.

From Greenwich proper the Thames Path can take you all the way to the bulge of the Greenwich Peninsula, which first came to national recognition as the home of the Millennium Dome. That structure is to become a sport and leisure complex at the heart of a brand new town, made up of thousands of homes, shops and other businesses. Until this happens, the Peninsula is busy enough with its own yacht club, a Holiday Inn, a UCI cinema multiplex and the **Greenwich Peninsula Ecology Park**. There are some lovely walks and bike rides hereabouts: for organised bike rides, contact Greenwich Cyclists (www.greenwichcyclists.org.uk).

Cutty Sark

King William Walk, SE10 9HT (8858 3445/www.cutty sark.org.uk). Cutty Sark DLR/Greenwich DLR/rail. **Open** 10am-5pm daily (last entry 4.30pm). Closed 24-26 Dec. *Tours* Mon-Fri; depending on availability. **Admission** (LP) £4.25; £2.95 concessions; £10.50 family (2+3); free under-5s. *Tours* free. **Credit** MC, V.
Launched in 1869 from Dumbarton on the Clyde, the *Cutty Sark* took tea to China and later wool to Australia. Now a museum, the lower hold contains a large collection of handsome figureheads from merchant ships. The old ship is the scene of many a jolly family event throughout the year, and is about to undergo a daring restoration adventure. *See also p122* **All hands on deck**.
Buggy storage. Nearest picnic place: Cutty Sark Gardens. Shop.

Fan Museum

12 Crooms Hill, SE10 8ER (8305 1441/www.fan-museum.org). Cutty Sark DLR/Greenwich DLR/rail. **Open** 11am-5pm Tue-Sat; noon-5pm Sun. Closed 25 Dec, 1 Jan, Easter. **Admission** £3.50; £2.50 concessions; free under-7s, OAPs, disabled 2-5pm Tue. **Credit** MC, V.
This pair of impeccably restored Georgian townhouses is home to more than 3,000 fans, although only a fraction of the collection is on display at any one time, with fans retired periodically to give them a rest. There are fantastically ornate and very old fans here, and they come from all over the world and every period since the 11th century. Give it a whirl if the children are interested in pretty things, fashion and design, but realistically it is one for the over-tens. Check the website for details of fan-making workshops. Until 19 September 2004, 'A Garden of Fans' (100 fans decorated with flowers) celebrates the Royal Horticultural Society's bicentenary.

Outside, there's an attractive oriental-style garden, and the breathtakingly elegant Orangery, with its beautiful murals, is open for afternoon tea on Tuesdays and Sundays.
Buggy access. Lift. Nearest picnic place: Greenwich Park. Shop.

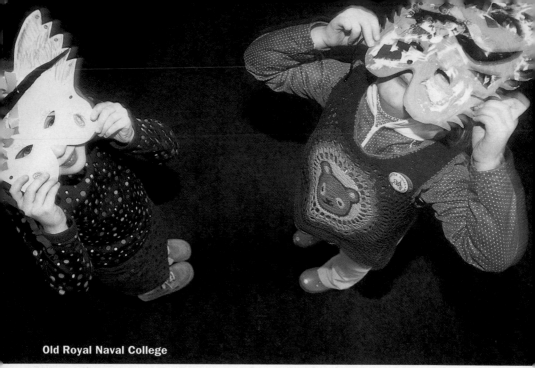

Old Royal Naval College

Greenwich Park

Blackheath Gate, Charlton Way, SE10 8QY (visitors centre 8293 0703/www.royalparks.gov.uk). Cutty Sark DLR/Greenwich DLR/rail/Maze Hill rail/1, 53, 177, 180, 188, 286 bus/riverboat to Greenwich Pier.
Open 6am-dusk daily.
The oldest Royal Park, dating from 1433, is a tree-hugger's paradise. Beeches, oaks and chestnuts line the great Tudor avenues and there are cedars, sweet chestnuts and Judas trees among the lawns and flowerbeds. One of the sweet chestnuts here is 400 years old, and the Queen Elizabeth oak (not far from the observatory) is thought to date from the 12th century. Henry VIII and Anne Boleyn danced round it, and for a time its hollow trunk was used as a lock-up for criminals. A storm brought down the long-dead husk in 1991, but next to its preserved remains stands an adolescent tree planted by Prince Phillip for the Queen's Golden Jubilee.

As well as a most beautiful collection of trees, the summit of this hilly park affords fabulous views and, just outside the top gates, donkey rides. The main café also stands at the top of the hill. At the bottom, there's a boating lake and fine playground, with a snack bar.

Being a Royal Park, there's extra children's fun during the summer holidays, with free theatrical performances and puppet shows (check the website for details).
Buggy access. Café.

Greenwich Peninsula Ecology Park

Thames Path, John Harrison Way, SE10 0QZ (8293 1904/www.urbanecology.org.uk). North Greenwich tube/ 108, 161, 188, 422, 472, 486 bus. **Open** 10am-5pm Wed-Sun. **Admission** free.
This nearly four-acre (2ha) wetland area with woodland, marsh, meadow, lakes and streams is the pretty side of the huge North Greenwich regeneration project. For a nature reserve that's only been established for three years, it's doing really well, supporting frogs, toads, dragonflies and a wide variety of birdlife. Run by the Trust for Urban Ecology for English Partnerships, it is as much an educational centre as a pleasant place to breathe. To that end, children are plied with quizzes and trails to follow as they explore, as well as regular activities that often involve pondlife, mud and gumboots. On Mondays and Tuesdays the park is reserved for schools and other prebooked groups. Check the website for details of July's Open Day and March's Grand Frog Day.
Buggy access. Nappy-changing facilities.

National Maritime Museum

Romney Road, SE10 9NF (8858 4422/8312 6565/tours 8312 6608/www.nmm.ac.uk). Cutty Sark DLR/Greenwich DLR/rail. **Open** *Summer (July-Aug)* 10am-6pm daily. *Winter* 10am-5pm daily. Closed 24-26 Dec. **Tours** phone for details. **Admission** free. **Credit** *Shop* MC, V.
Of Greenwich's many treasures, this beautiful museum is the place that pleases children – of all ages – the most. From look-don't-touch models of old galleons to the touch-everything-please 'All Hands' gallery, everything is beautifully presented and you're never far from a helpful visitor assistant.

The airy lobby presents 'Planet Ocean', where you can make waves and explore tides. The dark, atmospheric 'Explorers' gallery shows eerie film footage of the wreck of the *Titanic* at the bottom of the Atlantic. It is devoted to pioneers of sea travel, covering Columbus, the Vikings and the race to the Poles. 'Passengers' is a shrine to glamorous ocean liners of yore, 'Rank and Style' looks at the influence of climate and class on uniform design, and 'Maritime London' tells the capital's nautical history.

Upstairs, 'Seapower' covers naval battles from Gallipoli to the Falklands, and 'Hidden Treasures' is where to find the giant model ships. You'll also find the temporary Tintin exhibition – celebrating the adventures of tufty-haired boy journalist and the artwork of Hergé, who created him – which runs until 5 September 2004. Visitors to the exhibition (£5;

Lord Nelson was laid in state here while thousands came to pay their respects. In the chapel there are free organ recitals on the first Sunday of each month.

The Greenwich Gateway Visitor Centre, in the Pepys Building, has an exhibition on 2,000 years of Greenwich history, including the story of the Royal Hospital for Seamen, as well as background information on other Greenwich attractions such as the National Maritime Museum (*see p124*), the *Cutty Sark* (*see p123*) and the Ranger's House (*see below*).

At weekends and during school holidays, the College runs children's events, such as archaeology workshops or exciting re-enactments called things like 'Brave Knights of Old England'. Be sure to make a date in your diary for 'Cut and Thrust Tudor Duelling' (4-5 Sept, 11am-4pm).
Café. Nappy-changing facilities. Nearest picnic place: Naval College grounds. Shops.

Queen's House

Romney Road, SE10 9NF (8312 6565/www.nmm.ac.uk). Cutty Sark DLR/Greenwich DLR/rail. **Open** 10am-5pm daily. Closed 24-26 Dec. **Admission** free; occasional charge for temporary exhibitions. **Credit** *Shop* MC, V.
Designed in 1616 by Inigo Jones for James I's wife, Anne of Denmark, Queen's House so pleased its royal resident that she dubbed it the 'house of delights'. The house is now home to the National Maritime Museum's impressive art collection, which includes portraits of famous maritime figures and works by Hogarth and Gainsborough. More importantly, it's also home to a ghost, famously captured on film by a couple of Canadian visitors in 1966 but spotted as recently as 2002 by a gallery assistant. Family Sundays see party games, performances, dancing, and art and craft activities; no need to book, but ring before coming to check what's on.
Buggy access. Nappy-changing facilities. Nearest picnic place: Greenwich Park.

Ranger's House

Chesterfield Walk, SE10 8QX (8853 0035/www.english-heritage.org.uk). Blackheath rail or Greenwich DLR/rail/ 53 bus. **Open** *June-Aug* 10am-5pm Wed-Sun. *Sept-May* group bookings only. **Admission** (EH) £5; £3.80 concessions; £2.50 5-16s; free under-5s. **Credit** MC, V.
This red-brick villa – formerly the official residence of the Greenwich Park Ranger and, prior to that, a 'grace and favour' home to minor royals – was built in 1720. It now contains the magnificent collection of treasure amassed by millionaire diamond magnate Julius Wernher, who died in 1912. His priceless collection of 19th-century art, including jewellery, bronzes, tapestries, furniture, porcelain and paintings, is one of the most unusual in the world. Displayed in 12 elegant rooms, this glittering spectacle shows what Britain's richest man liked to spend his dosh on – enamelled skulls, miniature coffins and jewel-encrusted reptiles are just some of the unusual items that caught Wernher's eye.
Buggy storage. Lifts. Nearest picnic place: Greenwich Park. Shop.

Royal Observatory & Planetarium

Greenwich Park, SE10 9NF (8312 6565/www.rog. nmm.ac.uk). Cutty Sark DLR/Greenwich DLR/rail. **Open** 10am-5pm daily. Closed 24-26 Dec. **Tours** phone for details. **Admission** free.
Built for Charles II by Wren in 1675, this observatory now examines the lonely life of John Flamsteed, the Royal Astronomer, who was assigned the weighty task of mapping the heavens. A series of set-piece rooms evoke the Flamsteed household. Elsewhere, there are cases and cases of clocks and watches, from hourglasses to a mind-bogglingly accurate atomic clock. The dome houses the largest refracting

£4 concessions) follow the intrepid Tintin on the search for treasure in far-flung islands of the Caribbean and the snowy wastes of the North Pole.

Continuing up, Level 3 has the 'All Hands' gallery: all hands-on and interactive, and based on the lives of seafarers. Children can play with a variety of exhibits, including Morse code machines, ships' wheels and a cargo-handling model. 'Shipmates', an activity room off the gallery, is used for children's craft sessions. As usual, you can't leave without a sojourn in the extensive gift shop; here it runs the vaguely nautical gamut from £1.50 clockwork lobsters to large £70-scale models of the *Mary Rose*.

Scarcely a weekend or school holiday goes past without costumed actors and storytellers entertaining the children. There's also the 'Crows' Nest Adventure' (interactive tours for ages two to six), craft sessions, sailor-themed sing-songs and activities designed to complement current exhibitions – you can expect a lot of Tintin for summer 2004. Family Sundays (the last Sun every month), with their workshops and performances, are very popular.
Buggy access. Café. Nappy-changing facilities. Nearest picnic place: Greenwich Park. Restaurant. Shop.

Old Royal Naval College

King William Walk, SE10 9LW (8269 4747/tours 8269 4791/www.greenwichfoundation.org.uk). Cutty Sark DLR/Greenwich DLR/rail. **Open** 10am-5pm daily (last entry 4.15pm). Closed 25, 26 Dec. *Tours* by arrangement. **Admission** free. **Credit** MC, V.
The majestic Old Royal Naval College was built by Sir Christopher Wren in 1696. The buildings were originally a hospital, then a naval college and are now part of the University of Greenwich. The public are allowed into the rococo chapel and Painted Hall; the amazing painted tribute to William and Mary took beleaguered artist Sir James Thornhill 19 years to complete. For his efforts, he was paid £6,685 2s 4d – just £3 per square yard. In 1806 the body of

telescope in the country – and eighth largest in the world. In the courtyard is the Prime Meridian Line – star of a billion snaps of happy tourists with a foot in each hemisphere. You can pay £1 to receive a certificate marking your visit.

Just up the hill from the Observatory, the Planetarium offers a range of guided tours to the stars; these take place at 2.30pm and 3.30pm daily (£4; £2 children).

Family learning days are held on such topics as 'Getting Started in Astronomy' or 'The Red Planet'. The school holiday programme, meanwhile, features a range of workshops and stories (call 8312 6608 for details).

Buggy access (not in dome). Nappy-changing facilities. Nearest picnic place: Greenwich Park. Shop.

Blackheath & Lewisham

Windswept **Blackheath** is kite-flying central, and home to many of Britain's first sports clubs: the Royal Blackheath Golf Club (1745), the Blackheath Hockey Club (1861) and the Blackheath Football Club (1862), which actually plays Rugby Union. Nearby Blackheath village easily outdoes Dulwich (*see p131*), its rival in poshness, for shops and restaurants (there are several good children's shops here, notably Pares Shoes, 24 Tranquil Vale, SE3 0AX, 8297 0785), but the level of traffic pollution is shocking. Blackheath Halls (23 Lee Road, SE3 9RQ, 8318 9758, www.blackheathhalls.com) programmes plenty of children's activities: theatre productions, dance workshops, films, a young bands programme, a youth jazz orchestra and an all-ages community orchestra. On Sundays there's a farmers' market in Blackheath station car park.

South-west of Blackheath lies **Lewisham**, a world away from its exclusive neighbour, but enjoying easy access to town thanks to the DLR. The indoor shopping centre with its playground, and outdoor street market are bustling (if decidedly downmarket) community resources. If you keep walking down Lewisham Promenade and you'll end up in **Catford**, famed for its landmark black-and-white cat over an ugly shopping centre, the beautiful old art deco Broadway Theatre and trees lit up by blue light bulbs. Lewisham borough has a good number of parks. Mountsfield Park (Stainton Road, SE6) hosts People's Day (10 July), an annual summer festival that draws 30,000 people to enjoy circus acts, music, poetry and various stalls (call 8318 3986 for details). Other parks in the area include beautiful Sydenham Wells Park (Wells Park Road, SE26) and **Manor House & Gardens**.

Age Exchange Reminiscence Centre

11 Blackheath Village, SE3 9LA (8318 9105/www.age-exchange.org.uk). Blackheath rail. **Open** 10am-5pm Mon-Sat. **Admission** free.

It's like stepping into (great) granny's parlour. The centre has a little old-fashioned sweetie shop, with classics like rhubarb and custard and rosy apples in big jars, and a mock-up of a sitting room circa 1940s, with nostalgic toys, a stove and ancient furnishings and crockery. There's also a sweet little

café at the back. The centre's programme of exhibitions based around older people's memories is in 2004 likely to include its touring exhibition about the Merchant Navy, but check the website for dates of further attractions. *Café.*

Manor House & Gardens

34 Old Road, SE13 5SY (8318 1358). Hither Green rail. **Open** *Café & park* 9am-dusk daily. *House & library* 9.30am-5pm Mon, Sat; 9.30am-7pm Tue, Thur. **Admission** free.

This 1772 Manor House, once the gracious home of George Baring the illustrious banker, is now one of the grandest local libraries in London; the children's section is particularly sweet (the library has children's storytelling on Mondays). In the garden is an ancient ice house, which opens to the public occasionally. The park outside, with its large central lake, raised platform for wildfowl feeding and unchallenging play area, is Lewisham parents' favourite place to meet, have lunch and exercise their pre-schoolers. The park café, Pistachio's, specialises in exotic sandwiches, simple hot meals, ice-cream and childen's hot chocolate (£1). There's a parent-and-toddler session that takes place on Tuesday mornings. *Buggy access. Café.*

Woolwich

The riverscape at Woolwich may seem bleak and neglected, but this area, like much of the south-east's riverside, is in the throes of regeneration: the extension of the DLR will have a huge effect on the neighbourhood. Woolwich has a proud naval heritage, but its former role as anchorage for the hellish, overcrowded Victorian prison ships (as described by Charles Dickens in *Great Expectations*) is less of a source of pride.

The last prison ships were removed 150 years ago, but vessels to take note of nowadays are the splendid, free **Woolwich ferry** (8921 5786). These diesel-driven boats replaced a paddle steamer that had been in use until 1889. They take pedestrians and cars across the river every 15 minutes daily. If you take the ferry to the north shore, you disembark right by the North Woolwich Old Station Museum (*see p117*) and Royal Victoria Gardens. Just by the ferry terminal on the south bank is the **Waterfront Leisure Centre** (Woolwich High Street, SE18 6DL, 8317 5000), with flume-filled pools and an indoor adventure playground for children aged up to nine.

The Woolwich Arsenal was established in Tudor times as the country's main source of munitions. By World War I, it stretched 32 miles (51 kilometres) along the river, had its own internal railway system and employed 72,000 people. Much of the land was sold off during the 1960s, but thankfully the main section of the Arsenal, with its beautiful cluster of Georgian buildings, has been preserved. The grounds are now open to the public, as is **Firepower**, the artillery museum. South of here, the Royal Artillery Barracks is famous for having the longest Georgian façade in the country. For more on the Arsenal, visit the Greenwich Heritage Centre (Artillery Square, Royal Arsenal, SE18 4DX, 8854 2452, open 9am-5pm Tue-Sat). The centre has a large collection of historical sources – books, maps, drawings, and manuscripts – and an archaeological archive and natural history specimens. There are also historical displays concerning the Arsenal and Greenwich borough. Woolwich high street holds the dubious distinction of being home to the first McDonald's to open in Britain. In 1974, trivia fans.

Firepower
Royal Arsenal, SE18 4DX (8855 7755/www.firepower. org.uk). Woolwich Arsenal rail. **Open** *Nov-Mar* 10.30am-5pm Fri-Sun (last entry 3pm). *Apr-Oct* 10.30am-5pm Wed-Sun (last entry 4pm). Closed 25 Dec. **Admission** (LP) £5; £4.50 concessions; £2.50 5-16s; £12 family (2+2 or 1+3); free under-5s. **Credit** MC, V.
Young (and old) guns really go for Woolwich's major claim to family attention, the Royal Artillery Museum, which occupies some fine buildings in the heritage corner of the historic Royal Arsenal. Since the completion of Phase Two of the development, Firepower has become even more of a must-see for devotees of military hardware.

Exhibits trace the evolution of artillery from primitive catapults to nuclear warheads. By way of introduction to the Gunners and their history, there's an affecting seven-minute film in the Breech cinema, then visitors are bombarded on all sides by a multimedia presentation called 'Fields of Fire', which covers various 20th-century wars. Other galleries in this building include the Gunnery Hall (full of howitzers and tanks), the Real Weapon gallery (which shows you how guns work) and the medal gallery.

Phase Two, opened by Dame Vera Lynn on 31 March 2004, includes a huge collection of trophy guns and the Cold War gallery, which focuses on the 'monster bits' (ginormous tanks and guns used in military conflict from 1945 to the present). Each piece is in its own bay, surrounded by vast iconic photographs to give it its place in history. Of most interest to children, however, is the first-floor Command Post. It has a paintball range (ten balls for £1.50), a mock-up of an Andersen shelter and the Rolling Rock. This latter is a 12ft (3.7m) climbing wall with a moving surface. The challenge is to get to the top – and it's harder than it looks.

The big upcoming event for 2004 is 'Zulu' (20-21 Aug), which will mark the 125th anniversary of the death of the Prince Imperial with a special exhibition and a film about the making of the classic film of the same name. Other events will see the mounted King's Troop visit the museum and various armoury displays and demonstrations (duck!). Then there are the gun salutes for various royal occasions (duck again!), various musical nights and, of most interest to the children, special party packages for little birthday soldiers (call 8312 7111 for details).
Buggy access. Café. Lift. Nappy-changing facilities. Nearest picnic place: riverside. Shop.

Thames Barrier Information & Learning Centre
1 Unity Way, SE18 5NJ (8305 4188/www.environment-agency.gov.uk). North Greenwich tube/Charlton rail/ riverboats to & from Greenwich Pier (8305 0300) & Westminster Pier (7930 3373)/177, 180 bus. **Open** *Apr-late Sept* 10.30am-4.30pm daily. *End Sept-Mar* 11am-3.30pm daily. Closed 24 Dec-2 Jan. **Admission** *Exhibition* £1; 75p concessions; 50p 5-16s; free under-5s. **Credit** MC, V.
The key player in London's flood defence system looks like a cross between the Sydney Opera House and row of giant metallic shark's fins spanning the 1,700ft (520m) Woolwich Reach. The Barrier is the world's largest adjustable dam and was built in 1982 at a cost of £535million; since then it has saved London from flooding at least 67 times. The small but interesting Learning Centre explains how it all works and has a fascinating map that shows which parts of London would be submerged if it stopped working. Outside, there's a wetland centre and a wildlife garden, and there are plans to create a more extensive picnic and playground area, with a woodland walk and foreshore access. Time your visit to see the barrier in action: every September there's a full-scale testing, with a partial test closure once a month (ring for dates). The best way to see the barrier is by boat: Campion Cruises (8305 0300) runs trips from Greenwich.
Café. Shop.

Playtime at... the Horniman Museum

When Helen McDonald starts to strum an African mbela, the room falls silent. Children previously chattering among themselves are frozen cross-legged on the carpet as parents lean forward to listen; all are caught in a musical spell.

Workshops like this take place in the Hands On Base, an interactive gallery created as part of the 2002 Centenary Development of the fabulous **Horniman Museum** (*see p132*). Over the course of 45 minutes kids are introduced to various instruments from around the world and are encouraged to pass them and play with them. Indeed, exposing children to world music is a primary target in the Horniman's ongoing mission. Those who fall under the spell of the mbela can visit the African Worlds gallery, learning more about the role of music and festivities through a range of ceremonial exhibits that include a revolving Ijele masquerade costume the size of a small house. African instruments are among the hundreds on display in the Music gallery with its interactive listening stations. Weekly African drumming and dance workshops for five- to 12-year-olds are run by the Nzinga Dance Ensemble every Sunday in the Education Centre.

It's not all a song and dance. In the Natural History gallery a collection of specimens and skeletons watch the world go by from behind glass. Josh, one of the resident Saturday storytellers, uses them as a starting point for his stories. The animal theme is continued throughout. The Environment Room is home to a community of working bees. There's also an aquarium recreating a range of habitats for the fish collection. The current Dinomites exhibition, meanwhile, displays a bunch of baby dinosaurs (until November 2004).

Around Shooters Hill

Two centuries ago, highwaymen (including the notorious Dick Turpin) lurked in the woods between Shooters Hill and Charlton. Anyone travelling the Old Dover Road took a considerable risk – but then again, so did the robbers, who, if caught, were hanged on the gallows at the bottom of Shooters Hill. These days, Shooters Hill has more pleasant associations, particularly Hornfair Park, which during hot weather attracts sweaty Charltonians with its lido, although whether it will open for summer 2004 is unclear as we go to press. Many of the green spaces in this corner of London are connected by the Green Chain Walk (call 8921 5028 for maps), which takes in meadows and ancient woodlands such as Oxleas Wood (*see p134*).

Charlton House

Charlton Road, SE7 8RE (8856 3951/www.greenwich. gov.uk). Charlton rail/53, 54, 380, 422 bus. **Open** *Library* 2-7pm Mon, Thur; 10am-12.30pm, 1.30-5.30pm Tue, Fri; 10am-12.30pm, 1.30-5pm Sat. *Toy library* 10.30am-12.30pm, 1.30-3.30pm Mon, Tue, Fri. **Admission** free.
From the outside, this Jacobean manor house looks like the grandest of stately homes – which, once upon a time, it was. Built in 1612, it housed the tutor of Henry, eldest son of James I. These days it's a community centre and library, but glimpses of its glorious past can be seen in the creaky oak staircase, marble fireplaces and ornate plaster ceilings. The library has a good children's section, and is a rather delightful home to the Charlton Toy Library (8319 0055). Outside, the venerable mulberry tree, dating back to 1608, receives many visitors each year.
Buggy access. Café. Lifts. Nearest picnic area: Charlton House grounds.

Kennington & the Elephant

If initial impressions of Kennington turn off more bohemian folk, it's probably thanks to the Elephant and Castle – an unsightly architectural carbuncle whose days are numbered. A £1.5-billion regeneration project to create a market square and raze the eyesore has been approved by Southwark Council. Until this brave new town centre is established, the atmosphere is (to put it kindly) gritty. Nonetheless, some arty types like it here. The most notable artspace is the Gasworks (7582 6848, www.gasworks.org.uk), which engages local schoolchildren in various community art projects. Check the website for a post-refurb opening date.

Kennington Park, though not extensive, has a playground and a café. In the late 18th century the park formed a preaching ground for John Wesley, founder of the Methodists: these days the faithful flock to the **AMP Oval** cricket ground for inspiration of a different kind. Meanwhile, the excellent **Imperial War Museum** offers an insight into the history of modern conflict. Neighbouring St George's Cathedral – built by Pugin, who helped design the Houses of Parliament – has a programme of classical music concerts (tickets from £5).

AMP Oval

Kennington Oval, SE11 5SS (ticket office 7582 7764/ 6660/tours 7820 5750/www.surreycricket.com). Oval tube. **Open** *Ticket office* 9.30am-12.30pm, 1.30-4pm Mon-Fri. *Tours* by arrangement; phone for details. **Admission** varies; depending on match. **Credit** MC, V.
London's most famous skewed circle is also a landmark venue in the history of national and international cricket. With a £24-million redevelopment plan adding new terraces, a community education centre and even a swanky aerofoil roof as we go to press, it's also promising to play a clear role in cricket's future. The development will be completed in time for the Ashes Test in May 2005; until then, membership for under-18s is £10 per year, including free entry to all games (the last domestic match of 2004 is 3-6 Aug). The Oval continues to work with local kids, offering Outreach coaching for 250 London schools, as well as school tours, educational workshops and young people's tournaments (including a girls-only series). The club is currently developing a second community venue for young cricketers at Kennington Park; until then, the affiliated coaching programme offers a more intensive introduction to the sport, with sides from under-nines to under-17s and a Colts Cricket league for children.

Imperial War Museum

Lambeth Road, SE1 6HZ (7416 5000/www.iwm.org.uk). Lambeth North tube/Elephant & Castle tube/rail. **Open** 10am-6pm daily. Closed 24-26 Dec. **Admission** free. **Credit** *Shop* MC, V.
The IWM isn't for everyone: housed in an old lunatic asylum, the extensive collections of 'important' military weapons tend to send kids diving through halls and dodging imaginary machine-gun fire, which may rile some parents. Much more interesting – if no less disturbing – are the excellent First and Second World War galleries, displaying poetry by Wilfred Owen, Siegfried Sassoon and their contemporaries, as well as a reconstructed Somme trench and a look at life on the Home Front. The Secret War exhibition, meanwhile, takes aspiring Bonds on a whirlwind tour of British espionage. There's also a 200-seat cinema that shows a range of drama and documentary footage of conflicts through history. Most commendable – although not suitable for younger children – are the powerful and now permanent Holocaust and Crimes Against Humanity exhibitions: both use film, photographs and personal accounts to place the mechanics of genocide in a painfully human context.

Various temporary exhibitions operate throughout the year, and there is a rolling educational programme offering audio guides, workshops and talks by costumed actors.
Buggy access. Café. Lifts. Nappy-changing facilities. Nearest picnic place: Geraldine Mary Harmsworth Park. Shops.

Camberwell & Peckham

Camberwell is a continuing source of fascination and frustration for families in and around: until 1800 it was a picturesque farming village, but these days the colour of greatly diminished Camberwell Green is decidedly less verdant. It has a small children's playground, although health-conscious families may question the benefits of breathing in the fumes from

Look out duty at the **Imperial War Museum**.
See p128.

Village life in **Dulwich**. *See p131*.

one of London's most congested crossroads. Far better to retreat to the sanctuary of nearby **Burgess Park** or prettier **Ruskin Park**, near the top of Denmark Hill (the latter is one of the few London parks that still dares to fill up its large, shallow paddling pool for hot tots during the summer). Camberwell's fortunes have diminished significantly over the centuries: from the identification of a new species of butterfly, the Camberwell Beauty, in 1748 to infamous Camberwell Carrot of the 1987 hit film *Withnail and I*. Nowadays things are on the up, as the proliferation of swanky bars and cafés on Camberwell Church Street goes to prove.

Peckham is another place that's made some positive changes of late – although the cynics might suggest it couldn't have got any worse. When Will Alsop's terribly modern **Peckham Library** won the RIBA award for Britain's best new building in 2000, it was the first bit of good press the area had received since early reviews of *Only Fools and Horses*. Next door to the library, the Peckham Pulse health club (7525 4999, www.fusion-lifestlyle.com) is helping things along nicely: it's one of south London's best fitness centres and boasts excellent child and baby facilities, including health clinics and a resident homeopath, as well as a useful (if not over healthful) café. There are also after-school activities from community forums like New Peckham Varieties (7708 5401), which runs performance workshops with the Magic Eye Theatre (*see p229*).

Few would describe central Peckham, with its depressing numbers of bargain emporia, as picturesque, but the clutter of African and West Indian meat and fish stalls on Rye Lane lend the area plenty of colour – even if they pong a bit and leave ghoulish puddles of blood and ice underfoot. Further up, however, things are decidedly more beautiful: Peckham Rye Common is where William Blake claimed to have encountered his first angel as a child. It's still a heavenly place, with playgrounds alongside a shaded pond, and gardens, streams and leafy glades to explore. Overgrown **Nunhead Cemetery**, to the east, is a less cultivated but equally tranquil retreat.

Burgess Park

Albany Road, SE5 0RJ (park rangers 7525 1066). Elephant & Castle tube/rail, then 12, 42, 63, 68, 171, 343 bus. **Open** 24hrs daily. **Admission** free.
A certain amount of controversy surrounded the creation of this park. Planned in 1943, the construction involved demolishing terraced housing and led to large numbers of residents being uprooted and relocated to the nearby Aylesbury Estate. Thankfully, it's a gamble that appears to have been worth making, repaying the local community a thousand-fold for its patience. For a start, Burgess Park is a genuine breath of fresh air in an otherwise congested neighbourhood: not classically beautiful, perhaps, but large enough for kids to get lost in and boasting an adventure playground, an indoor games room (7277 1371), a kart track that also organises parties (7525 1101) and the ornamental Chumleigh Gardens, home to five different styles of exoticism: Mediterranean, Caribbean, Islamic, Oriental and… English Country. Best of all are the family and schools projects organised by Art in

the Park (7277 4297, www.artinthepark.co.uk). Recent efforts have resulted in the creation of the Heart Garden – a fruit and vegetable patch planted, tended and harvested by those with long-term illnesses – while, on Wednesdays and Thursdays throughout the year, the Peckham Sure Start programme organises creative outdoor games and activities for families with young children (phone for more information). *Café.*

Livesey Museum for Children

682 Old Kent Road, SE15 1JF (7639 5604/www.livesey museum.org.uk). Elephant & Castle tube/rail/53 bus. **Open** 10am-5pm Tue-Sat; last entry 4.30pm. Closed Sun, Mon, bank hols. **Admission** free.

The first library in Camberwell, the Livesey was turned into a local history museum in 1960. In the late '80s it became this sweet, very hands-on museum – one of the few in the country aimed at children under 12, their families, carers and teachers. There's an agreeable little courtyard area, specially designed for young children, with olde-worlde items (old milk churns, an ancient pillar box) salvaged from the museum's days as a bastion of local history. The Education Room is full of curiosities for little ones to explore. After the current exhibition of children's art – produced by Peckham Education Action Zone schools in collaboration with local artists – the museum closes for a couple of months over the summer holidays (July-Sept), reopening in September with 'Energy', which looks at all aspects of fuel and power, with interactive displays on forces, sustainability and nutrition. *Nappy-changing facilities.*

Nunhead Cemetery

Limesford Road or Linden Grove (entrances), SE15 3LD (information 7732 9535). Nunhead rail. **Open** *Summer* 8.30am-7pm daily. *Winter* 8.30am-4pm daily. **Tours** 2pm last Sun of mth. **Admission** free; donations to FONC appreciated.

Upstanding members of society tend to reserve a certain look for people who spend too much of their free time in grave-yards, but in a place as hectic as Peckham this stone garden is one of the few guaranteed portions of peace and quiet. It's truly an unsung beauty, one of the loveliest and least known of London's Victorian cemeteries, filled with broken statues and stone monuments that have been upturned over time by roots of trees and ivy. With an eerie and inspiring atmosphere, the cemetery is a nature reserve for various species of insect, bird and butterfly (make sure kids bring binoculars), and from its highest points offers some incredible views of the city – framed by tangled branches and fragmen-tary angels. There are guided tours on the last Sunday of each month, meeting at the Linden Grove gates at 2pm. *Buggy access.*

Peckham Library

122 Peckham Hill Street, SE15 5JR (7525 0200). Peckham Rye or Queen's Road rail/12, 36, 63, 171 bus. **Open** 9am-8pm Mon, Tue, Thur, Fri; 10am-8pm Wed; 9am-5pm Sat; noon-4pm Sun.

Will Alsop's award-winning design is all well and good, but it's the huge range of family activities inside the avant-garde exterior that makes Peckham Library such a pillar of the community. These include creative baby and toddler sessions every Tuesday morning (10.30am), with storytelling, songs and crafts on the cards, and the Sure Start reading group for under-fives the same afternoon (1.30pm). At both, kids are encouraged to make use of the wide selection of children's books on the fourth floor. Mondays and Fridays ring in the ominous Homework Club (3.30-7pm), and there are meetings of the Teenage Reading Group (TRG) on the second Tuesday

and Family Reading Group (FRG) on the last Thursday of each month, with an extended programme of holiday work-shops to make those precious summer days whizz by even faster. The square outside hosts a farmers' market on Sundays (9.30am-1.30pm): phone 7525 0856 for information. *Lift. Nappy-changing facilities. Shop.*

South London Gallery

65 Peckham Road, SE5 8UH (7703 6120/www.south londongallery.org). Bus 12, 36, 171. **Open** 11am-6pm Tue, Wed, Fri; 11am-7pm Thur; 2-6pm Sat, Sun. Closed 25, 26 Dec, bank hols. **Admission** free.

Some say Peckham is becoming the next Hoxton. While it's still mercifully short on ironic mullets, this excellent gallery goes some way towards supporting such claims. Work on display tends towards the cutting edge: artists including Tracey Emin and Gilbert and George have exhibited here in the past, and the gallery has a forward-thinking approach and futuristic atmosphere. Which is only appropriate: found-ed in 1868 as the South London Working Men's College, its original principal was biologist TH Huxley, grandfather of Aldous Huxley, the author of *Brave New World* and advocate of hallucinogenic experiences. The gallery was due to reopen in June 2004 following refurbishment; check the website for their comprehensive new education programme. *Buggy access. Nappy-changing facilities. Nearest picnic place: gallery garden (during summer).*

Dulwich & Herne Hill

At times it can feel like every well-heeled happy couple in London has relocated to **Dulwich** – but who can blame them? Its peaceful streets and leafy parks are some of the safest places for kids to blossom in the capital, as well as being home to a huge number of family restaurants, cafés and quaint little boozers (the latter often teeming with bleary-eyed young fathers swapping nappy-changing horror stories). Dulwich Village is the centre of attention: peppered around delightful **Dulwich Park** are the many grand buildings of Dulwich College, site of the Edward Alleyn Theatre and its public drama school (*see p221*). **Dulwich Picture Gallery** is lovely, and each May the village comes to life for the annual Dulwich Festival (8299 1011, www.dulwichfestival.co.uk), which positively bristles with children's activities. Sydenham Hill Wood – across the South Circular from Dulwich Park – is also worth a visit, if only to scope out the bird life. But the area's most amazing wildlife collection is at the **Horniman Museum** in nearby Forest Hill, the idyllic grounds and gardens of which also offer great views across the city.

East Dulwich isn't quite so picturesque, but it does have an excellent selection of child-friendly shops and cafés on colourful Lordship Lane – the Goose Green end of which is home to a good children's playground (opposite a mural of Blake's angelic vision). Nearby, the **London Wildlife Trust Centre for Wildlife Gardening** has turned a bus depot into a gardening mecca.

Herne Hill is a less-chaotic Brixton (*see p136*): the shops, pubs and restaurants of Half Moon Lane are popular with young families, and **Brockwell Park** is a great place for kids to put that new kite to the test. Adjoining Brockwell Lido (*see p267*) is the spot for young upstarts to be seen in summer.

Brockwell Park
Dulwich Road, SE24 0PA (7926 0105). Herne Hill rail. **Open** 7am-dusk daily.
This park offers year-round refuge from the chaos of Brixton (*see p136*), though it's just ten minutes' walk away. Family-friendly, Brockwell Park has football, BMX and basketball facilities, but its biggest claim to fame is the Lido, an outdoor pool that more than makes up for the cold water with its elegant 1930s architecture, exotic greenery and a good programme of children's activities in summer. The terrific First Come First Served Café (8671 5217), in an impressive Victorian house atop the hill, serves good little dinners and organises super parties. Another highlight is the annual Lambeth Country Show, held in July, which manages to defy the surrounding urban sprawl by charming kids silly with live music, animal displays, novelty vegetable competitions (no laughing at the back) and more.
Buggy access. Café. Nappy-changing facilities.

Dulwich Park
College Road, SE21 7BQ (park rangers 8693 5737). North Dulwich or West Dulwich rail. **Open** 8am-dusk daily.
Dulwich Park offers south Londoners a landscape as verdant as many of those framed in nearby Dulwich Picture Gallery (*see below*). It's always been a pretty place: the park was formally landscaped in 1890, but had served as a scenic retreat long before that. Queen Mary was a regular visitor (one of the park's four gates is named after her). Visitors today are treated to the Pavilion Café (*see p178*), a much-loved playground complete with 'spider's web' climbing frame, boat hire on the lake (£5.25 for 30mins) and a number of sculpted gardens (including the original American Garden, home to one of London's largest collections of rhododendrons and azaleas, as well as herons, cormorants and the occasional kingfisher). Those hoping to save their legs can borrow four from the Dulwich Riding School (8693 2944), which arranges riding lessons for over-tens and regularly makes use of the park's many sandy paths, while the eccentric London Recumbents (8299 6636, www.londonrecumbents.com) hire out and sell a host of obscure bikes including tandems, trikes and the eponymous horizontal cycles – lessons can be arranged for less steady little ones. Watch out for extensive refurbishments to the park, thanks to a sizeable Lottery grant: changes will include improved drainage, a new boating house and a comprehensive programme of children's activities in the refurbished cricket pavilion.
Buggy access. Café.

Dulwich Picture Gallery
Gallery Road, SE21 7AD (8693 5254/www.dulwich picturegallery.org.uk). North Dulwich or West Dulwich rail/P4 bus. **Open** 10am-5pm Tue-Fri; 11am-5pm Sat, Sun, bank hol Mon. Closed 24-26 Dec, 1 Jan, Good Friday. **Tours** 3pm Sat, Sun. **Admission** £4; £3 concessions; free under-16s. **Tours** free. **Credit** MC, V.
Widely held to be the first purpose-built art gallery in the country, this neo-classical building – designed by John Soane (*see p58* **Sir John the Collector**) in 1811 – also remains one of its best. Despite being anything but enormous, the gallery proudly houses an outstanding collection of work by

European Old Masters and offers a fine introduction to the baroque era through pieces by such as Rembrandt, Rubens, Poussin and – batting for the home team – the great Thomas Gainsborough.
Kids' activities are organised throughout the year. Popular Thursday after-school classes for ten to 13s run during term, and in April 2004 included a six-week exploration of portraiture across a range of media. Prices vary, but average £40 per term, while the Saturday Art School for 12- to 15-year-olds costs roughly £55 for five weeks, and involves more advanced classes such as printmaking, figure drawing and sculpture. Younger children (from age six) can get creative at individual half-day holiday workshops (week-long courses run throughout the summer) tied into seasonal themes like Nativity or Easter Egg making, while family group activities on the first Sunday of every month allow mums and dads to join the fun (2-4.30pm, free with entry ticket). The exhibition of Henry Moore's sculpture and painting (until Sept 2004) is followed with Old Master Drawings from the Capodimonte Museum in Naples (from 5 Oct).
Buggy access. Café. Nappy-changing facilities. Nearest picnic place: gallery gardens. Shop.

Horniman Museum
100 London Road, SE23 3PQ (8699 1872/www. horniman.ac.uk). Forest Hill rail/63, 122, 176, 185, 312, P4 bus. **Open** 10.30am-5.30pm daily. Closed 24-26 Dec. **Admission** free; donations appreciated. **Credit** *Shop* MC, V.
This lovely museum was founded in 1901 by tea trader and collector Frederick Horniman. It has nicely tended gardens with sweeping city views, an animal enclosure with a whole menagerie of rotund goats, grumpy turkeys, rabbits and guinea pigs, an environment room, natural history galleries and a music room. The museum's café is great for children, with low-priced hot meals (pasta, sausage and chips) in small portions, sandwiches, pastries and a full range of drinks. *See also p127* **Playtime at… the Horniman Museum**.
Café. Nappy-changing facilities. Nearest picnic place: Horniman Gardens. Shop.

London Wildlife Trust Centre for Wildlife Gardening
28 Marsden Road, SE15 4EE (7252 9186/ www.wildlondon.org.uk). East Dulwich rail. **Open** 10.30am-4.30pm Tue-Thur, Sun. **Admission** free.
The London Wildlife Trust has for more than 20 years been reclaiming derelict land for nature reserves, and this fantastic centre – created on a disused bus depot – is one of their best. Children can wander through a range of natural habitats, from wilderness to well-maintained, including woodland, marshland, a herb garden, a lovely pond area and a nursery for plants and trees. Local families fill their gardens with the native woodland and pond plants raised here, giving a donation to the LWT as payment. The whole area is teeming with wildlife, from the beehives to various birds, critters and creepy-crawlies that come and go as they please in the wildlife meadow. For children, there's a play area and sandpit, and the visitors' centre – where school parties congregate – has tanks of fish and stick insects.
Eight- to ten-year-olds can cement their relationship with Mother Nature by joining the Wildlife Watch club (£10 per year) and attending annual activities like pond dipping or bat walking, while conservation activities are open to all and organised throughout the year. Every March, families descend on the centre for Frog Day. To join, contact the centre or London Wildlife Trust (Harling House, 47-51 Great Suffolk Street, SE1 0BS, 7261 0447, www.wildlondon.org.uk).

Crystal Palace

The irony of Crystal Palace is the absence at its centre. Sir Joseph Paxton's incredible glass structure, which housed the era-defining Great Exhibition of 1851, was moved here from Hyde Park in 1853 and continued to pack in the punters until 1936, when it was destroyed by fire. These days the crumbling remains – ivy-tangled stone staircases to nowhere, sculpted lions covered with graffiti and giant plaster dinosaurs – lend the park the air of a lost civilisation. The aesthetically uninspired National Sports Centre, in the south-eastern corner of the park, continues to be a premier venue for national athletics (as well as the occasional rock concert), while the **Crystal Palace Museum** expounds the rise and fall of Paxton's testament to Victorian overachievement.

The **Horniman Museum**. *See p132.*

Crystal Palace Museum
Anerley Hill, SE19 2BA (8676 0700). Crystal Palace rail. **Open** 11am-5pm Sun, bank hol Mon. **Admission** free.
The displays at this nostalgic little museum are housed in the old engineering school where John Logie Baird invented the television – a development that too many children will consider more important than the erection of a great glass building. Thankfully (and despite irregular opening hours – the museum is run entirely by volunteers), this 'exhibition of an exhibition' puts the record straight: video and audio presentations and plenty of artefacts from the original Crystal Palace show just how monumental a show it was. The Crystal Palace Foundation, which operates the museum, has proposed plans for a more modern museum as part of the area's ongoing regeneration. Check www.crystalpalace foundation.org.uk for up-to-date information.
Nearest picnic place: Crystal Palace park. Shop.

Crystal Palace Park
Crystal Palace Information Centre, Thicket Road, SE20 8DT (8778 9496/www.bromley.gov.uk). Crystal Palace rail/2, 3, 63, 122, 157, 227 bus. **Open** *Information Centre* 9am-8pm in summer; 9am-dusk in winter. *Park* dawn-dusk daily. **Admission** free.
The most recent instalment in the 150-year-old Crystal Palace saga is the slow-going restoration of this strange and fabulous park. Once the landing site for Prince Albert's Great Exhibition – or at least the elaborate glass hall that housed it – these grounds were also home to some exquisitely landscaped gardens, an amusement park and life-sized model dinosaurs. That is, until a fire in 1936 brought one of British history's most extravagant chapters to an abrupt end.
Ironically, the dinosaurs survived: they've recently been repaired and now loom menacingly over various bits of the park as they did in the mid 19th century. It's all part of Bromley Council's £3.6-million restoration programme aimed at reversing the slow decay of this monumental place. The gardens are being restored (landscape gardeners planting scores of exotic plants not seen here since Victorian times), the lakes are being streamlined and a new rhododendron dell is in the works. Until the restoration is complete, visitors can make do with London's only maze, a playground, a small museum about the history of the palace and a café. Italianate stone terraces nod to the park's former grandeur, and the old lion statues make a good photo opportunity for the kids. The National Sports Centre, although shockingly ugly and in need of cosmetic attention, nonetheless has a busy programme of events for all ages and abilities.
Buggy access. Café. Nappy-changing facilities.

Further south-east

London's rough south-eastern suburbs conceal a surprising number of gems: grand old houses, ancient parkland and historic woodland lead you all the way into Kent, London's back garden. Those houses include William Morris's old place, the Red House (13 Red House Lane, Bexleyheath, Kent DA6 8JF, 01494 755588). Morris, the august founding father of the Arts & Crafts Movement, lived here for five years until 1864; now owned by the National Trust, the Red House contains some original furnishings, stained glass and paintings, and will be of interest to students of art and design, if not to small children.

Crystal Palace Park's strange palaeontology. *See p133*.

Between Bexleyheath and Welling, the huge and lovely Danson Park (attributed to the great landscape gardener 'Capability' Brown) contains the 18th-century Palladian villa, Danson Mansion; looked after by English Heritage, it opens occasionally for visits (check www.english-heritage.org for details). The park itself (Park Ranger Service 8304 2631) hosts annual summer fairs, dog shows, circuses and firework displays. Its 19.3-acre (7.8-hectare) lake provides for fishing, boating, sailing and other water-based sports; there are cafés, putting greens, playgrounds and tennis courts, as well as woodland and garden, and the two-centuries-old Charter Oak, one of the 'Great Trees of London'. More award-winning gardens, this time containing a stunning Tudor mansion, can be enjoyed at **Hall Place**, just up the road in Bexley.

The area around Eltham and Bexley is dotted with meadows and woodlands. Oxleas Wood (across the Shooters Hill Road from Falconwood rail station, in Welling, Kent) is an 8,000-year-old piece of woodland, dating to the Ice Age. The wood, famous for bluebells in May, was to be uprooted back in the mid '90s – until a campaign stopped the bulldozers. A gallows once stood at the entrance to the woods, ready to stretch the necks of the highwaymen who worked in the area. Paths link up with the Green Chain Walk (8921 5028, www.greenchain.com), a 40-mile (64-kilometre) network starting near the Thames Barrier (*see p127*) and ending at Crystal Palace (*see p133*). The Oxleas Wood path starts at Erith and takes in the remains of 12th-century Lesnes Abbey, a fine picnic place with toilets, information centre and views of the towerblocks to the north.

Organic **Woodlands Farm** is open to the public and can be found just off Shooters Hill (the name of this area of Kent as well as the road that leads to it from near Blackheath). Dick Turpin's cave is nearby. It's not much to see: just a small hole near Bostall Woods, so we doubt he spent much time there.

Another suburb worth visiting is Croydon, notable for its £200-million tram system and the Whitgift Centre for shopping. **Croydon Clocktower** has three galleries, a library, a theatre space, a cinema and a café. The Warehouse Theatre Company (62 Dingwall Road, Croydon, Surrey CR0 2NF, 8681 1257, www.warehousetheatre.co.uk) offers drama workshops and a different children's production every Saturday morning.

Pretty Chislehurst still has a nostalgic feel. It's also home to one of Kent's great geographical wonders, the **Chislehurst Caves**.

Chislehurst Caves

Chislehurst, Old Hill, Kent BR7 5NB (8467 3264/ www.chislehurstcaves.co.uk). Chislehurst rail. **Open** 10am-4pm Wed-Sun. **Admission** £4; £2 children, OAPs.
The spooky caves at Chislehurst were carved out of the hillside by Druids digging for chalk and flint (they also came here to make grisly human sacrifices). In due course the Romans were to extract chalk from here and, more recently, the caves were used as a World War I ammunition dump and a mushroom farm in the 1930s. But the caves only became famous during World War II, when they were Britain's largest bomb shelter.

The tour covers less than a mile (2km). It's not strenuous, but it isn't for the claustrophobic – at one point the lanterns are extinguished and you're engulfed by darkness. The tour captures the imagination: how those plucky Kentish folk could bunk down in all this damp and gloom is beyond us.
Café. Shop.

Croydon Clocktower

Katharine Street, Croydon, Surrey CR9 1ET (box office 8253 1030/tourist information 8253 1009/www.croydon. gov.uk/clocktower). East Croydon or West Croydon rail/ George Street tram. **Open** *Clocktower & library* 9am-7pm Mon; 9am-6pm Tue, Wed, Fri; 9.30am-6pm Thur; 9am-5pm Sat; 2-5pm Sun. *Café Opera* 9.30am 5.30pm Mon Sat; 1 5pm Sun. Closed bank hols. *Tourist Information Centre* 9am-6pm Mon, Wed, Fri; 9.30am-6pm Thur; 9am-5pm Sat; 2-5pm Sun. *Museum & galleries* 11am-5pm Mon-Sat; noon-5pm Sun. **Admission** free (check for exhibitions).
Croydon Clocktower, built in 1896, is a splendid Victorian building – a stark contrast to all the surrounding office blocks. It also has a corker of a museum, tracing the history and future of Croydon, with lots of interactive exhibits, stories about real-life Croydonites and a dressing-up corner. The museum offers children's workshops, ranging from sculpture and poetry to calligraphy and crafts (call 8253 1023 for details). The David Lean cinema is renowned for its Tick Tock children's club (11am Sat). The Clocktower also provides a Saturday crèche.

Braithwaite Hall, the centre's theatre, hosts weekend and holiday theatre productions for children. There's also an excellent library with regular story, music and art sessions.
Café. Nappy-changing facilities. Nearest picnic place: Queen's Gardens.

Eltham Palace

Court Yard, off Court Road, SE9 5QE (8294 2548/www. english-heritage.org.uk). Eltham rail. **Open** *Apr-Oct* 10am-5pm Wed-Fri, Sun. *Nov-Mar* 10am-4pm Wed-Fri, Sun. Closed 24 Dec-31 Jan. **Admission** (EH) *House & grounds* (incl audio tour) £7; £5.30 concessions; £3.50 5-16s; free under-5s. *Grounds only* £4.50; £3.40 concessions; £2.30 5-16s; free under-5s. **Credit** MC, V.
An art deco extravaganza, complete with medieval remains and a moat, Eltham Palace was rebuilt by Stephen Courtauld, a member of the textile family and patron of the arts. The house was bought by English Heritage and restored to its 1930s glory. The interior is all sensuous curves, polished veneer walls and modish abstract carpets, with a retro-glam entrance hall and swish bathrooms. Kids might be tickled by the specially designed quarters for the Courtaulds' pet lemur. By contrast, the great hall (all that remains of the original building) is a splendid example of medieval architecture. The garden is just lovely, especially at spring bulb time.

As well as quiz sheets and trails for children, the palace and gardens are used for open-air performances of Shakespeare during the summer, an Art Deco Fair (12 Sept 2004) and a carol concert (16 Dec 2004). Check the website for details.
Café. Lifts. Nappy-changing facilities. Nearest picnic place: palace grounds. Shop.

Hall Place & Gardens

Bourne Road, Bexley, Kent DA5 1PQ (01322 526 574/ www.hallplaceandgardens.com). Bexley rail/B15, 132, 229, 492 bus. **Open** *Apr-Oct* 10am-5pm Mon-Sat, 11am-5pm Sun, bank hols. *Nov-Mar* 10am-4pm Tue-Sat. **Admission** free.
This enchanting Tudor mansion was built nearly 500 years ago for the Lord Mayor of London, Sir John Champneys. Its fine panelled Great Hall, with minstrels' gallery, is a favourite venue for music societies and chamber groups, and a lone lutenist serenades visitors most Monday afternoons. In the Austen gallery a local archaeology display runs until 25 January 2005, and regular art and photography exhibitions take place in the Chapel and Dashwood galleries. Half term art and craft activities cater for children aged from three, and the Easter and summer holidays see egg trails, garden festivals and open-air theatre productions, while Christmas is celebrated with merry workshops, craft fairs and carols.
Buggy access. Café. Garden centre. Nappy-changing facilities.

Woodlands Farm

331 Shooters Hill, Welling, Kent DA16 3RP (8319 8900/www.thewoodlandsfarmtrust.org). Falconwood rail/89, 486 bus. **Open** 10am-4pm daily. **Admission** free; donations appreciated.
Spread out over 89 acres (36ha) on the border of Greenwich and Bexley, Woodlands Farm is a bittersweet reminder of the rural way of life once enjoyed in this area. In 1995 the farm was nearly bulldozed to make way for a proposed East London crossing. Fortunately, the Farm Trust, with the help of Lottery money, came to the rescue. It bought the derelict farmhouse and surrounding field, and turned them into a thriving organic enterprise. There are some noisy geese, hens, a flock of sheep, a cow and some Shetland ponies. A core staff keeps the place ticking over, but volunteers are welcome to don their gumboots and help out. The farm hosts school tours, giving lessons on farm-animal care, conservation, composting and the history of farming. In a few years, the newly planted orchard – echoing the Kent of yore – will yield the sweet fruits of the farmers' labour.
Buggy access. Nearest picnic place: farm grounds. Shop.

South-west London

The villages are long gone, but you're spoilt for parks, farms and palaces.

Vauxhall & Stockwell

The name **Vauxhall** is said to have come about through the union of noblewoman Margaret de Redvers, who had a house in the area, with an unscrupulous soldier called Fulk le Breant. Fulk acquired the house, which came to be known as Fulk's Hall and ultimately Vauxhall. By the 18th-century, this corner of London had developed into a swanky location: its famous Pleasure Gardens were a favourite with the well-to-do, but today the pocket-sized Spring Park is a poor reminder of former glories. Opposite Spring Park you'll find **Vauxhall City Farm**, but for park life try Vauxhall Park (South Lambeth Road, at the junction with Fentiman Road, SW8, wth its tennis courts, a bowling green, a play area, a One O'Clock Club and a fenced ball-game area. Another green space is Bonnington Square's Pleasure Garden. Starting life as a play area during the 1970s, it subsequently lay neglected for years until local residents unearthed a secret garden. Vauxhall Bridge gives the children an eyeful of the 'Spies' Building'. It's the MI6 building, once the target of a missile attack from the Real IRA, and much enlivened by imagining James Bond flirting with Miss Moneypenny within.

Places for playing in are few and far between in **Stockwell**, although Slade Gardens (on Robsart Street) is well set up for kids with an adventure playground and play areas, and, over on Stockwell's west side, Larkhall Park (on Larkhall Rise) is a peaceful open space, with picnic areas, a café, two ball-game areas, tennis courts, a walled garden, a playground and nappy-changing facilities. Each park has its own One O'Clock Club. Stockwell Park skate park (*see p261*), at the start of Stockwell Road as you leave Brixton, is a star attraction for gangs of kids, especially in summer. It's in dire need of a refurb, however, and its future looks uncertain.

Vauxhall City Farm

24 St Oswald's Place, Tyers Street, SE11 5JE (7582 4204). Vauxhall tube/rail/2, 36, 44, 77, 360 bus. **Open** 10.30am-4pm Tue-Thur, Sat, Sun. **Admission** free; donations appreciated.
Urban bumpkins can breathe in the sweet smell of manure here in this farm project, created from a couple of acres of derelict land back in 1977. The farmyard inhabitants include pigs, donkeys, goats, chickens, rabbits and guinea pigs, all thriving under the adoring gaze of visiting children. Vauxhall City Farm runs workshops and special needs riding sessions. *Buggy access. Disabled: toilet. Nappy-changing facilities.*

Brixton

Once a marshy wasteland, **Brixton** came into its own in 1816 when Vauxhall Bridge improved access to central London. From then on it developed rapidly as a suburb. One of Brixton's main thoroughfares, Electric Avenue (immortalised in the song by Eddy Grant) is so-named because it was one of the first shopping streets in London to be lit by electricity. Now the capital of liberal Lambeth, and south London's busiest area, Brixton is best known for its nightlife, but families visiting during daylight hours can have fun exploring nearby Brockwell Park (*see p132*) or the terrific Brixton Market (*see p184*), bursting with everything from exotic fruit to cheap electrical goods. It's hard to believe that during its respectable heyday – between 1900 and 1915 – the sedate suburb of Brixton boasted a greyhound track and nine cinemas. The **Ritzy** (*see p217*) cinema is the only one left, but it does boast a cracking Kids Club every Saturday morning.

Streatham

There's not much left – save the waggish appellation 'St Reatham' that some jokers attach to the place – to suggest that **Streatham** was once a village in the midst of a rural landscape. Trains and automobiles put paid to all that, with today's seemingly infinite High Road frequently a traffic-clogged nightmare. But the area does have its attractions: Streatham Megabowl (*see p266*), the Streatham Ice Arena (*see p259*) and Playscape Pro Racing (*see p238*) are all big players in the birthday treat stakes. What's more, there are plans afoot to launch a weekend market in the area in 2004, which should raise its profile as a visitor destination a little.

Another plus point for Streatham is that it's been designated a conservation area, with green sites like Streatham Common and the gorgeous hidden treasure of the formal garden known as the Rookery proving excellent landmarks for children and families. Perhaps that explains why so many young families choose to settle here. Certainly, the vegetarian meals at Cicero's Café (2 Rookery Road, SW4 9DD, 7498 0770) pull in the crowds. Sat snugly on the tip of the common, the café is all warm-coloured walls, flowers and fairy lights inside, and the outside tables are popular with toddlers who can play with scattered toys in the gated yard.

Vauxhall City Farm. *See p136.*

Battersea

There's been a settlement in **Battersea** for more than 1,000 years, but any notions of isolation from the city were swallowed up during the Industrial Revolution. Now annexed to Wandsworth, Battersea stakes its claim to individuality with gems like the Battersea Arts Centre (*see p221*); **Battersea Park**, which contains the now reopened **Battersea Children's Zoo** and an adventure playground; and Sir Giles Gilbert Scott's Battersea Power Station. Built in 1933, it has been closed for the last two decades, but the countdown is now under way for the next phase in its development. Construction is set to start in 2004 on the redevelopment, but it will be 2008 before Battersea Power Station reopens as a leisure complex, with shops, restaurants, cafés, bars and even green areas. (In the meantime, a new 14-screen Cineworld cinema was opening opposite Sainsbury's on Garrett Lane as we went to press.) The other major source of attraction to the area for kids lies between Battersea Park and the power station: **Battersea Dogs' Home**.

Battersea Children's Zoo
Battersea Park, SW11 4NJ (8871 7540/ www.wandsworth.gov.uk). Sloane Square tube, then 19, 137 bus/Battersea Park or Queenstown Road rail/156, 345 bus. **Open** 10am-5pm daily (last admissions 30mins before closing). **Admission** £2.50; £1.50 2-16s, concessions; £8.50 family (2+3); free under-2s. **Map** p315 F13.

In 2003 it looked like the Children's Zoo had reached the end of the road, but it seems the popular site has had a reprieve. The early part of 2004 saw a bit of an ad hoc restart in terms of opening hours (it was weekends only up until April), but the zoo is now back to its daily routine and we're hopeful that the series of children's activities – animal handling sessions, pony rides, Easter egg trails, World Parrot Day, Barnardo's Toddler events – will carry on throughout the year. Regardless of activities, the children love the squirrel monkeys and inquisitive meerkats, not to mention the porcupine. There are domestic animals here as well, including goats and a donkey, and the zoo offers pony rides.
Buggy access. Café. Disabled access. Nappy-changing facilities. Shop.

Battersea Dogs' Home
4 Battersea Park Road, SW8 4AA (7622 3626/ www.dogshome.org). Vauxhall tube/rail, then 44 bus/Battersea Park or Queenstown Road rail/344 bus. **Open** *Viewings* 10.30am-4.15pm Mon-Wed, Fri; 10.30am-3.15pm Sat, Sun, bank hols. Closed 25, 26 Dec, 1 Jan, Good Friday. **Admission** £1; 50p 5-16s, concessions; free under-5s. **Credit** *Shop* MC, V.

Dog lovers young and old visit this famous rescue centre regularly. It's more than just a shelter for lost pups, with its souvenir shop, café and wall of brass plaques to commemorate long-gone canines and their owners. Staff are usually happy to answer questions, but families looking for a four-legged addition to the household are always obliged to visit several times. Indeed, even with more than 300 cats and dogs to choose from, the process of acquiring a pet is appropriately thorough: potential owners are vetted as carefully as the animals. Children might go all gooey-eyed for the cutest canine, but finding a suitable match can be harder than potential adopters might imagine. The centre also offers Behaviour Hotline talks in your home. Sessions include how to choose the right puppy (or kitten), teaching your pet new tricks and dealing with bad behaviour. Phone for further details, or download factsheets on adopting a pet from the website.
Buggy access. Café. Disabled access: lift, ramp, toilet. Nearest picnic place: Battersea Park. Shop.

Battersea Park
SW11 4NJ (8871 7530/www.wandsworth.gov.uk). Sloane Square tube, then 19, 137 bus/Battersea Park or Queenstown Road rail. **Open** 7am-dusk daily. **Map** p315 F13.

Battersea Park was laid out in high Victorian style – all lakes and carriageways, subtropical gardens and wide open spaces. In 1951 it was the site for the Festival of Britain Pleasure Gardens, a lighter alternative to all that high culture on the South Bank a couple of miles further up the Thames. But by the end of the 20th century was left was a sorry tale of decline: the Festival Fun Fair became rickety and sad looking (it was closed in 1974), the fountains ran dry, were patched up and promptly ran dry again. Yet hope springs eternal, even when fountains do not, and from 2003 the park has been undergoing major restoration.

For starters, Battersea Park is well equipped for active fun. The Battersea Park Millennium Arena (8871 7537) has an eight-lane running track, 19 floodlit tennis courts, a netball court, an all-weather sports pitch and a state-of-the-art fitness centre with sauna. Tennis coaching is available to anyone over eight, and the children's summer tennis camp takes place over two weeks in August every year. You can take a rowing boat out from the Scandinavian-style boating house on to the picturesque Victorian lake (£3.50/hr, May-Sept). Nearby, London Recumbents (7498 6543; *see also p256*) offers low-down and funky pedal power. Hire a bike, tandem, trike

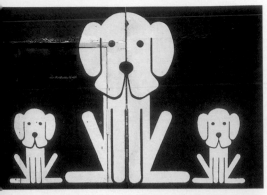

Battersea Dogs Home. *See p137.*

With two leisure pools and a wave machine it's small wonder the centre attracts legions of local children. It also offers junior activities, gathered under the brand name of the Fun House Club. Sessions include arts and crafts, a bouncy castle and competitions, many of them taking place during school holidays. There's a Playzone soft-play area too. *Buggy access. Café. Crèche. Disabled: ramps, lift, showers, toilets. Nappy-changing facilities. Nearest picnic place: Battersea Park.*

Clapham & Wandsworth

The pubs, bars and restaurants of modern **Clapham** are the big attraction nowadays, but the open grassed areas, tree-lined paths and little woods of Clapham Common are a better representation of the area's original character. It's a good spot for picnics, walking and cycling, as well as having three ponds, two with fishing areas. The expansive common existed way back in the Saxon era as grazing land and, although no one will be surprised to hear livestock are no longer fed here, eyebrows may be raised over the fact that the pasture was still in use in the early 20th century. The children will be more exhilarated by tales of the 17th-century highwaymen who made use of this patch. Most famous among them was cunning Robert Forrester, who found that wearing ladies' nighties worked for him on his mission to rob passing stagecoaches.

The area around **Wandsworth** and Clapham Common is known as 'Nappy Valley' – much to the annoyance of its residents – as it's generally considered one of the most desirable places in London to bring up a family. Accordingly, breezy Wandsworth Common adds to its ornamental areas, sports pitches, tennis courts, bowling areas and lake (you need membership for seasonal fishing) more child-focused activities like the **Nature Study Centre** and fabulous **Lady Allen Adventure Playground**. On Wandsworth borough's westerly reaches, across the railway tracks from the common, lies distant King George's Park, the **Kimber BMX/Adventure Playground** and the **Wandle Recreation Centre**. Both are a little off the beaten track, but they're worth travelling to if you're in charge of any two-wheel tearaways or a team of dedicated footie players.

Shopping in the Nappy Valley is terrific, thanks to **Northcote Road**, with its mixed bag of a market (Thur-Sat) that includes stalls for fresh bread, olives, cheese, herbs, plants, fruit and vegetables among its attractions. Other sources of childish fascination include the trendy little streetwear boutique known as Tomboy Kids (*see p200*). Don't miss the Hive Honey Shop (93 Northcote Road, SW11 6PL, 7924 6233, www.thehivehoneyshop.co.uk). Open 10am-5pm on weekdays and run by a beekeeper, the shop has an intriguing glass-walled hive at the back.

or banana bike for £5 and cruise the broad pathways for an hour. The chaps at London Recumbents also promise to teach you or the children to ride by their patent methods.

The Italian-styled, natch, Gondola al Parco café (7978 1677) has tables overlooking the boating lake for the indolent or exhausted. Tuesdays and Fridays have been jazz nights in recent years and, literal-minded as ever, the café owners added a Venetian gondola to the rowing fleet in 2002.

The south-west corner of the park has a large One O'Clock Club, toddlers' playground, play equipment for under-eights and adventure playground, one of London's biggest, for children aged eight to 15. Battersea's other famous landmark, the lofty Peace Pagoda, was built in 1985 by Japanese monks and nuns to commemorate Hiroshima Day. It stands proudly opposite the much loved Children's Zoo (*see p137*), in the centre of the park's northern edge. *Buggy access. Café. Disabled access: toilets. Nappy-changing facilities.*

Latchmere Leisure Centre

Latchmere Leisure Centre, Burns Road, SW11 2DY (7207 8004/www.kinetika.org). Vauxhall tube, then 44, 344 bus/Clapham Junction or Battersea Park rail/49, 319, 345 bus. **Open** 7am-10.30pm Mon-Thur; 7am-10pm Fri; 7am-8pm Sat; 7am-10pm Sun. *Crèche* 9.45-11.45am Mon-Fri. **Admission** 80p. *Crèche* £3.50.

Kimber BMX/Adventure Playground

King George's Park, Kimber Road, SW18 4NN (8870 2168). Earlsfield rail, then 44 or 270 bus. **Open** *Term-time* 3.30-7pm Tue-Fri; 11am-6pm Sat. *Holidays* 11am-6pm Mon-Sat.

Kimber has all the usual variously challenging platforms, ropes, tyres and ladders, big swings, little swings and monkey bars, plus the added attractions of a basketball court and a small BMX track. If you don't have your own bike to skid round on, you can usually hire one at the playground (though do phone ahead to check availability). For showery days there's also an indoor games room with table tennis, as well as kitchens and arts and crafts rooms.

Buggy access. Disabled access: ramp, toilet. Shop.

Lady Allen Adventure Playground

Chivalry Road, SW11 1HT (7228 0278/www.kids active.org.uk). Clapham Junction rail. **Open** *Term-time* 10am-5pm Tue; 3.30-5pm Wed-Thur; 10am-4pm Sat. *Holidays* 10am-4pm Mon-Fri.

On the north-west corner of Wandsworth Common, this well-designed playground lets children with special needs and disabilities swing, slide, climb ropes, dangle off monkey bars and generally muck about with their mates in a very safe, well-supervised environment. Children with disabilities can use this wonderful playground during all opening hours; non-disabled children are also admitted, but only at certain times (phone for details).

Disabled access: ramps, toilets.

Nature Study Centre

Wandsworth Common, Dorlcote Road, SW18 3RT (8871 3863/www.londonwildlifehospital.org). Wandsworth Common rail. **Open** 10am-dusk Sun; other times by appointment only. Check website hours during school hols. **Admission** free.

As we went to press, this study centre had just been taken over by charity London Wildcare. No need to worry: they plan to continue offering environmental arts and wildlife activities for children from the long-established wooden cabin on Wandsworth Common. There may even be cause for rejoicing: the centre should soon be able to offer more homes than ever for hedgehogs, rabbits and insects, especially the borough's populations of stag beetle.

Buggy access. Café. Shop.

Wandle Recreation Centre/Playzone

Mapleton Road, SW18 4DN (8871 1149/www.kinetika. org). Wandsworth Town rail/28, 44, 220, 270 bus. **Open** 7.30am-11pm Mon-Fri; 9am-8pm Sat; 9am-10pm Sun. *Crèche* 10am-noon Mon, Wed, Fri. **Admission** *Crèche* £2.90. **Credit** MC, V.

Along the banks of the Wandle and just outside the gates of King George Park, the Wandle has football pitches for local teams and also organises sports parties. The Kinetika fitness room is available for parents who need a workout, and just outside a padded room has been provided to oppress the kids – it's actually a play zone with full complement of climbing frames and sliding tubes, very popular with the under-eights.

Buggy access. Disabled: toilet. Nappy-changing facilities. Nearest picnic place: King George's Park.

Wandsworth Museum

The Courthouse, 11 Garratt Lane, SW18 4AQ (8871 7074/www.wandsworth.gov.uk). Clapham Junction, then 39, 77A, 156, 170, 337 bus/Wandsworth Town rail/ 28, 37, 44, 220, 270 bus. **Open** 10am-5pm Tue-Fri; 2-5pm Sat, Sun. Closed bank hols. **Admission** free. **Credit** *Shop* MC, V.

This tiny space has been lovingly preserved to offer temporary exhibitions throughout the year, as well as giving a history of Wandsworth from prehistoric times to the present

Magic Wandsworth

An original 1870 baker's handcart greets you at the entrance to the **Wandsworth Museum** (*see* p139), a remarkably child-friendly place where prehistoric to present-day highlights of the area's history are permanently or temporarily displayed.

The downstairs museum area is packed with all manner of objects. These range from an Iron Age sword and scabbard that was unearthed on the Thames foreshore at Wandsworth, cooking and farming tools from Wandsworth's Roman period, and swords, scabbards and sundry weaponry from the medieval villages of Batricesge (Battersea), Baelgeham (Balham), Puttenhythe (Putney), Totinge (Tooting) and Waendelesorde (Wandsworth). Interactive exhibits let children get hands on with an ancient flint hand-axe or a Roman helmet, or make a brass rubbing of a Putney knight. Potted histories giving the lowdown on Wandsworth life are displayed throughout, including the grim fact that Wandsworth succumbed to the plague 12 times between 1603 and 1666. There's also a small community gallery room that offers temporary exhibitions throughout the year, with displays for children usually taking place during the Easter and summer holidays.

The museum's own long history – it was, in a past life, a county court house – is just as interesting as the exhibits inside. The upstairs Education Centre was long ago used as a courtroom, so was the nearby exhibition room where today objects from the building's colourful past are displayed alongside an original judge's seat and ancient prison door from Wandsworth jail.

A favourite term-time trip for local schools and school holiday venue for families, the museum programmes year-round activities to suit all comers. These include storytelling for under-fives, as well as free craft sessions and workshops. Activities take place upstairs in the Education Centre – they're popular so you'd be well advised to book in advance. Creative sessions have included painting self-portraits using huge paper sheets and fun materials, as well as drop-in painting workshops – all providing plenty of excuses to make as much mess as possible. Storytelling sessions reveal the craft behind some of the monsters carved on Wandsworth's medieval churches, and workshops might involve making your own beasts and gargoyles out of clay or stained-glass window decorations.

day. Displays include an Ice Age fossil skull of a woolly rhino (found during the construction of Battersea Power Station), a model of Wandle mills, a World War II shelter and a Southfields chemist's shop. There is also an ample range of children's activities during both term-time and holidays (*see p139* **Magic Wandsworth**). The museum shop is good for gifts, cards and souvenirs.

Buggy access. Disabled access: toilet. Nappy-changing facilities. Nearest picnic place: King George's Park/ Old Burial Ground. Shop.

Tooting

As houses and flats in Clapham became too expensive for many people during the 1990s, Balham and neighbouring **Tooting** soaked up much of the overspill. Thanks to their resistance to wholesale gentrification, they may not be as pretty as their posher neighbour but they are more interesting. Their history goes back a good distance: Tooting High Street has been a thoroughfare since Roman times, once serving as the main road from Londinium to Regnum (Chichester).

Tooting Common (Tooting Bec Road, SW17) is a lovely wide open space with woods, tennis courts, ponds, football pitches and an athletics track. The common also offers the watery delights of Tooting Bec Lido (*see p283*), as well as the best under-eights playground for miles: it's not huge, but there are swings and wooden things to jump around on. Tooting is also home to a well-established Asian community, with October/November seeing the annual Diwali Festival of Light celebrated with a street party and lights strung along Tooting High Street and Upper Tooting Road. This also means there are several brilliant restaurants for South Asian food. Though their proprietors stop short of kiddie menus and balloons, babies and children are welcome; smaller portions are available on request.

Wimbledon

Best known for the two-week tennis celebrity fest that takes place every summer, there's a lot more to **Wimbledon** than June's unholy racket. It's a fine place to visit at any time of year. Tennis fans of all ages can have fun at the **Lawn Tennis Museum** even if they can't bag a ticket for the main event, but outdoorsy types are rewarded with all manner of sporting opportunities. One of London's best riding stables, Wimbledon Village Stables (*see p260*), really understands pony-mad children, and rambling, cycling, kite-flying, athletics and numerous team sports take place in the many parks and playgrounds all around the borough.

Wimbledon Common (look out for Wombles) is huge. It has nature trails, 16 miles (26 kilometres) of horse rides, cycle paths and sports grounds.

Whatever you choose to do, there's a rich selection of wildlife to look out for. The nature trail, which loops away from the windmill, is usually accessible to buggies – unless nature has decided to flood part of the trail. If that has happened, visit the **Windmill Museum** (Windmill Road, SW19 5NR, 8947 2825) instead and take a look at the small Robert Baden-Powell exhibition: the founder of the scout movement wrote *Scouting for Boys* here in 1908. Children can have a go at grinding grain to make flour as part of the weekend family activities. Elsewhere on the common there are no fewer than ten ponds, each one rich in water life, but the best (from a child's point of view) is **Seven Post Pond**, where a dipping platform lets you observe the creatures that lurk beneath the surface of the water without trampling their habitat.

Wimbledon's shopping centre, just near the rail and tube station, is clean, bright and family friendly. Special activities for children are often organised in the school holidays, and there's a crèche for parents who want to shop in peace. From the shopping centre, the main street (Wimbledon Broadway) takes you past the New Wimbledon Theatre, whose studio theatre regularly programmes children's productions. Further down toward South Wimbledon tube station is the much-loved Polka Theatre for Children, which has its own attractive café and small playground. It's a lovely place to pop into even if you're not seeing a show (*see also p224*), although we wouldn't want you to miss its consistently good productions for kids.

Deen City Farm

39 Windsor Avenue, SW19 2RR (8543 5300/ www.deencityfarm.co.uk). Colliers Wood tube, then 200 bus. **Open** 10am-4.30pm Tue-Sun. **Admission** free; donations welcome.

Here rarities – including Jacob sheep and a British White cow – join the more familiar pigs, goats, rabbits and fowl for petting (staff permitting). A tidy-sized community farm, Deen City works as an educational resource for all ages, with volunteer schemes for those who fancy getting their hands dirty. There's a riding school with facilities for the disabled. Children's activities include Young Farmer days for eight to 13s who can learn to feed, groom and clean out the animals. There are also Own a Pony Days and parent and toddler sessions with soft toys for under-fours.

Buggy access. Café. Disabled access: toilet. Nappy-changing facilities. Shop.

Tiger's Eye

42 Station Road, SW19 2LP (8543 1655). Colliers Wood or South Wimbledon tube. **Open** 10am-6pm Tue-Sun. **Closed** 25, 26 Dec, 1 Jan. **Admission** £4.50 2-10s; £2.25 under-2s. **Credit** MC, V.

The Tiger's Eye is an indoor playcentre for kids up to the age of ten. It's a vast barn of a place, so there's space to run. The soft play equipment includes stuff to climb on, slide down and bounce off. There's a height restriction of 1.44m (4ft 9in).

Buggy access. Café. Car park. Nappy-changing facilities. Nearest picnic place: Merton Abbey Park/Merton Park.

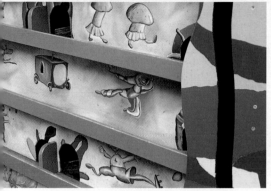

The ever-playful **Polka Theatre**. *See p140.*

Wimbledon Lawn Tennis Museum

Centre Court, All England Lawn Tennis Club, Church Road, SW19 5AE (8946 6131/www.wimbledon. org/museum). Southfields tube/39, 93, 200, 493 bus. **Open** 10.30am-5pm daily. Closed 24-26 Dec, 1 Jan. *During championships* spectators only. **Admission** £6; £5 concessions; £3.75 5-16s; free under-5s. **Credit** MC, V. What started off in the Victorian era as a mere pastime has, like many sports, now evolved into a million-dollar international business. The Wimbledon Lawn Tennis Museum, which originally opened in 1977, celebrates the glorious game by offering memorabilia from famous players, views of Centre Court and an education programme that puts on workshops, children's guided tours and educational visits. Café Centre Court, next to the museum, is open all year round. *See also p143* **A good sport**.
Buggy access. Café. Disabled access: lift, toilet. Nappychanging facilities. Shop.

Putney

Riverside **Putney** is the jewel in the crown around these parts. Familiar to millions as the starting point of the annual Varsity Boat Race, the river takes on a semi-rural aspect at Putney Bridge – looking back down the Thames you'll catch glimpses of London's skyline, but upstream the Putney treeline is pretty well all that the eye can see. Back from the river, and away from the busy high street, Putney is a peaceful, affluent spot. For a bit of the great outdoors, there

are a few options. Putney Heath is the eastern edge of the huge piece of common land (three times the size of Hampstead Heath, *see p95*) that eventually peters out where Wimbledon Common joins Richmond Park, but there are no areas set aside for children's play. Infinitely tamer – but with more for the kids – are King George's Park and Leaders Gardens at the end of Asilone Road. This dainty little riverside park is a delight for all the family, with two play areas and tennis courts.

Barnes, Mortlake & East Sheen

These are also pleasant residential areas, steeped in stately history and swathed in parks, commons and open spaces. The Varsity Boat Race traditionally finishes in Mortlake, and illustrious former inhabitants of these parts include former prime minister Earl Grey, composer Gustav Holst and writer Henry Fielding. Hints of a more reckless kind of fame can be found near Barnes Common, in the form of Marc Bolan's flower-bedecked memorial. The Mini he was travelling in hit a sycamore tree here on 16 September 1977, killing the young rock star. Of most interest to visiting families, however, is the award-winning **WWT Wetland Centre**, which makes a fantastic day out for twitchers and casual nature lovers alike.

East Sheen Common Nature Trail

East Sheen Common, Fife Road, SW14 (Ranger 8876 2382/Borough Ecology Officer 8831 6125). Hammersmith tube, then 33 bus/Mortlake rail, then 15min walk. **Open** dawn-dusk daily. **Admission** free.

Toads, frogs and diving beetles can all be found in the ponds of East Sheen Common, which is owned and managed by the National Trust. The small nature trail has 13 areas, marked with orange posts, that are split between woodlands, ponds and streams. Nature activities take place from time to time, helping all ages to learn about traditional woodland activities, and they don't cost a penny.

Buggy access. Disabled access.

WWT Wetland Centre

Queen Elizabeth's Walk, SW13 9WT (8409 4400/ www.wwt.org.uk). Hammersmith tube, then 33, 72, 209 (alight at Red Lion pub) or 283 (Duck Bus direct to Centre) bus. **Open** *Summer* 9.30am-6pm daily. *Winter* 9.30am-5pm daily. Last entry 1hr before closing. Closed 25 Dec. *Tours* 11am, 2.30pm daily. *Feeding tours* noon, 3.30pm daily. **Admission** £6.75; £5.50 concessions; £4 4-16s; £17.50 family (2+2); free under-4s. *Tours* free. *Feeding tours* free. **Credit** MC, V.

One of nine Wetland visitor centres, this London site opened in 2000 and had already notched up a Site of Special Scientific Interest award only two years later. Just 4 miles (6.5km) from central London, it has a bumper 42 hectares (105 acres) of specially created wetland where visitors can see rare or threatened wildlife, like the Hawaiian Goose, White-headed Duck, Red-breasted Goose and Blue Duck. The centre is divided into a permanent section, where the exotic and endangered waterfowl are given appropriate (notwithstanding the English weather) habitats to play in, and the open water lakes, reedbeds and mudflats that attract scores of insects and hence flocks migratory of birds – large numbers of lapwings were wheeling around the place when we last visited, as well as a woodpecker who'd clearly gone a bit astray.

If the weather's atrocious, it's possible to view parts of the reserve from indoors through CCTV cameras, but it's best to get outside with the binoculars (which can be rented here) and head for one of the three strategically placed hides. Young children might find it hard to keep quiet within the hides, and they won't be popular if they scare away their fellow birdwatchers within and wild birds without – so they're probably best sticking to the permanent habitats (watch out for the prehistoric-looking Magpie Geese) or joining one of the centre's impressively informed guides for a tour. The centre has a nice café, and it runs activities, like the Big Batty Walks or arts and crafts events.

Buggy access. Café. Car park. Disabled access: lifts, toilet. Nappy-changing facilities. Shop.

Richmond & Kew

Richmond, once known as Shene, was the seat of kings during the 12th century, when Henry I lived at Sheen Palace on the south-west corner of what is now Richmond Green. Edward III had a riverside palace here in the mid 1300s and Henry VII built Richmond Palace in 1501. There are few royal connections these days (though many famous folk live hereabouts), but this most royal of boroughs still retains enough attractions to make it a pleasure park for little princes and princesses.

Extensive Richmond Park is supreme ruler of local pleasures. Eight miles (13 kilometres) across at its widest point, it's the biggest city park in Europe and rivalled only by Epping Forest (*see p119*) as the nearest London gets to wild countryside. Picturesque herds of red and fallow deer roam freely, a source of much fascination to children, but do bear in mind that these seemingly shy and gentle wild animals can be fierce in autumn during the rutting season (that means paying heed to the signs that warn you not to get too close).

A great way to see the park is by bike: a well-kept cycle path rings the perimeter. If it's too much hassle to bring your own, hire as many bicycles as you need from Richmond Park Cycle Hire (07050 209249) at Roehampton Gate. Adult bikes with tag-alongs (for the over-fives) and child-seats are available, as are children's bikes for those who have already learnt how to ride without stabilisers.

Tucked away in the middle of the park is Isabella Plantation, a secluded and tranquil woodland garden. It's primarily home to acid-loving plants such as rhododendrons, azaleas and camelias, and is best seen in all its fabulous flowering glory in early summer or in late September, when it blazes with autumn colour. Criss-crossed with streams and ponds, stepping stones and wooden bridges make it fun walking for children. There are also plenty of benches and grassy glades where you can picnic.

While you're here, take a moment to stroll to King Henry VIII's Mound. Follow the twisting path up this leafy hillock and, from the top, you'll have a spectacular view right across London. On a clear day the London Eye and St Paul's Cathedral can easily be made out. Alternatively, you could stroll along Terrace Walk, a famous Victorian promenade that stretches all the way from the philosopher Bertrand Russell's childhood home, Pembroke Lodge (now a café, so a great place for lunch for the picnicless, *see p180*), and beyond the park to Richmond Hill, continuing the wonderful views of west London and beyond.

Museum of Richmond

Old Town Hall, Whittaker Avenue, Richmond, Surrey TW9 1TP (8332 1141/www.museumofrichmond.com). Richmond tube/rail. **Open** *May-Sept* 11am-5pm Tue-Sat; 1-4pm Sun. *Nov-Apr* 11am-5pm Tue-Sat. Closed 25, 26 Dec, 1 Jan. **Admission** free.

With so many royal connections, it's only fitting that Richmond should have a museum that loyally parades its regal history, detailing the lives of silver-spooned former residents from Henry I in the 12th century to Elizabeth I in the 16th century. There are permanent and temporary displays, and the museum's programme of children's activities include workshops for pre-schoolers. Harry the Herald's Saturday Club, for five- to 11-year-olds, takes place on the third Saturday of every month.

Buggy access. Disabled access: lift, toilets. Nearest picnic place: Richmond Green, riverside. Shop.

National Archives

*Kew, Richmond, Surrey TW9 4DU (8876 3444/
www.pro.gov.uk/education). Kew Gardens tube, then
10mins walk/65, 391 bus, then 5min walk.* **Open** 9am-
5pm Mon, Wed, Fri; 10am-7pm Tue; 9am-7pm Thur;
9.30am-5pm Sat. **Tours** 11pm, 2pm Sat (booking
necessary). **Admission** free. *Tours* free.

What was once known as the Public Record Office is now the
National Archives. Having been devoted to keeping the
records of 1,000 years of central government and the law
courts, the Archives have, unsurprisingly, a fascinating
Education and Visitor Centre. More surprising is its accessibility to families and children. The museum spans British history from the Domesday book to the Festival of Britain, and
there's an engaging online 'Secret and Spies' exhibition detailing the history of British espionage. The millions of historical documents here go back as far as the Norman Conquest,
some of them relating to the lives of everyday people.
*Buggy access. Café. Disabled access: lifts, toilet. Nappy-
changing facilities. Nearest picnic place: National Archives
grounds. Shop.*

Royal Botanic Gardens
(Kew Gardens)

*Richmond, Surrey TW9 3AB (switchboard 8332 5000/
info 8332 5655/www.kew.org.uk). Kew Gardens
tube/rail/Kew Bridge rail/riverboat to Kew Pier.* **Open**
Feb, Mar 9.30am-5.30pm daily. *Apr-Sept* 9.30am-6.30pm
Mon-Fri; 9.30am-7.30pm Sat, Sun. *Oct-Jan* 9.30am-4.15pm
daily. **Admission** (LP) £8.50; £6 concessions; free under-
16s. **Credit** AmEx, DC, MC, V.

The magnificent 300 acres (120 hectares) of Kew Gardens are
split into 47 areas, each of which are designed to provide two
or three hours of interest. That means it's usually best to take
some care over selecting your visiting areas, although
wandering from one beautifully composed garden to
another is, of course, a pleasure in itself.

The monuments, gardens, buildings and landscapes are
divided into eight zones. Most visitors start at the Entrance
Zone, which has the Broad Walk, Nash conservatory and the
Orangery, which now operates as an elegant café/restaurant.
This leads to the Pagoda Vista Zone, with the glorious
Japanese Gateway taking you to the serene gardens of Peace,
Activity and Harmony. Perhaps most popular of all is the
Palm House Zone. The famous glass-constructed building,
(designed by Decimus Burton and Richard Taylor in 1848)
has spectacular and enormous exotic plants from Africa, Asia
and America, and a series of spiral staircases that lets you
view them all from the gallery. The Palm House has its
resident record breakers in the form of the oldest pot plant in
the world and the tallest palm under glass. You can also enjoy
the prospect from Syon Vista Zone – dominated by an
artificial lake and providing views to Syon House (*see p154*)
across the Thames – or the Western Zone, which was once
part of Richmond Gardens and now has a bamboo garden
and traditional Japanese Minka House (used for workshops,
displays and events). The Riverside Zone runs alongside the
Thames. It contains the Dutch House (Kew Palace), as well
as the 17th-century-style Queen's Garden.

There are cafés, restaurants and snack areas dotted
throughout Kew Gardens, but on a fine day it's well worth
bringing your own food and picnicking in the gardens or
beside the ten-storey Pagoda, built in 1762 (unfortunately, it's
closed to the public, but that doesn't stop you looking from
the outside). An treetop walkway just to the west of here gives
you stunning views of the forest canopy.
*Buggy access. Cafés. Disabled access: ramps, toilets.
Nappy-changing facilities. Nearest picnic place: grounds.
Restaurants. Shop.*

A good sport

During Wimbledon's world famous lawn tennis
tournament, Centre Court has been graced over
the years by such skilful racket-wielders as Goran
Ivanisevic, sisters Serena and Venus Williams,
John McEnroe, Martina Navràtilovà, Andre Agassi…
frankly, all the game's greats. What better place,
then, to construct a museum dedicated to the
sport, with year round activities for all ages?

The Lawn Tennis Championships started life
here in 1877, with just a few hundred people
showing up to watch. A hundred years later, the
museum (*see p141*) was opened by the Duke of
Kent as part of the Centenary celebrations.
Champions that year were six-times winner Bjorn
Borg and Britain's Virginia Wade, who picked up
her trophy from the Queen – and has had 25 years
to celebrate being the most recent Brit to win it.

Since 1977 the growing and eclectic collection of
artefacts here has come to include memorabilia
such as Victorian flannels, racket presses and tea
sets, trophies from former champions, even 'I love
Wimbledon' T-shirts and stickers. There are also
videos of matches, an art gallery and an area
displaying the changing styles of women's tennis
gear since the game first began. Of course, the
numbers of visitors to the museum increase hugely
in the run-up to and during the Championships
(the date changes from year to year – but it's
always held six weeks before the first Monday
in August), but throughout the year there's more
than enough to see and do. School groups are
particularly well catered for, with the museum's
Education Unit running classroom activities and
workshops for childrenup to the age of 11, as
well as presiding over a developing programme
for secondary school or college-based visitors.
Family activities happen throughout the year; 2004
looks busy, with a number of crafts and drama
workshops, and in October the Big Draw ceramics
and painting event (part of the national Campaign
for Drawing; check the website for details).

There is another good reason to visit Wimbledon.
You can take a tour of the whole jolly complex,
including Court 1, the players' boards and the
hallowed Centre Court. Along the way your guide
explains how the astonishingly perfect grass
courts are kept pristine by dedicated groundstaff
who hand-weed and mow it to an eighth of an inch
in height, before lovingly rolling it in two directions
to give the players the splendidly solid bounce
they require. Small wonder the Back Lawn Tennis
Championships never caught on.

Further south-west

The pretty southern reaches of the river towards well-to-do **Twickenham** are lovely spots to ride a bike around, and there's the Thames Path for walkers. The area has a number of gracious historic buildings. Overlooking the river from Marble Hill Park, **Marble Hill House** is the perfect Palladian villa. Neighbouring Orleans House (Riverside, Twickenham, 8892 0221; *see also p213*) was built in 1710 for James Johnston, William III's secretary of state for Scotland, but later home to the exiled Duke of Orléans – hence the name. **Ham House** is another favourite: a handsome, red-brick, riverside mansion with a beautiful garden. Carrying on along the river past Twickenham, you'll eventually come to the **Museum of Rugby**.

From Twickers, the river passes the busy shopping centre of Kingston-upon-Thames, then curves around to **Hampton Court Palace**. Once the country seat of Cardinal Wolsey, the palace was taken over by Henry VIII who liked it so much he spent three honeymoons here.

Ham House

Ham Street, Ham, Richmond, Surrey TW10 7RS (8940 1950/www.nationaltrust.org.uk). Richmond tube/rail, then 371 bus. **Open** *House* late Mar-Oct 1-5pm Mon-Wed, Sat, Sun. *Gardens* 11am-6pm or dusk Mon-Wed, Sat, Sun. Closed 25, 26 Dec, 1 Jan. **Tours** (pre-booking essential) Wed. Phone for membership details & prices. **Admission** (NT) *House & gardens* £7; £3.50 5-15s; £17.50 family (2+3); free under-5s. *Gardens only* £3; £1.50 5-15s; £7.50 family (2+3); free under-5s. **Credit** AmEx, MC, V.
If you like snooping around other people's houses, there aren't many to better this riverside mansion, home to the Duke and Duchess of Lauderdale in the late 17th century. Built in 1610, it was occupied by the same family until 1948. Today the lavish interiors have original furniture, paintings and textiles. The grounds include the Cherry Garden with a central statue of Bacchus, the South Garden and the maze-like Wilderness. There's also an Orangery with a terrace café.

Children can take part in events ranging from Easter egg trails to craft workshops and music in the garden. The house itself is said to be haunted by the 17th-century duchess and a few other spirits, so it's always best to make sure you wipe your feet before entering.
Café (high chairs). Disabled access: lift, toilets. Nappy-changing facilities. Shop.

Hampton Court Palace

East Molesey, Surrey KT8 9AU (0870 751 5175/info 0870 752 7777/www.hrp.org.uk). Hampton Court rail/riverboat from Westminster or Richmond to Hampton Court Pier (Apr-Oct). **Open** *Palace* Apr-Oct 10.15am-6pm Mon; 9.30am-6pm Tue-Sun. Nov-Mar 10.15am-4.30pm Mon; 9.30am-4.30pm Tue-Sun. Last entry 45mins before closing. *Park* dawn-dusk daily. **Admission** *Palace, courtyard, cloister & maze* £11.80; £8.70 concessions; £7.70 5-15s; £35 family (2+3); free under-5s. *Gardens only* £4; £3 concessions; £2.50 5-16s; £12 family; free under-5s. *Maze only* £3.50; £2.50 5-15s. **Credit** AmEx, MC, V.
Surely the greatest of the historic royal palaces, Hampton Court's 500 years of history spans its creation in 1514 and

Henry VIII's notorious repo job in 1525 all the way through the 1986 fire in the King's Apartments. All is detailed in the palace's permanent exhibition and, once inside, you'll be awed by the grandiose State Apartments. They include the Georgian Rooms, preserved to look as they were in 1737; Henry VIII's apartments; the Queen's state apartments; the public dining room, with its huge marble fireplace; and the extensive Tudor Kitchens, which are set up as if in the middle of putting together the feast of John the Baptist in 1442. With over 60 acres (24 ha) of riverside gardens (including the famous maze with half a mile of paths), a series of courtyards and cloisters, costumed guides offering free palace tours, and daily events throughout the year, all ages are spoilt for choice. The events range from children's workshops to the Hampton Court Palace Music Festival, which takes place every June and the Hampton Court Flower Show (6-11 July 2004).

If all this splendour and activity gives you a bit of an appetite, the Privy Kitchen Coffee Shop is on hand for tea, coffee or a light lunch. Children's menus, snacks and sandwiches are available in the Tiltyard Café, which is in the palace gardens, or you can picnic in designated areas inside the palace or outside at picnic tables in the popular 20th-Century Garden.
Buggy access. Café. Car park. Disabled access: lift, toilets. Nappy-changing facilities. Nearest picnic place: palace gardens. Shop.

Marble Hill House

Twickenham Road, Middx TW1 2NL (8892 5115/ www.english-heritage.org.uk). Richmond tube/rail/33, 90, 290, H22, R70 bus. **Open** *Apr-Oct* 10am-2pm Sat; 10am-5pm Sun. Closed Nov-Mar. **Tours** by prior arrangement. **Admission** (EH, LP) £3.70; £2.80 concessions; £1.90 5-15s; free under-5s. **Credit** MC, V.
This is a beautiful Thameside villa that was once the home to Henrietta Howard, the mistress of King George II. Filled with original objects and paintings from the Georgian period, Marble Hill House also hosts events throughout the year that include Easter trails, house tours, craft workshops and open-air concerts. The house is surrounded by 66 acres (27 ha) of parkland, but if that's not enough the house is connected by ferry to Ham House just across the river.
Café (in park). Nearest picnic place: Marble Hill Park. Shop.

Museum of Rugby/ Twickenham Stadium

Twickenham Stadium, Rugby Road, Twickenham, Middx TW1 1DZ (8892 8877/www.rfu.com/microsites/museum). Hounslow East tube, then 281 bus/Twickenham rail. **Open** *Museum* 10am-5pm Tue-Sat; 11am-5pm Sun. Last entry 30mins before closing. **Tours** 10.30am, noon, 1.30pm, 3pm Tue-Sat; 1pm, 3pm Sun. Closed 24-26 Dec, 1 Jan, Easter Sun, Sun after match days. **Admission** *Combined ticket* £8; £5 concessions; £25 family. Advance booking advisable. **Credit** MC, V.
Since England's 2003 World Cup Rugby spectacular, there's been even more interest that usual in this already popular museum and sports venue. Non-match days see tours of the stadium, during which visitors can walk down the players' tunnel, look at the England dressing room and drop in on the Members Lounge, the Presidents Suite and the Royal Box. In the museum you can watch international footage of some of the greatest tries of all time or peruse artwork and rugby memorabilia dating all the way back to 1871. Temporary exhibitions change every six months or so.
Buggy access. Disabled access: toilet. Nappy-changing facilities. Restaurant. Shop.

Hampton Court Palace. *See p144.*

West London

Flutter by westerly through cool urban enclaves and balmier pastures with butterflies and bunnies.

Paddington & Bayswater

As 18th-century London extended westward, **Bayswater** was the obvious next choice for development into a posh new suburb. The only thing preventing the transformation was the shadow of the gallows of Tyburn. (The spot where the gallows stood is marked by a plaque on the ground at the junction of Bayswater Road and Edgware Road.) Huge and raucous crowds attended the public hangings, and a multitude of inns and street attractions lined Bayswater to serve them. So the trustees of the Bishop of London's Estate, owners of this prime stretch of land, had to bide their time until the last public hanging in 1763.

The eventual gentrification of Bayswater was the spur to development further west into the farmlands at **Paddington**. Unlike Bayswater, Paddington never really gained the suburban respectability that was envisaged and, with the arrival of the station, it became home to a large transient population. In the 1950s the area became a byword for overcrowding, poverty and vice. Yet now Paddington is back on the map, halfway through an ambitious regeneration project that is throwing new office blocks up along the canal like a mini-Docklands.

Nearby **Queensway** is named after the young Queen Victoria, who used to ride her horse down this road from Kensington Palace (see p87). The only real stop for kids here is Queens, the ten-pin bowling alley (see p270) and London's most famous ice rink, which now goes under the name of Leisurebox (see p260). Especially popular with young teens, both these attractions are busy at the weekends. Further down, where Queensway merges with Bayswater, **Whiteley's** shopping centre is popular with families. Special activities are laid on for kids in the foyer during half-term and holidays (check the website for details), with one of the regulars being Jumpzone – youngsters are strapped into a harness attached to elastic and bounced up as high as the first floor. Don't try that at home. The second floor has an eight-screen cinema and any number of child-friendly restaurants. There are loads of toyshops, and Gymboree (0800 092 0911) – purveyor of dance, music and all-round enjoyment to the under-fives – is an infant magnet.

Alexander Fleming Laboratory Museum

St Mary's Hospital, Praed Street, W2 1NY (7725 6528/www.st-marys.org.uk/about/fleming_museum). Paddington tube/rail/7, 15, 27, 36 bus. **Open** 10am-1pm Mon-Thur. *By appointment* 2-5pm Mon-Thur; 10am-5pm Fri. Closed 24 Dec-1 Jan, bank hols. **Admission** (LP) £2; £1 concessions, children. **No credit cards. Map** p313 D5.
Alexander Fleming made his momentous chance discovery of penicillin in this very room on 3 September 1928, when a Petri dish of bacteria became contaminated with some kind of mysterious mould. Fleming's laboratory has now been recreated, and displays and a video offer insights into both his life and the role of penicillin in fighting disease. The staff run special tours for family and school groups, and other visitors get a guided tour as part of the entrance fee. *Nearest picnic place: Hyde Park.* Shop.

Maida Vale, Kilburn & Queen's Park

Maida Vale is a sedate residential area, with little in the way of dedicated children's activities. It's an attractive district, characterised by white stucco houses, some perched romantically along the edge of the canal, but the only interest for visitors is the large, well-established houseboat community at Little Venice. Visit for the festival during the May Day bank holiday (see p32). The Puppet Theatre Barge (see p218), moored here during the winter, is another must-visit as far as the children are concerned. Next to Little Venice is a pretty park full of flowers, which is perfect for a summer picnic.

Walking along the canal from Little Venice to Camden is a popular family stroll. It takes about 45 minutes, passing London Zoo (see p66) on the right, with the Lord Snowdon Aviary to the left. If that's too far for little feet, the London Waterbus ticket office (Blomfield Road, W9) will get you on to a boat to the zoo or Camden Lock (see p91).

The best green space in the area is Paddington Recreation Ground, where Roger Bannister trained for his four-minute mile 50 years ago. Today's athletes have a proper running track to train on, and there are five-a-side football pitches, cricket nets and basketball courts. Play areas to suit all ages and a decent café make this a popular spot that buzzes with activity at the weekends. **Queen's Park** is run by the ever-efficient and impressively wealthy Corporation of London; it's well kept and a treat to visit with young children. Nearby **Kilburn**

Lisboa Patisserie, **Golborne Road**.

gets packed with families shopping at weekends. For children, the deservedly popular Tricycle Cinema & Theatre (*see p213*) is the area's saving grace; their café is a good place to revive flagging enthusiasm.

Queen's Park
Kingswood Avenue, NW6 6SG (park manager 8969 5661). Queen's Park tube/rail. **Open** 7.30am-dusk daily. **Admission** free.

Within 6 acres (2.5ha), Queen's Park has everything a park should have. There's a playground with an adjacent paddling pool (open in summer) and a small enclosure of goats, ducks and chickens, as well as rotund guinea pigs and rabbits that keep small children busy for ages. At the northern end of the park is a wild, overgrown area with a nature trail signposted with pictures of the mini-beasts you are likely to find there. There's a decent café, popular for alfresco eating, that keeps hunger pangs at bay, and active bodies can enjoy the pitch-and-putt area and six tennis courts. Occasional performances at the bandstand lend the place a carnival atmosphere in the summer months.

Buggy access. Café. Disabled access: toilet. Nappy-changing facilities.

Notting Hill

Notting Hill is now firmly established as a starry media playground, with only the well-heeled able to afford those characteristic white stuccoed buildings that took over the previously rural area – inhabited

mainly by pigs and cattle – in the early and mid 1800s. By the 1950s the area's fortunes had dipped, with racial tension flaring up between sectors of the white, working-class population and West Indian immigrants who moved in alongside them. What with poverty and the race riots, the streets around Notting Hill were considered dodgy for years, until the mid 1980s when the yuppies moved in.

Every August bank holiday for the last four decades the area has exploded with revelry for the world-famous Notting Hill Carnival (for details, *see p27*). At the southernmost end of Notting Hill is the Gate cinema (7727 4043), which has a Saturday kids' club with pre-show activities; the Electric Cinema (*see p216*) holds parent and baby screenings.

As well as the carnival, Notting Hill is famous for Portobello Road Market (*see p187*). One of the most popular street markets in the world, it starts off as an antiques market then gradually morphs into a fashion fair as it nears the Westway. It's best on Saturdays. The northern end where the market crosses Golborne Road is full of bric-a-brac, but there are lots of interesting cafés here where the trendy Portobello mums hang out. Just off Portobello Road, on Powis Square, young performers can join one of the numerous clubs run by the **Tabernacle**, and crafty kids can practise their skills at Art 4 Fun

Queen's Park.
See p146.

(*see p231*). Most Notting Hill parents needing a bit of fresh air will make a beeline for Kensington Gardens (*see p86*), but there are many smaller parks and city gardens dotted around the area. Avondale Park (Walmer Road) is one of the nicest, with a country feel and a small playground and football pitch; just off Kensal Road, at the northern end of Notting Hill, is another nice little park, albeit one with an unwieldy name: the **Emslie Horniman Pleasance Gardens**. Sadly, only children who live or go to school in the borough are allowed into the playground (Southern Row, W10 5BJ, 8969 5740). Once you reach Ladbroke Grove, there are many other excellent resources for youngsters. If your children aspire to a life behind the camera, check out YCTV (77 Barlby Road, W10 6AZ, 8964 4646), which provides training in camera, sound, editing and lighting for 11- to 20-year-olds.

The **Westway** is one of the less attractive landmarks of the area. This stretch of the A40 used to cast a rather grim shadow in its wake as it brutally sliced through the neighbourhood, but now the gloomy area beneath it has been successfully transformed into an extended children's zone. PlayStation Skate Park (*see p264*) has ramps for all levels and lessons for greenbacks. Further up, by Latimer Road, is the Westway Sports Centre (*see p256*), which has the highest climbing wall in the country. Just past the centre is Westway Stables, which organises rides in nearby Wormwood Scrubs,

a large green space more famous for its prison. Right next to Latimer Road tube station is Bramley's Big Adventure (*see p251*), the ever-popular play palace for youngsters up to 11 years old. A similar facility, Bumper's Back Yard, can be found at nearby Kensington Leisure Centre (Walmer Road, W11 4PQ, 7727 9747); it also has tubular slides for whizzing down into the pool (summer only). More adventurous water sports are the business of the **Canalside Activity Centre**.

Canalside Activity Centre
The Boat House, Canal Close, W10 5AY (8968 4500). Ladbroke Grove tube or Kensal Rise rail/52, 70, 295 bus. **Open** *Enquiries & bookings* 10am-5pm Mon-Fri; 10am-4pm Sat. Closed mid Dec-mid Jan, bank hols. **Admission** *Classes & sessions* members free; non-members from £4. *Membership* £60-£120/yr. **No credit cards.**
Canalside is an unpretentious urban watersports centre, open to families, carers and children. It aims to promote health and education through learning to row, canoe and be safe in the water. Qualified instructors run the courses and lessons. *Buggy access. Disabled access: lift, toilets. Nearest picnic place: Centre courtyard.*

The Tabernacle
Powis Square, W11 2AY (7565 7890/7800/www.tabernacle.org.uk). Ladbroke Grove or Westbourne Park tube/ 7, 23, 31, 52 bus. **Open** 8.30am-10.30pm daily; ring for details of late evening activities. **Admission** depends on activity; phone for details. **Credit** MC, V. **Map** p312 A6.
The community centre in this converted church has a packed programme of family events. There are parent and baby fitness sessions, Tiny Tots dance and music classes, and a

Holland Park

*Ilchester Place, W8 6LU (7471 9813/www.rbkc.gov.uk).
Holland Park tube/9, 27, 28, 49 bus.* **Open** 7.30am-dusk
daily. **Map** p314 A9.

Holland Park is a slice of countryside plonked in the city. A
series of paths through wild forested areas takes you past the
imperious peacocks and plenty of squirrels and rabbits. The
well-equipped Ecology Centre (7471 9809) provides site maps,
plus nets for pond dipping and information on local wildlife.
There's also a smart Italian park café, with modern glass
walls. Children can choose from a please-all menu that
includes pizza and pasta. The remains of Holland House
(it suffered irreparable damage from German bombers
during a World War II raid) are at the centre of the park, its
murals and fountains making it a lovely spot to sit. The
house's restored east wing contains the most dramatically
sited youth hostel in town, though one without family rooms,
sadly. It also provides the backdrop for the open-air theatre,
whose summer programme of opera and Shakespeare is
popular for family outings (see the website for details).

The pond of Koi carp in the Japanese Garden will entertain
the kids for a while, but there's also a noticeably well-to-do
One O'Clock Club at the other end of the park; next door, a
well-equipped adventure playground keeps the over-fives
entertained. Perhaps of most interest to youngsters is
Whippersnappers (7738 6633/whippersnappers@ukonline.
co.uk) who put on weekly musical and puppet workshops.
Buggy access. Café. Nappy-changing facilities. Restaurant.

Linley Sambourne House

*18 Stafford Terrace, W8 7BH (7602 3316 ext 305 Mon-
Fri/07976 060160 Sat, Sun/www.rbkc.gov.uk/linley
sambournehouse). High Street Kensington tube.* **Tours**
10am, 11.15am, 1pm, 2.15pm, 3.30pm Sat, Sun (with the
curator). Maximum of 12 on each tour. **Admission** £6;
£4 concessions; £1 under-18s. **Map** p314 A9.

Edward Linley Sambourne was a Victorian cartoonist, famous
for his work in *Punch*. His house, which contains almost all
the original fittings and furniture, can only be visited in
the context of the terrific tours. The first tour is by a conventional guide, but the others are each guided by a costumed actor
(*see p150* **Tales from... a Victorian house**). On Sundays
holders of a Kensington and Chelsea library card are
admitted free if they make an advance booking.

Earl's Court & Fulham

Earl's Court has long been associated with
entertainment and its huge exhibition centre is
its best-known landmark. It was built in 1887,
and hosted Buffalo Bill's Wild West Show in 1891.
Nowadays the centre is used mainly for conferences
and consumer exhibitions, such as the annual Boat
Show and the Ideal Home Exhibition.

In the post-war years, the area surrounding Earl's
Court went into decline and large houses previously
owned by wealthy Victorians were gradually
converted into flats for poorer residents. In the
1960s and '70s the area became known as 'Kangaroo
Valley', as Australian and New Zealand travellers
descended in search of cheap accommodation. The
area is still full of bedsits and hostels, and there's
a dearth of open spaces (the nearest is Brompton
Cemetery – a last resort in more ways than one).

community education breakdancing project for young
and old. Youngsters who want to take part in the carnival
can join a steel-pan class here, as well. Music technology and
new-media classes are popular, and the 8am yoga classes
attract all ages.
*Buggy access. Café. Disabled access: toilets. Nappy-
changing facilities.*

Holland Park

In Holland Park there's a marked ratcheting up of
gentility. While Notting Hill still has a bohemian air,
with independent mums shoving their three-wheeler
buggies around, people who can afford the beautiful
mansion houses in Holland Park are more likely to
have traditional navy perambulators, uniformed
nannies and chauffeur-driven cars. The area's name
comes from Holland House, the remains of which are
in the park. Duels took place in meadows to the west
and when Cromwell was a visitor he used the
gardens to talk with his general so as to avoid
eavesdroppers at the house.

There are several other interesting buildings
around the park. **Leighton House** (12 Holland
Park Road, W14 8LZ, 7602 3316) is worth an
ogle to get a sense of the grandeur of its former
inhabitant Lord Leighton, but nearby **Linley
Sambourne House** demands a visit from anyone
interested in Victoriana. If you are looking for
refreshment hereabouts, your best bet is to take a
short walk to Notting Hill or Kensington High Street.

Around Town

Tales from... a Victorian house

At 18 Stafford Terrace (*see p149*), the daily life of eccentric cartoonist Edward **Linley Sambourne** and his family is faithfully recreated by actor guides. Marion, the lady of the house, her son Roy and housekeeper Mrs Reffle all lead tours round their former home, chatting to the visitors as if they are expected guests. Each of them provides a lively introduction to the Victorian era, which, of course, is a Key Stage 2 essential, but Mrs Reffle is the guide of choice for kids.

After a short slide show, the children are introduced to Mrs R, a gossipy character who steers her young visitors round the house as she dispenses an account of the family's life. Being a servant she can be very informal, making lots of jokes and cheeky asides, whereas other family members are a little aloofThe part is played so convincingly that, without realising it, the youngsters find themselves participants in a wonderful piece of improvised theatre. Younger members of the tour groups have been known to conclude the housekeeper is a real live ghost.

The tour is dictated by the children's interest and this usually means the focus is on the lives of young Roy and his sister Maude. Mrs Reffle is full of pertinent information on how much pocket money the children got, what they spent it on, where they went for entertainment and the household chores that had to be done. Kids learn about the fog that seeped into houses, covering furniture with grease, and the problem of living with endless fleas attracted by the horse manure that clogged the streets. All the rooms have little points of interest, from the gun kept under the master's bed and the collection of hair from Marion's brush (used to supplement her own on special occasions) to the tiny bed in the servants' quarters at the top of the house in which two maids slept top to toe.

Kids love the cartoons that cover the walls and are fascinated by Linley's method of tracing his photographs to draw the cartoon figures ('Cheating!' declares a disapproving Mrs Reffle). He sometimes even took photographs of people in secret: you can see a camera disguised as a pair of binoculars that takes photos from the side.

After the tour the kids have a look at some real Victorian toys and replica costumes. They get busy working out which layer went where in the frocks and which shoes belonged to the servants and which were the family's.

Some tours also include a craftwork session. The children choose an object from the house and a photo of it is taken. Then, in the visitors' centre downstairs, they have a go at making it. It's all good, educational – if rather dotty – fun.

Most parents rely instead on Hammersmith and Fulham, where there are plentiful parks and activities. The most obvious destination, if you're seeking an antidote to bustling London life, is the river. **Bishop's Park** runs alongside the Thames Path and has a small boating lake for summer, as well as two playgrounds and a basketball pitch. It also has a One O'Clock Club (Bishops Rainbow Playhouse) for under-fives, with a thrilling (for three-year-olds) selection of trikes and bikes. The café has pleasant outside seating and the ice-cream van on Stevenage Road serves the nicest cornets for miles around. **Fulham Palace**, on the edge of Bishop's Park, has lovely grounds and a walled kitchen garden, an ideal spot for lazy riverside picnics. On the opposite side of the park you'll find **Fulham FC**'s football ground; it can be reached along the Thames Path. The stadium is expected to be renovated in time for the 2004-05 season. Just down the Fulham Road at **Chelsea**'s ground Stamford Bridge, you can book on a tour of the stadium or pick up kit and souvenirs from the Chelsea Village megastore.

The South Kensington end of Fulham Road has a number of posh clothes shops (there are clothing ranges for tots at agnès b and children at Replay), while the Fulham Broadway end has entertainment in the form of the Pottery Café (735 Fulham Road, SW6 5UL, 7736 2157). Smart families join the exclusive Hurlingham Club for its beautiful grounds and great outdoor sports facilities, but those without a trust fund can enjoy Hurlingham Park (Hurlingham Road, SW6). It's open to the public, but the emphasis is on sport, with a number of rugby and football pitches.

Fulham Palace
Bishop's Avenue, off Fulham Palace Road, SW6 6EA (7736 3233). Hammersmith or Putney Bridge tube/220, 414, 430 bus. **Open** *Museum* Mar-Oct 2-5pm Wed-Sun. Nov-Feb 1-4pm Thur-Sun. Closed 24-31 Dec. **Tours** 2pm 3rd Wed, 2nd & 4th Sun of mth. **Admission** (LP) *Museum* free. *Tours* £4-£5; free under-16s.
The official residence of the Bishops of London from 704 until 1973, Fulham Palace has some buildings dating back to 1480, although the main house is 16th century. The moat is gone, but some of its trench is still visible. The museum traces the buildings' history and has some funny exhibits, not least a mummified rat. Imaginative staff organise children's workshops (suitable for six- to 14-year-olds) during the school holidays; a recent workshop series was based on wartime Britain, but most relate to Roman, Tudor and Victorian eras. Ring to check what's coming up or ask for regular email updates. Leave plenty of time to admire the lovely grounds, planted with rare trees, which provide a sanctuary off the busy Fulham Palace Road. There's a walled kitchen garden, too, full of herbs and rare plants. As we went to press, Fulham Palace was awaiting the outcome of a bid for Lottery funding.

If the bid is successful, the palace will be out of bounds for 15 months probably from January 2005 (although the gardens will remain open). Ring to check before you visit. *Buggy access. Disabled access: toilet. Shop.*

Shepherd's Bush & Hammersmith

There would have been plenty of sheep in **Shepherd's Bush** up until the 19th century. Stockmen on their way to Smithfield Market regularly grazed their flocks on the roundabout site, which is an ancient piece of common land. These days, you're only likely to see them as you enter the tube station – there's a huge photo of a local shepherd and his flock. The transition from rural serenity to urban sprawl was rapid and the population of the area multiplied after the introduction of the railway in the early 1900s. In recent years, Hammersmith and Shepherd's Bush have experienced a gradual gentrification to become popular places for young families to set up home.

Other than sheep, Shepherd's Bush has a long association with music and theatre. The **Empire** at Shepherd's Bush roundabout has been a popular venue for concerts and many big names (the Rolling Stones, the Who, Eric Clapton) have graced its stage. The BBC once used it as a studio (*Crackerjack* was broadcast from here, parents). Much-needed recent improvements include a new shopping centre with a multi-screen cinema. Future plans include landscaping Shepherd's Bush Green, which should make better use of what is now little more than an oversized traffic island. The Music House at Bush Hall (*see p232*) provides tuition and workshops for all ages. For a different kind of culture, Loftus Road Stadium, home to **Queen's Park Rangers** and, until their new stadium is complete, Fulham is just west of Shepherd's Bush.

Closer to **Hammersmith** are a few more well-respected arts venues. The Riverside Studio is used by Dramatic Dreams Theatre Company (8741 1809, www.dramaticdreams.com) and Young Blood youth theatre company (01473 430395) as a venue for children's theatre projects during holidays and half-term. Another popular haunt is the Albert & Friends Instant Circus workshop (Ealing, Hammersmith & West London College, Glidden Road, W14 9BL, 8237 1170; *see also p254*), where apprentice clowns can master juggling, unicycling and acrobatics. Courses are run for children from 15 months to 18 years. The Lyric Theatre also runs acting workshops for all ages, particularly during the summer months. If you're still seeking inspiration, go to Wood Lane, where the BBC studios invite groups to take backstage tours (tickets need to be booked in advance and the minimum age is nine years; call 0870 603 0304 to book a ticket).

Around Hammersmith, the best spot to let off steam is **Ravenscourt Park**, off Chiswick High Road. On the other side of the shopping mall cum transport hub that is Hammersmith roundabout you'll find Brook Green, which has in recent years become a congregating point for parents with pushchairs – the interactive play area makes it ideal for toddlers. The Frank Banfield Park on Distillery Lane is another good option. It has an after-school kids' club for over-fives that gives members use of an adventure playground; parents need to register to join the waiting list. There are plans to expand this park as far as the river. Hammersmith also boasts the Ceramic Café (215 King Street, W6 9JP, 8741 4140), which holds mums and babies sessions at which you can record your baby's footprints for posterity in a ceramic plate or bowl.

Queen's Park Rangers Football Club
Loftus Road Stadium, South Africa Road, W12 7PA (8743 0262/www.qpr.co.uk). White City tube. **Open** *Shop* 9am-5pm Mon-Fri; 9am-1pm Sat. **Tours** by appointment only. **Admission** *Tours* £4; £2 under-16s. **Credit** MC, V.
Loftus Road, home to QPR, is also a hub of community football for young people. The match-day coaching package for children aged five to 16 gives them an exhausting morning of football training, followed by a welcome sit-down to see QPR play at home. The match-day birthday party includes a tour of the ground, two hours of outdoor football training, a £5 lunch voucher to spend in the ground, a ticket to see the match and a goodie bag, all for £21 per head. For more information, phone 8740 2509.
Buggy access. Disabled access: toilet. Nearest picnic place: Hammersmith Park. Shop.

Ravenscourt Park
Ravenscourt Road, W6 0UL (www.lbhf.gov.uk). Ravenscourt Park tube. **Open** 7.30am-dusk daily. **Admission** free.
In summer the packed paddling pool is the most popular part of this family-friendly park, but it also has three play areas and a One O'Clock Club (8748 3180) for under-fives. There's a big pond, a nature trail and an exotic scented garden for the visually impaired. Kids with spare energy can use the skateboarding ramp or enjoy a game of tennis. The nicely appointed café (*see p182*) is open all year round and the children's play area outside allows parents to enjoy a bit of a sit-down while keeping an eye on things. There's an annual flower show and children's fair in July, and the fun day with bouncy castles and face painting is also worth checking out.
Buggy access. Café. Nappy-changing facilities.

Chiswick

Chiswick is a stylish riverside suburb with a relaxed village feel. A prehistoric hammer and chisel found near Syon House suggest that some of the city's earliest human inhabitants lived here, and the part of Chiswick High Road running from Turnham Green towards Brentford is the remnants of a Roman road that stretched into the West Country. In the 18th century *Ceswican*, as it was known, was an area famous for cheesemaking, but most modern

Chiswickians know of a lovely little deli where they can buy theirs. As well as chi-chi food shops and boutiques, proximity to the M4 and Heathrow airport are also modern benefits of living here, and wealthy families have been attracted to the area's large red-brick houses and acres of green space.

Turnham Green epitomises Chiswick's villagey atmosphere. **Acton Green Common**, just off Chiswick High Road, has a church at the centre and local teams play cricket on the pristine lawns during the summer months. However, there are no facilities for anything other than a picnic and a bit of exercise. Just opposite Turnham Green is a branch of the arts café Art 4 Fun (see p231).

A stroll along the riverbank's Mall is popular with families on a Sunday. Over-eights can have a go at canoe polo on the Thames with the Chiswick Pier Canoe Club (The Pier House, Corney Reach Way, W4 2UG, www.chiswickcanoeclub.co.uk). Next door is Pissarro's on the River (Corney Reach Way, W4 2TR, 8994 3111), a popular stop for family lunches after working up an appetite on the riverbank. **Duke's Meadows** is one of the first green spaces you reach: it has tennis courts, boat houses, cricket pitches and a nine-hole golf course. Junior golf coaching is organised on Saturday afternoons: contact Duke's Meadow Golf Club (8995 0537). If you continue further along the river, you'll soon forget that you are in London at all. During the 18th century **Strand-on-the-Green** was a fishing community; now it's a particularly picturesque strolling spot, with a couple of child-friendly pubs with riverside terraces that serve food all day.

Further adventures can be had beyond Strand-on-the-Green on Brentford High Street. The **Kew Bridge Steam Museum** (best visited at weekends) can be identified by its huge chimney. Nearby, the unusual **Musical Museum** (368 High Street, Brentford, Middx TW8 0BD, 8560 8108, www.musical museum.co.uk) is a fantastic collection of organs and self-playing keyboard instruments. Open 2-5pm on Saturdays and Sundays from 3 April to 31 October, it is in the process of relocating (for up-to-date information, check the website). **Watermans** (40 High Street, Middx TW8 0DS, 8232 1010) is a riverside arts venue with children's theatre productions and art and drama workshops, and sporting urges can be satisfied at the Fountain Leisure Centre (658 Chiswick High Road, Middx TW8 0HJ, 0845 456 2935), renowned for its huge pool complex with waterslide and wave machine. For kids there is also the popular new play centre, a similar facility to Bumper's Back Yard (see p148).

One of the best places in west London for fresh air and fluttery fun is **Syon Park**. The grand house, owned by the Duke of Northumberland, may not be top of many children's lists of fun days out, but the surrounding grounds are full of child-friendly activities. The **Butterfly House** has over 1,000 live butterflies; there's also the fab **Aquatic Experience** with its rescued reptiles and a huge indoor adventure playground, Snakes and Ladders.

Further into the suburban expanses beyond Brentford you come to **Gunnersbury Park**, home to the fascinating Gunnersbury Park Local History Museum, (8992 1612; open 1-5pm Mon-Fri, 1-6pm weekends). This museum opens its splendid Victorian kitchens to the public on irregular summer weekends (call to check dates). More fun in the kitchen can be had year round at the **Kids' Cookery School** (107 Gunnersbury Lane, W3 8HQ, 8992 8882), where chefs aged three to 16 learn new culinary techniques.

Chiswick House

Burlington Lane, W4 2RP (8995 0508/www.english-heritage.org.uk). Turnham Green tube, then E3 bus to Edensor Road/Chiswick rail or Hammersmith tube/rail, then 190 bus. **Open** *Apr-Oct* 10am-5pm daily. *Nov-Mar* pre-booked appointments only. Last entry 30mins before closing. Closed 24-26 Dec, Jan, Feb. **Tours** by arrangement; phone for details. **Admission** (EH/LP) incl audio guide £3.70; £2.80 concessions; £1.90 5-16s; under-5s free. **Credit** MC, V.

Walking through the picturesque gardens of Chiswick House you'll come across various delights: obelisks hidden among the trees, a classical temple, a lake and a cascading waterfall. Lots of families come here on summer days for a picnic or to play cricket on the well-maintained grounds. You can also take a jaunt along the river, which is only a stone's throw away. Burlington's Café (see p181), in the grounds of Chiswick House, is a splendid place for lunch. English Heritage sometimes stages family activity days and even occasional re-enactments here: check its website for details. *Buggy access. Café. Disabled access: toilet. Nappy-changing facilities. Nearest picnic place: Chiswick Park. Shop.*

Gunnersbury Triangle Nature Reserve

Bollo Lane, W4 5LW (8747 3881/www.wildlondon.org.uk). Chiswick Park tube. **Open** *Reserve* 24hrs daily. *Info* Apr-Aug 10am-4.30pm Tue-Sun. Sept-Mar 10am-4pm Tue; 1-4pm Sun. **Admission** free.

In the late 19th century this area of land was enclosed by railway tracks and unfit for human habitation. As the woodland grew up and wildlife took over, it became one of the most important sites for urban wildlife in this part of the city. Following the trail today, visitors can admire the pond and meadowland, and try to spot all 19 species of butterfly that have been recorded here. The warden (full-time during the summer) has produced a wonderful programme of free, drop-in activities – craft workshops, mini-beast safaris and so on – for youngsters. The reserve's open day is usually in June: to find out more, call and ask for a programme. When the small information cabin is open you can ask the staff questions about urban ecology, pick up trail leaflets, find out about guided tours (summer only) or hire a net for pond dipping.

Kew Bridge Steam Museum

Green Dragon Lane, Brentford, Middx TW8 0EN (8568 4757/www.kbsm.org). Gunnersbury tube, then 237 or 267 bus/Kew Bridge rail/65, 391 bus. **Open** 11am-5pm daily. Closed 20 Dec-4 Jan, Good Friday.

Syon House.
See p154.

Tours by arrangement; phone for details. **Admission** (LP) *Mon-Fri* £3.60; £3 concessions; £2 5-15s; £10 family (2+3); free under-5s. *Sat, Sun* £5.20; £4.20 concessions; £3 5-15s; £15 family (2+3); free under-5s. Free to all after 4pm Mon-Fri. Under-13s must be accompanied by an adult. **Credit** MC, V.

Visit this Victorian riverside pumping station on high days and holidays and it's all sound and fury, but the engines are only in steam on specific days, so ring before you set out. The Cornish beam engine is fired up at 3pm most weekends and holiday periods, and there are usually a couple of others powering away. During the school holidays and bank holidays, there's a lot of action, because the Education Department and friendly volunteers run all kinds of family activities. The 'Water for Life' exhibition gives the lowdown on the history of London's sewers. This includes walking through a section of the city's water ring main, just to show how much water flows around this city all the time. Don't worry about getting wet, though – the section is for demonstration only, so there's no water in it. The website has up-to-date details on special events and exhibitions at the museum. Events need to be booked ahead to guarantee you'll get a place.

Buggy access. Café. Disabled access: toilet. Nearest picnic place: Kew Green. Shop.

Syon House

Syon Park, Brentford, Middx TW8 8JF (8560 0882/ London Butterfly House 8560 0378/Aquatic Experience 8847 4730/Snakes & Ladders 8847 0946/www.syon park.co.uk). Gunnersbury tube/rail, then 237, 267 bus. **Open** *House* mid Mar-late Oct 11am-5pm Wed, Thur, Sun, bank hol Mon. Last entry 4.15pm. *Gardens* closed 25, 26 Dec. **Tours** by arrangement; phone for details. **Admission** *House & gardens* £7.25; £5.95 concessions, 5-16s; £16 family (2+2); free under-5s. *Gardens only* £3.75; £2.50 concessions, 5-16s; £9 family (2+2); free under-5s. *Aquatic Experience* £4; £3.50 3-15s; free under-3s; £12.50 family (2+3). *Butterfly House* £4.95; £4.25 concessions; £3.95 3-16s; £15 family (2+3). *Snakes & Ladders* £3 under-2s; £4.00 under-5s; £5.00 over-5s; adults free. School hols & weekends £3.90 under-5s; £5 over-5s. No adults unaccompanied by children. **Credit** MC, V.

While parents love Syon House for its gracious location, many children find other attractions more enjoyable: the London Butterfly House, say, or the Aquatic Experience (*see p155* **Close encounters of the creepy-crawly kind**). Most children yearn for Snakes and Ladders, an indoor adventure playground designed like a castle, with three tiers of play areas, including slides, hanging ropes and masses of huge balls. There's also an indoor motorised bike track (£1/ride) and, for the parents, a café. This place positively heaves with boisterous kids of a weekend. Bring a picnic in summer, as the nicest eating locations are outside. In winter, the cafeteria has a selection of hot meals and a junior menu.

If you do find the time and finances to visit the house and grounds as well as forking out for all the child-pleasers, you can easily spend half a day here. This turreted Tudor mansion – developed from a building once dedicated to the Bridgettine Order, until the Dissolution of the Monasteries, when it was dedicated to providing Henry VIII with another country seat – is quite an adventure. Each room seems more impressive than the last, from the grand Roman hallway to the crimson silk walls and Roman statues of the Red Drawing Room – and on Sundays a wooden mini-steam railway travels through the trees and around the flowerbeds.

Buggy access. Café. Nappy-changing facilities. Nearest picnic place: Syon House Gardens/Syon Park. Shop.

Further west

In the comfortable suburb of **Ealing**, at the westerly end of the District and Central lines, you're never more than a toddler's ramble from a park or open space, many of them distinctly rural in character. The largest open spaces are nestled around the Brent river, where you can find golf courses, fields of ponies and acres of common land. **Brent Lodge Park**, or 'Bunny Park' as locals refer to it, is a good place to start. It has a lovely playground, maze and small zoo for the bunnies and other cuddleworthy residents. From here you can wander for hours along the river in either direction. Other green spots include Horsenden Hill, the highest point in Ealing borough, with great views over the whole of London; Ealing Common, close to the busy high road; and Osterley Park on the outskirts of Hanwell. **Osterley House** is a gorgeous place to visit, with a brilliant café. In summer there are all sorts of events for children around the grounds.

The central green lung, where most parents congregate, is **Walpole Park**. During July and August the park hosts the majority of events at the Ealing Summer Festival, with lots of child-friendly activities; phone Ealing council for details (8579 2424). The playground here is up and running with a new range of play equipment, and the park contains sumptuous **Pitshanger Manor**. Ealing Town Hall is the venue for parent and toddler groups throughout the year, and also organises half-term children's discos. The busy Questors Theatre (Mattock Lane, W5 5BQ, 8567 0011, www.questors.org.uk) runs acting workshops for all ages, and a playgroup for six to tens.

Ealing has a number of sports centres; the most interesting is the Gurnell Leisure Centre (*see p266*), which boasts an Olympic-sized pool. Riders tack up at Ealing Riding School (*see p262*), and Brent Valley Golf Course (Church Road, Hanwell, W7 3BE, 8567 1287) is a good place for beginner golfers.

Further west of Ealing is **Southall**, home to London's largest Asian community. This is the venue for London's only surviving agricultural market, auctioning horses each Wednesday. It is also a great place to pick up saris, bangles, sandals and other bits and bobs at bargain prices. The largest Sikh temple outside India opened in nearby Hounslow in spring 2003. The Sri Guru Singh Sabha Gurdwara temple (Alice Way, Hanworth Road, Hounslow, TW3 3UA), second in size only to the Golden Temple in Amritsar, has a capacity of 3,000 people. The glorious **Shri Swaminarayan Mandir Temple**, to the north of Southall, is a breathtakingly beautiful monument to Hinduism.

Carry on west and you come to **Heathrow**, but there's more to the airport than departures and arrivals. There's an excellent visitors' centre with

Close encounters of the creepy-crawly kind

There's more to the **Aquatic Experience** at **Syon House** (*see p154*) than fish and amphibians: rescued pets and exotic specimens donated by the friendly customs man at nearby Heathrow airport have expanded the animal collection. It is these that are introduced at the regular Animal Encounters sessions, during which children get a rare opportunity to get up close. It certainly beats gawping at the beasts in cages or aquaria. The lecture starts at the smaller end of the animal spectrum, introducing Jump the grasshopper, and progresses through steadily larger creatures to the finale: ten feet (three metres) of a boa constrictor called Amy. As well as the children, the audience includes some large parrots and a cockatoo, nonchalantly perched without cage or chain.

Everyone who wants to can hold the creatures and, for their part, the animals seem quite unfazed – only rescued pets that are accustomed to human contact are used for this part of the event. The best bit is watching the children, who have queued up expecting to gingerly touch Amy one by one, when the great snake is actually draped over everybody's shoulders – a great video opportunity.

The young tutors encourage plenty of participation, which means there's hardly any sitting around passively listening and the children strain to be first to answer questions. It is quite unnerving to find such a high proportion of studious arachnophiles in one room. Parents shouldn't be bored, either, as there is plenty of wildlife trivia to enjoy. Did you know, for example, that the daddy-long-legs's venom is more poisonous than that of the tarantula or

even the scorpion? Luckily, their fangs aren't strong enough to pierce human skin. The sessions are very relaxed, with a fair amount of coming and going, but it's not hard to sit through the whole hour as the guides are experienced in the art of stretching short attention spans.

At the neighbouring **Butterfly House**, where many species of elegant lepidoptera flutter past and land on entranced visitors to their steamy, jungly enclosure, you can enjoy a similar talk on the lifestyle of butterflies and moths. Throughout the lecture, the creatures in question swirl around little heads and congregate on sponges soaked in sugar. Rows of pupa in every stage of growth fill special cabinets and butterflies freshly emerged from their cocoons hover, ready to fly out as soon as the door is opened. There is also a talk on mini-beasts. Curious youngsters are given contacts of insect societies where they can nurture their interest, hopefully in butterflies rather than cockroaches. In the shop there are grow-your-own-butterfly kits (after the butterfly has emerged, you are advised to let it go), lots of plastic creepy-crawlies and wildlife gardening books and activities.

Unfortunately, the Butterfly House's lease runs out in autumn 2004 and the owners have not yet found new premises, though they are looking at a space in nearby Gunnersbury Park. With luck, the collection won't flutter far away, as there are few experiences more therapeutic on a grey winter's day than sitting in a tropically heated garden, contemplating the beating of butterfly wings all around.

plenty to entertain the children and a viewing area for plane spotting. Still, the best thing about Heathrow and the Hounslow area is the huge amount of open space. The heath (450 Staines Road, Hounslow, TW4 5AB, 8577 3664, www.cip.com) is an enormous nature reserve, complete with information centre, a bird hide, nature trails, a bridle path and a children's play area. A visit to the warden will yield plenty of information on local wildlife. For more beastly stuff, **Hounslow Urban Farm** houses endangered breeds of livestock and breeds guinea pigs for sale.

Brent Lodge Park

Church Road, W7 3LB (8825 7529). Hanwell rail. **Open** 7.30am-dusk daily. *Maze & animals* Apr-Sept 10.30am-5pm daily. Sept-Mar 10.30am-4pm daily. **Admission** £1; 50p concessions, 3-16s; free under-3s. **No credit cards.**
The Millennium Maze, planted here in 1999, continues to bulk up. Young explorers love standing triumphantly on the central tower once they've worked their way round, and anxious parents can stand on the viewing platform outside to locate squawking progeny. Walk up the hill from the maze for the hub of activities in this sweet local park: there's a café for ice-cream and sandwiches, a playground and an animal centre. The centre (25p children, 50p adults, 8758 5019) houses a handful of squirrel monkeys, a pair of sleepy geckos and some scary spiders, along with a few birds and the odd bunny.
Buggy access (no access to animal area). Café. Disabled access: toilet.

Heathrow Airport Visitor Centre

Newall Road, Middx UB3 5AP (8745 6655/www.ba. com). Hatton Cross tube, then 285, 555, 556, 557 bus/ Heathrow Terminal 1, 2 & 3 tube, then 81, 105, 111, 140, 222, 285, 555, 556, 557 bus to Bath Road. **Open** 10am-5pm daily. Closed 25-26 Dec. **Admission** free.
This small but rewarding centre explains how Heathrow has grown over 50 years into the world's busiest airport. Once you've collected your picture Eye Spy for tiny ones and fun quizzes for the six and overs, plus paper and crayons for brass rubbings, the first thing you come to is a check-in desk with scales for you to weigh your 'luggage'. The staff are quite relaxed about small children weighing themselves (but do draw the line at adults trying the same!). Further amusement is to be had testing the Archway Metal Detectors by setting off the alarms. You can also see a bag as viewed through the X-ray. Two aircraft seats are great for practising before a family's first flight: you can show the kids how to buckle in with the seat belts. Most fun, though, is the flight simulator, which lands (of course) at Heathrow. At the far end of the ground floor there is a collection of illegal items intercepted by customs, including some endangered species. You will also find interactive displays on what the airport is doing for the environment, covering everything from public transport to noise management and local wildlife. Finally, you can visit the café, and watch the planes take off and land through the enormous panoramic window.
Buggy access. Café. Disabled access: toilet. Nappy-changing facilities. Shop.

Hounslow Urban Farm

A312 at Faggs Road, Feltham, Middx TW14 OLZ (8751 0850/www.cip.com). Hatton Cross tube, then 25min walk or 90, 285, 490 bus. **Open** *early Feb-Oct* 10am-4pm Tue-Fri; 10am-5pm Sat, Sun, school hols. Closed Nov-early Feb. **Admission** £3; £2.25 concessions; £1.50 children; free under-2s.

At 29 acres (11.7ha) this is London's largest community farm. There are pigs, goats, ducks, Exmoor ponies and more – feeding time is 3.30pm daily. The farm has a conservation programme – endangered breeds of domestic livestock are reared here. Most fascinating is a visit during lambing season: turn up at the right time and you could be lucky enough to see a lamb, goat or piglet being born. Orphan lambs need to be bottle-fed and kids are allowed to help. There's a playground (with, we're delighted to report, pedal tractors), a picnic area and a café.
Buggy access. Café. Disabled access: toilet. Kiosk. Nappy-changing facility.

Osterley House

Osterley Park, off Jersey Road, Isleworth, Middx TW7 4RB (8232 5050/recorded info 01494 755566/www.national trust.org.uk/osterley). Osterley tube. **Open** *House* late Mar-Oct 1-4.30pm Wed-Sun. *Park* 9am-dusk daily. **Tours** by arrangement; minimum 15 people. **Admission** (NT) *House* £4.70; £2.30 5-15s; £11.70 family (2+3); free under-5s. *Park* free. **Credit** (tearoom/shop only) MC, V.
Osterley House was built for Sir Thomas Gresham (founder of the Royal Exchange) in 1576, but transformed by Robert Adam in 1761. Adam's revamp is dominated by the imposing colonnade of white pillars before the courtyard of the house's red-brick body. The splendour of the state rooms alone makes the house worth the visit, but the still-used Tudor stables, the vast parkland walks and the ghost said to be lurking in the basement add to Osterley's allure. Children can pick up a house trail from the office to help them explore these delightful surroundings. In August children can get in free, and every Monday in August is a Funday.
Café. Car park (£3/day, NT members free). Disabled access: lift, toilet. Nappy-changing facilities. Nearest picnic place: front lawn/picnic benches in grounds. Shop.

Pitshanger Manor & Gallery

Walpole Park, Mattock Lane, W5 5EQ (8567 1227/ www.ealing.gov.uk/pmgallery&house). Ealing Broadway tube/rail/65 bus. **Open** *May-Sept* 1-5pm Tue-Fri; 11am-5pm Sat; 1-5pm Sun. *Oct-Apr* 1-5pm Tue-Sat. Closed 25, 26 Dec, 1 Jan, bank hols. **Tours** by arrangement; phone for details. **Admission** free.
Most of Pitshanger, a beautiful Regency villa, was rebuilt in 1801-3 by Sir John Soane (*see p58* **Sir John the Collector**). His individual ideas in design and decoration make this a very special place. Among the exhibits is the Hull Grundy Martinware collection of pottery, and there is an art gallery (8567 1227) where contemporary exhibitions are held, plus a lecture and workshop programme for all ages. Realistically, though, most children would rather be in the park.
Buggy access. Disabled access: lift, toilet. Nearest picnic place: Walpole Park. Shop.

Shri Swaminarayan Mandir Temple

105-115 Brentfield Road, NW10 8LD (8965 2651/ www.swaminarayan.org). Wembley Park tube, then BR2 bus. **Open** 9.30am-6pm daily. **Admission** (LP) free. *Exhibition* £2; £1.50 6-15s; free under-6s.
Built in 1995, this Hindu temple is an extraordinary structure, intricately carved by master sculptors. Much of the stone was sent to India to be carved and then brought back to Neasden at a cost of more than £10 million. It also has a permanent exhibition, with a video, called 'Understanding Hinduism'; it's particularly useful for Year Sixes studying world religion. Stock up on incense sticks at the shop and you can try to recreate the temple's serenity at home.
Buggy access. Café. Disabled access: lift, toilet. Nappy-changing facilities. Shop.

Around Town

Consumer

Eating

Great food for children, not despite them.

Slurptastic **Wagamama**.
See p163.

Very few restaurants, in these politically correct times, refuse to admit babies and children. But before we all go for a family celebration in the Savoy Grill, it's worth sorting out those that welcome, from those that merely tolerate, children. The only way we've managed to come up with our list is by eating our way round town – accompanied by babies, toddlers, infants, an under-11s football team and a couple of teenagers. It's been exhausting, but we can promise that each place mentioned has been tested. We know our favourites, but would love to hear from you if we've missed somewhere great or included a place you loathe.

Some of the restaurants we tried we could not include. Either because the food was awful, but too often – despite a big show of high chairs, kiddie menus, crayons and the rest – the less obvious signs of child-friendliness were lacking. By the same token, we've listed places that can't be doing with high chairs and whose chefs wouldn't let a chicken nugget or kiddie burger anywhere near their kitchen, but where the staff have been sweetness itself, asking the kitchen for half portions, say, or providing spare plates or plain pasta for fussy small eaters. Pleasant service, decent grub – it's all we ask, really. And the ketchup, please.

Where possible, we've included contact details for other branches of the restaurants we list, but bear in mind that not all branches have the same facilities. For useful places to eat in a particular area, *see* the **Pit stops** boxes in **Around Town** (*pp34-156*).

South Bank & Bankside

Cantina del Ponte
Butlers Wharf Building, 36C Shad Thames, SE1 2YE (7403 5403/www.conran.com). Tower Hill tube/London Bridge tube/rail. **Lunch served** noon-3pm daily. **Dinner served** 6-11pm Mon-Sat; 6-10pm Sun. **Main courses** £5.95-£15.50. **Credit** AmEx, DC, MC, V. **Map** p321 R8.
This clattery, spacious Cantina is laid-back about under-fives cluttering up the place. The menu, provided you don't go down the Italian peasant food route (we didn't think much of the osso bucco or the cannelloni) is attractive to young diners. There are great pizzas from £5.50, lovely soups and breads, and some appealing set menus. The children's menu includes soup, salads, pizzas, spaghetti and grilled chicken.
Buggy access. Children's menu. Nappy-changing facilities. Tables outdoors (terrace).

fish!
Cathedral Street, Borough Market, SE1 9DE (7407 3803/ www.fishdiner.co.uk). London Bridge tube/rail. **Meals served** 11.30am-3pm, 5-10.45pm Mon-Fri; noon-11pm Sat; noon-10.30pm Sun. **Main courses** £8.90-£16.95. **Credit** AmEx, MC, V. **Map** p319 M8.
The last outpost of the fish! chain sits in a plum tourist location, attracting choristers and clergy from Southwark Cathedral and gourmands from Borough Market. It's a shame the friendly staff haven't quite got used to the crowds descending at weekends, and that their memories are rather fish-like when it comes to requests like 'may we order now?' The food is great, if pricey (the firm and lovely halibut cost £17.50). You choose from the fish list of the day and persuade the children to partake of the £6.95 kid menu, which includes a drink and ice-cream. The fish cakes are fabulous and cod and chips with mushy peas a huge portion.
Buggy access. Children's menu (£6.95). Crayons. High chairs. No-smoking tables (not Sat). Tables outdoors (24, pavement).
Branch: Loco, County Hall, Belvedere Road, SE1 7GP (7401 6734).

Konditor & Cook

*Young Vic Theatre, 66 The Cut, SE1 8LZ (7620 2700/
www.konditorandcook.co.uk). Waterloo tube/rail.* **Meals
served** 11.30am-2.30pm daily. **Main courses** £3.75-
£7.25. **Credit** MC, V. **Map** p320 N8.
This is the theatre bar/café branch of one of the city's most
talented purveyors of great cakes and confectionery. Here you
can sit and choose from a savouries list that might include
tortellini, club sandwiches or sausages and mash, or just concentrate on the cake department: lemon cake, rich nutty fruit
cake or the famous chocolate tart. The menu changes daily,
so you might not find the K&C cake you're dreaming of; if
this is the case, scuttle over to one of the shops (the nearest
is on Cornwall Road, where there are cakes, brownies, chocolate novelties and all kinds of delights.
Buggy access. Disabled access: toilets.
Branches: 22 Cornwall Road, SE1 8TW (7261 0456); 46
Gray's Inn Road, WC1X 8LR (7404 6300); 10 Stoney Street,
SE1 9AD (7407 5100).

The People's Palace

*Level 3, Royal Festival Hall, South Bank Centre, SE1 8XX
(7928 9999/www.peoplespalace.co.uk). Embankment tube/
Charing Cross or Waterloo tube/rail.* **Lunch served**
noon-2.30pm, **dinner served** 5-11pm daily. **Main
courses** £12.50-£17. **Set lunch** £14 2 courses, £18.50
3 courses. **Set dinner** (5-7pm Mon-Sat, all day Sun) £18
2 courses, £23 3 courses. **Credit** AmEx, DC, MC, V.
Map p319 M8.
There are other places on the South Bank where you can eat
well and enjoy river views, but few are as appealing as this.

A combination of gracious staff, loads of space and a
top modern European menu make the People's Palace a huge
favourite for a family treat. And treat it must remain, as it's
not cheap. The set lunches represent good value, though: the
menu for adults changes regularly, but usually includes an
excellent, light vegetarian tarte, a tender braised meat dish
and fabulous fish specials. There's a children's menu, listing
chicken and chips, vegetarian pasta, pizza or sausage and
mash, or simple staples such as beans on toast, followed by
banana and custard, ice-cream or sorbet. But you'd be barmy
to spend a tenner on beans on toast with ice-cream for afters.
*Buggy access. Children's menu (£10 2 courses). High
chairs. No-smoking tables.*

The City

Carluccio's Caffè

*12 West Smithfield, EC1A 9JR (7329 5904/
www.carluccios.co.uk). Farringdon tube/rail.* **Meals
served** 8am-11pm Mon-Fri; 10am-11pm Sat; 10am-10pm
Sun. **Main courses** £4.95-£8.95. **Credit** AmEx, MC, V.
Map p320 O5.
This ever-expanding chain does not compromise on quality,
despite its ubiquity, combining high standards with relaxed
service. Fine Italian ingredients are used to create wonderful
pasta, salads, soups and impressive adaptations of standards,
such as a risotto with radicchio and borlotti beans or char-
grilled lamb with spinach. The bread baskets are legendary,
the coffees and puddings worth lingering over, and the wel-

Chains u like

Some restaurant chains are like old family friends.
You can rely on them to look after the children,
as well as providing a decent meal and a glass of
wine for the adults. What's more, you just know
they're going to have high chairs if you need them,
affordable favourite dishes to suit all ages,
nappy-changing facilities and a generally unfazed
approach to requests for extra plates, more
ketchup and 'napkins to mop that up, please'.

Most parents would agree that the family lunch
stalwart, the place where grown-ups eat as
enthusiastically as the children, is **Pizza Express**
(www.pizzaexpress.co.uk). It doesn't hurt that
Pizza Express is ubiquitous; you're always likely
to find one in a heavily touristed part of town –
there are four in the South Bank and Bankside
area alone. Noticeably cheaper, but rather less
refined, is **Pizza Hut** (www.pizzahut.co.uk). Children
certainly agitate for the latest Hut promotion,
whether it be a stuffed-crust pizza, a big square
for the family to share, the sickly sweetie-laden
ice-cream factory or decorate-your-own cookie
cake. And before we leave the subject of pizza,
both **ASK** (www.askcentral.co.uk) and **Strada**
(www.strada.co.uk; *see also p166*) do good-
quality, thin-crust, well topped spherical lunches.

Alongside pizza on a child's top ten favourite
foods comes pasta – handily, it's often the
healthy option on a kiddie menu. **Caffè Uno**
(www.caffeuno.co.uk) lists a number of pasta

dishes on its £3.95 Arthur's Menu: you can
choose tomato, bolognese, carbonara or cheese
sauce, and ice-cream and a soft drink are included.
The ever-fresh pasta at good old **Spaghetti House**
(www.spaghetti-house.co.uk) also comes up
trumps when feeding a family, with £5 children's
meals including a soft drink and ice-cream.

Prefer French? The reasonably priced children's
menu at **Café Rouge** (www.caferouge.co.uk) has
been praised by many readers. For £3.95 kids get
a drink, a choice of fish cake, croque monsieur,
sausage or chicken, with chips, salad or healthy
green beans. Chicken goujons with fries is the
most popular dish on this jolly menu, with its word
searches and quiz questions, which is why...

...most links in the **Nando's** (www.nandos.co.uk)
chain are inundated with families. Nine out of
ten carnivorous children rate chicken above all
other meat, and chicken is the main ingredient
here. Nandinos (kids) can choose from a children's
menu priced £3.75 for wings, strips of breast or
chicken burger, chips, plus unlimited soft drinks
and refillable frozen flavoured yoghurts.

But the chain we rate highest, because the
food is great and the children get a nutritious
dinner whatever they choose from the big noodly
menu, is **Wagamama** (www.wagamama.com; *see
also p160*). It's a no-smoking restaurant, where
healthy juices and fresh veg come as standard,
and kids all enjoy a chopstick challenge.

come for children genuine. Our kids always enjoy the junior menu, which includes grissini (breadsticks) and a soft drink, mains of spaghetti with tomato or bolognese sauce, breaded chicken or a focaccia sandwich, followed by terrific ice-cream. Carluccio's hot chocolate is really somethingspecial.
Buggy access. Delicatessen. Children's menu (£4.50). No-smoking tables. Tables outdoors (8, pavement).
Branches: throughout town. Call or check the website.

The Place Below
St Mary le Bow Church, Cheapside, EC2V 6AU (7329 0789/www.theplacebelow.co.uk). St Paul's tube/Bank tube/DLR. **Breakfast served** 7.30-10.30am, **lunch served** 11.30am-2.30pm, **snacks served** 7.30am-3.30pm Mon-Fri. **Main courses** £5-£7.50. **Credit** MC, V. **Map** p320 P6.
If you don't want to fight disapproving City workers for a table in this crypt restaurant, come for elevenses or for a late lunch when everyone's back in the office. The vegetarian menu changes daily, but there's always a great main-meal salad. We're keen on the lentil soup and vegetarian lasagne, but whatever you choose, leave room for the Comptoir Gason pastries, rich flapjacks or – every child's favourite – chocolate brownies from heaven (not really… they're by Valrhona, £1.55). There aren't any high chairs and space is limited, so it's not the most brilliant place for toddlers.
No smoking. Tables outdoors (20, courtyard). Takeaway service. Vegan dishes.

Smiths of Smithfield
67-77 Charterhouse Street, EC1M 6HJ (7251 7950/ www.smithsofsmithfield.co.uk). Farringdon tube/rail. **Meals served** *Ground-floor bar/café* 7am-5pm Mon-Fri; 10am-5pm Sat; 9.30am-5pm Sun. **Main courses** £3.50-£8.50. **Credit** AmEx, MC, V. **Map** p320 O5.
Downstairs at Smith's – a capacious multi-function venue with a cool warehouse look – the vibe is relaxed. It's a favourite brunching place for media folk, but it's also a cool place to bring the kids for lunch. Many of the ingredients are organic (or free range where appropriate) and stalwarts such as the all-day breakfast fry-up (for about £4), porridge and honey, scrambled eggs, chicken or salmon sandwiches and perfect, crispchips mean everyone is happy. Don't go without sampling one of the milkshakes – they make great puds.
Buggy access. High chairs. Tables outdoors (6, pavement).

Holborn & Clerkenwell

Bank Aldwych
1 Kingsway, WC2B 6XF (7379 9797/ www.bankrestaurants.com). Holborn tube or Temple tube. **Breakfast served** 7-10.30am Mon-Fri. **Brunch served** 11.30am-3.30pm Sat, Sun. **Lunch served** noon-3pm Mon-Fri. **Dinner served** 5.30-11pm Mon-Sat; 5.30-9.30pm Sun. **Main courses** £9.50-£32. **Set meal** (lunch, 5.30-7pm, 10-11pm) £12.50 2 courses, £15 3 courses. **Credit** AmEx, DC, MC, V. **Map** p317 M6.
A business-lunching place, but staff are happy to provide high chairs and spare plates for family groups during the day. Brunch-time at weekends clears most of the suits away and brings an activities table with crayons, paper, puzzles and toys for children. The portions are vast on the children's menu: linguine with tomato sauce, chipolatas with chips and beans, breaded chicken or beefburger with chips can be followed by ice-cream, sticky toffee pudding or a milkshake.
Buggy access. Booking advisable. Children's menu (£7.25). Crayons. High chairs. Nappy-changing facilities.

Bloomsbury & Fitzrovia

Bertorelli's
19-23 Charlotte Street, W1T 1RL (7636 4174). Goodge Street tube. **Meals served** noon-11pm Mon-Sat. **Main courses** £4.95-£14.95. **Credit** AmEx, DC, MC, V. **Map** p316 J5.
Often noisy and crowded in the evenings, the ground-floor café area at Bertorelli's, one of London's oldest Italian restaurants, is a useful lunching place for families. Children who are past the need for toys, high chairs and balloons appreciate the slick modern decor, the metropolitan buzz and the pretty terrific Italian menu. Ultra-thin pizzas start at £5.95, the same price as a small portion of spaghetti bolognese. The pasta is delightfully presented and dressed, the meat dishes lean and accompanied by delicate little salads, cheesy polenta, baby vegetables or, if you prefer, a side order of chips for £2. Service is brisk and efficient, but friendly, and the loos, with grand marble slabs instead of basins, are something else.
Buggy access. High chair. No-smoking tables. Tables outside (5, pavement).

Cigala
54 Lamb's Conduit Street, WC1N 3LW (7405 1717/ www.cigala.co.uk). Holborn or Russell Square tube. **Lunch served** noon-3pm Mon-Fri; 12.30-3.45pm Sat. **Dinner served** 6-10.45pm Mon-Sat. **Meals served** 12.30-9.30pm Sun. **Main courses** £10-£17. **Tapas** £2-£8. **Credit** AmEx, DC, MC, V. **Map** p317 M4.
The basement area of this smart, slick Spanish restaurant is the place for sophisticated tapas options, such as oak-smoked beef, which are listed alongside more familiar salads, olives, prawns and chicken. The own-made bread is really delicious.
Buggy access. Crayons. High chairs. Tables outside (10, pavement).

Navarro's
67 Charlotte Street, W1T 4PH (7637 7713/www. navarros.co.uk). Goodge Street tube. **Lunch served** noon-3pm Mon-Fri. **Dinner served** 6-10pm Mon-Sat. **Tapas** £3-£15. **Credit** AmEx, MC, V. **Map** p316 J5.
A beautiful little Spanish restaurant, Navarro's brightly painted furniture and Moorish tiling are a feast for the eyes, but it's the stomach that gets the real pleasure here. The tapas is what eveyone raves about, and it's certainly the menu to stick with if you're here with children. With dishes starting at £1.50, you'd do well to order as many as you can and give the family a chance both to taste the classics (tortilla, fried potatoes, olives and grilled chicken) and to experience the unusual (chicken with prawns in sherry and paprika sauce, wild mushrooms, chickpeas in sauce and meaty chorizo).
Buggy access. High chairs.

North Sea Fish Restaurant
7-8 Leigh Street, WC1H 9EW (7387 5892). Russell Square tube/King's Cross tube/rail/68, 168 bus. **Lunch served** noon-2.30pm, **dinner served** 5.30-10.30pm Mon-Sat. **Main courses** £7.90-£16.95. **Credit** AmEx, MC, V. **Map** p317 L3/4.
A friendly little chippie near the British Library, North Sea is very popular with American tourists and, although the atmosphere is pretty sedate, staff are accommodating toward family groups, unearthing the high chair where necessary. The chips are fantastic; a portion of cod or haddock and same is extremely filling. If you want to make the national dish a bit healthier, you can opt for grilled fish, but anyone who can choose boiled spuds over those chips must be a bit wanting.
Buggy access. High chair. Takeaway service.

Parking space

The average park café menu tends to be sandwiches in cellophane, microwaved jacket potatoes and suspiciously big, dry scones with inadequate butter portions. There are plenty, however, that are a cut above. Some, like the all-new **Inn The Park** (*see p171*), which opened in St James's Park in April 2004, seem determined to take parkside eating to new heights of sophistication. Run by Oliver Peyton, it's in an eco-friendly building designed by Sir Michael Hopkins (designer of the Mound Stand at Lord's cricket ground). Made of wood, with a turf roof and an elegant terrace that's visited by occasional ducks, Inn The Park divides neatly into a restaurant beside the windows and a spacious self-service café. The latter is very child-friendly, with organic Pots for Tots and packed lunches (crusts off the bread) alongside gorgeous cakes and pastries. In the restaurant part, the tables beside the windows are a bit tight for less mobile family units, but the menu is an all-day mouth-waterer for grown-ups – the sophisticated ploughman's lunch an unlikely sensation – with kids catered for with a couple of options, including the likes of shepherd's pie. Some may say it's a little highfalutin for families, but we love the notion of expense-accounters getting their besuited elbows in melted ice-cream all summer.

Ice-cream is the main draw at **Golders Hill Park Refreshment House** (*see p172*). Famous for Arte Gelato ice-creams, many made by the proprietor, the Refreshment House is heavenly on a hot summer's day. On winter ones, hot soups and pasta provide a warm welcome. Another sunny delight, **Oshobasho Café** (*see p173*) draws big crowds when school's out: expect queues at weekends and consider yourself blessed if you can bag a table on the terrace. The menu is usually short and on a blackboard, listing crowd-pleasing exotica like focaccia sandwiches, salads, pastas and own-made cakes.

One of the most child-friendly park cafés we know is the **Ravenscourt Park Teahouse** (*see p182*). Refurbished a year ago and still looking great, it's a pleasant surprise to those who remember the old place. Apart from coffees and own-made cakes, the daily changing menu has hot food, including delicious salady and vegetarian dishes. There's a special menu for kids that offers organic burgers and tomato pasta.

The **Brew House** (*see p172*), in the former coach house of Kenwood House, has a country-kitchen feel and a full organic or free-range brief. Sadly, this means it's almost impossible to grab a seat on sunny weekends, but if you're willing to do battle with the crowds you can expect about three hot dishes of the day and big trays of delectable cakes, including enormous profiteroles.

A delightfully homely café, much loved by dog-walkers and visitors to Chiswick House, **Burlington's Café** (*see p181*) does a children's menu (chips, pasta, beans on toast) and far more attractive fresh sandwiches and moist cakes.

The **Pavilion Café** (*see p178*) in Dulwich Park is run by a family and always full of families. The proprietors have sensitively separated the seating areas, so one side – with the toy corner – is for those accompanied by small children and the other is reserved for those who want a bit of peace. The food is simple. Children can choose from their own menu (burgers, pasta) or go for sandwiches. Everything on the menu, including the cakes, is made on the premises.

Pembroke Lodge (*see p180*) stands in Richmond Park and affords stunning views over the Thames Valley. On mild days you can sit on the terrace while kids roam the gardens. In colder weather, enjoy the view from the former drawing rooms. The cooks provide a children's lunch; there are weekend roasts and usually four hot dishes of the day, as well as cream teas, ice-creams and cakes.

Wagamama

4A Streatham Street, WC1A 1JB (7323 9223/www.wagamama.com). Tottenham Court Road tube. **Meals served** noon-11pm Mon-Sat; 12.30-10pm Sun. **Main courses** £5.50-£9.25. **Credit** AmEx, DC, MC, V. **Map** p317 K/L5.

A great place for a quick, family meal, Wagamama is wholesome, but not bland. Free green tea, no smoking, no fizzy pop and large amounts of purifying garlic, ginger and green vegetables mean it's easy to steer the kids toward healthy choices. Noodles and rice dishes, particularly those served with lean, stir-fried chicken or big char-grilled king prawns are highly acceptable. Dishes are big, so grab an extra pair of chopsticks and let children pick their favourite bits out of yaki soba or fried ramen with beef, salmon, egg or tofu.
Buggy access. Children's menu. High chairs. No smoking. **Branches**: throughout town. Call or check the website.

Marylebone

Fairuz

3 Blandford Street, W1H 3AA (7486 8108/8182). Baker Street or Bond Street tube. **Meals served** noon-11.30pm Mon-Sat; noon-10.30pm Sun. **Main courses** £9.95-£12.95. **Set meals** £17.95 meze, £24.95 3 courses. **Cover** £1.50. **Credit** AmEx, MC, V. **Map** p316 G5.

Fairuz is an attractive, homely Middle Eastern restaurant, named after a famous Lebanese songstress, where the ambience is relaxed and the staff are reserved but always polite. The meze is prepared and presented with great attention to detail and it's fun to select as many as you can for a colourful and varied family meal. You can choose from about 50 dishes – houmous, small sausages, aubergine purée, falafel, chicken – all accompanied by warm, soft flatbread. The barbecued lamb and mixed fish grill main dishes are also good and the sticky, nutty baklavá pastries a sugary delight.
Booking advisable. High chairs. Tables outside (4, pavement).

La Galette

56 Puddington Street, W1U 4HY (7935 1554/ www.lagalette.com). Baker Street or Bond Street tube. **Breakfast served** 9.30am-noon Mon-Fri. **Meals served** 10am-11pm Sat, Sun. **Main courses** £3.95-£8.95. **Set lunch** (noon-5pm Mon-Fri) £6.95 2 courses. **Credit** AmEx, MC, V. **Map** p316 G5.

A galette is the savoury, buckwheat flour crêpe made traditionally served in crêperies in Brittany. This bright, modern crêperie does regular pancakes as well, served sweet with lemon and sugar, bananas and chocolate sauce or maple syrup, which is what many young children love best. The galette is more suited to savoury toppings: the complète (ham, cheese and egg) makes a substantial meal.
Bookings not accepted for fewer than 6 people. Buggy access. High chairs. No smoking. Tables outdoors (2, terrace).

Giraffe

6-8 Blandford Street, W1H 3HA (7935 2333/ www.giraffe.net). Baker Street or Bond Street tube. **Open** 8am-4pm, 5-11.30pm Mon-Fri; 9am-11.30pm Sat; 9am-10.30pm Sun. Only drinks & desserts served 4-5pm Mon-Fri; 4-5.30pm Sat, Sun. **Main courses** £7-£10. **Set dinner** (5-7pm Mon-Fri) £6.95 2 courses; (7-10.45pm Mon-Fri) £9.95. **Credit** AmEx, MC, V. **Map** p316 G5.

The staff here are always cheery and ready with a balloon, so Giraffe remains our favourite place to eat with the children. Although there are quite a few Giraffes around (and we've tried them all), the excellent 'global' menu (meaning 'a bit of everything') doesn't give off a chainy vibe. Everything, from delightful brunch options to lunch and dinner specials of noodles, grilled fish dishes, burgers, curries and excellent puddings, is well presented and carefully cooked. The children's menu lists veggie noodles, cod cakes, salads, lovely potato wedges and various items on toast. Whatever you have, leave room for pudding: how can you not when there's sticky toffee and banana pudding, rhubarb and apple skillet crumble and honeycomb chewchew cheesecake to try?
Buggy access. Children's menu (£2.95-£4.95). Crayons. High chairs. No smoking. Tables outdoors (5, pavement patio). Toys.
Branches: throughout town. Call or check the website.

West End

Amato

14 Old Compton Street, W1D 4TH (7734 5733/ www.amato.co.uk). Leicester Square or Tottenham Court Road tube. **Open** 8am-10pm Mon-Sat; 10am-8pm Sun. **Main courses** £5.50-£8.50. **Credit** AmEx, DC, MC, V. **Map** p317 K6.

This atmospheric Italian brasserie, with old movie posters on the walls and cheerful staff, is a fine place for a comforting lunch of well-made pasta. There are also quiches and salads, as well as breakfast staples such as scrambled eggs and salmon or brioche. Most people, however, come for the perfect coffee and pasticcerie – huge creamy creations with sponge and sweet cream, or light pastry and fruit. There are also more restrained fruit tartes, florentines and light pastries. Cakes and pudding cost from £1.30 for a gentle Danish up to very much more if you want a whole cake; *see p238.*
Bookings not accepted. Buggy access. Takeaway service.

Benihana

37 Sackville Street, W1S 3DQ (7494 2525/www.benihana. co.uk). Piccadilly Circus tube. **Lunch served** noon-3pm daily. **Dinner served** 5.30-10.30pm Mon-Sat; 5-10pm Sun. **Set meals** Lunch £8.75-£25 4 courses. Dinner £17-£50 6 courses. **Credit** AmEx, DC, MC, V. **Map** p318 J7.

There's no children's menu at Rocky Aoki's Japanese-style restaurants, but kids will happily share, entranced by the sight of their steaks and seafood being cooked at the table by chefs as well trained in the dramatic arts as they are in the culinary ones. Golden chicken, prawns, steak and vegetables are served fresh and sizzling. Sushi, sashimi and tempura are also on the menu, and the set menus are good: teppan specials include green tea, onion soup, salad, rice, prawn roll and ice-cream to follow. The Samurai lunchbox with chicken beef and salmon, plus rice, miso soup and green tea costs £9.25.
Buggy access. High chairs. Nappy-changing facilities. Takeaway service.
Branches: 77 King's Road, SW3 4NX (7376 7799); 100 Avenue Road, NW3 3HF (7586 9508).

Ed's Easy Diner

12 Moor Street, W1V 5LH (7439 1955). Leicester Square or Tottenham Court Road tube. **Meals served** Winter 11.30am-11.30pm Mon-Thur; 11.30am-midnight Fri, Sat; 11.30am-11pm Sun. Summer 11.30am-midnight Mon-Thur; 11.30am-1am Fri, Sat; 11.30am-11.30pm Sun. **Main courses** £4.40-£7.90. Minimum (at peak hours) main course. **Credit** AmEx, MC, V. **Map** p317 K6.

Ed's retro filling stations are just great. The quality of the thick burgers, chunky fries (try the cheesy ones for those

added calories) and gloriously gloopy malts and milkshakes. You sit at the bar to feed your face, with a mini-jukebox ('70s hits) in front of you. The stools are high, so don't bring babies or toddlers, but for over-fours the music, great grub (served in Junior Bite portions for mini-appetites), jelly-bean vending machines and smiley staff make Ed's easy heaven.
Buggy access. Children's menu (£4.45 incl drink). Crayons. No smoking. Tables outdoors (4, pavement). Takeaway service.
Branches: 362 King's Road, SW3 5BT (7352 1956); 19 Rupert Street, W1D 7PA (7287 1951); O2 Centre, 255 Finchley Road, NW3 5UZ (7431 1958).

The Fountain
Ground floor, Fortnum & Mason, 181 Piccadilly, W1A 1ER (7734 8040). Piccadilly Circus tube. **Meals served** 8.30am-7.30pm Mon-Sat. **Main courses** £8.95-£25. **Credit** AmEx, DC, MC, V. **Map** p318 J7.
See p174 **Scoff till you drop**.
Buggy access. Children's menu (£4.25-£5.25). Crayons. High chairs. Nappy-changing facilities (in shop, until 6.30pm). No-smoking tables.

Hamleys Café
Fifth floor, Hamleys, 188-96 Regent Street, W1B 5BT (7479 8016/general info 0870 333 2450/www.hamleys. com). Oxford Circus tube. **Open** 10am-8pm Mon-Sat; noon-6pm Sun. **Credit** AmEx, MC, V. **Map** p316 J6.
See p174 **Scoff till you drop**.
Buggy access. Children's menu. Nappy-changing facilities. No smoking.

Harbour City
46 Gerrard Street, W1D 7QH (7439 7859). Leicester Square or Piccadilly Circus tube. **Dim sum served** noon-5pm Mon-Sat; 11am-5pm Sun. **Meals served** noon-11.30pm Mon-Thur; noon-midnight Fri, Sat; 11am-10.30pm Sun. **Main courses** £6-£20. **Map** p319 K7.
Not all the restaurants in Chinatown are friendly. Some, like the Wong Kei on Wardour Street, are famous for their rude staff, but Harbour City is notably accommodating towards family groups. The menu is very long, with some unusual Hakka dishes, but all the family favourites (fried rice, king prawns, spring rolls, fried chicken) can be found. Come at lunchtime for dim sum, an array of dumplings and other tit-bits, served with a pot of tea.
Buggy access. No-smoking tables. Takeaway service .

Hard Rock Café
150 Old Park Lane, W1K 1QR (7629 0382/www. hardrock.com). Hyde Park Corner tube. **Meals served** 11.30am-12.30am Mon-Thur, Sun; 11.30am-1am Fri, Sat. **Main courses** £7.95-£14.95. *Minimum* (when busy) main course. **Credit** AmEx, DC, MC, V. **Map** p318 H8.
Don't be alarmed if you see a man-sized guitar bearing down on you along Old Park Lane. This is Rocky, the guitar mascot adopted by the Hard Rock to get children into the rock 'n' roll mood. Food critics grumble that this loud and lively place is only good for tourists and children, and the latter certainly get the full gamut of kiddie-friendly accoutrements: a large play area with toys, Rocky, children's menu, children's parties (these are bookable, costing £6.95 a head) and themed activities for the holidays, such as Little Monsters Hallowe'en events and twinkly Christmas parties. The food is, on the whole, enjoyable and hearty. We like the chicken fajitas, the filling cheesy nachos, the quality burgers and the amusing Lil' Rocker menu and activity book for children, the price of which includes refillable soft drinks (in a souvenir 'kiddie cup'). Mains include a small version of the excellent Hard

Rock cheeseburger or 'Foo Fighting fish sticks' with chips and beans. The hot fudge sundae costs just 95p.
Buggy access. Children's menu (£4.25). Entertainment: occasional face-painting Sat, Sun. High chairs. No-smoking tables. Tables outdoors (10, pavement). Toys.

Harry Ramsden's
The Regent Palace Hotel, Sherwood Street, W1A 4BZ (7287 3148/www.harryramsdens.co.uk). Piccadilly Circus tube. **Open** 11am-11pm daily. **Credit** AmEx, DC, MC, V. **Map** p318 J7.
A name that will always be associated with the 'great' British seaside holiday (when extreme cold forces you into the nearest chippie to the beach), Harry Ramsden's is now delivering fish in batter and potatoes that cheer to hungry Londoners. This restaurant looks a bit impersonal, but the food is fab and children very welcome. Our cod in batter was flakily fresh, the chips golden and not too dry. For children aged up to eight, the junior menu provides nuggets or sausage instead of fish for £2.99; nine to 12s pay £1 more for theirs.
Buggy access. Children's menu (£3.99). High chairs. Nappy-changing facilities. No-smoking tables. Takeaway service.

Hong Kong
6-7 Lisle Street, WC2H 7BG (7287 0352). Leicester Square or Piccadilly Circus tube. **Dim sum served** noon-5pm daily. **Meals served** noon-11.30pm Mon-Thur; noon-midnight Fri, Sat; 11am-11pm Sun. **Main courses** £5.50-£10.50. **Set lunch** £10 3 courses. **Map** p319 K7.
Sunday lunchtimes see the Hong Kong full of families, both Chinese and foreign, enjoying slap-up meals from the ginormous dim sum list, with its numerous light little dumplings with prawn, pork and scallops within. The cooked-at-table sizzling dishes go down especially well, but so do the seafood specials. Hong Kong isn't cheap, but it's fine for a treat.
Buggy access. High chairs. Nappy-changing facilities.

Masala Zone
9 Marshall Street, W1F 7ER (7287 9966/ www.realindianfood.com). Oxford Circus tube. **Lunch served** noon-3pm Mon-Fri; 12.30-3.30pm Sun. **Dinner served** 5.30-11pm Mon-Fri; 6-10.30pm Sun. **Meals served** 12.30-11pm Sat. **Main courses** £6-£12. **Credit** MC, V. **Map** p316 J6.
The nicest thing about this pretty, spacious pan-Indian restaurant is that you can taste lots of little dishes for next to nothing: just 75p buys a little pot of dahl, or pickle, or vegetable curry to try. Otherwise children can have a child-sized thali, with various little dips, crunchy bits, rice and pickles – excellent value for money. The Masala Zone special lunch is put together with the eater's health in mind, and there are even Ayurveda-inspired special thalis for diabetics. As well as the more snacky spreads, there are slow-cooked, beautifully detailed curries, stews and noodle bowls. Service is kind and encouraging to children, especially when it's not too busy.
Buggy access. Children's menu (£3.50). High chairs. No smoking. Takeaway service.

Planet Hollywood
13 Coventry Street, W1D 7DH (7287 1000/ www.planethollywoodlondon.com). Piccadilly Circus tube. **Meals served** noon-1am Mon-Sat; noon-12.30am Sun. **Main courses** £8.50-£19.95. **Credit** AmEx, DC, MC, V. **Map** p319 K7.
Early teens are crazy about this place: we know many who have celebrated birthdays with refillable pop and massive burgers in its starry environs, getting a real kick out of see-

Rock & Sole Plaice. *See p167.*

ing themselves on the wall of video screens. Parents tend to find the barrage of noise and *Rambo/Die Hard* memorabilia bewildering, so it's best to leave the kids to it. If that's not possible, the grown-ups can at least take comfort in the tasty American stalwarts: lovely spinach and cheese dip with tortillas, or buffalo wings with a fancy blue cheese dressing or salads to start, then excellent lean burgers, massive plates of ribs and golden fried chicken, with crisp, medium-cut fries. (If you want to escape the red meat, there are good and very large salads, seafood and fish dishes.) Service is friendly and amusingly indulgent towards children.
Balloons. Booking advisable (weekends; no reservations Sat). Buggy access. Children's menu (£7.95). Crayons. High chairs. Nappy-changing facilities. No-smoking tables.

Quod Restaurant & Bar

57 Haymarket, SW1Y 4QX (7925 1234/www.quod.co.uk). Piccadilly Circus tube. **Open** noon-midnight Mon-Sat; 5-10.30pm Sun. **Main courses** £7.95-£14.95. **Credit** AmEx, DC, MC, V. **Map** p319 K7.
Quod is a big, friendly and efficient restaurant in an enormous space. Noise levels climb in the evenings, but for lunch or afternoon tea (scones, cream, jam and a restorative cuppa are served 3-5pm) it's very pleasant. The menu is mostly Italian, with plenty of pasta and risottos, as well as good grilled fish, cold meats and salads, and tempting puddings. The children's menu lists cheese and tomato pizza, spaghettini and burger or nuggets with chips. Ice-cream follows.
Buggy access. Children's menu (£3.95). High chairs. No-smoking area.

Rainforest Café

20 Shaftesbury Avenue, W1D 7EU (7434 3111/ www.therainforestcafe.co.uk). Piccadilly Circus tube. **Meals served** noon-10pm Mon-Thur; noon-8pm Fri; 11.30am-8pm Sat. **Main courses** £9.95-£15.95. **Credit** AmEx, DC, MC, V. **Map** p319 K7.

The minute they walk into this steamy rainforest emporium, children are saucer-eyed with wonder – tinies get the screaming ab-dabs when the animatronic crocodile in the doorway swamp snaps and moves towards them. On the ground floor, the shop has mountains of soft toys, plastic reptiles, clothing and stationery. Usher the children past polystyrene rocky outcrops and bubbling swamps to the downstairs restaurant, with its chattering, cawing and roaring sound effects, waterpools and animatronic animals lurking in shadowy glades. It's a warm welcome, without a doubt, but at a price: the Rainforest Rascals menu for children costs nearly a tenner, and an adult's chicken salad costs £11.25. Portions of interestingly named burgers, ribs, pizza, chicken and pasta are unfailingly generous, so there's a lot of waste if the children are young; order a starter and help them with their chips. This is the city's largest no-smoking restaurant.
Buggy access. Children's menu (£9.95). Crayons. High chairs. Nappy-changing facilities. No smoking.

RIBA Café

66 Portland Place, W1B 1AD (7631 0467). Great Portland Street or Oxford Circus tube. **Open** 8am-6pm Mon-Fri; 9am-4pm Sat. **Credit** AmEx, DC, MC, V. **Map** p316 H5.
It's so amazingly grand around this neck of the woods, and the Royal Institute of British Architects looks forbidding with its lofty portals, marble staircases and towering columns, but venture upstairs to the café and you'll be pleasantly surprised. It's spacious, so you can sit away from the bespectacled designer types earnestly discussing RSJs, and enjoy the view from the massive windows and elegant roof terrace. Coffees and drinks are reasonably priced, the sandwiches, cakes and light lunches delicious. No one minds if you want to share a chocolate croissant or brownie with your toddler or bring the family for a pre-shopping breakfast.
High chairs. Tables outdoors (20, terrace). Nappy-changing facilities. No smoking.

Smollenskys on the Strand. *See p168.*

Royal Dragon

30 Gerrard Street, W1D 6JS (7734 1388). Leicester Square or Piccadilly Circus tube. **Dim sum served** noon-5pm daily. **Meals served** noon-3am Mon-Sat; 11am-3am Sun. **Main courses** £6.30-£23. **Map** p319 K7.

We're fond of the Dragon, because it serves some of the area's finest dim sum from a menu that is long and quite daunting. Go for the good value dim sum deal, which gives you a tableful of the traditional breakfast and lunchtime snacks of little dumplings and other tasty morsels to try. The noodle dishes are also good. Service is patient and child-friendly.

High chair. Takeaway service.

Stanleys

6 Little Portland Street, W1W 7JE (7462 0099). Oxford Circus tube. **Meals served** noon-11pm Mon-Sat. **Main courses** £8.50-£10.95. **Credit** AmEx, DC, MC, V. **Map** p316 J5.

Rather hidden away, and giving more than a suggestion of a softly lit gents' club, Stanleys is nonetheless exceedingly friendly toward families, particularly during the day and early evening. The stolidly British menu has stalwarts like steak and fish cakes or posh dishes such as seared tuna and pan-fried scallops, but its main draw is the range of sausages. There are lamb ones, turkey ones, sausages with beef and beer, or simple Stanley pork. They're served with mash, veg and gravy flavoured to suit your choice of meat. Kids can have small portions of anything on the menu for a fiver, which is fair enough, especially if the full-size dish is £15.

Buggy access. High chairs. Nappy-changing facilities. No-smoking tables. Reduced-price children's portions.

Strada

15-16 New Burlington Street, W1S 3BJ (7287 5967/ www.strada.co.uk). Oxford Circus or Piccadilly Circus tube. **Meals served** noon-11pm Mon-Sat; noon-10.30pm Sun. **Credit** AmEx, DC, MC, V. **Map** p318 J7.

There are 15 Stradas in London, which is great news for devotees of simple Italian food. The menu changes but you can always rely on great pizzas from the wood-fired ovens. They're thin of crust and top heavy with delights such as buffalo mozzarella with tomato and basil, salami, spinach and Parma ham. There are seven or so pasta dishes and risottos and a range of daily specials, with half portions for kids.

Buggy access. High chairs. No-smoking tables. Tables outdoors (6, pavement). Takeaway service.

Branches: throughout town. Call or check the website.

Yo! Sushi

52 Poland Street, W1V 3DF (7287 0443/www.yosushi. co.uk). Oxford Circus tube. **Meals served** noon-11pm Mon-Thur; noon-midnight Fri, Sat; noon-10.30pm Sun. **Credit** AmEx, DC, MC, V. **Map** p316 J6.

Though an acquired taste – the famous conveyor-belt (kaiten) sushi bar is great entertainment, and encourages healthy habits. Not only do the plates (colour coded) include tuna and seaweed-and-rice combos, but there's unlimited mineral water (£1) and green tea. Sushi aficionados may complain that the salmon, mackerel and tuna nigiri are bland, but our reviewers, aged 11 and 14, loved the grub.

Balloons and stickers. Booster seats. No smoking.

Branches: throughout town. Call or check the website.

Covent Garden

Belgo Centraal

50 Earlham Street, WC2H 9LJ (7813 2233/www.belgo-restaurants.com). Covent Garden tube. **Meals served** noon-11pm Mon-Thur; noon-11.30pm Fri, Sat; noon-10.30pm Sun. **Main courses** £9.95-£18.95. **Set lunch** (noon-5.30pm) £5.95 1 course. **Credit** AmEx, DC, MC, V. **Map** p317 L6.

We like the fact that Belgo's children's menu has the healthy option of a flavoursome bowl of garlicky moules as well as more usual fish and chips or sausages; many kids love the rotisserie chicken. But the best thing about the food is that it's all free if the adult in the party chooses a dish from the menu (the great-value set lunches don't count in this deal). *See also p179* **Cheap as chips**.
Buggy access. Children's menu (free with paying adult). Crayons. Disabled access: lift. High chairs.
Branches: Belgo Bierodrome, 173-4 Upper Street, N1 1XS (7226 5835); Belgo Noord, 72 Chalk Farm Road, NW1 8AN (7267 0718).

Browns

82-4 St Martin's Lane, WC2N 4AA (7497 5050/www.browns-restaurants.com). Leicester Square tube. **Meals served** noon-10.30pm Mon, Sun; noon-11.30pm Tue-Sat. **Main courses** £7.95-£16.95. **Set meals** (noon-6.30pm Mon-Sat) £10.95 2 courses. **Credit** AmEx, DC, MC, V. **Map** p319 L7.
An after-the-office sort of place, with ceiling fans and potted palms, where Theatreland workers come to let their hair down and save a bit of money on a set menu (available before 6pm) that offers steak sandwiches, soup, pasta, chicken and burgers. The surroundings are spacious and pleasant enough, and the children's menu is useful if unimaginative, with meat- or tomato-sauce-based pasta, burgers or rather nice chicken strips, pork and leek sausages or salmon fish cakes with either chips or mash. A ice-cream pudding is included in the price, but drinks, sadly, aren't.
Children's menu (£4.95). High chairs. Nappy-changing facilities. No-smoking tables.

Café Pacifico

5 Langley Street, WC2H 9JA (7379 7728/ www.cafepacifico-laperla.com). Covent Garden or Leicester Square tube. **Meals served** noon-11.45pm Mon-Sat; noon-10.45pm Sun. **Main courses** £6-£14.95. **Credit** AmEx, MC, V. **Map** p317 L6.
We love this homely cantina, where the staff are always good natured and the chicken quesadillas, full of avocado and moist, smoky meat, are delicious. Families can share a spread of street tacos, nachos and enchiladas or can interest the children in their own, ridiculously cheap, menu. Nuggets (*pepitas de pollo*) and chips and fish fingers (*dedos de pescado*) are listed, but the Mexican option is best: a platter of cheese-filled quesadillas with rice, avocado and mayo. The price includes pop and an ice-cream. Parents driving prams might have to forgo the Margarita jugs in favour of delicious alcohol-free cocktails (which children also love). Our favourite is the Cancun Cooler, all crushed strawberries and citrus (£2.90). *See also p179* **Cheap as chips**.
Buggy access. Children's menu (£2.95). Crayons. High chairs.

Food for Thought

31 Neal Street, WC2H 9PR (7836 0239). Covent Garden tube. **Breakfast served** 9.30-11.30am Mon-Sat. **Lunch served** noon-3.30pm Mon-Sat; noon-5pm Sun. **Dinner served** 5-8.15pm Mon-Sat. **Main courses** £4-£6. *Minimum* (noon-3pm, 6-7.30pm) £2.50. **No credit cards**. **Map** p317 L6.
There aren't many successful restaurants in town that (a) first opened in the 1970s and (b) have never stopped being successful. The venerable veggie FfT is one such. Come before the lunchtime rush and you can bag a table (though you'll still be rubbing shoulders with your neighbours); if it's full (and it nearly always is), use the takeaway counter and take your meal to St Paul's Churchyard (*see p76*) or on the piaz-

za. The food is legendary – and filling. Slabs of quiche are vast, salads interestingly put together, puddings fruit- and fibre-rich with splendid creamy toppings; flapjacks are fruit-filled oaty sensation. Expect to spend about £6 on a square meal for lunch and not fancy any tea.
No smoking.

Hamburger Union

4 Garrick Street, WC2E 9BH (7379 0412/www.hamburgerunion.com). Leicester Square tube. **Meals served** 11.30am-10pm Mon-Wed; 11.30am-10.30pm Thur-Sat; 11.30am-9.30pm Sun. **Main courses** £3.95-£6.95. **Credit** MC, V. **Map** p319 L7.
Gourmet hamburgers are the way to go these days, this is one of the most recent exponents. The Union has plain bench seating (one high chair), perfect char-grilled and juicy burgers, own-made chips, fabulous malts. The burgers come as a filling surprise to children accustomed to fast-food patties. They're made with naturally reared beef and the grilled breastmeat in the chunky chicken sandwich is free range. With burgers from £3.95 and chips £2, prices are reasonable for such top-quality grub, and it's so filling you'll hardly have room for your nutritious, creamy malt shake (£2.95).
Buggy access. High chairs. No smoking. Takeaway service.

Maxwell's

8-9 James Street, WC2E 8BH (7836 0303/ www.maxwells.co.uk). Covent Garden tube. **Meals served** noon-11pm daily. **Main courses** £7.25-£14.14.45. *Minimum* (when busy) main course. **Credit** AmEx, DC, MC, V. **Map** p317 L6.
Maxwell's is a long-established American burger/rib/steak joint that prides itself on its family- (in fact everybody-) friendliness. It is most geared up for babies, children and bewildered parents at lunch-times, as during the evening it can get very crowded and noisy. Whatever the time of day, staff greet you like long-lost friends and make a fuss of the children partaking of the kiddie menu, which includes an ice-creamy pud and soft drink alongside its nice lean mini-burgers, hot dogs or chicken strips. Fries are particularly good, thick, crispy and golden. Adult portions are whopping and fattening, even the salads, which aren't easy on the oil.
Buggy access. Children's menu (£7.25). Crayons. High chairs. Nappy-changing facilities. No-smoking tables. Tables outdoors (6, pavement).
Branch: 76 Heath Street, NW3 1DN (7794 5450).

The Mediterranean Kitchen

50-51 St Martin's Lane, WC2N 4EA (7836 8289). Charing Cross tube/rail. **Meals served** 11am-11.30pm Mon-Sat; 11am-10.30pm Sun. **Main courses** £5.95-£13.95. **Credit** AmEx, DC, MC, V. **Map** p319 L7.
A restrained-looking restaurant, the Med kitchen endears itself to families by providing a decent £5 children's menu. The options are hearty and pan-European, with simple starters like olives, oil and delectable fresh-baked Pugliese bread (a Med Kitchen speciality) and more complicated numbers such as spinach, mushrooms and goat's cheese with bruschetta. A deliciously seasoned chopped steak burger comes with a huge pile of the nicest own-made thin fries we've tasted in a long while. Pasta and risotto strike a reliable Italian chord, but lamb tagines, marinated chicken and pan-fried fish add a touch of exotica. Most of the dishes on the main menu can be served in smaller portions if the kids cock a snook at the menu dedicated to them.
Buggy access. Children's menu (£5). Crayons. High chairs. Tables outdoors (2, pavement).
Branches: 127-9 Kensington Church Street, W8 7LP (7727 8142); 334 Upper Street, N1 0PB (7226 7916).

Neal's Yard Bakery & Tearoom

6 Neal's Yard, WC2H 9DP (7836 5199). Covent Garden tube. **Meals served** 10.30am-4.30pm Mon-Sat. **Main courses** £3.50-£5. Minimum (noon-2pm Mon-Fri; 10.30am-4.30pm Sat) £2.50. **No credit cards.** **Map** p317 L6.

This sweet tearoom has views over the lovely, colourful yard full of interesting-looking bohemian types. There are rejuvenating pots of tea (juices or milk for the kids) to be taken with fantastic cakes, or lunchtime specials such as mushroom risotto, a sweet potato bake that looks a bit messy but tastes heavenly, and lovely salady bean burgers. Most children will choose cakes over hearty hot-pots, but that's kids for you. Those who are wheat-, milk- or yeast-sensitive can pop across to Neal's Yard Salad Bar for dairy- and gluten-free dishes. *No smoking. Tables outdoors (2, courtyard; 5, patio).*

Paul

29 Bedford Street, WC2E 9ED (7836 3304). Covent Garden tube. **Open** 7.30am-9pm Mon-Fri; 9am-9pm Sat, Sun. **Credit** AmEx, MC, V. **Map** p319 L7.

This most attractive of cafés has a shop in the front and cool, dark, nostalgic seating area beyond. It's a lovely place for morning coffee or afternoon tea, and though it looks a bit elegant for sticky-fingered children, the staff are indulgent. As well as light lunches (omelettes, salads, crêpes, tarts), there are fabulous, light pastries, tartes and pains au chocolat. *See also p177* **Let them eat cake.** *Buggy access. Children's menu.*

PJ's Grill

30 Wellington Street, WC2E 7BD (7240 7529). Covent Garden tube. **Brunch served** noon-4pm daily. **Meals served** noon-1am Mon-Sat; noon-4pm Sun. **Main courses** £8.95-£13.95. **Credit** AmEx, DC, MC, V. **Map** p319 L6.

Smart, slick PJ's eschews full-on US pumped-up volume in favour of Theatreland elegance. Staff are all American cheeriness, however. The adult-sized steaks are legendary and children's menu has pasta, with or without tomato sauce, chicken or fish and chips, and very fine burgers. *Buggy access. Children's menu (£4.95). High chairs. No-smoking tables.*

Rock & Sole Plaice

47 Endell Street, WC2H 9AJ (7836 3785). Covent Garden or Leicester Square tube. **Meals served** 11.30am-10.30pm Mon-Sat; noon-9.30pm Sun. **Main courses** £7-£13. **Credit** MC, V. **Map** p317 L6.

There's a pleasant Mediterranean influence at work on this, London's oldest surviving chip shop. The Turkish proprietors have included pitta, taramasalata and Efe's beer in a nod to their homeland, but most people come for fish and chips – huge platefuls that children with modest appetites do well to share. As well as increasingly expensive cod, there's mackerel, haddock, plaice and tuna to go with the thick-cut chips. Come on a summer evening to eat at a pavement table. *Buggy access. Tables outdoors (10, pavement). Takeaway service.*

Smollensky's on the Strand

105 Strand, WC2R 0AB (7497 2101/ www.smollenskys.co.uk). Embankment tube/Charing Cross tube/rail. **Meals served** noon-midnight Mon-Wed; noon-12.30am Thur-Sat; noon-5.30pm, 6.30-10.30pm Sun. **Main courses** £8.85-£19.95. **Set meal** (noon-7pm, after 10pm Mon-Fri) £10 2 courses, £12 3 courses. **Credit** AmEx, DC, MC, V. **Map** p319 L7.

Saturdays and Sundays are family affairs at Smollensky's. On these days smoking is banned and the flustered staff grin winningly at the children underfoot; it sometimes feels as if everyone in town has come for lunch, and the entertainers – balloon-modelling clowns, jolly jesters and face-painters – are

Well chuffed at **Blue Kangaroo**. *See p171.*

as rushed off their feet as the waiting staff. Children who can be persuaded to sit down instead of diving into the play areas choose between slightly anaemic hot dogs, fish, chicken or burgers with curly fries, or go for pasta or pizza. A drink is included. For adults there are steaks, seafood and veggie choices. Puddings are fab; for £2.25 children can choose between a pancakes, chocolate and ice-cream combo, gingerbread man and ice-cream, mousse, sundaes or brownies. *Booking advisable. Buggy access. Children's menu (£4.99). Crayons. Entertainment: clown, magic show, Nintendo games, face-painting (Sat, Sun). High chairs. No smoking. Play area (under-7s). Toys.*

TGI Friday's

6 Bedford Street, WC2E 9HZ (7379 0585/www.tgifridays. co.uk). Covent Garden or Embankment tube/Charing Cross tube/rail. **Meals served** noon-11.30pm Mon-Sat; noon-11pm Sun. **Main courses** £7.15-£15.45. **Credit** AmEx, MC, V. **Map** p319 L7.

With their badge-festooned braces and friendlier than thou welcome, the TGI staff are programmed to make customers feel special. Children are plied with balloons, activity sheets and crayons as soon as they sit down, and there are occasional entertainers (ring for details). The whole TGI experience is a delight for small people, if a tad headachey for parents. The food is consistently enjoyable. There are nachos, potato skins, ribs, corn cobs and seafood on the kids' menu, alongside favourites like burgers, chicken wings, steaks and pasta. The price includes drinks and puddings with whizz-poppy ice-creams and rich brownies. Kinder Eggs thrown in after, as if the children want anything more after all that. *Balloons. Buggy access. Children's menu (£6.25-£8.25). Crayons. Entertainment: occasional face-painting (Sat, Sun). High chairs. Nappy-changing facilities. No-smoking tables.* **Branches**: throughout town. Call or check the website.

World Food Café

Neal's Yard Dining Room, 1st floor, 14 Neal's Yard, WC2H 9DP (7379 0298/www.worldfoodcafe.com). Covent Garden or Leicester Square tube. **Meals served** 11.30am-4.30pm Mon-Fri; 11.30am-5pm Sat. **Main courses** £4.65-£7.95. **Minimum** (noon-2pm Mon-Fri; 11.30am-5pm Sat) £5. **Credit** MC, V. **Map** p317 L6.

A bustling, tourist-attractive place, the World Food Café has an open kitchen and long, wooden tables. The menu constitutes a vegetarian jaunt around the globe: Egyptian falafel, Middle Eastern meze, Thai stir-fries, Greek salads, Mexican refried beans and loads of interesting hot and cold meat-free snacks, meals and teatime treats (yummy cheesecake). The staff, when they're not rushing, are smiley and chatty to kids. *High chairs. No smoking.*

Westminster

Café in the Crypt

Crypt of St-Martin-in-the-Fields, Duncannon Street, WC2N 4JJ (7839 4342/www.stmartin-in-the-fields.org). Embankment tube/Charing Cross tube/rail. **Lunch served** 11.30am-3pm Mon-Sat; noon-3pm Sun. **Dinner served** 5-7.30pm Mon-Wed; 5-10.30pm Thur-Sat. **Main courses** £5.95-£7.50. **Set meal** £5.25 2 courses. **No credit cards. Map** p319 L7.

If you're after an honest-to-goodness square meal in the centre of town, with helpful staff and an unpretentious atmosphere, choose this subterranean café with its stone pillars and handy brass-rubbing centre (*see p82*). The hot dishes of the day, served with two veg, come in meaty or vegetarian form and may include shepherd's pie, meaty stews or beany bakes. Puddings, such as apple crumble and custard, fill any gaps, and there are lovely cakes. *High chairs. No-smoking tables. Takeaway service (drinks).*

Consumer

Inn The Park

*St James's Park, SW1A 2BA (7451 9999/www.innthe
park.com). St James's Park tube.* **Open** 8am-11pm daily.
Credit AmEx, MC, V. **Map** p319 K8.
See p162 **Parking space.**
*Buggy access. Children's menu (£4-£6). Disabled access:
toilets. High chairs. No smoking (inside). Tables outdoors
(40, terrace). Takeaway service.*

Texas Embassy Cantina

*1 Cockspur Street, SW1Y 5DL (7925
0077/www.texasembassy.com). Embankment
tube/Charing Cross tube/rail.* **Meals served** noon-11pm
Mon-Wed; noon-midnight Thur-Sat; noon-10.30pm Sun.
Main courses £7.50-£16.95. **Credit** AmEx, DC, MC, V.
Map p319 K7.
An exceptionally friendly restaurant, whose staff provide a
warm welcome for tourists looking for sustenance after a
morning in the National Gallery (*see p81*), the Texas
Embassy (there was one here, when Texas was a country in
its own right) is equally good with children, serving Tex-Mex
grub with a big smile and a stack of colouring-in materials.
Expect big burgers, T-bone steaks and Mexican staples, such
as nachos, fajitas and, interestingly, chicken breast with mole
(the bitter chocolate sauce). Dishes on the children's menu
include nachos, grilled cheese quesadillas, hot dogs and burgers, all at £4.50. Ice-cream or apple pie costs £1.75-£2.
*Balloons. Buggy access. Children's menu (main meals
£4.50). Crayons. High chairs. Nappy-changing facilities.
Tables outdoors (8, pavement).*

Kensington & Chelsea

Big Easy

*332-4 King's Road, SW3 5UR (7352 4071/www.big
easy.uk.com). Sloane Square tube, then 11, 19, 22 bus.*
Meals served noon-11.30pm Mon-Thur; noon-12.30am
Fri; 11am-12.30am Sat; 11am-11.30pm Sun. **Main
courses** £7.95-£14.50. **Set lunch** (noon-5pm Mon-Fri)
£7.95 2 courses. **Credit** AmEx, MC, V. **Map** p315 E12.
Vast plates of chicken wings, giant prawns, huge ribeye
steaks… this Southern-style joint serves food in Homer
Simpson-style portions. Children's helpings of hot dogs,
chicken dippers and burgers are more modest, though most
kids are hard-pushed to do justice to their pudding, whether
milkshake, ice-cream float, chocolate cake or baked
cheesecake. But try stopping them.
*Children's menu (£5.45, dessert £2-£3.95). Balloons.
Crayons. High chairs. Nappy changing facilities. No-
smoking tables. Tables outdoors (5, pavement).*

Bluebird

*350 King's Road, SW3 5UU (7559 1000/www.conran.
com). Sloane Square tube, then 11, 19, 22 bus.* **Brunch**
served noon-3.30pm Sat, Sun. **Lunch served** 12.30-3pm
Mon-Fri. **Dinner served** 6-11pm daily. **Main courses**
£7.95-£23. **Set lunch** (Mon-Fri) £15 2 courses, £20 3
courses. **Credit** AmEx, DC, MC, V. **Map** p315 D12.
The large-windowed Bluebird, with its fine summer
courtyard and courteous staff, is a delightful place to eat en
famille – if you can afford it. There's no pecuniary problem
with the children's menu of linguine in tomato sauce, fish and
chips or bangers and creamy mash. The set lunch also gives
reasonably good value, but à la carte sadly less so.
*Buggy access. Children's menu (£5.25-£6.25). High
chairs. Lift. Nappy-changing facilities. Tables outdoors
(25, courtyard).*

Blue Kangaroo

*555 King's Road, SW6 2EB (7371 7622/www.theblue
kangaroo.co.uk). Fulham Broadway tube/Sloane Square
tube, then 11, 19, 22 bus.* **Meals served** 9.30am-7pm
Mon-Fri; 9.30am-8.30pm Sat, Sun. **Main courses** £8-£16.
Credit AmEx, MC, V. **Map** p314 C13.
The fact that the bouncy Blue Kangaroo is sitting on a
frenetic indoor playground makes it an obvious contender for
this section and for the 2004 *Time Out* Best Family
Restaurant award, but the play apparatus would mean nothing if the staff weren't so sweet and the food so good. The
ingredients used for the dishes on the wipe-clean menu are
organic, the poultry free-range and the salmon wild. The children's menu (£4.95 with a drink) lists own-made all-breast
chicken nuggets, chunky real burgers and crud-free organic
sausages; a mixed-leaf salad can replace chips, if required.
The food for adults is equally encouraging: terrific, own-made
soups (our broccoli soup was beautifully fresh and flavoursome); a chicken sandwich of juicy breast meat, coated with
melted cheese and snug in fresh ciabatta; salmon fish cakes
with salad and buttery asparagus; or crunchy beer-battered
fish and chips. Parents whose children are too young to be
left can take coffee, meals and pastries downstairs by the play
equipment, but should be prepared for hideous noise levels.
*Buggy access. Children's menu (£4.95). High chairs.
Nappy-changing facilities. No smoking. Toys.*

Sticky Fingers

*1A Phillimore Gardens, W8 7EG (7938 5338/
www.stickyfingers.co.uk). High Street Kensington tube.*
Meals served noon-11pm Mon-Thur, Sun; noon-11.30pm
Fri, Sat. **Main courses** £8.45-£15.95. **Credit** AmEx, DC,
MC, V. **Map** p314 A9.
Too bad if your children have never heard of the Rolling
Stones or find them embarrassingly antique – Bill Wyman
has filled his restaurant with Stones memorabilia. But
parents (and grandparents) are usually thrilled by the posters,
mag covers, portraits, gold discs and guitars covering every
wall. You can buy T-shirts, caps, a souvenir menu… sad,
really. This rock 'n' roll diner is a treat, though. The young,
hip staff are welcoming to all ages (when we visited a
mother and baby group were installed, enjoying burgers and
milkshakes and breastfeeding happily). Children can choose
from their own burger/pasta/nugget menu, which includes
drinks and an ice-cream with sauce, or help out the grown-
ups. The food is good: the steaks juicy, the burgers lean and
smoky, own-made onion rings light and crunchy, chips fabulous and a hot chocolate brownie a stodgy delight.
*Buggy access. Children's menu (£7.25). Entertainment:
face-painting 1-4pm Sun. High chairs. No-smoking tables
(weekends).*

Top Floor at Peter Jones

*Peter Jones, Sloane Square, SW1W 8EL (7730 3434/
www.johnlewis.com). Sloane Square tube.* **Open** 9.30am-
6.30pm Mon-Sat. **Credit** MC, V.
See p174 **Scoff till you drop.**
*Buggy access. Children's menu (free-£2.50). Disabled: lift,
toilets. High chairs. Nappy changing facilities. No smoking.*

North London

Afghan Kitchen

*35 Islington Green, Islington, N1 8DU (7359 8019).
Angel tube.* **Lunch served** noon-3.30pm Tue-Sat.
Dinner served 5.30-11pm Tue-Sat. **Main courses**
£4.50-£6. **No credit cards.**

Sticky Fingers.
See p171.

This is a tiny and minimalist restaurant where you sit on very high stools to eat big plates of stew. There are four meat and four veggie choices on the menu, so it's quite easy to order the whole repertoire if you're in a hungry family group. The food is delicious: the mains are wholesome and well prepared, and the baklavá light, sweet and flaky. To aid digestion, staff offer Wrigley's chewing gum with the bill. Exotic, eh?
High chairs. Takeaway service.

Banners

21 Park Road, Finsbury Park, N8 8TE (8292 0001/ booking line 8348 2930). Finsbury Park tube/rail, then W7 bus. **Meals served** *9am-11.30pm Mon-Thur; 9am-midnight Fri; 10am-midnight Sat; 10am-11pm Sun.* **Main courses** *£7.95-£11.95.* **Set lunch** *£5.50 1 course.* **Credit** MC, V.
Banners does an amazing trick: it appeals to both kids and adults with huge plates of food and a noise level that drowns out any crying. Mid afternoon it has a crèche-like atmosphere, because children are tempted in with free popcorn, colouring books and toys. Portions are generous, and though the food isn't exactly refined – jerk chicken, steak sandwiches, fajitas, burgers and globetrotting specialities – it's served in hearty portions with always delicious fat-cut chips and cornbread.
Buggy access. Children's menu (£2-£5). High chairs.
Branch: 83 Hazelville Road, N19 3NB (7686 2944).

Brew House

Kenwood, Hampstead Lane, Hampstead Heath, NW3 7JR (8341 5384). 210, 214 bus. **Open** *Oct-Mar 9am-dusk daily. Apr-Sept 9am-6pm daily (7.30pm on concert nights).* **Credit** *(over £10)* MC, V.
See p162 **Parking space**.
Buggy access. Children's menu (£2.50-£3.95). High chairs. Nappy-changing facilities. No smoking (inside). Tables outside (seating for 400, garden). Takeaway service.

Café Mozart

17 Swains Lane, Highgate, N6 6QS (8348 1384). Highgate tube/Gospel Oak rail/C11 bus. **Meals served** *9am-10pm daily.* **Main courses** *£6.75-£11.* **Credit** *(over £5)* MC, V.
Cakes are a speciality at this Viennese-themed café, so cosy after a bracing yomp on Parliament Hill. Opt for the baked cheesecake or sachertorte if you have any sense, though the fruit tarts, pastries and cakes are all amazing. If you want a full meal, Mozart obliges with goulash, cold meats, pickles and bread, or a decent fry-up. The interior can be a bit cramped for buggies. Be prepared to queue at weekends. *See also p177* **Let them eat cake**.
Buggy access. High chair. No smoking. Reduced-price children's portions. Tables outdoors (8, courtyard).

Fine Burger Co.

256 Muswell Hill Broadway, Muswell Hill, N10 3SH (8815 9292/www.fineburger.co.uk). Highgate tube, then 43, 134 bus. **Meals served** *noon-11pm daily.* **Main courses** *£4.95-£8.20.* **Credit** AmEx, MC, V.
FBC burgers have been praised far and wide, which is just as well, since the menu is dominated by them – lamb, beef, chicken, vegetarian and even fish ones. The tuna burger is excellent, but the star is made from Scottish Highland Aberdeen Angus beef, eaten with cheese on top and big fat chips. The children's menu consists of 4oz beef or veggie burger, char-grilled chicken breast or breaded plaice goujons, all with chips and salad, but often children eat free when accompanied by a main-course burger-eating adult. (*See also p179* **Cheap as chips**.)
Buggy access. Children's menu (£4.95). Crayons. High chairs. Nappy-changing facilities. No smoking (until 7pm).
Branch: 37 Bedford Hill, SW12 9EY (8772 0266).

Golders Hill Park Refreshment House

North End Road, Golders Green, NW3 7HD (8455 8010). Golders Green or Hampstead tube. **Open** *10am-dusk daily.* **No credit cards**.
See p162 **Parking space**.
Children's menu (£2-£3.90). High chairs. Nappy-changing facilities. No smoking. Tables outdoors (25, terrace). Takeaway service.

Iznik

19 Highbury Park, Highbury, N5 1QJ (7354 5697). Highbury & Islington tube/rail. **Meals served** *10am-4pm daily.* **Dinner served** *6.30pm-midnight daily.* **Main courses** *£7.50-£9.50.* **Credit** MC, V.
After a run around in Highbury Fields, many families come to this Turkish restaurant for a long lunch. It's easy to see why: it looks exotic, with screens, candles and Ottoman lamps, and the menu is authentic and affordable. Stews and bakes are a speciality, but for lighter meals, try the salads, fresh bread and kebabs with yoghurt. Puddings are lovely.
Booking advisable (weekends).

Lemonia

89 Regent's Park Road, Chalk Farm, NW1 8UY (7586 7454). Chalk Farm tube/31, 168 bus. **Lunch served** *noon-3pm Mon-Fri; noon-3.30pm Sun.* **Dinner served** *6-11.30pm Mon-Sat.* **Main courses** *£8.75-£14.50.* **Set lunch** *£7.25 2 courses incl coffee; £8.50 3 courses.* **Credit** MC, V.
Some parents complain that Lemonia has become slightly too glamorous in recent years. Its popularity with famous folk of Regent's Park, and the consequent difficulties in booking a

weekend table, can be frustrating. Nevertheless, it's popular for many reasons, all still in evidence. The Greek menu is first rate, the ingredients fresh and lovely, and the staff good-natured. The lovely surroundings have a light and airy feel and the hanging baskets lend a holiday atmosphere. Choose from favourites, such as aubergine salads, kalamari, kléftiko and keftédes, or something rather more unusual from the daily specials. Don't miss out the rich, honeyed baklavá. *Buggy access. Tables outdoors (4, pavement).*

Mangal II
4 Stoke Newington High Street, Dalston, N16 8BH (7254 7888). Stoke Newington rail/76, 149, 243 bus. **Meals served** noon-1am Mon-Thur, Sun; noon-2am Fri, Sat. **Main courses** £7-£12. **No credit cards**.
This is the main jewel in the Mangal crown, where trendy Stokey families enjoy big meze meals safe in the knowledge that their children will find plenty to enjoy in the spread – chicken or lamb kebabs, rice, salads, soft breads and pleasantly sugary desserts all appeal to the young. The staff are as sweet as their puddings and ever eager to please. *High chairs. Takeaway service.*

Marine Ices
8 Haverstock Hill, Chalk Farm, NW3 2BL (7482 9003). Chalk Farm tube/31 bus. **Meals served** noon-3pm, 6-11pm Mon-Fri; noon-11pm Sat; noon-10pm Sun. **Main courses** £5.20-£9.60. **Credit** MC, V.
A family restaurant in every respect, this institution was founded by the Mansi family, whose ice-cream know-how quickly turned the place into a north London institution. Nowadays the gelateria comes with a light, bright, spacious restaurant, whose walls are adorned by compliments and signatures from satisfied celebrity customers. You'll struggle to get your children away from the ice-cream window – the delicious pistachio and outrageous tiramisu are our favourite flavours – but bag a table (book at weekends) and you'll find the menu also offers a good range of Italian pasta and pizza. *Buggy access. High chairs. No-smoking area (restaurant).*

Mosaica @ the factory
The Chocolate Factory, Wood Green Business Centre, Clarendon Road (off Coburg Road), Wood Green, N22 6XJ (8889 2400). Wood Green tube. **Open** 10am-10pm Tue-Fri; 7-10pm Sat; noon-4pm Sun. **Lunch served** noon-2pm Tue-Fri; 12.30-3pm Sun. **Dinner served** 7-10pm Tue-Sat. **Main courses** £10.75-£15.95. **Credit** AmEx, MC, V.
Runner-up in the Best Local Restaurant category in the 2003 *Time Out* Eating Awards, Mosaica charms all Londoners who brave the industrial wastes of Wood Green to reach it. Children get over their initial disappointment at Willy Wonka's absence and enjoy the courtyard area, and small portions from the brasserie-style menu. This usually lists a selection of appetisers, such as soups, warm salads and seafood, followed by well-made pasta specials, fish steaks with salad and char-grilled, roast or braised meat dishes. Puddings, such as our favourite chocolate mousse, are large. *Buggy access. High chairs. No-smoking tables. Tables outdoors (15, courtyard).*

Oshobasho Café
Highgate Wood, Muswell Hill Road, Highgate, N10 3JN (8444 1505). Highgate tube/43, 134 bus. **Open** 11am-3pm Mon (no food served); 8.30am-30mins before dusk Tue-Sun. **No credit cards**.
See p162 **Parking space**.
Children's menu (£2.80). Nappy-changing facilities. Tables outdoors (40, garden). Takeaway service.

Pukkabar
40 Chalcot Road, Chalk Farm, NW1 8LF (7483 0077). Chalk Farm tube. **Dinner served** 6.30-11pm Mon-Sat. **Meals served** 12.30-10.30pm Sun. **Main courses** £6.95-£10.95. **Credit** AmEx, MC, V.
This new-wave Indian restaurant in a quiet residential area looks sophisticated with its modern-looking ground-floor mezzanine and trendy basement, but it's child-friendly place. The children's menu is a selection of spicy little treats, such as Indianised fish fingers or little chicken kebabs with rice balls. The curries, baked meats and vegetable dishes here are incredibly good and perfectly spiced. *Buggy access. Children's menu (£1.50-£1.95). Tables outdoors (8, pavement). Takeaway service.*

Five perfect burgers

Our perfect burger isn't a flat, rubbery disc of low-grade meat, scored with fake char-grill lines and encased in a dried-out bap with limp iceberg garnish. A proper burger is a thick, juicy patty of minced meat (and nothing else) served in a fresh, doughy bun. If salads or gherkins are to be involved, they should be crisp and fresh. Thick-cut chips and interesting garnishes should be available. Where can you get such a feast? In many places; these days the gourmet burger means business. Our favourites are found at:

Ed's Easy Diner
See p163.

Fine Burger Co.
See p172.

The Gourmet Burger Kitchen
See p180.

Hamburger Union
See p167.

Tootsie's
See p182.

Santa Fe

75 Upper Street, Islington, N1 0NU (7288 2288/ www.santafe.co.uk). Angel tube. **Meals served** noon-10.30pm Mon-Thur, Sun; noon-11pm Fri, Sat. **Main courses** £6.95-£12.95. **Credit** AmEx, DC, MC, V.
Housed in Islington's old Electric Theatre, Santa Fe's child-friendliness isn't of the balloon-wielding variety. In fact, when we last visited the staff seemed a little bewildered by our small party of infants. Nevertheless, they were friendly and happy enough to dig out crayons and a big pile of paper, cheerfully arranging high chairs and warming bottles as they unearthed the children's menu. This lists quesadillas, pasta with cheese or tomato sauce, and (over)grilled chicken breast or burgers, plus a drink of choice. Portions are large. Adult meals are also generous: the chunky guacamole and various salsa starters are delicious. Mains include grilled lime salmon on rösti, spicy pork dishes and salads – the meaty ranch salad (chicken, leaves, grapes, parmesan and a creamy dressing) and a nutty one with goat's cheese. We've had issues with overcooked dishes, but this is an amiable enough place. *Booking advisable (weekends). Buggy access. Children's menu (£3.95). Crayons. High chairs. No-smoking tables.*

S&M Café

4-6 Essex Road, Islington, N1 8LN (7359 5361). Angel tube/19, 38 bus. **Meals served** 8.30am-11.30pm Mon-Thur; 9am-midnight Fri, Sat; 9am-10.30pm Sun. **Main courses** £2.50-£5.95. **Credit** MC, V.
This branch of the sausage café is attractive to adults who appreciate art deco tiling and aged wood counters. Children don't know what all the fuss is about but – if they like sausage and mash – they love it here too. There is an inventive selection of sausages: trad pork, some with healthy sun-dried tomato, even meat-free basil and mozzarella, although it's

Scoff till you drop

You've been dragging the children round the shops all morning. You're tired, hungry and the pushchair keeps upending itself because it's so laden with bulging carrier bags. Now you've got to find a restaurant that (a) accommodates aforementioned pushchair, (b) offers grub the kids might fancy, and (c) tolerates, er, spirited behaviour.

The good news is that London's top department stores have restaurants that not only cater for children, but positively encourage them. Top of the list is the self-styled child heaven of **Hamleys**, whose fifth-floor café (*see p164*) is a fitting finale to four floors of over stimulation. Nothing the children eat here will cost more than £3.95, so your credit card can take a bit of breather while you tuck into the Hamleys Monster Burger with cheese, salad and chips (£3.70 for kids; £6.95 for the adult equivalent, served with spicy potato wedges). Simpler lunches can be made of peanut butter and jelly sandwiches, own-made soup, panini, salads, pizzas, baked potatoes or pasta of the day. What's more, there are table-top games and a children's corner with plasma screen showing CBBC and children's films.

At **Planet Harrods** (guess where that is... *see p183*) a frantic wall of video screens play constant Cartoon Network to distract the children from the booty in those distinctive olive-green carrier bags. For £5.75 the children's menu provides burgers, beans and fried chicken dinners. If the dedicated children's restaurant doesn't appeal, there are Italian gelati made from double cream and real eggs in **Morelli's** in the food hall or American-style burgers, shakes and fries at **Mo's Diner**. The biggest noise to hit the Harrods food hall in the last year, however, is the first **Krispy Kreme Doughnuts** store in Europe.

Such calorie-laden kitsch is de trop for **Top Floor at Peter Jones** (*see p171*), a brasserie – that affords lovely views toward Hyde Park. This may be where lunching ladies come for sandwiches and a glass of chilled white, but it's also where they bring their children. Staff are very friendly and the children's menu caters for junior tastes, whether they tend to sausage and mash, a half portion of the pasta of the day or the special lunchbox, which contains sandwiches, juice or milk, fruit and a cake or biscuit (it costs from £2.50).

You have to herd the children past the amazing chocolatier in **Fortnum & Mason** (free chocs are sometimes available on the counter top) to take them downstairs to the frightfully old-fashioned **Fountain** (*see p163*). There, staff in black and white uniforms – the women spotless in maid's aprons and caps, the men starched in collars and ties – sashay from table to table, presenting high chairs and extra plates and spoons to the little masters and misses. The children's menu is great value in comparison to the gulp-inducing adult prices: for adults the impeccable soup with own-made cheese straw is £8 and Welsh rarebit costs £11, whereas children's mains (including a junior version of that lovely rarebit with beans and bacon on the side) are just £4.25. Quality ice-creams or shakes for pudding cost £2-£4.95.

At **Selfridge's** (*see p184*) there are so many chow-down choices you'll find a lunch spot wherever you are in the store. The self-service **Food Garden Café** on the fourth floor is billed as the family restaurant. Good choices from the griddle include child's size hamburgers or chicken. Vegetable stroganoff, fish and chips, and chicken nuggets with chips or veg come in children's portions for £3.75. Other offerings include Thai and Indian food, soups, fresh juices and Häagen-Dazs for afters. There's ample seating (350 places) too. Away from the Garden, there are perhaps 20 cafés and restaurants. For obvious reasons neither Momo, the exotic Moroccan café (with hookah pipes and thick coffee) on the third floor, nor the Balcony wine bar (no under-14s) are good for children, but **Yo! Sushi** (in the Food Hall), hot drinks and pastries from **Siena** (lower ground) and the soups and sandwiches on the first floor are all worth checking out.

hard to imagine the latter going with any of the varieties of mashed potato on offer (bubble and squeak suit you, or leek and cheddar, or do you prefer mash with cream and butter?), let alone the gravy. Though sausages are the draw, there's a menu of other comfort food, such as the All Day Breakfast and Crumble of the Day (with custard, natch).
Buggy access. Children's menu (£3.50).
Branches: 268 Portobello Road, W10 5TY (8968 8898); 48 Brushfield Street, E1 6AG (7247 2252); 231 High Street, Acton, W3 9BY (8992 7345).

Shish
2-6 Station Parade, Willesden Green, NW2 4NH (8208 9290). Willesden Green tube/260, 266 bus. **Meals served** 11.30am-11.45pm Mon-Sat; 10.30am-10.30pm Sun. **Main courses** £3.95-£8.95. **Credit** MC, V.
The novelty value of this sophisticated-looking place, with its proud 'Silk Road' menu (food from Turkey to Indonesia), long winding bar and trendy young staff, is as attractive to children as the grub. They like to sit on high stools at the bar, operating the pumps for unlimited mineral water (£1) and watching the Willesden cool cats sup their healthy mixes from the juice bar (apple, melon and cucumber is nice). Food-wise, the shish kebabs are a winner: try marinated chicken, salmon teriyaki or juicy lamb. Or ditch the shish and go for fries, bread and dips, spicy couscous, juices, sticky honey-drenched baklavá and ice-creams.
Buggy access. Children's menu (£4.25). High chairs. No-smoking tables (downstairs).
Branch: 313 Old Street, EC1V 9LE (7749 0990).

Toff's
38 Muswell Hill Broadway, Muswell Hill, N10 3RT (8883 8656). Highgate tube, then 43, 134 bus. **Meals served** 11.30am-10pm Mon-Sat. **Main courses** £8.95-£17.50. **Set meals** (11.30am-5.30pm Mon-Sat) £7.95 1 course. **Credit** AmEx, MC, V.
Time was when the Wild West saloon-style double doors here would have been enough to excite little children, but these days crayons, pictures and a dedicated menu are provided to keep the ankle-biters occupied. All too often they get stuck into the excellent chips and forget their colouring-in, such is the quality of the food. A child's portion of cod and chips costs £3; adults pay a bit more for large platters of battered, firm white cod, surrounded by chunky chips and optional mushy peas. Perfection on a plate, the whole family agreed.
Buggy access. Children's menu (£2.95-£3.50). High chairs. Takeaway service.

East London

Arkansas Café
Unit 12, Old Spitalfields Market, Whitechapel, E1 6AA (7377 6999). Liverpool Street tube/rail. **Lunch served** noon-2.30pm Mon-Fri; noon-4pm Sun. **Dinner served** party bookings only, by arrangement. **Main courses** £5-£14. **Credit** MC, V. **Map** p321 R5.
You'll smell this place long before you see it, which is a good thing when that smell is barbecued steaks, chicken and ribs. They taste as good as they smell, too, with plenty of sauce to squidge out of the bun as soon as the nearest launderer has turned away. Friendly and busy, Arkansas serves huge portions – chicken with mash and own-baked beans, gooey great slabs of cake and pecan pie – at makeshift tables with mismatched chairs. No chips, it states on the menu. No need.
No-smoking tables. Tables outdoors (terrace inside market).

Space to play at **Santa Fe**. *See p174.*

Faulkner's

424-6 Kingsland Road, Dalston, E8 4AA (7254 6152).
Dalston Kingsland rail/67, 76, 149, 242, 243 bus. **Lunch
served** noon-2pm Mon-Fri. **Dinner served** 5-10pm
Mon-Thur; 4.15-10pm Fri. **Meals served** 11.30am-10pm
Sat; noon-9pm Sun. **Main courses** £8.50-£13. **Minimum**
£4. **Credit** MC, V.

Dalston isn't in a part of London that's exactly attractive to
tourists, but if you find yourself hungry here, Faulkner's
gives you cheery service and decor that evokes seaside chippies circa 1964 (one for the grannies, then). Portions are large,
if not exactly cheap given the area. Children's servings of
scampi or nuggets and chips keep them happy while adults
tuck in to lovely fish cake balls, juicy pickled herring, followed by mountainous plates of battered cod, rock and haddock or rock salmon with chips, followed by fruit pie and
custard, while admiring the old pictures on the walls.
*Buggy access. Children's menu (£4.50). Disabled access:
toilet. High chairs. No-smoking tables.*

Frizzante at City Farm

1A Goldsmith's Row, Hackney, E2 8QA (7739 2266).
Bethnal Green tube, then 55, 106 bus. **Meals served**
10am-5.30pm Tue-Sun. **Main courses** £4.50-£6.50.
No credit cards.

Located in the free-range chicken heaven of Hackney City
Farm, this Italian café has a real community-hall feel to it: it's
a large room filled with benches and wooden tables bedecked
with red check tablecloths, the walls adorned with noticeboards. You order your food from the kitchen hatch – steak
sandwiches, vegetarian or meaty pies and quiches, big
nutritious salads, and a children's menu of either pasta (pesto
or tomato sauce) or ultra-thin, delicious pizzas (£2.50). Or you
can choose from the daily specials, reasonably priced (£4-
£7.50). The chefs use high-quality ingredients to create dishes such as gnocchi with wild mushroom sauce, served with
rocket salad, fabulous grilled chicken and vegetable skewers
with fried potatoes and salad, and spaghetti with mussels
and tomato sauce. Desserts, like the light pineapple cake and
tiramisu, are own-made and prepared fresh daily. The food's
attention to detail belies the rustic surroundings. You'll have
a job bagging outdoor seats on a sunny Sunday, so popular
is Frizzante with dressed-down, well-spoken nouveau
Hackney families.
*Buggy access. High chairs. Children's menu (£2.50-
£3.50). Tables outdoors (7, garden). Toys.*

Hadley House

27 High Street, Wanstead, E11 2AA (8989 8855).
Snaresbrook or Wanstead tube. **Lunch served** 11.30am-
2.30pm Mon-Sat. **Dinner served** 7-10.30pm Mon-Sat.
Meals served 10.30am-9pm Sun. **Main courses** £8.95-
£16.95. **Set dinner** (Mon) £16.95 3 courses.
Credit MC, V.

If you've made the pilgrimage way out east to lovely
Wanstead Park (*see p118*) or ancient Epping Forest (*see
p119*), you should reward your efforts with a blowout at
Hadley House. The menu is international, but there are
always a number of comforting dishes such as roast lamb or
seafood linguine, with cheesecakes and crumbles for pudding.
*Buggy access. High chairs. Reduced-price children's
portions. Tables outdoors (6, patio).*

Jones Dairy Café

23 Ezra Street, Bethnal Green, E2 7RH (7739 5372).
Old Street tube/rail, then 55 bus. **Open** 9am-3pm Fri, Sat;
8am-2pm Sun. **Main courses** £2-£6. **No credit cards.**
Jones is an institution for the early birds who made it to
Columbia Road Flower Market on a Sunday. No wonder: the
plain brunch-style food – omelettes, scrambled egg and
smoked salmon, tomatoes on toast – is excellent, the cakes
all but irresistible. It's only a small place, which means that
it's full to bursting on market days. No matter: you can
always get a takeaway from the bakery.
*Buggy access. High chair. No smoking. Tables outdoors (3,
patio). Takeaway service.*

Laxeiro

93 Columbia Road, Bethnal Green, E2 7RG (7729 1147).
Bethnal Green tube, then 8 bus/bus 26, 48, 55. **Lunch
served** noon-3pm, **dinner served** 7-11pm Tue-Sat.
Meals served 9am-3pm Sun. **Tapas** £2.95-£7.50.
Credit MC, V.

If you're driving (buggies, that is), you're not going to
manage cramped Laxeiro; for everyone else, the squeeze
enhances the sociable atmosphere. You'll find the typical
Spanish tapas – barbecued sardines, patatas bravas, chorizo, garlic mushrooms – at affordable rates. The Columbia
Road rule applies, though: make sure you book for Sunday
lunch, as the lovely Flower Market makes things extra busy.
*Booking advisable (dinner). Tables outdoors (2,
pavement). Takeaway service.*

Royal China

30 Westferry Circus, Docklands, E14 8RR (7719 0888).
Canary Wharf tube/DLR/Westferry DLR. **Meals served**
noon-11pm Mon-Thur; noon-11.30pm Fri, Sat; 11am-10pm
Sun. **Dim sum** noon-4.45pm daily. **Main courses** £6-
£40. **Dim sum** £2.20-£4.50. **Set meal** £28 per person
(minimum 2). **Credit** AmEx, DC, MC, V.

Docklands is making bolder and bolder claims on the attentions of visitors, with the Museum in Docklands (*see p116*)
only the most visible attraction here. It's a shame that, with
the exception of some chain branches, bargain eating needs
aren't dealt with better. Nonetheless, if a treat is what you
have in mind, the riverside location makes Royal China a joy.
The pleasure doesn't come cheap, but the dim sum menu is
justly famous, starring light and lovely seafood dumplings.
The rest of the menu lists the usual stir-fried meat and vegetable main dishes, noodles and rice – all delicious and beautifully prepared. Fabulous teas are served in little gold pots
– actually cardboard, they can be taken away as a souvenir.
Disabled: toilet. High chairs. Tables outdoors (23, garden).
Branches: 13 Queensway, W2 4QJ (7221 2535); 40 Baker
Street, W1M 1BA (7487 4688); 68 Queen's Grove, NW8
6ER (7586 4280).

Royal Inn on the Park

*111 Lauriston Road, E9 7HJ (8985 3321). Mile End tube,
then 277 bus.* **Open** noon-11pm Mon-Fri; noon-midnight
Sat; noon-10.30pm Sun. **Lunch served** noon-3pm, Mon-
Fri. **Dinner served** 6-9.30pm Mon-Fri. **Meals served**
noon-9.30pm Sat; noon-6pm Sun. **Credit** MC, V.

A popular pub right on Victoria Park (*see p114*), with ample
outdoor seating, has to be a boon for post-playground refuelling. The Royal heaves at Sunday lunchtimes, as the roast
lunch brigade head in to enjoy the specials, which come with
the tallest Yorkshires, roasties and veg (£9) – all served until
5pm. Puds include a splendidly squidgy jam sponge or
cherry pie with custard (£4). At other times, all sorts of choices are chalked up on the menu blackboards (the pub was
changing chefs as we went to press, but we're told to expect
no dramatic changes, thank goodness). There's a dedicated
dining room, plus a heated tent area out the back, but you
can eat your food anywhere.
*Buggy access. High chair. Nappy-changing facilities. No-
smoking area (restaurant). Tables outdoors (30, garden).*

Sông Quê

134 Kingsland Road, Shoreditch, E2 8DY (7613 3222).
Bus 26, 48, 55, 67, 149, 242, 243. **Meals served** noon-
3pm, 5.30-11pm Mon-Sat; noon-11pm Sun. **Main courses**
£4-£8.50. **Credit** MC, V.
This was *Time Out*'s favourite cheap eat in 2003, so it's a
great place to come for a big family repast. If there ever were
such a thing as a gregarious restaurant, this is it: the plain,
café style and high ceiling practically beg to be filled up with
friends and in-laws. You'd struggle to spend more than a tenner a head if everyone shares dishes chosen from the bewildering 170-plus item menu. As well as the brilliance of the
Vietnamese food – lots of noodles, stir-fries, little pancakes,
seafood, spicy soups, rice and chicken – the sweet-natured
staff and vast portions make every visit a delight.
Buggy access. High chairs. No-smoking tables. Takeaway
service.

South-east London

Beachcomber

34 Greenwich Church Street, Greenwich, SE10 9BJ (8853
0055). **Meals served** 11am-11pm Mon-Sat; 11am-10pm
Sun. **Main courses** £6.90-£22. **Credit** AmEx, MC, V.
Along with most of the restaurants in Greenwich,
Beachcomber has to keep a weather eye on the tourist trade.

Indeed, it pulls in many a hungry visitor with generous
portions of fish and chips. Yet this quirky, cluttered little
place is extremely friendly and staff are only too pleased to
provide small portions for children. As well as the traditional battered fish, seafood specialities include a mixed seafood
'dipper', octopus and Dover sole, served with new or sautéd
potatoes or chunky chips.
Children's menu (£3.90-£4.90). High chairs. No-smoking
tables. Takeaway service.

Chapter Two Coffee Shop

43-5 Montpelier Vale, Blackheath, SE3 0TJ (8333 2666/
www.chaptersrestaurants.co.uk). Blackheath rail. **Lunch**
served 8.30am-5.30pm daily. **Main courses** £3.95-
£5.95. **Credit** AmEx, MC, V.
This smart little café is attached to a posher modern
European restaurant. The cakes, bakes, puddings pastries
and pies is just what a body needs after a spot of football on
Blackheath. They're wonderfully child-friendly in here: the
kids can have a babycino (that's an espresso cup of milk, froth
and a sprinkling of chocolate powder for 30p) and little junior
blueberry muffins. Otherwise try fab pains au chocolat,
gâteaux and scrumptious sandwiches. The coffee shop's Just
Desserts display lets customers invest in whole fruit tartes
and tatins for their own dinner parties.
Buggy access. Disabled access: toilet. High chairs. Nappy-
changing facilities. No-smoking tables.

Let them eat cake

We're talking the sort of sticky cakes that
Paddington Bear famously paddled in on
the tabletop of a station café while Mr
Brown stirred his tea and wondered what
he was getting himself into. Big treat
cakes, all fluffy with cream and delicate
chocolatey flakes, with feather-light
sponge and melt-in-the-mouth pastry. The
sort you just can't make yourself, even if
you've bought every Nigella book on the
market. The sort you only find in an
effortlessly stylish French pâtisserie like
Paul (*see p169*), which smells of freshly
baked bread and has eclairs, meringues
and millefeuilles piled up on the counter
that really taste as good as they look.

For big, creamy gâteaux and delicate
glazed fruit tartes there's nowhere better
than Soho's **Patisserie Valerie** (44 Old
Compton Street, W1D 4TY, 7437 3466). Unless,
of course, it's **Patisserie Valerie at Sagne** (105
Marylebone High Street, W1U 4RS, 7935 6240),
the rather more child-friendly of the central London
Valeries. **Maison Bertaux** (28 Greek Street, Soho,
W1V 5LL, 7437 6007) is the croissant lover's
bakery of choice, although children usually
choose a pain au chocolat. As far as its cakes
are concerned, think creamy, fruity, chocolatey,
custardy French pâtisserie. For a plate of cakes
and a pot of tea after a run on Hampstead Heath,
try the legendary sachertorte at **Café Mozart** (*see*
p172) or enter cake heaven at **Maison Blanc** (62
Hampstead High Street, NW3 1QH, 7431 8338).

Less French finesse, more yankee doodle – with
a fragrance to make your tummy rumble – the
branch of **Krispy Kreme** in Harrods (*see p183*) is
pure doughnut-making theatre: you can watch the
snacks emerge from the fat to receive their sugar
glazing. A large carton of 15 varieties – iced and
spiced – will have the family doing Homer's
doughnut drool all over the posh food hall.

Our favourite cakes, however, are in branches
of **Konditor & Cook** (*see p159*). The bestsellers
include the outstanding chocolate curly whirly
cake, a dark chocolate sandwich, coffee walnut
cake and the little brightly iced individual magic
cakes, which look so pretty in their selection box,
almost too beautiful to bite into.

Chips ahoy! **Cutty Sark**.

Cutty Sark

Ballast Quay, off Lassell Street, Greenwich, SE10 9PD (8858 3146). Cutty Sark DLR/Maze Hill rail. **Open** 11am-11pm Mon-Sat; noon-10.30pm Sun. **Food served** noon-9pm Mon-Fri; noon-6pm Sat, Sun. **Credit** MC, V.

Walk about ten minutes along the Thames Path east from the famous tea clipper (*see p123*) and you get to this lovely old pub, perfect for pre- and post-riverside walks or park play. Inside, it's all dark wood and maritime memorabilia, with plenty of secluded tables where families can spread out. The picnic tables outside look over to the Dome on the peninsula and Canary Wharf across the water. An extensive menu chalked up on boards includes traditional warmers such as liver and bacon casserole, vegetable lasagne and some excellent fish, including everyone's favourite cod and chips that tends to sell out pretty quickly. The children's menu is bog standard sausage, nuggets or fish tiddlers and chips. *Children's menu (£2.75). Tables outdoors (10, riverside).*

Domali Café

38 Westow Street, Crystal Palace, SE19 3AH (8768 0096/www.domali.co.uk). Gypsy Hill rail. **Meals served** 9.30am-6pm Mon, Tue; 9.30am-11pm Wed-Sun. **Main courses** (9.30am-6pm Mon-Fri) £3.90-£4.90; (6-11pm Wed-Fri; 9.30am-11pm Sat, Sun) £5.90-£9.50. **Credit** MC, V.

Domali is a pleasant and laid-back local where families with young children fresh from an encounter with the local park's dinosaurs come for nursery meals of beans or scrambled egg on toast, huge peanut butter and banana sandwiches, and healthful fruit smoothies. There's a nice little garden to enjoy on sunny days and, if you're in the market for a big breakfast, Domali does the best meat-free fry-up for miles around. *Buggy access. High chairs. No-smoking tables. Tables outdoors (8, garden). Reduced portions for children (£1.45-£3.50).*

Escape

214-16 Railton Road, Herne Hill, SE24 0JT (7737 0333). **Meals served** noon-10pm daily. **Main courses** £4.50-£6. **Credit** AmEx, MC, V.

Escape to this art gallery and spacious refuelling spot. Its daytime popularity with the buggy brigade is assured: here are sofas to loll about on, or trendy tables, topped with pebbles cast in laminate. The Italian-slanted menu lists a handful of antipasti (bresaola carpaccio, £6.50), four salads (goat's cheese and roasted vegetables, £5.50), a dozen varieties of pizza (the pepperoni and roasted red onions is recommended) and ten types of hot ciabatta sandwiches (try the brie with mushrooms, sun-dried tomatoes and rocket). *Buggy access. High chairs. Tables outdoors (3, pavement).*

Olley's

67-9 Norwood Road, Herne Hill, SE24 9AA (8671 8259/ www.olleys.info). Herne Hill rail/3, 68 bus. **Meals served** noon-10.30pm Tue-Sat. **Dinner served** 5-10.30pm Mon, Sun. **Main courses** £5.75-£18.25. **Credit** AmEx, MC, V.

It may just be a little local fish and chip restaurant with a big pot-plant collection, but the Olley's Fish Experience is legendary. Its fish and chips are second to none, and the menu has amused food critics across the capital. Fish can be grilled or steamed if you're batter-unfriendly, and there's a huge range – from tuna (a big herby steak) to scampi (crisp and tender, but a tad salty), as well as more workaday cod, haddock and salmon. Chips are large, double-fried, crisp, golden and gorgeous. The children's menu (£4) lists cod and chips, scampi, plaice goujons or prawns and chips, and soft drinks are included. Leave room for apple pie and custard. *Children's menu (£4). High chairs. Tables outdoors (12, pavement).*

Pavilion Café

Dulwich Park, off College Road, Dulwich, SE21 7BQ (8299 1383). North Dulwich or West Dulwich rail. **Open** *Summer* 9am-6pm (with some late evenings) daily. *Winter* 9am-dusk daily. **No credit cards.** *See p162* **Parking space.** *Buggy access. Children's menu (£1.50-£3). Disabled access: toilet. High chairs. Nappy-changing facilities. Tables outdoors (8, terrace). Takeaway. Toys.*

El Pirata

15-16 Royal Parade, Blackheath, SE3 0TL (8297 1770/ 1880). Blackheath rail. **Meals served** noon-midnight daily. **Main courses** £8-£13. **Tapas** £2-£7. **Credit** AmEx, DC, MC, V.

The location right opposite the heath, great prices and an extensive tapas menu all add up to a timber-shivering family lunch venue. Children appreciate the crossed cutlass and ships' wheel decor, and their parents are touched by the benevolent attitude of the staff toward marauding young hearties. Choose tapas for lunch: you can have three for £6.95 or two for £4.95, so families can mix and match fried potatoes, avocado and mozzarella salad, sardines, marinated chicken, prawns or soup. Unlimited baskets of fresh bread keep everyone content, and the chocolate cake and ice-cream on the pudding menu have the kids dancing with joy. *Buggy access. High chairs. Tables outdoors (5, pavement).*

Tai Won Mein

39 Greenwich Church Street, Greenwich, SE10 9BL (8858 2688). Greenwich Cutty Sark DLR/Greenwich rail. **Meals served** 11.30am-11.30pm daily. **Main courses** £3.20-£3.80. **No credit cards.**

The policy at these Chinese cafés seems to be pack 'em in and stuff 'em full. The menu is displayed in vibrant glossy photo

form around the walls, and the food looks uncannily like the lurid depictions. You sit on benches at long tables to eat vast portions of thick, thin, soupy or fried noodles, loaded with stir-fried veg, beef, prawn, egg, tofu and duck. Each dish costs about a fiver and they generally defeat young appetites. Get children to share big helpings of prawn crackers, yummy prawn toast, ribs, spring rolls, egg-fried rice and noodles, and try to do a Cleversticks with their chopsticks (spoons are provided for the hungry and frustrated). The Greenwich branch is our favourite as it's just near the *Cutty Sark (see p123)*. *Buggy access.*
Branches: 90-92 Rushey Green, SE6 4HW (8690 8238); 14 Walworth Road, SE1 6SE (7277 1918).

South-west London

Blue Elephant
4-6 Fulham Broadway, Fulham, SW6 1AA (7385 6595/ www.blueelephant.com). Fulham Broadway tube. **Lunch served** noon-2.30pm Mon-Fri; noon-4pm Sun. **Dinner served** 7pm-midnight Mon-Thur; 6.30pm-midnight Fri, Sat; 7-10.30pm Sun. **Main courses** £9.50-£28. **Set meals** £35-£59 3 courses. **Set buffet** (Sun lunch) £22 adults, £11 children. **Credit** AmEx, DC, MC, V.
Really, this amazing Thai restaurant is a bit like an oriental theme park, but that doesn't stop wide-eyed children loving the fish ponds, dense foliage and elegant pavilions where people tuck into the specialities. Blue Elephant isn't cheap, but the Sunday buffet of Thai staples, such as spring rolls, pad Thai, spicy curry, fish cakes and kitschily carved fruits, makes the cost bearable. An even bigger draw on the Sabbath

is the range of activities for children (£2), which may include face-painting and sugar-spinning (making sweet curly decorations out of melted sugar). Great fun.
Buggy access. High chairs. Takeaway service.

Boiled Egg & Soldiers
63 Northcote Road, Battersea, SW11 1ND (7223 4894). Clapham Junction rail, then 219 bus. **Open** 9am-6pm Mon-Sat; 10am-4.30pm Sun. **Main courses** £3.95-£4.95. **No credit cards.**
On weekdays, after nursery, or Saturday afternoons, after the park, the café is packed with young families, with the odd dog chained up outside. Sunday mornings see the hollow-eyed hangover crew – rather tarnished young things recovering from last night's excesses. Breakfasts are lovely, from smart smoked salmon and scrambled egg with a glass of bubbly for the rich through whopping great full English fry-ups for the hungry to humble five-minute eggs, with toastie soldiers, for dads with toddlers. Afternoon teas, with cucumber sandwiches, own-made cakes and cookies are another big attraction. *See also p179* **Cheap as chips**.
Buggy access. Children's menu (from £1.50). Crayons. High chairs. Tables outdoors (3, pavement; 8, garden). Toys.

The Depot
Tideway Yard, Mortlake High Street, Barnes, SW14 8SN (8878 9462). Mortlake rail/209 bus. **Open** 10am-11pm Mon-Sat; 10am-10.30pm Sun. **Lunch served** noon-3pm Mon-Thur; noon-3pm Fri, noon-4pm Sat; noon-4pm Sun. **Dinner served** 6-10.30pm Mon-Thur, Sun; 6pm-midnight Fri; 6-11pm Sat. **Main courses** £9.95-£15. **Set meal** (Mon-Fri lunch) £10.95 2 courses. **Credit** AmEx, DC, MC, V.

Cheap as chips

We wish we could afford to eat in the sophisticated People's Palace (*see p159* and Julie's (*see p182*) every day, but sometimes there's that overdraft to mollycoddle. If we're feeling the pinch, our favourite destination is the rather noisy brothers **Belgo Centraal** (*see p166*) and **Bierodrome** (67 Kingsway, WC2B 6TD, 7242 7469), where junior mussel fans can enjoy a free lunch if they're accompanied by an adult who's eating a main course. (If they don't like shellfish, the chicken or fish goujons and chips are nice too.) Other places where children can eat free include the swanky **Bush Bar & Grill** (*see p181*) and the very fine **Fine Burger Co.** (*see p172*), whose 'kids eat free' offer (noon-7pm Mon-Fri, provided their adult pays for a burger) has found favour with Muswell Hill's large appetites. The offer isn't constant, though, so do ring to check before venturing north.

There are also those places where junior portions aren't quite free, but they are cheerily cheap. These include our favourite **Giraffe** (*see p163*), which has the added benefit of being no smoking, and **Café Pacifico** (*see p167*), the Mexican cantina where children get a full meal for £2.95. If that's too exotic, try boiled egg and soldiers at, er, **Boiled Egg & Soldiers** (*see p179*) for £2.25, or beans on toast at the sweet little **Bush Garden Café** (*see p182*) for a miserly £1.50.

Of course, many a child's favourite cheap treat is to be found at **McDonald's**. Don't scream. Now the burger giant's global domination is on the wane (it failed to make a profit last year), it's been adding apple slices, yoghurt, organic milk and salads to the children's menu. And anyway, a little of what they fancy doesn't always do them harm.

For river views and tempting menus, this brasserie can't be beat. That it's a firm favourite with moneyed family groups is largely because of a hugely successful menu, with some perfect vegetarian dishes as well as juicy ribeye steaks, char-grilled swordfish, cod and crab cakes, and rack of lamb. While adults indulge themselves in such fare, children can work their way through their own simple menu: penne served plain, with butter and cheese, or with a napolitana or bolognese sauce, salmon fish cakes and chips, or sausage and mash. Service is good-natured toward young diners.
Buggy access. Children's menu (£3.50 incl free ice-cream). Crayons. High chairs. No-smoking tables. Tables outdoors (6, courtyard).

Dexter's Grill
20 Bellevue Road, Wandsworth, SW17 7EB (8767 1858). Wandsworth Common rail. **Meals served** noon-11pm Mon-Fri; 10am-11pm Sat, Sun. **Main courses** £6.50-£14. **Credit** AmEx, MC, V.
Since awarding Dexter's the gong for Best Family Restaurant in 2003, we've received mixed reports about it. Most people are of the opinion that this American-influenced burger-and-grills restaurant is just too popular, with children milling around and waiting staff tending to lose the plot somewhat at busy weekend lunchtimes. We weren't impressed by its smokiness on the busy Sunday that we ate here, lured by the promise of a magician, who was indeed very good. Come at a quieter time and you'll be able to appreciate the friendliness of the staff, the lavish provision for young children, and the usually well-executed dishes. The good-quality nursery food available for young children (shepherd's pie, cheesy broccoli pasta and bangers and mash, made with some organic ingredients) is another big plus in our opinion. Kids with more fast-food inclinations can have small-sized burgers, baby back ribs, hot dogs, fish and chips or all-day breakfasts. Puddings include a sundae with loads of extra topping served separately, so children can make an almighty mess 'building their own' with the raspberry fizz sherbet, chocolate knobbles, sticky sauces and other delightful garnishes.
Buggy access. Children's menu (£4.95 2 courses & drink). Crayons. High chairs. Nappy-changing facilities. No-smoking area. Tables outdoors (8, balcony terrace).

Don Fernando's
27F The Quadrant, Richmond, Surrey TW9 1DN (8948 6447/www.donfernando.co.uk). Richmond tube/rail. **Meals served** noon-3pm, 6-11pm Mon, Tue; noon-11pm Wed-Sat; noon-10pm Sun. **Main courses** £7.25-£13.25. **Tapas** £3-£5. **Set meals** £15-£19 2 courses. **Credit** AmEx, MC, V.
Just by Richmond station, this cosy and traditional Spanish restaurant is owned and run by the Izquierdo family of Andalucia. In the evenings it's a lively Latin hangout for local families, but those with small children may prefer the delightfully solicitous service of a weekday lunchtime. Whenever you come, the welcome is warm. It's worth ordering a selection of favourites from the extensive vegetarian, meat or seafood tapas lists: fussy children go for bread and chips, adventurous ones like the spicy chicken wings, squid, Spanish sausage or *caracoles granadina* (snails). If there are people in the party after a Spanish holiday memory, try the seafood, meat or vegetarian paella (minimum two people).
Buggy access. High chairs. No-smoking tables.

Gourmet Burger Kitchen
44 Northcote Road, Battersea, SW11 1NZ (7228 3309/ www.gbkinfo.co.uk). Clapham Junction rail. **Meals served** noon-11pm Mon-Fri; 11am-11pm Sat; 11am-10pm Sun. **Main courses** £4.95-£6.95. **Credit** MC, V.

These burgers aren't fast, and they're not American. The menu was dreamed up by a New Zealander with a flair for fusion cooking, and the resultant patties aren't all about beef (although the 100% Aberdeen Angus ones are delicious). Vegetarians might fancy a burger made of portabello mushrooms, peppers and pesto, or a bun filled with falafel, houmous and salad. Avoiders of red meat have a choice of chicken numbers, and game samplers might fancy venison. For under-tens there's a junior burger, in either beef or chicken, at £3.80; most children prefer the cheeseburger, with chunky chips, salad and fries. All the burgers come in a sourdough bun – very gourmet kitchen.
Buggy access. High chairs. No smoking. Tables outdoors (4, pavement).
Branches: 331 West End Lane, NW6 1RS (7794 5455); 131 Chiswick High Road, W4 2ED (8995 4548); 333 Putney Bridge Road, SW15 2PG (8789 1199); 49 Fulham Broadway, SW6 1AE (7381 4242).

Newton's
33-5 Abbeville Road, Clapham, SW4 9LA (8673 0977/ www.newtonsrestaurants.co.uk). Clapham South tube. **Meals served** noon-11.30pm Mon-Fri; 10am-11.30pm Sat; 10am-10.30pm Sun. **Main courses** £7.50-£15. **Set lunch** (noon-3pm Mon-Sat) £6 2 courses, £8.50 3 courses. **Credit** AmEx, MC, V.
This is a smart little restaurant in the increasingly posh, villagey bit of Clapham. There's plenty of outside seating for long, lazy summer lunches from a simple but impressive brasserie-style menu, with great Sunday roasts or smartly detailed à la carte dishes (crispy squid rings, say, or halibut). Children are made very welcome, and can choose a small portion of whatever the grown-ups are having or get pasta and tomato sauce or chicken nuggets. Ice-cream is included in the price, which is £5 regardless.
High chairs. Children's menu (£5). No-smoking tables. Tables outdoors (7, terrace).

Pembroke Lodge Cafeteria
Richmond Park, Richmond, Surrey TW10 5HX (8948 7371). Richmond tube/rail. **Open** 10am-5.30pm daily. **Main courses** £3-£5.99. **Credit** (over £10) MC, V. *See p162* **Parking space.**
Buggy access. Children's menu (£3). High chairs. Nappy-changing facilities. No-smoking tables. Tables outdoors (20, terrace).

Tiger Lil's
16A Clapham Common South Side, SW4 7AB (7720 5433/www.tigerlils.com). Clapham Common tube. **Lunch served** noon-3pm Fri. **Dinner served** 6-11.30pm Mon-Thur; 6pm-midnight Fri. **Meals served** noon-midnight Sat; noon-11pm Sun. **Unlimited stir-fry** £12.50; £5.50 5-12s; free under-5s. **Credit** AmEx, MC, V.
A very popular venue, especially for large groups and families with young children, Tiger Lil's has as its central concept the DIY stir-fry, which sounds like fun even before you see the chefs making the burner flames leap up under their woks. There's a selection of chopped vegetables, meats and seafood to select in their raw state. These you take to your chair, select a sauce for the stir-fry, and watch the lot sizzle. Children love being in charge of their dinner, selecting colourful vegetable items without thinking to make a fuss about their nutritious qualities. Additional plus points are the free prawn crackers little 'uns can guzzle while waiting, and the choice of child-pleasing starters such as barbecued ribs and spring rolls.
Buggy access. Crayons. High chairs. Toys.
Branches: 270 Upper Street, N1 2UH (7226 1118); 75 Bishop's Bridge Road, W2 6BQ (7221 2622).

Victoria

*West Temple Sheen, SW14 7RT (8876 4238/
www.thevictoria.net). Mortlake rail/33, 337 bus.* **Open**
7.30am-11pm daily. **Breakfast served** 7.30-9.30am Mon-
Fri; 8-10am Sat, Sun. **Lunch served** noon-2.30pm Mon-
Fri; noon-3pm Sat, Sun. **Dinner served** 7-10pm daily.
Credit AmEx, MC, V.

There's something very restful about the Victoria. Maybe it's
because the children always make a beeline for the end of the
patio garden, where play equipment waits under a canopy of
pine trees and there are usually other kids about. But it might
also be the fact that, when we come for a weekend lunch, it's
full of equal measures of families and unencumbered couples
doing the same as us… enjoying a pint, choosing from the
lovely menu and chatting to the well-mannered staff. The
food is unfailingly good. The menu changes regularly, but
we have loved the risottos, wild boar and apple sausages, and
chicken club sandwich with french fries. On the pudding
front, the chocolate and seville orange tart is delightful and
even something simple, such as an apple pie or a chocolate
pudding is is served with enormous attention to detail. On
Sunday the options might be roast beef with Yorkshire pud,
onion tart or grilled salmon, all of which we can recommend.
Small portions of grilled chicken, sausages, risottos and roast
meats can be arranged for the children.
*Buggy access. High chairs. Nappy changing facilities.
Tables outdoors (9, garden & play area).*

West London

Burlington's Café

*Chiswick House, off Burlington Lane, Chiswick, W4 2RP
(8987 9431). Turnham Green tube/Chiswick rail.* **Open**
Oct-Mar 10am-4pm Thur-Sun. *Apr-Sept* 9.30am-5pm
daily. **No credit cards.**
See p162 **Parking space.**
*Buggy access. Children's menu (£2-£3.50). High chairs.
Nappy-changing facilities. No smoking. Tables outdoors
(10, garden).*

Bush Bar & Grill

*45A Goldhawk Road, Shepherd's Bush, W12 8QP (8746
2111/www.bushbar.co.uk). Goldhawk Road tube.* **Lunch
served** noon-3pm Mon-Sat; noon-4pm Sun. **Dinner
served** 5.30-11.30pm Mon-Sat, 6.30-10.20pm Sun **Main
courses** £9.75-£15.50. **Set lunch** (Mon-Sat) £12.50 2
courses, £15 3 courses. **Credit** AmEx, MC, V.

Set back from the road in a cool courtyard, this is a favourite
lunching spot for families, especially at weekends (it's a bit
expense-account during the week, although the children's
menu is always available). There's loads of space (those
without children find it easy to escape those with), but the
plant-filled outside seating is always at a premium on sunny
Sundays. There is no disputing the quality of the daily
changing modern European menu, with its organic wild
salmon, organic Aberdeen Angus steaks and similarly pure
free-range chicken. The two-course set (£12.50) usually offers
an interesting fish dish (sea bream when we went) alongside
grilled meat or a vegetarian option and magnificent
puddings (recent examples included white chocolate and
cherry torte, caramelised lemon tarte and a superior sort of
bread and butter pudding). The children's menu is entirely
organic, and gives them sausages or chicken, fish goujons or
some sort of pasta. What's more, at lunchtimes under-eights
eat free (one child per adult). *See also p179* **Cheap as chips**.
*Buggy access. Children's menu (£5 1 course). High chairs.
Tables outdoors (8, pavement).*

Moroccan Tagine.
See p182.

Bush Garden Café

59 Goldhawk Road, Shepherd's Bush, W12 8EG (8743 6372). Goldhawk Road tube. **Open** 8am-6pm Mon-Sat. **Main courses** £3.90-£4.60. **Credit** (minimum £10) AmEx, MC, V.

This wholesome café and quality grocery shop has a strong family-friendly vibe. With its white tongue-and-groove walls, mismatched furniture, antique chandelier and laden shelves of organic pasta sauces, oils, spices, cakes and confectionery, it's a homely, stylish place for lunch. The back garden has an outdoor heater, many more tables and chairs, a grassy knoll for picnics, and a plastic playhouse, while the fare is all health-giving produce: shots of wheatgrass for £1.50; big beakers of celery, ginger, carrot or fruit juice, pressed to order (£2.20); salads and quiches; veg hot-pots, soups and bean salads. The Bush Breakfast is a pile of buttery free-range scrambled eggs or puffy almond croissants and mugs of hot chocolate. For children, there's Marmite on toast, beans on toast and boiled eggs served with same, all priced at £1.50. Konditor & Cook provide the cakes. *See also p179* **Cheap as chips.**

Buggy access. High chairs. Nappy-changing facilities. No smoking. Tables outdoors (4, garden).

Julie's Restaurant

135-7 Portland Road, Holland Park, W11 4LW (7229 8331/www.juliesrestaurant.com). Holland Park tube. **Lunch served** 12.30-2.45pm Mon-Sat; 12.30-3pm Sun. **Dinner served** 7-11.30pm Mon-Sat; 7-10.30pm Sun. **Set meal** (Sun lunch) £22 2 courses, £26 3 courses. **Main courses** £11.50-£17. **Credit** AmEx, MC, V.

This was one of the first restaurants in London to offer a Sunday lunchtime crèche, and very popular it is too. The price includes a child-sized lunch of organic chicken pieces with roast potatoes and vegetables, or own-made sausages with chips, or organic pasta with sauce. Meanwhile, grown-ups tuck in to a lunch menu that may include Dublin Bay prawns or soup for starters, and mains of roast beef with Yorkshire pud, lamb with mint sauce, roast pork with apple sauce or salmon with seared lime. Puddings often include a lemon and lime meringue, a warm brownie or light mousse. Ingredients are carefully sourced and organic where possible.

Buggy access. Children's menu (Sun, £10.95). Crèche (1-4pm Sun). High chairs. Tables outdoors (12, pavement).

Moroccan Tagine

95 Golborne Road, Ladbroke Grove, W10 5NL (8968 8055). Ladbroke Grove or Westbourne Park tube/23 bus. **Meals served** noon-11pm daily. **Main courses** £5.50-£7.90. **Credit** MC, V.

This plain, genial Moroccan restaurant is in the heart of London's North African community, and does the best couscous in the city. The coarse-grained semolina, often popular with children, is served properly light and fluffy here, and may come with grilled meats and fish, colourful salads or chunky vegetable stews. Children need to be guided towards the less spicy options, but they're assured of a very warm welcome and a wide choice of wholesome dishes.

High chairs. No-smoking tables. Table outdoors (8, pavement). Takeaway service.

Branches: throughout town. Check the phone book for your nearest.

Old Ship

25 Upper Mall, Hammersmith, W6 9TD (8748 2593/ www.oldshipw6.co.uk). Hammersmith, Ravenscourt Park or Stamford Brook tube. **Open** 9am-11pm Mon-Sat; 9am-10.30pm Sun. **Meals served** 9am-10.30pm Mon-Sat; 9am-10pm Sun. **Credit** AmEx, MC, V.

There has been a Ship pub on this site since at least 1722. Restoration and rebuilds over the centuries have resulted in the Old Ship looking quite new, and its balcony, terrace and walkway are the very best place from which to watch the Oxford and Cambridge boat race. There are canoes hanging from the ceiling, and staff are quite relaxed about the children running about on the waterfront veranda (which is where everybody goes, given half a chance). Children have their own menu (available at all times), which lists not especially exciting nuggets, panini, fish fingers, pasta and so on. On Sundays things look up: children can have smaller portions of adult Sunday roasts; own-made ice-creams also go down a treat. Expect weekends to be pretty hectic round here if the weather's good. There's a play area (with swings and a roundabout) on the green right next to the pub, which makes it even more of a draw for young families.

Buggy access. Children's menu (£2.95). High chairs. Nappy-changing facilities. Tables outdoors (10, terrace).

Ravenscourt Park Teahouse

Paddenswick Road, Hammersmith, W6 0UL (8748 1945). Ravenscourt Park tube. **Open** 9am-5pm daily. Closing varies, call to confirm. **No credit cards.** *See p162* **Parking space.**

Buggy access. Children's menu (£3). High chairs. Nappy-changing facilities. No smoking. Tables outdoors (seating for 100, terrace). Takeaway service. Toys.

Rotisserie Jules

133A Notting Hill Gate, Notting Hill, W11 3LB (7221 3331/www.rotisseriejules.com). Notting Hill Gate tube. **Meals served** noon-11pm daily. **Main courses** £5.75-£10.75. **Credit** AmEx, MC, V.

Roast chicken has to be near the top of any (meat-eating) child's culinary wish list, so this clean and bright restaurant, with its golden and delicious spit-roasted poultry (a whole chicken with gravy for a small family costs £11.50), served with crisp french fries and pleasantly appointed salads, is a treat. Especially if you pair your chicken and chips with some corn on the cob and follow it with a chocolatey mousse or Ben & Jerry's ice-cream. Staff are extremely friendly.

Buggy access. Children's menu (£4.25). High chairs. Table outdoors (1, pavement). Takeaway service.

Tootsies

120 Holland Park Avenue, Holland Park, W11 4UA (7229 8567/www.tootsiesrestaurants.co.uk). Holland Park tube. **Meals served** 11am-11pm Mon-Thur; 11am-11.30pm Fri; 9am-11.30pm Sat; 9am-11pm Sun. **Main courses** £5.95-£14.95. **Credit** AmEx, MC, V.

There are a number of Tootsies restaurants around London, but they avoid corporate chaininess. This branch, always our favourite, has lovely big windows looking out on the avenue. The food has American predictability – burgers, ribs, chicken and giant crustaceans – but it's well presented and delicious. One burly burger with emmenthal cheese, optional bacon, onions and salad for £7.95 is a filling meal, but you just have to have crisp chips with it (only £1.50). The lamb and rosemary burger is an interesting variation on a theme, and the China salad, loaded with vitamin-packed watercress, sugar snap peas and crunchy greens, then dressed to thrill, is wonderfully wholesome. The children's menu gives them their burger in a 3oz incarnation with chips, or they can have salmon fish cakes or a chicken sandwich.

Balloons. Buggy access. Children's menu (£4.95 incl drink & dessert). Crayons. High chairs. No-smoking tables. Tables outdoors (4, pavement).

Branches: throughout town. Check the phone book for your nearest.

Consumer

Shopping

Go on, blow your Child Benefit...

For diversity, style, playfulness and classic good taste, London's shops for children are the best in the world. You'll note we've left value for money off that list: you're likely to make full use of the credit card when buying for the kids, and pester power sees to it that shopping with the children sees you even further out of pocket. We can at least show you how to have fun while you're being bled dry.

Fun and frolics are in short supply on the street most commonly held to be shoppers' paradise – Oxford Street. We'd advise staying well away, were it not for the department stores round here, the best of which are stolid, reliable **John Lewis** and the rather confusing, flighty and always entertaining **Selfridges** (for both, see p184).

Much more gratifying are the buzzy, chain-filled but uncluttered shopping hubs of High Street Kensington, and Chelsea's main street, the once cutting-edge, now just comfortably off, King's Road. Then there are the much vaunted urban villages, with their cosy organic butchers, bakers and trad toymakers. Areas such as **Marylebone** (see p66), **Highgate** (see p96), Clapham's **Northcote Road** (toys, fashion, food, a market and and even a specialist honey shop, see p138) all have a vaguely smug, but pleasant, old-fashioned air. North London's finest child-centred enclave, however, is **Fortis Green**, with its Children's Bookshop (see p188), Never Never Land (see p205) and Early Clothing (see p192). Only in London could such fiercely independent community stores thrive.

London's Euroswank boutiques, with their mini-Versace and Gucci, coexist happily with unashamedly traditional purveyors of classic christening gowns and lined party frocks or the street markets with cheapo trackie bottoms and Britney T shirts. We've listed our favourites in all categories, but had most fun checking out the toyshops – once again the independents have the edge on the chains when it comes to jolly shopping experiences. Indeed, some toyshops have so much fun in store for young visitors (see p185 **Child's play**) that you can play for hours there without spending a penny.

Talking of which, we've mentioned essential facilities, such as toilets and nappy-changing areas, alongside less essential ones like play areas, in our reviews. Do bear in mind that not all branches of a shop have the same facilities or opening hours. Always ring before making a special journey.

All-rounders

First stop

Daisy & Tom
181-3 King's Road, Chelsea, SW3 5EB (7352 5000/ www.daisyandtom.com). Sloane Square tube, then 11, 19, 22, 49 bus. **Open** 9.30am-6pm Mon-Wed, Fri; 10am-7pm Thur, Sat; 11am-5pm Sun. **Credit** AmEx, MC, V. **Map** p315 E12.
D&T is a lovely place to shop for the children, and one where the objects of your labours will be as entertained as you. It has clothes (plentiful designer labels), equipment, toys and accessories. Children can read in the great book department, ride the carousel, get haircuts or be diverted by the regular events and activities. *See also p185* **Child's play**.
Buggy access. Delivery service. Disabled access. Mail order. Nappy-changing facilities. Play area.

Mothercare
461 Oxford Street, Oxford Circus, W1C 2EB (7629 6621/www.mothercare.com). Marble Arch tube. **Open** 10am-8pm Mon-Fri; 10am-7pm Sat; noon-6pm Sun. **Credit** AmEx, MC, V. **Map** p316 G6.
The byword for shopping with baby, or pre-baby, Mothercare's fortunes have taken a dive, thanks to those cost-cutters Tesco and Toys R Us (see p206), but this main London branch is still a good browse. For breast feeding bras, babywipes, muslin squares and terry nappies, it's a reliable first stop, and the high chairs, cots and easy-fold buggies are competitively priced and pleasantly designed.
Buggy access. Delivery service. Disabled access: toilet. Mail order. Nappy-changing facilities.
Branches: throughout town. Check website for details.

Department stores

Harrods
87-135 Brompton Road, Knightsbridge, SW1X 7XL (7730 1234/www.harrods.com). Knightsbridge tube. **Open** 10am-7pm Mon-Sat. **Credit** AmEx, DC, MC, V. **Map** p315 F9.
The fourth floor is kid country, its capital undoubtedly Toy Kingdom, which most children want to visit and many refuse to leave (see p185 **Child's play**). There's also an overwhelming choice of fashion here. Leading designer brands include Armani Junior, Kenzo and Monnalisa in every age from newborn to 16. Harrods' own collection, whether mini-me designer suits or sturdy and sensible woollen coats in muted colours, is all top quality. The more casual wear Ben Sherman, Quiksilver and Animalgoes down better with streetwise kids. Shoes include Tod's and Start-Rite, but lean towards fancy Italian labels such as Missouri and Mirella. Other departments, such as nursery furniture, run the gamut from fantasy four posters for little princesses to plain pine cot/babybed conversions. See *also p174* **Scoff till you drop**.
Buggy access. Café. Car park. Delivery service. Disabled access: lift, toilet. Mail order. Nappy-changing facilities.

John Lewis

278-306 Oxford Street, Oxford Circus, W1A 1EX (7629 7711/www.johnlewis.co.uk). Bond Street or Oxford Circus tube. **Open** 9.30am-7pm Mon-Wed, Fri; 9.30am-8pm Thur; 9.30am-7pm Sat; noon-6pm Sun. **Credit** MC, V. **Map** p316 H6.

Covering the whole of the fourth floor, the John Lewis children's department is practical and convenient; you can wander through the clothes department picking up own-label pyjamas, swim- or ski-suits (this is definitely the best place for children's ski-wear) while waiting for the pager to beep with your shoe-fitting appointment. The school uniform department is second to none. Nursery equipment is carefully chosen and advice is patient and sensible. It may be hard to keep the kids out of the adjacent toy department, but at least aisles are wide and everything is logically set out with clear signs and prices. You'll appreciate levels of service most at busy times – even when children throw tantrums or hi-jack diggers, good humour and efficiency prevails.

Buggy access. Café. Delivery service. Disabled access: lifts, toilets. Mail order. Nappy-changing facilities. Play area.

Selfridges

400 Oxford Street, Oxford Circus, W1A 1AB (0870 837 7377/www.selfridges.com). Bond Street tube. **Open** 10am-8pm Mon-Fri; 9.30am-8pm Sat; noon-6pm Sun. **Credit** AmEx, MC, V. **Map** p316 G6.

There are two good reasons to visit here as a family. The first is a teenage enclave on the first floor, where aspirational beach bum labels (O'Neill, Quiksilver) are offered in an environment dominated by sportswear, bikes and skateboards. The second is Kids' Universe, a self-consciously funky retail 'concept' on the third floor, where designer clothes (up to eight years) and edited toy collections are displayed in floating white plastic pods. The department is a gratifyingly open space, so see everything from your seat on a padded mushroom. A small party section does glitzy hats, sparkly fairy dresses and a few magic tricks, and Buckle My Shoe provides footwear. Create & Play inspires stationery-mad children.

Buggy access. Cafés. Car park. Delivery service. Disabled access: toilet. Mail order. Nappy-changing facilities. Play area.

Markets

Every borough in London has its own street markets. We've listed the few we like best as family destinations. If you're a market addict and want to visit some good local ones, try **Northcote Road Market** in Battersea (9am-5pm Thur-Sat; *see also p138*) or Hackney's **Ridley Road Market** (7am-5pm Mon-Sat). **Walthamstow Market** (*see p118*) is apparently Europe's longest street market.

Brick Lane Market

Brick Lane (north of railway bridge), Cygnet Street, Sclater Street, E1; Bacon Street, Cheshire Street, Chilton Street, E2. Aldgate East or Shoreditch tube/Liverpool Street tube/rail. **Open** 8am-2pm Sun. **Map** p321 S4.

The traditional flea market, selling cheap soaps and razors, magazines, bagels, bric-a-brac, second-hand clothes, old furniture and seafood, contrasts nicely with the trendy boutiques and expensive home-accessory stores that have become increasingly familiar along these narrow streets. The most browsable bit of the market is the warehouse on Cheshire Street, which is full of microwaves, TVs, CDs, DVDs, glasses and everything else under the sun.

Brixton Market

Electric Avenue, Pope's Road, Brixton Station Road, Atlantic Road, SW9 8PA (7926 2530). Brixton tube/rail. **Open** 8am-6pm Mon, Tue, Thur, Sat; 8am-3pm Wed; 8am-7pm Fri.

Visiting Brixton's thronged market is like being plunged into another country. Electric Avenue is packed with stalls piled high with exotic fruit and vegetables, while permanent stores are packed with halal meats and fish. As the market moves into Atlantic Road it turns towards various consumer durables – clothes, towels, toys, cheap wallets and mobile phone covers. On Saturdays a few stalls of rather jumbly clothes appear along Brixton Station Road.

Camden Market

Camden High Street *junction with Buck Street, Camden Town, NW1 (7278 4444).* **Open** 9am-5.30pm daily.
Camden Lock *off Chalk Farm Road, NW1 8AF (7485 3459).* **Open** 10am-6pm daily.
Stables Market *off Chalk Farm Road, opposite junction with Hartland Road, NW1 8AH (7485 5511).* **Open** 9am-6pm daily.
Camden Canal Market *off Chalk Farm Road, south of junction with Castlehaven Road, NW1 9XJ (7485 8355).* **Open** 9.30am-6.30pm Fri-Sun.
Electric Market *184 Camden High Street, south of junction with Dewsbury Terrace, NW1 8QP (7485 9006/9007).* **Open** 10am-5pm Sun.
All *Camden Town tube.*

It's all paradise for the over 12s, but trendy parents, who still remember the hotbed of anarchic fashion it used to be in the 1980s, moan that Camden Market isn't as cutting edge as it once was. The section just next to the tube station continues to sell clubby T-shirts and bondage wear, trendy platform shoes and cheap interpretations of current fashions. The Electric Market sells plenty of second-hand clothes and young designers' wares of varying quality. In the building beside the Lock and its courtyard are a range of crafty goods including jewellery, funky handmade boxes, candles, picture frames and mirrors. The Stables Yard is full of permanent clothing sellers and food huts. Upmarket, permanent retro stalls and clubwear outlets have taken over in the railway arches, while an avenue of food stalls and craft stalls sits beside the canal.

Columbia Road Market

Columbia Road, between Gosset Street & the Royal Oak pub, Bethnal Green, E2. Bus 26, 48, 55. **Open** 8am-2pm Sun. **No credit cards**.

This Sundays-only flower market is pretty hectic but there are always families with tots in tow. There is usually some kind of street music during fine summer weather and plenty of little brunch places ensure no one goes hungry. If you've come here to shop for the garden, balcony or window box, be prepared to get up early, as the healthiest, bushiest and most unusual specimens are snapped up by 9am. Half the stalls are dedicated to cut flowers, the rest to potted plants, bedding plants and trees, but it's the little shops along the road that contain most of interest for children. Infancy Retail (140 Columbia Road, E2 7RG, 7739 4737, 9am-2.30pm Sun, Sat in Dec) is the best: a colourful little toyshop with a selection of nursery accessories, such as witty nightlights and ornaments. A small musical instrument range includes plenty of things to shake, strum, rattle 'n' roll. There's also a limited but rather lovely selection of clothes (including the Fruity range of dresses and swimwear), some tie-dye babygros, and beautiful books and accessories.

Child's play

Look, don't touch. That's not what you want and it's certainly not what the kids want, but where can you go for a truly hands-on shopping trip?

If you only make it to one shop, it has to be **Daisy & Tom** (*see p183*), five floors of bouncing retail fun and games. On the first floor you'll find puppet shows every 25 minutes, while a carousel operates at regular intervals throughout the day (11am, 1pm, 3pm, 5pm Mon-Sat; 11am, 3pm Sun) – it only takes ten children at a time, but fret not: the carousel won't stop until the queue has disappeared. Should you pop in outside carousel times, kids can create circles of their own on one of the many tricycles dotted about the store. The book department has regular colouring-in competitions, and a central area, padded out with big bean bags and cushions, offers all ages the opportunity to snuggle down with a book. A programme of events (posted on www.daisyandtom.com) features face-painting, storytelling and visits from characters like Maisie.

Majestic **Harrods** (*see p183*) also has plenty to keep the kids entertained. Before you hit the fourth-floor Toy Kingdom, be sure to wind your way through the elaborate interiors and plenteous counters of the Food Hall – don't miss the delectable ice-creams at Marino's. The vine chandeliers, life-sized statues of game and displays of exotic fruits never fail to delight. Ascend on the Egyptian escalator and stop off at the pet department to visit Harry the blue and gold macaw, Harrods' parrot in residence. He is sometimes let out of his cage to fly about the livestock area and his repertoire of squawks includes a convincing 'woof!'. The toy department itself is a million miles from the frenetic chaos of Hamleys. There's ample room to manoeuvre between the toy-laden aisles and to try out everything from arcade games to big wooden chess sets and the latest in remote-controlled spinning tops. You can watch Marvin's Magic displays, belt out karaoke around the pop video wall, play table football, or just sit on the crayon settees in the babies' clothing department to watch cartoons. Sulky teenagers can mooch

around the young designer lines and hang out in Mo's Diner, while smaller kids enjoy the child-friendly menu and atmosphere at the Acme-like Planet Harrods café-restaurant (*see also p174* **Scoff till you drop**). If all that's not enough, schedule your visit to coincide with one of the frequent in-store events: face-painting, say, or the exclusive toy launches, author signings, puppet shows and storytelling. Such goings-on are often organised at short notice, so call or check the website if you're going to be in the area.

And, of course, there's **Hamleys** (*see p206*) – absolute mayhem on a Saturday and not exactly empty any other day of the week. For good reason, too. Hit the basement for blaring video arcade games, where kids can become a break-dancer or champion racing driver for a pound or two. Or, once you've exhausted the toy demos – magic, the latest paper planes, the next big toy craze – wind your way up the Harry Potter staircase, which gains new additions to its magical form with each film (the latest updates are top secret, we're told). In the third-floor girls' department, little misses can take a walk down Barbie fashion avenue or they can pout at the spotlit mirror in the dressing-up section and check their profile from beneath a huge bright-pink afro wig. The Scalextric track on the next floor up makes the one at Harrods look poxy, while a large test area for remote-controlled cars and toys offers less competitive automated diversions. Keep your eye on www.hamleys.com for details of the 1760 Day anniversary events on and around 14 August 2004 – yes, apparently Hamleys has been in operation since the 18th century, and staff will be wearing doublet and hose to celebrate, and not showing a bit of embarrassment, we're sure. Special guests at the store this year include Harlem Globetrotter Otis Key, Toffee the Highland Cow and the Cabbage Patch Dolls.

Aside from the big-time consumer extravaganzas in central London, going local can be just as playful. Bookworms love burrowing into the chairs at **Bookworm** (*see p187*) to read new publications and old favourites, as well as joining in the regular storytelling sessions (2pm Tue, Thur). Staff at The **Golden Treasury** (*see p188*) also take turns at storytelling hour (4pm Fri) and have ample books to amuse the kids at other times. Join its mailing list for news of face-painting, finger-painting, author signings and other in-store events. At north and south-east London's fabulous **Soup Dragon** (*see p205*) stores, kids will find playhouses to crash about in, as well as other madness in the Saturday rush and on special clown days. Staff are wonderfully tolerant, as are those at Kensington's **Their Nibs** (*see p195*), with its well-equipped play area, gallery and blackboard for visitors' scribbles, and at Stoke Newington's delightful little children cornucopia **Route 73 Kids** (*see p202*), where they're always pleased to see you.

Spitalfields Market.

Greenwich Market

Antiques Market *Greenwich High Road, SE10 9HZ.* Open 9am-5pm Sat, Sun.
Central Market *off Stockwell Street, opposite Hotel Ibis, SE10 9BP.* **Open** *Outdoor* 7am-6pm Sat; 7am-5pm Sun. *Indoor* 10am-5pm Fri, Sat; 10am-6pm Sun.
Crafts Market *College Approach, SE10 9HZ.* **Open** *Antiques & collectibles* 7.30am 5.30pm Thur. *Arts& crafts* 9.30am-5.30pm Thur-Sun.
Food Market *off Stockwell Street, opposite Hotel Ibis, SE10 9BQ.* **Open** 10am 4pm Sat.
All *Greenwich rail/DLR.*

Heading into the town centre from the station you come first to the Antiques Market, a collection of bric-a-brac and junk. Next is the Central Market for second-hand clothes and home furnishings. Passing the food court, you come to the covered Crafts Market, Greenwich's jewel in the crown. Ideal for gift-hunting, it sells all manner of crafts and has a number of stalls that will appeal to children. There's a whole table of magnetic insects made of delicately painted metal for a couple of quid each; Ray and Cathy Daley's sweet traditional toy stall with pop guns, picture bricks, models cars and craft kits; original print shirts and dresses by Beaumont Childrenswear; and jolly clothing by the Cuddley [sic] Crew. A traditional sweets and fudge stall also attracts attention.

Portobello Road Market

Portobello Road, W10, W11; Golborne Road, W10. Ladbroke Grove, Notting Hill Gate or Westbourne Park tube. **Open** *General* 8am-6pm Mon-Wed; 9am-1pm Thur; 8am-7pm Fri, Sat. *Antiques* 4am-6pm Sat.
Portobello Road is like several markets in one. At the Notting Hill end you'll mainly find antiques and general Victoriana. Further up you come to food stalls, then clothes and jewellery. A favourite for rocking families is Jelli (Sat only), which sells hip clothes for tots too tiny to notice exactly how hip they're looking: never mind, the bibs, babygros and T-shirts featuring the Sex Pistols' *God Save the Queen* album cover and other iconic images make trendy parents feel rebellious. Hendrix, Motörhead, Elvis and the Ramones are alternative images if the punk's too strong. Cafés under the Westway are a good place to refuel before taking on the new designer clothes and vintage wear on the walkway to Ladbroke Grove.

Spitalfields Market

Commercial Street, between Lamb Street & Brushfield Street, Spitalfields, E1 6AA (7247 8556). Liverpool Street tube/rail. **Open** *General market* 10.30am-4.30pm Mon-Fri; 9am-5pm Sun. *Fashion market* 10am-3pm Thur. *Antique market* 10am-4pm Thur. **Map** p321 R5.
Cool parents in the first flushes of parenthood tout their couthly papoosed young round this fashionable market in search of baby massage oils, organic breadsticks and one-off babyclothes. They also like the handsome traditional wooden toys sold by Leslie Bobrow of Wood 'n' Things and the cute T-shirts by Natty Kids (www.nattykids.co.uk). The stalls run by Blue Skin (8672 4465, www.blueskin.com) and Gayle Haddock of Carry Me Home (07771 996 768, www.car-rymehome.co.uk) are also worth a look.
Bars. Buggy access. Cafés. Disabled access: toilet. Nappy-changing facilities. Restaurants. Takeaways.

Educational

Books

Bookseller Crow on the Hill

50 Westow Street, Crystal Palace, SE19 3AF (8771 8831/www.booksellercrow.com). Gypsy Hill rail. **Open** 9am-7.30pm Mon Fri; 9am-6.30pm Sat; 11am-5pm Sun. **Credit** AmEx, MC, V.
This full, busy shop is run by a couple who have a young family of their own and are a mine of information on baby, toddler, child, teen, fretful parent and grandparent literature. Modern classics by Michael Morpurgo, Anthony Horowitz, Jaqueline Wilson and, of course, JK Rowling form a fraction of the vast stock, but the Crows are happy to recomend something if your child wants to branch out from the bestseller list. Kids can browse at the shop's tables and chairs.
Buggy access. Mail order. Play area.

Bookworm

1177 Finchley Road, Temple Fortune, NW11 0AA (8201 9811). Golders Green tube. **Open** 9.30am-5.30pm Mon-Sat; 10am-1.30pm Sun. **Credit** MC, V.
Bookworm has a central rotunda full of cushions and bean bags, and a cubbyhole with tables and chairs for quiet reading/playing at the back. The stock is exemplary: shelf after shelf of everything from reference books for projects such as 'The Victorians' or 'The Romans' to the latest fiction. Twice-weekly storytelling sessions take place on Tuesdays and Thursdays (2pm) for under-fives, when badges and stickers are handed out and not-so-literary friendships forged. Local authors, including Katherine Holabird (Angelina Ballerina) and Anthony Horowitz, often come by for signings.
Buggy access. Disabled access. Mail order.

Children's Book Centre

237 Kensington High Street, Kensington, W8 6SA (7937 7497/www.childrensbookcentre.co.uk). High Street Kensington tube. **Open** 9.30am-6.30pm Mon, Wed, Fri, Sat; 9.30am-6pm Tue; 9.30am-7pm Thur; noon-6pm Sun. **Credit** AmEx, MC, V. **Map** p314 A9.
A visit to this two-storey treasure trove will yield far more than books. On the ground level are clothes, including the trendy Punky Fish label, accessories and toys at pocket money prices. There is a PC set up at the back for children to try out new games. Downstairs is mainly toys and family games. The range of books covers all ages and includes classic teen reads such as Stephen King.
Buggy access. Mail order.

Consumer

Children's Bookshop

29 Fortis Green Road, Fortis Green, N10 3HP (8444 5500). Highgate tube, then 43, 134 bus. **Open** 9.15am-5.45pm Mon-Sat; 11am-4pm Sun. **Credit** AmEx, MC, V.
This epicentre of children's literature still never fails to impress. Below an ancient painting of a hot-air balloon are row upon row of neatly ordered shelves, full of colour and interest. There are small themed displays and a children's corner with picture books at floor level. Book related events are publicised in the quarterly newsletter, which carries helpful, personal reviews of new titles.
Buggy access. Mail order. Play area.

The Golden Treasury

29 Replingham Road, Southfields, SW18 5LT (8333 0167). Southfields tube. **Open** 9.30am-6pm Mon-Fri; 9.30am-5.30pm Sat. **Credit** MC, V.
Staff can offer friendly advice on the best reads for children from tinies to teens. Fun publications include pop-ups and books for colouring; less fun but significant is the educational range for schools. Harry Potter's popularity having eased off a bit, the current must-haves include the thriller *Across the Nightingale Floor* by Lian Hearn.
Buggy access. Delivery service. Nappy-changing facilities. Play area.

Little green warriors

Ethical concerns are no longert the sole preserve of parents in stripy hippie trousers touting bare-bottom babies in rainbow jumpers. Going organic and supporting fair trade have greater benefits than salving your conscience. They're about looking after fragile young skin with unbleached cottons, providing tiny tums with optimum nutrition and buying toys that haven't been made from toxic materials by child labour. So, for those green souls who want eco-nappies organic baby food, or environmentally sustainable children's parties, read on.

If you're about to pop or you've just dropped, make **Green Baby** (*see p190*) your first port of call. It has clothing basics for the newborn and sheets made from 100 per cent organic cotton, nappy balms and baby lotions based on sweet almond oil and cocoa butter, and nursery furniture made of beech from sustainable forests. Green Baby clothing is made in South India, on a community project that supports the education and employment of young girls. Another source of funky fair-traded threads is **People Tree** (Studio 7, Units 8-13, New Inn Street, EC2A 3PY, 7739 0660, www.peopletree.co.uk), whose clothes for children are both covetable and affordable.

If you're thinking of a washable nappy system, Green Baby's helpful staff can offer advice. Go for a shaped nappy that pops into place to avoid wrestling with terry towelling and giant nappy pins. Washable nappies are kinder to your coffers, too. An initial outlay of about £400 sets you up for one or two kids, saving you over a grand in the long run compared with using disposables. **Bambino Mio** (01604 883777, www.bambinomio.co.uk), the **Ellie Nappie Company** (0151 200 5012, www.elliepants.co.uk) and **Little Green Earthlets** (01825 873301, www.earthlets.co.uk) also sell real nappies and environmentally friendly cleaning products. For further infomation, check out www.realnappy.com.

But, before it comes out the other end, what are you putting in the little darling in the first place? **Bumble Bee** (30-32 Brecknock Road, N7 0DD, 7607 1936, www.bumblebee.co.uk) in Kentish Town, Bayswater's excellent **Planet Organic**

(42 Westbourne Grove, W2 5SH, 7221 7171, www.planetorganic.com) and the friendly, informative **Oliver's Wholefoods Store** (5 Station Approach, Kew, Surrey TW9 3QB, 8948 3990) are all recommended. So is **Here** (7351 4321) in Chelsea Farmers' Market, which keeps fresh, refrigerated pots of Chow Baby organic baby food.

When getting to the shops is a problem handle, you can always buy from **www.foodferry.com** (7498 0827) or **www.goodnessdirect.co.uk** (0871 871 6611), who will deliver to your door. For organic cookery books, among them the *Organic Baby Book* by Tanya Maxted-Frost, the best online shop is **www.greenbooks.co.uk** (01803 863 260), while **www.borndirect.com** (0117 924 5080) has alternative health products for childhood ailments.

When it comes to keeping children amused, the **Natural Collection** (0870 331 3333, www.natural collection.com) sells everything from plant-based paints to wooden jigsaws made with non-toxic paints by a Sri Lankan craft enterprise. A wonderful company specialising in fair-traded multicultural toys such as Thai shadow puppet kits and jaipuri paper kites is **www.parrotfish.co.uk** (01621 858940), while **www.greenboardgames.com** (01494 538999) makes and sells games to inspire. Try Walking with Dinosaurs to drum up excitement before a trip to the Natural History Museum. The **British Association of Fair Trade Shops** (7739 4197, www.bafts.org.uk) can provide you with info on other ethical toy companies.

If you want to recycle old toys or buy second-hand, visit **Chocolate Crocodile** recycling centre (39 Morpeth Road, Hackney, E9 7LD, 8985 3330), buy and sell online at **www.baby-things.com** or join your local **toy library** (see p 297).

The fun doesn't stop with toys, however. When it's party time call on those green **Red Sisters** (07947 478 414, helenarigg@yahoo.co.uk). Based in north London, Red Sisters is a teacher-and-artist collaboration whose Jungle Arts parties for kids aged four to ten use a diverse range of recycled materials to help children to create their own dance mask and jungle rainsticks. Each party culminates in a choreographed dance and song, and kids take home everything they've made.

Rub a Dub Dub.
See *p190*.

The Lion & Unicorn
19 King Street, Richmond, Surrey TW9 1ND (8940 0483/www.lionunicornbooks.co.uk). Richmond tube/rail. **Open** 9.30am-5.30pm Mon-Fri; 9.30am-6pm Sat; noon-5pm Sun. **Credit** MC, V.
This is a tiny space, dressed top to toe in children's books, which has been around for over 25 years. It hosts Saturday events that have attracted a fine stable of visiting writers: Jaqueline Wilson, Anthony Horowitz and Eoin Colfer.
Buggy access. Mail order. Play area.

Owl Bookshop
209 Kentish Town Road, Kentish Town, NW5 2JU (7485 7793). Kentish Town tube. **Open** 9.30am-6pm Mon-Sat; noon-4.30pm Sun. **Credit** AmEx, MC, V.
The Owl continues its very locally oriented literary offerings. Adult fiction blends into psychology, women's and babies' health, and children's titles, with all sections clearly labelled by age and interest. There's even a local version of chainstore largesse: 'Owl Value' offers three for two on picture books.
Buggy access. Mail order.

Musical instruments

Chappell of Bond Street
50 New Bond Street, Oxford Circus, W1S 1RD (7491 2777/www.chappellofbondstreet.co.uk). Bond Street tube. **Open** 9.30am-6pm Mon-Fri; 9.30am-5pm Sat. **Credit** AmEx, MC, V. **Map** p318 H6.
A famous music store, Chappell is especially good for sheet music and keyboards – many musicians drop in to tickle the

ivories. Certain instruments (typically flutes, saxes, clarinets, trumpets) may be hired on a rent-to-buy scheme, but quarter- and half-size instruments must be purchased, the child is measured beforehand. Recorders are the most popular starting position; Yamaha does colourful ones for £5.50.
Delivery service. Mail order.

Dot's
132 St Pancras Way, Camden Town, NW1 9NB (7482 5424/www.dotsonline.co.uk). Camden Town tube/Camden Road rail. **Open** 9am-5.30pm Mon-Sat. **Credit** MC, V.
Run and staffed by an experienced music teacher, Dot's has new instruments – mostly stringed and wind – costing from, say, £5 for a recorder, £40 for a guitar and £59 for a violin. There's also a rent-to-buy scheme, with hire costs eventually offsetting the purchase price should a child show consistent interest. The great joy here is receiving unpressured advice in a friendly setting. Ads for tuition and second-hand instruments are complemented by Dot's own recorder club, and you can get your instrument repaired.
Mail order.

Dulwich Music Shop
2 Croxted Road, Dulwich, SE21 8SW (8766 0202). West Dulwich rail. **Open** 9.30am-5.30pm Mon, Tue, Thur-Sat; 9.30am-7.30pm Wed. **Credit** AmEx, MC, V.
This excellent shop dispenses brass, wind and string instruments, as well as sheet music (particularly strong on classical, although all musical tastes are catered for). Reeds, strings and cleaning cloths are also sold, alongside knick-knacks, gifts, CDs and stationery. There's also a repair service.
Buggy access. Delivery service. Mail order.

Northcote Music

155C Northcote Road, Clapham, SW11 6QB (7228 0074). Clapham Junction rail. **Open** 10.30am-6pm Mon-Sat. **Credit** MC, V.
String, brass and digital equipment is here for music lovers, as well as an on-site workshop for any instrumental mishaps. Classical sheet music is sold, as well as a great selection of other music, ranging from *Thoroughly Modern Millie* for vocals to the Paul McCartney chord songbook or Christine Aguilera's *Stripped* album for vocals, piano and guitar.
Buggy access. Delivery service. Mail order.

Equipment & accessories

Dragons of Walton Street

23 Walton Street, South Kensington, SW3 2HX (7589 3795/www.dragonsofwaltonstreet.com). Knightsbridge or South Kensington tube. **Open** 9.30am-5.30pm Mon-Fri; 10am-5pm Sat. **Credit** AmEx, MC, V. **Map** p315 E10.
Purveyor of beautiful hand-made children's furniture to the well-to-do for more than 25 years, Dragons has carved a niche for itself as a smart but friendly venue for parents to buy nursery items that are designed to last. Prettily decorated items, such as miniaturised rocking chairs, tables and chairs, sofas and beds and the large wooden toy chests, are adorned with pictures of various playthings. The toys themselves include rocking horses and magnificent dolls' houses, chunky wooden Routemaster buses and teddy bears.
Buggy access. Delivery service. Mail order.

Green Baby

345 Upper Street, Islington, N1 0PD (7359 7037/mail order 0870 240 6894/www.greenbabyco.com). Angel tube. **Open** 10am-5pm Mon-Fri; 10am-6pm Sat. **Credit** MC, V. *See p188* **Little Green Warriors**.
Buggy access. Delivery service. Mail order.
Branch: 5 Elgin Crescent, W11 2JA (7792 8140).

Humla Children's Shop

13 Flask Walk, Hampstead, NW3 1HJ (7794 7877). Hampstead tube. **Open** 10.30am-6pm Tue-Sat; noon-6pm Sun. **Credit** AmEx, MC, V.
Since Humla's West End outlet closed, this is now the place for both its own label handknits (cute baby cardigans, £25.95), designer label clothes (such as hand-embroidered Malala or hand-painted Balu) and the traditional wooden toys that no middle-class nursery should be without. Sit-upon cars and trains are always popular, but the cow (with leather ears and pink-painted udder, £59.95) is more fun. Rarely seen soft musical toys are also available. The least expensive items here are hand-knitted finger puppets (£3.50) in the shape of camels, elephants and so on.
Buggy access.

Lilliput

255-9 Queenstown Road, Battersea, SW8 3NP (7720 5554/0800 783 0886/www.lilliput.com). Queenstown Road rail. **Open** 9.30am-5.30pm Mon, Tue, Thur, Fri; 9.30am-7pm Wed; 9am-6pm Sat; 11am-4pm Sun. **Credit** MC, V.
Nursery equipment – cots, high chairs, bags, mattresses – and toys fill the kingdom of Lilliput. The store's own range includes sturdy pine nursery furniture; there are also Tripp Trapp high chairs (from £99) and Bébé Confort prams.
Buggy access. Delivery service. Mail order. Nappy-changing facilities. Play area.
Branch: 100 Haydons Road, SW19 1AW (8542 3542).

Mini Kin

22 Broadway Parade, Crouch End, N8 9DE (8341 6898). Finsbury Park tube, then W7 bus/41 bus. **Open** 1-5.30pm Mon; 9.30am-5.30pm Tue-Sat; 11am-5pm Sun. **Credit** MC, V.
Mini Kin has one important advantage in competition with all the other Crouch End baby shops: a children's hairdressing salon, with animal-themed seats and the possibility of mini-makeovers. Baby haircuts start at £10; the full princess treatment costs £29.95. Otherwise this sizeable venue caters for the caring parent's desire for natural bath and hygiene products (including the SOS range for eczema), sells Bugaboo buggies, Baby Björn potties and stools, cute goldfish- or cowboy-decorated bibs and changers, adorable bootees and Nurtured by Nature merino wool babygros. A new line for 2004 is Angulus shoes (from £46.95). A snip.
Buggy access. Disabled access: toilet. Nappy-changing facilities. Play area.

Nursery Window

83 Walton Street, South Kensington, SW3 2HP (7581 3358/www.nurserywindow.co.uk). South Kensington tube. **Open** 10am-6pm Mon-Sat. **Credit** AmEx, MC, V. **Map** p315 E10.
Look through the Nursery Window for bedlinen, fabrics, furniture and wallpaper. Friendly staff are on hand to help parents select lap-of-luxury nursery essentials such as cashmere blankets (£89.95), hanging nappy stackers (£36.95) and a Moses basket set (£139.95). For toddlers and older children, designs tend to be bold and traditional (trains and racing cars for boys, delicate pink roses for girls), but with some unusual designs such as new world maps or Imperial garden motifs. The shop offers a made-to-measure curtain service.
Buggy access. Delivery service. Mail order.

Rub a Dub Dub

15 Park Road, Crouch End, N8 8TE (8342 9898). Finsbury Park tube, then W7, 41 bus. **Open** 10am-5.30pm Mon-Fri; 9.30am-5.30pm Sat. **Credit** MC, V.
Nursery requisites – many impressively high-tech – are the forte here. Nomad (£125) is a travel cot that folds to backpack size and doubles as a UV tent; Stokke's Xploryy baby buggy is an amazingly space age, multi-position buggy that elevates your little darling above nasty car fumes (£499). Every conceivable brand of eco-friendly nappy and bottom cream is stocked, while baby toys range from quaintly retro wooden bricks to award-winning learning blankets. The funny old giraffe outside is still the kids' favourite ride (50p for two gos).
Buggy access. Disabled access. Mail order.

Fashion

Budget

Adams

Unit 11, Surrey Quays Centre, Redriff Road, Rotherhithe, SE16 7LL (7252 3208/www.adams.co.uk). Surrey Quays tube. **Open** 9.30am-6.30pm Mon-Thur, Sat; 9.30am-8pm Fri; 11am-5pm Sun. **Credit** AmEx, MC, V.
Best for everyday essentials: decent-quality underwear, T-shirts, tights, jellies for summer, gumboots for winter, and lots of naff sparkly stuff come Christmas. It's also useful for school uniforms in small sizes, swimming stuff and inexpensive, workaday anoraks. Adams concessions can be found in larger branches of Sainsbury's.
Buggy access. Mail order. Play area.
Branches: throughout town. Check website for details.

H&M

*103-11 Kensington High Street, Kensington, W8 5SF
(7368 3920/www.hm.com). High Street Kensington tube.*
Open 10am-7pm Mon-Wed, Fri, Sat; 10am-8pm Thur;
noon-6pm Sun. **Credit** AmEx, MC, V. **Map** p314 A9.
The kids section of the budget fashion store has its finger on
the pulse. Mini-outfits echo what is selling on the grown-up
levels, everything is affordable, and the jewellery (for both
sexes), wallets and accessories are much loved by Father
Christmas. Boy's clothes are very 'street': cut-off trousers and
sports Ts (from £5.99), with ID tags to finish the look. Little
girls look gorgeous in denim pinnies and floral sundresses
*Buggy access. Disabled access: lift, toilet. Nappy-changing
facilities. Play area.*
Branches: throughout town. Check website for details.

Primark

*King's Mall, King Street, Hammersmith, W6 0QM (8748
7119/www.primark.co.uk). Hammersmith tube.* **Open**
9am-7pm Mon-Sat; 11am-5pm Sun. **Credit** MC, V.
Why be snobbish? This Irish bargain store has plenty of uses.
If you need white tights (£1) for the Nativity play, inexpensive knickers (£2 for five pairs) for a child being potty trained,
baby vests for a mewling puker (£2), T-shirts for mummy
and daddy, play clothes for the sandpit and bright fleece blankets for the pram and nursery, you need look no further.
Buggy access. Disabled access.
Branches: throughout town. Check website for details.

Designer

Barney's

*6 Church Road, Wimbledon, SW19 5DL (8944 2915).
Wimbledon tube/rail, then 93 bus.* **Open** 10am-6pm Mon-
Sat; noon-5pm Sun. **Credit** MC, V.
Smart designer wear for babies to teens, with labels Petit
Bateau, Catimini and Les Robes taking pride of place. Since
last year Timberland, Kenzo, Guess and Replay have been
added to the stock, which also includes some lovely gifts and
accessories like bags, wallets, baby teddies and watches.
Quiksilver and O'Neill streetwear sells well.
Buggy access. Play area.

Breezy Stores

*142 Crouch Hill, Crouch End, N8 9DX (8341 2020).
Finsbury Park tube, then W7/11 bus.* **Open** 10am-6pm
Mon-Fri; 9.30am-6pm Sat; noon-4pm Sun. **Credit** MC, V.
A sure bet if you're looking for a baby present, Breezy Stores
makes the most of its small space with floor-to-ceiling displays of cool T shirts (typical rubric: 'I don't do greens...';
£14.95), furry hot-water bottle covers, fleece blankets, novelty wellies, flowery flip-flops and boxed babygros. There are
toys, including Dr Seuss characters, but the store is famed
for fine merino handknits. It generally errs on the stylish side.
Buggy access.

Caramel

*291 Brompton Road, South Kensington, SW3 2DY (7589
7001). South Kensington tube.* **Open** 10am-6.30pm Mon-
Sat; noon-5pm Sun. **Credit** AmEx, MC, V. **Map** p315 E10.
Ring the bell to enter this chicer-than-chic designer outlet for
tots whose parents have both good taste and bulging wallets.
The deliciously cuddly stripy cashmere pullover for babies
of six months (£95) and teeny Prada trainers (£90) are for
seriously label-led yummy mums. There are rompers, skirts
and trousers for children up to ten, plus miniature wellies,
lambswool-lined papooses and a finger puppet set (£40).
Buggy access. Delivery service.

Catimini

*52 South Molton Street, Mayfair, W1Y 1HF (7629
8099/www.catimini.com). Bond Street tube.* **Open** 10am-
6.30pm Mon-Wed, Fri, Sat; 10am-7pm Thur; noon-5pm
Sun. **Credit** AmEx, MC, V. **Map** p316 H6.
This is the only London outpost of the sophisticated French
label for babies and children up to ten. Classic, good-looking
casuals for boys and girls include striped summer three
quarter length trousers and long-sleeved T-shirts, layered
sundresses and vests, and a range of tasteful formalwear. It
all looks delightfully European and effortlessly chic Prices
are on the high side (expect to pay £53.95 for a cotton-only
sundress for a four-year-old). Young shoppers are sometimes
given a balloon on a stick as they leave.
Buggy access. Disabled access. Mail order. Play area.

Decisions, decisions. **H&M**.

Clementine
73 Ledbury Road, Notting Hill, W11 2AG (7243 6331).
Notting Hill Gate tube. **Open** 10am-6pm Mon-Sat. **Credit**
AmEx, MC, V. **Map** p312 A6.
This store stocks 95% Petit Bateau – the label that was the
coolest when we were children still produces underwear as
cute as ever. The assistant is French and the shop full of
French customers on our visit. The pastel-striped velour
babygros (£28) are as soft as soft and will raise any baby's
ooo-factor. Loose print dresses pull off a certain well-bred
style in suntanned little girls, as only the French know how.
Boys get a selection of similarly understated quality casuals,
such as long baggy shorts and soft, coloured shirts. The
basement stocks prams, buggies and Stokke beds.
*Buggy access. Delivery service. Mail order. Nappy-
changing facilities.*

The Cross
141 Portland Road, Notting Hill, W11 4LR (7727 6760).
Holland Park or Notting Hill Gate tube. **Open** 11am-
5.30pm Mon-Sat. **Credit** AmEx, MC, V.
An adult designer store, with a tiny but significant range of
childish treasures. The emphasis for accessories is on the
hand made – woollen rugs are beautifully stitched with nursery rhymes, for example – but quality doesn't come cheap:
expect to pay £400 for a blanket or £100 for a cushion. The
quirkily charming rag dolls and knitted sequinned fish are
also pricey. There's a range of merino wool knitted babygros
and tops, appliquéd sweatshirts for hip toddlers, and long
cotton tunics and Moroccan-style slippers for little hippies.
Some surprisingly cheap toys soften the blow to the wallet.
Buggy access. Delivery service. Mail order.

Early Clothing
*79-85 Fortis Green Road, Fortis Green, N10 3HP (8444
9309). Highgate tube.* **Open** 9.30am-5.30pm Mon-Sat.
Credit AmEx, MC, V.
Polished floorboards and old-fashioned shopfittings set the
shabby-chic tone in this independent store. Flowery tights lie
in wooden hosiery drawers; church pews are used to seat
fidgety children while their feet are measured; and little
wooden stands display adorable floppy sunhats. There's a
good range of clothes for women and children, including Petit
Bateau, French Connection, Ali Bali, Jean Bourget and Balu,
plus shoes in both classic and deeply fashionable styles from
Start-Rite and D&G Junior.
Buggy access. Disabled access. Play area.

Little Willie's
*16 The Pavement, Clapham Common, SW4 0HY (7498
7899). Clapham Common tube.* **Open** 11am-6pm Mon-Fri;
10am-5.30pm Sat. **Credit** MC, V.
Little Willie's, a funky-looking venue overlooking Clapham
Common, doubles as both hairdresser and boutique for
children up to the age of 15. The colourful clothes – mainly
bright T-shirts, fleeces, hoodies, pretty summery tops and
accessories such as canvas shoes, witty tights and hats – are
sized with under-tens in mind.
Buggy access. Nappy-changing facilities. Play area.

Membery's
1 Church Road, Barnes, SW13 9HE (8876 2910).
Barnes Bridge rail. **Open** 10am-5pm Mon-Sat. **Credit**
AmEx, MC, V.
Made-to-measure bridesmaids' dresses are available for all
ages at this shop, where Sally Membery's own label shares
space with Catimini, IKKS and Petit Bateau. Nought to eight
is the general age range; both boys and girls are catered for.
Buggy access. Delivery service. Play area.

MikiHouse
*107 Walton Street, South Kensington, W3 2HP (7838
0006/www.mikihouse.co.uk). South Kensington tube.*
Open 10am-6pm Mon-Sat. **Credit** AmEx, MC, V.
Map p315 E10.
This shop stocks the Japanese label's clothes for babies and
children up to seven, as well as colourful designer outfits from
Italy and France. Toddler sundresses are £51.50, dungarees
£45 and a T-shirt and shorts set with aeroplane motif £48.
You'll also find accessories such as bootees and bibs, wood-
en toys, colourful shoes, sun hats and changing bags.
Buggy access. Delivery service. Mail order.

Notsobig
*31A Highgate High Street, Highgate, N6 5JT (8340
4455). Archway or Highgate tube.* **Open** 9.30am-6pm
Mon-Fri; 10am-6pm Sat; 11am-5pm Sun. **Credit** MC, V.
The harder you look in this tiny jewel box of a shop, the more
delights you see. Tiny outfits by Cacharel, Braez, Diesel and
No Angel hang on the walls; there is Wright and Teague silver jewellery for babies (from £40 for a chain with bell), and
Little Chums T-shirts sit in organza bags alongside hand
crocheted monkeys. Down the windy stairs are fancy-dress
costumes by Bandicoot Lapin (from £60) and the basement
has vintage ranges, including Miss Hollywood multicoloured
chenille robes and adjustable dressing-up gear by Childhood
Enchantment. Notsocheap.
Buggy access. Delivery service. Play area.

Oilily
*9 Sloane Street, Knightsbridge, SW1X 9LE (7823 2505/
www.oilily-world.com). Knightsbridge tube.* **Open** 10am-
6pm Mon, Tue, Thur-Sat; 10am-7pm Wed. **Credit** AmEx,
MC, V. **Map** p315 F9.
This large, white shop gets its colour from vibrant, funky
gear for girls and boys, newborn to 12 years old; there's a
range of similarly summery, happy-feeling women's garments. A Spanish dancer swing skirt is £79, while a green
dragon T-shirt for boys is £27.50. Babywear is similarly bold.
Buggy access. Mail order. Play area.

Patrizia Wigan
*19 Walton Street, South Kensington, SW3 2HX (7823
7080/www.patriziawigan.com). Knightsbridge or South
Kensington tube.* **Open** 10.30am-6.30pm Mon-Fri;
10.30am-6pm Sat. **Credit** AmEx, MC, V. **Map** p315 E10.
Attractive to royals and heads of state, this smart shop is full
of conservative formal wear for 12s and under. Babies get
stunning christening gowns with matching bootees, or any
of a range of trad gifts for newborns. You'll also find smocked
dresses, kilts, party dresses and velvet frocks, and can get
pageboy and bridesmaid outfits made or altered.
*Buggy access. Delivery service. Nappy-changing facilities.
Play area.*

Rachel Riley
*82 Marylebone High Street, Marylebone, W1 4QW (7935
7007/www.rachelriley.com). Baker Street or Bond Street
tube.* **Open** 10am-6pm Mon-Sat. **Credit** AmEx, MC, V.
Map p316 5G.
RR has a well-established mail-order business, and her
unmistakeable '50s retro look is predictable enough to make
ordering from the catalogue a cinch. But a visit allows you to
wallow in antique French chic. For children, hand-smocked
dresses (£85), Harris tweeds with velvet collars (£95) and tiny
ruched bikinis in Liberty print (£45) are staples, along with
Start-Rite shoes.
Buggy access. Delivery service. Mail order.
Branch: 14 Pont Street, SW1X 9EN (7259 5969).

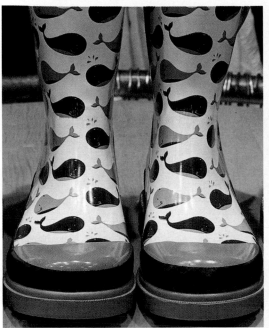

Consumer

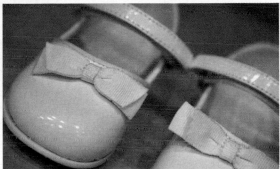

Gymboree.
See p195.

Sasti

*8 Portobello Green Arcade, 281 Portobello Road,
Ladbroke Grove, W10 5TZ (8960 1125/www.sasti.co.uk).
Ladbroke Grove tube.* **Open** 10am 6pm Mon-Sat. **Credit**
AmEx, MC, V.

Children with flamboyant tastes like it here. Little prima don-
nas love body warmers in pink fake fur or leopard-skin print
and fluffy red coats with pink hearts. Boys like the POW!
and ZAP! T-shirts. We like the cowboy-style fringed denims
and cute knickers with three layers of frilly netting.
*Buggy access. Delivery service. Mail order. Nappy-
changing facilities. Play area.*

Semmalina

*225 Ebury Street, Pimlico, SW1W 8UT (7730 9333/
www.semmalina.co.uk). Sloane Square tube.* **Open**
9.30am-5.30pm Mon-Sat. **Credit** AmEx, MC, V.
Map p318 G11.

A sweet little place to visit, with its fantasy drawbridge and
prettily presented gifts. The shop's own label is sold alongside Triple Star, Pipsie and Lucy Lockett, with gypsy-style
tops and embroidered cotton cropped trousers popular with
small girls. Toys, gifts and party paraphernalia include £1.50
going-home bags and a range of piñatas.
*Buggy access. Delivery service. Nappy-changing facilities.
Play area.*

Tartine et Chocolat

*66 South Molton Street, Mayfair, W1Y 1HH (7629
7233). Bond Street tube.* **Open** 10am-6pm Mon-Sat.
Credit AmEx, MC, V. **Map** p316 H6.

The trademark sky-blue or pink stripes of the fragrant T&C
brand date back to 1977; now there's a whole range of products for babies and under-11s, including clothes, perfumes,
soft toys and gifts. The pink and blue/feminine and mascu-
line detailing may offend, but you can always opt for the
snowy white sleepsuits and little dresses.
Mail order.

Their Nibs

*214 Kensington Park Road, Notting Hill, W11 1NR
(7221 4263/www.theirnibs.com). Ladbroke Grove or
Notting Hill Gate tube.* **Open** 9.30am-6pm Mon-Fri;
10am-6pm Sat. **Credit** MC, V.

Celebrity tots are flocking to Fiona Bell's stylish clothes shop.
For all its popularity with the rich and famous, Their Nibs is
a friendly and child-centred place. The gorgeous floaty
dresses, fairy dresses, party dresses and baby dresses (£20-
£35) are most eye-catching, but boys like the print shirts and
combats embroidered with red dragons, and there are shoes
by Angulus and Ugg boots. An amusing vintage rail has stuff
from the '40s to the '60s: dinky little psychedelic dungarees
and flash boys' suits, pinafores and sweet print shirts for
cowlicked little faces. Prices aren't very vintage – from £30.
The play area is refreshingly large for a boutique, with a
hopscotch mat, blackboards for chalk graffiti and lots of toys.
You can also get a haircut (4-6pm Mon, Tue).
*Buggy access. Disabled access: ramps. Mail order. Play
area.*

Tots

*39 Turnham Green Terrace, Chiswick, W4 1RG (8995
0520/www.totschiswick.com). Turnham Green tube.* **Open**
10am-6pm Mon-Sat; noon-5pm Sun. **Credit** AmEx, MC, V.
The clothes here, catering for boys and girls up to 12 years
old, include the Babar the Elephant range for little 'uns and
Timberland and Quiksilver for bigger 'uns. The latter
includes some bright print shirts that stand out from the
usual sea of navy and khaki on the boy's rails. Girls get

dungaree dresses in denim from Oilily, pink baseball boots
and cool accessories. There are Roobeey soft leather shoes
for babies and cute one-off designs like the lovely terry cape,
which has a bear-shaped pocket with little bear inside.
Buggy access. Mail order. Play area.

Trendys

*72 Chapel Market, Islington, N1 9ER (7837 9070). Angel
tube.* **Open** 9.30am-6pm Mon-Sat; 9.30am-4pm Sun.
Credit AmEx, MC, V.

A well-established designer kidswear shop, with a small
range of shoes and a large collection of cute clothes by the
likes of French Connection, Oilily, Elle, Cacharel and Diesel.
Buggy access.

Mid-range & high street

Biff

*41-3 Dulwich Village, Dulwich, SE21 7BN (8299 0911).
North Dulwich rail.* **Open** 9.30am-5.30pm Mon-Fri; 10am-
6pm Sat. **Credit** MC, V.

Two adjoining shops cater for Dulwich surfer dudes, and
their baby bro', sister and mum. Expect excellent-quality
casual and formal wear, including a fabulous stock of striped
tights and tops for winter toddling, superb babywear by Coco
and Petit Bateau and an irresistible swimwear range.
Buggy access. Play area.

Gap Kids

*122 King's Road, Chelsea, SW3 4TR (7823 7272/
www.gap.com). Sloane Square tube.* **Open** 10am-7pm
Mon-Sat; noon-6pm Sun. **Credit** AmEx, MC, V.
This is our favourite branch of the ubiquitous chain with its
always browsable sale rails. Gap has provided fashion
conscious children with toasty hoodies, puffas, striped tights
and cardies for years, and prices aren't bad: the jeans (from
£25) and khakis (from £20) are as well made. The babywear
is of a high standard and softly stylish.
Buggy access. Nappy-changing facilities.
Branches: throughout town. Check website for details.

Gymboree

*198 Regent Street, Oxford Circus, W1D 5TP (7494
1110/www.gymboree.com). Oxford Circus tube.* **Open**
10am-7pm Mon-Wed, Fri, Sat; 10am-8pm Thur; 11.30am-
5.30pm Sun. **Credit** AmEx, MC, V. **Map** p316 J6.
The clothing here (for under eights) sits midway between
French conservative and US casual. Quality is good and
prices affordable, especially during the frequent sales. Buying
outfits is a breeze, too, with clothes designed to co-ordinate.
*Buggy access. Delivery service. Disabled access: lift.
Play area.*
Branches: throughout town. Check website for details.

Iana

*186 King's Road, Chelsea, SW3 5XP (7352 0060/www.
iana.it). Sloane Square tube.* **Open** 10am-6pm Mon, Tue,
Thur, Fri; 10am-7pm Wed; 10am-6.30pm Sat; 11am-6pm
Sun. **Credit** AmEx, DC, MC, V. **Map** p315 F11.
Cool Italian outfits for children up to age 14 include, for girls,
little tops and skirts in pale pinks, blues and khaki or, for
boys, bold blue and red tops to team with shorts or trousers.
Prices are reasonable: a baby's top might cost £11.50, a light
summer coat for a three-year-old £16, and combats £25. The
staff are friendly and happy to help.
Buggy access. Delivery service.
Branch: Putney Exchange Shopping Centre, Putney High
Street, SW15 1TW (8789 2022).

Jigsaw Junior

190-92 Westbourne Grove, Notting Hill, W11 2RH (7727 0322/www.jigsaw-online.com). Notting Hill Gate tube. **Open** 10am-6.30pm Mon-Wed, Sat; 10am-7pm Thur, Fri; noon-6pm Sun. **Credit** AmEx, MC, V. **Map** p312 A6.
A beautiful shop, decorated in shabby-chic style. Half the staircase has been cut away to make way for a children's metal slide, allowing them to scoot down to the lower level where they'll find a beautiful antique mirrored dressing table draped with vintage embroidered silk cushions. The girls' clothes are versions of grown-up styles: a suede A-line skirt with embroidery (£79.95), say, or print sundresses (£38).
Buggy access. Play area.
Branches: throughout town. Check website for details.

Monsoon Girl

Unit 25, The Market, Covent Garden, WC2 8AH (7497 9325/www.monsoon.co.uk). Covent Garden tube. **Open** 10am-8pm Mon-Sat; 11am-6pm Sun. **Credit** AmEx, MC, V. **Map** p319 L7.
Little girls look adorable in Monsoon's winsome styles, while the baby range (two months upwards) includes delicate little dresses (about £20) and cardies in beautiful shades of raspberry, mauve and green. The T-shirts have attractive detailing (from £12) and the lined dresses (from £30) are superb.
Buggy access.

Petit Bateau

62 South Molton Street, Mayfair, W1K 5SR (7491 4498/ www.petit-bateau.com). Bond Street tube. **Open** 10am-6.30pm Mon-Wed, Fri, Sat; 10am-7pm Thur; noon-6pm Sun. **Credit** AmEx, MC, V. **Map** p316 H6.
This French brand makes stylish comfortable casuals. Best known in the UK for its fine cotton underwear, Petit Bateau's whole range will find favour with those who like discreet luxury and subtle colours. Prices are middling to high, but quality is top notch and the service always obliging.
Buggy access. Delivery service. Mail order. Play area.
Branches: 106-8 King's Road, SW3 4TZ (7838 0818); 19 Hampstead High Street, NW3 1PX (7794 3254); 188 Chiswick High Road, W4 1BB (8987 0288); 56-8 Hill Street, Twickenham, TW9 1TW (8332 6956).

Quackers

155D Northcote Road, Clapham, SW11 6QB (7978 4235). Clapham Junction rail, then 319 bus. **Open** 9.30am-5.30pm Mon-Fri; 10am-5.30pm Sat. **Credit** MC, V.
Veronica McNaught's bright and cheerful children's clothing store offers a fine selection of fun items. Labels include OshKosh, Alphabet, Petit Bateau and Carnet de Voyage. Accessories include pink secret diaries, hair grips and slides, but our personal favourites are the multicoloured wellies.
Buggy access. Play area.

Trotters

34 King's Road, Chelsea, SW3 4UD (7259 9620/www. trotters.co.uk). Sloane Square tube. **Open** 9am-7pm Mon-Sat; 10.30am-6.30pm Sun. **Credit** MC, V. **Map** p315 F11.
This lively establishment caters for babies (romper suits £23) to ten year olds (Tommy Hilfiger T-shirts £15). Professional fitters ensure Start-Rite shoes are the perfect size (there is a 40% discount for the sixth pair purchased), and children's haircuts cost from £10.50. A good selection of toys and books makes for perfect gifts.
Buggy access. Delivery service. Hairdressing. Mail order. Nappy-changing facilities. Play area.
Branches: 127 Kensington High Street, W8 5SF (7937 9373); Unit A6, Brent Cross Shopping Centre, Hendon, NW4 3FP (8202 1888).

Second-hand

Boomerang

69 Blythe Road, Olympia, W14 0HP (7610 5232). Olympia tube. **Open** 9.30am-6pm Tue-Sat. **Credit** AmEx, DC, MC, V.
This jolly shop is crammed with babies' and children's clothes and toys. There's a good selection of babygros, kids' separates and shoes, and loads of generally useful baby paraphernalia. Judging by the plethora of French labels (look no further if you're hunting for Petit Bateau classics), there's a sizeable Gallic presence in this villagey neighbourhood. Stock changes every season and you can off-load your children's hand-me-downs for a share of the asking price. To save time trawling through the rails, let the owner know what sort of thing you're after.
Buggy access. Mail order. Nappy-changing facilities.

The Little Trading Company

7 Bedford Corner, The Avenue, Chiswick, W4 1LD (8742 3152). Turnham Green tube. **Open** 9am-5pm Mon-Fri; 9am-4.30pm Sat. **No credit cards.**
This Tardis-like shop is packed to the rafters with stock. With not an inch of space unfilled, the stackers have been ingenious – car seats dangle from the upper reaches of the walls, and baby chairs, toys, cots, swimmers, buggies and beds jostle for space with clothes and books. Practically every kiddie need can be met, but it's a good idea to enlist the help of the assistant to find things. Handing over your own children's cast-offs will get you 50% off.
Buggy access. Play area.

Merry-Go-Round

12 Clarence Road, Hackney, E5 8HB (8985 6308). Hackney Central rail. **Open** 10am-5.30pm Mon-Sat. **Credit** AmEx, MC, V.
One of the largest kids' second-hand agencies still trading in London, Merry-Go-Round thrives in the absence of any local kids' clothing or toy store. It's spacious and ordered by type: items for under-twos are on the ground floor, stuff for twos to teenagers in the basement, and toys, buggies and baby walkers spill on to the pavement. High shelves hold bottle sterilisers and wellie boots (£2.50-£4), baby bootees (£2), even football and skating boots are strung from the ceiling. You'll find the odd designer-label item on the racks, but Next, Gap and Hennes aplenty, plus Fisher Price and Chad Valley toys. Videos, books, car seats and cycling helmets are here in impressive quantities.
Buggy access. Nappy-changing facilities. Play area.

Pixies

14 Fauconberg Road, Chiswick, W4 3JY (8995 1568/ www.pixiesonline.co.uk). Chiswick Park or Turnham Green tube. **Open** 10am-4.30pm Tue-Fri; 10am-3pm Sat. **Credit** MC, V.
People come from all over to visit this little shop in a quiet Chiswick parade. As well as nearly new clothes, Pixies sells top-quality baby and tots equipment of the kind that isn't easily found on the high street. Savvy parents love brands like Stokke, whose high chairs, cots and changing tables convert into proper-sized furniture for a longer life. Other desirables include HandySitt travel chairs. The shop manages to squeeze in a summer range, too – pram shades or UV bodysuits to make swimming safe in even the hottest sunshine. Fretful mothers-to-be can sign up for the consultancy service (£40/hr) for advice on what they need and what they can just as well do without. An unnecessary luxury? It all depends how fretful you are.
Buggy access. Mail order.

They rule at **Their Nibs**.
See p195.

Rainbow

253 Archway Road, Highgate, N6 5BS (8340 9700/www. rainbow-toys.co.uk). Highgate tube. **Open** 10.30am-5.30pm Mon-Sat. **Credit** MC, V.

The Rainbow toy shop's proximity to both Highgate Wood (*see p97*) and Jackson's Lane (*see p223*) have always ensured a great deal of attention from north London children on a family jaunt with their Saturday pocket money. New owners have spruced up the once shabby premises. The traditional wooden toys (Plan and Pin fire engines, farms, painted forts, wonderfully des res dolls' houses) are shown off against a cool white background. A few more sparkly things have crept in (Lucy Locket dresses from £23, plus sequin-studded wands and bags), as have rather adorable cloth dolls, Sylvanian Families and irresistibly cute pull-along rabbits and dogs (£14.95). The table of party toys remains firmly at the centre, of course – for everything from dolls' house accessories to practical jokes – and a new service can make up party bags. *Buggy access. Delivery service. Mail order service*

Swallows & Amazons

91 Nightingale Lane, Clapham, SW12 8 Clapham South tube. **Open** 10am-5.15pm **credit cards**.

Two floors of second-hand clothes for boys to 12, at encouragingly nifty prices. Labels street to designer, and kids' haircuts can also *Buggy access. Play area.*

Shoes

Brian's Shoes

2 Halleswelle Parade, Finchley Road, Temple Fortune, NW11 0DL (8455 7001/www.briansshoes.com). Finchley Central or Golders Green tube. **Open** 9.15am-5.30pm Mon-Wed, Fri, Sat; 10.30am-1.30pm Sun. *School holidays only* 9.15am-5.30pm Thur. **Credit** MC, V.

A boon for busy parents, this dedicated children's shoe shop is close to the Bookworm (*see p187*) and offers Timberland, Start-Rite, Ricosta, Skechers, Babybotte, Nike and Kickers in a helpful, calm atmosphere. Registering on the website brings updates on sales and special offers. *Buggy access. Disabled access.*

Instep

45 St John's Wood High Street, NW8 7NJ (7722 7634). St John's Wood tube. **Open** 9.30am-5.30pm Mon-Sat; 11am-5pm Sun. **Credit** AmEx, MC, V.

Close to Regent's Park, this sizeable shoe store has a huge stock of good-looking footwear and mature, helpful staff. Expect to pay around £30 for expertly fitted baby shoes, £40 for school shoes and from £50 for Italian-made, fantasy oriented delights in pastel-coloured leather. Ballet shoes and tights can also be picked up here. *Buggy access. Disabled access.* **Branches**: 47 High Street, Wimbledon Village, SW19 5AX (8946 9735).

Look Who's Walking

78 Heath Street, Hampstead, NW3 1DN (7433 3855). Hampstead tube. **Open** 10am-5.30pm Mon-Sat; noon-6pm Sun. **Credit** AmEx, MC, V.

This tiny boutique is crammed with clothes by Replay, Roberto Cavalli, Maharishi, Juicy and Oilily, and D&G, Mod8, Naturino and Skechers shoes. Staff are friendly and cope well with brat attacks; prices for shoes range from £35 to £70. The Loughton branch has a range of more sparkly stuff. *Buggy access.* **Branch**: 166A High Road, Loughton, IG10 1DN (8508 7472).

Pom d'Api

3 Blenheim Crescent, Ladbroke Grove, W11 2EE (7243 0535). Ladbroke Grove or Notting Hill Gate tube. **Open** 9.30am-6pm Mon-Sat. **Credit** MC, V.

Here children sow the seeds of a lifelong shoe obsession. The styles can't fail to get small feet noticed, many of them miniatures of covetable adult fashions. Chocolate-brown leather trainers (£55), pink silk boxing boots (£60), open-toe crisscross sandals (£58) and sandals with multicoloured leather flowers covering the bar are just a small sample. All are beautifully made in quality leather, in designs children will remember fondly for years. There is plenty of room for buggies and the kid-size sofa is a cute touch. Every purchase comes with a little present in the box for smiles all round. *Buggy access. Mail order. Nappy-changing facilities. Play area.*

Jigsaw Junior. *See p196.*

The Shoe Station

3 Station Approach, Kew, Surrey TW9 3QB (8940 9905/ www.theshoestation.co.uk). Kew Gardens tube. **Open** 10am-6pm Mon-Sat. **Credit** MC, V.
A colourful range of baby and child shoes in leather, suede and canvas, including Buckle My Shoe, Pom d'Api and witty little numbers by Ricosta and Elefanten. Staff, always friendly and patient with the grottiest of children, are trained Start-Rite fitters.
Buggy access. Play area.

Stepping Out

106 Pitshanger Lane, Ealing, W5 1QX (8810 6141). Ealing Broadway tube. **Open** 10am-5.30pm Mon-Fri; 9am-5.30pm Sat. **Credit** MC, V.
This much-loved local shop has many loyal customers. It's a Start-Rite agent first and foremost, but stocks plenty of Ricosta, Mod8 and Kenzo as well. There are big shoes, too, so parents can get in a bit of retail therapy. Experienced assistants specialise in advising on shoes for children with mobility problems, with local GPs often referring kids here; lots of styles provide extra support, but manage to be fashionable too (Le Loup Blanc, for example, is perfect for kids with weak ankles). At the back is an area with toys and games for kiddies to look through as parents pay.
Buggy access. Delivery service. Mail order. Play area.

Sportswear

Ace Sports & Leisure

341 Kentish Town Road, Kentish Town, NW5 2TJ (7485 5367). Kentish Town tube. **Open** 9.30am-6pm Mon-Wed, Fri, Sat; 9.30am-7pm Thur. **Credit** AmEx, DC, MC, V.
Why schlep into town for trainers and sports gear when you can pop across the road from Kentish Town tube to this excellent little store, with its calm atmosphere and helpful staff? Apart from the endless footwear (Puma, Adidas, Reebok and Nike, with lots of cool new astroboots from £16.99), there are small baseball mitts (£20) and the latest footballs (£14 for Euro 2004; £5.99 in appealing mini-sizes), children's cricket balls and bats, junior tennis racquets, ping-pong balls in bright colours, tracksuits, swim nappies, goggles, earplugs and nose clips – everything, in fact, to get kids active.
Buggy access. Disabled access.

Decathlon

Canada Water Retail Park, Surrey Quays Road, SE16 2XU (7394 2000/www.decathlon.co.uk). Canada Water tube. **Open** 10am-7.30pm Mon-Thur; 10am 8pm Fri; 9am-7pm Sat; 11am-5pm Sun. **Credit** MC, V.
Europe's biggest sports superstores have clothes and equipment for more than 60 types of sport, including football, rugby, tennis, golf, riding and swimming. Beware that they don't always have children's sizes in clothes, but for bikes, this is one of the cheapest places around. Frequent sales make it a useful focus for birthday and Christmas present-buying to suit sporty family members. Prices are reasonable; expect to pay about £26 for a replica football shirt.
Buggy access. Delivery service.

Lillywhites

24-36 Regent Street, SW1Y 4QF (0870 333 9600). Oxford Circus tube. **Open** 10am-8pm Mon-Wed, Fri; 10am-9pm Thur, Sat; noon-6pm Sun. **Credit** AmEx, MC, V. **Map** p319 K7.
This may be the first name that crosses the mind of a busy parent with sporting requests to satisfy, and it does still supply skiwear and cricket gear in their respective seasons,

as well as swimsuits, football and tennis kit all yea▮
But the store's layout over several half-levels is confusing, and our impression is of a store noticeably understocked, understaffed and worryingly full of sale rails.
Buggy access. Disabled access: lift, toilet.

Ocean Leisure

11-14 Northumberland Avenue, WC2N 5AQ (7930 5050). Embankment tube. **Open** 9.30am-6pm Mon-Wed, Fri; 9.30am-7pm Thur; 9.30am-5.30pm Sat. **Credit** MC, V.
Fancy body boarding in Cornwall with the kids? To spare them teeth-chattering misery, they'll need short-sleeved wet-suits (£44) in summer or a full steamer suit (£74.99) in winter. Boards may be purchased more cheaply at the seaside than here, but there's a good range of Reef sandals and neoprene Aquashoes (£6) in small sizes, as well as baby life jackets for sailing, fins (£11.95), masks and snorkels (set £21.95), and even scuba equipment (from age eight).
Buggy access. Disabled access. Mail order.

Selfridges

400 Oxford Street, Oxford Circus, W1A 1AB (0870 837 7377/www.selfridges.com). Bond Street tube. **Open** 10am-8pm Mon-Fri; 9.30am-8pm Sat; noon-6pm Sun. **Credit** AmEx, MC, V. **Map** p316 G6.
Second floor on Selfridges is sportwear, but it's Fitness Network on the first floor that most people sprint to. Concessions include CycleSurgery (7318 2448), which has small crash helmets and bikes by Ridgeback, Specialised and Trek suitable for over-eights. Skateboards hang from the ceiling and there's even a tiny climbing wall that kids find impossible to resist. If you want a taste of the frustration you may experience beyond Selfridges, a JD Sports concession, with thumping music and a very limited range for small feet, reminds you why most sensible parents avoid high-street trainer stores like the plague. For more on Selfridges, *see p184.*
Buggy access. Cafés. Car park. Delivery service. Disabled access: toilet. Mail order. Nappy-changing facilities. Play area.

Soccerscene

56-7 Carnaby Street, W1F 9QF (7439 0778/www.soccer scene.co.uk). Oxford Circus tube. **Open** 9.30am-7pm Mon-Sat; 11.30am-5.30pm Sun. **Credit** AmEx, MC, V. **Map** p316 J6.
Footie fans and rugger... fans converge on this sizeable store devoted to both the games of gentlemen and ruffians. Scaled-down replica kits are available for most of the popular teams, especially the sainted Arsenal and ever-popular ManU, with sales of white rugby shirts with a red rose logo having shot up last winter. As well as kit, there are balls, boots, shinpads, trainers, socks, boxes, scarves and hats. Service is friendly.
Buggy access. Delivery service. Mail order.

Speedo

41-3 Neal Street, Covent Garden, WC2H 9BJ (7497 0950). **Open** 10am-7pm Mon-Wed, Fri, Sat; 10am-8pm Thur; noon-6pm Sun. **Credit** AmEx, MC, V. **Map** p317 L6.
This outlet makes you feel proud to be a water baby. As a brand, Speedo has traditionally catered for lane swimmers after comfort and coverage, but it also sells beachwear, towelling capes, sun-tops and knee-length sun-suits (£23) with up to 98% UV protection. The regular range lets kids look cool in their swimming lessons (the elongated 'tankini' bikinis are lovely for little girls). There are more and more kids' accessories here: come for aquanappies, armbands, snorkels, goggles and caps that match your swimsuit.
Delivery service. Mail order.

Wigmore

79-83 Wigmore Street, Marylebone, W1U 1QQ (7486 7761/www.wigmoresports.co.uk). **Open** 10am-6pm Mon-Wed, Fri, Sat; 10am-7pm Thur. **Credit** AmEx, MC, V. **Map** p316 G6.

Service is always polite and knowledgeable in this racket specialist, a boon for adult tennis, squash and badminton players. Its huge range extends to junior players and there's plenty of expert advice on offer. If you have a child who has decided to rise to this desperate nation's challenge to find a new Tim Henman or, er, Virginia Wade, buy the necessary kit to help them succeed here. Excellent tennis shoes by K-Swiss, Adidas, Nike and others, £30-£40) are stocked in half sizes from 12 up, but more important for children are the shorter rackets (from 50cm/19in, £15-£100) and softer balls, which together prevent young beginners getting discouraged on court.

Buggy access. Delivery service. Disabled access. Mail order. **Branches**: Selfridges, 400 Oxford Street, W1A 1AB (7318 2498); Harrods, 87-135 Brompton Road, SW1X 7XL (7730 1234).

Street

O'Neill

5-7 Carnaby Street, W1F 9PB (7734 3778/www.oneill europe.com). Oxford Circus tube. **Open** 10am-7pm Mon-Wed, Fri, Sat; 10am-8pm Thur; noon-6pm Sun. **Credit** AmEx, MC, V. **Map** p318 J6.

Lovely surfer fashions that look great on sun-kissed boys and girls. This season's baggy shorts, bright button-through shirts, tough flip-flops, miniskirts, vests and cropped trousers are perfect for the summer hols. Prices range from £15 for a T-shirt; for autumn, tough, chunky hoodies start at £40.

Buggy access. Mail order.
Branch: Bluewater Shopping Centre, Kent DA9 9SJ (01322 623300); 9-15 Neal Street, WC2H 9PU (7836 7686).

Quiksilver

Units 1 & 23, Thomas Neal Centre, Earlham Street, Covent Garden, WC2H 9LD (7836 5371/www.quiksilver. com). Covent Garden tube. **Open** 10am-7pm Mon-Sat; noon-6pm Sun. **Credit** AmEx, MC, V. **Map** p317 L6.

This iconic label, started in the 1960s in Torquay (that's Torquay, Australia) by surfers Alan Green and John Law and a pair of revolutionary board shorts, is a label of choice even for those who never ride the waves. Snow- and skateboarders choose from hardwearing loose-cut jeans, T-shirts, shorts, shoes and sweats, paying from £15 for T-shirts, £30 for jeans.

Buggy access.
Branch: Unit 7, 12 North Piazza, WC2E 8HD (7240 5886); 11-12 Carnaby Street, W1F 9PH (7439 0436).

Skate of Mind

Unit 26, Thomas Neal Centre, Earlham Street, Covent Garden, WC2H 9LD (7836 9060). Covent Garden tube. **Open** 10am-7pm Mon-Sat; noon-6pm Sun. **Credit** AmEx, MC, V. **Map** p317 L6.

If the kids are minded to skate and want to look the part, the lads here can usually find smallish T-shirts with the right logos or 26-inch waist baggy pants and small-size skate shoes by, perhaps, DC. Junior skateboards are available as well: a complete rig by Blind costs £120.

Buggy access. Disabled access.
Branches: 4 Marlborough Court, W1F 7EQ (7434 0295); Unit 3, Camden Wharf, James Town Road, Camden High Street, NW1 7BX (7485 9384); 7 The Quadrant, Richmond, TW9 1BP (8940 5778).

Slam City Skates

16 Neal's Yard, Covent Garden, WC2H 9DP (7240 0928/ www.slamcity.com). Covent Garden tube. **Open** 10am-6.30pm Mon-Sat; 1-5pm Sun. **Credit** AmEx, MC, V. **Map** p317 L6.

Decks, T-shirts, the skate shoes of the moment (the smallest is UK size three, so no good for the very young), rucksacks and accessories are all sold here. Although there's no stock dedicated to children, most are happy to buy the 'Small' Slam City T-shirt and grow into it. Shoes include chunky Nikes (the Dunk was the deal when we visited), Carroll, Vans and Lakai.

Buggy access. Delivery service. Mail order (0870 420 4146)

Tomboy Kids

176 Northcote Road, Clapham, SW11 1RE (7223 8030/ www.tomboykids.com). Clapham Junction rail. **Open** 10am-5pm Mon; 10am-5.30pm Tue-Sat. **Credit** MC, V.

A funky little boutique is perfect for youngsters who like to make a statement with their clothes. There's an eclectic mix of styles, ranging from flowery hippie summer tops and nicely printed summer dresses with matching hats for girls to Paisley-esque shirts for boys, plus combats, red or green Hunter Spanish wellies, parkas and chunky Canadian jumpers. Rockmount, Birkenstock, Quiksilver, Oxbow and IKKS are names to look for.

Buggy access. Play area.

Toyshops

Bikes

Chamberlaine & Son

75-7 Kentish Town Road, Camden, NW1 8NY (7485 4488/www.chamberlainecycles.co.uk). Camden Town tube. **Open** 8.30am-6pm Mon-Sat. **Credit** MC, V.

Hundreds of bikes, suspended from the ceiling and walls. New for 2004 is the revamped Raleigh 'Chopper' (£200), while other requisites are reclinable Hamax baby seats (£69.99), a Phillips trailer buggy for two (£215), and a Giant 'halfwheeler' trailer (£179) for children who are old enough to pedal diligently behind a parent. Expect to pay £100 for a new child's bike; the first service is free.

Buggy access. Delivery service. Mail order.

Edwardes

221-5 Camberwell Road, Camberwell, SE5 0HG (7703 3676/5720). Elephant & Castle tube/rail, then P3, 12, 68, 176 bus. **Open** 8.30am-6pm Mon-Sat. **Credit** AmEx, MC, V.

Bikes for children aged two to 12, including Pro Bike, Bronx and Giant ranges. Repairs for slipped chains, punctured tyres and damaged wheels are all dextrously carried out.

Buggy access. Delivery service. Mail order.

Hills

58 Fortis Green Road, Muswell Hill, N10 3HN (8883 4644). Highgate tube, then bus. **Open** 9am-5.30pm Mon-Fri; 9am-5pm Sat. **Credit** MC, V.

Little girls' bikes, complete with streamers and flower stickers, cost £89.99 (there's a boy's equivalent painted in combat colours.) Depth of stock is not so much in evidence as other stores, but breadth is. Proximity to Alexandra palace ice rink means there's a handy sideline in ice skates (by Bauer, from £59.99), plus roller skates, unicycles, skateboards (from £25), crash helmets (£20) and tagalongs (by Allycat, £149).

Buggy access. Disabled access.

Shops by area

Covent Garden & St Giles's
Benjamin Pollock's Toyshop (Traditional toys, *p205*); **Quiksilver** (Street, *p200*); **Slam City Skates** (Street, *p200*); **Skate of Mind** (Street, *p200*).

Kensington & Chelsea
Caramel (Designer, *p191*); **Daisy & Tom** (All-rounders, *p183*); **Children's Book Centre** (Books, *p187*)' **Dragons of Walton Street** (Equipment & accessories, *p190*); **Early Learning Centre** (Fun & games, *p206*); **Gap Kids** (Mid-range, *p195*); **Harrods** (Department Stores, *p183*); **H&M** (Budget, *p191*); **Iana** (Mid range and high street, *p195*); **MikiHouse** (Designer, *p192*); **Nursery Window** (Equipment, *p190*); **Oilily** (Designer, *p192*); **Patrizia Wigan** (Designer, *p192*); **Semmalina** (Designer, *p195*); **Traditional Toys** (Traditional toys, *p205*); **Tridias** (Traditional toys, *p206*); **Trotters** (Mid-range & high street, *p196*)

West End
Catimini (Designer, *p191*); **Chappell of Bond Street** (Musical instruments, *p189*); **Disney Store** (Fun & games, *p206*); **Gymboree** (Mid-range & high street, *p195*; **Hamleys** (Fun & games, *p206*); **Iana** (Mid-range, *p191*); **John Lewis** (Department stores, *p184*); **Lillywhite's** (Sportswear, *p199*); **Monsoon Girl** (Mid-range & high street, *p196*); **Mothercare** (All-rounders, *p183*); **Ocean Leisure** (Sportswear, *p199*); **O'Neill** (Street, *p197*); **Petit Bateau** (Mid-range & high street, *p196*); **Selfridges** (Department stores, *p183*); **Soccerscene** (Sportswear, *p199*); **Speedo** (Sportswear, *p199*); **Tartine et Chocolat** (Designer, *p195*); **Wigmore** (Sportswear, *p200*).

Marylebone
Rachel Riley (Designer, *p192*).

North London
Ace Sports & Leisure (Sportswear, *p199*); **Baby Munchkins** (Equipment, *p198*; **Bookworm** (Books, *p187*); **Breezy Stores** (Designer, *p191*); **Brent Cross** (Bargain centres, *p200*); **Brian's Shoes** (Shoes, *p197*); **Camden Market** (Markets, *p184*); **Chamberlaine & Son** (Bikes, *p200*); **Children's Bookshop** (Books, *p188*); **Dot's** (Musical instruments, *p189*); **Early Clothing** (Designer, *p192*); **Fagin's Toys** (Local toyshops, *p202*); **Frederick Beck** (Local toyshops, *p203*); **Green Baby** (Equipment, *p190*); **Happy Returns** (Local toyshops, *p202*); **Hills** (Bikes, *p200*); **Humla Children's Shop** (Equipment, *p190*); **Infantasia** (Bargain centres, *p200*); **Instep** (Shoes, *p197*); **Kristen Baybars** (Traditional toys, *p205*); **Look Who's Walking** (Shoes, *p197*); **Mini Kin** (Equipment, *p190*); **Mystical Fairies** (Fun & games, *p206*); **Never Never Land** (Traditional toys, *p205*); **Notsobig** (Designer, *p192*); **Owl Bookshop** (Books, *p189*); **Rainbow** (Second-hand, *p205*);

Route 73 Kids (Local toyshops, *p2032*); **Rub-a-Dub-Dub** (Second-hand, *p190*); **Soup Dragon** (Traditional toys, *p205*; **Toy Wonderland** (Local toyshops, *p203*); **Trendys** (Designer, *p195*); **Two Wheels Good** (Bikes, *p201*); **Word Play** (Local toyshops, *p203*).

East London
Baby This 'n' Baby That (Equipment & accessories, *p198*); **Brick Lane Market** (Street markets, p184); **Chocolate Crocodile** (Second-hand, *p192*); **Columbia Road Market** (Street markets, p184); **Family Care** (Equipment, *p198*); **M&G Junior Fashions** (Budget, *p185*); **Merry-Go-Round** (Second-hand, *p196*).

South-east London
Adams (Budget, *p190*); **Biff** (Mid-range & high street, *p195*); **Bookseller Crow on the Hill** (Books, *p187*); **Compendia Traditional Games** (Traditional toys, *p205*); **Decathlon** (Sportswear & trainers, *p199*); **Dulwich Music Shop** (Musical instruments, *p189*; **Edwardes** (Bikes, *p200*); Greenwich Market (Street markets, *p187*); **London Recumbents** (Bikes, *p201*); **Toys R Us** (Fun & games, *p206*).

South-west London
Barney's (Designer, *p191*); **Brixton Market** (Street markets, *p184*); **Bunnies** (Second-hand, *p192*); **Centre Court** (Bargain centres, *p200*); **The Farmyard** (Traditional toys, *p205*); **Fun Learning** (Fun & games, *p206*); **The Golden Treasury** (Books, *p188*; **Havana's Toy Box** (Local toyshops, *p202*); **Lilliput** (Equipment, *p190*); **The Lion & Unicorn** (Books, see *p184*); **Little Willie's** (Designer, *p192*); **Membery's** (Designer, *p192*); **Northcote Music** (Musical instruments, *p185*); **Patrick's Toys & Models** (Local toyshops, *p202*); **QT Toys** (Local toyshops, *p202*); **Quackers** (Mid-range, *p196*); **The Shoe Station** (Shoes, *p199*; **Stock House** (Clothes, *p203*); **Swallows & Amazons** (Second-hand, *p197*); **Tiny Set Toys** (Local toyshops, *p203*); **Tomboy Kids** (Street, *p200*; **The Toy Station** (Local toyshops, *p204*).

West London
Boomerang (Second-hand, *p192*); **Cheeky Monkeys** (Fun & games, *p206*); **Children's Book Centre** (Books, *p183*); **Children's Book Company** (Books, *p194*); **Clementine** (Designer, *p192*); **The Cross** (Designer, *p192*); **Jigsaw Junior** (Mid-range, *p196*); **The Little Trading Company** (Second-hand, *p196*); Petit Bateau (Clothes, *p201*); **Pixies** (Second-hand, *p196*); **Pom d'Api** (Shoes, *p197*); Portobello Road Market (Markets, p187); **Primark** (Budget, *p191*); **Sasti** (Designer, *p195*); **Snap Dragon** (Local toyshops, *p202*); **Stepping Out** (Shoes, *p199*); **Their Nibs** (Designer, *p195*); **Tots** (Designer, *p195*).

London Recumbents

Dulwich Park (access from College Road), Dulwich, SE21 7BQ (8299 6636). **Open** 10am-5pm Mon-Fri; 10am-6pm Sat, Sun. **Credit** MC, V.

Must a kid's bike always be sit-up-and-beg? A three-year-old can learn to ride a foot-steered recumbent – terrific fun and extremely cool. This company hires out (£5/hr) and sells (around £200) an astonishing variety of two- and three-wheel machines. Stock includes superior tag-alongs that clip into a rear carrier (rather than the seat stem) and offer gears to the secondary pedaller (£250).

Buggy access. Mail order.
Branch: Battersea Park, East Carriage Drive, SW11 4NJ (7498 6543).

Two Wheels Good

143 Crouch Hill, Crouch End, N8 9QH (8340 4284/www. twowheelsgood.co.uk). Finsbury Park tube, then W7 bus. **Open** 8.30am-6pm Mon-Sat, 11am-5pm Sun. **Credit** AmEx, MC, V.

Funkier than most bike shops, this one combines the cool, sporty side of adult biking with a good range of kids' equipment – perhaps the children's versions of Trek, Ridgeback and Puky, which cost from £100 like most other makes but look smarter. There are helmets (by Met, £20) with lovely designs and Trek trailers (£250, converts to a stroller) and tag-alongs (from £120, geared and ungeared), plus Bobike child seats (£70), one of them perfect for older passengers (it has no sides and folds into a parcel rack). Neat.

Buggy access.
Branch: 165 Stoke Newington Church Street, N16 0UL (7249 2200).

Local toyshops

Fagin's Toys

84 Fortis Green Road, Muswell Hill, N10 3HN (8444 0282). East Finchley tube, then 102 bus. **Open** 9am-5.30pm Mon-Sat; 10am-3pm Sun. **Credit** MC, V.

This is the sister shop of Word Play in Crouch End and has a similar feel: fixtures are tatty, but who cares when the space is so big and the toys so sensibly chosen? There is almost nothing faddy here, just yards and yards of Galt, Orchard, Brio, Lego, Playmobil, Sylvanian Families and other good-quality children's products that encourage creative play. A large table at the front always has lots of novelties, from masks to mouse keyrings, all pitched at pocket money prices.

Buggy access.

Happy Returns

36 Rosslyn Hill, Hampstead, NW3 1NH (7435 2431). Hampstead tube. **Open** 9.30am-5.30pm Mon-Fri; 10am-6pm Sat; noon-5.30pm Sun. **Credit** MC, V.

Locals return happily and regularly to this little shop, which doubles as local party supplier (stationery, helium balloons, cards, giftwrap). A good range of Galt crafts, from Octons and paints to hair art, is complemented by Crayola art equipment. There are cheap and cheerful items like police helmets, swords and feather boas, but otherwise it's all proper boxed toys – Sylvanian Families (£10.99), bubble machines (£9.99), sailing yachts, Wolfhammer games and action figures.

Buggy access. Play area.

Havana's Toy Box

Ground floor, Putney Exchange Shopping Centre, Putney High Street, Putney, SW15 1TF (8780 3722). Putney Bridge tube/Putney rail. **Open** 9am-6pm Mon-Sat; 11am-5pm Sun. **Credit** AmEx, MC, V.

Traditional wooden toys for under-eights are just one part of this shop's range of gifts and accessories, with fairy dresses, snuggle sacks, cuddly toys and night lights all cosily displayed in the bijou premises.

Patrick's Toys & Games

107-11 Lillie Road, Fulham, SW6 7FX (7385 9864/ www.patrickstoys.co.uk). Fulham Broadway tube. **Open** 9.15am-5.45pm Mon-Sat. **Credit** MC, V.

This cavernous shop has something to suit every pocket and for once boys get the lion's share of the goods. It's the main service agent for Hornby and Scalextric, so expect lots of tracks and model trains – everything for everyone from novices to adults with the whole shebang in their attic. Outdoor sports get a look in with kites, bikes and garden games, while war buffs will find enough to engage in full-scale combat. Girls have a choice of dolls' houses with all the furniture miniature Victorians could wish for. Among the dolls downstairs is Ken, in the guise of *Swan Lake*'s lead dancer, and a pregnant Sindy, which makes for quite a broad range. There is also a large selection of cheap party gifts.

Buggy access. Delivery service (local).

QT Toys

90 Northcote Road, Clapham Junction, SW11 6QN (7223 8637). Clapham Junction rail. **Open** 9.30am-5.30pm Mon-Sat. **Credit** MC, V.

This low-ceilinged shop is a mini-labyrinth, with toys packed into every nook and cranny. Reliable stalwarts Lego, Duplo, Brio and Meccano and of course Barbie with her endless accessories, all sell like billy-o, but there are other dollies, dressing-up, art and craft materials, models, ride-on and push-along toys too. Outdoor toys for the small London garden include paddling pools and simple swings. The pocket money-priced items change frequently to prevent boredom.

Buggy access.

Route 73 Kids

92 Stoke Newington Church Street, Stoke Newington, N16 0AP (7923 7873/www.route73kids.com). Finsbury Park tube/rail, then 106 bus/73, 393, 476 bus. **Open** 10am-5.30pm Tue-Sat; 11am-5pm Sun. **Credit** AmEx, MC, V.

Still the sole repository of children's fun in Stokey, the shop-behind-the-bus-stop excels in its own brightly coloured, personable way. There are lots of traditional toys, ranging from the wooden Plan range (the hot favourite locally is a dear little humpty-back pull-along snail, £14) through Brio train sets to more cerebral playthings, such as chess setsand solitaire. Route 73 is strong on crafts (face-paints, friendship bracelets) and not so big on dressing up. But piñatas and pocket money novelties are here in spades (or rather buckets) and, in summer, you can buy either play sand or the sandpit toys necessary for a trip to the park.

Buggy access. Delivery service (local). Mail order.

Snap Dragon

56 Turnham Green Terrace, Chiswick, W4 1QP (8995 6618). Turnham Green tube. **Open** 9.30am-6pm Mon-Sat; noon-5pm Sun. **Credit** MC, V.

Children are well served in Turnham Green it seems, with a designer clothes store, a second-hand outlet and this toy store all in one street. Snap Dragon is a colourful and busy shop. There's a lot of cute stationery and fashionable accessories for teens, plus all the tots' favourite figures (including rodent stars Angelina and Maisie). Add family games, kites and model castles to the mix, and you should be able to find all the presents you need in a single trip.

Buggy access. Delivery service (local). Mail order.

Pet subjects at **Tridias**. *See p206.*

Pet subjects at **Tridias**. *See p206.*

Consumer

Tiny Set Toys

54 Lower Richmond Road, Putney, SW15 1JT (8788 0392). Putney Bridge tube/22 bus. **Open** 9.30am-5.30pm Mon-Sat; 10am-2pm Sun. **Credit** MC, V.

Playtime equipment at Tiny Set Toys features swings, climbing frames and paddling pools for those who are feeling athletic, and jigsaws, puzzles and board games for those who want more stationary fun.

Buggy access. Delivery service. Mail order.

The Toy Station

6 Eton Street, Richmond, Surrey TW9 1EE (8940 4896). Richmond tube/rail. **Open** 10am-6pm Mon-Fri; 9.30am-6pm Sat; noon-5pm Sun. **Credit** Over £8 MC, V.

A well-stocked little place, spread over two floors, with Brio, Meccano, Lego, Airfix and radio-controlled toys sold alongside dollies, craft sets, paints, plasticine and toys at pocket money prices.

Buggy access.

Toystop

80-82 St John's Road, Clapham Junction, SW11 1PX (7228 9079). Clapham Junction rail. **Open** 9.30am-6pm Mon-Sat; 11am-5pm Sun. **Credit** MC, V.

Toys and games galore at this yellow-fronted shop. Everything from stuffed monkeys (this being the Chinese year of that particular primate) to pink Angelina Ballerina tutus for tinies. All ages will find something they want to take home in here; the two expansive rooms are full to bursting with new or classic board games, puzzles, a small selection of books, make-up cases, novelty stationery. mini-racing cars, and beads, bangles and baubles.

Buggy access.

Toy Wonderland

10-11 Northways Parade, Finchley Road, Swiss Cottage, NW3 5EN (7722 9821/www.toywonderland.co.uk). Swiss Cottage tube. **Open** 10am-6pm Mon-Sat; 11am-4pm Sun. **Credit** MC, V.

Not especially atmospheric, but friendly and in a convenient location for Swiss Cottage, this family-run store has some of everything and always attempts to cater for the latest craze – in trading cards (Yu-Gi-Oh!), character dolls (Thunderbirds) and so on. All the branded dolls are here, from Barbie and those rather hard-faced Bratz creatures to Baby Björn. In winter you'll find stacks of board games, puzzles, Playmobil and Tomy activity toys; in summer, some of them make way for footballs, kites, and tennis or badminton sets. Prices are fair: you can pick up a pretty useful remote controlled car for £25, or a plane for £100.

Buggy access. Delivery service. Mail order.

Word Play

1 Broadway Parade, Crouch End, N8 9TN (8347 6700). Finsbury Park tube/rail, then W7 bus/11 bus. **Open** 9am-5pm Mon-Sat; 11am-5pm Sun. **Credit** MC, V.

Slightly shabby on the outside, Word Play is nonetheless a sincere and well-loved Crouch End fixture. One reason is that a good half of its display space is devoted to children's books, from nursery rhymes to history and reference. Then it has lots of craft supplies for rainy days, plus popular building toys such as Bionicles or Geomag at sensible prices. A set of wooden draughts costs £7.99, a Total Soldier kit £9.99 and nicely formed pocket money dolls £1.99. A low table has penny dreadfuls, and cuddly toys are suspended, neatly out of reach, in a hammock above the till.

Buggy access.

It's in the post

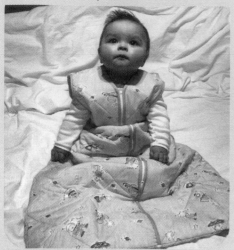

Traffic, parking-space stress, negotiating child-hostile West End shops... who needs it? Sometimes it's best to stay in your pyjamas and shop comfortably from home, making the most of a growing number of companies that sell by mail order through catalogues or via the internet.

Bump to 3
0870 606 0276/www.bumpto3.com
Wakeful nights from kicked-off bedding? Grobag's cosy sleeping bags were a godsend for our review wriggler (*pictured*, in his Grobag) – and his mum. These are available in sizes newborn to six years (£17.95-£29.95). Outdoor gear and UV-protective swimwear are also sold.

The Children's Audio Company
www.kidsmusic.co.uk
Available on various formats, you'll find a good range here: a five-tape karaoke box set (with lyrics leaflet, £14.99) is good for wannabe pop idols, or there are more traditional soothers, such as nursery rhymes, stories and party games.

Dormitory
1.14 Oxo Tower Wharf, Barge House Street, SE1 9PH (7928 0404/sales@dormitoryuk.com).
The stylish nursery range includes gingham cotton and Mogul-embroidered bedlinen, hooded towels and robes, pyjamas and gorgeous baby blankets.

Hawkin's Bazaar
0870 429 4000/www.hawkin.com
A fun-to-read catalogue of 'astonishing curiosities', nostalgic and interesting toys, amusing tricks, and puzzles and games that don't need batteries, bleep infuriatingly or require remortgaging the house (prices start at 30p).

J&M Toys
01274 599314/www.jandmtoys.co.uk
Birthday parties, school plays, a visit to granny... you never know when a mermaid/Roman centurion/purple dragon costume will be called for. J&M supplies sensibly priced dressing-up outfits for ages three to eight.

Letterbox
www.letterbox.co.uk
Good for posh presents and personalised items, you'll also find glittery girlie stuff, traditional toys, scooters and – yay! – foam rockets. The website has tempting 'special offers' and 'under £6' sections for bargainhunters.

Manufactum
0800 096 0937/www.manufactum.co.uk
This range of practical and stylishly designed products veer towards pricey, but be assured that you're paying for high-quality items, traditionally crafted from durable materials. The sturdy kitchen- and cookware, furniture, innovative camping gear and garden utensils should last long enough to pass on toyour progeny, while toys that include table football, construction and wooden puzzle kits, steel kazoos, and a crossbow and rubber arrows will keep them busy until then.

Mini Boden
0845 677 5000/www.boden.co.uk
Good-looking and easy-to-wear casuals, beach gear, nightwear and shoes for 0- to 14-year-olds. Colourful retro prints mix with cosy stripy hoodies, camouflage cargo pants, fun logo T-shirts, hotchpotch pinafores, pretty vintage-design dresses and bright sumer shoes.

Mulberry Bush
www.mulberrybush.co.uk
Handsome traditional toys are Mulberry's forte. We loved the 100-piece wooden train set (£39.99), sold alongside squirty bath stuff, trinket boxes, dolls, puppet theatres and a whole host of other fun and traditional ideas for babies and children.

Science Museum
www.sciencemuseumstore.com
Outgrown Pingu and Postman Pat? There are state-of-the-art gadgets, how-to books and creative kits here – walkie-talkie watches are £24.99 and the motorised telescope at £499 will send parents starry-eyed.

The Talking Book Shop
7491 4117/www.talkingbooks.co.uk
Offering the personal stereo alternative to torch-under-the-duvet reading, this shop stocks a wide range on tape and CD, from favourite sports and animal stories, traditional folk tales and sci-fi to children's classics.

Traditional toys

Benjamin Pollock's Toyshop
44 The Market, Covent Garden, WC2E 8RF (7379 7866/ www.pollocks-coventgarden.co.uk). Covent Garden tube. **Open** 10.30am-6pm Mon-Sat; 11am-4pm Sun. **Credit** AmEx, MC, V. **Map** p319 L7.
Best known for its toy theatres, Pollock's is an educational wonderland for young thesps and hugely enjoyed, on a more superficial level, by other kids. The most popular paper theatre for kids to assemble is Jackson's (£5.95), with its set and characters for the ballet *Cinderella*. The Victorian Gothic version features a nativity play and there's an Elizabethan one (£8.95) that puts on *A Midsummer Night's Dream*. Other items on sale include marionettes, glove and finger puppets and French musical boxes (£37.50). If the history of paper theatres sparks an interest, there are books on the subject. Collectors pop in for antiques and hand made bears (from £82), but there are quirky pocketmoney toys too.
Mail order.

Compendia Traditional Games
10 The Market, Greenwich, SE10 9HZ (8293 6616/ www.compendia.co.uk). Cutty Sark DLR/Greenwich rail. **Open** 11am-5.30pm daily. **Credit** MC, V.
The ultimate shop for a rainy day, Compendia has the traditionals – chess, backgammon, dominos – as well as an appealing range of games from around the world to suit all ages. If you've had enough Cluedo, check out Champagne Murders (a murder-mystery game for ages eight to adult). Little ones have fun with Coppit – a wobbly hat game – but the drug-smuggling board game Grass is, natch, adults only.
Buggy access. Disabled access. Delivery service. Mail order.

The Farmyard
63 Barnes High Street, Barnes, SW13 9LF (8878 7338). Barnes or Barnes Bridge rail. **Open** 10am-5.30pm Mon-Fri; 9.30am-5.30pm Sat. **Credit** MC, V.
The Farmyard stocks traditional toys and games for newborns to eight-year-olds, including its own personalised range of wooden toys, models and kits. There are, indeed, mini-farm animals and the farmyards to keep them in, although dairy stock isn't a particular specialism. Small and large gifts include puzzles, games, wooden toys, dolls and puppets. Dressing up for that all important party could also cue a trip here, as it stocks princess dresses and other costumes.
Buggy access. Play area.
Branch: 54 Friar's Stile Road, Richmond, Surrey TW10 6NQ (8332 0038).

Kristin Baybars
7 Mansfield Road, Gospel Oak, NW3 2JD (7267 0934). Kentish Town tube/Gospel Oak rail/C2, C12 bus. **Open** 11am-6pm Tue-Sat. **No credit cards.**
Alleged to be a showcase for collectors' items, this miniaturist's paradise is also a fairytale come true for any child capable of looking without touching. You have to knock to gain entry ('mysterious' is a preferred adjective of Ms Kristin Baybars herself), but what you'll see inside is the biggest, most jaw-dropping array of tiny scenes and houses outside a craft fair. Show enough interest and decorum, and you'll be ushered into the inner sanctum – room after room of amazing little worlds, including a house full of dogs, a macabre execution scenario and an old-fashioned store for mourning jewellery. The dolls' house kits aren't prohibitively expensive (£70 for a massive Regency affair), and it's well worth investing a few pounds in a tiny picnic hamper and contents (food items from 15p).
Buggy access.

Never Never Land
3 Midhurst Parade, Fortis Green, N10 3EJ (8883 3997). East Finchley tube. **Open** 10am-5pm Tue, Wed, Fri, Sat. **Credit** MC, V.
It's easy to forget that this teensy shop (three customers feels like a crowd) is not merely a supplier of dolls' houses and their contents. This it does supremely well, recommending only kits that really do fit together (from £85) and modest alternatives such as conservatories (£20) and shops (£57.50). But the energetic owner is also adept at sourcing unusual wooden toys (such as dancing musical frogs, £11.99) and has many inspired gifts, including winged 'wish bears'.
Buggy access. Mail order.

Rainbow
253 Archway Road, N6 5BS (8340 9700/www.rainbow-toys.co.uk). Highgate tube. **Open** 10.30am-5.30pm Mon-Sat. **Credit** MC, V.
Still distinguished by its rainbow-painted window, this shop has something of a hippie-dippie aura, but it's a real treasure trove. Mobiles and paper lampshades got up as hot air balloons (£5.75) hang from the ceiling, and wooden toys and puppets are much in evidence. Beanie Buddies are heaped in a corner, while display counters nearest the till offer assorted glass and clay marbles, practical jokes, kids' jewellery and such dolls' house furnishings as tiny plates of food, coat-hangers or books (from 15p, often bought on their own). The back room has a useful variety of dressing-up costumes, dolls, balloons and little plastic figures on and off horseback.
Buggy access. Delivery service. Mail order (toys only). Nappy-changing facilities.

Soup Dragon
27 Topsfield Parade, Tottenham Lane, Crouch End, N8 8PT (8348 0224/www.soup-dragon.co.uk). Finsbury Park tube/rail, then W7, 41 bus. **Open** 9.30am-6pm Mon-Sat; 11am-5pm Sun. **Credit** MC, V.
Successive generations of Crouch End children are weaned on this quirky little shop, which specialises in wooden and traditional toys, plus faintly hippie-ish clothes. More nursery products have crept in of late – buggies, snuggles, high chairs and slings. It's also a stockist of removable wall art (paint your own background, then stick on flowers, fish, rockets or whatever, £43). Then there are the Groovy Girl dolls (£8.90), an endearingly flat-chested alternative to Barbie; Balu hand-painted dresses; pretty dolls' houses (£79 for an impressive Georgian) and a mini-kitchen play area that survives its perennial popularity. The free community noticeboard is excellent, and bargain-hunters may leave an email address to be advised of the bi-monthly, half-price warehouse sales.
Buggy access. Play area.
Branch: 106 Lordship Lane, Dulwich, SE22 8HF (8693 5575).

Traditional Toys
53 Godfrey Street, Chelsea, SW3 3SX (7352 1718). Sloane Square tube, then 11, 19, 22 bus/49 bus. **Open** 10am-5.30pm Mon-Fri; 10am-6pm Sat. **Credit** AmEx, MC, V. **Map** p315 E11.
Every nook and cranny here is filled with games, books and toys. There's a wide range of toys at pocket money prices – farm animals, dolls' house furniture and soldiers – plus larger items such as a smart wooden tricycle (£74) and a bright-red wooden fire engine (£63). Shelves hold Julip model ponies; Brio train sets, boats, dolls, teddies and much more. Don't miss the fantastic fancy dress: sheriffs and fairies, plus accessories for imaginative games, such as like shields, swords, a miniature bow and arrows set and hobbyhorses (£45).
Buggy access. Delivery service.

Tridias

25 Bute Street, South Kensington, SW7 3EY (7584 2330/www.tridias.co.uk). South Kensington tube. **Open** 9.30am-5.30pm Mon-Sat. **Credit** MC, V. **Map** p315 D10.
The proximity of Tridias to the museums shows in the several shelves stocking intriguing chemistry and science experiment sets (for about £30), but there's also a corner devoted to party equipment. Outdoor toys include croquet and swingball sets. Dressing-up clothes, Brio, tool kits, garages and cars, dolls' houses, plenty of educational books and board games fill the spaces. Favourites include a stage for puppet shows (£34.99), wizard puppets (£6.99 each) and an ace wooden rocking horse (£759, inc delivery).
Buggy access. Mail order (0870 443130).
Branch: 6 Lichfield Terrace, Richmond, Surrey TW9 1AS (8948 3459).

Fun & games

Cheeky Monkeys

202 Kensington Park Road, W11 1NR (7792 9022/ www.cheekymonkeys.com). Notting Hill Gate tube, then 52 bus. **Open** 9.30am-5.30pm Mon-Fri; 10am-5.30pm Sat. **Credit** MC, V. **Map** p312 A6.
These lovely modern toyshops are strong on presentation and good at stocking unusual, attractive and fun products. Monkeys have some of London's best fancy dress (from smart soldiers to tigers and frogs, alongside Angelina Ballerina tutus). Then there's Playstack, a brilliant vertical puzzle system that comes with a book telling the story of, say, Jack in the Beanstalk. Pocket money toys and small gifts (for around £1.99) tend to be offbeat; we like the coloured bath bombs and raggy dolls, and children could spend ages deciding what to spend their weekly stipends on in here.
Buggy access. Delivery service. Disabled access. Mail order (website only).
Branches: throughout town. Check website for details.

Disney Store

360-66 Oxford Street, W1N 9HA (7491 9136/www. disneystore.co.uk). Bond Street tube. **Open** 10am-8pm Mon-Sat; noon-6pm Sun. **Credit** AmEx, MC, V. **Map** p316 J6.
Fancy-dress costumes (Disney's Snow White and Woody the Cowboy are favourites), stationery, tableware, videos, dolls and cuddly toys are the bestsellers in this animated shop. There are brash mounds of soft toys, and the famous characters have also been fashioned into covetable twirly straws, beach towels and pencil cases (from £3.99).
Buggy access. Mail order.
Branches: 9 The Piazza, Covent Garden, WC2E 8HD (7836 5037); 22A & 26 The Broadway Shopping Centre, Hammersmith, W6 9YD (8748 8886).

Early Learning Centre

36 King's Road, Chelsea, SW3 4HD (7581 5764/www. elc.co.uk). Sloane Square tube. **Open** 9am-6pm Mon, Tue, Thur-Sat; 9am-7pm Wed; 11am-5pm Sun. **Credit** AmEx, MC, V. **Map** p315 F11.
ELC's wide range of toys, games and art materials is dedicated to imaginative play for babies and young children. Here you'll find chunky musical instruments, play food and cookware, plus plastic animals, dinosaurs, play houses, swings, sand pits, wooden train sets, science sets and arty-crafty sets. Every branch has its own play space, and this one holds play sessions for little ones on Tuesdays (9.30-11am).
Buggy access. Delivery service. Mail order. Play area.
Branches: throughout town. Check website for details.

Fun Learning

Bentall's Centre, Clarence Street, Kingston-upon-Thames, Surrey KT1 1TP (8974 8900). Kingston rail. **Open** 9am-6pm Mon-Wed, Fri, Sat; 9am-8pm Thur; 11am-5pm Sun. **Credit** MC, V.
Fun Learning has toys for everyone from fives to 15s, including some brain-teasers and puzzles that will flummox even grown-ups. Eager learners can try out the educational software at the computer table in the centre, while others head straight to the toys and books, encompassing themes such as the night sky and the animal kingdom, that are arranged around the edges. Crafty toys allow children to make lovely things with pipe-cleaners, tissue paper and Hama Beads. There are plenty of outdoor toys too.
Buggy access. Nappy-changing facilities.
Branch: Brent Cross Shopping Centre, Hendon, NW4 3FP (8203 1473).

Hamleys

188-96 Regent Street, W1E 5BT (0870 333 2450/www. hamleys.com). Oxford Circus tube. **Open** 10am-8pm Mon-Sat; noon-6pm Sun. **Credit** AmEx, MC, V. **Map** p316 J6.
The largest toyshop in the world (allegedly) is a loud, frenetic, exciting experience. You can get most of the products you're looking for here, though prices tend to build in a margin for the convenience. The ground floor is where the latest fun toys are demonstrated This floor also accommodates a mountain of soft toys. The basement is the Cyberzone, full of games consoles and high-tech gadget. The first floor has items of a scientific bent, plus a lurid sweet factory and bear depot. On second is everything for pre schoolers. Third is girlie heaven – Barbie World, Sylvanian Families and departments for dressing up, make-up and so on. Fourth has some large and pricey remote-controlled vehicles, plus die-cast models. Fifth is Lego World, which has its own café. Kids can have their birthday party here – typically on a Sunday morning – and Hamleys also arranges Christmas parties and other events. *See also p185* **Child's play**, *p174* **Scoff till you drop**.
Buggy access. Café. Delivery service. Disabled access: lift, toilet. Nappy-changing facilities. Mail order. Play areas.

Mystical Fairies

12 Flask Walk, Hampstead, NW3 1HE (7431 1888/www. mysticalfairies.co.uk). Hampstead tube. **Open** 10am-6pm Mon-Sat; 11am-6pm Sun. **Credit** MC, V.
Fairy creatures hang from the ceiling on beaded swings, endure being shaken inside glitter-storm bubbles and lend their wings to little girls' rucksacks. Is there anything in this shop that doesn't sparkle in a magical-mystical-most-amazing way? What's more, fairy costumes and ballet wear are available in great profusion and the basement is an atmospheric party venue (*see p247*).
Buggy access.

Toys R Us

760 Old Kent Road, SE15 1NJ (7732 7322/www.toysrus. co.uk). Elephant & Castle tube/rail, then 21, 56, 172 bus. **Open** 9am-8pm Mon-Fri; 9am-7pm Sat; 11am-5pm Sun. **Credit** AmEx, MC, V.
Geoffrey's spacious toy warehouses – usually buried in retail parks – may be rather soulless, but they stock industrial quantities of the toy of the moment. Inexpensive bikes, trikes, ride-on tractors and go karts, car seats, baby accessories and buggies are another attraction, and the party paraphernalia is pretty good: themed paperware, silly hats, balloons and party bags with their various plasticky fillings.
Buggy access. Car park. Delivery service. Disabled access: toilet. Nappy-changing facilities.
Branches: throughout town. Check website for details.

Stuck in at **Hamleys**. *See p206.*

Where to Stay

Staying over? London's got plenty of guest rooms...

A s one of the most popular city-break venues in Europe, London has had to look to its accommodation options for leisure travellers with children in tow. Until fairly recently, choices were limited, to say the least. There were the famous names – Ritz, Dorchester, Savoy, Claridge's – all gorgeous, of course, but with the cost of a family suite upwards of £500 per night, not really a serious option for the average family on a city break. There were swanky boutique hotels with witty lobbies and spas – think Sanderson, St Martin's and myhotel – but again, not great for the family budget. Then there were the cheap and cheerfuls – affordable, yes, but with rooms so poky and service so offhand you'd be better off camping in Crystal Palace (yes, there really is a campsite there; call 8778 7155 for details).

This unsatisfactory situation is slowly changing. A series of bad years following the Iraq war, SARS anxiety and continuing terrorism threats have resulted in a drop in US visitor numbers. This has made hoteliers hungry for business. Hotels all over town have special offers and short-break packages

for the discerning traveller. To find out about them, ring Visit London's hotel booking line or log on to Superbreak, which has a huge range of family packages, including lots of 'Kids Go Free' deals.

INFORMATION AND BOOKING
The staff at Visit London will look for hotels within your selected area and price range for a £5 fee. You can also check availability and reserve rooms on its website. Superbreak can organise theme park packages to Legoland Windsor (*see p292*) and Theatrebreak packages for those who want to take in a show and a theatre tour; its website and brochure are also available through Visit London.
Visit London Booking Line *0845 644 3020/ www.visitlondon.com*. **Open** 8am-11pm daily.
Superbreak *01904 679 999/www.superbreak.com*
London Rooms *www.londonrooms.biz*

PRICES AND CLASSIFICATION
British hotels are classified according to a star system agreed by the English Tourism Council, the AA and the RAC. We don't list star ratings, as they tend to reflect facilities rather than quality; instead, we've classified hotels according to the price of the cheapest double room per night.

The hotels listed below extend a warm welcome to children. We've even included a couple of well-placed, luxury independents that allow children to kip on a sofabed in their parents' room; most expensive hotels would insist families book suites (and pay a packet for the privilege).

A lot of hotels that attract business travellers offer discounted rates on weekends, with deals often available via their websites. Also check online for special offers, facilities and accessibility, and phone ahead if you require a particular service, such as babysitting: many hotels will make arrangements on your behalf.

Luxury hotels

Charlotte Street Hotel
15-17 Charlotte Street, Fitzrovia, W1T 1RJ (7806 2000/ fax 7806 2002/www.firmdale.com). Tottenham Court Road tube. **Rates** (breakfast not incl) £230-£240 single; £270-£335 double; £388-£934 suite. **Credit** AmEx, MC, V. **Map** p316 J5.
This delicious boutique hotel (*pictured above*) is the ultimate in 'modern English' style. Despite its poshness, the hotel has extremely sweet management when it comes to families and will happily put a sofabed in one of the deluxe double rooms for the children to share. If you're willing to shell out a little-

more, the loft mezzanine room (£411) lets parents sleep on a different level to their progeny. The bedrooms are all in English country-house style, with quirky touches and transatlantic treats: shiny granite bathrooms, bulging mini-bars and technological conveniences.

The Gore
190 Queen's Gate, Knightsbridge, SW7 5EX (7584 6601/ fax 7589 8127/www.gorehotel.com). Gloucester Road tube. **Rates** (breakfast not incl) £182-£199 single; £223-£335 double; £346 suite. **Credit** AmEx, DC, MC, V. **Map** p315 D9.

This wonderfully atmospheric, antique-filled hotel may be expensive, but it's beautiful. All the rooms have massive 18th-century four-poster beds, Persian rugs and any number of handsome antiques; the bathrooms feature Victorian clawfoot tubs. Best of all, there are rather sweet, aged leather couches, which fold out into sofabeds where children can sleep. So you can stay in this characterful, elegant hotel and save a bit of cash by having your kids in the same room. If you can, take a look at the Tudor Room, which has a 15th-century bed, a minstrel's gallery and atmospheric beamed ceilings. The whole place has a delightful air of shabby chic, from the worn leather sofas to the casual, wood-panelled bar.

Amsterdam Hotel
7 Trebovir Road, Earl's Court, SW5 9LS (0800 279 9132/fax 7244 7608/www.amsterdam-hotel.com). Earl's Court tube. **Rates** £78-£86 single; £88-£100 double; £112-£135 triple. **Credit** AmEx, DC, MC, V. **Map** p314 B11.

Earl's Court is popular with families for its affordable prices and easy access to the centre of town. The Amsterdam Hotel is a jolly choice. The whole place feels like a Florida condo, with a palm-filled lobby, tropical upholstery and Caribbean prints. The comfortable and modern rooms are done up in Key West pastels, and the breakfast room feels more Gulf of Mexico than Earl's Court, replete with furniture made of white wicker and bamboo. All that cheery decor is great for coming home to on a grey London day. For longer stays, there is also a wing of private apartments.

Sherlock Holmes Hotel
108 Baker Street, Marylebone, W1U 6LJ (7486 6161/ fax 7958 5211/www.sherlockholmeshotel.com). Baker Street tube. **Rates** (breakfast not incl weekdays) £128-£145 double; £186 suites. **Credit** AmEx, DC, MC, V. **Map** p316 G5.

This is a chilled boutique hotel with a surprisingly laid-back attitude to children, who can be given a double sofabed in their parents' double bedroom. The lobby is a casual, New York-style cocktail bar, with wood floors, cream walls and brown leather furniture. The rooms are like hip bachelor pads: beige, brown and wood, leather headboards, pinstripe sheets and swanky bathrooms. There's a gym, sauna and steamroom, and an award-winning restaurant, Sherlock's Grill. There's a babysitting service too.

Arran House Hotel
77-9 Gower Street, Bloomsbury, WC1E 6HJ (7636 2186/fax 7436 5328). Goodge Street tube. **Rates** £45-£55 single; £62-£85 double. **Credit** MC, V. **Map** p317 K4.

The Arran House is a small family-run hotel in a 200-year-old Georgian townhouse in the heart of Bloomsbury (within walking distance of the British Museum). Kids are welcome, and any child small enough to sleep in a cot or share a bed with their parents can stay free of charge. Special events, such as Easter egg hunts, are laid on during holidays; otherwise children can play in the gardens or avail themselves of the art materials and paints. The breakfast room has a high chair.

Garden Court Hotel
30-31 Kensington Gardens Square, Bayswater, W2 4BG (7229 2553/fax 7727 2749/www.gardencourthotel.co.uk). Bayswater or Queensway tube. **Rates** £39 £62 single; £58-£92 double; £72-£114 triple; £82-£135 quad. **Credit** MC, V. **Map** p312 B6.

Garden Court is also a small townhouse hotel but, unlike so many in London, it has a bit of panache: that becomes clear as soon as you enter the lobby, with its giant Beefeater statue, marble busts and bonsai trees. It's been run by the same family for 50 years, and you can tell they take pride in their business. The rooms are cheery, with wooden furniture and comfy beds, and there's an attractive lounge decorated with oil paintings and greenery. Guests have access to the square's pretty garden, and the hotel is handy for Kensington Gardens.

Hotel chains

Many global chains have branches in London. Don't, as a rule, expect a great deal of individual character, but rest assured you'll get a reliable standard of service and comfort. One great attraction is that chain hotels are far more likely to have a swimming pool than private townhouse hotels: Holiday Inn King's Cross and the Regent's Park and Swiss Cottage Marriotts all have indoor pools; check the websites below for details.

Novotel (www.novotel.com) has branches in the City, near Tower Bridge, Waterloo, Euston, Hammersmith and Heathrow, and offers frequent 'Children Go Free' deals. Among the innumerable London **Marriotts** (consult www.marriott.com) are branches in Belgravia and Mayfair, as well as at County Hall. On a budget? You could do worse than **Holiday Inn**. The global chain has many hotels scattered around London, from fashionable Hoxton to rarefied Hampstead via bustling Oxford Circus (57-9 Welbeck Street, W1G 9BL, 7935 4442), though our hands-down favourite is the County Hall branch (*see p210*); consult www.holiday-inn.com for a full list.

If you want a little London pad of your own for a night or two, right in the heart of things, you could do worse than book a **Citadines** studio. This French chain has four branches in central London (Barbican, Trafalgar Square, Kensington and Holborn). Each studio or apartment has a fully equipped kitchen, satellite television, a stereo and a phone. A two-room place, with a double bedroom for the parents and twin sofabeds in the lounge for the kids, costs from about £170 per night, although the Citadines website (www.citadines.com) often advertises special offers for inexpensive family breaks.

Kensington Gardens Hotel

*9 Kensington Gardens Square, Bayswater, W2 4BH
(7221 7790/fax 7792 8612/www.kensingtongardens
hotel.co.uk). Bayswater or Queensway tube.* **Rates**
£40-£55 single; £75 double; £95 triple. **Credit**
AmEx, DC, MC, V. **Map** p312 B6.
The same pretty Victorian square, another small townhouse
hotel. This one has an elegant lobby, staffed 24 hours a day,
and it's only a short walk from Hyde Park or fashionable
Westbourne Grove and Notting Hill. The rooms are clean and
comfortable, if unspectacular, but with such a great location
you won't be spending much time in them. The triples are
great for families, and baby cots can be provided.

London County Hall
Travel Inn Capital

*County Hall, Belvedere Road, South Bank, SE1 7PB
(0870 238 3300/fax 7902 1619/www.travelinn.co.uk).
Waterloo tube/rail.* **Rates** £79.95-£84.95 double. **Credit**
AmEx, DC, MC, V. **Map** p319 M9.
This branch of the Travel Inn chain has three things going
for it: location, location, location. Across the river from the
Houses of Parliament, it's right next to the London Eye and
within walking distance of the Eurostar and Tate Modern.
Unabashedly tourist-friendly and good value, the restaurant
has a children's menu and the rooms, if plain, are inoffensive.
You won't find a better deal in London.

Rushmore Hotel

*11 Trebovir Road, Earl's Court, SW5 9LS (7370 3839/
fax 7370 0274/www.rushmore-hotel.co.uk). Earl's Court
tube.* **Rates** from £55 single; from £65 double; from £85
triple. **Credit** AmEx, DC, MC, V. **Map** p314 B11.
The Rushmore is of that rare breed of budget hotels with
a bit of flair. The hotel's biggest talking point is the trompe
l'oeil paintings, depicting everything from pastoral Tuscany
to tranquil oceans. The Italianate breakfast room, with its
granite surfaces and glass tables, is also extremely stylish.

St George's Hotel

*25 Belgrave Road, Pimlico, SW1V 1RB (7828 2061/
fax 7828 3605). Victoria tube/rail.* **Rates** from £35
single; from £45 double; from £60 triple. **Credit**
AmEx, DC, MC, V. **Map** p318 J11.
Children stay free up to and including the age of six at St
George's (although once they're seven they're classed as
adults). This friendly, family-run budget hotel offers basic,
comfortable, clean rooms with colour tellies and a full English
breakfast. Cots and high chairs are available on request.

Windermere Hotel

*142/4 Warwick Way, Pimlico, SW1V 4JE (7834 5163/
fax 7630 8831/www.windermere-hotel.co.uk). Victoria
tube/rail.* **Rates** £69-£99 single; £89-£145 double; £129-
£149 family. **Credit** AmEx, MC, V. **Map** p318 H11.
Winner of Best B&B in the 2003 London Tourism Awards,
the Windermere is a top-notch small hotel. London's first ever
B&B opened here in 1881, and the current hotel's owners have
continued the proud legacy. Rooms are comfortable and
decorated in reasonably tasteful English chintz with classy
touches: mother-of-pearl tea trays, say, or chrome fans and
the odd coronet bed. Bathrooms are clean and modern, with
power showers. For a small hotel, there are plenty of luxuries,
such as room service, modem points and satellite TV. Another
rarity for a budget hotel is a basement restaurant with
sophisticated, decently priced menu. The staff can provide
cribs for babies. Do book ahead, as the excellent Windermere
family rooms are frequently oversubscribed.

The gorgeous **Gore**. *See p209.*

Youth hostels

The following hostels are all geared up for
children and their adults, with high chairs,
baby baths, cots and pushchairs for hire, and the
excellent-value family rooms sleep up to six. There's
plenty of space to run around in the garden at the
Hampstead hostel, and the modern Rotherhithe
one has a games room and children's library.

If you're not a member of the International
Youth Hostel Federation (IYHF), you'll pay £2 extra
a night (after six nights you automatically become
a member). Alternatively, join the IYHF for £13
(£6.50 for under-18s) at any hostel or through www.
yha.org.uk, which also allows you to book rooms.
Always phone ahead for availability. These hostels
all take MasterCard and Visa; breakfast is included.

City of London *36-8 Carter Lane, EC4V 5AB (0870
770 5764). St Paul's tube/Blackfriars tube/rail.* **Open**
24hr access. *Reception* 7am-11pm daily. **Rates** £15-£32;
£15-£20.50 under-18s. **Map** p320 O6.
Hampstead Heath *4 Wellgarth Road, Golders Green,
NW11 7HR (0870 770 5846). Golders Green tube.* **Open**
24hr access. *Reception* 6.45am-11pm daily. **Rates** £21;
£18.50 under-18s.
Rotherhithe *Island Yard, Salter Road, SE16 5PR (0870
770 6010). Canada Water or Rotherhithe tube.* **Open**
24hr access. *Reception* 7am-11pm daily. **Rates** £24.60;
£20.50 under-18s.
St Pancras *79-81 Euston Road, NW1 2QS (0870
770 6044). King's Cross tube/rail.* **Open** 24hr access.
Reception 7am-11pm daily. **Rates** £24.60; £20.50 under-
18s. **Map** p317 L3.

Activities

Arts & Entertainment

No excuses – it's time to get out and have some fun.

Watching This Space, outside the **Royal National Theatre**. *See p224.*

From Bollywood to the Bard, sometimes it feels like there isn't a dull corner in the capital. Children could try their hand at something each day without ever covering the same ground, and yet too many of them sit out the best years of their lives staring at the goggle box, blistering their thumbs playing video games or – worst of all – complaining that they're bored. Bored? Next time suggest they take up Indonesian percussion or Indian cookery or DJing or ballet. It would be possible to fill a whole book just with London's entertainment venues, but you'll find enough over the next few pages to keep the kids occupied.

Many of the organisations listed below have facilities to support disabled children; double-check before you book, though. Also bear in mind that seasonal programmes alter throughout the year – and expand significantly in school holidays – so get on as many mailing lists as possible and keep an eye on council websites for arts fairs and festivals.

Arts centres

Barbican Centre
Silk Street, The City, EC2Y 8DS (box office 7638 8891/ cinema hotline 7382 7000/arts education programme 7382 2333/www.barbican.org.uk). Barbican tube/ Moorgate tube/rail. **Open** *Box office* 10am-8pm Mon-Sat; noon-8pm Sun, bank hols. *Gallery* 10am-6pm Mon, Tue, Thur-Sat; 10am-9pm Wed; noon-6pm Sun, bank hols. **Admission** *Library* free. *Exhibitions, films, shows, workshops* phone for details. **Membership** (BarbicanCard) £10/yr. *Film Club* £7.50/yr per family. **Credit** AmEx, MC, V. **Map** p320 P5.
Both parents and children are pleased by the original and well-organised range of family activities staged here throughout the year. Central to this is the Family Film Club. Since the 1980s it has been screening a diverse mix of movies from around the world to kids aged five to 11. Less regularly, the Barbican hosts festivals and events for families. The Children's Classic Concerts are excellent: this year Sing a Song of Opera offered a light-hearted introduction to a genre that tends to be anything but.
Buggy access. Café. Disabled access: lift, toilet. Nappy-changing facilities. Shop.

The South Bank Centre

Belvedere Road, South Bank, SE1 8XX (7960 4242/box office 0870 380 0400/www.rfh.org.uk). Waterloo tube/rail. **Open** *Box office phone bookings 9am-8pm daily. Personal callers* 11am-9pm daily. **Credit** AmEx, MC, V. **Map** p319 M8.

Families are more than welcome here; indeed, most big events involve a simultaneous flurry of related children's activities. The permanent Ballroom Interactive floor (in the foyer of the Royal Festival Hall) is home to a rolling programme of colourful displays, like the touchy-feely Enchanted Room, which was inspired by an adjoining performance of *Swan Lake* and perfect for younger children. Also bringing classical music to life for younger audiences are occasional FUNharmonics concerts, for which the London Philharmonic replace their sombre ties with kid gloves and mix masterpieces with tribal dance rhythms and famous theme tunes. Face-painting and performance art in summer spills out on to the river terraces. More obscure musical treats await members of the Saturday Gong Club (for over-sevens; 11am-12.30pm), a rare window into Indonesian percussion instruments (gamelan), with public performances for those who see it through.

Buggy access. Cafés. Disabled access: lift, toilet. Nappy-changing facilities. Restaurant. Shops.

Tricycle Theatre & Cinema

269 Kilburn High Road, Kilburn, NW6 7JR (box office 7328 1000/www.tricycle.co.uk). Kilburn tube/Brondesbury rail. **Open** *Box office* 10am-9pm Mon-Sat; 2-9pm Sun. *Children's shows* 11.30am, 2pm Sat. *Children's films* 1pm Sat. **Tickets** *Theatre* (Sat) £5; £4 advance bookings. *Films* (Sat) £4; £3 under-16s. **Credit** MC, V.

The Tricycle's range of term-time and holiday workshops incorporates various after-school classes spread through the week (£20/term). Included are drama, dance and the ever-popular Hopscotch classes, which provide an introduction to performance through simple music, movement and storytelling exercises for children as young as 18 months. Half-term and holiday workshops allow kids to get creative with everything from scrap sculpture to urban street dance. Prices and age groups vary from class to class, but an up-to-date leaflet can be downloaded from the website – it also gives details of the regular Saturday film screenings and stage shows. While the former lean towards more mainstream spectacles, the programme of theatrical performances is diverse indeed. The Tricycle's popularity has led to an increased degree of control over advance bookings to ensure that kids from across the city can attend. The parental migration to Kilburn, however, continues unabated.

Buggy access. Disabled access: lift, toilet. Nappy-changing facilities. Restaurant. Shop.

Art galleries

Check **Around Town** *(pp34-156)* for information on workshops, events and activities in other big-name galleries, including the South Bank's **Tate Modern** *(see p45)* and **Hayward Gallery** *(see p38)*, Westminster's **National Gallery** *(see p81)*, the grand **Royal Academy of Arts** in Piccadilly *(see p74)*, the popular armour workshops that take place at the **Wallace Collection** in Marylebone *(see p70)*, **Dulwich Picture Gallery** down in south-east London *(see p132)* and east London's **Whitechapel Art Gallery** *(see p105)*.

Courtauld Institute Gallery

Somerset House, Strand, WC2R 0RN (7848 2526/ education 7848 2922/www.courtauld.ac.uk). Covent Garden, Holborn or Temple (closed Sun) tube. **Open** *Gallery* 10am-6pm daily (last entry 5.15pm); 10am-4pm 31 Dec; noon-6pm 1 Jan. Closed 24-26 Dec. **Tours** pre-booked groups only; phone for details. **Admission** *Gallery* £5; £4 concessions; free under-18s, students. Free to all 10am-2pm Mon (not bank hols). **Credit** MC, V. **Map** p319 M7.

A brilliant new Learning Centre in the gallery offers a range of activities to make the displays accessible to all ages. Instrumental in this are the Saturday workshops, which are free, run throughout the year and open up various exhibits with child-friendly adventures including mystery tours and storytelling. Half-term and holiday activities are more hands-on, and a small fee may be charged for materials – fashion design classes, for example, are inspired by portrayals of historical clothing throughout the gallery. An occasional series of Art Start events for under-sevens includes Sculpture Safaris, while Art Extra talks – for 13- to 18-year-olds – illuminate more obscure corners of the Courtauld, including contemporary works in the East Wing Collection. Art packs and paper trails are available behind the desk all year round; more advanced students may prefer the programme of Spring and Summer Schools (March and June respectively), which concentrate on art history, last for one week and cost £350 per person (over 16): phone 7848 2678 for more information.

Buggy access. Café. Disabled access: lift, toilet. Nappy-changing facilities. Shop.

London International Gallery of Children's Art

O2 Centre, 255 Finchley Road, Finchley, NW3 6LU (7435 0903/www.ligca.org). Finchley Road tube. **Open** *Gallery* 4-6pm Tue-Thur; noon-6pm Fri-Sun. **Admission** *Gallery* free; donations requested. **No credit cards.**

LIGCA is a neutral space uniting the world's children through the universal language of art. Exhibitions often stem from more troubled corners of the globe: recent displays have included work from schools in Chernobyl and South Africa. They're used as reference points for educational workshops (from £8 per session, running in six-week courses from £40), which encourage kids to respond with their own drawings and paintings. The best of their work is shown in the gallery, and all proceeds are sent to relevant charities. Saturday morning classes for under-fives (10.30-11.30am; £10) offer simple arts activities based on storytelling. After the mess has been cleared away, children over five can dabble in creative techniques such as mural design, monoprinting and self-portraiture (2-3.30pm; £10). For creative birthday parties *(see p234)*.

Buggy access. Disabled access: lift.

Orleans House Gallery

Riverside, Twickenham, Middx TW1 3DJ (8831 6000/ www.richmond.gov.uk/orleanshouse). St Margaret's or Twickenham rail/33, 490, H22, R68, R70 bus. **Open** *Gallery* Apr-Sept 1-5.30pm Tue-Sat; 2-5.30pm Sun, bank hols. Oct-Mar 1-4.30pm Tue-Sat; 2-4.30pm Sun, bank hols. **Admission** *Gallery* free. **Credit** MC, V.

The house is accessed by a secluded riverside path, surrounded by acres of woodland, and it looks more like a decaying country seat than a centre for living arts. That said, the collections are less stuffy than you might imagine: alongside an abundance of paintings and prints of scenic Richmond-on-Thames is a lively programme of temporary exhibitions, which until October 2004 will include Asian and African domestic crafts and a colourful display of

Activities

Tricycle Theatre. See p213.

various printmaking techniques. Tied in with the exhibitions is a similarly upbeat series of year-round activity workshops for kids, with after-school sessions (3.45-5pm Wed, Thur) for five to nine year olds available alongside the recently established Star Club (4-5.30pm Tue), the latter offering those aged seven to ten a place to try their hands (and feet) at dance and drama. Both are £5.50 per session, and worth booking in advance. During half-term these workshops run for two hours twice daily (10am-noon; 2-4pm), and once a month Orleans House is home to a Family Funday (2-4.30pm) at which creative minds of all ages unite, using the gallery's displays and materials as starting points for pieces of their own. *Buggy access. Disabled access: ramp, toilet. Nappy-changing facilities. Nearest picnic place: Marble Hill Park or riverside benches. Shop.*

Tate Britain

Millbank, SW1P 4RG (7887 8000/recorded info 7887 8008/family events 7887 3959/www.tate.org.uk). Pimlico tube/88, 77A, C10 bus. **Open** *Gallery* 10am-5.50pm daily. **Admission** *Gallery* free. *Temporary exhibitions* prices vary; phone for details. **Credit** MC, V. **Map** p319 L11.

It may seem a little bespectacled beside its more Modern partner in culture, but the 'old' Tate is still one of London's most child-friendly galleries, knowing exactly how to turn down stress levels on a family day out. For example, the Artspace studio (1-5pm Sat, Sun) is a handsome cross between a crèche and a chill-out room, replete with creative toys and games. Equally charming is the time-honoured but constantly changing Art Trolley, wheeled out every Saturday and Sunday (noon-5pm) and packed with a wide range of making and doing activities tied neatly into surrounding displays:

everything from solving clues and finding characters in the background of particular paintings to writing the stories that brought them there. Sometimes the job is done for them: Tate Tales, on the first Sunday of each month, sees resident storytellers spin yarns about individual works – kids can even have their own stories added to the Tate Tales Storybook as part of the online activity page. There's a Tate Forum for educational talks for over-15s, events for schools and themed workshops during holidays (during which time the Art Trolley and Artspace studio are more frequently available), as well as activity bags, audio tours and paper trails awaiting little explorers behind the information desk. *Buggy access. Café. Disabled access: lift, toilet. Nappy-changing facilities. Restaurant. Shop.*

Cinemas

When it comes to the silver screen, London is best known for the behemoths battling it out in **Leicester Square**, the city's première capital and home to the Empire (0870 010 2030, www.uci-cinemas.co.uk), Warner Village West End (7437 4347, www.warnervillage.co.uk) and the Odeon (0870 505 0007, www.odeon.co.uk). Prices are high in such places, but the **Prince Charles Cinema** (7494 3654, www.princecharlescinema.com) offers a cheap and cheerful alternative. Or visit one of the picture palaces (*see p216*), where kids' clubs and workshops to make film-going more family-friendly.

Film studies at **Clapham Picturehouse.**

Clapham Picturehouse

76 Venn Street, Clapham, SW4 0AT (7498 3323/
www.picturehouse-cinemas.co.uk). Clapham Common
tube/35, 37 bus. **Open** *Box office* (phone bookings)
10am-8.30pm daily. *Film Club* (activities) 11.15am,
(screening) 11.45am Sat. **Tickets** £3; members £2.
Membership £4/yr. **Credit** MC, V.

One of the capital's original kids' clubs is also a pioneer of
screenings for babies: parents can bring children under one
to the Big Scream! club at 10.30am every Thursday and take
in a movie from the current roster of blockbuster and
art-house films without having to worry about disturbing the
audience. Nappy-changing facilities are within dummy-spit-
ting distance. Meanwhile, the more conventional Kids' Club
offers Saturday matinées for three- to ten-year-olds, with
activity workshops preceding the show and three questions
to answer afterwards – pay attention, win a prize!
Buggy access. Café. Disabled access: toilet. Nappy-
changing facilities.

Electric Cinema

191 Portobello Road, W11 2ED (7908 9696/www.electric
house.com). Ladbroke Grove or Notting Hill Gate tube/52
bus. **Open** *Box office* 9am-8pm Mon-Sat; 10am-8pm Sun.
Children's screenings 11am, 1pm Sat. **Tickets** £4.50.
Credit AmEx, MC, V. **Map** p312 A7.

For membership to the Electric you must apply in writing,
be accepted by a committee made up of local residents and
businessmen, and then pay up to the tune of £250 per year.

It has its advantages, however – parents on the books receive
two free tickets for every Kids' Club screening. These show
classic films and preview new releases in a truly luxurious
environment, recently renovated from a historical fleapit to
one of the best cinemas in the country, red leather armchairs,
lovingly restored wall friezes and all. The Saturday movies
alternate between those suitable for over-fours and those for
over-nines, although there's no official restriction on entry.
Parents and their babies (up to one year old) can enjoy special 'Electric Scream' screenings on Mondays at 3pm.
Buggy access. Disabled access: lift, toilet. Kiosk.

Movie Magic at the NFT

NFT3, National Film Theatre, South Bank, SE1 8XT
(box office 7928 3232/www.bfi.org.uk/moviemagic).
Waterloo tube/rail. **Open** *Box office* phone bookings
11.30am-8.30pm daily; personal callers 5-8.30pm Mon-
Thur, 11.30am-8.30pm Fri-Sun. *Film Club* times vary Sat,
Sun, school hols. **Tickets** *Children* £1 film, £5.50
workshop & film. *Adults* £4. Prices may change, phone to
confirm. **Credit** AmEx, MC, V. **Map** p319 M8.

If you're keen on turning square eyes into widescreens, at
weekends and during school holidays you should get the
children down to Movie Magic, the NFT's programme of
films for kids under 16. Sometimes, the movies in question
are classics of yesteryear, so nostalgic parents might want to
tag along. At other times Movie Magic previews the new film
of the moment (*Shrek II* was a recent crowd-puller). Children
aged between six and 12 can take part in themed activity
workshops on the last Saturday of every month – perhaps

making papier-mâché Harry Potter masks, trying out scriptwriting and prop design, or even using a movie camera. School holidays give rise to two-day Movie Magic schools with more in-depth activities on offer. Booking in advance is advisable; phone for a list of upcoming events. *Buggy access. Café. Disabled access: ramp, toilet.*

Rio Cinema

103-7 Kingsland High Street, Dalston, E8 2PB (7241 9410/www.riocinema.co.uk). Dalston Kingsland rail/ Liverpool Street tube/rail, then 67, 77, 149 bus. **Open** *Box office* 2-9pm daily. Opening times vary depending on programme. *Film Club* 4.15pm Tue (term-time only); 11am Sat. **Tickets** £3.50; £2.50 under-15s. **Credit** AmEx, MC, V.

The Rio is a fun, friendly place where children can sample something a bit different from Hollywood blockbusters. The Saturday Morning Kids' Club intersperses major new releases with occasional classics like *The Seventh Voyage of Sinbad*, with a repeat performance – the Playcentre Matinée – at 4.15pm every Tuesday afternoon during term. Membership of the club is free, and comes with a card that's stamped on each visit. Ten stamps are worth a free movie, 25 reward faithful young film-goers with a free movie poster. Kids under five must be accompanied throughout the movie. *Café. Disabled access: toilet. Nappy-changing facilities.*

Ritzy Cinema

Brixton Oval, Coldharbour Lane, Brixton, SW2 1JG (7733 2229/www.ritzycinema.co.uk). Brixton tube/rail. **Open** *Box office* 10am-8pm Mon-Sat; 11.55am-8pm Sun. *Film Club* 10.30am Sat. **Tickets** £3; £1 under-16s. **Credit** MC, V.

The grand old Ritzy opened in 1911 as one of the UK's first purpose-built cinemas; since then it has survived various owners, near demolition and – most recently – significant development to become one of London's finest. Age is no restriction: two Kids' Club films are shown each Saturday – the first aimed at under-sevens and the second at over sevens – and accompanying adults get free newspapers, tea and coffee thrown in. During school holidays the club also runs on Tuesdays and Thursdays, with related activity sessions, competitions and special events often set up at short notice (phone for details). Like its sister Picturehouse in Clapham (*see p216*), the Ritzy has a programme of matinées open to parents with babies under one; phone for details of these occasional Watch With Baby screenings. *Buggy access. Café. Disabled access: lift, toilet. Nappy-changing facilities.*

Music venues

Royal Albert Hall

Kensington Gore, South Kensington, SW7 2AP (7589 8212/www.royalalberthall.com). South Kensington tube. **Open** *Box office* 9am-9pm daily. **Credit** AmEx, MC, V. **Map** p315 D9.

After nine years of ongoing cosmetic refurbishment, the Royal Albert Hall is finally happy with its appearance. The installation of new facilities including bars, toilets and dressing rooms has created a more modern venue, while a brand new education department opens this marvellous auditorium up to younger audiences with a series of family events throughout the year. A specially commissioned Jason and the Argonauts concert (27 June) sets the tone for things to come, with a story-based approach to organ-driven classical music that's anything but snooty. In November the Royal Philharmonic Orchestra will be laying on one of their patented and celebrated Noisy Kids performances, renowned for encouraging audience participation and TV and movie themes, and there's always the annual Blue Peter concert, given as part of the BBC Proms, which offers a pint-sized variation on pomp and circumstance. The Royal Albert's work with schools is also commendable. To coincide with National Poetry Day, staff are running the Storyquest event, at which children wander around the building hearing snatches of narrative from poets and storytellers, before taking part in a number of creative workshops. Phone or check the website for more information. *Buggy access. Café. Disabled access: lift, ramp, toilet. Nappy-changing facilities. Restaurant (booking necessary). Shop.*

Royal College of Music

Prince Consort Road, South Kensington, SW7 2BS (7589 3643/www.rcm.ac.uk). South Kensington tube/9, 10, 52 bus. **Map** p315 D9. **Map** p315 D9.

It may have turned out ex-Hear'say hottie Myleene Klass, but sculpting pop stars isn't what the Royal College of Music does on a regular basis. Indeed, its tuition is tailored to 'extremely talented people', which pretty much rules out most of today's teen idols. Applications are by audition alone, heavily oversubscribed, of course, and lessons – which run in conjunction with the school term (8am-5pm Sat) – focus almost exclusively on classical instruments. Families are perhaps best off keeping an eye on the programme of performances staged by pupils throughout the year, they're usually free (check the website for details). *Café. Disabled access: lift, toilet.*

Wigmore Hall

36 Wigmore Street, Marylebone, W1U 2BP (7935 2141/ education 7258 8240/www.wigmore-hall.org.uk). Bond Street tube. **Open** *Box office* 10am-7pm Mon-Sat; 10.30am-6.30pm Sun. **Credit** AmEx, DC, MC, V. **Map** p316 H5.

The beautiful, art deco Wigmore Hall was built in 1901 by the German piano manufacturers Bechstein, although barely 15 years later they were made to sell it to Debenhams (for a song, natch) when the First World War forced German businesses up against the wall. Thankfully, the interior of this stunning venue remains virtually unaltered, with marble, warm wood panelling and plush red seating setting it a cut above most other small venues in the capital. Best of all is the mural above the stage – a Blakean vision of the Soul of Music by Frank Lynn Jenkins. Performances take place daily, and are uniformly classical, although occasional schools concerts present work with relevance to the National Curriculum at heavily reduced rates. There's also a programme of interesting family events, starting with the sadly oversubscribed Chamber Tots classes, which encourage two- to five-year-olds to create music after listening to a mini-concert (£5 children, adults free). From there the only way, in terms of age at least, is up: Young People's Day workshops occur during half-terms and on occasional term-time Saturdays (£8 children, £10 adults), covering everything from song and story-writing (five- to six-year-olds) to more challenging jazz classes for older kids. The workshops are held in various rooms, even the stunning main hall itself. There are also two family concerts each term (£3 children, £6 adults). The Wigmore will be closing for essential repair work for 16 weeks from 14 June 2004 and opens on 9 October 2004 with a grand reopening performance of Mahler with the Nash Ensemble . *Buggy access. Disabled access: toilet. Nappy-changing facilities. Restaurant.*

Activities

Theatre

Puppets

Little Angel Theatre

14 Dagmar Passage, off Cross Street, Islington, N1 2DN (7226 1787/www.littleangeltheatre.com). Angel tube/ Highbury & Islington tube/rail, then 4, 19, 30, 43 bus. **Open** *Box office* 10am-6pm Mon-Fri; 9.30am-4.30pm Sat, Sun. **Tickets** £7.50-£8.50; £5-£6 children. **Credit** MC, V. Established in 1961, the Little Angel remains London's only permanent puppet theatre. Performances cover a huge range of styles and just about every kind of puppet under the sun, with the annual calendar peppered with shows by touring companies from across the country eager to work with the theatre's rare proscenium arch. Most productions – including an excellent in-house production of Lewis Carroll's *Jabberwocky* earlier in 2004 – are aimed at audiences aged five and over, but *Stuff and Nonsense*, the follow-up to *Jabberwocky*, was the first Little Angel show to cater for kids aged two to five. It took the work of artist Paul Klee as inspiration for a carnival of shapes and colours. A Saturday Puppet Club runs in conjunction with most major productions, although jealous mums and dads must wait for one of a number of family fun days – held during school breaks – for their own chance to play with the puppets.
Buggy access. Kiosk. Shop.

Puppet Theatre Barge

Opposite 35 Blomfield Road, Little Venice, W9 2PF (7249 6876/www.puppetbarge.com). Warwick Avenue tube. **Open** *Box office* 10am-8pm daily. Closed 25 Dec, 1 Jan. *Children's shows* term-time Sat, Sun; school hols daily. **Tickets** £7; £6.50 under-16s, concessions. **Credit** MC, V. One of the capital's most enchanting assets since its creation in 1982, to this day the barge's combination of high-quality puppet shows – courtesy of Movingstage Productions – and the loveliness of the location remains unique. Small and cosy (there are just 60 seats), the barge is moored on the towpath in Little Venice between November and June, with a variety of performances held on Saturday and Sunday afternoons (3pm) and a more comprehensive programme of weekday and even evening slots during school holidays. Shows in 2004 have already pitted several classic characters against new and unusual situations: *Brer Rabbit Visits Africa*, which opened in February, is a particular favourite. Between July and October, the barge chugs merrily off on a summer tour of the Thames, stopping off to perform at picturesque riverside towns Henley, Clifton, Marlow and Richmond along the way. During this period, shows take place at 2.30pm and 4.30pm, and there's a special Saturday evening performance (7.30pm) aimed at adults.

Touring companies

Younger audiences need shows that suit their developing senses; dealing with subjects that are relevant to them in a language they understand. That's what these theatre companies provide.

Oily Cart

8672 6329/www.oilycart.org.uk
If all the world's a stage, then Oily Cart's role is more essential than most. Their motivation is simple: to fire the imaginations of two theatrically excluded groups – very young children and children with special needs – with bold, innovative productions. Touring since 1981 to great critical acclaim, the company's work has developed into a truly interactive art form, utilising large multi-sensory spaces or 'Wonderlands', where groups of children can not only watch, but also take part in performances. Even more commendable is the fun they inject into each show – *Boing!*, for disabled kids, was based around trampolines, while the follow-up, *Moving Pictures*, projected individual reactions on to giant movie screens. *Baking Time* was exactly that – delicious.

Pop-Up Theatre

7609 3339/www.pop-up.net
Pop-Up have pioneered a range of theatrical media that are respectful of younger children's intelligence and responsive to their needs. For example, the Dramatic Links workshops (held at the Robert Blair School in north London) let writers work with kids, drawing inspiration from one another to produce uniquely relevant scripts. The Equal Voice sessions tour schools across the city engaging pupils in theatrical dialogues that explore emotional issues and build self-esteem. In 2005 the company will tour a study of the Seven Deadly Sins, with the new Offstreet mobile stage allowing certain shows to take place on any flat 20sq ft (6sq m), allowing for almost limitless performance possibilities.

Quicksilver Theatre

7241 2942/www.quicksilvertheatre.org
Quicksilver productions are engaging rather than self consciously educational, encouraging kids to develop emotionally by letting go of their fears and having fun. Over 25 years the theatre group have worked at building a rapport with young audiences that, in 2004, was seen in a national tour of *Upstairs in the Sky* (ages three to five; until 19 June). Next up is a revival of *Little Victories*, a sensitive study of renewal and death as seen through the eyes of a child, which will be in theatres across the country later in 2004.

Theatre Centre

7377 0379/www.theatre-centre.co.uk
Theatre Centre has not only secured a reputation for on-stage excellence and technical invention, but also champions more challenging writing when many of its contemporaries are just rehashing the same old stuff. Recent productions have dealt with missing persons (*Missing*) and female boxing (*Glow*), while last year's Christmas play, *A Spell of Cold Weather*, was anything but the usual carol fodder.

Theatre-rites

8946 2236/www.theatre-rites.co.uk
Founded by the late Penny Bernand in 1995, Theatre-rites generated a whirlwind of positive reviews for its site-specific *Houseworks* project a year later. A similar project – *Finders Keepers* – ran, in collaboration with the Unicorn Theatre (*see below*), at the Livesey Museum for Children (*see p131*) until May 2004, while 2003's *Catch Your Breath* was more stage-based, if no less ingenious. A project for three- to six-year-olds is planned in association with the Lyric (*see p223*): check the website for details.

Unicorn Theatre for Children

7700 0702/www.unicorntheatre.com
The Unicorn's brand new purpose-built youth theatre in the heart of Southwark will open in 2005 (*see p22*). The plans are looking good, with separate main and studio auditoriums, an education centre and a rehearsal studio all part and parcel. Until then, this renowned company will continue to tour an exciting programme of theatre for children, which in March included the première of *Clockwork*, an inspirational opera based on an award-winning short story by *His Dark Materials* author Philip Pullman.

Venues

Several of the places listed below are children's theatres: most, however, are adult venues with family programmes. Phone to check the suitability of any show before you book tickets. Most venues put on extra performances in school holidays.

artsdepot/The Bull

The Bull *(until July 2004)* 68 High Street, Barnet, Herts EN5 5SJ. High Barnet tube. **Open** Box office 10am-5.30pm Mon-Sat.
artsdepot *(from Oct 2004)* 5 Nether Street, North Finchley, N12 0GA (8449 0048/tours 8275 5375/ www.artsdepot.co.uk). Finchley Central or Woodside Park tube. **Open** Box office 10am-8pm daily.
Both Tickets free-£8. **Credit** MC, V.

When we checked just before going to press, the opening of this formidable North Finchley centre for the arts had been delayed until October 2004 (check the website for updated information). As well as housing the relocated Bull Theatre, the new building will be home to Community Focus (an arts activity centre for disabled people and the elderly) and the Performing and Public Arts arm of Barnet College. College students will take classes and perform for the public in the theatre, with its two auditoriums (most children's theatre will take place in the smaller 150-seat studio, although larger shows will be held in the 400-seater main hall). Kids' shows will run on Sundays at 3pm. Also, with the comprehensive Learning Ladder programme, young ones can tread the boards before they've learned to walk: classes cover all ages from one-year-olds to adults, with courses – from the intriguing Dinky Depot through to the Bull's Youth Theatre and beyond – running throughout term-time and ending with the participants putting on a play of their own. Performances at the old Bull ceased in April, but its reopening weekend, *Play!* (24 Oct), will be business as usual – a packed programme of free family activities and workshops, and the first children's performance (*The Owl and the Pussycat*, by Tall Stories) will begin its run from that date.
Buggy access. Café. Disabled access: ramp, lift, toilet.

Sing it loud

As a medium, opera has never been famous for occupying the middle ground. Back in 1998 a pre-performance picnic at Glyndebourne was disrupted by a mass socialist trespass that had to be broken up by police, while Vienna's glamorous Opera Ball at the State Opera House has been known to attract demonstrations and riots by disaffected Austrian workers. In short, the last time the genre made any significant inroads into the public consciousness was when snatches of 'Nessun Dorma' accompanied slow-motion replays of the 1990 World Cup.

So it's refreshing to see a revitalised opera scene in London, where a whole host of operatic resources are being made available to children, many for the first time. Not least of these is the new Clore Education Room at the recently reopened **Coliseum** (St Martin's Lane, WC2N 4ES, 7632 8300, www.eno.org, map p319 L7), Covent Garden's largest theatre and home to the English National Opera. To mark the development, ENO's education team, Baylis, has expanded its range of open events, which include workshops, courses and child-oriented performances. One of the latter is *The Early Earth Operas*, John Browne's trilogy based on children's responses to the Book of Genesis. These are being performed on the main stage by pupils from schools across the capital (10.30am 28-29 June; £5 adults, £2.50 children). In October 2004 comes a concert entitled For the Public Good; 500 amateur singers will be auditioned for this one. There's also a Saturday Live! group that gives nine- to 18-year-olds a weekly dose of all things performance-based, including dance, drama and, of course, opera. Auditions for the group are held at the end of each academic year in preparation for the next, and classes, leading to a public performance, are held on Saturdays during term.

Also shedding some of its notorious formality is Covent Garden's **Royal Opera House** (*see p75*), which this June ran its first week-long series of activities for families; phone for details of similar events later in the year. The ROH also runs programmes of unticketed open-air screenings, with in-house shows relayed live to parks and public spaces in and around the capital. On 17 June 2004 the Royal Ballet's performance of *Onegin* will be simultaneously beamed to temporary silver screens in Trafalgar Square and Victoria Park (7.40pm), with *Faust* relayed live to the Covent Garden piazza in the evening of 19 June and *Tosca* to both the piazza and Canary Wharf on 13 July (ring for times of performances). An equally fresh introduction to the genre can be found at the **Handel House Museum** (*see p73* **Getting a Handel on London**), where regular concerts take place in the composer's own rehearsal room, and opera is mixed with other classical music and even jazz. Even better for kids is the museum's series of storytelling workshops that combine pared-down performances of Handel's *Magic Operas* with retellings of the fantastic tales that inspired them.

Speaking of fantastic tales, Whitbread winner Philip Pullman's spine-tingling short story about wolves and mechanical characters *Clockwork* was given the operatic treatment by the **Unicorn Theatre Company** (*see p218*), with its première at the Royal Opera House's Lindbury Studio Theatre in March 2004. There are already plans for a revival later in 2004, not that it should come as any surprise: 2002's family-friendly production of *The Wind in the Willows* enjoyed a second sell-out run on the same stage in Christmas 2003. Kids, it would seem, have nothing against high culture – so long as they're given the opportunity to find out about it for themselves.

Activities

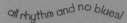

BAC (Battersea Arts Centre)

Lavender Hill, Battersea, SW11 5TN (7223 2223/ www.bac.org.uk). Clapham Common tube, then 345 bus/Clapham Junction rail/77, 77A, 156 bus. **Open** *Box office* 10.30am-6pm Mon-Sat; 4-6pm Sun. *Puppet Centre* 2-6pm Mon, Wed, Sat. **Tickets** £5.75; £4.50 under-16s, concessions; £3.50 Young BAC members; £16 family (2+2). **Membership** £10.75/yr; £16.50 family (2+2). **Credit** AmEx, MC, V.

The cash-strapped but hugely respected BAC constantly challenges established notions of what is and isn't 'proper' theatre: the popular Scratch sessions, for example, allow writers to air work in progress and develop it with the participation of their audiences (this is where *Jerry Springer the Opera* began). Drama queens (and kings) aged three to 11 take part in the Arts Express workshops, which run in conjunction with the school term and develop performance skills through improvisation and role-play exercises (from £38.50/term). The next rung on the ladder comes courtesy of the (oversubscribed) Young People's Theatre, which takes kids from the age of 12 (an older version is run for over-17s) and works towards an end-of-term performance (Wed evenings; £30/term). The Saturday children's theatre, for four- to seven-year-olds (2.30pm), airs the work of touring companies: phone or check the website for details.
Buggy access. Café. Disabled access: lift, toilet.

Broadway Theatre

Catford Broadway, Catford, SE6 4RU (8690 0002/ www.broadwaytheatre.org.uk). Catford or Catford Bridge rail/75, 181, 185, 202, 660 bus. **Open** *Box office* 10am-6pm Mon-Sat. **Tickets** £3.50-£20. **Credit** AmEx, MC, V.
This handsome, art deco building is scruffy Catford's pride and joy. Regular Saturday morning shows at the Broadway Theatre cater for children from the age of three, showcasing work from all the major touring companies. At other times, the youth programme is less well developed, although occasional performances by teen-idol impersonators appease screaming adolescents. There are also family-friendly shows like holiday favourite *The Wizard of Oz* dotted through the annual calendar, (and the Christmas panto is always a rowdy delight). More educational are the occasional Shakespeare 4 Kids events, which combine loud and energetic performances with fun seminars in a commendable effort to make the Bard more appealing to young audiences.
Buggy access. Café. Disabled access: lift, toilet. Nappy-changing facilities.

Chicken Shed Theatre

Chase Side, Southgate, N14 4PE (8292 9222/www. chickenshed.org.uk). Cockfosters or Oakwood tube. **Open** *Box office* 10am-7pm Mon-Fri; Sat varies. **Tickets** *Workshops* £2.50/hr. *Shows* £4.40-£10.80. **Credit** MC, V.
Chicken Shed offers so inclusive an admissions policy that at any given time its 800 members will represent as many ages, races, backgrounds and abilities as possible. The result is productions that are among the liveliest in London, and with a range of groups for younger players – from Tales From The Shed (under-fives) to the Youth Theatre (12- to 19-year-olds) – there's nothing stopping little ones getting involved except, of course, the enormous waiting lists. Performances take place in one of four creative spaces, including a 250-seat main auditorium and an outdoor amphitheatre for the summer months. Best of all is the unprecedented cross-pollination between various groups: toddlers act up alongside adults, and everyone mucks in for the annual Christmas show.
Buggy access. Café. Disabled access: lift, toilets. Nappy-changing facilities. Restaurant. Shop.

Colour House Theatre

Merton Abbey Mills, Watermill Way, Merton, SW19 2RD (box office 8640 5111/www.wheelhouse.org.uk). Colliers Wood tube. **Open** *Box office* 10am-5pm Mon-Fri; 1hr before show. *Shows* 2pm, 4pm Sat, Sun. **Tickets** £7; £6 for parties of 4 or more. **No credit cards**.
Colour is the operative word at this delightful little theatre, tucked into a quiet corner of riverside South Wimbledon. Each year a number of fairytale classics get the Colour House treatment, rendering them anything but predictable and as amusing to parents as their offspring. In 2004 you'll see *Hansel and Gretel* (until Sept), with *Robin Hood* to follow and *Snow White* in time for Christmas. Plays run every Saturday and Sunday afternoon (2pm, 4pm). Little ones can get more involved by joining the Colour House Theatre School, which takes four- to 16-year-olds and develops their singing, dancing and acting techniques, culminating in twice-yearly shows that let the kids perform to an audience – indispensable experience. Classes are held on Saturday mornings and Monday, Tuesday and Wednesday evenings (phone for prices).
Buggy access. Disabled access. Shop.

The Edward Alleyn Theatre

Dulwich College, Dulwich Common, SE21 7LD (8299 9232/www.dulwich.org.uk). West Dulwich rail/Brixton tube, then 3, P4, P13 bus. **Tickets** £5; £3.50 under-16s, concessions. **No credit cards**.
The theatre is named after the founder of Dulwich College, himself one of the great actors of Shakespeare's day. There are a number of shows from touring companies to engage literary brains (February 2004's *After Juliet* was a hypothetical postscript to the Bard's tragedy), but there are also 12 annual performances aimed more directly at younger audiences (such as the charmed puppetry of *Three Singing Pigs* in April 2004). The Edward Alleyn also runs week-long theatre schools over Easter, the summer holidays and October half-terms: two separate classes cater to seven- to 11-year-olds and 12- to 16-year-olds, and although neither demand auditions those attending the senior group are expected to commit to the whole course. Booking is required well in advance: phone for prices.
Buggy access. Disabled access: toilets. Nappy-changing facilities.

Hackney Empire

Mare Street, Hackney, E8 1EJ (8510 4500/box office 8985 2424/www.hackneyempire.co.uk). Bethnal Green tube, then 106, 253, D6 bus. **Open** *Box office* 10am-8pm Mon-Sat; 1hr before show on Sun. On non-performance days, 10am-6pm. **Tours** 1st Sat of mth; phone for times. **Tickets** prices vary, phone for details. *Tours* £5; £4 concessions. **Credit** AmEx, MC, V.
After an extended hiatus, a fully restored and refurbished Hackney Empire opened its Matcham auditorium in January 2004, a stage that has echoed with the footsteps of everyone from Chas Chaplin to Chas 'n' Dave. The Empire's educational programme is impressive. This year's Get Ahead programme runs dance and musical performance courses for seven- to 11-year-olds (24 Apr-10 July; from £27.50/ person), culminating in a performance for the old folks. For 12- to 16-year-olds, the fourth Artist Development programme (Sept-Nov) shapes the talents of 40 of east London's youngsters (auditions required: check the website); there are less intensive Saturday workshops for seven- to ten-year-olds and 11- to 16-year-olds, providing everything from guidance on scriptwriting to role-play exercises.
Buggy access. Disabled access: toilet. Nappy-changing facilities.

Having a laugh

Teachers have, since time immemorial, thus admonished the classroom wag: 'Children who tell jokes are popular at school. Children who study are popular for the rest of their lives.' It's a load of cobblers. James Campbell (*pictured*) has been the class joker for most of his 30-odd years, and everyone thinks he's the business. Even his teachers recognised his talent: as a seven-year-old he was called on every Friday to regale the class with his latest adventures, and that's pretty much what he's been doing ever since.

These days James is billed as 'the only children's stand-up comedian in the universe', but don't let that put you off. His act isn't all novelty hats and 'he's behind you' routines; it has been honed over ten years and more than 1,000 school performances (for which he started on a flat rate of £5 per hour), and these days the twists of his surreal narrative owe more to the Milligans and Mertons of this world than anything else. Into a 45-minute performance he'll cram everything from inflating cows to steadily shrinking elderly folk – some of it written, some of it pulled out of thin air – with plenty of poetry and tangential songs along the way. His ease with children – and theirs with him – is something to behold: under-age hecklers would be most adults' worst nightmare, but Campbell seems to revel in using their spontaneous outbursts as platforms for his own.

Campbell passes on what he disparagingly refers to as the 'primary colours syndrome', choosing to perform in the dark shirts and trousers beloved of more adult performers. Indeed, when he's up there bouncing around and looking every bit the lithe fringe-festival performer, you could easily forget the average age of the audience, especially when the venue is one as big as the Criterion, on Charing Cross Road. This was where Campbell's Comedy 4 Kids tour played in late 2003, where it reduced a packed house to 'helpless, infectious fits of hysterics', according to one *Mail on Sunday* reviewer. His wacky flights of fancy proved so popular he was transplanted to the Arts Theatre, on Great Newport Street, for a handful of extended Christmas shows that earned Campbell plaudits as one to watch on the stand-up circuit.

We aren't just talking about the 'children's stand-up comedy circuit' either – primarily because there's no such thing, but also because adults are as enraptured by James Campbell as their kids. In fact, he was in the process of writing his first adult shows when Graham Norton's So! Television asked him to star in his own children's TV series. 'I've been told I'm not allowed to swear ever again,' he quipped in a recent interview, and a nation of parents simultaneously sighed with relief. *Check www.jamescampbell.info for details of upcoming shows across the capital.*

Half Moon Young People's Theatre

43 White Horse Road, Stepney, E1 0ND (7709 8900/ www.halfmoon.org.uk). Limehouse DLR/rail. **Open** *Box office* 10am-6pm Mon-Fri; 10am-4pm Sat. **Tickets** £5; £3.50 under-18s, concessions. **Credit** MC, V.

In an area sadly lacking in artistic outlets, the Half Moon is a pillar of creativity, uniting young people regardless of race, gender or financial situation. Its fully accessible, purpose-converted theatre is home to two studios, between them offering an annual calendar of performances for kids from six months old. *Baa Moo Yellow Dog*, for two- to five-year-olds, is one of two in-house productions for the year. Children hoping to get involved in similar ventures can join up with one of eight youth theatre groups, catering to five- to 17-year-olds. The groups meet weekly during term (£1.50 per session) and put on a show at the end of it all. The aim is to improve self-expression and build confidence, although the more committed participants may end up filtering into the Half Moon's larger productions. Staff also work with schools both in Tower Hamlets and across London, organising workshops and occasionally setting up residencies.

Buggy access. Disabled access: toilets. Nappy-changing facilities.

Jackson's Lane

269A Archway Road, Highgate, N6 5AA (box office 8341 4421/administration 8340 5226/www.jacksonslane.org. uk). Highgate tube. **Open** *Box office* 10am-10pm daily. **Tickets** £4.50; £3.50 members. **Membership** £25/yr, £15/yr children. **Credit** MC, V.

The comprehensive range of classes and courses on offer at this much loved arts centre housed in an old church are a constant source of delight to local families. They run from the After School Club for five- to 11-year-olds (Mon-Fri, 3.30-6pm; £7 per session) to off-the-cuff sessions with visiting groups like Kaos! Organisation, with everything from ballet to breakdance and tap to trapeze in between. Prices vary: an 11-week course might cost £77, while a drop-in afternoon class with dance impresario Debbie Campbell just £5, but all events are oversubscribed, so phone in advance. The diary of children's shows at Jackson's Lane offers a family treat every weekend during term (and on occasional weekdays during school breaks), with performances by touring companies like Tam Tam Theatre, Pekko's Puppets and the Half Moon.

Buggy access. Café. Disabled access: toilet. Nappy-changing facilities. Nearest picnic place: Highgate Wood.

Lauderdale House

Highgate Hill, Waterlow Park, Highgate, N6 5HG (8348 8716/www.lauderdale.org.uk). Archway tube, then 143, 210, 271, W5 bus. **Open** *Box office* 30mins before performance; bookings not accepted. **Tickets** £4; £3 concessions. **No credit cards.**

Set in a rustic 16th-century manor house that backs on to tranquil Waterlow Park (*see p96*), this arts centre is a more traditionally magnificent creative hotbed than most. Theatrical flowers may flourish in any environment, but the beauty of Lauderdale House certainly won't stunt artistic development – as the huge range of highly popular activities and classes suggests. Weekly dance and drama courses cater to ages three and upwards, as do drawing, painting and music workshops (phone or check the website for details). There's also an excellent variety of puppetry, music and magic brought to the stage by professional touring companies (10am, 11.30am Sat), while school holidays give rise to a number of ad hoc family days, including the annual Halloween Walk and a Jazz in the Park festival.

Buggy access. Café. Disabled access: toilet.

Lyric Theatre

King Street, Hammersmith, W6 0QL (0870 050 0511/ www.lyric.co.uk). Hammersmith tube. **Open** *Box office* 10am-6pm Mon-Sat (until 8pm during showtimes). **Tickets** from £8 adults; £6 concessions, students, under-16s; £5 16-25s (restrictions apply). **Credit** AmEx, DC, MC, V.

Outside it looks modern, but inside the main auditorium it's antique…and the proscenium-arch stage looks out on to a Victorian seating plan that wasn't exactly designed to accommodate children's fields of vision. Nonetheless the Lyric is one of London's most future-focused theatres when it comes to engaging young imaginations. Most kids' events take place in a purpose-built, 120-seat studio (although many spill into the foyer or the stalls) and a large proportion are done in conjunction with schools. They range from pre-performance workshops to Activate and Start Up classes that offer creative guidance to socially excluded five- to 13-year-olds and 14- to 25-year-olds respectively. An open series of weekend workshops, meanwhile, offers insights into the Essentials of Acting, Storytelling and – in June 2004 – Singing and Voice coaching. These are aimed at seven- to 11-year-olds (£6), and run concurrently with the weekly Saturday kids' show, which are consistently of the highest calibre: June sees Tam Tam Theatre's *Ling Chung the Dragon* (three- to eight-year-olds) and Heather Imani's *Crick! Crack!* (three- to six-year-olds), among others. Finally, during the annual Catch festival in April, children's performers from around the world descend on the Lyric for a free weekend of magic and mayhem, with an extended week of Easter shows to follow.

Buggy access. Café. Disabled access: lift, toilet. Nappy-changing facilities. Nearest picnic place: riverside.

Nettlefold Theatre

West Norwood Library, 1 Norwood High Street, SE27 9JX (7926 8070/www.lambeth.gov.uk). West Norwood rail/2, 68, 196, 468 bus. **Open** *Box office* 9am-4pm Mon-Fri. **Tickets** £3. **Credit** (advance only) MC, V.

It's not enormous but, with its purpose-built 200-seat theatre (built into West Norwood Library), the Nettlefold is an excellent resource for the neighbourhood's creatively curious. One show per month is child-oriented: in 2004 the excellent Kazzum have returned with *The Mermaid's Tale*, while magician Ian Saville conjured up the inspired *Three Bananas* in April (phone for a list of upcoming performances). More regularly, the Bigfoot Theatre Company (8761 5447, www.bigfoot-theatre.co.uk) runs drama, dance and singing classes here for eight-year-olds and up; they take place every Saturday morning during school terms, with plenty of half-term and holiday activities organised on an ad hoc basis.

Buggy access. Nappy-changing facilities.

New Wimbledon Theatre

The Broadway, Wimbledon, SW19 1QG (0870 060 6646/ www.wimbledontheatre.com). Wimbledon tube/rail. **Open** *Box office* 10am-8pm Mon-Sat; also Sun during shows. **Credit** AmEx, MC, V.

After being acquired and refurbished by the Ambassador Theatre Group, the New Wimbledon opened its newly polished doors on 11 February 2004. The debut performance was *The Nutcracker Suite*. In the coming season many productions are suitable for families: the Reduced Shakespeare Company makes a welcome appearance (15 June) and there's a short run of *Cats* (2-20 Nov). More a great theatre with children's entertainment than a great children's theatre, then, although staff promise a more comprehensive youth programme will be up and running soon.

Disabled access: lift, toilet. Shop.

Activities

Open Air Theatre

Inner Circle, Regent's Park, NW1 4NU (box office 0870 060 1811/www.openairtheatre.org). Baker Street tube. **Tickets** free-£11. **Credit** AmEx, MC, V. **Map** p316 G3.
Here seldom a summer goes by without an outdoor performance of *A Midsummer Night's Dream*, and this summer is thankfully no exception. For children there's no better introduction to Shakespeare than seeing this other-worldly work played out beneath a canopy of sky. This summer, you even get to enjoy Russ Abbot as Bottom (2.30pm or 8pm, 10 June-8 Sept). Younger children, however, might get more from the animal antics in this year's family show, *The Wind in the Willows* (11am or 2.30pm, 27 July-21 Aug), while a Midsummer Night Concert is scheduled for 26 June (phone for details). Tickets start at £10 (although all seats for *The Wind in the Willows* are £11 and the Midsummer Night Concert is free) and need to be booked well in advance. The weather may, quite literally, stop play, although your tickets will be exchanged for a later performance – subject to availability – in the event of cancellation.
Café. Disabled access: toilet.

Polka Theatre

240 The Broadway, Wimbledon, SW19 1SB (8543 4888/www.polkatheatre.com). South Wimbledon tube/Wimbledon tube/rail, then 57, 93, 219, 493 bus. **Open** *Phone bookings* 9.30am-4.30pm Mon; 9am-6pm Tue-Fri; 10am-5pm Sat. *Personal callers* 9.30am-4.30pm Tue-Fri; 10am-5pm Sat. **Tickets** £5-£10. **Credit** AmEx, MC, V.
Polka, a dedicated young persons' theatre, has one of the most highly praised programmes of children's events in London. Daily shows are staged by touring companies in the main auditorium (10.30am, 2pm), with weekly performances – rarely featuring more than two actors, and often puppet-based – taking place in the Adventure Theatre for those younger than four. The theatre diligently seeks out new writers and performers, whose work is then added to the Polka's wide programme of productions, drama workshops and storytelling for families and schools across London. It's worth booking for half-term, Easter and summer workshops, as well as getting involved in the Polka Youth Theatre, where directors, choreographers, actors and musicians help young people to put on their own shows. After-school drama workshops for three- to 11-year-olds cost from £55 per term; half-term and holiday workshops tied to current productions vary in price. Drama parties can be booked for up to 20 children to take part in role-playing, dressing up, magic and games. There's a complimentary ice-cream for every child taking part in the free monthly World of Stories drop-in event.
Buggy access. Café. Disabled access: lift, toilet. Nappy-changing facilities.

Royal National Theatre

South Bank, SE1 9PX (box office 7452 3000/info 7452 3400/www.nationaltheatre.org.uk). Waterloo tube/rail. **Open** *Box office* 10am-8pm Mon-Sat. **Credit** AmEx, DC, MC, V. **Map** p319 M8.
Kids have been flocking to the Olivier Theatre in recent months. The reason? A two-part adaptation of Philip Pullman's *His Dark Materials* series, which ran until 27 March 2004. If you missed it, fear not: a revival of both parts will be shown between 20 November 2004 and 2 April 2005 (check the website for details). For the rest of the year, the NT's calendar is more traditionally adult-oriented (although occasional productions – such as February's performance of *Dr Faustus* in the Cottesloe – are aimed at children) and it's only in the school holidays that things really open up to all ages. Then the theatre puts on numerous free concerts and

activities in cordoned-off areas of the foyer, or when the weather permits – out by the river. This summer sees a half-term Word Alive! storytelling festival bringing tales as timeless as *The Iliad* up to speed for modern seven- to 11-year-olds and their adults (11-15 June 2004), while the free outdoor Watch This Space festival kicks off again soon after, with a mix of musicians, actors and physical performers from around the world drawing family crowds on a daily basis.
Cafés. Disabled access: lift, toilet. Restaurant. Shop.

Shakespeare's Globe

21 New Globe Walk, Bankside, SE1 9DT (7401 9919/tours 7902 1500/www.shakespeares-globe.org). Mansion House tube/London Bridge tube/rail. **Open** *Box office* (theatre bookings, May-Sept 2004) 10am-6pm daily. **Tours** *Oct-Apr* 10.30am-5pm daily. **Tickets** £5-£29. *Tours* £8; £6.50 concessions; £5.50 5-15s; free under-5s; £24 family (2+3). **Credit** AmEx, MC, V. **Map** p320 O7.
Young audiences at the Globe can take advantage of the new Childsplay scheme, which engages eight- to 11-year-olds in theatrical workshops while their parents enjoy the first half of the play, before reuniting the family for the second half (selected Saturdays; £10 per child). A huge range of talks, tours and activities – many of them conducted by staff in full period costume – are conducted with schools throughout term, with holiday workshops opening the floor to families (phone for more information).
Café. Disabled access: lift, toilet. Nappy-changing facilities. Restaurant. Shop.

The Warehouse Theatre

Dingwall Road, Croydon, Surrey CR0 2NF (8680 4060/www.warehousetheatre.co.uk). East Croydon rail. **Open** *Box office* 10am-5pm Mon-Fri; 10am-1pm Sat; extended opening hours during shows. **Tickets** £5; £4 2-16s. **Credit** AmEx, MC, V.
Housed in a converted Victorian warehouse set back from the main thoroughfare, those not looking out for this place might easily walk straight past it – and it's not somewhere that families want to miss. Theatre4Kidz shows are aired every Saturday morning at 11am (£4.50 adults, £3.50 children), while a variety of touring shows are hosted for those as young as two. Perhaps most commendable, however, is the ongoing success of the Croydon Young People's Theatre (CRYPT), which for 20 years now has been offering a creative forum for 13- to 16-year-olds, many of whom have gone on to tread the Warehouse boards under harsher lights. CRYPT meets from 2pm to 5pm every Saturday during term-time, and puts on an annual show in July. The fee per term is just £10, and application forms are available on the website.

Young Vic

66 The Cut, Waterloo, SE1 8LZ (box office 7928 6363/www.youngvic.org). Southwark or Waterloo tube/rail. **Open** *Box office* 10am-7pm Mon-Sat. **Tickets** prices vary; phone for details. **Credit** MC, V. **Map** p320 N8.
The Young Vic was never meant to be permanent: built in 1970 to last five years, the fact that it has held out until now is a sign of just how valuable a theatrical asset it is. Finally, this groundbreaking venue is undergoing a period of closure for essential repair work. A fully rejuvenated auditorium will reopen in 2006, complete with a new foyer, new dressing rooms and a 130-seat studio theatre. Parents can rest assured that the Young Vic's reputation for infamously left-field Christmas shows won't be hindered by its temporary homelessness, although a venue for 2004's instalment has yet to be confirmed: phone or check the website for updates.
Buggy access. Café. Disabled access: lift, toilet.

Kickin'. **Half Moon Young People's Theatre.** *See p223.*

West End shows

This year's big West End opening takes place in December: *Mary Poppins* (altogether now, supercalifragilisticexpialidocious!) should be great family entertainment. Below we've listed the best of the current shows. With the exception of *Chicago*, they're suitable for children of all ages. Less developed attention spans may find some more suitable than others (many clock in at over two hours), and very young children are advised to avoid the West End and go instead to one of the more intimate kid-specific venues in other parts of town (*see p219*), where plays are shorter, lights brighter and the bangs less likely to scare.

For an alternative introduction to Theatreland, contact the Society of London Theatres (7557 6700, www.officiallondontheatre.co.uk): every August, the SOLT organises a **Kids Week** during which juniors get in free (with accompanying adults) to West End shows. Best of all are the pre-performance workshops – recent highlights have ranged from making some noise with boots, bins, brooms and the cast of *Stomp* and working with the Children's Director of *Chitty Chitty Bang Bang*. For more on Kids Week and the best family friendly theatre information in London, subscribe to the free family bulletin on the SOLT website. SOLT's Kids Club also runs a Saturday morning theatre club at the Theatre Museum in Covent Garden (*see p76*), but you have to book, as places are limited.

Blood Brothers
Phoenix Theatre, Charing Cross Road, St Giles, WC2H 0JP (7369 1733). Leicester Square or Tottenham Court Road tube. **Times** 7.45pm Mon-Sat. *Matinée* 3pm Thur; 4pm Sat. **Tickets** £17.50-£42.50. **Credit** AmEx, MC, V. **Map** p317 K6.
A powerful folk-opera, *Blood Brothers* is first and foremost a rousing show with ultimately tragic lead characters – and some great tunes. It tells the story of separated twins reunited in later life and deals with issues of family ties and class divisions. The ending may upset very young children.

Chicago
Adelphi Theatre, Strand, Covent Garden, WC2E 7NA (Ticketmaster 08704 030303). Charing Cross tube/ rail. **Times** 8pm Mon-Thur, Sat, 8.30pm Fri. *Matinée* 5pm Fri; 3pm Sat. **Tickets** £15-£40. **Credit** AmEx, MC, V. **Map** p319 L7.
Since the likes of Richard Gere, Renée Zellweger and Catherine Zeta-Jones appeared in its big-screen incarnation, there's been a huge resurgence in the popularity of this effortlessly slick, sexy and criminally minded musical. It's certainly not suitable for under-12s, but older children looking for anti-role models need look no further.

Chitty Chitty Bang Bang
Palladium, Argyll Street, W1A 3AB (7494 5020/box office 0870 890 1108/www.chittythemusical.co.uk). Oxford Circus tube. **Times** 7pm Tue; 7.30pm Wed-Sat. *Matinée* 2.30pm Wed, Sat, Sun. **Tickets** £19.50-£45. **Credit** AmEx, MC, V. **Map** p316 J6.
A flying car and a nice, clean fight between good and evil: there's really very little about this lavish production of Ian Fleming's classic novel that doesn't go down well with children. The whole thing is ingeniously designed – it's said to be the most expensive West End musical ever – but it's also well acted and utterly engaging.

Dancing days at **Laban**. *See p228.*

The Complete Works of William Shakespeare (Abridged)

Criterion Theatre, Piccadilly Circus, W1V 9LB (7413 1437/www.ticketmaster.co.uk). Piccadilly Circus tube. **Times** 8pm Tue-Sat. *Matinée* 3pm Thur; 5pm Sat; 4pm Sun. **Tickets** £10-£34.50. **Credit** AmEx, MC, V. **Map** p319 K7.

Culturally aligned parents may disagree, but this is a joy for kids (and adults) who find the Bard a bit of a bore. All 37 plays are hilariously edited, spliced together and spat out in under two hours. If the irreverent approach appeals, you can follow on with *The Complete History of America (Abridged)* on Tuesdays at 8pm, or *The Bible – Complete Word of God (Abridged)* on Thursdays at 8pm.

Fame: The Musical

Aldwych Theatre, Aldwych, WC2B 4DF (0870 400 0805/ www.famethemusical.co.uk). Charing Cross tube/rail. **Times** 8pm Mon-Thur; 8.30pm Fri; 7.30pm Sat. *Matinée* 5.30pm Fri; 3pm Sat. **Tickets** £15-£39.50. **Credit** AmEx, MC, V. **Map** p319 M6.

Fame may not live forever, but it's certainly having a good stab at learning how to fly: you should catch this unfeasibly energetic show before it dances itself into an early grave. The story – revolving around a bunch of leotard-clad, tantrum-throwing wannabes at New York's High School of the Performing Arts – will appeal to drama queens of all ages.

Joseph and the Amazing Technicolor Dreamcoat

New London Theatre, Drury Lane, Covent Garden, WC2B 5PW (0870 890 1110). Holborn tube. **Times** 7.30pm Mon-Fri; 8pm Sat. *Matinée* 2.30pm Wed; 2pm, 5pm Sat. **Tickets** £27.50-£42.50 (£5 reduction for children). **Credit** AmEx, MC, V. **Map** p317 L6.

Darren Day heads a revival of Andrew Lloyd-Webber's *Joseph* in the theatre that still smells of *Cats*. Children love the songs, many having sung them with great gusto in school singing lessons but tend not to leave wanting a tech-nicoloured dreamcoat of their own to wear, as we did in the '80s. We blame puffa jackets.

Les Misérables

Queen's Theatre, Shaftesbury Avenue, Soho, W1V 8BA (0870 154 4040). Leicester Square tube. **Times** 7.30pm Mon-Sat. *Matinée* 2.30pm Wed, Sat. **Tickets** £15-£45. **Credit** AmEx, DC, MC, V. **Map** p317 K6.

An enduring adaptation of Victor Hugo's tale of revolution in 19th-century France: almost 20 years since its London pre-mière, Les Mis is still impressive. The Les Mis Kids' Club pro-vides a backstage tour, drama and singing workshops, a meeting with a cast member, a commemorative certificate – and a matinée ticket for the show (there are several permu-tations of this package available: call 7439 3062 for details).

The Lion King

Lyceum Theatre, Wellington Street, Covent Garden, WC2E 7RQ (0870 243 9000). Covent Garden tube. **Times** 7.30pm Tue-Sat. *Matinée* 2pm Wed, Sat; 3pm Sun. **Tickets** £10-£45. **Credit** AmEx, MC, V. **Map** p319 L7.

Few children will be unfamiliar with the film version of this charming Disney classic, so following the storyline will be no problem. This means they can concentrate on the beauty of this production, the elaborate staging of which lives up to the unprecedented hype that surrounded its opening more than four years ago. Expect awesome set designs, a combination of puppetry and live actors, and a cocktail of West End cho-ruses and African rhythms: it's a delight.

Mamma Mia!

Prince of Wales Theatre, Coventry Street, Soho, W1V 8AS (0870 154 4040). Piccadilly Circus tube. **Times** 7.30pm Mon-Thur, Sat; 8.30pm Fri. *Matinée* 5pm Fri; 3pm Sat. **Tickets** £25-£45. **Credit** AmEx, MC, V. **Map** p319 K7.

It may be thin on story, but what Mamma Mia! lacks in dra-matic development it more than makes up for with feel-good musical numbers – the children will be singing ABBA's greatest hits for days afterwards.

Stomp

Vaudeville Theatre, Strand, Covent Garden, WC2R 0NH (0870 890 0511). Charing Cross tube/rail. **Times** 8pm Tue-Sun. *Matinée* 3pm Thur, Sat. **Tickets** £15-£37.50. **Credit** AmEx, MC, V. **Map** p319 L7.

Kids that like smashing pans together will be in seventh heav-en at this hyperactive show. The cast finds music in the most obscure objects – including the kitchen sink – and the whole thing feels as vital as it did when it opened ten years ago. Just remember to hide the bin lids before you leave home.

Performance workshops

Centrestage

Office: 7 Cavendish Square, Fitzrovia, W1G 0PE (7328 0788/www.centrestageschool.co.uk). **Classes** Sat mornings, afternoons. **Fees** £235 12wk term. **Credit** AmEx, MC, V.

The Holland Park, Harley Street and Hampstead branches offer a range of theatrical activities for four- to 15-year-olds. Workshops take place on Saturdays during term (10am-1pm, 2-5pm), developing a range of skills that can be capitalised on during a number of holiday courses. These are a week long, and all culminate in a show of some sort: younger kids are taught basic performance skills (including simple magic), while more developed thesps tackle plays and musicals.

Dance Attic

368 North End Road, Fulham, SW6 1LY (7610 2055). Fulham Broadway tube. **Fees** from £50 11wk term; phone for individual class prices. **No credit cards.**

The original Fulham Fame Academy: the range of perfor-mance classes at Dance Attic is staggering, setting it apart from less serious studios. Children under ten are encouraged to take part in Saturday morning workshops on tap (for over-fives) and ballet (for over-threes), the second of which work towards the prestigious RADA exams. Both cost £5 per hour-long session between 9am and 3pm.

Dramarama

Holiday courses *South Hampstead High School, Maresfield Gardens, NW3 5SS.* **Term-time classes** *South Hampstead Junior School, Netherhall Gardens, NW3 5RN.* **Both** *(8446 0891) Finchley Road tube.* **Fees** prices available on request from Jessica Grant.

OFSTED-affiliated Dramarama is the work of Jessica Grant, who has been turning north London's little extras into leading boys and girls since 1987, with a number of theatrical workshops for kids aged three and up on Saturdays during term. More intensive tuition leads eleven- to 14-year-olds confidently into their Guildhall speech and drama exams. Jessica's half-term and holiday workshops last five days and see participants devising and performing a play of their own. Four courses will be held over the summer in 2004, starting on 12 July. Dramarama can also organise theatrical parties at specified venues: phone for details.

Activities

Helen O'Grady's Children's Drama Academy

Headquarters: Northside Vale, Guernsey, GY3 5TX (01481 200 250/www.helenogrady.co.uk). **Classes** times vary; phone for details. **Fees** £63 12wk term. **No credit cards.**

Helen O'Grady's theatrical empire runs to over 37 academies across Britain and many more in other countries. The eight in London work out of one of a number of schools across the capital. The curtains come down once the books have been put away, with children aged five to 17 attending a one-hour workshop each week, with courses spread across three terms. Skills are developed depending on age – the Lower Primary group (five to eight) is concerned with nurturing self-esteem through clear speech and fluent delivery. The Youth Theatre (13- to 17-year-olds) studies more advanced techniques including improvisation and monologues. A production is devised and performed at the end of every third term.

Hoxton Hall

130 Hoxton Street, Hoxton, N1 6SH (7684 0060/ www.hoxtonhall.co.uk). Old Street tube/rail (exit 2). **Classes** times vary; phone for details. **Fees** £1.50 session. **Credit** MC, V.

The refurbished music venue offers a Junior Music Class (4.30-6.30pm Tue), in which eight- to 11-year-olds can experiment and compose at their own pace, with the choice of working individually or with others. They can also eternalise their endeavours in the hearts and souls of a live audience – or just on a CD. The parallel Junior Arts Class, meanwhile, encourages artistic expression using a range of resources and materials. Both the Junior Drama (4-5.30pm Mon) and Youth Theatre (7.15-9pm Wed) groups – for eight- to 11-year-olds and 11- to 18-year-olds respectively – give kids a free hand in writing and producing a piece for performance in the main hall. All classes run in term-time, costing £15 for the course.

Laban

Creekside, Deptford, SE8 3DZ (8691 8600/www.laban. co.uk). Deptford rail. **Classes** Sat. **Fees** from £38 12wk term. **No credit cards.**

This most recent incarnation of Laban, although barely two years old, is already a creative oasis in this neglected area, offering a variety of children's performance classes that is as refreshing and open-minded as its programme of contemporary dance and music. Across 13 separate studios and housed in an architecturally progressive building, Laban's creative dance courses cater for a number of groups – from four to 14 years old, as well as a carers and toddlers class. Last year the centre merged with Trinity College of Music, and the two continue to work in collaboration with local schools. Touring performances in the theatre are combined with lectures and educational workshops, many of them for younger audiences: check the website for a list of upcoming events.

Lewisham Youth Theatre

Broadway Theatre, Catford Broadway, Catford, SE6 4RU (8690 3428/www.broadwaytheatre.org.uk). Catford or Catford Bridge rail. **Classes** *1hr lessons* 10.30am Sat (8-11s); 11.45am Sat (11-13s). *Youth theatre* 6-8pm Mon, Thur (14-21s). *Children's theatre performances* 11.30am Sat. **Fees** *Performances* £3.50. *Workshops* free, refundable deposit required.

The free, no-auditions concept behind the Lewisham Youth Theatre can be misleading. The programmes may be open to all, but the standard is so impressive and the theatre so well respected that it has just received another nomination at the prestigious International Connections festival. A more spacious home in the Broadway Theatre, Catford has allowed for expansion, which means they can now take workshops after school as well as at weekends. Classes give classical texts a modern edge, reinterpreting the likes of *A Midsummer Night's Dream* for a final performance in the 100-seat studio theatre. Junior Youth Theatre is divided into two groups, catering for eight- to 11-year-olds and 11- to 13-year-olds respectively, but there is cross-pollination with the Senior Youth Theatre for young people aged between 14 and 21. *Café. Nappy-changing facilities.*

London Bubble Theatre Company

5 Elephant Lane, Rotherhithe, SE16 4JD (7237 4434/ www.londonbubble.org.uk). Bermondsey or Rotherhithe tube. **Open** *Box office* 10am-6pm Mon-Fri. **Classes** (term-time) 4.30pm, 6.30pm Mon. **Fees** £33 11wk term. **Credit** MC, V.

Bubble TC works with groups traditionally marginalised by mainstream theatre in a way that is challenging and refreshing. Its Open Performance Theatre (OPT) projects mix actors of all ages, backgrounds and dramatic experience in a show that tours the city's less conventional stages: last year's *Punchkin, Enchanter* involved 150 players, and was shown in parks and woods around the capital. The next OPT project takes place in 2006, and this summer London Bubble's production of *Alice Through the Looking Glass* will be popping up in some similarly unexpected places. Already in 2004 the company has pioneered the Intergenerational Project, which teamed up the Bubble Youth Theatre with elderly and disabled members of Entelechy Arts to write and perform a play about cultural difference, and the Southwark Youth Council Project, which brought kids together on a weekly basis and resulted in a performance in March. The Youth Theatre is open to kids aged eight to 18 and meets every Monday at 4.30pm (from £16.50/term), while a variety of open workshops offer guidance in everything from choral singing to MCing (from £2/ person).

Millfield Theatre School

Silver Street, Edmonton, N18 1PJ (box office 8807 6680/ www.millfieldtheatre.co.uk). Silver Street rail, then 34, 102, 144 bus/217, 231, W6 bus. **Classes/fees** £85 10wk term (4-5s) 10.30am-noon Sun. £85 10wk term (6-7s) 12.30-2pm Sun. £165 10wk term (8-16s) 11am-2pm Sun. £100 10wk term (14-21s) 6.30-9pm Fri. **Credit** MC, V.

Tucked into its calendar of musicals, comedies and mainstream dramatic events, Edmonton's 362-seat Millfield Theatre also shows a lively selection of children's theatre. The in-house Silver Street Youth Theatre, develops the dramatic instinct of local luvvies aged 14 to 21. The group runs courses throughout term-time, meeting on Fridays or Sundays, with performances throughout the year.

National Youth Music Theatre

www.nymt.org.uk

For the NYMT, 2003 was a far from satisfactory year: a critical lack of funding almost forced closure of what Andrew Lloyd-Webber once called 'the best youth music theatre company in the world'. This would have been an awful shame. For more than 27 years now, the NYMT has been discovering untold numbers of talented kids in London and beyond and whisking them away on whirlwind national and even international tours. Auditions are notoriously serious – on the potential rewards tend to swell even the most gentle ambitions – but Lab courses (ages ten to 19) across the country last year offered a less intimidating introduction to this historic organisation. Details of future productions are still unavailable, but a fund-raising gala is planned for later in the year: keep an eye on the website for updated information.

New Peckham Varieties

New Peckham Varieties at Magic Eye Theatre, Havil Street, Camberwell, SE5 7SD (venue 7703 5838/office 7708 5401). Elephant & Castle tube/rail, then 12, 171, 45A bus. **Classes** times vary; phone for details. **Fees** £2-£3.50. **Credit** MC, V.

The waiting list for New Peckham Varieties has not been much reduced by the decision to offer more places by dividing the classes between the Magic Eye Theatre and the Sojourner Truth centre on Sumner Road. With an activity line-up to match the diversity of central Peckham, it's little wonder that spaces are so coveted. Lively drama groups for four- to 18-year-olds run on Mondays from 4pm to 9pm, there's tap-dancing from 4.30pm on Tuesdays, Musical Theatre for Beginners on Wednesdays, and jazz lessons on Thursdays. The highlight of the weekend is the 'Boys Project' on Sunday afternoon, which has been successful in luring usually reluctant seven- to 14-year-old males into trying their hands at anything from stage-fighting to break-dancing. The drama team's four annual performances on the Magic Eye's main stage are open to members of any age, and these are supplemented by one-off concerts. Check *Time Out* magazine's Children listings for details of public shows for families; they're always a great showcase for local young acting talent and lots of fun to watch. Classes cost £1-£3 on top of an initial membership fee of £15 per year or £6 per term.

Perform

66 Churchway, Somers Town, NW1 1LT (7209 3805/ www.perform.org.uk). **Classes** times vary; phone for details. **Fees** £110 10wk term (weekday); £165 10wk term (weekends). **Credit** MC, V.

From humble beginnings, Lucy Quick's Perform is fast becoming one of the brightest lights in bringing the dramatic arts to children across the capital. Not that her aim is to groom the next Jude Law or Kate Winslet: central to Perform's mission is developing self-esteem and cultivating sociable attributes in even the most reclusive children, working on how they feel about themselves rather than the effect they may be having on adoring audiences. Quick's workshops – which run for 90 minutes at weekends and an hour during the week – are aimed at four- to seven-year-olds only, the age group she believes is most receptive to those all-important Cs: Confidence, Communication, Concentration and Co-ordination. Sessions include movement games, singing and improvisation, and each term focuses on a new theme: Fairytale Forest, for example, or The Magician's Workshop. A child's first class is free, so you can test for keenness before making a financial commitment. There are also week-long Experience workshops during the school holidays, which help children devise, rehearse and finally showcase a mini-performance of their own. Perform runs at dozens of venues: check the website for your nearest.

Not so fast, foodies

It's official: our porky children are eating less healthily than ever before. The popularity of certain multinational burger chains may be on the wane, but processed food is available in so many places – from corner shops to supermarkets – that the notion of 'fast' food is, to all intents and purposes, redundant: all food, it would seem, is fast these days. Not so at the **Kids Cookery School** (*see p232*), which attempts to reintroduce London's children to the joys of a well-stocked kitchen. The school doesn't encourage playing at grown-ups in the kitchen, nor whisk fights at ten paces, and though these purpose-built kitchens have marked many a culinary beginning there's no prescribed end to proceedings. 'Food therapy', as staff call it, is the very definition of life-learning.

That's not to say it isn't fun. No ten-year-old wants to waste a sun-drenched Saturday afternoon hand-making houmous. Instead, the menu changes to accommodate various age groups and attention spans (children as young as three can take part): younger children will get busy with simple, colourful ingredients, turning out sweetcorn fritters and funny-face pizzas by the dozen, while older kids turn their attention to more complicated dishes, experimenting with seasonings and sauces, and thus laying the foundations for a healthy lifelong relationship with the kitchen. All classes end with an introduction to various fruits and vegetables, may of which might otherwise be off the average youngster's radar (easy to understand when you realise that most kids these days think vegetables grow in the freezer), with plenty of taste-testing and a fun quiz to tie it all together.

What makes this school really stand out, however, is its open and inclusive attitude: more than 60 per cent of the kids who come through its doors do so on an assisted-places scheme, allowing participants to pay whatever they can on a sliding scale starting at 50p per session (although no one is ever turned away for having empty pockets). The ease with which financially deprived kids fall into bad eating habits is just another reason to ensure they get their slice of the action – and eat it too. Food therapy has been shown to help kids overcome eating disorders, and the school works with a large number of children affected by attention deficit and hyperactivity disorders. On top of that, one of the three in-house kitchens is fully equipped to accommodate disabled children and wheelchair users: no one, it would seem, is to be left out of KCS's ongoing mission to (in its own words) 'empower young people to take responsibility for their own health and well-being, through gaining cookery as a vital life skill'.

KCS offers after-school cookery classes in term-time (75mins; £15), as well as a range of lively cookery workshops (135mins; £30) and five-hour study days (£50 including lunch) in the school holidays. Classes are small (no more than 12 children to each fully trained and ably assisted cookery teacher), and staff organise ingenious children's birthday parties at weekends (prices for parties start from £28 per child) on a range of international culinary themes (Italian, Indian). Without so much as a cocktail sausage in sight.

Activities

The Place to aim high.

Pineapple Performing Arts School

7 Langley Street, Covent Garden, WC2H 9JA (8351 8839/www.pineapplearts.com). Covent Garden tube. **Classes** (8-11s) 1-2pm, (12-16s) 2-3pm, (over-17s) 3-4pm Sat; (3-4s) 11am-noon, (5-12s) 11am-2pm, (13-14s) 1-4pm, (15-18s) 2-5pm Sun. **Fees** *12wk term* £226. *Trial class* £20. *Registration fee* £30. **Credit** MC, V. **Map** p317 L6. One of the nation's premier schools for the performing arts, Pineapple, with its desirable location in the heart of London's theatreland, offers some of the most oversubscribed courses in the country. These are for students aged five to 18, and fall into three categories – Dance, Drama and Singing – each broken down into three-hour workshops over the course of three terms. It's not cheap, but the advantage of having experienced staff on hand – not to mention big-name shows – means that students receive more coverage than they would elsewhere, be it performing as part of the CBBC Proms in the Park or dancing for *Top of the Pops*. Requiring less commitment (and cash) are the Young and Boomin' street dance workshops, held every Saturday, while three- to four-year-olds can take part in the Pineapple Chunks classes (11am-noon Sun), a gentle introduction to the PPAS programme.

Nifty Feet!

8879 1618.
Lynn Page is best known for turning young actor Jamie Bell's two left feet into the twinkle-toed performance engines of Billy Elliot for the 2000 blockbuster of the same name. Soon after that she was swamped by young males hoping to effect a similarly spectacular transformation, and so Nifty Feet! was born, bringing ballet to the capital's two- to 16-year-olds by way of vibrant, mixed classes that defy the medium's somewhat dusty stereotype. The key to her success is cunning:

Page hooks the kids in with urban dance tuition using popular tunes that only slowly, and with her subjects hardly noticing it, turns into ballet lessons without the slippers. These classes run on Tuesdays for fives to eights (4-6pm) and Thursdays for twos to fives (11am-noon) at the Southfields Baptist Church. They also take place on Saturdays for ages nine to 12 (2-4pm) and 12 to 16 (4-6pm) at the Wimbledon Theatre. For more information, call the number above.

The Place

16 Flaxman Terrace, Bloomsbury, WC1H 9AB (box office 7387 0031/classes 7387 7669/www.theplace. org.uk). Euston tube/rail. **Classes** times vary, phone for details. **Fees** from £65-£75 11wk term; £5 discount for siblings. **Credit** MC, V.
A hub of contemporary dance, the refurbished Place provides a home to both the London Contemporary Dance School and the touring Richard Alston Dance Company; an extensive programme of shows runs throughout the year. The Place is also known for its policy of open education: the centre is fully accessible to all ages, as well as to the disabled. There is a daunting waiting list. The majority of classes take place on Saturdays and run concurrently with school terms. These take children aged five and over, striking a balance between creative expression and imparting more technical dance technique, and lead to occasional 'Offspring' performances in the adjoining Robin Howard Dance Theatre. These performances tend to be of challenging pieces, ranging from Virgilio Sieni's fairytale *Cappux Red* to Protein Dance's more recent *Banquet*. Considerable work is also done with schools in Camden: there are Breakfast Clubs and after-school workshops, as well as the Camden Dance Festival, which involves 16 schools each summer and results in three annual performances.

Royal Academy of Dance

36 Battersea Square, Battersea, SW11 3RA (7326 8000/www.rad.org.uk). **Classes** variable, call for details. **Fees** call for details.

The RAD offers a diverse range of activities for children aged from two and a half. Activities range from ballet, jazz and contemporary dance, to drama, singing, creative movement, musical theatre and classes in excerpts from ballets. Prices vary according to the length of the course. Discounts are available if 2 or more siblings are enrolled.

Stagecoach Theatre Arts

Head office: The Courthouse, Elm Grove, Walton-on-Thames, Surrey KT12 1LZ (01932 254333/www.stage coach.co.uk). **Fees** *Term-time classes* £270 (£135 for 4-7s). **No credit cards.**

With over 450 venues between Edinburgh and Exeter (more than 60 of them in London alone) and many more in other countries in Europe and beyond, Stagecoach is most prolific part-time theatre school in the world. Courses run parallel to the school term, and break down into three hours of professional tuition per week (one of dance, one of drama and one of singing). Two performances are given annually to family and friends, medals are awarded for continued achievement, and there's an in-house agency to represent the most promising talents in each division. All schools take kids aged six to 16, and most run Early Stages schools for ages four to seven.

Sylvia Young Theatre School

Rossmore Road, Marylebone, NW1 6NJ (7402 0673/ www.sylviayoungtheatreschool.co.uk). Marylebone tube. **Classes** times vary, phone for details. **Fees** *Classes* £75 13wk term. *Summer school* (10-18s) £250/1wk. **No credit cards.**

Sylvia Young's alumni are an intimidating list of plastic pop idols (Emma Bunton, Matt from Busted) and soap stars (Dean Gaffney, Tamzin Outhwaite). But the tuition encourages an interest in all aspects of performance art, and as many end up scaling the dizzy heights of the Royal Shakespeare Company as supping pints in the Old Vic. It's a full-time school, a Saturday school and it runs a programme of holiday courses. The full-time school is, of course, oversubscribed (roughly 150 pupils are on the roll at any one time). It accommodates boys and girls aged ten to 16 and supplements three days of National Curriculum studies with two of vocational dance, music and drama classes at a very high standard. The Saturday school caters for kids aged four to 18 and covers a range of performance styles. A holiday school operates out of term-time, with a Theatre Skills course for eight- to 18-year-olds in July and a five-day Musical Theatre Workshop for ten- to 18-year-olds in August.

Workshops

For **Performance workshops**, *see p227.*

Archaeology

LAARC

Mortimer Wheeler House, 46 Eagle Wharf Road, Hoxton, N1 7ED (7410 2200).

Archaeology hasn't had much of a hold over this nation's children since the adventures of Indiana Jones in the '80s – but that could soon change. As a storehouse for the Museum of London (*see p53*), the LAARC is a library of London's past, home to artefacts gathered from over 5,000 archaeological digs in and around the capital over the last century or so.

Public entry (9am-8.30pm Mon-Fri) is by appointment, and only legitimate research requests will gain you access, but there are family days, held roughly once a month, that bring the archive to life for explorers of all ages. National Archaeology Day is being marked with a weekend of open activities (17-18 July), with tours through the archives and demonstrations on a range of topics. Ring for details.

Art

Art 4 Fun

Various venues (head office 8449 6500/www.art4fun. com). **Fees** *Workshops* £15. *Half-day course* £25.85. *Full-day course* £38.80. **Credit** MC, V.

Children choose a ceramic item (from £2.50 for a small tile) and get busy painting. Pieces are fired and glazed in the café, to be picked up at a later date: a studio fee (£4.95 per person) covers the process and provides materials. A range of workshops run throughout the year, the most popular of which are seasonal events for four- to 14-year-olds, plus a range of daily half-term workshops. On a more regular basis, daily Painting with the Master classes offer after-school activities for kids aged six and up (£12.74/two hour session). Also daily is the Little Artists Club for one-to four-year-olds (£8.95/one hour session), while weekend clubs let families muck in together (£12.75/two hour session). *See also p233.*

The Art Yard

318 Upper Richmond Road West, Mortlake, SW14 7JN (8878 1336). Mortlake rail/33, 33, 493 bus. **Open** *Classes* term-time 9am-6pm Mon-Fri; school holidays 9.30am-3.30pm Mon-Fri. **No credit cards.**

The busy Art Yard provides a welcome artistic outlet for children (aged from five) starved of messy, painty and gluey fun at boring old SATs-obsessed schools. Many children come for two-day workshops (9.30am-3.30pm, bring a packed lunch and wear old clothes) every school holidays, and have a whale of a time making improvised art works, listening to music and making friends. Staff help children through creative crises. The birthday party package lets kids choose what they'd like to make from a list then have lots of fun creating. Objects range from papier-mâché mirrors to decorative treasure chests. Parties cost £15 per child (minimum 8 children in a party); ring for workshop prices. *Buggy access.*

Ceramics Café

215 King Street, Hammersmith, W6 9JP (8741 4140/ www.ceramicscafe.com). Ravenscourt Park tube. **Open** 10am-6pm Tue, Wed, Fri, Sat; 10am-10pm Thur; 11am-6pm Sun. **Fees** £2. **Credit** MC, V.

With three venues across London, staff at the Ceramics Café have their hands full with Young Masters on a daily basis, each of them choosing a piece from the selection of unfired ceramics, decorating it with a range of coloured underglazes in any style they choose and screaming with glee when they pick it up, two to four days later, all shiny and professional looking. But it's not just fun on the agenda: a more embedded mission statement involves reviving the value of individualism in an age where mass production is king. This particular branch is big, so well suited to one of the Café's celebrated arts parties (ring for details of party packages). For serial decorators, membership club offers free studio sessions and special offers throughout the year. *Buggy access. Café. Disabled access.*

Branches: 6 Argyle Road, West Ealing, W13 8AB, 8810 4422; 1A Mortlake Terrace, Kew Green, TW9 3DT, 8332 6661.

Activities

Cooking

The Kids' Cookery School

*107 Gunnersbury Lane, W3 8HQ (8992 8882/www.
thekidscookeryschool.co.uk). Acton Town tube.*
Open *Office* 9am-5.30pm Mon-Fri. **Fees** £15 75mins.
No credit cards.
West London's children's cookery school, the first to have
achieved charitable status, is an innovative project aimed at
promoting culinary skills, healthy eating and food awareness
among children from all social backgrounds and age groups.
Events and classes aim to teach kids in a deliciously hands-
on way, about new ingredients and equipment, and are
encouraged to touch, smell and feel different foods. *See also
p229* **Not so fast, foodies**.

French

Le Club Tricolore

*10 Ballingdon Road, Wandsworth, SW11 6AJ (7924
4649/www.leclubtricolore.co.uk).* **Fees** vary; £100 10wk
term. **No credit cards.**
Kids might dispute the logic of listing French lessons under
'Entertainment', but Le Club Tricolore isn't a French lesson
in the conventional sense. There are no verb tables, no
grammar exercises and no tests. Instead, everything is learnt
orally, by means of light-hearted role-playing or old fashioned
singalongs. After-school classes are complemented by
Saturday morning ones, while a range of holiday workshops
dish up cookery, craft activities and treasure hunts. The club
is aimed at children aged three to 11, and operates in venues
across London – phone for details of your nearest.

1.2.3 Soleil

Head office: 0845 085 0048/www.123-soleil.co.uk.
1.2.3 Soleil gives children from eight months old to 11 years
a fun, informal introduction to French at a number of venues
across London (more are opening all the time, so check the
website for your nearest). They participate in small classes
where they engage in a variety of French-led activities, from
singing and storytelling to arts and craft sessions.

Music

London Suzuki Group

Various venues (01372 720088/www.suzukimusic.net).
Fees vary; phone for details. **No credit cards.**
The LSG takes the principles of Dr Shinichi Suzuki as its
starting point. The good doctor's belief that talent was
inherent in all newborn children led to him establishing a
revolutionary school of music in Japan. In London the Suzuki
Method is expounded by 18 teachers (ten violin, five cello and
three piano), each of whom work with children as young as
three to develop their natural ability. The key is learning
through listening, and then playing for pleasure: no previous
musical experience is necessary (there is pre-instrument training for the very young) and, while the course is aimed at fostering excellence, fun is seen as a natural by-product. Classes
are held after school and on weekends, and are for members
only (although occasional holiday workshops encourage non-
members to join in; check the online diary).

Music House for Children

*Bush Hall, 310 Uxbridge Road, Shepherd's Bush, W12
7LJ (8932 2652/www.musichouseforchildren.co.uk).
Shepherd's Bush tube.* **Classes/fees** vary; phone for
details. **Credit** MC, V.

Everything about the Music House is aimed at developing
musical talent by bringing out the fun in performing. It's an
incredible institution. Despite being primarily concerned with
classical tuition when it opened its doors in 1994, the
organisation these days seeks to engage a wide range of
musical interests 'from Mozart to Primal Scream' and use
them as the starting points for a lifelong relationship with a
musical instrument. Nor are we talking about an either/or
decision between the violin and the oboe: lessons in
saxophone, guitar and drum are, predictably enough, the
most popular run by the Music House. The staff choose a professional teacher (from the more than 200 on their books)
based on the individual needs of the child in question, and
arrange lessons at times convenient to both parties. These
are usually held in the pupil's home. Meanwhile, those
seeking a more sociable environment to rock in can make
their way to the company headquarters in Bush Hall, where
group sessions are held every day after school and
expanded musical workshops take place during half-terms
and holidays. These group sessions help children appreciate
the sociability and co-operation required in musical
performance, and give them a valuable hands-on
introduction to a range of instruments.

Ocean

*270 Mare Street, Hackney, E8 1HE (box office 0870 400
820/info 8533 0111/www.ocean.org.uk). Hackney Central
or Hackney Downs rail.* **Open** *Education centre* 10am-6pm
Mon-Fri. **Fees** vary; phone for details. **Credit** *Box office*
AmEx, MC, V.
Starchy types might huff and mutter, but Ocean's lively
programme for musical development is entirely appropriate
given the venue's gritty surroundings. The staff recognise
and nurture creative interests in all forms, many of them
leaning heavily towards the urban end of the musical
spectrum. The Rising Tide project caters for youngsters aged
between 15 and 18, with practical DJing, drum programming
and songwriting courses run by trained professionals like
Richy 'Fingas' Hughes and DJ Obsession. Not the sort of
names you'd ordinarily associate with music lessons, but that
very difference is half of the £2.3-million Ocean project's
success. Inclusivity is the other half: Ocean offers assisted
places to financially disadvantaged local schoolchildren, and
children with disabilities can make music with electronic
interfaces housed in the specially designed RTC studio. Check
the website for a list of upcoming classes and events.
Disabled access: toilet.

Wildlife

Roots & Shoots

*The Vauxhall Centre, Walnut Tree Walk, Lambeth, SE11
6DN (7582 1800). Lambeth North tube.* **Open** *July-Apr*
9.30am-5.30pm Mon-Fri. *May, June* 9.30am-4pm Mon-Fri;
10am-2pm Sat. Phone before visiting. **Admission** free;
donations welcome.
Roots & Shoots organises a range of outdoor activities around
a one-acre (half-hectare) patch of south London. Over the
years it has introduced the pleasures of tending a simple garden to a large number of the city's weary offspring, many of
them children with disadvantages and disabilities. The site
is also a popular destination for school groups, where David
(the wildlife outreach worker) takes children dipping ponds
while telling them all about Lambeth's streetwise frogs,
hunting bugs and collecting honey (the centre is home to the
London Beekeepers Association), as well as informing them
about surrounding flora and fauna. Phone for details of the
next in a series of ad hoc seasonal family days.

Parties

Twice the fun for them – half the effort for you.

There are people all over London who make it their business to make a song and dance of your progeny's birthday. Party organisers run the whole show – sorting out invitations, a venue, entertainers, balloon numbers, party bags, cakes and clearing up – and all parents have to do is flash the cash. If it's true that we live in an increasingly cash-rich but time-poor society, leaving everything in the hands of professionals might just be the best way to approach the sticky problem of infant entertaining.

Such professionals come in many guises. Creative types from all walks of life are party animals these days: resting actors specialise in drama parties, paint-spattered artists lead jolly craft workshops, chefs encourage groups of children to have fun while preparing their own birthday tea. Arts and crafts parties are reassuringly and increasingly popular, with kids getting busy with everything from paint to clay, and infants as young as three learning about famous artists while constructing madcap creations alongside their friends. Another growth area is sports parties – several venues are listed below, or you could contact YogaBugs® (see p272) if you think the kids might enjoy making like a cobra.

Following the cliché that children grow up too fast these days, you may also have noticed increasing interest in makeover parties and pop-star or model transformations. These can vary greatly in price, starting with one-person entertainers who set up the whole event, complete with mini-stage and the usual party trimmings, to party organisers that supply disco sound systems, a couple of entertainers to run the show and a bubble machine if-that's-what-madam-requires. Parents may feel pressured to spend loads of money to keep up with the latest trends, but don't panic. For one thing, good entertainers add their own new ideas and contemporary themes to their acts, and may negotiate a price to fit your budget. For another, ideas that are inexpensive and simple can prove just as successful as the elaborate and expensive ones, especially if the budget won't stretch to an entertainer. You could just organise your own special trip to the park for a mini-sports day, and a visit to one of London's many museums and venues (for inspiration, see pp34-156 **Around Town**) may please kids as much as turning your home into a party zone.

THE BEST Parties

For burning rubber
Playscape Pro Racing. See p238.

For clowning around
Juggling John. See p243.

For crafty art
Nellie's Art Parties. See p242.

For mini-models
Teeny Boppers Dance Parties. See p246 **Girls aloud**.

For pop princesses
popKidz. See p246.

For sticky fingers
Cookie Crumbles. See p235.

Activities

Arts & crafts

Art 4 Fun
172 West End Lane, West Hampstead, NW6 1SD (8449 6500/www.art4fun.com). West Hampstead tube/rail/139, 311 bus. **Open** 10am-6pm daily; by appointment until 10pm. **Credit** AmEx, DC, MC, V.
Along with the joy of creating a unique work of art to add to the family mantelpiece, Art 4 Fun staff let parents take a back seat while they take care of the messy stuff with the kids. Party themes vary and cater for all ages (motto: 'you're never too young or old to give it a try'). It isn't limited to ceramic activities, either; there's face-painting (£5 per head), making and decorating a plaster model (£10) or T-shirt painting (£8). To round the day off, staff will happily clear the tables to make way for a birthday cake, drinks or even a takeaway if you wish. See also p231.
Buggy access. Café (snacks only). Disabled access. Nappy-changing facilities. Shop.
Branches: 444 Chiswick High Road, W4 5TT (8994 4100); 212 Fortis Green Road, N10 3DU (8444 4333); 196 Kensington Park Road, W11 2EF (7792 4567).

Crawley Studios
39 Wood Vale, Forest Hill, SE23 3DS (8516 0002). Forest Hill rail. **Open** daily (by appointment only). **No credit cards.**
Although artist Marie Lou runs her weekend pottery painting parties for small groups of children, the parents are more than welcome to have a dabble too. Held in a small art and antique restoration studio, the young artists are supplied with paints, stencils, aprons and Marie's guidance. The cost is usually no more than a tenner a head, but depends on what's to be painted – selections range from popular animal plaques and

ornaments (around £8) to the usual cups and bowls (£3-£5). Although there is no set studio fee, firing is charged at £3 per item and usually takes around a week. After you've completed your masterpieces and while the creative shrapnel in the studio is being swept away, a conservatory area is available for a tea party to round off the session (£3 a head).

London International Gallery of Children's Art

O₂ Centre, 255 Finchley Road, Finchley, NW3 6LU (7435 0903/www.ligca.org). Finchley Road tube. **Open** *Gallery* 4-6pm Tue-Thur; noon-6pm Fri-Sun. **Admission** *Gallery* free; donations requested. **No credit cards**.
This small gallery (*see p213*) presents a diverse range of parties for five- to 12-year-olds. Contemporary themes, such as designing sculptures from scrap and wire, are offered alongside familiar art party favourites – mask-making and painting portraits. Older children with a little more patience can learn origami or mobile-making, and new ideas can be devised if you aren't too taken with the workshops currently on offer. Prices start at £125 (plus material expenses), with fees increasing if there are more than ten heads to entertain. *Buggy access. Disabled access: lift.*

Pottery Café

735 Fulham Road, Parsons Green, SW6 5UL (7736 2157/ www.pottery-cafe.com). Parsons Green tube/14, 414 bus. **Open** 11am-6pm Mon; 10am-6pm Tue-Wed, Fri, Sat; 10am-9.45pm Thur; 11am-5pm Sun. **Credit** MC, V.

At Pottery Café an all-inclusive party package (£17 per child) covers the necessary craft materials – everything from aprons and animal-shaped sponges – and the sandwiches, crisps and a drink each, plus all invitations and decorations. The ready to paint ceramics come as a variety of objects, ranging up to £10.50 in value. Items can be collected later, once they've been glazed and fired. The popularity of the parties here means they must be arranged well in advance, especially if the birthday in question falls on a weekend – for weekends the maximum permitted stay is two hours.
Buggy access. Café. Nappy-changing facilities. Shop.
Branch: 332 Richmond Road, TW1 2DU (8744 3000).

Tulse Hill Pottery Studios

93 Palace Road, Tulse Hill, SW2 3LB (8674 2400). Tulse Hill rail/2, 68, 196, 432 bus. **Open** by appointment only. **No credit cards**.
Pottery teacher Caroline Dekosta is happy to fill her studio up with as many as 14 children for a party, but she'll also visit your house or a hired venue to hold the session if you wish. Although more of an art lesson than a party as such, plenty of fun is had and the bonus is that children learn real skills and techniques using grown-up tools. Probably best suited for ages six and up, prices for a studio party start at £100 plus £5 per child, which covers materials, firing and use of equipment (older children can use the wheel). Most young guests walk away from a party having made a professional-looking (well, almost) wet-painted vase or an animal-face mask or model.

Gill's Cookery Workshop. *See p235.*

Claiming their independents

There's no question that London's independent cinemas make a better choice for a film party than one of those characterless multiplexes. Some of them – like the **Ritzy** (*see p217*), the **Rio** (*see p217*), and both **Clapham** (*see p216*) and **Stratford Picture Houses** (Theatre Square, Salway Road, E15 1BX, 8555 3366) – run popular kids' clubs on a Saturday morning, which are a good first option. The birthday child sometimes even gets invited up to the projection room to start the film, and it all works out rather economical if you're entertaining a gang: the price rarely exceeds £3.50 per child or adult. Refreshments are usually no problem, either. Many of these venues have small café bars for cakes and snacks, but it's always a good idea to check with the cinema first in case there's nowhere suitable for an invasion of revellers (in some places birthday-cake candles contravene fire regulations, for instance).

For the right price, some cinemas will organise a more private bash. Sessions at the **Phoenix** (52 High Street, Finchley, N2 9PJ, 8444 6789) usually begin in the mornings with your own film screening, continuing afterwards with up to an hour of art- or drama-based activity. Prices start at around £175 for groups of up to 35 people, but at least one adult must accompany every eight children. An alternative plan is to visit the **Prince Charles** (7 Leicester Place, off Leicester Square, WC2H 7BY, 7734 9127) to experience the joy that is *Sing-a-Long-a-Sound-of-Music*. There's a compère to ensure the whole crowd croons lustily, with the prodigious panto hissing and cheering always going down well with kids. Held on the last Saturday of every month at 8.30pm (earlier matinées are held during half-terms) this fusion of theatre and film is a real giggle. Tickets, costing £13.50 per person, should be booked in advance.

Cookery

Cookie Crumbles
8876 9912/0845 601 4173/www.cookie crumbles.net. **Credit** MC, V.
As long as the idea of your kitchen being overrun by children doesn't scare you, these parties are a great introduction to cooking. Cordon bleu chef Carola Weymouth can help up to 30 kids create their own special tea, instigating foodie party games into the bargain. Menus have been tailored to suit children from as young as four and include all sorts of treats, from animal biscuits to potato footballs. For older children, there are 'disco diva' and 'pirate bounty' themes. Drinks are fruit punches, cola floats or just plain old apple juice. A two-hour party starts at £165 for six kids; the price covers everything from shopping to mopping up.

Gill's Cookery Workshop
7 North Square, Golders Green, NW11 7AA (8458 2608). Golders Green tube. **No credit cards.**
Gill Roberts' cookery parties take place in her Hampstead home on Saturdays (10am-1pm or 2-5pm; £225). They cater for 12 children (£10 per extra child, up to a maximum of 20). Parents leave offspring in Gill's capable hands, and are charmed by the results when they return: animal bread rolls, home-made ice-cream, funny-face pizzas and replete children. To make it all the more fun, children can decide on their own themes or menus to make on the day. Gill's two-day holiday classes for six- to 13-year-olds cost £85, and Saturday morning sessions for three- to eight-year-olds are £25.

Drama

Club Dramatika!
8883 1554. **No credit cards.**
Club Dramatika! is run by former drama-school teacher Vicky Levy, who offers fun-packed drama parties for birthday kids with thespian proclivities. The workshop-based sessions bring classic tales of magic and mystery to life. Parties follow the format of her popular workshops, starting with voice exercises and ending in a full-blown production. Parties are £80 for one hour, £150 for two.

Dramarama
Jessica Grant: 8446 0891. **No credit cards.**
Dramarama attendees can expect to be transported into fairy-lands, a Harry Potter adventure or their own version of *Oliver!* Older children get a more general drama session, with games, role-play and the chance to act to an audience at the end (prices vary according to venue and group-size). Drama classes are also available on Saturday mornings for three- to ten-year-olds and in school holidays for three- or 14-year-olds.

Fairy Tale Theatre
01727 759661. **No credit cards.**
Two leading ladies travel to living rooms across the land to perform their adaptations of children's storybook favourites (such as *Rapunzel* and *Little Red Riding Hood*). In true panto style, the audience are encouraged to hiss or cheer the plot along. All props are provided – mainly a screen behind which the actors change costume while the kids indulge in cupcakes and crisps. The two-hour parties also include theatrical takes on traditional party games (Pass the Parcel becomes Pass the Prickly Hedgehog); it all costs £190 for up to 25 children.

Lydie Children's Parties
7622 2540. **No credit cards.**
Lydie's themed parties, for children aged four to nine, turn living rooms into fantasy lands filled with decorations, as up to 26 kids take on roles from popular tales like *Peter Pan*. There are also plenty of ingenious games, funny songs and special goody bags: prices start at £355 for a two-hour party.

Marvellous Productions
8679 0917/www.marvellousproductions.org.uk. **No credit cards.**
Old Mother Marvel, aka drama therapist Roya Hamid, whisks children away on her magic carpet to other worlds and times – Hogwarts, Narnia or Ancient Egypt – with interactive storytelling sessions that have her audiences enthralled. A professional face-painter is on hand to get kids in character. Alternatively, Make and Take workshops offer the chance to make puppets, masks or toys based on the story (all materials provided, any mess removed). Prices vary, ranging from £150 for a magic carpet ride with up to 20 children.

Activities

NICKELODEON
12
PECKHAM
SMK 733F
nick.co.uk
©Viacom International Inc. All rights reserved.

Perform

7209 3805/www.perform.org.uk. **Credit** MC, V.
The respected drama workshop specialists bring a unique element of interaction to their largely improvised parties. Parents liaise with performers in advance to pick a theme that most suits the kids in question, but the possibilities are endless: discos for pop princesses or dramatic escape scenes for young action heroes. The show is set in a pre-arranged venue – usually a living room – and costs £115 per high-octane hour. Specially commissioned songs can also be written if the staff are given enough notice.

Tiddleywinks

8964 5490/www.tiddleywinks.co.uk. **No credit cards**.
All the living room's a stage at Kate Gielgud's parties. The fun starts when she turns up at a house in character (and in costume) to narrate and direct traditional tales (*Sleeping Beauty* is a favourite with girls, boys prefer *Peter Pan*), with kids aged three to seven acting out various roles. Later, traditional party games offer themed prizes, while older kids (eights and over) are treated to three hours of rehearsals for a 15-minute murder mystery – starring the children – that slowly turns into a comedy. *Bugsy Malone* and *Annie* have been added to the repertoire this year, with help from a musical theatre coach. Prices start at £200 for two hours; all costumes and props are provided.

Face-painting & make-up

Magical Makeovers

01932 244347/07957 681824/www. magicalmakeovers.com. **No credit cards**.
The Magical Makeovers team of beauty specialists comes to your house to offer light-hearted but sound advice on everything from skincare to general grooming, with hair accessories for girls to keep when the party's over. The service caters to girls aged six to 18. Small kids have make-up applied for them (which keeps lipstick off the sheepskin rug); older girls get a practical, hands on tutorial. Prices start at £150 for eight kids; all materials are provided.

Mini Makeovers

8398 0107/www.minimakeovers.com. **No credit cards**.
Diamonds may be a girl's best friend, but a load of glitter, make-up and hair accessories will certainly do in the interim. Mini Makeovers bring a vast supply of hypoallergenic, age-appropriate cosmetics to your home for five- to 12-year-olds to raid. They'll get anything from nail treatments to temporary tattoos, either as part of a sleepover or before the girls head off elsewhere else for an evening out; if it's the latter, Mini Makeovers also offers a limo service. Other options include dance tuition, goody bags and mounted photographs of the new young stars.

Sport

Alexandra Palace Ice Rink

Alexandra Palace Way, Wood Green, N22 7AY (8365 2121/www.alexandrapalace.com). Wood Green tube/ Alexandra Palace rail/W3 bus. **Open** 11am-5.30pm Mon-Fri; 10.30am-12.30pm, 2-4.30pm Sat, Sun. **Admission** *Mon-Fri* £4.20; £3.50 concessions; £17.50 family (2+2). *Sat, Sun* £5.50; £4.50 concessions; £17.50 family (2+2). **Credit** MC, V.
The Palace is a wonderful place for kids who like to get their skates on: it feels a million miles away from the out-of-town warehouses that rinks usually inhabit. Parties are equally

special, with between ten and 20 kids getting 15 minutes of good-humoured tuition before taking off for an hour on the ice. Prices are £7.95 per head including a cold snack, or £8.95 including a hot meal, and parties take place weekends only at 10.30am, 11am, 2pm, 2.30pm. Booking is essential. *Buggy access. Café. Disabled access: toilet. Nappy-changing facilities.*

The Elms Soccer School Parties

The Elms, Pinnacles Close, Stanmore, Middx HA7 4AF (8954 8787/www.theelms.co.uk/schools). **Open** *Enquiries* 9am-6pm Mon-Fri. **Credit** AmEx, MC, V.
It's a game of two halves at the Elms. They'll send an FA-qualified football coach to your garden, your local park or some other pre-arranged venue, and there the kids will get professional tuition (without the abusive shouting), followed by a mini-game with the birthday boy or girl as captain. The whole shebang costs from £95 for up to 20 kids and lasts 90 minutes. Of course.

League One Sports Academy

8446 0891. **No credit cards**.
League One coach Danny Grant organises sporty activities for children aged between five and 11, ranging from football and cricket to full-blown mini-Olympics. Varying skill levels don't generally prove an issue, as the coaches will cater for everyone's needs. Parties (starting at around £150) cover all equipment, the coaches' fees and a winner's trophy for the birthday boy or girl. Venue hire can be arranged for an extra charge. League One also offers an after-school programme and holiday courses in the Hampstead area.

Mallinson Sports Centre

Bishopswood Road, Highgate, N6 4NY (8342 7272). Highgate tube. **Credit** MC, V.
Facilities at Mallinson – attached to the highly sporty Highgate school for boys – are first rate. Kids have two party packages to choose from. The first, on Saturday mornings, gives little ones an hour on a bouncy castle (from £145), while the second, held throughout the weekend, offers seven- to 15-year-olds a more comprehensive sporting experience (from £185). Whether they choose basketball, hockey, football or some other favourite sport, kids get an hour of supervised team play, followed by half an hour in the pool and then 45 minutes in the social room, giving them a chance to reflect on the day's highlights over whatever party food parents care to supply. Party packages are available at weekends and also during school holidays.

Michael Sobell Leisure Centre

*Hornsey Road, Finsbury Park, N7 7NY (7686 2362/
www.aquaterra.org). Finsbury Park tube/rail.* **Open**
7.15am-10.30pm Mon-Fri; 8.45am-5.30pm Sat; 8.45am-
8.30pm Sun. **Credit** MC, V.
This complex has a good range of entertainments for young
party-goers. Four- to eight-year-olds can take over Safari, the
centre's indoor playground facilities (£65 Mon-Wed; £130
Thur-Sun) or they can enjoy an all-round sports party that
includes basketball, badminton and netball – such a party
caters for up to 15 children and costs £60. Trampolining and
ice-skating parties (costing £85 and £111 respectively) are
available for the over-eights, with equipment (skates) and
tuition provided: all last 90 minutes, and parents bring
refreshments for their own offspring.
*Buggy access. Café. Disabled access: lift, toilet.
Nappy-changing facilities. Shop.*

Mile End Climbing Wall

*Haverfield Road, Mile End, E3 5BE (8980 0289/www.
mileendwall.org.uk). Mile End tube.* **Open** noon-9.30pm
Mon-Thur; noon-9pm Fri; 10am-6pm Sat, Sun. **Credit**
AmEx, MC, V.
Mile End's extensive indoor facilities may not be as swanky
as those in the more recently developed Westway climbing
centre (*see p256*), but they're designed to allow those who are
still learning the ropes greater freedom and flexibility. Parties
are hosted here for over-eights, putting beginners under the
wing of an experienced instructor (one instructor to eight
children costs £50; for each additional instructor you'll pay
an extra £40) and laying on climbing and abseiling for an
adrenalin-filled 90 minutes. Parties end in the Monkey Room
– imagine a fully padded squash court with a sloping ceiling
and holds everywhere – after which the little monkeys
will probably sleep all the way home. Refreshments aren't
included, but you're welcome to supply your own food.
Otherwise, the café serves basic snacks and the centre backs
right on to Mile End Park (*see p112*).
Buggy access. Disabled access: toilets. Shop.

Playscape Pro Racing

*Streatham Kart Raceway, 390 Streatham High Road,
Streatham, SW16 6HX (8677 8677/www.playscape.
co.uk). Streatham rail/50, 109, 255 bus.* **Open** 10am-
10pm daily. **Credit** MC, V.
The capital's favourite karting circuit really burns rubber.
Parties are held for eight- to 16-year-olds (10am-5pm Mon-
Fri; 10am-1pm Sat, Sun), with an hour on the track for up to
ten kids (£195), 90 minutes for 15 (£292.50) and two hours
for 20 kids (£390). Full training and safety gear are provided,
and there's a trophy presented to every 'driver of the day' –
usually the birthday boy or girl, however shaky his or her
three-point turns may have been.
Buggy access. Café.

Pro-Active 4 Parties & Entertainment

8381 5005/www.magicalparties.net. **No credit cards.**
Alongside a range of less strenuous theme parties, Pro-Active
organises high-energy activities such as the 'mayhem' party.
This involves magic, dancing, games and parachute play, all
in one hugely energetic blast. The Premier Football theme is
in a league of its own, putting small teams through a series
of tournaments and shootouts, while the Sports Combo
parties and Mini-Olympics cover everything from basketball
to Ultimate Frisbee. Older kids tend to go for Junior
Gladiators (over-sixes only) or *Crystal Maze*-style challenges.
Pro-Active can set up events in your own garden if you're
lucky enough to have one that's big enough, but recommends
you hire a hall (and will find one near you).

Westway Sports Centre

*1 Crowthorne Road, North Kensington, W10 5RP (8969
0992/www.nkat.org.uk). Latimer Road tube/7, 295, 316
bus.* **Open** 8am-10pm Mon-Fri; 8am-8pm Sat; 10am-10pm
Sun. **Credit** AmEx, MC, V.
The Westway is expansive, relatively inexpensive and well
equipped. Activities available to party animals include
tennis, football and the capital's largest (if least well heated)
indoor rock-climbing wall. Invitations and decorations are
provided, as well as equipment and any relevant training
(how not to look down, for example), with catering available
as an optional extra. Prices start at £96 for 12 children, with
a maximum of 24 kids permitted (phone for more details).
*Buggy access. Café. Disabled: toilet. Nappy-changing
facilities.*

Cakes

Nothing can beat a home-made cake topped with
candy-striped candles and chocolate buttons, but
those parents who don't have the inclination to
slave over a hot tin can leave it to the experts.
The baking professionals we recommend will
add all the personal touches at your request.
Though more expensive than a supermarket
offering, the quality and individuality of these
beauties make them worth the extra cost. If you
prefer to make your own, inspiration can be found
in Carol Deacon's *Party Cakes for Children* and
her latest *Two-Hour Party Cakes*.

Amato Caffè/Pasticceria

*14 Old Compton Street, Soho, W1D 4TH (7734 5733/
www.amato.co.uk). Leicester Square/Tottenham Court
Road tube.* **Open** 8am-10pm Mon-Sat; 10am-8pm Sun.
Credit AmEx, DC, MC, V. **Map** p317 K6.
Amato, one of the more technically advanced bakers in the
capital, can feed designs into a computer, manipulate them
on screen and then print, for example, an image of your little
angel at the wheel of a tractor on to sugar sheet paper for a
truly personalised design (charging you from £30 for the
pleasure). If you're after something more elaborate, the chefs
can shape cakes that stagger the imagination: their free-
standing *Star Wars* droids are impressive, the five-month
Starship Enterprise project outstanding (prices vary).

Choccywoccydoodah

*47 Harrowby Street, Lisson Grove, W1H 5EA (7724
5465/www.choccywoccydoodah.com). Edgware Road or
Marble Arch tube.* **Open** 11am-6pm Fri, Sat; or contact
Brighton branch daily on 01273 329462. **Credit** MC, V.
Map p313 F5.
Layered with fresh Belgian truffles, Choccy creations can be
coated in white, plain, milk or cunningly dyed chocolate to
match your party's colour scheme. Eight to ten portions cost
from £19.50, up to 70 portions cost £90; hand-moulded
figures can be added for extra cash, and cakes tailored to the
most demanding imaginations. For party table extras, there
are also a range of novelty chocs.
Buggy access.

Chorak

*122 High Road, East Finchley, N2 9ED (8365 3330).
East Finchley tube/263 bus.* **Open** 8.30am-6.30pm daily.
No credit cards.

Playscape Pro Racing. *See p238.*

Alongside the usual range of gâteaux, cream pies and cheesecakes in all shapes and sizes, Chorak specialises in handmaking party cakes with iced designs, from well-known TV characters to tractors, toys and nursery-rhyme stars. Cakes come in two sizes, with the price depending on whether you opt for a flat cut-out design or a 3D shape. Small cakes cost from £48 to £55 and large creations from £60 to £65. *Buggy access. Disabled access.*

Dunn's
6 The Broadway, Crouch Hill, N8 9SN (8340 1614/ www.dunns-bakery.co.uk). Finsbury Park tube/rail, then W7 bus/Crouch Hill rail/41, 91 bus. **Open** 7am-6pm Mon-Sat. **Credit** MC, V.
For five generations Dunn's has been turning out cakes of the highest quality, available in a huge number of prepared designs, including 3D football pitches and snooker tables (£39.60). Bespoke designs can be iced to order – a popular cartoon character, perhaps – or maybe a photo-quality image of the birthday child (from £34.30).
Buggy access. Disabled access.

Jane Asher Party Cakes
22-4 Cale Street, South Kensington, SW3 3QU (7584 6177/ www.jane-asher.co.uk). South Kensington tube/11, 19, 211 bus. **Open** 9.30am-5.30pm Mon-Sat. **Credit** AmEx, MC, V. **Map** p315 E11.
Ms Asher's seasonal collection of mail-order cakes is quite something. For kids, designs include 3D books, GameBoys, teddy bears (*pictured*) and an all-too-realistic hamburger, with a choice of fruit or sponge bases and a variety of fillings (£35-£55). A (more expensive) bespoke service is available: recent work has included ladybirds, sleeping lions and beloved ponies. Cake mixes and Jane Asher sugar-craft materials are also available, should you prefer to bake your own.
Buggy access. Disabled access.

Maison Blanc
102 Holland Park Avenue, Holland Park, W11 4UA (7221 2494/www.maisonblanc.co.uk). Holland Park tube. **Open** 8am-7pm Mon-Thur, Sat; 8am-7.30pm Fri; 8.30am-6pm Sun. **Credit** MC, V.
Any of the gâteaux from this chain of pâtisseries can be personalised with a handwritten message for an extra 20p per portion (cakes start at around £10), or a marzipan plaque popped on it for £2.25. If that doesn't sound elaborate enough, more deluxe creations can be whipped up – perhaps child-pleasing cartoon characters or a more distinguished design. *Buggy access.*
Branches: throughout town. Check website for details.

Margaret's Cakes of Distinction
224 Camberwell Road, Camberwell, SE5 0ED (7701 1940/www.purple-pages.com/margarets). Elephant & Castle tube/rail, then 12, 45, 35, 68, 171, 176 bus. **Open** 9am-5pm Mon-Sat. **No credit cards.**
Got a sweet tooth? The distinctive creations that are hand-crafted at this West Indian bakery are icing heaven. A simple round sponge cake sandwiched with buttercream or jam can be embellished with cute little marzipan figurines or perhaps a

flat design of your choice (from £43.93). Alternatively, a 12in (30cm) cake in the shape of a favourite animal or colourful cartoon character can be ordered for £80.52.

Pierre Péchon
127 Queensway, Bayswater, W2 4XJ (7229 0746). Bayswater or Queensway tube. **Open** 7am-7pm Mon-Wed; 7am-8pm Thur-Sat; 8am-7pm Sun. **Credit** MC, V. **Map** p312 C6.
The staff can shape your child's dream cake – plane? Shetland pony? Easy-peasy – from vanilla or chocolate sponge with fresh cream or buttercream, with the option of iced messages, characters or printed designs. If you're low on ideas yourself, a catalogue of past work is available. Prices for a 12in (30cm) cake start at £56.30; it provides 30 portions. Photographic images on the icing cost £10 extra.

Costumes

Mail order

Hill Toy Company
Unit 1, The Tavern, Lower Green, Higham, Bury-St-Edmonds, Suffolk IP12 6NL (0870 607 1248/www.hilltoy.co.uk). **Open** *Phone orders* 10am-4pm Mon-Fri. **Credit** MC, V.
The greatness of the Hill Toy Company isn't limited to just dressing up but, as well as an excellent range of toys and games, it stocks a selection of outfits that are impossible to ignore. Forget realism: most of the costumes – from the Indian brave (£24.95) to an unbelievably huggable all-in-one lamb suit (£21.95) – are designed to make kids look cute, and they do it with style. Accessories run from impressive medical kits (£12.95) to wigwams (£44.95), and their online ordering system is top notch.

Hopscotch
Summer Wood, Puttenham Heath Road, Compton, Guildford, Surrey GU3 1DU (01483 813728/ www.hopscotchdressingup.co.uk). **Open** *Phone orders* 9.30am-5.30pm Mon-Fri. **Credit** MC, V.
There's something charming about the way Hopscotch outfits fit the kids so well: maybe it's because each one is assessed for comfort and ease of use by a rigorous group of young testers. The costumes are first rate, with plenty of unusual takes on the traditional faves: cowboy suits, for example, come with sheepskin chaps and cowhide waistcoats (£32.95). There are plenty of extras as well, if you're on the hunt for those all-important accessories.

J&M Toys
46 Finsbury Drive, Wrose, Bradford, W Yorks BD2 1QA (01274 599314/fax 01274 591887/ www.jandmtoys.co.uk). **Open** *Phone enquiries* 9am-5.30pm Mon-Fri. **Credit** MC, V.
The costume catalogue for J&M Toys is organised by profession: firemen, lollipop men and ladies, and enough medical outfits and paraphernalia to kit out a hospital. Owners Jim and Melanie are also medieval enthusiasts, so regal robes, Robin Hoods and a nice range of knights' armour are also among the options. It's all surprisingly cheap: most outfits cost little more than £15 in the first place, with discounts on group purchases. Orders are taken by internet, post or fax. *See also p204* **It's in the post.**

Activities

Nellie's Art Parties

Over the last decade Fenella Shepherd has shared her talents with around 10,000 children through both her studio art classes and her innovative parties. Originally, her workshops were held in a small studio in Camden, but that studio was threatened with closure and she was forced to move out, despite parents rallying in support (Jonathan Ross was a devoted leader of the 'Save Nellie Campaign'). Fenella still runs the art classes, but has most successfully channelled her talents into **Nellie's Art Parties** (07710 479852/01298 872752).

Nellie and her crew of professional artist and actor friends transform various themes (thought up by the birthday boy or girl) into a 'very over the top and magical' reality. Any idea can be brought to life, from unicorns, mermaids and magic to Salvador Dalí and Picasso parties, during which children construct bizarre Dalí sculptures and give their personal Picasso interpretations on giant painting boards. Certainly, nothing is done by half, with hours spent preparing and perfecting the scene: for a recent 'cyber-delic' party, hundreds of white balloons were strung up and the entire house and garden covered in sparkling plastic.

If you're worried that not everyone will share her enthusiasm for art, Nellie is happy to reassure you, guaranteeing she will win any attendee over.

'When running children's parties, you need to create a successful formula. Over the years I've learnt the formula that ensures that even if children start off by saying they don't like art, they end up loving it by the end of the party.'

Nellie's reputation for enthusing children has spread far and wide, even unto the ivory towers of celebrity parents: she was called on to design and organise an art party for the launch of Madonna's book *The English Roses*. Nor was this Nellie's first encounter with the rich and famous – she's taught the sons and daughters of many a film, telly and pop star in her workshops over the years, and seen a fair number enjoying her parties too.

Nellie often brings crafty ideas and characters from her own books into an event (aficionados will recognise Bingo Flamingo and Percy the Parrot), and her various inspirations for arty parties are to be set out in a new publication, *My Party Art Class*, due to be published in September 2004. The book will be full of colourful new characters to create, most of them made, *Blue Peter*-style, with household objects, glitter, paint and pipe-cleaners. Nellie is also preparing a television show, but she's still got plenty of inventive ideas for future parties up the sleeves of her overall – the latest development is helium-powered flying broomsticks, tried and tested on children of course.

Shops

Angels
*119 Shaftesbury Avenue, St Giles's, WC2H 8AE
(7836 5678/www.littleangels.co.uk). Leicester Square
or Tottenham Court Road tube.* **Open** 9am-5.30pm
Mon-Fri. **Credit** AmEx, MC, V.
Already an established venue for those who require some
adult fancy-dress, Angels now has a growing collection of
costumes for children aged three to 11. As well as current
favourites such as the Hulk and (still) Power Rangers,
you'll find all sorts of superheroes, Disney characters and
traditional outfits, with prices ranging from £12 (for a
doctor) to £39 for a rather unusual 'Pretty Witch' costume.
The 'Costume Treasure Chests' on offer are a great gift idea,
coming filled with dressing-up outfits and accessories for
both boys and girls (from £33.50 for three outfits).

Escapade
*150 Camden High Street, Camden Town, NW1 0NE
(7485 7384/www.escapade.co.uk). Camden Town tube.*
Open 10am-7pm Mon-Fri; 10am-6pm Sat; noon-5pm Sun.
Credit AmEx, MC, V.
Most of these costumes are made in-store, which makes them
unique but also means that they can't, for reasons of copyright, supply popular Disney characters. Instead, Escapade
is home to animals (kittens are popular with girls, bears with
boys) and well-rendered Cinderellas, Prince Charmings and
oodles of accessories, hats and wigs. Three-day hire costs
£15-£20 after a £50 deposit. There is now also a range of
ready-made kits featuring comic-book heroes – prices start
at around £10 for a Robin Hood outfit and span £25-£30 for
the Power Rangers, Spiderman and Batman sets.

Harlequin
*254 Lee High Road, Lewisham, SE13 5PR (8852 0193).
Hither Green rail/Lewisham rail/DLR/21, 261 bus.* **Open**
10am-5.30pm Mon, Tue, Thur-Sat; 10am-1pm Wed.
Credit MC, V.
Snow White, Peter Pan, Cinderella? You name the hero and
Harlequin will supply the kit that fits. There are other, more
generic outfits if you opt out of fairytale land. Prices start at
£9.95 for a king's robe and go up to £28 for more elaborate
animal suits or costumes made of finer materials. If the
budget's tight, just get the bare minimum: £3.95 will buy you
a pirate's patch, bandanna, moustache and earring.

Deals on wheels

The Party Bus
07836 605032/www.childrenspartybus.co.uk
The bus is a colourful, converted single-decker that holds up
to 24 children and runs on pure fun. Onboard events are
tailored to the age group in question (from four to nine year
olds), with games and comedy magic for younger ones
giving way to London's most mobile disco venue for older
kids. £300/£350 brings it to your house, and provides all
catering except the cake. Best of all, when the music stops,
the mess just drives off into the sunset.

The Wonder Years
0700 012 3455/www.limousinehireheathrow.com
You need a chauffeur-driven stretch limo with leather seats,
fairy lights and mirrored ceilings? Look no further. Soft
drinks are provided (parents can even supply non-alcoholic
champagne if they see fit) and each car seats up to eight
people; hire starts at £175 for three hours.

Entertainers
More information on the seasoned entertainers we've
listed can be found on their websites, if they have
them, and their prices coaxed out of them by phone.

Ali Do Lali
01494 774300.
With over 30 years perfecting his magic tricks and illusions,
Ali Do Lali can grip all ages with his individual and quirky
style of entertaining. Younger party-goers enjoy storytelling
and more gentle trickery; fire-eating and sawing in half of
parents are saved for the older kids.

Billy the Disco DJ
8471 8616/www.billythediscodj.co.uk
Billy's disco for party people aged four to 11 includes limbo
contests, disco lights, pop quizzes and karaoke. He also has
a bubble machine, and will oversee hand-painting and games.
He charges £150 for a two-hour do.

Blueberry Playsongs Parties
8677 6871/www.blueberry.clara.co.uk
A parent-and-toddler music group with nine branches in
London, Blueberry sends entertainers to kids' parties (one to
six years old) for 45 minutes of guitar-led singing, dancing
and fun. Prices start at £75 for 20 children, and include
Blueberry balloons and a present for the birthday boy or girl.

Boo Boo
7727 3817/www.mr-booboo.co.uk
Boo Boo is part clown, part magician, part comic. His popular
shows for three- to eight-year-olds incorporate music, balloon-
modelling, dancing and general buffoonery, while older kids
get to shake their tail feathers to more contemporary tunes in
a Boo Boo disco party. Most shows last for two hours.

Chris Howell
7376 1083/www.christopherhowell.net
Chris is a member of the School of American Conjuring (and
the Magic Circle). Sometimes he's the one who seems slightly
out of his depth, letting the audience think he's fluffed a trick
before pulling it off with flair. Hour-long parties for four- to
eight-year-olds are woven through with a story in which the
kids play an active part, and there's balloon-modelling to
round things off. Prices start at £85.

Foxy the Funky Genie
8461 1223/www.foxythefunkygenie.com
Funky Foxy goes down a storm. He offers four separate party
packages for children aged two and up, involving conjuring
and balloon shows or games, puppetry and full-blown discos
– all tied together with his brand of comedy magic and
irrepressible '70s cool. Prices start at £95 for 45 minutes.

Jenty the Gentle Clown
8207 0437/07957 121764.
A favourite in Great Ormond Street Hospital, Jenty's parties
for children aged two to 11 include singing, banjo music,
puppets, storytelling, balloon-modelling, face-painting and
limbo dancing. Choose the activities to suit your child,
and know that Jenty charges £150 for two hours.

Juggling John
8938 3218/www.jugglersetc.com
John Haynes is Juggling John, master of slapstick and mime
for kids' parties and corporate events. Success led to him
launching Jugglers Etc agency, which supplies unicyclists,

stilt-walkers, storytellers and fire-eaters. John is available himself for children's parties in several guises, including Reggie the Raccoon, Ronnie the Robot and good old JJ. One- or two-hour shows (depending on age, kids aged from as young as one year old and up can be catered for) start at around £140-£180.

Lee Warren
8670 2729/www.sorcery.org.uk
Lee's brilliant shows combine deft sorcery with audience participation. Boys and girls dress up, often as pirates and princesses, to take part in stories as they unfold, with plenty of conjuring, illusion and amusing calamity along the way. The hour-long shows – for four- to eight-year-olds – cost £110 for a home performance or £120 in a hired hall, and Lee will deal with nearly any size of audience (eight minimum).

Lisa the Disco Diva
07778 122277.
Lisa's collection of mobile DJ and disco equipment includes bubble and smoke machines, fancy lights and mirrorballs. She can design a party according to a child's desires and choreograph a whole dance routine to a favourite tune; kids can then do their new grooves for grown-ups, or just party the rest of the afternoon away in peace. Events cater for boys and girls aged four and upwards, with games and competitions, magic and more in the high-energy, two-hour package.

Little Blisters
8948 3874.
Actress Ava Desouza uses her dramatic skills to make parties sparkle for three- to seven-year-olds. As Flossie the Fairy, Sea Lily the Mermaid or Kitty the Magical Pussy Cat, she tells an entrancing story, with plenty of song and dance along the way. Shows last one or two hours (£100-£220), with games, prizes and face-painting.

Merlin Entertainments
8866 6327/www.merlinents.co.uk
Choose from a long list of performers, with everything from caricaturists and comedy waiters to fortune-tellers and fire-eaters on Merlin's books. Prices start at £115 for a one-hour performance, or £145 for a more interactive two-hour show. Merlin also organises circus and clown workshops or parties for ages six upwards; they'll bring the necessary equipment to a suitable venue of your choice.

Mr Squash
8808 1415/www.mr-squash.co.uk
Parents of pre-schoolers are fond of Mr Squash, who travels all over London with his musical puppet show, balloon tricks, singalongs and funny stories. Well known on the playgroup circuit, he's experienced in engaging the very young (two- and three-year-olds) but his parties are suitable for children aged up to six. His puppet friends, performing in a booth, invite audience participation, especially from the birthday boy or girl. Mr Squash charges from £140 for a one-hour set.

Pekko's Puppets
8575 2311/www.pekkospuppets.co.uk
Veteran of the touring circuit and regular at both Jackson's Lane and the Lyric Hammersmith (for both, *see p223*), Stephen Novy is also an old hand at birthday parties. His puppet plays are aimed at kids aged three to 11, with shows for under-fives packing in two shorter tales with lots of singing and audience participation, while older children get a full performance from a repertoire that runs to Celtic folk tales, popular classics and chillers like Dracula, all enacted from one of two mobile booths (from £130 for one hour).

Peter McKenna
7703 2254/07956 200572.
Magic Circle member Peter McKenna appears in a variety of guises to suit various age groups – and performs tricks with a degree of competence rarely seen at kids' parties. Illusions might include levitating, sawing parents in half and decapitating audience members, but there are always less alarming routines for little ones. Discos, party games and goody bags are all available by arrangement. Prices start at £90 for one hour, £145 for two hours.

Professor Fumble
01395 579523.
Professor Fumble's routine involves repeatedly bungling his tricks, juggling like a seasoned amateur and sitting down in his own custard pies. Shows can last one or two hours (£100 or £145 respectively); the former include balloon animals for the kids and – where space permits – a chance for party-goers to have a crack at spinning plates or walking on small stilts. Longer performances allow for Fumbling versions of old party games, with the mad Professor providing the prizes.

Equipment hire
Disco
Young's Disco Centre
20 Malden Road, Chalk Farm, NW5 3HN (7485 1115/www.youngsdisco.com). Chalk Farm tube.
Open by appointment only Mon-Fri; 11am-5pm Sat. **Credit** AmEx, MC, V.
Everything you need for the groove can be hired at Young's: a state-of-the-art sound system comes with a DJ, from £180 for a two-hour weekday party (£250 at weekends), and karaoke set-ups are available from £80; further refinements include a smoke machine (from £20) or industrial bubble blower (from £15), popcorn and candy-floss makers (from £50 each), and even fake snow machines (£30).
Branch: 2 Malden Road, NW5 3HN (7485 1115).

Fairground
PK Entertainments
07771 546676/www.fairandfete.co.uk. **No credit cards.**
What do you get for the child who has everything? An indoor fairground might be a start. PK Entertainments can set up a basic package (from £200) in your living room, with mini-bouncy castle, bucking bronco and stalls of the pop-gun variety; those with more capacious lounges can even request a toboggan run. Outdoor events start at about £250 for 20 kids, though a fully blown fair can be built for roughly £500: roundabouts, swingboats and all.

Marquees
Sunset Marquees
20 Bradmore Park Road, Hammersmith, W6 0DT (8741 2777/www.sunsetmarquees.com). Hammersmith tube.
Open *Enquiries* 24hrs daily. **No credit cards.**
A marquee can localise the next round of birthday madness to a clearly defined and disposable space. Basic 3m by 3m (10ft by 10ft) packages start from £190 and go up (literally) from there. With the advent of double- and triple-decker marquees, the sky is the limit. If you need lighting, heating and underfoot carpeting, they can be supplied but cost extra. Phone for further details.

Girls aloud

Depending on the birthday princess in question, there are several paths you could follow when organising her party. Be warned: they're likely to involve a great deal of twirly girlie stuff. In fact, if you've got anything against glitter and lip gloss, read no further.

These days six-going-on-26-year-olds are no longer content to raid their mothers' bedrooms for high heels and lipstick. Parties providing 'pampering' and fashion-oriented fun – inspired by all those telly makeover programmes – are gaining in popularity. Children's make-up specialists **Magical Makeovers** and **Mini Makeovers** (*see p237*) teach all ages a thing or two about applying eye shadow and nail polish; they also make sure plenty of freebies are thrown in. Magical Makeovers now also organise spa parties for older girls, including facials, manicures and advice on skincare. You could, of course, organise your own party beauty salon, but using an expert makes sure all the supplies (including child-friendly cosmetics) are provided, with parents only having to do the birthday cake and refreshments.

If your eardrums can handle it, a teeny-bopper party organised by the friendly folk at **Popstarz Parties** (8428 1983, www.popstarzparties.co.uk) may be a hot ticket for ages six and up. The venue is transformed for two hours into a catwalk show or dance stage, with optional mirrorballs and smoke machines. The girls (and boys if they are willing) are then taught a simple dance routine to perform later, or they learn the peacock strut of a catwalk

model. Games, makeovers and glamorous attire are all part of the package. Prices start at £180 for weekday parties. Alternatively, two hours of glitter and glamour can be brought to you by ex-backing dancer turned dance tutor Michaela Dicker, at her energetic **Teeny Boppers Dance Parties** (8352 6471, www.teenyboppers.org.uk). The stage – a canvas backdrop, fairy lights, balloons and fluorescent tubes – is filled with Haribo-fuelled boppers, sporting glitter make-up and tattoos, with photos taken throughout. For more boy appeal, Michaela has introduced body-popping and break-dancing. She also runs fashion parties, with lots of make-up, photographs and a catwalk lesson. Prices start at £240 for 6-20 children aged six and above, with discounts for smaller groups. For other performance parties, check the listings for **Perform** (*see p237*), **popKidz** (*see p246*) and **Lisa the Disco Diva** (*see p245*).

While everyone is feeling grown up, bring on the champers. We're talking about **Children's Bubbly**, a non-alcoholic beverage in appealing fruity flavours that pops like the real thing but costs only a fraction of the price (£20 for a case of six).

Of course, some children are happy just being children, and they're made up at the prospect of **Mystical Fairies** (*see p247*), whose fairy godmothers transform your home into a woodland grotto or enchanted garden. But it will come as no surprise, however, that even these fairy circles have karaoke discos and enough magic glitter to go around twice.

Organisers

Action Station
0870 770 2705/www.theactionstation.co.uk
The Action Station agency is a fine resource for any parent on the verge of last-minute planning meltdown. Its books are bursting with entertainers, jugglers and clowns. There are storytellers who give children acting parts as the tale unfolds. Two-hour drama parties are available (kids pick a theme and perform for parents), while face-painters and film make-up parties between them create everything from tiger faces to fake scars, warts and boils. Most activities cost £135 for one hour or £190 for two, and staff also organise discos and karting events (phone for more information).

Adam Ant's
8959 1045/www.adamantsparties.com
Adam Ant stands and delivers music and dancing, magic and balloon sculpture... general jollity, in fact, all courtesy of a wide range of entertainers. Depending on the length of the party (prices start at £85 for one hour), activities can be stopped for a birthday lunch: Adam also caters, though parents tend to provide the cake. Increasingly popular are the kid-o-gram characters who turn up to wow the party for half an hour (from £85): Cinderella, for example, tells a gentle story, while Batman chases bad guys round the garden. Party accessories, including ball ponds and bouncy castles, may be hired (from £45).

Crechendo
8772 8140/www.crechendo.co.uk
The events arm of this childcare company creates bespoke theme parties, covering everything from Peter Pan's Never Never Land to a glamorous 'model' party, complete with catwalk and cameras. All ages are catered for and extras include stretch limos, celebrity lookalikes or entertainers. If you require just the entertainer, prices start at around £250. Prices for the bespoke service, however, don't come with a fairytale receipt: they start at £1,500.

Kasimira
29 South Terrace, South Kensington, SW7 2TB (7581 8313/www.kasimira.com). **Open** *Phone enquiries* 10am-6pm Mon-Fri.
Kasimira's database lists entertainers, face-painters, magicians and other party experts, all interviewed, referenced and police-checked. Harry Potter parties, with potions classes and Quidditch lessons, are a big fave. Kasimira sets great store by its personal service and tailor-made parties.

popKidz
07929 218987.
Staff at popKidz know how to treat fledgling pop stars. Their recording equipment can be set up in any living room, as the party-goers get made-up and spend three hours preparing for the five-minute final take – which comes back a week later, professionally edited on VHS or DVD with special effects and a five-minute 'bloopers' reel. There's a list of contemporary

tunes for boys and girls aged between seven and 11, and the package costs £500, including two VHS or DVD copies of the performance (extra copies are £7 per VHS and £15 per DVD).

Laurie Temple & the Party Wizard Company

8840 5293/www.thepartywizard.co.uk
Entertainer Laurie Temple runs a host of parties for kids of all ages. With his talented team, he offers fun-filled parties that include magic, balloons, juggling, junior discos, puppetry, storytelling and face-painting. Parties can last for one or two hours, and themes vary from pop-star discos to circus workshops that teach kids how to stilt-walk and spin plates. Party Wizard also offers full party organisation, and can supply entertainers to suit a wide range of budgets. Prices can vary from £100-£150 (one hour) to £150-£240 (two hours).

Mystical Fairies

12 Flask Walk, Hampstead, NW3 1HE (7431 1888/ www.mysticalfairies.co.uk). Hampstead tube.
The parties organised here are asparkle with fairy dust, disco lights and glittering entertainers, with the children able to borrow gauzy outfits from the shop as part of the package. Prices depend on whether you want to have your mystical party at home or in the Enchanted Garden in Flask Walk. A home party (which lasts two hours and includes a fairytale character) costs £180 plus VAT; a glitter disco and karaoke package in the Enchanted Garden, complete with makeover or face-painter, party supplies and invitations, costs £395 plus VAT. If you'd like the good fairies to tailor a party to your child's needs, ask for a quotation.

Puddleduck Parties

8893 8998/www.puddleduckparties.co.uk
Quacking good party themes for children of all ages: Teddy Bears' Picnics for the youngest, perhaps, or Batman birthdays for the more heroically inclined. PP also does drama, sport and disco parties; phone for more details.

Splodge

7350 1477/www.planetsplodge.com
Actors run the fantasy parties that are Splodge's speciality, including quests for unicorns, the Ring of Fear, inner peace and more. They immerse groups of children in a choice of environments: animal magic at Battersea Children's Zoo (*see p137*), enchanted unicorn hunts at Holland Park (*see p149*) Orangery; wildlife games and explorations at Wandsworth's Nature Study Centre (*see p139*); military manoeuvres at the National Army Museum (*see p87*), or – one for the lads and dads – mystical makeovers with yoga and aromatherapy at Lotus Lifestyle (Design Centre, Chelsea Harbour, SW10 OXE). Tailor-made packages might include themed party teas, party bags, decorations, a video and a face-painter, personalised according to the family's wishes. For 20 kids, such parties cost from £330 and last two hours.

Twizzle Parties

8789 3232/www.twizzle.co.uk
Twizzle puts on different events for different ages. While toddlers will enjoy a giant bubble-blowing party (£240), there are circus, princess and beach themes for infants or a creepy-crawly party for elder siblings (£280). Wannabe pop stars can cut their own CD and video in a studio (from £350 for two hours, up to 16 kids), taking a copy away to play at home.

The Non-Stop Party Shop. *See p249.*

Talk about it, man to man

If your knowledge of ventriloquism begins and ends with Keith Harris and Orville, you may not have considered hiring a voice-thrower for your child's birthday party. Ventriloquism is, after all, a rather specialised form of party entertaining, and true professionals are still something of a rarity. The disappearance of the old Vaudeville shows, however, has not completely silenced the ventriloquists. Indeed, adult comedy acts Nina Conti and Paul Zerdin are helping to raise the profile of a fading art.

Recently awarded the MBE for his contribution to entertainment, long-established ventriloquist **John Styles** (8300 3579, www.johnstylesentertainer. co.uk; *pictured*) declares through clenched teeth: 'To become a vent you have to be willing to lose your dignity and be insulted by a doll.' As he has done in many appearances on children's telly – he even had a role in the movie *Time Bandits*. Like many vents, John started young, when he joined a magic club, before finding his first job in a Baker Street shop that was owned by a busy party entertainer in need of an apprentice. It was also here that John met his first dummy.

Peter Brough was the celebrity vent of the 1950s and '60s. His radio show, *Educating Archie*, proved so popular you could buy your own Archie Andrews dummy in Hamleys, and Brough was the inspiration for many a self-taught vent, including the young **Len Belmont** (7254 8300). Len now has been entertaining with voice-throwing and magic for 50 years, and has built up a collection of character dolls to suit all situations, from talking birds and pop stars (Shaun Ryder and Kylie are always popular) to his favourite showbiz partner Charlie Cherrywood. Best suited to three- to eight-year-olds, Len's children's party entertaining is not the only thing to keep him busy these days. Two years ago he helped set up the **British Association of Ventriloquists** (contact Trevor Burch on 01246 270653), an organisation that is dedicated to reviving the ancient art.

Parents looking to save money may fancy trying to master the art themselves, using Association secretary Trevor Burch's *The Art of Ventriloquism* (published by Litton Books and available at www.countrybookshop.co.uk), but to avoid lockjawed embarrassment you'd be better off calling on **Merlin Entertainments** (*see p245*) to find a vent for your party. Mr Geoff (a vent himself) has run this well-respected agency for the magically minded for over 25 years and will sort you out with the ideal entertainer. His recommendation for entertaining an unruly party of children? 'Adopt a dual personality for ten minutes and argue with yourself'. It's a winner! Oh yes it is!

Paraphernalia

Mail order

Baker Ross

Unit 53, Millmead Industrial Estate, Millmead Road, N17 9QU (enquiries 8808 6948/orders 0870 770 7030/ www.bakerross.co.uk). **Open** *Shop* Jan-Sept 9am-5pm Mon-Fri. Oct-Dec 9am-5pm Mon-Fri; 9am-1pm Sat. *Phone orders* 24hrs daily. **Credit** MC, V.
This wholesaler of educational materials and novelty gifts for schools is also supplier to the general public. One way to make a favourable impression on young party guests would be to give each boy and girl a teddy bear bearing his or her name on a printed sash (£1.85 each for 12 or more). The vast range of toys is equally appealing, running from stretchy aliens (£1.32 for six) to glitter-filled water bracelets (£2.64 for 12). Phone or visit the website for a catalogue.

Party Directory

14 Woodbourne, Farnham, Surrey GU9 9EF (01252 336100/www.partydirectory4kids.co.uk). **Open** *Phone orders* 9.30am-6pm Mon-Fri. **Credit** MC, V.
This mail-order catalogue (available by phone or online) contains everything you need for a celebration. Themed tableware includes paper plates, cups and tablecloths, matching balloons, and invitations in styles such as Pirate's Treasure, Prehistoric or Party Girl (items sold separately). Accessories like conical hats (eight for £1.65), animal masks (50p) and Happy Birthday banners (£1.75) can also be supplied.

Party Pieces

Child's Court Farm, Ashampstead Common, Berks RG8 8QT (01635 201844/www.partypieces.co.uk). **Credit** MC, V.
PP is possibly the best supplier of activities and accessories we've found. Its huge range of themed tableware includes famous faces like the Boohbah and unstoppable Harry Potter (items sold separately), while themes for older kids offer ingenious spins on ever-popular themes: the Action Man jeep-shaped cup holder, for example, or a girlie version in the shape of a stagecoach (both 55p each). There are loads of party-bag fillers, traditional games (the Pin the Tail on the Donkey costs a very reasonable £1.95), and a whopping range of banners, balloons and assorted decorations.

Shops

Balloon & Kite Company

613 Garratt Lane, Earlsfield, SW18 4SU (8946 5962/ www.balloonandkite.com). Tooting Broadway tube/ Earlsfield rail. **Open** 9am-5.30pm Mon-Sat. **Credit** AmEx, MC, V.
Balloons are available in rubber or foil (£1 or £2.99 apiece), bearing pics of screen heroes, names can be added to Happy Birthday variants while you wait (£3.25 each). There's themed paper tableware and banners, while kites (from £10) make good last-minute gifts. Goody-bag stuff starts at 99p for a packet. London delivery is available for orders over £10.

Balloonland

12 Hale Lane, Mill Hill, NW7 3NX (8906 3302/www. balloonland.co.uk). Edgware tube/Mill Hill Broadway rail/ 221, 240 bus. **Open** 9.30am-5.30pm Mon-Fri; 10am-5.30pm Sat. **Credit** MC, V.
Offers a range of products to make children's parties look spectacular. Regular balloons start from 17p each (if bought in bulk) and come in a staggering variety of shapes and sizes.

The choice is inflated further by designer creations (balloon clusters, jumbo balloon trees, balloons attached to soft toys or choc boxes), as well as themed tableware and decorations.

Circus Circus

176 Wandsworth Bridge Road, Fulham, SW6 2UQ (7731 4128/www.circuscircus.co.uk). Fulham Broadway tube. **Open** 10am-6pm Mon-Sat. **Credit** AmEx, MC, V.
If you have a particular kids' party theme in mind, Circus Circus will supply everything that's needed to bring the whole thing to life, from the style of background music to the decorations; staff will even bake the right sort of cake, blow up the right balloons and bring the right entertainer to your home. Individual items are available for those who trust their own event co-ordination skills, including children's costumes from £10.99, invitations, bouncy castles and balloons.

Just Balloons

127 Wilton Road, Victoria, SW1V 1JZ (7434 3039/www. justballoons.com). Victoria tube/rail. **Open** 9am-6pm Mon-Fri; 10am-5pm Sat. **Credit** AmEx, MC, V. **Map** p318 J10.
A thoroughly misleading name: this store offers the complete party package – bunting, bubble blowers, face paints, party poppers et al. Still, the name does give a good indication of the inflatable empire lying behind the tiny doors. Foil balloons come in a range of styles from £2.95 each; balloons can also be printed with personalised messages, although more extravagant types may want to relive some more memorable moment with a printed photograph balloon (£76.38 for 50).

Mexicolore

28 Warriner Gardens, Battersea, SW11 4EB (7622 9577/www.pinata.co.uk). Battersea Park or Queenstown Road rail/44, 137 bus. **Open** by appointment only. **No credit cards.**
Pinatas, smashable targets that are a traditional feature of a Mexican Christmas, are now popular at children's parties in this country. Made of beautifully decorated papier-mâché, they can be filled with fruit, sweets or small toys and are available in various animal forms, from a small fish (£15.95) to a large elephant (£41.95). When you see it you may well feel a pang to think that, come party time, blindfolded guests will queue to whack it with a stick until it's smashed to bits.

The Non-Stop Party Shop

214-16 Kensington High Street, W8 7RG (7937 7200/ www.nonstopparty.co.uk). High Street Kensington tube/ 10, 27, 391 bus. **Open** 9.30am-6pm Mon-Sat; 11am-5pm Sun. **Credit** MC, V. **Map** p314 A9.
A fully operational fun factory, the Non-Stop has themed tableware and dressing-up materials. Hats from around the world (from starchy would-be aristo top hats to the battered Australian bushwhacker headpiece, starting at 99p) are a speciality, otherwise there are plastic animal masks (£2.50) and – to complete the look – face-crayons.

Oscar's Den

127 9 Abbey Road, St John's Wood, NW6 4SL (7328 6683/ www.oscarsden.com). Swiss Cottage tube/West Hampstead tube/rail/28, 31, 139, 189 bus. **Open** 9.30am-5.30pm Mon-Sat; 10am-2pm Sun. **Credit** AmEx, MC, V.
Oscar's Den has a sturdy reputation for excellence, even organising parties for the Prime Minister's children. They don't only co-ordinate grand affairs for the rich and famous, however: celebrations can be tailored to your budget, and their range of services runs from face-paints to year-round firework displays. Ball ponds, bouncy castles (from £40) and big toys (see-saws, slides, pedal cars and more, from £10) are permanently for hire; individual items are always on sale.

Party Party

*11 Southampton Road, Gospel Oak, NW5 4JS
(7267 9084/www.partypartyuk.com). Chalk Farm
tube/Gospel Oak rail/46 bus.* **Open** 9.30am-5.30pm
Mon-Sat. **Credit** MC, V.

Party Party has a bespoke piñata service, offering any
character, animal or object you desire, and a whole catalogue
of party bag fillers, from 15p star stickers to £5 soft toys and
beyond. Fireworks are sold all year round, the decorations
cover everything from themed tableware to mirrorballs, and
there are dressing-up costumes (with prices starting at
around £10) that come with all the usual accessories – pirate
swords, devil forks and angel wings.

Party Superstore

*268 Lavender Hill, Clapham, SW11 1LJ (7924 3210/
www.partysuperstore.co.uk). Clapham Junction rail/
39, 77, 345 bus.* **Open** 9am-6pm Mon-Wed, Fri, Sat;
9am-7pm Thur; 10.30am-4.30pm Sun. **Credit** AmEx,
MC, V.

The first floor of the Superstore is children's party accessories,
fancy-dress costumes (from £7.99), novelty hats (from £1.99)
and wigs (from £2.99); most items are available for hire. There
are also more than 50 themed tableware collections, many of
which are suitable for children, as well as practical jokes,
hundreds of balloons, mock jewellery and a lovely collection
of cake decorations and candles.
Branch: 43 Times Square, High Street, Sutton,
Surrey SM1 1LF (8661 7323).

Purple Planet

*Greenhouse Garden Centre, Birchen Grove, Kingsbury,
NW9 8SA (8205 2200/www.purpleplanet.co.uk). Wembley
Park Station, then 182, 297 bus.* **Open** 10am-5pm Mon-
Sat; 10.30am-4.30pm Sun. **Credit** AmEx, MC, V.

The Purple Planet shop has a vast art and craft section, and
runs regular card-making workshops and free in-store demos.
Many party items are available: helium balloons from 90p, a
good selection of themed tableware and, most importantly,
the fine selection of sugarcraft accessories and cookie cutters
(90p-£19.99) for which the Planet is known. When it comes
to the birthday centrepiece, there's everything you could
think of for a truly magnificent cake, from opulent fountain
candles (£2.50 each) to edible paint.

Venues

All aboard

Golden Hinde

*St Mary Overie Dock, Cathedral Street, Southwark,
SE1 9DE (0870 011 8700/www.goldenhinde.co.uk).
London Bridge tube/rail/21, 35, 43, 133, 214 bus.*
Credit AmEx, MC, V. **Map** p321 P8.

The Golden Hinde has two costumed crew members ready
to greet and lead evil little birthday pirates on a series of
shipshape activities. These include treasure hunts and
storytelling. After that, a sailor's meal of pemmican and
dry biscuits is provided... or rather crisps, sandwiches
and sausage rolls – all you provide is the cake. The
minimum charge is £250 for 15 children (extra kids board
for £15 each), and party bags can be provided. Children
are encouraged to come in costume – preferably as pirates
(cowboys will be made to walk the plank). Regular
sleepovers are organised for more dedicated ocean-goers
looking to rough it in the ship's hold: phone for details.
Shop.

HMS Belfast

*Morgan's Lane, Tooley Street, Bankside, SE1 2JH
(7940 6320/www.iwm.org.uk/belfast). London Bridge
tube/rail.* **Credit** MC, V. **Map** p321 R8.

Who would have thought that the warship *Belfast* would one
day be boarded by armies of under-16s armed with cakes and
fizzy pop? It happens regularly, because, for £75, up to 26
kids (one adult per five children) can take over a party room
within the hull. Parents can provide their own refreshments
or, for an extra £5 per head, on-board caterers supply basic
food and drink (you bring along the cake). A private tour of
the *Belfast*, led by Captain Corky, can be arranged for an extra
£100, during which children can man the bridge, marvel at
the gun turrets and even dress up in costume.
*Café. Nappy-changing facilities. Nearest picnic place:
Potters Fields. Shop.*

London Waterbus Company

*58 Camden Lock Place, Camden Town, NW1 8AF
(7482 2550). Camden Town tube.* **No credit cards.**

With the London Waterbus Company up to 20 children can
take to the water for two hours (£210) or three (£275), with
parents allowed to bring their own food, decorations and
whatever entertainment they see fit (even a clown, providing
he's seaworthy). The route is a return journey between
Camden Lock and Little Venice: which end you start from is
entirely up to you. Parents who can't afford that needn't
resign themselves to dry land: small parties can just buy
standard return fares (£4 kids, £6.20 adults), and break up
the trip with a picnic at one end. Even better, special reduced
rate tickets are available that combine a return boat ride with
entry to London Zoo (£10.70 kids, £14.50 adults).

Cinemas

BFI London IMAX Cinema

*1 Charlie Chaplin Walk, South Bank, Waterloo, SE1 8XR
(0870 787 2525/www.bfi.org.uk). Waterloo tube/rail.*
Credit AmEx, MC, V. **Map** p319 M8.

The sheer scale of this place makes it a dramatic party venue,
and any group of ten or more gets a discounted ticket rate
(kids £4.20, adults £6.20). There are usually four or five films
to choose from at any given time (most tend to last an hour),
all of them suitable for children.
*Buggy access. Café. Disabled access: lift, toilet.
Nappy-changing facilities. Nearest picnic place:
Jubilee Gardens.*

Screen West

*The New Boat House, 136-42 Bramley Road, North
Kensington, W10 6SR (bookings 7565 3102/www.screen
west.co.uk). Latimer Road tube/295 bus.* **Credit** MC, V.

This 74-seat screening room is hired out for parties, with
children bringing along their favourite video or DVD to
watch. A separate function room, complete with sofas, tables,
chairs and a CD player, is used for the tea; it seats up to 30
children. Phone for further information, but expect prices to
start at around £200 for up to two hours.

Museums

Museum of Childhood
at Bethnal Green

*Cambridge Heath Road, Bethnal Green, E2 9PA (8983
5200/recorded info 8980 2415/www.museumofchildhood.
org.uk). Bethnal Green tube/rail/106, 253, 309, 388 bus.*
Credit MC, V.

It's a bomb!
Campaign Paintball

The facilities here include a specially decorated party room, with kitchen facilities and tableware for parents who are bringing food (there's no catering, although staff will take care of the clean-up operations afterwards). More importantly, you can get exclusive use of the soft play area as an optional extra (from 2.55pm). Parents provide their own entertainment, although galleries and exhibits are free to the group until closing (5.50pm), which means dinner may be best left till later. Hire of the party room is £50 for a maximum of 12 kids, with 40 minutes in the soft play area for an extra £30. *Buggy access. Café. Disabled access: toilet. Nappy-changing facilities. Shop. Nearest picnic place: museum grounds.*

Science Museum
Exhibition Road, South Kensington, SW7 2DD (0870 870 4868/science night info 7942 4747/www.science museum.org.uk). South Kensington tube/9, 49, 74, 345 bus. **Admission** free. **Credit** *Café/restaurant* AmEx, MC, V. **Map** p315 D9.
The Science Museum is well known for its child friendliness, and its party options are suitably many and various. Young children can spend a few hours in The Garden (*see p89* **Scient'rific**) before lunch at the Deep Blue restaurant (mini-pizzas or pasta, then jelly and ice-cream) for £4 a head. An extra £24 buys a personalised cake. Older children like IMAX cinema parties: the big-screen birthday includes a meal (£9 per head) and, for the more daring, the 'extreme birthday' involves simulator rides, a film and dinner. For £30 per child, a minimum of five children (and one adult, £25) can book a sleepover with entertainment. An early breakfast is provided. *Buggy access. Cafés. Disabled: lift, toilet. Nappy-changing facilities. Restaurant. Shop.*

Playgrounds & games

Bramley's Big Adventure
136 Bramley Road, North Kensington, W10 6TJ (8960 1515/www.bramleysbig.co.uk). Latimer Road tube/295 bus. **Open** 10am-6pm Mon-Fri; 10am-6.30pm Sat, Sun. Closed 25 Dec, 1 Jan, Aug bank hol. **Credit** AmEx, MC, V.
The sheer quantity of attractions crammed into Bramley's indoor adventure playground (slides, ball ponds, monkey swings) provokes almost deafening chaos when packs of feral children are let loose. Parties cost from £7 per little monster on weekdays and £10 at weekends, offering 75 minutes in the playground followed by 45 minutes in the party room (the party room gets divided by a curtain to separate smaller parties, which is hardly ideal). A choice of hot or cold food is provided (vegetarians are catered for), as are party bags. Silver and gold packages are available (£12 and £14 per child respectively), with extra-large party bags, helium balloons and other treats, and for £12.50 Bramley the Brontosaur spends 15 minutes amusing the kids.
Buggy storage. Café. Disabled access: toilet. Nappy-changing facilities. Shop.

Campaign Paintball
Old Lane, Cobham, Surrey KT11 1NH (01932 865999/ www.campaignpaintball.com). Effingham Junction rail. **Credit** MC, V.
Campaign Paintball is a 200-acre (80ha) playground for the gung-ho, whose owners insist that warlike combat is just a cover for the centre's primary objective: team-building. But children prefer to be lone heroes and infiltrate enemy camps. By planning a Sunday attack, they get the centre when it's

free of City types, and a party package (£25.50 per head) offers kids 300 paintballs to fire at will between 9.30am and 4pm, with a barbecue lunch and awards ceremony after.

Clown Town
222 Green Lanes, Southgate, N13 5UD (8886 7520). Southgate tube/W6, 121, 329 bus. **Open** 10am-7pm daily. **No credit cards.**
Clown Town has all the climbing nets, tree houses and Tarzan ropes needed to help parties go with a swing. For £8.50 each, up to 35 kids (minimum of ten in the week, 12 at weekends) spend an hour clambering, then a second hour in the party room upstairs, where food, drink and going-home bags are provided. There's no top age limit, but there is a 1.45m (4ft 9in) height restriction on entry.
Buggy access. Café. Disabled access: toilet. Nappy-changing facilities. Nearest picnic place: Broomfield Park.

Coram's Fields
93 Guilford Street, Bloomsbury, WC1N 1DN (7837 6138). Russell Square tube. **Open** 9am-dusk daily. **Admission** free (adults admitted only if accompanied by a child under 16). **No credit cards. Map** p317 L4.
The Fields, with their sand pit, climbing frames, a helter-skelter, summer paddling pool and small animal pen (sheep, goats and rabbits), are fabulous for a party. At weekends rooms – with kitchen facilities – may be rented, costing from £32. Parents provide food and entertainment.
Buggy access. Café. Disabled access. Nappy-changing facilities.

Discovery Planet
Surrey Quays Shopping Centre, Redriff Road, Rotherhithe, SE16 7LL (7237 2388/www.discovery-planet.co.uk). Surrey Quays tube. **Open** 10am-6pm Mon-Sat; 11am-5pm Sun. **Credit** (over £10) MC, V.
Parties at Discovery Planet come in gold, silver or bronze packages (£11.99, £9.99 or £7.99 per child, with reduced rates Mon-Thur). Kids get 75 minutes on the extensive indoor playground, followed by 45 minutes in a private party room. The bronze option includes ice-cream, balloons and party bags, silver throws in food from Burger King, and the gold goes large with the party bags, plus foil balloons and a cake.
Buggy access. Disabled access: lift, toilet (nearby in shopping centre). Nappy-changing facilities. Nearest picnic place: Southwark Park.

Kidzmania
28 Powell Road, Clapton, E5 8DJ (8533 5556/www.kidzmania.net). Clapton rail/38, 55, 56, 106, 253 bus. **Open** 10am-6.30pm daily. **No credit cards.**
Kidzmania parties combine 90 minutes on the usual slides, chutes and ropes with another 40 minutes of food and fun in a party room. The price is £8 per child aged one to 12, with a minimum of 12 and a maximum of 40 children involved. As if anyone could possibly have more than 40 friends.
Buggy access. Café. Car park. Nappy-changing facilities.

Laserquest
155 Clarence Street, Kingston-upon-Thames, Surrey KT1 1QT (8974 8484/www.laserquest.co.uk). Kingston rail/65, 131, 281, 418 bus. **Open** noon-10pm Mon-Fri; 10am-10pm Sat, Sun. **No credit cards.**
At Laserquest, two 20-minute games for up to 20 kids (over six years old) cost from £7.30 to £7.90 per child, depending on when they play (weekends are more expensive). Bringing birthday grub is up to you: just make sure the cake isn't of a style that would embarrass a highly decorated space marine.

Paintball Centre
Tithebarns Farm, Tithebarns Lane, Woking, Surrey GU23 7LE (0800 917 0821/www.paintballgames.co.uk). **Open** *Phone enquiries* 9am-5.30pm Mon-Fri; 9am-3pm Sat, Sun. **Credit** MC, V.
Each soldier gets 150 paintballs to fire off during a morning and early afternoon, with a barbecue lunch laid on while the young guns debrief. The day runs from 9.15am to 4pm, with helmets and overalls provided, and prices starting at £17.50 per head (12-17s, minimum of 20 kids on weekdays).

Snakes & Ladders
Syon Park, Brentford, Middx TW8 8JF (8847 0946/ www.syonpark.co.uk). Gunnersbury tube, then 237, 267 bus. **Open** 10am-6pm daily (last entry 5.15pm). **Credit** MC, V.
Children get 90 minutes of madness in the three-tier playground, then half an hour of food and fun in the party room, with a private host to oversee proceedings. Party bags and invitations are provided, and the price is £7.95 per head with cold food (sausage rolls, crisps, sandwiches) or £8.95 with hot food (nuggets, pizza or burger and chips).
Buggy access. Café. Disabled access: toilet. Nappy-changing facilities. Nearest picnic place: Syon Park.

Take in a show

Jackson's Lane
269A Archway Road, Highgate, N6 5AA (Matthew Rose: 8340 5226/www.jacksonslane.org.uk). Highgate tube. **Open** 10am-11pm daily. **Tickets** *Children's shows* £4.50 per person. **Credit** MC, V.
Party rooms can be rented out for after-show dos from £50 for three hours. Catering can be provided by Chef Kwaks at the Veggie House theatre café (8348 7666), though you can also bring your own. Tickets for a performance are reduced to £3.50 for party bookings.
Buggy access. Café. Disabled access: toilets. Nappy-changing facilities. Nearest picnic place: Highgate Wood.

Lyric Theatre
King Street, Hammersmith, W6 0QL (0870 050 0511/ www.lyric.co.uk). Hammersmith tube. **Open** *Enquiries* 10am-6pm Mon-Sat. **Tickets** from £8 adults; £6 concessions, students, under-16s; £5 16-25s (restrictions apply). **Credit** AmEx, DC, MC, V.
The Lyric programmes great birthday entertainment, and parties can be held in the foyer at Café Brera (8741 9291). Two menus are available: a cold one of sandwiches, biscuits and fruit (£4.50 per child), or a hot option of pizza or pasta (£5.50 per child). Parents usually bring the cake. Parties are for a minimum of five and a maximum of 30 kids, and food served at noon or 2pm to coincide with 11am or 1pm performances.
Buggy access. Café. Disabled access: lift, toilet. Nappy-changing facilities. Nearest picnic place: riverside.

Puppet Theatre Barge
Opposite 35 Blomfield Road, Little Venice, W9 2PF (7249 6876/www.puppetbarge.com). Warwick Avenue tube. **Open** Nov-June 3pm Sat, Sun, school hols. July-Oct 2.30pm daily. **Credit** MC, V. **Map** p312 C4.
The barge is a brilliant place for a birthday party. Tickets for the children's performances are £6.50 for kids and £7 for adults, and for £50 extra the boat can be rented out for an hour of fun and feasting once the rest of the audience has left (parents bring the food). Kids can be treated to a private performance, with an hour on the barge afterwards, for £295.
Kiosk (drinks). Nearest picnic place: Rembrandt Gardens.

Sport & Leisure

Shake those potatoes off the couch.

A recent study of more than 24,000 children aged between 12 and 16 carried out at Exeter University's Schools' Health Education Unit found that nearly half the girls and one-third of the boys took less exercise than the equivalent of a brisk ten-minute walk per week. While reports that highlight the increasing levels of obesity among British children have tended to concentrate on the quantity of saturated fat, sugar and salt contained in their food, attention is now shifting to the balance between nutrition and activity. After all, the key to a healthy lifestyle and to effective weight management – for all ages – is simple: calories out must equal calories in.

The Fitness Industry Association's project, Adopt-A-School, which links private gyms to local primary schools, has been piloted in ten areas around the UK. Pupils on the scheme use the exercise equipment and enjoy a healthy breakfast before joining a 'walking bus' to school. The FIA hopes to extend the scheme to 1,600 schools during 2004.

Adopt-A-School recognises not all children enjoy competitive team games, and London offers sport and fitness options to suit all tastes. Where children are concerned, the overwhelming priority has to be a three-letter word: not 'win', but 'fun'.

Many sports have introduced a Sport England-accredited quality assurance scheme, to show that a club is 'safe, effective and child-friendly'. Any organisation holding a 'Clubmark' award, or working to it, will operate to high ethical standards and offer structured coaching and matchplay with qualified instructors and a supportive ethos.

The capital is a great place to watch sport too. London teams boast some of the best footballers and rugby players – union and league – in the world. But the biggest inspiration for children to get sporty must be the tantalising thought that the 2012 Olympic Games might be staged on our doorstep. Now that really would make future generations lace up their trainers and start to exercise!

THINGS TO DO

Athletics

A 2003 survey found the British public thought athletics rather than football should be given the highest sporting profile. That's partly a reflection of achievements by such stars as Paula Radcliffe, but it also shows that track and field is a vibrant sport at grass-roots level. There are 18 different disciplines in athletics; most children, no matter their physical dimensions, will find at least one they're good at.

Athletics coach Maureen Jones (8224 7579, 07956 807689) organises 'Run, Jump, Throw' courses during the school holidays. Aimed at eight- to 15-year-olds, the courses run from 10am to 3pm and cost £13 per day.

South of England Athletics Association

4th Floor, Marathon House, 115 Southwark Street, SE1 0JF (7021 0988/www.seaa.org.uk).
Contact the SEAA for details of clubs around London; otherwise, you can access a national directory at www. british-athletics.co.uk.

The following clubs have sections for young athletes:

Belgrave Harriers *Roger Alsop (until Sept 2005, 8870 5148/www.belgraveharriers.com).*
Blackheath & Bromley Harriers *J Baldwin (01825 768193/www.bandbhac.org.uk).*
Enfield & Haringey AC *Ray Gibbins (8805 6543/www.enfield-haringeyac.co.uk).*
Havering Mayesbrook AC *Jean Tierney (01708 341547/www.havering-mayesbrook.org).*
Newham & Essex Beagles AC *Dave Green (01708 349597).*
Shaftesbury Barnet Harriers *Joyce Smith (01923 672945/www.sbharriers.co.uk).*
Thames Valley Harriers *Kathy Davidson (01895 676513/www.thamesvalleyharriers.com).*
Victoria Park Harriers & Tower Hamlets AC *Brenda Puech (7249 2590/www.vphthac.org.uk).*
Windsor, Slough, Eton & Hounslow AC *Dennis Daly (01753 686169/www.wseac.org.uk).*
Woodford Green AC with Essex Ladies *Keith Hopson (8524 1959/www.woodfordgac-essexl.org.uk).*

Orienteering

The aim of this 'cunning running' is to navigate around a course from one control point to the next with the aid of a special map. For children, it's a great way to make country walks fun. There are nine permanent courses in London and more than 40 in the surrounding countryside. You can proceed at your own pace and most are suitable for buggies. For details of more courses, contact the **British Orienteering Federation** (01629 734042, www.britishorienteering.org.uk); if you're after details of local events, call the **South Eastern Orienteering Association** (8948 6056).

Activities

Badminton & squash

To find the nearest junior development programme, contact the **Badminton Association of England** (01908 268400, www.baofe.co.uk) or **England Squash** (0161 2314499, www.englandsquash.co.uk).

The following all have junior badminton and/or squash departments; phone for prices and times:

Dulwich Sports Club *Giant Arches Road, Burbage Road, SE24 9HP (7274 1242). Herne Hill rail.*
New Grampian Squash Club *Shepherd's Bush Road, W6 7LN (7603 4255). Hammersmith tube.*
New Malden Tennis, Squash & Badminton Club *Somerset Close, New Malden, Surrey KT3 5RG (8942 0539/www.newmaldenclub.co.uk). Malden Manor rail.*
Southgate Squash Club *Walker Cricket Ground, Waterfall Road, N14 7JZ (8886 8381/www.thewalker ground.org.uk). Southgate tube.*
Wimbledon Racquets & Fitness Club *Cranbrook Road, SW19 4HD (8947 5806/ www.wsbc.co.uk). Wimbledon tube/rail.*

Baseball & softball

A single agency, **BaseballSoftballUK** (7453 7055, www.baseballsoftballuk.com), governs the two games. Windsor is an established centre for junior baseball: based at Windsor Boys School, the 12-year-old Little League run by the Windsor Bears attracts some 500 players aged six to 16. For the **London Area Youth League**, contact Ron Pasch (Ron.Pasch@occ.treas.gov); to find a club with junior teams, contact one of the following:

Essex Arrow Juniors *Phil Chesterton (01376 551254) or Geoff Hare (8440 6219).*
London Baseball Association *www.londonsports.com*
London Meteors Baseball & Softball Club *Neil Warne (07770 381308/www.londonmeteors.co.uk).*
South London Ravens *Robin Webb (8251 7050).*
Thames Valley Softball Club *John Middlemist (01189 628469/www.tvsoftball.com).*
Windsor Baseball & Softball Club *John Boyd (07769 655496).*

Basketball

The sport is well organised at junior level, with local leagues all over London and competitions right up to national standard. For clubs, contact regional development manager Steven Alexander (8968 0051) or the **English Basketball Association** (0870 774 4225, www.basketballengland.org.uk). If you're in Hampstead, **NYC Basketball** (8445 2952) runs courses for eight to 16s during the school holidays.

The following clubs have junior programmes:

Brixton Topcats *Brixton Recreation Centre, Station Road, SW9 8QQ (7737 3354).*
Jimmy Rodgers runs mixed sessions from schools and the recreation centre, with players starting as young as six.
Croydon Flyers *Lewis Sports Centre, Maberley Road, SE19 2JH (www.croydonflyers.com).*

A girls' club offering weekend training sessions and matches for nine- to 16-year-olds.
Hackney Academy *SPACE Centre, Hackney Community College, Falkirk St, N1 6HF (01702 298613).* The Academy has 11 teams and some of the best facilities and coaching in the capital. Under-13s upwards welcome.
London United *Harrow High School, Gayton Road, Harrow HA1 2JG (07710 578346).*
This new club has an academy for under-12s upwards. There are plans to establish basketball scholarships at Brunel University for outstanding players.

Boxing

At amateur level, boxing has an impressive safety record; youngsters are simply not powerful enough to inflict the sort of damage that has disfigured the professional game. Nor is the sport, as is so often claimed, only for those seeking 'a way out of the gutter': heavyweight hope Audley Harrison is a university graduate and boxing has returned to some schools. To find a local club, contact the **Amateur Boxing Association of England** (8778 0251, www.abae.org.uk).

Circus skills

The idea of teaching kids to perform potentially dangerous tricks and stunts might strike fear into parents' hearts. Rest assured, safety is always given the highest priority at circus schools.

Albert & Friends Instant Circus

8237 1170/www.albertandfriendsinstantcircus.co.uk.
Albert the Clown (aka Ian Owen) has more than 20 years' experience as a teacher and performer. His Instant Circus workshops teach stilt-, ball- or wire-walking to children with little or no experience. More than 200 kids of all ages and backgrounds attend each week, many of whom go on to join the Albert & Friends' performing troupe – the UK's largest children's circus theatre; it also tours abroad. A&FIC also runs occasional masterclasses in specific disciplines.

Jackson's Lane Community Circus

269A Archway Road, N6 5AA (8340 5226/www.jacksons lane.org.uk). Highgate tube.
Kids' classes include trapeze, rope-climbing and acrobatics.

The Circus Space

Coronet Street, N1 6HD (7613 4141/www.thecircus space.co.uk). Old Street tube/rail.
This powerhouse of contemporary circus runs ten-week courses for over-sevens on Sunday mornings, teaching static and flying trapeze, juggling, club-swinging, diabolo, tumbling, unicycling, stilt-walking and clowning.

Climbing

Climbing demands a unique combination of physical and mental agility, which explains why reaching the top of a wall brings such enormous satisfaction, and a well-structured session with a nurturing instructor

Get up, get on up: **Westway Climbing Complex**. *See p256.*

can help overcome a fear of heights. London's indoor centres cater for children aged around eight-plus. If you want general information on climbing, contact the **British Mountaineering Council** (0870 010 4878).

Castle Climbing Centre
Green Lanes, N4 2HA (8211 7000/
www.castle-climbing.co.uk). Manor House tube.
This atmospheric Grade II-listed Victorian pumping station offers a 120ft (394m) drop for aspiring spiderboys and girls. The centre's children's club, the Geckos, meets on Friday evenings and weekend mornings, plus midweek afternoons in the school holidays. A two-hour session costs £16. The minimum age (unaccompanied) is eight; with a climbing adult, children can be any age (the centre has harnesses for kids aged from about four).

Mile End Climbing Wall
Haverfield Road, E3 5BE (8980 0289/
www.mileendwall.org.uk). Mile End tube.
Located in a converted pipe-bending factory, this centre runs children's sessions every Friday evening and Saturday morning, as well as birthday parties and a holiday programme.

Westway Climbing Complex
Westway Sports Centre, 1 Crowthorne Road, W10 5RP
(8969 0992/www.nkat.org.uk). Latimer Road tube.
Recently upgraded, this indoor centre challenges the best but inspires novices. Its big, chunky holds are perfect for kids.

Cricket

Clubs around the capital have stepped in to develop the game for boys and girls aged six upwards. Many run junior sections, with 11-year-olds and under playing an adapted form of the game called 'terrier cricket', in which everyone gets an equal chance to bat, bowl and field. Safety is to the fore: all under-16s must wear a helmet when batting, keeping wicket or fielding close to the bat against a hard ball. Most clubs will provide all the essential protective equipment until a youngster decides whether they want to play regularly. To find your nearest club, contact the relevant County Board:
Essex *Graham Jelley (01245 254026/*
www.essexcricket.org.uk).
Hertfordshire *Derek Dredge (01707 658377/*
www.hertscricket.org).
Kent *Jamie Clifford (01227 456886).*
Middlesex *Phil Knappett (07768 558090/*
http://middlesexcb.play-cricket.com).
Surrey *Dave Sheppard (7820 5734/*
www.surreycricket.com).

Coaching courses and workshops are available at the following indoor centres:
Ken Barrington Cricket Centre *Brit Oval, SE11 5SS*
(7820 5739). Oval tube.
MCC Indoor School *Lord's Cricket Ground, NW8 8QN*
(7432 1014/www.mcc.org.uk). St John's Wood tube.
Middlesex County Cricket Centre *East End Road,*
N3 2TA (8346 8020). Finchley Central tube.
Peter May Centre *135 Wadham Road, E17 4HR*
(8531 9358). Highams Park rail.

Cycling

In this country, barely two per cent of children cycle to school – a statistic that should raise serious questions about our attitudes both to green transport and to road safety. In response, **Safe Routes to Schools** (01179 150100, www. saferoutestoschools.org.uk) supports projects that encourage children to cycle and walk to school by improving street design, calming traffic and linking with the National Cycle Network, which opened in 2000. Sustrans (www.sustrans.org.uk) is a sustainable transport charity working to create a safer environment for cycling, while the **London Cycling Campaign** (Unit 228, 30 Great Guildford Street, SE1 0HS, 7928 7220, www.lcc.org.uk) acts as an umbrella organisation for local groups. Indeed, the LCC has compiled 19 maps showing cycling routes throughout Greater London. They're free, and available from train stations and sports centres, or from the 24-Hour Travel Information Line on 7222 1234. The best guide to family rides around the capital is the *London Cycle Guide* (Haynes, £8.99), published in association with the LCC.

Cycle sport

For details of kids' clubs, phone the venues.

Herne Hill Velodrome
Burbage Road, SE24 9HE (7737 4647/www.hernehill
velodrome.org.uk). Herne Hill or North Dulwich rail.
Opened in 1892 and used for the 1948 Olympics, the quarter-mile (450m) banked concrete track is among the fastest in the country – and the capital's sole purpose-built velodrome. There's also a new mountain bike track for dramatic bunny-hopping. Pedal Posse mountain-bike camps, cycling skills and proficiency courses are run in the school holidays.

Hillingdon Cycle Circuit
Minet Country Park, Springfield Road, Hayes, Middx
UB4 0LT (8737 7797). Hayes & Harlington rail.
This is a tarmac track, used for both racing and tuition.

Lee Valley Cycle Circuit
Quarter Mile Lane, E10 5PD (8534 6085/
www.leevalleypark.com/cyclecircuit). Leyton tube.
This 45-acre (18ha) site has a tarmac track and mountain bike/BMX circuit. There are Saturday morning sessions for kids aged four to 16.

Cycle training

Cycle Training UK
7582 3535/www.cycletraining.co.uk
Male and female instructors offer individual tuition anywhere in Greater London. The emphasis is on safe, confident road cycling. Accompanied journeys to school are also available.

London Recumbents
7498 6543.
Specialists in off-road training. Special bikes are available so that people of all abilities can enjoy learning to cycle.

London School of Cycling

7249 3779.
Private tuition for adults, teenagers accompanied by adults and people with special needs.

Dance

An exceedingly useful resource for would-be dancers and their parents is the **London Dance Network** (www.londondance.com), which has an extensive directory of dance venues and organisations. The following offer a range of classes for children:
Chisenhale Dance Space *64-84 Chisenhale Road, E3 5QZ (8981 6617/www.chisenhaledancespace.co.uk). Mile End tube.*
Danceworks *16 Balderton Street, W1K 6TN (7629 6183/www.danceworks.co.uk). Bond Street tube.*
Drill Hall *16 Chenies Street, WC1E 7EX (7307 5060/ www.drillhall.co.uk). Goodge Street tube.*
Greenwich Dance Agency (gDA) *Borough Hall, Royal Hill, SE10 8RE (8293 9741/www.greenwich dance.org.uk). Greenwich rail.*
The Place *17 Duke's Road, WC1H 9PY (7387 7669/ www.theplace.org.uk). Euston tube/rail.*
Ravenscourt Theatre School *30-40 Dalling Road, W6 0JB (8741 0707/www.dramaschoollondon.com). Hammersmith tube.*
Rona Hart School of Dance *Rosslyn Hall, Willoughby Road, NW3 1SB (7435 7073). Hampstead tube.*
Tricycle Theatre *269 Kilburn High Road, NW6 7JR (7328 1000/www.tricycle.co.uk). Kilburn tube.*

While some children love the formality of ballet, others prefer the freedom of unusual techniques. **Capoeira**, the Brazilian martial art/dance combo is taught at the Place (*see above*), Amazonas Capoeira (7263 5291, www.amazonas.org.uk) and the London School of Capoeira (7281 2020) to youngsters from the age of eight. **Biodanza** (7485 2369), an expressive form of dance created by psychologist Rolando Toro, is taught in Camden, Hampstead and Covent Garden, while **Dalcroze Eurhythmics** (Hannah Biss, 7794 5119), a whole-body technique used by the Royal Ballet School, is taught to five- to nine-year-olds in north London. There are also the **Chantraine Dance of Expression** (Patricia Woodall, 7435 4247; Kate Green, 8989 8604), taught to over-fours, and the **Medau Society** (01372 729056, www.medau.org.uk), which teaches a natural whole-body dance using hoops, balls, clubs and scarves to emphasise flowing movement.

Fencing

Physically demanding and very skilful, fencing is a cool alternative for those children who don't like team games. Most junior classes comprise warm-ups to develop co-ordination, flexibility and balance, formal work towards the nine fencing grades, and finally the bit everyone enjoys best: free fighting.

Disability sport

As the success of the Paralympic movement and personalities like Tanni Grey-Thompson have shown, disability sport is finally getting the recognition it deserves. The Lottery-funded Integrated Fitness Initiative is helping with the redevelopment of public sports facilities to include accessible equipment.

An interesting scheme involves Wimbledon Football Club, the **Limbless Association** and the One2One Ability Counts programme operated by the English Federation of Disability Sport, along with Surrey FA and the borough of Wandsworth. The partnership provides regular training sessions with qualified coaches for those who have lost one or more limbs, along with opportunities to play in tournaments. The junior squad welcomes players aged seven to 14. For more details, phone 8788 1777 or email football@limbless-association.org.

Meanwhile, the **Back-Up Trust**, a national charity working with people paralysed through spinal cord injury, runs multi-activity weeks for kids aged 13 to 17. Canoeing, abseiling, wheelchair basketball and rugby are included on the programme. A week-long course costs £395 to the charity, with parents asked to contribute the full cost or as much as they can afford. Further information is available from 8875 1805 or www.backuptrust.org.uk.

In addition to the organisations listed below, the following offer sports programmes for children: **British Blind Sport** (01926 424247, www.british blindsport.org.uk), **British Deaf Sports Council** (www.britishdeafsportscouncil.org.uk) and **English Sports Association for People with Learning Disability** (01924 267555, www.esapld.co.uk).

British Wheelchair Sports Foundation

01296 395995/www.britishwheelchairsports.org
The umbrella body for 17 wheelchair sports, from archery to rugby, this foundation organises a number of major events at the National Wheelchair Sports Centre in Stoke Mandeville, Buckinghamshire. It also provides a comprehensive information service and is developing regional sports camps for children with disabilities aged six-plus.

English Federation of Disability Sport

0161 247 5294/www.efds.co.uk
This is the umbrella organisation for disability sport. Its local office is the London Sports Forum for Disabled People (7354 8666, minicom 7354 9554, www.londonsportsforum.org.uk).

Olympic dreams

On 6 July 2005 the 126 members of the International Olympic Committee will cast their votes to decide the venue of the 2012 Games – and one of the world's great cities will never be the same again. London and Paris are reckoned the front-runners, with French hopes bolstered by the fact that the showpiece Stade de France has already hosted football's World Cup final and the World Athletics Championships. However, London's bid leader Barbara Cassani (www.london 2012.org) has pledged that a Games in the capital would be about regeneration and creating a sporting legacy for generations to come.

Despite London's image as a key sporting location, the reality is somewhat different following three decades of underfunding and lack of direction. Unlike many European cities, there is no public ownership of major stadia so top football clubs such as Arsenal and Chelsea have no obligation to allow community access to their facilities. Meanwhile, the project to build a new Wembley Stadium was bedevilled by delays and political wrangling (although it is now on target for completion in early 2006 and is sure to be earmarked for the Olympic football finals). In addition, the abandoned plan to stage the 2005 World Athletics Championships at Picketts Lock is an embarrassment some IOC members will not forget. More apparent to Londoners is the fact that the 33 boroughs have just two Olympic-size (50-metre or 160-foot) swimming pools – one of which is at Crystal Palace, the 40-year-old national sports centre whose survival has long been uncertain.

Undaunted, Tony Blair has pledged absolute support for the £2.5-billion project, which will be paid for by the government, the Mayor of London and the National Lottery. At its launch in January 2004, Mayor Ken Livingstone described London as a city 'representing the Olympic ideal of destroying the barriers that divide us and bringing people together'. If the bid were to succeed, there's little doubt that it would have a huge positive impact on the hitherto neglected boroughs of Newham, Hackney, Tower Hamlets and Waltham Forest.

Seventeen of the 28 sports would be held at sites within a 15-minute bus journey of Stratford, the planned epicentre, utilising largely derelict land and ensuring uses for the facilities after the Games are clearly defined so as to ensure permanent regeneration for one of the poorest areas of the UK. The 80,000-seat Olympic Stadium would become the country's main athletics centre, perhaps with a football club also moving in. An aquatic centre, including an Olympic-sized pool, is to be built even if London doesn't get the Games. In addition, a velodrome, BMX track and three indoor arenas are planned for the 500-acre (200-hectare) Olympic Park. Many of London's other major locations are set to play their part, ensuring that the bid represents the whole of the capital rather than just one part of it. Archery at Lord's, baseball at the Oval, tennis at Wimbledon, triathlon in Hyde Park and equestrian events in Greenwich Park are among the options.

It's a bold and imaginative strategy that, mindful of the need to invest in facilities to help tackle Britain's obesity timebomb, promises improvement to London's sporting infrastructure even if the Games go elsewhere. Should the bid to host the 2012 Olympics actually succeed, though, our children will never have a better chance to take part in sport – and to dream of going for gold.

The sport has a reassuringly strong safety ethic – no one is allowed to participate without a qualified instructor present, and everyone wears protective clothing and a mask. For details of clubs and regional organisers, contact the **British Fencing Association** (8742 3032, www.britishfencing.com). The following clubs offer regular junior sessions:

Egham Fencing Club *Egham Sports Centre, Vicarage Road, Egham, Surrey TW20 8NL (Mick Johnson 01483 504770). Egham rail.*

Finchley Foil Fencing Club *Copthall School, Pursley Road, Mill Hill, NW7 2EP (Clare Halsted 7485 1498). Mill Hill East tube, then 221 bus.*

Haverstock Fencing Club *Haverstock School, Haverstock Hill, NW1 8AS (Jackie Harvey 07811 077048). Belsize Park tube.*

King's College School & Wimbledon High School Joint Fencing Club *Southside Common, SW19 4TT (8255 5300). Wimbledon tube/rail.*

Richmond & Twickenham Fencing Club *Clifden Centre, Clifden Road, Twickenham, Middx TW1 4LT (8843 7921). Twickenham rail.*

Salle Paul Fencing Club *Highgate School, The Old Gym, Hampstead Road, N6 4AY (Ziemek Wojciechowski 07889 014376). Highgate tube.*

Streatham Fencing Club *Dunraven Lower School, Mount Nod Road, SW16 2QB (Roger Barnes 8677 6207/www.streathamfencing.org). Streatham Hill rail.*

Football

Football dominates the British sporting scene. More than 45,000 clubs cater for all standards and ages, and both sexes. When helping your child to find a team to play for, ask about:

● Whether the club holds or is working towards the FA Charter Mark and whether its coaches hold FA qualifications. If possible, watch a session to see how well organised it is.

● The number of children in each age group. Some clubs have large memberships, which may mean only the best get to play regularly.

• The atmosphere and ethos: is it a club where winning is all that matters, or is 'sport for all' the priority? Are parents and supporters encouraged to lend a hand, and is their contribution valued?

If you're looking for a girls' team, phone the **Football Association** (7745 4545) or check their website (www.TheFA.com/women).

Coaching

All the professional clubs in London run **Football in the Community** coaching courses, fun days and skills clinics. These are suitable for boys and girls of all standards, aged from about six, and are staffed by FA-qualified coaches. Phone the numbers below or check the club websites (*see p273*) for details: **Arsenal** (7704 4140); **Brentford** (8758 9430); **Charlton Athletic** (8850 2866); **Chelsea** (0870 300 2322); **Crystal Palace** (8768 6000); **Fulham** (7384 4759); **Leyton Orient** (8556 5973); **Millwall** (7740 0503); **Queens Park Rangers** (8740 2509); **Tottenham Hotspur** (8365 5000); **Watford** (01923 440449); **West Ham United** (7473 7720).

Similar schemes operate through the **County FAs.** Call the following for details: **Essex** (01245 357727); **Hertfordshire** (01462 677622); **Kent** (01634 843824); **London** (0870 774 3010); **Middlesex** (8424 8524); **Surrey** (01372 373543).

A highly rated scheme is run by former QPR goalkeeper **Peter Hucker.** This is based in Newham, Barking and Wanstead, and offers weekly coaching, matchplay and football parties for all abilities aged five to 16. Hucker also founded the **East London & Essex Small-Sided Soccer League.** Details are available from 07931 901140, www.peterhucker-soccer.com.

There are plenty of commercial football clinics to choose from. An **Ian St John Soccer Camp** (0845 230 0133, www.soccercamps.co.uk), for example, costs £70 for five days (10am-3.45pm) and caters for children aged eight to 15. **European Football Camps** (www.footballcamps.co.uk) is also worth checking out, and there are eight **Powerleague** (www.powerleague.co.uk) centres around London, all of which have regular leagues for under-12s, -14s and -16s, as well as courses and a party package.

Golf

The English Golf Union (01526 354500, www.english golfunion.org) has realised that golf needs to do more to encourage youngsters. Accordingly, they've developed **Tri-Golf** for six- to 12-year-olds, and are working to introduce the game in primary schools. A driving range is a great place to introduce the basics and the professional based there will offer lessons.

Beckenham Place Park
The Mansion, Beckenham Place Park, Beckenham, Kent BR3 2BP (8650 2292).
Juniors can use this course at any time. Lessons are available on Saturdays at 11am and cost £2 (booking essential). It costs £6.50 to play a round or £4.50 for nine holes.

Regent's Park Golf & Tennis School
North Gate, Outer Circle, Regent's Park, NW1 4RL (7724 0643/www.rpgts.co.uk).
Children who are 'old enough to take instruction' are welcome (the coaches have taught golf-mad kids as young as five). Junior membership is £30; the Saturday afternoon clinic costs £5 per hour (book in advance); club hire is £1.

Driving ranges

A1 Golf Driving Range *Rowley Lane, Arkley, Herts EN5 3HW (8447 1411). Elstree & Borehamwood rail.*
Chingford Golf Range *Waltham Way, E4 8AQ (8529 2409). Chingford rail, then 313 bus.*
Chiswick Bridge Golf Range *Great Chertsey Road, W4 2SH (8995 0537/www.golflessons.co.uk). Hammersmith tube, then 190 bus.*
Cranfield Golf Academy *Fairways Golf Centre, Southend Road, E4 8TA (8527 7692/www.cga-golf.com). Walthamstow Central tube/rail.*
Croydon Golf Driving Range *175 Long Lane, Addiscombe, Croydon, Surrey CRO 7TE (8656 1690/ www.golfinsurrey.com). East Croydon or Elmers End rail.*
Ealing Golf Range *Rowdell Road, Northolt, Middx UB5 6AG (8845 4967). Northolt tube.*
Warren Park Golf Centre *Whalebone Lane North, Chadwell Heath, Essex RM6 6SB (8597 1120/www.jjb. co.uk). Dagenham Heathway tube.*
World of Golf *Kingston Bypass, New Malden, Surrey KT3 4PH (8949 9200/www.worldofgolf-uk.co.uk). New Malden or Raynes Park rail.*

Gymnastics & trampolining

The **British Amateur Gymnastics Association** (01952 820330, www.baga.co.uk) has around 100,000 members. Its clubs and schools run sessions for four-year-olds and under, based around soft-play equipment and simple games, leading to a series of proficiency awards. The **British Trampoline Federation** (same contact) has a similar structure.

How and when should small children be taught using adult equipment? Bill Cosgrove, a former national gymnastics coach, answered the question by creating **TumbleTots** and, later, **Gymbabes** and **Gymbobs**. Gymbabes is for babies from six months to the crawling stage, TumbleTots is for walkers, and Gymbobs is for school age up to seven. For details of centres around the country, call 0121 585 7003 or contact www.tumbletots.com.

The following clubs offer a range of activities. Be sure that any club you choose displays a current certificate of inspection by BAGA or the London Gymnastics Federation (8529 1142).

Avondale Gymnastics Club *Hollyfield Road, Surbiton, Surrey KT5 9AL (8399 3386). Surbiton rail.*

Hillingdon School of Gymnastics *Victoria Road, South Ruislip, Middx HA4 0JE (8841 6666). South Ruislip tube.*
IGC *King's Hall Leisure Centre, 39 Lower Clapton Road, Hackney, E5 0NU (8983 6799). Hackney Central rail.*
North-East London Gymnastics Club *Newham Leisure Centre, 281 Prince Regent's Lane, Newham, E13 8SD (8983 6799). Prince Regent DLR.*
Plumstead Leisure Centre *Speranza Street, SE18 1NX (8855 8289). Plumstead rail.*
Redbridge School of Gymnastics *Pulteney Road, E18 1AP (8530 3810). South Woodford tube.*
Richmond Gymnastics Centre *Townmead Road, Kew, Surrey TW9 4EL (8878 8682). Kew Gardens rail.*

Ice skating

Ice rink session times vary from day to day (the ice needs regular refreezing and sweeping), but venues generally open from 10am until 10pm. Prices below include skate hire, unless otherwise stated. For more information about the sport, contact the **National Ice Skating Association** (0115 853 3100, www.iceskating.org.uk).

Alexandra Palace Ice Rink
Alexandra Palace Way, N22 7AY (8365 4386). Wood Green tube/Alexandra Palace rail/W3 bus.
A six-week course of lessons at this international-size rink costs from £44. Parties are also available.

Broadgate Ice Arena
Broadgate Circle, Eldon Street, EC2M 2QS (7505 4068/ www.broadgateestates.co.uk). Liverpool Street tube/rail. **Admission** £7; £4 under-16s.
This tiny outdoor rink is open from late October to April.

Lee Valley Ice Centre
Lea Bridge Road, E10 7QL (8533 3154). Clapton rail. **Admission** *Mon-Thur* £4.70; £3.70 under-15s. *Fri-Sun* £4.80; £3.70 under-15s. *Skate hire* £1.30.
Rink management says Lee Valley has high-quality ice (it certainly feels hard enough when you land on it) and the warmest skating environment in the UK.

Leisurebox
17 Queensway, W2 4QP (7229 0172). Bayswater or Queensway tube. **Admission** £5.50. *Skate hire* £1.
The most famous rink in London, where top skaters have learned their moves. The disco nights are legendary, but beginners are also well looked after.

Michael Sobell Leisure Centre
Hornsey Road, N7 7NY (7609 2166/www.aquaterra.org). Finsbury Park tube/rail. **Admission** £3.20; £3 parent & toddler session.
Children from four upwards are welcome at this small rink, which runs popular after-school sessions. A six-week course of lessons costs £33. You can also hold parties here.

Somerset House
Strand, WC2R 1LA (7845 4600/www.somerset-house.org. uk). Holborn or Temple tube (closed Sun). **Admission** *Courtyard & terrace* free. *Skating* phone to check.
Every December (ring for the exact date), the courtyard here is iced over for a limited season; the ice has usually melted by mid January. Be prepared to queue.

Streatham Ice Arena
386 Streatham High Road, SW16 6HT (8769 7771/ www.streathamicearena.co.uk). Streatham rail. **Admission** £6.80.
A six-week course of lessons costs £45 for adults, £40 for children and £35 for 'toddlers' aged up to four.

Karting & motor sports

Instruction is given at all tracks, but modern karts are easy to grasp, consisting of just two pedals (an accelerator on the right, a brake on the left). There is no gearbox, so all your child needs to do is concentrate on steering, braking and accelerating.

The karting venues listed below welcome children and can be booked for parties. Watch out for others, which are geared towards the corporate market and not so friendly to kids. Brands Hatch is arguably Britain's most complete motor-sports centre.

Brands Hatch
Fawkham, Longfield, Kent DA3 8NG (01474 872331/ www.motorsportvision.co.uk).
Since being taken over by Motor Sport Vision Ltd, Brands Hatch has become the country's most impressive on-track activity venue. There are almost too many things to do here, on two and four wheels, including 'Early Drive', which puts your youngster in control of an Audi A2 – a quite brilliant educational concept that should be adopted everywhere.

F1 City
Gate 119, Connaught Bridge, Royal Victoria Dock, E16 2BS (7476 5678/www.f1city.co.uk). Royal Albert DLR.
This kart track is the widest in London and nearly half a mile (800m) long. Children who meet the minimum height requirement (1.57m or 5ft 2in) are given their own track times, while the Cadet Club provides a place to learn how to kart safely.

Playscape Pro Racing
390 Streatham High Road, SW16 6HX (8677 8677/ www.playscape.co.uk). Streatham rail.
This centre can be booked for children's parties (aged eight-plus) or for half-hour taster sessions. Those who become addicted can find out about the Playscape Cadet School, a founder member of the RAC's Association of Racing Kart Schools. The school operates on the first Saturday of each month (8.30am-12.30pm; cost £30) and students are put through their paces before gaining an RAC racing licence.

Martial arts

See also p264 **Martial lore.**

Bob Breen Academy
16 Hoxton Square, N1 6NT (7729 5789/www.bobbreen. co.uk). Old Street tube.
This excellent centre runs Saturday morning kung fu classes for children aged seven upwards.

The Budokwai
4 Gilston Road, SW10 9SL (7370 1000). Gloucester Road/South Kensington tube.
The Budokwai is one of Britain's premier martial arts clubs. For children, it runs programmes of judo tuition for the six to 12 age group.

Hwarang Academy... pow!

Hwarang Academy
The Place, 17 Duke's Road, WC1H 9PY (7348 3963/ hwarangacademy.com). Euston tube.
Tae kwondo, a martial art that originated in Korea, is now an Olympic sport. Youngsters aged from eight to 18 can learn its spectacular kicks here.

Jackson's Lane Community Centre
269A Archway Road, N6 5AA (8340 5226/ www.jacksonslane.org.uk). Highgate tube.
Drop-in kung fu classes for six- to 12-year-olds.

School of Japanese Karate (Shotokan International)
Various venues in north London (8368 6249).
Karate is the most popular Japanese martial art in this country. There are no holds or grappling, just strikes and kicks. David and Lilian Alleyn run this well-established school, teaching children aged five and over at venues in Southgate, Arnos Grove and Enfield.

Riding

The riding schools listed below all welcome children. Some run 'Own a Pony' events, which involve a lucky rider's parents paying about £40 (for a day) or more than £100 (for a week) for the privilege of looking after their favourite pony in the school: mucking out, grooming, feeding and watering, exercising and schooling. Riding is usually included. Many places offer birthday party packages, while most also cater for riders with disabilities.

Riding lessons and hacks must be booked in advance: it's often worth asking whether there are 'taster' sessions for newcomers. Riders, whatever their age, should always wear a hard hat (establishments can usually provide one if you don't have your own, sometimes for a small fee) and boots with a small heel, rather than trainers or wellies. Your child's bottom will thank you for being made to wear sturdy trousers or jodhpurs. The rates given are for children, per hour.

Aldersbrook Riding School
Empress Avenue, E12 5HW (8530 4648). Manor Park rail. **Lessons** from £7.
This is a small, friendly school with a countryside feel to it. There are eight ponies and four horses working here. Lessons take place in an outdoor manège, hacking on Wanstead Flats.

Ealing Riding School
Gunnersbury Avenue, W5 3XD (8992 3808). Ealing Common tube. **Lessons** £18.

This school is benevolent towards children. Riders, from as young as five, even take part in occasional gymkhanas.

Hyde Park & Kensington Stables
Hyde Park Stables, 63 Bathurst Mews, W2 2SB (7723 2813/www.hydeparkstables.com). Lancaster Gate tube. **Lessons** *Individual £50 Mon-Fri; £60 Sat, Sun. Course of 10 £425-£495.*
From the age of five, kids can enjoy hour-long instruction sessions with patient, streetwise ponies in the glamorous surroundings of Hyde Park. All rides must be booked in advance.

Lee Valley Riding Centre
71 Lea Bridge Road, Leyton, E10 7QL (8556 2629). Clapton rail/48, 55, 56 bus. **Lessons** (1hr) £17 4-6.30pm Mon-Fri, all day Sat, Sun; (30mins) £11 beginners Sat, Sun.
A well-appointed school, where 28 placid horses and ponies enjoy the open spaces of Walthamstow Marshes. During hot weather some hacking out is available to regulars.

London Equestrian Centre
Lullington Garth, N12 7BP (8349 1345). Mill Hill East tube, then 221 bus. **Lessons** *from £10.*
This busy yard in North Finchley has 30 assorted horses and ponies; some are delightfully placid and deservedly popular with local children (minimum age four). There's a junior members' club for regulars, who may be able to take part in informal gymkhanas. There's also a restaurant on site.

Mudchute Equestrian Centre
Pier Street, E14 9HP (7515 0749). Crossharbour & London Arena or Mudchute DLR. **Lessons** £16/hr; £1.50 under-7s.
Members of the Mudchute arm of the Pony Club take part in club activities and gymkhanas. All new clients join the waiting list. As part of a city farm, Mudchute's birthday package involves both fun on the farm and a pony ride.

Ross Nye's Riding Stables
8 Bathurst Mews, W2 2SB (7262 3791). Lancaster Gate tube. **Lessons** £40/hr.
Children aged from six can learn here (instructional rides take place in Hyde Park), with club members able to join in good-value Pony Club Days in Christmas holidays (from £30/day) and take part in week-long pony camps at a Surrey farm.

Trent Park Equestrian Centre
Bramley Road, N14 4XS (8363 9005). Oakwood tube. **Lessons** £19/hr.
A benevolent attitude towards young riders (aged from four) and excellent hacking out in Trent Park (£25/hr) make this a fabulous place to ride.

Willowtree Riding Establishment
The Stables, Ronver Road, SE12 0NG (8857 6438). Grove Park or Lee rail, then 261 bus. **Lessons** *from £8.20/30mins; from £14.50/hr.*

Scrum on down

The exploits of the England rugby team at the 2003 World Cup certainly brought the 15-a-side game to wide attention. What's more, after Jonny Wilkinson's last-minute drop-kick won the final, thousands of children stopped trying to bend it like Beckham and instead began clasping their hands in front of them and copying the England hero's unique kicking style. The following weekend, the 100-plus rugby clubs around London reported hordes of new arrivals at their junior coaching sessions, many wearing pristine England shirts with number 10 on the back.

Already one of the most proactive of governing bodies, in a sport with established programmes for kids, the **Rugby Football Union** (Twickenham Stadium, Whitton Road, Twickenham, Middx TW1 1DZ, 8892 2000, www.rfu.com) moved quickly to capitalise on this surge of interest. Within days, its website was offering a postcode-based search facility for clubs, and this remains the best way to find out what's available in your area.

Most rugby union clubs cater for boys and girls with 'minis' from around six years old, 'midi rugby' at under-11 and 'youth rugby' from 13. Great emphasis is placed on the fun skills of handling, passing and running, while tackling, scrummaging and kicking are gradually introduced and carefully controlled. Primary-age children usually play non-contact 'tag' rugby, using a belt worn around the waist with two 'tags' attached. If an opponent removes a tag, possession switches to the other team. This is an ideal game for both sexes to play

together. Women's and girls' rugby have made rapid progress in recent years – England's women are the 2004 Six Nations champions – and many clubs are now fully integrated with training sessions and programmes of matches. Again, the RFU is an excellent source of information.

WATCHING RUGBY UNION
Twickenham is one of the biggest and most magnificent stadia in the country. However, you'll need to be a rugby club member or have the right connections to get tickets for internationals – although admission is easier to lesser games such as the Powergen Cup final, County Championship final and Zurich Premiership final in April and May each year. A tour of the stadium or visit to the **Museum of Rugby** (see p144) is also worthwhile.

London Wasps and London Irish retain a link with the capital in their name, but have moved to High Wycombe and Reading respectively. That leaves Saracens and Harlequins as the only two fully professional clubs in London. Both play in the Zurich Premiership and European competitions. Unlike top-flight football, you can 'pay on the day' at all but the biggest matches, and ticket prices are much more affordable than the ground-ball alternative – children are treated as future fans rather than a discounted inconvenience. Below the Zurich Premiership is the National League, which offers a high standard of play but fewer spectators and a traditional atmosphere. The season runs from late August to May.

For details of the London teams, *see p274.*

Activities

Mudchute Equestrian Centre: every young girl's dream. *See p262.*

Activities

The team of shaggy Shetlands at this friendly local venue are great for small children to sit on. Little learners dream of moving on to the more glamorous Arab ponies.

Wimbledon Village Stables

24A-B High Street, SW19 5DX (8946 8579/www.wv stables.com). Wimbledon tube/rail. Lessons from £30/hr Wimbledon's riding club (phone for membership details) allows children all sorts of perks to feed their pony habit, including gymkhanas, newsletters and special events. Riding is on Wimbledon Common.

Rugby league

The 13-a-side game is finally building a profile in the capital. The London Broncos (*see p274*) are drawing bigger and bigger crowds to their Super League matches, while much development is taking place at a lower level. The London Skolars and South London Storm compete in the National League and are working alongside the Broncos to introduce rugby league in schools around London. To find out more about the sport, contact the **Rugby Football League** (0113 232 9111, www.rfl.uk.com).

Greenwich Admirals *14 Mulgrave Road, Woolwich, SE18 5TY (Alan Bacon 07734 082754/ www.greenwichrl.com).*
London Skolars *New River Stadium, White Hart Lane, N22 8QW (8888 8488/www.skolars.com).*
South London Storm *Streatham-Croydon Rugby Club, 159 Brigstock Road, Thornton Heath, Surrey CR7 4JP (Dave Bold 8650 0691/www.southlondonstorm.co.uk).*

Rugby union

See p262 **Scrum on down**; for details of London teams, *see p274.*

Skateboarding & BMXing

That fewer and fewer parents fail to recognise terms like 'hot-dogging', 'double deckers' and 'hanging ten' is a testament to skateboarding's continuing popularity with kids. The sport retains its cool and radical edge, with children skating for free at traditional haunts like the South Bank, Shell Centre and beneath the Westway, but the centres listed below offer a more structured environment.

Harrow Skatepark

Christchurch Avenue (behind the leisure centre), Harrow, Middx HA3 5BD (8424 1754/www.harrowskatepark. co.uk). Harrow & Wealdstone tube/rail.
Years of abuse have resulted in the slow deterioration of Harrow's many obstacles, but there's still plenty here to keep dedicated riders happy. The cloverleaf and kidney bowls are always popular, while the unforgiving concrete half-pipe remains a monumental and irresistible challenge for more fearless urban athletes.

Meanwhile 3

Meanwhile Gardens, off Great Western Road, W10 5BN (no phone). Westbourne Park tube.
There are three concrete bowls of varying size and steepness, but no flatland for practising the basics, so beginners may be better off at the PlayStation Skate Park round the corner. Still,

there's huge potential for more accomplished riders: the bowls are linked from high ground to low, offering the possibility of long, technical lines as well as suicidal transfer attempts.

PlayStation Skate Park
Bay 65-6, Acklam Road, W10 5YU (8969 4669/ www.pssp.co.uk). Ladbroke Grove tube.
PS:SP has revolutionised the London scene. Sheltered beneath the A40, and lent an apocalyptic air by the artics thundering overhead, this enormous park includes two half-pipes, a long mini-ramp plus funboxes, grind boxes, ledges and rails.

Stockwell Park
Stockwell Road (next to Brixton Cycles), SW9 9TN (no phone). Brixton tube/rail.
A concrete wonderland constituting a single, unbroken series of bumps, hips, waves, bowls and lips, perfect for sequences of tricks or just good old-fashioned carve-ups. The park offers grand scope for riders of varying ability. The lack of rails and ledges might put off more technical skaters, but those seeking fun, pure and simple, have to try pretty hard not to fall for this place, for all that it needs serious refurbishment.

Skiing & snowboarding

Practice on a dry slope makes excellent preparation for the real thing, but gloves, long sleeves and trousers are compulsory if you want to avoid nasty burns when you fall. If you're taking a mixed-ability group out for an open recreational session, perhaps a birthday party, each group member must be able to perform a controlled snowplough turn and use the ski lift. A spate of closures has left just a handful of ski centres within reach of the capital, but the much-vaunted redevelopment of the 'Beckton Alp' into London's own real-snow centre is still a possibility. Contact the **Ski Club of Great Britain** (8410 2000, www.skiclub.co.uk) for developments.

Bromley Ski Centre
Sandy Lane, St Paul's Cray, Orpington, Kent BR5 3HY (01689 876812). St Mary Cray rail.
Three lifts serve the 120m (394ft) main slope; there's also a mogul field and nursery slope. Skiing and snowboarding taster sessions cost £15 for half an hour; book in advance.

Sandown Sports Club
More Lane, Esher, Surrey KT10 8AN (01372 467132/ www.sandownsports.co.uk). Esher rail.
The 120m (394ft) main slope, 80m (262ft) nursery area and 90m (295ft) snowboarding slope close during horse racing meetings. This is a lessons-only venue: tuition is available for seven-year-olds upwards, although special half-hour classes can be arranged for children as young as four.

Snozone
Xscape, 602 Marlborough Gate, Milton Keynes MK9 3XS (0871 222 5670/www.xscape.co.uk). Milton Keynes Central rail.
Before the opening of the Castleford Xscape (just outside Leeds) in October 2003, this was the UK's largest indoor snow dome. It has three slopes (in reality they are joined, so they resemble one wide slope): two at 170m (549ft) and one at 135m (443ft), with button lifts running all the way to the top. *See also p289* **The future's white**.

Martial lore

The fabled Sonshan Shaolin Temple in China's Henan province is where *gong fu* (kung fu) comes from, dating back more than 1,500 years. However, there is worldwide interest in Shaolin culture and monks are now sent by the temple to teach and promote their way of life. In 1998 the 34th-generation fighting monk Shifu Shi Yanzi was dispatched to dreary old London to set up the first European branch of the temple. **Shaolin Temple UK** (207A Junction Road, N19 5QA, 7687 8333, www.shaolintempleuk.org; annual membership £60 or £40 for under-12s, plus £3 per class) is based in Tufnell Park. There, Shi Yanzi and several other Shaolin masters now teach Shaolin *gong fu*, meditation and t'ai chi, with weekly classes for children included on the programme.

Every weekday at 5pm and on Sunday mornings at 9.30am you'll find Shi Yanzi and his team adapting *gong fu*'s powerful kicks and moves to suit young bodies aged from six to 15. The emphasis in the one-hour classes is on boosting confidence and self-discipline by developing balance, flexibility and co-ordination, plus basic self-defence skills. Improved fitness is a natural by-product – along with the chance to boast about working out with some of the coolest monks this side of the Great Wall of China.

It's hardly surprising that all martial arts are appealing to kids – after all, they feature in countless computer games. They're exotic, offering a glimpse of cultures that children may have studied at school. They require interesting clothes (often supplied by a club as part of the membership fee). Many have grading systems with belts and badges, while some offer tournaments and demonstrations. But most importantly, martial arts impart valuable skills for children learning to cope with life's rough and tumble.

Most sports centres will be home to at least one martial arts club; many more are based in church halls and community centres. Look for evidence of a disciplined atmosphere, with well-organised and age-appropriate teaching. Ask the instructor about his or her qualifications – the grading systems used in judo and karate, for example, help to ensure that teachers are of a suitable standard. However, note that a black belt is not a teaching qualification. Also ask for proof of insurance cover: martial arts usually involve physical contact and accidents can happen. What's more, few community facilities extend their insurance to the instructors who rent them.

For details of venues that offer martial arts classes for children, *see p260*.

Activities

Airborne at **PlayStation Skate Park**.
See p264.

Swimming

Swimming can be a matter of life and death, yet one in five children leave primary school unable to swim. Most local authority pools run lessons for kids aged from around three upwards, plus parent and baby sessions to develop water confidence from as young as three months. These can be oversubscribed, however, with long waiting lists. Ask at your local pool for a timetable and booking details.

When children are past the lesson stage, joining a club is the best way to improve, meet like-minded friends and, perhaps, swim competitively. Again, look on the noticeboards and ask at your local pool, or contact the **Amateur Swimming Association** (01509 618700, www.britishswimming.co.uk) for a list of clubs in your area.

Dolphin Swimming Club
University of London Pool, Malet Street, WC1E 7HY (8349 1844). Goodge Street tube. **Class times** 9.15am-3.45pm Sat; 9.15am-12.45pm Sun. **Cost** £214.50/11 individual 30min lessons; £73.70/11 30min small-group sessions (max 5/group).
The Dolphin Swimming Club teaches aquaphobic children (and adults) to overcome their fear, and takes children from about three years old all the way to gold standard. The club also teaches diving and life-saving.

Leander Swimming Club
Balham Leisure Centre, Elmfield Road, SW17 8AN (Sarah Cannell 7733 1071/www.leanderswimming club.org.uk). Balham tube/rail. **Class times** phone for details. **Membership** £26-£37/mth; £4.75/session.
Named after a Greek mythological character who swam huge distances to visit his lover, Leander offers a programme for children from seven years old and hosts sessions in Balham, Tooting, Crystal Palace and Dulwich.

Swimming Nature
0870 900 8002/www.swimmingnature.co.uk
Since 1992 Swimming Nature has taught thousands of London children to swim using a controlled, progressive, hands-on method. Lessons are held in Brondesbury, Chelsea, Paddington, Regent's Park, Twickenham and Victoria, with courses held to coincide with school terms.

Cool pools

Most pools are 25-metre-long (80-foot) rectangles. For different reasons, these are a little bit special:
Barnet Copthall Pools *Great North Way, NW4 1PS (8457 9900). Mill Hill East tube.*
Three pools and a diving area, with coaching and clubs to join if you fancy taking the plunge.

Finchley Lido.

Crystal Palace National Sports Centre *Ledrington Road, SE19 2BB (8778 0131). Crystal Palace rail.*
The city only has two Olympic-sized (50m/160ft) pools, this being one. It also has excellent diving facilities. The centre's future now looks secure.
Finchley Lido *Great North Leisure Park, High Road, N12 0AE (8343 9830). East Finchley tube.* **Open** *May-Sept* 9am-9.30pm Mon-Fri; 9am-4.30pm Sat, Sun.
Admission £3.10; £1.85 concessions.
There are two indoor pools here, and in the summer a small outdoor terrace and pool are a magnet for kids. Closed for refurbishment until 24 July 2004.
Gurnell Leisure Centre *Ruislip Road East, W13 0AL (8998 3241). Ealing Broadway tube, then E2, E7, E9 bus.*
This is the other Olympic-sized pool.
Ironmonger Row Baths *1-11 Ironmonger Row, EC1V 3QF (7253 4011/www.aquaterra.org). Old Street tube.*
Take a trip back in time at this 1930s 30m (100ft) pool and Turkish baths (one of only three remaining in London).
Kingfisher Leisure Centre *Fairfield Road, Kingston, Surrey KT1 2PY (8546 1042). Kingston rail.*
Super-friendly, Kingfisher has a teaching pool and main pool with beach and wave machine. Won 'best for families' in 2004's *Time Out* Sport, Health & Fitness Awards.

Latchmere Leisure Centre *Burns Road, Battersea, SW11 5AD (7207 8004). Clapham Junction rail.*
In addition to the lane-swimming main pool, Latchmere has a teaching pool and beach area with wave machine and slide to laze about in.
Queen Mother Sports Centre *223 Vauxhall Bridge Road, SW1V 1EL (7630 5522). Victoria tube.*
Three excellent pools in this recently refurbished centre, always popular with schoolkids.
Tottenham Green Leisure Centre *1 Philip Lane, N15 4JA (8489 5322). Seven Sisters tube.*
Lane-swimming and diving in the main pool or splashing amid the waves and slides in the 'beach pool'.
York Hall Leisure Centre *Old Ford Road, E2 9PJ (8980 2243). Bethnal Green tube.*
Built in the 1920s as a bath house, York Hall still houses Turkish and Russian baths. The 33m (110ft) main pool and separate children's pool have real East End character.

Out in the open

Have a dip, have a sunbathe, eat an ice-cream… London's open-air pools have a lot to recommend them when it's sweltering in the city.

Evian Lido *Brockwell Park, Dulwich Road,*
SE24 0PA (7274 3088). Herne Hill rail.
The future of this wonderful '30s lido is constantly
in doubt. Enjoy it while you can.
Hampstead Heath Swimming Ponds *(7485 4491)*
Men's & women's ponds *Millfield Lane, N6.*
Gospel Oak rail.
Mixed pond *Southend Green, NW3. Hampstead Heath rail.*
Open to children over eight who can swim at least 25m
(80ft) and are accompanied by an adult. Admission is free
and the setting simply lovely.
Hampton Pool *High Street, Hampton, Middx TW12*
2ST (8255 1116). Hampton rail.
This 36m (120ft) outdoor pool has a small slide, diving
board and, thank your lucky stars, heating! What's more,
it's open 365 days a year – the annual Christmas Day dip
is a popular local attraction.
Oasis Sports Centre *32 Endell Street, WC2H 9AG*
(7831 1804). Tottenham Court Road tube.
The 28m (92ft) outdoor pool is, as the name suggests, a
real oasis in the heart of the capital. Open year round.
Parliament Hill Lido *Gordon House Road, NW5 2LT*
(7485 3873). Gospel Oak rail.
You can swim free before 9am, after that a family ticket
costs £7.50. Full refurbishment is planned for late 2004.

Pools on the Park *Springhealth Leisure Club,*
Old Deer Park, Twickenham Road, Richmond, Surrey
TW9 2SF (8940 0561). Richmond rail.
A 33m (110ft) heated indoor pool, with one the same
size and temperature outside, plus a sunbathing area.
Tooting Bec Lido *Tooting Bec Road, SW16 1RU*
(8871 7198). Tooting Bec tube.
At 94m long and 25m wide (310ft by 80ft), this art deco
lido is the second largest open-air pool in Europe.

Water games

The leisure centres that we've listed below all
have flumes, wave machines or other devices that
should keep the children (and the young at heart)
properly entertained:

Brentford Fountain Leisure Centre

658 Chiswick High Road, Brentford, Middx TW8 0HJ
(0845 456 2933). Gunnersbury tube, then 237 bus.
Open 9am-7pm Mon; 10am-9.45pm Tue, Thur;
noon-6pm, 8-9.45pm Wed; noon-9pm Fri; 9am-5.30pm
Sat, Sun. **Admission** £3.40; £1.60 12-16s; £1.40 5-11s;
free under-5s.

Leisure pool with a 40m (130ft) aquaslide, underwater lights and wave machine, alongside a conventional teaching pool.

Goresbrook Leisure Centre
Ripple Road, Dagenham, Essex RM9 6XW (8593 3570). Becontree tube. **Open** 12.15-10pm Mon; 9am-6.30pm Tue; 9am-12.15pm, 1.15-8.30pm Wed; 9am-10pm Thur; 10am-10pm Fri; 11.15am-5pm Sat; 9am-6pm Sun. **Admission** £3.60; £2 3-16s; free under-3s.
Fountains, cascades and a 60m (200ft) flume, plus a small area for swimming lengths.

Leyton Leisure Lagoon
763 Leyton High Road, E10 5AB (8558 4860). Leyton tube. **Open** 9am-9pm Mon; noon-7pm Tue; 10am-5.30pm Wed; 1-8pm Thur; 9am-6.30pm Fri; 10.30am-4.30pm Sat; 9.30am-6pm Sun. **Admission** *Peak* £3.75; £1.65 children. *Off-peak* £2.40; 80p children.
All the exotic appeal of a flume, slides, fountains, rapids and cascades in a tropical island setting – in nondescript Leyton.

Northolt Swimarama
Eastcote Lane North, Northolt, Middx UB5 4AB (8422 1176). Northolt tube. **Open** 7am-7pm Mon, Fri; 7am-10pm Tue; 9am-10pm Wed; 7am-7.30pm Thur; 8am-4pm Sat, Sun. **Admission** £2.60; £1.45 children.
Three pools, a 60m (200ft) slide and diving boards.

Pavilion Leisure Centre
Kentish Way, Bromley, Kent BR1 3EF (8313 9911). Bromley South rail. **Open** 11am-7pm Mon; 11am-3.30pm, 6-8pm Tue, Thur; 11am-3.30pm Wed ; noon-6pm Fri; 10am-7pm Sat, Sun. **Admission** *Peak* £3.80; £2.50 children. *Off-peak* £3.20; £2.30 children.
Large leisure pool with gentle shallows, flumes, a wave machine at weekends and a separate toddlers' pool.

Waterfront Leisure Centre
Woolwich High Street, SE18 6DL (8317 5000). Woolwich Arsenal rail. **Open** 3-8pm Mon-Thur; 3-6pm Fri; 9am-5pm Sat, Sun. **Admission** £4.65; £3.25 children.

In the family way

Amid the horror stories about children's expanding waistlines, it's often forgotten that research has shown incontrovertibly that active parents tend to produce active children. If kids are brought up in an environment where physical exercise is valued, there's less chance they will slump into a lifestyle of PlayStation, pizzas and porkiness.

Many of London's fitness clubs and leisure centres have made the connection and developed programmes for the whole family. At one extreme is the **Park Club** (East Acton Lane, W3 7HB, 8743 4321, www.theparkclub.co.uk), which for £1,299 per year plus a joining fee of £90-£250 per person, provides the well-heeled of west London with facilities more akin to a posh country club. At the other extreme, Easter 2004 saw a **Kids Swim Free** initiative in five of the capital's poorest boroughs (Newham, Tower Hamlets, Waltham Forest, Greenwich and Hackney). This not only brought a 500 per cent increase in pool use, it also saw 34 per cent of parents go swimming more often than usual – and, crucially, most have continued to swim since the scheme ended. The aim is to extend the project to all London boroughs (details from the Greater London Authority on 7983 4100, www.london.gov.uk).

If you're looking to join a club as a family, don't assume that your offspring will receive a universally warm welcome. Some of the chains are geared towards all ages – although this may not be the case at all clubs within a chain – while others are essentially adults-only operations. **Esporta** (0870 739 0039, www.esporta.com) has the best family-friendly provision of all: at Hounslow, for example, there's a crèche, nursery, D-Zone indoor adventure playground, sports activities and special restaurant and café. Yet Esporta Islington doesn't permit kids at any time. **David Lloyd** clubs (0870 888 3015, www.davidlloydleisure.co.uk) give children their own membership, which is

particularly useful if they're keen on racket sports, while **LivingWell** (0870 600 7001, www.livingwell. com) has fitness and dance classes for kids, plus a crèche in some locations. If you're looking for help during holidays, **Cannons** (0870 780 8182, www.cannons.co.uk) runs Easter and summer camps at its more suburban centres.

Elsewhere, the picture is more patchy. **Fitness Exchange** (0800 298 3606, www.fitness-exchange. net) will allow kids in the pools during restricted hours but there are no crèches or activities, while at **Fitness First** (01202 845000, www.fitnessfirst. com) and **Profiles for Women** (01444 449161, www.profileswomen.com) you'll only find the occasional crèche. **Holmes Place** (www.holmes place.com) has crèches at all its clubs, while older children have some access to the pools and there are activity and educational programmes at larger centres. Meanwhile, the emphasis at **LA Fitness** (7366 8080, www.lafitness.co.uk) is on adults, but their children are not entirely excluded. At the Kensington club, for example, there are crèche facilities, kids' dance classes for age six to 13-plus, while the adults-and-kids-combined karate classes are incredibly popular – they provide a rare chance for children to kick the stuffing out of their parents without being sent to their room afterwards.

At all these centres, the focus is on having fun. Thankfully, Britain has yet to follow the American model of 'fat camps' and junior gyms, where overweight children are subjected to demeaning exercise and dietary restrictions, or shoved on treadmills in an appalling imitation of adults. In television programmes about such activities in the States, it's apparent that most of the obese children featured have equally obese and inactive parents. Let's hope that the growing trend towards family fitness on this side of the Atlantic proves a lasting one.

Four pools, six slides, waves, rapids and a water 'volcano' in Greenwich's flagship centre, the recent beneficiary of a £1-million upgrade.

Wavelengths Leisure Centre
Griffin Street, SE8 4RJ (8694 1134). Deptford rail.
Open times change regularly, ring for details.
Admission *Peak* £3; £1.55 children. *Off-peak* £2.40; £1.30 children.
Expect to find flumes, waves, wild water and cannons in the flashiest building on the edges of Deptford Market.

Water polo

'Aquagoal' is a version of this fast and furious game with amended rules for ten-year-olds upwards. Like handball, the aim is to score goals in your opponent's net – but without touching the side or bottom of the pool. It's a great challenge, then, for children who are already good swimmers. Contact the **Amateur Swimming Association** (01509 618700, www.britishswimming.org) for general information about the sport. The **National Water Polo League** website (www.nwpl.co.uk) has useful club contacts.

Table tennis

Twenty weekend junior leagues are now running in the capital and several clubs offer coaching for youngsters, and a competitive system to feed into. Alternatively, most sports centres will have at least one table and many will host a club. For more information contact the **English Table Tennis Association** (01424 722525, www.englishtabletennis.org.uk) or regional development officer Brian Spicer (7815 7808).

Tennis

Despite this country's high status in the game – which is due to our hosting the greatest of the four Grand Slam tournaments – our general playing standards are pathetic. This is because the sport has yet to shed its cosy middle-class reputation – and in some areas is desperate to maintain that image at all costs.

When looking for a club that values children rather than seeing them as an inconvenience, check that there is a range of coaching courses for all standards, times set aside for kids to play casually and that equipment is available for first-timers. Alternatively, most London boroughs run holiday courses: contact your local sports development team (details in the phone book or on the council website) or public library for details.

The **Lawn Tennis Association** (7381 7000/ www.lta.org.uk) publishes free, comprehensive guides giving contacts for hundreds of private clubs and public courts, listed by borough or county, along with contact details for local development officers. Details of tennis holidays are also available.

Clissold Park Junior Tennis Club
Clissold Park Mansion House, c/o Rangers' Office, Stoke Newington Church Street, N16 5HJ (court bookings 7923 3660/Tennis Club 8318 4856). Stoke Newington rail/73 bus. **Open** 5-8pm daily. **Court hire** £5.50/hr.
The LTA paid to resurface the four hard courts and four mini-tennis courts at this, Britain's first City Tennis Centre. Rackets and balls can be borrowed without charge, and the club is very active, with squads, coaching, club competitions and teams participating in the Middlesex League. Another City Tennis Centre is in Highbury Fields (contact Robert Achille on 7697 1206).

David Lloyd Leisure
0870 888 3015/www.davidlloydleisure.co.uk
There are 11 David Lloyd clubs in the London area, each of which combines tennis with upmarket fitness facilities. Although they're not cheap, they are all very family-friendly. Check the website or phone for your nearest venue and for membership details.

Islington Tennis Centre
Market Road, N7 9PL (7700 1370/www.aquaterra.org). Caledonian Road tube. **Open** 7am-11pm Mon-Thur; 7am-10pm Fri; 8am-10pm Sat, Sun. **Court hire** *Outdoors* £3.80/hr. *Indoors* £7.60/hr.
Developed under the LTA's Indoor Tennis Initiative, this centre offers excellent subsidised coaching on a membership or a 'pay as you play' basis. Short tennis and transitional tennis for youngsters learning the basics are also available.

Redbridge Sports & Leisure Centre
Forest Road, Barkingside, Essex IG6 3HD (8498 1000/ booking line 8498 1010/www.rslonline.co.uk). Fairlop tube.
Developed over 32 years and nine phases by an independent charitable trust, this outstanding multi sports centre has eight indoor and 18 outdoor courts – you can use them as a member or 'pay as you play'. It runs holiday activities for six- to 14-year-olds and a short tennis club for eights and unders. The centre also has an excellent development programme.

Sutton Junior Tennis Centre
Rose Hill Recreation Ground, Rose Hill, Sutton, Surrey SM1 3HD (8641 6611/www.sjtc.org). Morden tube, then 154, 280 bus. **Open** 7am-11pm Mon-Thur; 7am-10pm Fri; 7.30am-8pm Sat; 7.30am-10pm Sun. **Membership** £75/yr.
Set up more than a decade ago, this is now the top tennis school in Britain. Its performance coaches include Davis Cup captain Roger Taylor. There are residential courses for full-time players and a scholarship scheme linked with Cheam High School. Children can start at three with Tiny Tots classes, move on to short tennis and join in holiday programmes. There are six clay, ten acrylic and 11 indoor courts, so the centre is accessible all year round. Membership enables you to book cheaper courts in advance.

Westway Tennis Centre
1 Crowthorne Road, W10 6RP (8969 0992/www.westway. org). Latimer Road tube. **Open** 10am-10pm Mon-Fri, Sun; 8am-8pm Sat. **Court hire** £8-£19/hr.
Also the product of the LTA's Indoor Tennis Initiative, Westway follows a similar model to Islington – excellent subsidised coaching, short tennis and transitional tennis.

Tenpin bowling

Bowling is ideal for a fun (and relatively cheap) birthday party or family day out. Side bumpers and ball rollers help the very young to get involved, while computerised scoring has made the game less complicated. There's a network of regional and national youth tournaments and leagues; for more information, contact the **British Tenpin Bowling Association** (8478 1745, www.btba.org.uk).

All the centres listed are open seven days a week, typically 10am to midnight. Admission prices vary according to the time of day, but average around £5 per game – which includes the hire of soft-soled bowling shoes. Phone for children's party options.

Acton Mega Bowl *Royale Leisure Park, Western Avenue, W3 0PA (8896 0707). Park Royal tube.*
Airport Bowl *Bath Road, Harlington, Middx UB3 5AL (8759 1396). Hatton Cross tube.*
Dagenham Bowling *Cook Road, Dagenham, Essex RM9 6XW (8593 2888/www.dagenhambowling.co.uk). Becontree tube.*
Funland *Pepsi Trocadero, 1 Piccadilly Circus, W1D 7DH (7439 1914/www.funland.co.uk). Piccadilly Circus tube.*
Harrow Bowl *Pinner Road, North Harrow, Middx HA2 6DZ (8863 3491). North Harrow tube.*
Hollywood Bowl *Finchley Leisure Way, High Road, N12 0QZ (8446 6667/www.hollywoodbowl.co.uk). East Finchley tube, then 263 bus.*
Leisurebox *17 Queensway, W2 4QP (7229 0172). Bayswater tube.*
Rowans Bowl *10 Stroud Green Rd, N4 2DF (8800 1950/www.rowans.co.uk). Finsbury Park tube.*
Streatham MegaBowl *142 Streatham Hill, SW2 4RU (8678 6007/www.megabowl.co.uk). Streatham Hill rail.*

Volleyball

Though a minor sport in this country, volleyball is great fun for children aged nine upwards. Many clubs around the capital run junior teams, with nine- to 14-year-old beginners playing three-a-side 'mini volley' on a badminton-sized court with a lower net. To find your nearest set-up, contact the **London Volleyball Association** (07951 727595).

Water sports

Boating

Going round in circles in a rowing boat or bumbling along in a pedalo makes for a fun family afternoon.

Battersea Park Boating Lake
Battersea Park, SW11 4NJ (8871 7530). Battersea Park rail. **Open** *Oct-May* noon-5.30pm Sat, Sun, bank hols. *June-Sept* noon-5.30pm daily. **Prices** £5/hr; £3.50/30mins.
You'll find a varied crowd, ranging from families to solitary foreign students, piloting these sturdy vessels in the pleasant surroundings of the park. A new contractor is due to take over in 2004, so make sure you phone first to confirm opening hours and prices.

Finsbury Park Boating Lake
Finsbury Park, N4 2NQ (7263 5001). Finsbury Park tube/ rail. **Open** *Easter-Sept* noon-7pm daily. **Prices** £3/30mins.
There are around 20 rowing boats for hire in this north London park. Under-11s are obliged to wear life jackets and must be accompanied by an adult.

Regent's Park Lake
Regent's Park, Hanover Gate, NW1 4NU (7724 4069). Baker Street tube. **Open** *Mid Mar-Oct* 10.30am-dusk or 7pm (whichever is earlier) daily. **Prices** (per person) £2.50-£6/hr; £2-£4.50/30mins; family (2+3) £18.
With more than 50 rowing boats, this elegant lake in Regent's Park has plenty of opportunity for oars-play. Pedal boats are for children only.

Richmond Bridge Rowing Boat Hire
1-3 Bridge Boathouse, Richmond, Surrey TW9 1TH (8948 8270). Richmond tube/rail. **Open** *Easter-Oct* 9am-6pm daily. **Prices** (per person) £4/1st hr, then £2 each hr thereafter; £12/day.
Located on a tranquil stretch of the Thames, this thriving boating centre has doubled the size of its fleet and had its old boats refurbished. As well as the wooden rowing boats, single and double skiffs are available. A £20 deposit is required when hiring a boat.

Serpentine Boating Lake
The Boat House, Serpentine Road, W2 2UH (7262 1330/ www.royalparks.gov.uk). Hyde Park Corner tube. **Open** *Feb-Oct* 10am-4pm or 8pm, depending on weather. **Prices** (per person) £2.50-£6/hr; £1.50-£4/30mins.
The Serpentine can have anaconda-like queues for boats on sunny weekends, even with more than 100 craft available for hire. It's worth the wait, though.

Westminster Boating Base
136 Grosvenor Road, SW1V 3JY (7821 7389/www. westminsterboatingbase.co.uk). Pimlico tube. **Open** *Apr-Oct* 6-9pm Mon-Wed; 10am-1pm, 2-5pm Sun. Some session are canoeing or sailing only; check website for details. **Prices** £240/yr (or £10/3hr); £10/yr 10-23s.
Beautifully set in Pimlico Gardens, this charitable training centre offers low-cost sailing and canoeing for children aged ten and over. The venue is available for hire.

Rowing

Despite its upper-crust image, rowing is far from being an elitist sport. Children can start joining in from the age of 11. For details of clubs, contact the **Amateur Rowing Association** (8237 6700, www.ara-rowing.org).

Globe Rowing Club
Trafalgar Rowing Centre, Crane Street, SE10 9NP (8858 2106/www.globe.cwc.net). Cutty Sark DLR/Maze Hill rail. **Open** 6-9pm Mon, Wed; 8am-noon Sat, Sun, depending on tides. **Membership** £240/yr.
This friendly Greenwich-based club is particularly good value, with membership for under-16s costing just £4 a month.

Sailing

Children can start off learning the basics in a one-person dinghy such as a Topper or Laser Pico. Clubs will usually supply all the necessary kit, from vessel to wetsuit. A beginners' course recognised by the **Royal Yachting Association** (0845 345 0400, www.rya.org.uk) can be covered in a weekend.

Albany Park Canoe & Sailing Centre

Albany Mews, Albany Park Road, Kingston-upon-Thames, Surrey KT2 5SL (8549 3066/www.albanypark. co.uk). Kingston rail. **Open** 9am-5pm daily (phone to check, times vary). **Prices** vary; phone for details.
This friendly Kingston sailing centre hires out both single and crew dinghies. Training courses are available for adults and children, as are kayaking and open canoeing.

Fairlop Sailing Centre

Forest Road, Hainault, Ilford, Essex IG6 3HN (8500 1468/www.fairlop.org.uk). Fairlop tube. **Open** 9am-5.30pm, 7-9pm Mon-Fri; 10am-1pm, 2-4pm Sat. **Prices** vary; phone for details.
This RYA- and British Canoe Union-approved centre offers 40 acres (16ha) of water with two islands, situated in a very pleasant country park. An open aspect right across Fairlop Plain ensures a clean breeze. Windsurfing, dinghy sailing, canoeing and powerboating courses are available for adults and children from April to October, and the friendly staff run great kids' birthday parties (£82.20 for up to 12 children aged at least eight) using open canoes or bellboats; everyone usually ends up splashing about in the water.

Queen Mary Sailing Club & Sailsports

Queen Mary Reservoir, Ashford Road, Ashford, Middx TW15 1UA (01784 248881/www.queenmary.org.uk). Ashford rail. **Open** *Mar-Sept* 9am-1hr before sunset Wed-Sun. *Summer hols* 9am-1hr before sunset daily. *Oct-Mar* 9am-5pm Wed-Sun. **Prices** vary; phone for details.
This expanse of water is huge and the club that uses it well run, with a sailing school and a wide range of dinghies to hire out. There's an active youth programme, as well as sailing facilities for people with disabilities.

Royal Victoria Dock Watersports Centre

Gate 5, Tidal Basin Road, off Silvertown Way, E16 1AF (7511 2326/www.victoria-dock.com). Royal Victoria Dock DLR. **Open** *May-Oct* 4.30-6pm, 6.30-8pm Tue-Thur; 9.45am-1pm Sat; 9.15-10.45am, 11am-12.30pm, 1.30-3pm, 3.15-4.45pm Sun. *Nov-Apr* 9.15-10.45am, 11am-12.30pm, 1.30-3pm, 3.15-4.45pm Sun. **Prices** vary; phone for details.
The calm waters of Victoria Dock are a great place to set about mastering the art of dinghy sailing. A two-day Royal Yachting Association course for beginners will cost £105 (a four-day course costs £180), while a single session with a Laser or Wayfarer would cost £6 per hour. Children (aged

Westminster Boating Base. *See p270.*

between eight and 16) who have managed to secure a place on the 'Youth on H$_2$O' scholarship scheme are able to train here for free.

Shadwell Basin Outdoor Activity Centre
3-4 Shadwell Pierhead, Glamis Road, E1W 3TD (7481 4210/www.shadwell-basin.org.uk). Wapping tube. **Open** 9am-9pm Mon-Thur; 9am-5pm Fri; 10am-5pm Sun. **Prices** vary; phone for details.
Downriver from Tower Bridge, this multi-activity centre offers fairly priced summer sailing and canoeing for children aged from nine to 18.

Surrey Docks Watersports Centre
Greenland Dock, Rope Street, SE16 7SX (7237 4009). Surrey Quays tube. **Open** 9am-5pm Mon-Sun. **Prices** vary; phone for details.
Sailing, windsurfing and canoeing for eight-year-olds upwards takes place in the sheltered dock throughout school holidays and half-terms. Children take part in the RYA's structured sailing courses, which take three days to complete. Once the juniors have their certificates, they can join in Thursday and Friday 'Splashday' activities.

West Reservoir Centre
Stoke Newington West Reservoir, Green Lanes, N4 2HA (8442 8116). Manor House tube. **Open** 9am-5pm Mon-Fri; times vary, depending on course, Sat, Sun. **Prices** vary; phone for details.
Another good place for aspiring young dinghy-sailors to learn the basics.

Waterskiing

John Battleday Waterski
Thorpe Road, Chertsey, Surrey KT16 8PH (0870 606 1270/www.jbwaterski.com). Chertsey or Virginia Water rail. **Open** *Apr-Oct* 9am-dusk daily. *Nov-Mar* 11am-dusk Wed, Sat, Sun (subject to change, phone to check). **Prices** vary; phone for details.
Three times a world championship medallist, John Battleday knows a thing or two about waterskiing. And that makes his kids' club (catering for children aged five to 12) is understandably popular.

Weightlifting

Bethnal Green Technology College
Gosset Street, E2 6NW (7920 7937). Bethnal Green tube/rail. **Classes** 5.30pm Wed, Fri. **Cost** £1/class.
This East End venue is the only place in London offering boys and girls a chance to learn the basics and safety rules of weightlifting. The bulk of the work is targeted at technique (although participants do also enter competitions). Given the location it's mainly Tower Hamlets kids at present, but anyone is welcome.

Yoga

An expressive art that uses the whole body, yoga is ideal for children. Many of its postures are drawn from the movements of animals or take their names: the cobra pose, for example, expands the chest and strengthens the back – and the children can have

lots of fun slithering around and hissing. Each posture has an underlying physical or emotional benefit to a child.

This approach began at the Art of Health and Yoga Centre in Balham, where Fenella Lindsell created YogaBugs® for three- to seven-year-olds by integrating postures into creative stories. There are now more than 200 trained YogaBugs® teachers working in schools. Even though the Art of Health no longer exists as a centre, **YogaBugs Limited** (6 Fontenoy Road, SW12 9LU, 8772 1800, www.yogabugs.com) runs classes at several venues. YogaBugs® has also been developed to support those children with special needs.

Yoga Junction in Finsbury Park offers sessions for children with special needs, including Down's Syndrome, autism and ADD. Meanwhile, the therapeutic aspect of yoga is explored at the **Yoga Therapy Centre**, which runs weekly sessions for children with asthma. The big stretches of some positions help to unknot the chest muscles and assist with controlled breathing and relaxation.

The following centres offer classes for kids of different ages:
Holistic Health *64 Broadway Market, E8 4QJ (7275 8434/www.holistic-health-hackney.co.uk). London Fields rail.*
Iyengar Institute *223A Randolph Avenue, W9 1NL (7624 3080/www.iyi.org.uk). Maida Vale tube.*
Sivananda Yoga Vedanta Centre *51 Felsham Road, SW15 1AZ (8780 0160/www.sivananda.org/london). Putney rail.*
Triyoga *6 Erskine Road, NW3 3AJ (7483 3344/ www.triyoga.co.uk). Chalk Farm tube.*
Yoga Junction *Unit 24, City North, Fonthill Road, N4 3HF (7263 3113/www.yogajunction.co.uk). Finsbury Park tube/rail.*
Yoga Therapy Centre *90-92 Pentonville Road, N1 9HS (7689 3040/www.yogatherapy.org). Angel tube.*

THINGS TO WATCH

Basketball

London Towers
Crystal Palace National Sports Centre, Ledrington Road, SE19 2BB (8776 7755/www.london-towers.co.uk). Crystal Palace rail. **Admission** £8; £6 children.
The London Towers are one of the top teams in the country, competing in the British Basketball League (BBL). There's a game played most weekends from October to April and the atmosphere is loud, street-cool and very family-friendly.

Cricket

In addition to the four-day County Championship and one-day National League, 2003 saw the introduction of the Twenty20 Cup. This proved hugely successful at attracting a new, younger audience to cricket, with the 20 overs-a-side matches played in a noisy, family-oriented atmosphere. The tournament will be repeated during July and August 2004: for details of this and other matches during the summer click on the **England & Wales Cricket Board** website (www.ecb.co.uk). The season runs from mid April to mid September.

The grounds listed below stage at least one Test Match and a one-day international each summer. To get tickets for these games you'll have to book in advance (unlike county matches, where you can pay on the gate), but information is usually released the preceding winter. Call the ECB Ticketline on 0870 533 8833 or check the ECB website for details.

Middlesex

St John's Wood Rd, NW8 8QN (7289 1300/ www.middlesexccc.com). St John's Wood tube. **Admission** £10-£13; £5-£6.50 children.
In the First Division of the County Championship and the Second Division of the National League, Middlesex is blessed with a crop of exciting young players and, in Lord's, a magnificent venue to watch a game. Any child interested in cricket will be thrilled to attend a match here.

Surrey

Brit Oval, SE11 5SS (7582 7764/www.surreycricket.com). Oval tube. **Admission** £5-£10; children free.
Currently undergoing a major redevelopment programme, the Oval is an excellent ground with fewer airs and graces than Lord's. What's more, Surrey are among the best in the country – in both the County Championship and National League. Their squad is crammed with internationals, although the likes of Graham Thorpe and Mark Butcher are able to turn out for their county only rarely.

Football

If your child supports a Premiership team, becoming a junior member certainly doesn't mean a steady supply of match tickets. A top club may have three or four times as many members as the capacity of their ground; Arsenal has a waiting list for season tickets. In the Nationwide League, it's easier to get in to games. Lower-division clubs positively encourage families with cheap tickets and special deals.

Ticket prices and membership packages are too numerous to list for each club: call for details or check out the club's website. As a rule, a seat at a Premiership match will cost £25-£40 for an adult, around half that for kids, with a discount for club members. Nationwide League prices are around £15-£35, again with reductions for children and club members. The season runs from August to May.

Barclaycard Premiership

Arsenal *Arsenal Stadium, Avenell Road, N5 1BU (0870 906 3366/www.arsenal.com). Arsenal tube.*
Charlton Athletic *The Valley, Floyd Road, SE7 8BL (8333 4010/www.cafc.co.uk). Charlton rail.*

Chelsea *Stamford Bridge, Fulham Road, SW6 1HS (0870 300 2322/www.chelseafc.co.uk). Fulham Broadway tube.*
Fulham *Craven Cottage, Stevenage Road, SW6 6HH (0870 442 1234/www.fulhamfc.co.uk). Putney Bridge tube.*
Fulham have been playing at Queens Park Rangers ground for the last two years, but plan a return to their traditional Craven Cottage home for the 2004-05 season.
Tottenham Hotspur *Bill Nicholson Way, 748 High Road, N17 0AP (0870 420 5000/www.spurs.co.uk). White Hart Lane rail.*

Nationwide League

Brentford *Griffin Park, Braemar Road, Brentford, Middx TW8 0NT (8847 2511/www.brentfordfc.co.uk). Brentford rail.*
Division 2.
Crystal Palace *Selhurst Park Stadium, SE25 6PU (8771 8841/www.cpfc.co.uk). Selhurst rail.*
Play-offs for Premiership.
Leyton Orient *Matchroom Stadium, Brisbane Road, E10 5NE (8926 1010/www.leytonorient.com). Leyton tube.* Division 3.
Millwall *The Den, Zampa Road, SE16 3LN (7231 9999/www.millwallfc.co.uk). South Bermondsey rail.* Division 1.
Queens Park Rangers *Rangers Stadium, South Africa Road, W12 7PA (0870 112 1967/www.qpr.co.uk). White City tube.*
Division 1.
Watford *Vicarage Road, Watford, WD18 0ER (01923 496010/www.watfordfc.com). Watford High Street rail.* Division 1.
West Ham United *Boleyn Ground, Green Street, E13 9AZ (0870 112 2700/www.whufc.com). Upton Park tube.* Play-offs for Premiership.

Greyhound racing

'Monday Funday' at the 'Stow (Walthamstow Stadium, *see p274*) sees some 2,000 spectators, benefiting from free admission and parking, prove that greyhound racing is definitely not on its way to the knackers' yard.

On days other than Bank Holidays, you'll usually find morning or evening meetings at each of the four tracks around the capital. Kids are well catered for at all the tracks, both inside and out. Special occasions are marked with bouncy castles and playground fun (check websites for details), and the burger bars and restaurants are always good value. Meanwhile, the formalities of racing itself are fascinating: the parade of the dogs led by a gent in a red hunting jacket, installing the hounds in the traps, the buzz of excitement as the hare makes its progress round the circuit before the gates spring open and the chase is on. By which time, of course, favourites will have been chosen and wagers made with either the Tote or an independent bookmaker. A tip: look out for the dog that does a poo just before it goes into the starting stalls!

Activities

Admission's cheap, you can bet with small change and, if your greyhound romps home first, the next round of ice-creams is on you.

Crayford Stadium
Stadium Way, Crayford, Kent DA1 4HR (01322 557836/www.crayford.com). Crayford rail. **Admission** £5. **Racing** 7.30pm Mon; 1.45pm Tue; 2pm Thur; 11am, 7.30pm Sat.

Romford Stadium
London Road, Romford, Essex RM7 9DU (01708 762345/www.trap6.com/romford). Romford rail. **Admission** £1.50-£6. **Racing** 7.30pm Mon, Wed, Fri; 11am, 7.30pm Sat. Times may alter during summer, phone to check.

Walthamstow Stadium
Chingford Road, E4 8SJ (8531 4255/www.wsgrey hound.co.uk). Walthamstow tube/rail, then W11, 357 bus. **Admission** £1-£6. **Racing** 1.58-6.04pm Mon; 7.45pm Tue, Thur; 11.34am-1.44pm Fri; 7.30pm Sat.

Wimbledon Stadium
Plough Lane, SW17 0BL (8946 8000/www.wimbledon stadium.co.uk). Tooting Broadway tube. **Admission** £5.50. **Racing** 7.30pm Tue, Fri, Sat.

Horse racing

All of Britain's 59 courses welcome children, with free admission for under-16s at the majority of meetings. Many racecourses stage special 'family days', and there is a growing number of Sunday meetings designed to draw in a new clientele.

The Racecourse Association publishes a free guide, *Come Racing*, available from 01344 625912 or online at www.comeracing.co.uk. The RCA website has details of and links to all the British courses, a calendar and previews of major meetings.

Admission prices stated below are for adults attending regular meetings; children usually go free.

Ascot *High Street, Ascot, Berks SL5 7JX (01344 622211/www.ascot.co.uk). Ascot rail.* **Admission** £7-£20.
Epsom Downs *Racecourse Paddock, Epsom, Surrey KT18 5LQ (01372 726311/www.epsomderby.co.uk). Epsom Downs rail.* **Admission** £5-£18.
Kempton Park *Staines Road East, Sunbury-on-Thames, Middx TW16 5AQ (01932 782292/www.kempton.co.uk). Kempton Park rail (race days only).* **Admission** £8-£19.
Sandown Park *Esher Station Road, Esher, Surrey KT10 9AJ (01372 470047/www.sandown.co.uk). Esher rail.* **Admission** £14-£20.
Windsor *Maidenhead Road, Windsor, Berks SL4 5JJ (0870 220 0024/www.windsor-racecourse.co.uk). Windsor & Eton Riverside rail.* **Admission** £6-£18.

Ice hockey

London Racers
Lee Valley Ice Centre, Lea Bridge Rd, E10 7QU (7420 5900/www.londonracers.com). Walthamstow Central tube/rail, then 48 bus. **Admission** £12; £8 concessions; £5 children.

Following the demise of the London Knights, once based in the London Arena in Docklands, the Racers took over as the senior ice-hockey club in the capital. They play in the Elite League, but in 2003-04 suffered a disastrous first season: they played 56 games, with only three wins and two draws to their name. Here's hoping for a marked improvement in the coming season. Match night is an upbeat, family-oriented affair, with plenty of rough, tough action to relish. Kids love it – even those who've never seen the game before. The season runs from September to April.

Rugby league

London Broncos
Griffin Park, Braemar Road, Brentford, Middx TW8 0NT (0871 222 1132/www.londonbroncos.co.uk). Brentford rail. **Admission** £12-£15 (£10-£13 in advance); £3-£5 children.
The Broncos are doing a good job of proving that rugby league can succeed outside its northern heartland. Games here are always fun: a host of family-oriented entertainments are put on, so there's always something to enjoy even if the action fails to inspire. The Broncos play in the Tetley's Bitter Super League; the season runs from March to October.

Rugby union

For more details on playing and watching rugby union, *see p262* **Scrum on down**.

Zurich Premiership
Harlequins *Stoop Memorial Ground, Langhorn Drive, Twickenham, Middx TW2 7SX (8410 6000/www.quins. co.uk). Twickenham rail.* **Admission** £12-£30; £5-£10 children.
Saracens *Vicarage Road, Watford, Herts WD18 0EP (01923 475222/www.saracens.com). Watford High Street rail.* **Admission** £13-£25; £7-£10 children.

National League
Esher *369 Molesey Road, Hersham, Surrey KT12 3PF (01932 220295/www.esherrfc.org). Hersham rail.* **Admission** £8; children free.
London Welsh *Old Deer Park, 187 Kew Road, Richmond, Middx TW9 2AZ (8940 2368/www. london-welsh.co.uk). Richmond tube.* **Admission** £10-£14; under-15s free if accompanied by adult.
Rosslyn Park *Priory Lane, SW15 5JH (8876 6044/ www.rosslynpark.co.uk). Barnes rail.* **Admission** £8; £4 children.

Stock car & banger racing

Wimbledon Stadium
Plough Lane, SW17 0BL (8946 8000/www.spedeworth. co.uk). Wimbledon Park tube. **Admission** £11; £5 children.
Sunday-night meetings at Wimbledon Stadium are terrific entertainment for all ages. 'Racing' is not the most important thing for the drivers of stock cars and bangers – nor for the spectators, either. What matters are the crashes, for which look no further than the cataclysmic figure-of-eight finales.

Days Out

Days Out

© Copyright Time Out Group 2004

Days Out

Have a nice trip, and take all day about it.

You don't have to travel far from London to get a helping of country air, which means you can be back in the city in time for supper. Just half an hour to an Area of Outstanding Natural Beauty in Surrey (**Surrey Hills Llamas**). About 40 minutes out of Victoria and you're beside the seaside in **Brighton**. Strike out in a north-easterly direction from Liverpool Street Station and you could be a storming Norman at Stansted's **Mountfitchet Castle** within the hour. If you fancy staying away, *Time Out Weekend Breaks from London* (£12.99) covers the getaways in more depth.

For the main entries listed in this chapter we've included details of opening times, admission and transport details, but these can change without notice. If you're planning a trip around one particular sight, phone first to check that it's open. Most places have websites that list closures, events and special occasions.

To find out about more attractions, visit the offices or website of the **Britain Visitor Centre** (1 Regent Street, SW1Y 4NX, www.visitbritain.com). For opening hours for personal callers, *see p298*.

Travel from London

By train

Information on train times and ticket prices is available from National Rail Enquiries (0845 748 4950, www.nationalrail.co.uk), including the lowdown on the **Family Railcard**. This costs £20, and lasts one year. Valid across Britain, it gives travellers with children one year of discounts from standard rail fares (a third off adult fares, 60 per cent off child fares, £1 minimum fare). Under-fives travel free. Up to two adults can be named as cardholders and use the card – and they do not have to be related. The minimum group size is one cardholder and one child aged five to 15; maximum group size is two cardholders, two other adults and four children. To pick up a form for the Family Railcard, visit your local staffed station.

London's mainline stations

Charing Cross *Strand, WC2N 5LR*. **Map** p319 L7.
For trains to and from south-east England (including Dover, Folkestone and Ramsgate).
Euston *Euston Road, NW1 2RS*. **Map** p317 K3.
For trains to and from north and north-west England and Scotland, and a suburban line north to Watford.

King's Cross *Euston Road, N1 9AP*. **Map** p317 L2.
For trains to and from north and north-east England and Scotland, and suburban lines to north Londone.
Liverpool Street *Liverpool Street, EC2M 7PD*. **Map** p321 R5.
For trains to and from the east coast, Stansted airportand East Anglia, and services to east and north-east London.
London Bridge *London Bridge Street, SE1 9SP*. **Map** p321 Q8.
For trains to Kent, Sussex, Surrey and south London suburbs.
Paddington *Praed Street, W2 1HB*. **Map** p313 D5.
For trains to and from west and south-west England, south Wales and the Midlands.
Victoria *Terminus Place, SW1V 1JU*. **Map** p318 H10.
For fast trains to and from the channel ports (Folkestone, Dover, Newhaven); for trains to and from Gatwick Airport, and suburban services to south and south-east London.
Waterloo *York Road, SE1 7ND*. **Map** p319 M9.
For fast trains to and from the south and south-west of England (Portsmouth, Southampton, Dorset, Devon), and suburban services to south London.

By coach

Coach and bus travel is cheaper, if slower, than rail travel. **National Express** (0870 580 8080) runs routes to most parts of the country; coaches depart from **Victoria Coach Station**, a five-minute walk from Victoria rail and tube stations. **Green Line** (0870 608 7261) operates within an approximate 40-mile (64-kilometre) radius of London. Most buses depart from **Eccleston Bridge** (Colonnades Coach Station, behind Victoria Coach Station).

Victoria Coach Station

164 Buckingham Palace Road, SW1V 9TP (7730 3466). Victoria tube/rail. **Map** p318 H1.
National Express, which travels to the Continent as Eurolines, is based at Victoria Coach Station. It's also used by other companies operating to and from London.

By car

Check out your route for possible roadworks and delays, and avoid the morning rush hour (roughly 7-10am on a weekday). Travelling into London after about 4pm on a Sunday evening is often ghastly too.

Though we've given basic transport information for the listed sights (nearest rail station, which motorway and junction you should take if coming by car), it's always best to check on a detailed map first. Drivers can check out the free routeplanner service available from both the **Automobile Association** (AA, www.theaa.co.uk) and the **Royal Automobile Association** (RAC, www.rac.co.uk).

Farms

Barleylands Farm Centre

Barleylands Road, Billericay, Essex CM11 2UD (01268 532253/290029/www.barleylands.co.uk). **Getting there** *By train* Billericay or Basildon rail. *By car* J29 off M25. **Open** *End Mar-Oct* 10am-5pm daily. **Admission** £2.50; prices vary for special events. **Credit** MC, V.

Part agricultural museum, part farm-animal petting centre, Barleylands scores highly on our Old Macdonald register of cuddlesome farm theme parks. It doesn't cost much to get in, and the museum has plenty of vintage tractors, a pair of original Fowler plough engines, and generally a huge range of agricultural machinery and memorabilia.

Children love the chickens, rabbits and turkeys near the picnic area, and there are larger animals including ponies, cows and pigs further out towards the pond. There's also an activity playground, working stables and a restaurant. The miniature steam train runs on summer Sundays and bank holidays, and there are mini-tractors to ride around the farm.

The Essex Steam and Country Show takes place here each year (11-12 Sept 2004), with a steam fair, heavy horses, demonstrations of rural crafts such as wood turning and willow weaving, food stalls and all kinds of amusements for kids. *Buggy access. Café. Car park. Disabled access: toilet. Nappy-changing facilities. Nearest picnic place: grounds.*

Bocketts Farm Park

Young Street, Fetcham, nr Leatherhead, Surrey KT22 9BS (01372 363764/www.bockettsfarm.co.uk). **Getting there** *By train* Leatherhead rail, then taxi. *By car* J9 off M25/26. **Open** 10am-6pm daily. Closed 25, 26 Dec, 1 Jan. **Admission** £4.75; £4.25 concessions, 3-17s; £3.75 2s; free under-2s. **Credit** MC, V.

Sitting pretty in a valley in the glorious North Downs, Bocketts is a working farm that goes a bundle on play. This means that straw bales are also climbing mountains, sheep-dogs take time out from sheep work to show off their agility, and lambs, chicks and calves stagger about winsomely, eliciting 'aahs' from adoring children. Other attractions include pony rides, tractor rides, astroslides, sand pits, ride-on tractors in the play barn and a children's birthday party service. The café, in an 18th-century building, is a fine place for lunch. *Buggy access. Café. Car parking (free). Disabled access: toilet. Nappy-changing facilities. Nearest picnic place: grounds. Shop.*

Fishers Farm

New Pound Lane, Wisborough Green, West Sussex RH14 0EG (01403 700063/www.fishersfarmpark.co.uk). **Getting there** *By train* Billingshurst rail, then taxi. *By car* J10 off M25. **Open** 10am-5pm daily; ring for times during special events. **Admission** *Nov-Mar* £6.25; £4.75 OAPs; £5.75 3-16s; £2.50 2s. *Mar-Oct* £7.25; £5.75 OAPs; £6.75 3-16s; £3.50 2s. *Summer hols* £9.25; £7.75 OAPs; £8.75 3-16s; £5.50 2s. Free under-2s. **Credit** MC, V.

Less a farm and more a vast family fun area with added animals, Fishers has a well-appointed Barn Theatre, where there are magic, clown and marionette shows every day (Mon-Fri) of the school holidays and an annual panto. All shows are included in the Farm Park entrance price. The theatre is most usually used for 'meet the animal' sessions, with feeding and veterinary demonstrations given on a daily basis.

Among the various animals to pet, feed and ride, Ben the lofty shire horse stands out a mile. At just three years old, he's already one of the biggest horses in the world and has joined stablemates Seth and Danny as an all-round entertainer. Once all the animals have been given the attention due to them, children can make the most of the playgrounds, trampolines and bouncy castles. There are also slides in all shapes and sizes, miniaturised pedal tractors and, in summer months, a giant paddling pool with sandy shores. *Buggy access. Cafés. Car park. Disabled access: toilet. Nappy-changing facilities. Nearest picnic place: grounds. Restaurants. Shops.*

Godstone Farm

Tilburstow Hill Road, Godstone, Surrey RH9 8LX (01883 742546/www.godstonefarm.co.uk). **Getting there** *By train* Caterham rail, then 409 bus. *By car* J6 off M25. **Open** *Mar-Oct* 10am-6pm daily. *Nov-Feb* 10am-5pm daily. Closed 25, 26 Dec. **Admission** £4.80 2-16s (accompanying adult free); free under-2s. **Credit** MC, V.

A small (40-acre/16ha) farm, Godstone is especially well suited to the very young. It's teeming with cute and cuddly animal characters, and their various enclosures can be as enlightening as they are heart-warming. Eggs from the farm's large range of fowl are held in an incubator, for example, where hatching takes place before an audience, giving plenty of pre-schoolers their first peek at the miracle of life.

Children with their hearts set on something altogether less profound can chase each other across the adventure playground, while under-nines lose themselves in the ball pools and on the walkways that make up the play barn. There's also a mini dry slope toboggan run. The proximity to London of Godstone, like its sister farm Horton Park (*see below*), makes it ideal for giving grimy urban youngsters not only fresh air, but a fresh perspective. *Buggy access. Café. Car park (free). Disabled access: toilet. Nappy-changing facilities. Nearest picnic place: grounds. Shop.*

Horton Park Children's Farm

Horton Lane, Epsom, Surrey KT19 8PT (01372 743984/www.hortonpark.co.uk). **Getting there** *By train* Ewell West rail, then 467 bus. *By car* J9 off M25. **Open** *Apr-Oct* 10am-6pm daily. *Nov-Mar* 10am-5pm daily. Last entry 1hr before closing. **Admission** £4.85 over-2s (accompanying adult free). **Credit** MC, V.

The emphasis at this farm is on simple entertainment for smaller children (it's probably best for under-eights). Most of the enclosures are designed for close encounters of the furred kind: kids are encouraged to pet gentle animals like rabbits, chicks and hamsters, with non-venomous lizards and snakes for more intrepid handlers. Related activities are similarly unthreatening, including a maze, soft-toy barn and a climbing structure (Fort Horton), and all help kids work up an appetite for the café or a packed lunch dutifully prepared for the designated picnic area. *Buggy access. Café. Car park (free). Disabled access: toilet. Nappy-changing facilities. Nearest picnic place: grounds. Shop.*

Odds Farm Park

Wooburn Common, nr High Wycombe, Bucks HP10 0LX (01628 520188/www.oddsfarm.co.uk). **Getting there** *By train* Beaconsfield rail, then taxi. *By car* J2 off M40 or J7 off M4. **Open** *Early Feb-May, early Sept-late Oct* 10am-5.30pm daily. *June-early Sept* 10am-6pm daily. *Late Oct-mid Feb* 10am-4.30pm daily. **Admission** £6; £5 2-16s, OAPs; free under-2s. **Credit** MC, V.

Meet all your farmyard favourites – lambs, pigs, goats, horses and baby chicks – at Odds. The park was created with small children in mind, so there's plenty of interest for them: feeding the chickens and egg collection; rabbit world; piggies'

Fishers Farm.
See p278.

snakes through ancient woodland. This is complemented by the Great Oak Sky Ways, two long aerial runways for speed freaks. A special events timetable runs throughout the year, including themed picnics, classic car rallies and an annual carol service in the barn (for details, check the website).
Buggy access. Café. Car park (free). Disabled access: toilet. Nappy-changing facilities. Nearest picnic place: grounds. Shop.

Treks

Surrey Hills Llamas
12 Pit Farm Road, Guildford, Surrey GU1 2JH (01483 560831/www.surrey-hills-llamas.co.uk). **Getting there** *By train* Guildford rail, then transport arranged for trekkers. **Admission** *Day Picnic treks* from £49.50 adults, £25 over-8s. *Family Picnic trek* £125 (2+2).
Fancy taking a llama for a walk? Go on a Surrey Hills trek and your companion will be affectionate, well groomed and South American. These smaller, humpless camels are traditionally beasts of burden, but these live the life of pampered pets, with only your picnic (included in the price) to carry. They wear a headcollar and you hold the lead rope, walking beside them on a day-long guided tour through woods and pastures in an Area of Outstanding Natural Beauty. Llamas are affectionate creatures, and you become quite attached to them – particularly on one of the camping trips.

Wildlife reserves

Birdworld
Holt Pound, Farnham, Surrey GU10 4LD (01420 22140/ www.birdworld.co.uk). **Getting there** *By train* Farnham rail, then taxi or 18 bus. *By car* J4 off M3, then A325 & follow signs. **Open** *Mid Feb-Oct* 10am-6pm daily. *Nov-mid Feb* 10am-4.30pm daily. Closed 25, 26 Dec.
Admission £9.95; £7.95 concessions; £7.25 3-14s; £31 family (2+2); free under-3s. **Credit** MC, V.
Britain's biggest bird park also goes underwater and down the farm, so once you've exhausted the feathered highlights, there are still lots of exotic fish and domesticated beasts to admire. The best way to get an overview of all the residents in this 26-acre (11ha) site is on a guided Safari train. Penguin feeding displays take place 11.30am and 3.30pm daily. The Heron Theatre, meanwhile, takes birds from their enclosures to perform natural tricks for a seated audience (1pm, 3pm). At the Jenny Wren farm, children get to see (possibly even handle) new arrivals, including baby rabbits and lambs. There's a café, snack kiosks and plenty of idyllic spots for a picnic. Special events take place throughout the year, including the Wild West Funday (17 Aug) and Hallowe'en Activity Week in the October half-term.
Buggy access. Café. Car park (free). Disabled access: toilet. Nappy-changing facilities. Nearest picnic place: grounds. Restaurant. Shop.

Drusillas Park
Alfriston, East Sussex BN26 5QS (01323 874100/ www.drusillas.co.uk). **Getting there** *By train* Polgate or Berwick rail, then taxi. *By car* M23, then A23, then A27. **Open** *Apr-Oct* 10am-6pm daily. *Oct-Mar* 10am-5pm daily. Last entry 1hr before closing. Closed 24-26 Dec.
Admission £9.99; £9.49 2-12s; free under-2s.
Credit MC, V.
One of the best-loved bits of this fun park and zoological garden is the Meerkat Mound, where you can climb inside the dome to stare them out. In fact, low-level viewing booths

teatime; and tractor and trailer rides. Some activities are dependent on the time of year (sheep shearing, for example, is between May and July). Seasonal events – notably Easter egg hunts, Hallowe'en pumpkin carving and an encounter with Father Christmas – take place in the relevant school hols.
Several outdoor play areas (including a sand pit and plenty of log walkways, swings and slides) form focal points for the many birthday parties held at Odds all year round (phone for more information), but also make a nice spot for kids to amuse themselves while parents linger over a picnic.
Buggy access. Café. Car park. Disabled access: toilet. Nappy-changing facilities. Nearest picnic place: grounds. Shop.

South of England
Rare Breeds Centre
Highlands Farm, Woodchurch, nr Ashford, Kent TN26 3RJ (01233 861493/www.rarebreeds.org.uk). **Getting there** *By train* Ashford rail, then taxi. *By car* J10 off M20. **Open** *Apr-Sept* 10.30am-5.30pm daily. *Oct-Mar* 10.30am-4.30pm Tue-Sun. Closed 24, 25 Dec, 1 Jan. **Admission** £5.50 3-15s; free under-3s. **Credit** MC, V.
Owned and operated by the Canterbury Oast Trust, a charity dedicated to the care and occupational development of adults with physical and learning difficulties, the Rare Breeds Centre is a special sort of place. Animals once common to the British Isles, but now sadly endangered, are bred and left to roam the wonderful woodland acreage in peace. There are unusual species of goat, cattle and poultry to spot – and pet if you're lucky – but the stars are undoubtedly porcine. Butch and Sundance, the pigs otherwise known as the Tamworth Two, escaped from an abattoir and went on the run in January 1998. Half wild boar, with long snouts and curly coats, the pair are currently eating their heads off in this splendid home and occasionally acknowledge their adoring public.
Other attractions include special pens where children can play with piglets and small animals, as well as any number of play activities. The Mysterious Marsh Woodland Adventure is an off-ground adventure circuit of wire walkways, tree swings, balance beams and stepping stones that

ensure that children get a great view of all the animal residents: the latest arrivals at Drusillas include blue-and-gold macaws and silvery marmosets. It's intriguing to walk through the Rodrigues fruit bats enclosure, and lovely cuddling up to lambs and kids in the petting barn.

Other attractions range from slides, swings and things to climb to more informative activities at the Discovery Centre, such as the Maasai workshops or Mokomo's animatronic Jungle Rock exhibit, which explains the process of natural selection. Check the website for details of party packages, animal-adoption schemes and the unbeatable experience of letting your child be a junior keeper for the day.
Buggy access. Cafés. Car park (free). Disabled access: toilet. Nappy-changing facilities. Nearest picnic place: grounds. Restaurant. Shops.

Howletts

Bekesbourne, nr Canterbury, Kent CT4 5EL (01227 721286/www.howletts.net). **Getting there** *By train* Bekesbourne rail, then 30min walk (no taxis); or Canterbury East rail, then taxi. *By car* M2, then A2. **Open** *Nov-Mar* 10am-dusk daily (last entry 3pm). *Apr-Oct* 10am-6pm daily (last entry 4.30pm). Closed 25 Dec. **Admission** £11.95; £8.95 concessions, 4-14s; £34 family (2+2); £39 family (2+3); free under-4s. **Credit** AmEx, MC, V.
The late John Aspinall opened his beautiful Howletts estate to the public in 1975 to fund his beloved animal collection. Almost 30 years later, Howletts still operates his famous policy of non-containment, ensuring that contact between animals and their handlers is close (so close that, over the years, fatal mishaps have been 'unavoidable'), and that enclosures replicate specific environments as far as is humanly possible. Almost 50 gorillas are housed here (the largest group in care, with the mighty Kifu the dominant male), as well as African elephants, Siberian tigers and many more.

Many of the species of wolves, tapirs and antelopes kept at Howletts are endangered species, and Howletts is one of the few zoos in the world to run a commendable programme reintroducing such species into the wild. So if you find the park low on waterslides and seesaws, that's because the animals come first. Port Lympne (*see below*) is Howletts' sister zoo.
Buggy access. Café. Car park. Disabled access: toilet. Nappy-changing facilities. Nearest picnic place: grounds. Restaurant. Shop.

Port Lympne Wild Animal Park

Lympne, nr Hythe, Kent CT21 4PD (01303 264647/ www.howletts.net). **Getting there** *By train* Ashford rail, then link bus. *By car* J11 off M20. **Open** *Oct-Mar* 10am-dusk daily (last entry 3pm). *Apr-Sept* 10am-6pm daily (last entry 4.30pm). Closed 25 Dec. **Admission** £11.95; £8.95 4-14s, disabled adults; £6.95 disabled children; £34 family (2+2); £39 family (2+3); free under-4s. **Credit** AmEx, MC, V.
Even larger than sister site Howletts (*see above*), Port Lympne consists of a spectacular mansion overlooking 350 acres (142ha) of wilderness, where animals coexist in the closest thing this country has to an uninterrupted nature reserve. To which extent, the easiest way to see everything is on a safari trailer tour (£2 adults, £1 children). Still, expeditions on foot (a round trip of the amphitheatre-shaped park covers roughly three miles or 5km) can be far more rewarding – just make sure you have all day. Don't miss Palace of the Apes, the largest family gorilla house in the world, with its two bachelor gorilla groups. Other wild animals to look out for include black rhinos, lions, tigers, elephants, wolves and monkeys. As at Howlett's, most of the animals have a close social bond with their keepers.

The manor itself is also worth a visit. Although less than a century old, it radiates grandeur, with murals, fountains and plenty of fine art. The 125 Trojan Steps lead to one of the most breathtaking views in the South-east. This and the 'back-to-basics' attitude towards the animals (all of whom are treated with the same affection as at Howletts, and with the same record of conservation achievement) makes the atmosphere at Port Lympne unique.
Buggy access. Café. Car park. Disabled access: toilet. Nappy-changing facilities. Restaurant. Shop.

Whipsnade Wild Animal Park

Whipsnade, Dunstable, Beds LU6 2LF (01582 872171/ www.whipsnade.co.uk). **Getting there** *By train* Hemel Hempstead rail, then 43 bus from coach station (taxi between rail and coach station advised, check bus times before leaving). *By car* J21 off M25, then J9 off M1. **Open** *9 Mar-4 Oct* 10am-6pm Mon-Sat; 10am-7pm Sun. *5 Oct-8 Mar* 10am-4pm daily. Last entry 1hr before closing. Times subject to change, so phone to check. **Tours** free bus around the park; phone for times. **Admission** £13.50; £11.50 concessions; £10.10 3-15s; £42.50 family (2+2); free under-3s. *Cars* £10 (members £5). **Credit** AmEx, MC, V.
The ZSL (Zoological Society of London) bought this 600-acre (250ha) site for the study of large animals in 1926. Nowadays it's the permanent home for elephants moved from London Zoo (*see p66*): 2004 was a big year for the Asian elephants – a new baby daughter was born unto them on 1 March – and she's growing up fast. As well as the tuskers, there are plenty of other giants, notably giraffes, bears, tigers, rhinos and hippos. Many can be viewed only from a vehicle, either the Safari bus or (Apr-Oct) Excelsior, a traditional blue steam train with five open-sided carriages, or Hector, a green, black and red diesel engine with carriages. Train rides cost £2/child and £2.50/adult. A daily programme of activities keeps family groups busy all day, and there are frequent special events scheduled for school holidays – Whitsun saw a teddy bears' picnic with related activity sessions; children got in free, so long as they brought a bear of their own. At other times you can watch long-tailed lemurs leap and learn all about them in the 'acrobat in action' session, then there are birds of prey flying displays, bear talks, sea lion capers in the new Splashzone area, feeding time for the penguins, chimp chats and giraffe encounters. There's also a children's farm with marmosets, goats, alpacas and ponies. Arrive early during the summer holidays so that you can find out what's going on and make the most of the place.
Buggy access. Café. Car park (£3). Disabled access: toilet. Nappy-changing facilities. Restaurant. Shop.

Woburn Safari Park

Woburn Park, Beds MK17 9QN (01525 290407/www. woburnsafari.co.uk). **Getting there** *By car* J13 off M1. **Open** *Late Mar-2 Nov* 10am-5pm daily. *2 Nov-early Mar* 11am-3pm Sat, Sun. Closed 25 Dec. **Admission** £13.50-£15.50; £10.50-£13 concessions; £10-£12 3-15s. Prices vary during peak season; phone for details. **Credit** MC, V. No soft-top cars or convertibles.
It's car drivers only in the 40 acres (16ha) that make up the Duke of Bedford's Woburn spread. You watch the ranging elephants, giraffes, camels, black bears, monkeys, lions, tigers and a pack of lively wolves – all from the safety of the family jalopy. And when that rhino comes up close, you'll be glad of the electric windows. You don't have to strap the children into the car for long, though, as you can always break off the drive and stretch your legs in the Wild World Leisure Area. Here the free attractions include demonstrations of birds of prey and keeper talks on penguins,

Big savings
with the 'extended' Family Railcard

Family size savings are waiting for you with a Family Railcard. Kids get 60% off and adults save 1/3 on most rail fares throughout Britain. It costs just £20 for a whole year and up to 4 adults and 4 children can travel on one card – they don't even have to be related. Pick up a leaflet at any staffed ticket office or call 08457 48 49 50 for the telesales number of your local Train Company.

National Rail   www.family-railcard.co.uk   Family RAILCARD

lemurs and sea lions, and the free land-train, with its open carriages, takes you past grazing zebras and impressively horned oryx. The latest attraction, Land of the Lemurs, has raised walkways to help you commune with the primates. At Rainbow Landing (an indoor aviary) you can buy nectar (60p), attracting colourful lorikeets to land on your hand to drink (it opens four times a day). The sea-lion pool, with views above and below the waterline, is another must-see. Once you've exchanged pleasantries with the animals, there's fun for human young: the Tree Tops Action Trail with its aerial runway and 70m (230ft) Bobcat Run – six lanes of wavy descent – test their bottle, while the Tiny Tots Safari Trail and Badger Valley please under-fives. An indoor soft-play centre is the wet weather option.

Buggy access. Café, snack bar. Car park. Disabled access: toilet. Nappy-changing facilities. Restaurant. Shop.

Go off to camp

Sometimes children need to be able to get on with the fun and games without aged parents slowing them down. Day and residential camps over the school holidays let them do just that, and the range of sports and activities that kids can join in with ensures that all tastes are catered for. The best-known companies are listed below. All like to take bookings for a week (Mon-Fri) except Camp Hamilton, whose activity days are one-offs.

If you're not ready to let the kids go off too far, you can combine a day out at **Painshill Landscape Garden** (*see p285*) with an adult-free adventure for the kids. **Camp Hamilton** is a series of stimulating activity days for eight- to 12-year-olds, run by Painshill Education staff. They involve a whole day (9.30am-3.30pm) of fresh air and fun, with teams competing to build a safe and effective survival shelter in the woods. A sausage and marshallow roast over a camp fire is their reward. Ring Painshill for dates.

For those London children who don't want to travel too far out of town to lose their parents for the day, Finchley's **Cross Keys** Camps may be the answer. Camps for children aged from four to 12 take place in Christ College School in East Finchley and in Brookland School, just around the corner. Both schools have plenty of green space and swimming pools, with opportunities for football, tennis, judo, drama and art. Camps run from 9.30am to 3.30pm, Monday to Friday. Cross Keys and its sister camps Mini Minors also have a residential arm, known as **XUK**, which runs week-long camps in a boarding school in rural Norfolk.

Barracudas, a big name in activity camps, has 25 sites in country schools near the M25. The day camps take children from four-and-a-half right up to age 16. Activities they can enjoy include swimming, go-karting, cricket and circus skills, plus all sorts of creative and arts fun for the more sedentary child.

eac does day and residential camps for children aged five to 16. They have large, rambling countryside sites across the land, but the places of most interest to Londoners are the multi-activity day camps in independent day schools in Croydon (Croham Hurst School), which is especially good for football and tennis specialists, and in Canterbury (Kent College Junior School), where there are riding and golf options. Even better for working parents, eac offers a door-to-door transport service.

For children who love the high-energy atmosphere of day camps, the next step is staying away for the week. A big noise in activity holidays for children is **PGL**. This company specialises in weeks of riding, canoeing, football and pure fantasy, such as the frenetic Indiana Jones adventure (with a day spent at Alton Towers theme park). Less outdoorsy holidaymakers will prefer the art, drama or pop-star themed breaks. Young people aged 13 to 16 can even participate in a six-day learner-driver and car-maintenance course. PGL has centres in France, Austria and Switzerland in addition to its ten places across the United Kingdom.

A smaller player on the activity holiday scene, **Wickedly Wonderful** takes groups of eight- to 13-year-olds to the Sussex coast, for weeks of swimming, canoeing, riding, tennis and singing round camp fires with marshmallows on sticks (an essential activity for any child, we reckon).

All the camps mentioned are safety-conscious, and have been inspected by the British Activities Holidays Association (BAHA) or OfSTED – or both.

Barracudas
Young World Leisure Group Ltd, Bridge House, Bridge Street, St Ives, Cambs PE27 5EH (0845 123 5299/www.barracudas.co.uk).

Camp Hamilton
Painshill Park Trust, Portsmouth Road, Cobham, Surrey KT11 1JE (01932 868113/www.painshill.co.uk).

Cross Keys
48 Fitzalan Road, Finchley, London N3 3PE (8371 9686/www.xkeys.co.uk/www.miniminors.co.uk).

eac activity camps ltd
59 George Street, Edinburgh EH2 2JG (0131 477 7574/www.activitycamps.com).

PGL Travel Ltd
Alton Court, Penyard Lane, Ross-on-Wye HR9 5GL (0870 050 7507/www.pgl.co.uk).

Wickedly Wonderful
5 Daisy Lane, Fulham, SW6 3DD (0790 686 9062/ www.wickedlywonderful.com).

XUK
48 Fitzalan Road, Finchley, N3 3PE (8922 9739/ www.experienceuk.co.uk).

Outdoors is best at **Hever Castle**.

Castles

Bodiam Castle

Nr Robertsbridge, East Sussex TN32 5UA (01580 830436/www.nationaltrust.org.uk). **Getting there** *By train* Robertsbridge rail, then taxi or local rider bus (Sat only). *By car* J5 off M25. **Open** *Mid Feb-Oct* 10am-6pm or dusk daily. *Nov-mid Feb* 10am-4pm or dusk Sat, Sun. Last entry 1hr before closing. Closed 24-26 Dec. **Tours** groups of 15 or more only, by arrangement; phone for details. **Admission** (NT) £4.20; £2.10 5-16s; £10.50 family (2+3); free under-5s. **Credit** AmEx, MC, V.

Originally built in 1385 by Edward Dalyngrigge, Bodiam Castle was ransacked during the Civil War and, until the 20th century, its overgrown ruins were attended by no one but a handful of Romantic painters and poets. There's no roof to speak of, which should discourage visits in the driving rain, but the towers and turrets still offer sweeping views across the Rother Valley.

While the mere sight of these looming battlements is enough to send kids' imaginations into overdrive, Bodiam Bat Packs contain creative trails and even a tabard for younger knights of the realm to wear on their travels (£10 refundable deposit). There's also a Discovery Centre, giving children the chance to dress in armour and try their hand at medieval games and musical instruments: it's usually reserved for school tours, but is occasionally open to the public (check the website for dates) or it can be hired for historical kids' birthday parties. Otherwise, aim to visit in the school hols: the castle will be busier, but also buzzing with themed events and teeming with staff dressed in period costume. *Buggy access. Café. Car park (£2). Disabled access: toilet. Nappy-changing facilities. Nearest picnic place: castle grounds. Restaurant. Shop.*

Hever Castle

Nr Edenbridge, Kent TN8 7NG (01732 865224/www.hevercastle.co.uk). **Getting there** *By train* Edenbridge Town rail, then taxi; or Hever rail, then 1-mile walk. *By car* J5 or J6 off M25. **Open** *Gardens* Mar-Oct 11am-6pm daily (last entry 5pm). Nov 11am-4pm daily. *Castle* Mar-Oct noon-6pm (last entry 5pm daily). Nov noon-4pm daily.

Tours groups (min 20 people) by prior arrangement. **Admission** *Castle & gardens* £8.80; £7.40 concessions; £4.80 5-14s; £22.40 family (2+2); free under-5s. *Gardens only* £7; £6 concessions; £4.60 5-14s; £18.60 family (2+2); free under-5s. **Credit** MC, V.

Her inability to bear Henry VIII a male heir may have led to an unpleasant end in the Tower, but Anne Boleyn's childhood home is anything but gruesome. Replete with Tudor furnishings, it is open for the public to peruse at leisure. Kids might find the interiors a little formal, but then here the attraction is the great outdoors: Hever's idyllic gardens are home to an enormous yew maze, and there's an ingenious water maze on Sixteen Acre Island that is composed of precarious walkways and unpredictable fountains (bring a change of clothes). New for this year is Henry VIII's Tower Maze, a physical form of snakes and ladders with learning along the way and an adventure playground at the centre. Best of all are the family events taking place throughout the year: Easter sees egg hunts with chocolate prizes, May Day brings incostumed dancers and musicians, and there are half-term storytelling sessions in the castle grounds. Most popular with kids, however, are the jousting and archery displays in July, the former especially – it allows younger audiences to cheer on their favourite knight (and boo the bad guy) in a full throttle fight on horseback, lances and all. *Buggy access (grounds only). Car park. Disabled access: ramps, toilet (grounds only). Nappy-changing facilities. Restaurants. Shops.*

Leeds Castle

Maidstone, Kent ME17 1PL (01622 765400/www.leeds-castle.com). **Getting there** *By train* Bearsted rail, then coach service to castle. *By car* J8 off M20. **Open** *Castle* Apr-Oct 10am-5.30pm daily. Nov-Mar 10am-3.30pm daily. Last entry 1hr before closing. *Gardens* Nov-Mar 10am-3pm daily. Apr-Oct 10am-5pm daily. Closed 25 Dec, open-air concert days 26 June, 3 July, 6 Nov 2004. **Tours** pre-booked groups only. **Admission** *Castle, gardens & Dog Collar Museum* Mid Mar-Oct £12.50; £11 concessions; £9 4-15s; £39 family (2+3); free under-4s. Nov-mid Mar £10.50; £9 concessions; £7 4-15s; £33 family (2+3); free under-4s. **Credit** MC, V.

Sailing at **Bewl Water**. *See p285.*

Leeds Castle isn't proclaimed 'the loveliest castle in the world' without reason: erected soon after the Norman Conquest, the building itself has been immaculately maintained throughout the ages, and to this day the sight of its towers reflected in the moat is as evocative as it was centuries ago. Inside, a multitude of magnificent halls and chambers awaits, as do various historical displays (from the Heraldry Room to the unique Dog Collar Museum), but it's the less restrictive outdoor wonderland that tends to steal younger hearts. A simple walk around the grounds is grand enough, the riverside pathways bustling with black swans and even the occasional peacock (more exotic bird life can be pondered in the on-site aviary). Leave time to explore the gardens, greenhouses and a vineyard, and take a while to lose the kids in the yew maze, at the centre of which is a secret grotto decorated with mythical beasts and fashioned in stone and shell mosaics. Check the website for a list of annual family events held in the castle grounds, including open-air theatre, children's classical concerts, firework displays and a hot-air ballooning weekend in September. Also worth a look is the Museum of Kent Life (01622 763936, www.museum-kentlife.co.uk), just a short drive up the M20 (J6).
Buggy access. Cafés. Car park. Disabled access: lift, toilet. Nappy-changing facilities. Nearest picnic place: grounds. Restaurants. Shop.

Mountfitchet Castle & Norman Village

Stansted Mountfitchet, Essex CM24 8SP (01279 813237/24hr info line 0906 470 0898/www.mount fichetcastle.com). **Getting there** *By train* Stansted Mountfitchet rail. *By car* J8 off M11. **Open** *14 Mar-14 Nov 2004, 12 Mar-12 Nov 2005* 10am-5pm daily. **Admission** £6; £5.50 concessions; £5 2-14s; free under-2s.

House on the Hill Toy Museum (address, phone & website as above). **Open** 10am-5pm daily. Closed 24-26 Dec. **Admission** £4; £3.50 concessions; £3.20 2-14s; free under-2s.

10% discount if visiting both on same day. **Credit** MC, V.
Despite being built in the 11th century, Mountfitchet Castle today is less a medieval monument than a sort of museum. All that remains of the original construction are isolated piles of rubble, and a 'working' Norman Village has been constructed on the original site to give some indication of life more than 900 years ago. Thus the many buildings scattered around the original motte date from the 1980s – they're the work of archaeologically minded entrepreneur Alan

Goldsmith – and they are populated by wax figures going about their daily business: from the cook preparing a banquet in the castle kitchen to the criminal swinging from the village gallows. Indeed, gore is a regular feature – the severed head of an invader is stuck on a spike at the entrance, and the local surgeon hovers over a bloody corpse – but to there are less grotesque characters (brewer, blacksmith, carpenter, candle-maker) and a host of tame animals, such as sheep and fallow deer, wandering the extensive grounds.
The adjoining House on the Hill Toy Museum is also great for younger kids, with over 80,000 exhibits from the Victorian era through to the '80s, from spinning tops to space stations. *Buggy access. Café (castle). Car park. Disabled access: toilet (castle). Nappy-changing facilities. Nearest picnic place: grounds. Shops.*

Windsor Castle

Windsor, Berks SL4 1NJ (7766 7304/www.royal.gov.uk). **Getting there** *By train* Windsor & Eton Riverside rail. *By car* J6 off M4. **Open** *Mar-Oct* 9.45am-5.15pm daily (last entry 4pm). *Nov-Feb* 9.45am-4.15pm daily (last entry 3pm). Closed 25, 26 Dec. **Admission** (LP) £12; £10 concessions; £6 5-16s; £30 family (2+3); free under-5s. *Audio guide* £3.50. **Credit** AmEx, MC, V.
As a working royal residence, Windsor Castle is more formal (if less crumbly) than other seats across the country, and the often overwhelming queues can put a dampener on younger imaginations. Kids with any kind of historical interest will be rewarded, however, as the castle houses a unique collection of art and artefacts. The State Apartments are furnished with works by Rembrandt, Gainsborough and Rubens, and a unique collection of medieval weaponry is on display in the Grand Vestibule, the Queen's Guard Chamber and St George's Hall. Unfortunately, the biggest queue tends to be reserved for the exhibit most likely to appeal to younger kids: the unfeasibly intricate Queen Mary's Dolls' House, created by Sir Edward Lutyens in 1924 on a scale of one to 12. It's perfect from the working water and electric system to the handmade wool rugs and genuine vintage wine, bottled in miniature in the cellar.
For a moment's peace head outside for the Jubilee Garden, St George's Chapel (it contains the tombs of ten monarchs including Henry VIII and, more recently, the Queen Mum) or Windsor Great Park, whence the view of the castle is just stunning. But keep the proximity of Legoland (*see p292*) a secret, or peace will become pestering in a trice.
Buggy access. Disabled access: lift, toilet. Garden. Nappy-changing facilities. Nearest picnic place: grounds. Shop.

Country parks

Bewl Water

*Lamberhurst, nr Tunbridge Wells, Kent TN3 8JH
(01892 890661/www.bewl.co.uk).* **Getting there** *By train*
Wadhurst rail, then taxi. *By car* J5 off M25. **Open** 9am-
dusk daily. Closed 25 Dec, 10 July. **Admission** *per vehicle*
Apr-Oct £4 Mon-Fri; £5 Sat, Sun. Nov-Mar £2.50 daily.
Concert tickets phone for details. **Credit** MC, V.
The largest lake in the south-east, with more than 15 miles
(24km) of shoreline and 450 acres (180ha) of surrounding
woodland, Bewl Water is perfect for ramblers, bikers and
picnickers. Weather permitting, ferryboats leave every hour
(11am-4pm Apr-Oct), so families can cruise the whole
circumference or get off halfway and walk the rest (£3.50-£4
adults, £2.50 children).

Bewl is perhaps most famously a fisherman's paradise:
boat hire costs from £18 per angler per day, while daily fishing permits cost £17.60 for eight fish or £11 for two (an
Environment Agency licence is also required, available at
Bewl), and an afternoon permit (four fish after 3pm) costs
£13.20. Windsurfing tuition is given by qualified RYA (Royal
Yachting Association) instructors, with all equipment
provided; kids with a taste for water sports can then
graduate on to rowing and powerboat lessons, also given on
the premises (phone the Outdoor Centre on 01892 890716).

Events take place throughout the year. There are pirate
parties planned for July and August (01892 890171), a kite
festival (11-12 Sept) and dragon-boat racing (18 Sept; check
www.funraisers.org.uk for details).
*Café. Car park. Disabled access: toilet. Nappy-changing
facilities. Nearest picnic place: grounds. Restaurant. Shop.*

The Hop Farm Country Park

*Beltring, Paddock Wood, Kent TN12 6PY (01622
872068).* **Getting there** *By train* Paddock Wood rail,
then (peak times only) shuttle bus. *By car* J5 off M25,
then A21 south. **Open** 10am-5pm daily. Closed 25, 26 Dec
2004, 23 May 2005. **Admission** £7.50; £6.50 concessions;
£27 family (2+2); free under-4s. Prices vary on event days.
Credit MC, V.
Look out for little Noddy and his friends at the Hop Farm on
30 July; he'll be there for a couple of days to kick off a frantic programme of events for families that lasts all summer.
Themed weekly fun until September includes a variety of
punning titles: Fluff 'n' Stuff, On the Beach, Hoplympic
Games, Aquatic Antics, Aloha Ahopa and Hop Idol. Theatre
shows, singalongs and craft activities are all on the menu.

In fact, every school holidays sees something exciting for
children at this former Whitbread hop farm. It's home to the
largest collection of oast houses in the world, with a
permanent exhibition called the Decades Experience, a
walk-through guide to the last 100 years. The Hop Story
Museum has lovely old photos of the hop-pickers who used
to come to Kent for seasonal work. There's a permanent
military vehicle display, but tank and armoured car enthusiasts should set aside 21-25 July for the annual KM War and
Peace Show, the largest military vehicle event in the world.

Animal encounters come courtesy of the shire horse stables,
with rides in dray carts (low carriages used to haul beer)
available for a small fee. There's also an animal farm, and a
petting zoo with guinea pigs and rabbits. Smaller children
bounce off the walls in the Happy Hoppers soft-play barn,
and for putters there's a free, nine-hole crazy golf course,
based around local landmarks.
*Buggy access. Car park (free). Cafés. Disabled access:
toilet. Nappy-changing facilities. Nearest picnic place:
grounds. Shop.*

Painshill Landscape Garden

*Painshill Park Trust, Portsmouth Road, Cobham, Surrey
KT11 1JE (01932 868113/www.painshill.co.uk).* **Getting
there** *By train* Cobham or Esher rail. *By car* J10 off M25.
Open *Mar-Oct* 10.30am-6pm Tue-Sun, bank hols (last
entry 4.30pm). *Nov-Feb* 11am-4pm Wed-Sun, bank hols
(last entry 3pm). Closed 25 Dec. **Tours** groups of 10
or more, by arrangement only. **Admission** £6; £5.25
concessions; £18 family (2+2); £3.50 5-16s; free under-5s.
Season ticket £30 single; £45 joint (2 adults); £60 family
(2+2). **Credit** MC, V.
The gardens at Painshill were originally intended as a
Romantic retreat for culturally enlightened, high-society
Londoners. These days anyone can enjoy the lakes, exotic
foliage and a series of refurbished follies (including a Gothic
temple, a grotto and a water wheel) along the way. Children
are especially well catered for in school holidays, when a
range of family events takes place every Sunday through the
summer (£6 adults, £3.50 5-16s). The other big attraction is
the Camp Hamilton days (*see also p282* **Go off to camp**).
*Buggy access. Café. Car park. Disabled access: toilet. Nappy-
changing facilities. Nearest picnic place: grounds. Shop.*

Wildwood Wildlife Park

*Herne Common, Herne Bay, Kent CT6 7LQ (01227
712111/www.wildwoodtrust.org).* **Getting there** *By train*
Herne Bay rail, then 4 bus. *By car* J7 off M2. **Open** *May-
Sept* 10am-6pm daily (last entry 5pm). *Nov-Apr* 10am-5pm
daily (last entry 4pm). **Admission** *June-Aug* £8; £6.50
concessions; £6 3-15s. *Sept-May* £6.50; £5.75 concessions;
£5 3-15s; £20-£24 family (2+2); free under-3s, disabled
carers. **Credit** MC, V.
There are about 50 different species of animal and bird
waiting to spot the children roaming through Wildwood's 40
acres (16ha) of Kentish woodland. The enclosures for wild
cats, beavers, badgers, otters, red squirrels, owls, even
wolves and wild boar are designed to blend into the
countryside. Special events, daily talks and feeding
programmes take place around the park, both for school
groups and casual young visitors during the school holidays.
There's a restaurant for snacks and hot meals, and an
adventure playground for aspiring monkeys of all ages and
sizes. Check the website for a list of upcoming events, and
know that the proximity of Wildwood to Herne Bay means
that visits can besupplemented with a short trip to the beach.
*Buggy access. Car park. Disabled access: toilet. Nappy-
changing facilities. Restaurant. Shop.*

Grand gardens

Bedgebury, the National Pinetum

*Nr Cranbrook, Kent TN17 2SL (01580 211044/www.
bedgeburypinetum.org.uk).* **Getting there** *By train*
Etchingham or Tunbridge Wells rail, then taxi. *By car* J5
off M25. **Open** *Apr-Oct* 10am-6pm daily. *Nov-Jan* 10am-
4pm daily. *Feb-late Mar* 10am-5pm daily. Last entry 1hr
before closing. **Admission** £3.50; £3 concessions; £1.50
5-16s; £9 family (2+4); free under-5s. **Credit** MC, V.
This, one of the finest collections of conifers in the world,
provides a year-round habitat for all kinds of plant and
animal life. It's also a stunning backdrop for an afternoon's
leisurely strolling, from the water lilies on Marshal's Lake to
the 'Old Man of Kent', a 160ft-high (50m) silver fir that is the
tallest tree in the county. Open 365 days a year, the pleasures
of the Pinetum alter with the passing seasons: summer brings
orchids and 19 species of dragonfly; autumn is a dazzling
display of reds and oranges, with plenty of obscure fungi

underfoot. There's a café, the Pinetum Pantry (closed Mon), or bring a picnic to make the most of your surroundings. Family events and walks are organised throughout the year, including bat-watching (2 July), dragonfly-spotting (10 July) and Dormouse Awareness (17 July); phone for details. *Buggy access. Café. Car park (free). Nearest picnic place: grounds. Shop.*

Borde Hill

Balcombe Road, Haywards Heath, West Sussex RH16 1XP (01444 450326). **Getting there** *By train* Haywards Heath rail, then taxi. **Open** 10am-6pm or dusk (if earlier) daily. **Admission** £6; £5 concessions; £3.50 3-15s; free under-3s. *Season ticket* £16.50; £10 3-15s. **Credit** AmEx, MC, V.

It may be a 200-acre (80ha) country estate with one of the UK's most comprehensive collections of trees and shrubs from around the world, but Borde won't leave the children bored. As well as rare plants from China, Burma and the Himalayas, the Garden of Allah and nearby Azalea Ring, and a traditional English rose garden, there's an extensive adventure playground, with a Wild West-style fort, swings, slides and an obstacle course. A pond is set aside for children's fishing classes during weekends and school holidays (1-5pm; £4/hr including equipment hire), and various family events are organised at Borde Hill throughout the year, with a different Summer Fun activity every day during August (check the website for a complete list). *Buggy access. Café. Disabled access: toilet. Nappy-changing facilities. Nearest picnic place: grounds. Restaurant. Shop.*

Capel Manor

Bullsmoor Lane, Enfield, Middx EN1 4RQ (8366 4442/ www.capel.ac.uk). **Getting there** *By train* Turkey Street. *By car* J25 off M25. **Open** *Mar-Oct* 10am-6pm daily (last entry 4.30pm). *Nov-Feb* 10am-5pm Mon-Fri (last entry 4pm). **Admission** £5; £4 concessions; £2 3-16s; free under-3s; £12 family (2+2). **Credit** MC, V.

This is the only college specialising in horticulture and floral design in the whole of Greater London, and its 30 acres (12ha) of sculpted gardens are some of the best in the city. Formally landscaped areas include a Japanese garden and an Italianate maze, although most children are more excited by the prospect of getting up close with squeaky, furry and feathered friends, including poultry, pygmy goats and Kune Kune pigs, in the animal centre (10am-5pm Sat, Sun). The college is also home to some magnificent Clydesdale horses, often to be seen working and exercising around the grounds. Disabled access is excellent throughout, with wheelchairs bookable in advance and sensory gardens for physically handicapped visitors. The programme of events (including occasional Kiddie Caper Weekends) cater for families. *Buggy access. Café. Car park (free). Disabled access: toilet. Nappy changing facilities. Nearest picnic place: grounds. Shop.*

Groombridge Place Gardens

Groombridge Place, Groombridge, nr Tunbridge Wells, Kent TN3 9QG (01892 861444/recorded info 01892 863999/www.groombridge.co.uk). **Getting there** *By train* Tunbridge Wells, then 290, 291 bus or taxi. *By car* B2110 off A264 off A21. **Open** *Easter-early Nov* 9.30am-6pm or dusk (if earlier) daily. **Admission** £8.50; £7.20 concessions; £7 3-12s; free under-3s; £28.50 family (2+2). **Credit** MC, V.

The 17th-century country house at Groombridge is off limits to visitors, but the adjoining landscaped gardens were opened to the public in 1994, and over the years have developed into

a fine day out for families. No small part of this is due to the Enchanted Forest, a sculpted wonderland for children, split into areas including the crazy Wild Wood with its giant swings, the Dark Walk adventure trail and Jurassic Valley, peppered with dinosaur footprints. Elsewhere are more formal gardens, but they're no less playful: the Drunken Garden has asymmetrical topiary leaning as if intoxicated, there's a giant chessboard with oversized pieces, and a Knot Garden where wicker figures recline in the shade. Family events occur throughout the year and include a recreated skirmish by the Medieval Siege Society (18-19 Sept) and a spooky Hallowe'en wander through the shadowy Enchanted Forest (30-31 Oct). Not far away is Eddie's Raptor Centre (www.raptorcentre.co.uk), a bird of prey sanctuary with daily falconry demonstrations, and a small museum dedicated to the writer Sir Arthur Conan Doyle, a local resident, who was a regular visitor to the gardens. *Buggy access. Café. Car park (free). Nappy-changing facilities. Nearest picnic place: grounds. Shop.*

RHS Gardens, Wisley

Nr Woking, Surrey GU23 6QB (01483 224234/www.rhs. org.uk). **Getting there** *By train* Woking rail, then taxi or bus (Wisley Bus runs between Woking & Wisley May-Sept; call 01483 224 234 for times). *By car* J10 off M25. **Open** *Mar-Oct* 10am-6pm Mon-Fri; 9am-6pm Sat, Sun. *Nov-Feb* 10am-4.30pm Mon-Fri; 9am-4.30pm Sat, Sun. Last entry 1hr before closing. Closed 25 Dec. **Tours** by arrangement; phone for details. **Admission** £7; £2 6-16s; free under-6s, disabled carers. **Credit** MC, V.

The flagship garden for the Royal Horticultural Society, this is a beautiful place to wander and inspirational to gardeners of all ages. Little ones in particular enjoy the vegetable plots (reminiscent of Mr MacGregor's) and the broad sweeping grassy paths and orchards. Various greenhouses contain otherworldly displays of exotic fruit plants, cacti, jungle vines and orchids. There are paper trails for various age groups, while tinies can marvel at the animal life across several ponds, including frogs, ducks and colourful Koi carp. *Buggy access. Cafés. Car park (free). Disabled access: toilet. Nappy-changing facilities. Nearest picnic place: grounds. Plant centre. Restaurant. Shop.*

Seaside

Brighton

Getting there *By train* Brighton rail. *By car* M23/A23, follow A23/A27 into Brighton. **Tourist information** *10 Bartholomew Square, Brighton, East Sussex BN1 1JS (0906 711 2255/ www.visitbrighton.com).*

Brighton's progressive clutter of clubs, bars and restaurants may justify the 'London on Sea' tag, but kids will be most interested in the 'Sea' part of the equation – especially when it's London they're trying to escap. The Palace Pier (01273 609361) is still the centre of attention, an expansive tract of arcades with an amusement park at one end, although more tranquil entertainment can be found on the wooden promenade, peppered with bizarre sculpture and a popular haunt for local skaters and performance artists. Or there's the personable Volks Railway (01273 292718) – Britain's oldest electric train, running 1.25 miles (2km) between the Palace Pier and the Marina. Children make use of a free play area near the ill-fated West Pier, while the Sea Life Centre (01273 604234, www.sealifeeurope.com), big enough to pass an afternoon of wet weather, is home to a new octopus display that's both enlightening and utterly hypnotic.

Broadstairs

Getting there *By train* Broadstairs rail. *By car* J5 off M2.
Tourist information *6B High Street, Broadstairs, Kent CT10 1LH (01843 583334/www.tourism.thanet.gov.uk).*
Thanks to Charles Dickens (who, from 1837, visited regularly and wrote the greater part of *David Copperfield* here), Broadstairs enjoys a literary reputation. For eight days each June the annual Dickens Festival (01843 861827) devotees from across the country for a range of events, while the Dickens House Museum (01843 861232) offers an insight into the writer's world. The popularity of Broadstairs derives from its seven beaches, the largest of which is Viking Bay, a crescent shoreline with a picturesque harbour and a cluster of shops and stalls. Joss Bay is a good bet for aspiring surfers, and also offers views of England's oldest lighthouse. Tots love the tidal paddling pool created periodically between Viking and Louisa Bay. Check the website for a calendar of cultural get-togethers: the Water Gala and Folk Festival (both Aug) are regular highlights.

Eastbourne

Getting there *By train* Eastbourne rail. *By car* J7 off M25. **Tourist information** *Cornfield Road, Eastbourne, East Sussex BN21 4QL (01323 411400/ www.eastbourne.org).*
Eastbourne's most spectacular attraction is also tinged with tragedy: the views from Beachy Head are unforgettable, but its sheer 575ft (175m) drop is a notorious suicide spot. Beyond that, however, Eastbourne is an idyllic seaside retreat with a celebrated pier (01323 410466), along which traditional cafés snuggle up to a games arcade, a late bar and the Atlantis nightclub. Holywell is the most family-friendly beach; the coast path goes all the way to Seaford. High-octane thrills can be had on the rides and coasters at Fort Fun amusement park (01323 642833). Small children love the Railway Adventure Park (01323 520229) in Lottbridge Drove, or riding the electric Dotto Trains (01323 641984) up and down the seafront.

Littlehampton

Getting there *By train* Littlehampton rail. *By car* J6 off M25. **Tourist information** *63-5 Surrey Street, Littlehampton, West Sussex BN17 5AW (01903 721866/www.sussexbythesea.com).*
Each year the beaches here win the highest accolades when it comes to cleanliness, making them ideal for fair-weather swimming. Of the two main beaches, the East Beach is by far the busier, a sandy paradise teeming with peak season crowds, while the less cultivated West Beach is better for families – it lacks shops and services, but more than makes up for it as a Site of Specific Scientific Interest and hence a haven for rare plant and animal life. Beyond the sedative pace of the promenade land train, there's little to fill the time, although further west Bognor Regis has entertainment (including a Butlins). There's also a Norman castle at nearby Arundel.

Margate

Getting there *By train* Margate rail. *By car* M2, then A2. **Tourist information** *12-13 The Parade, Margate, Kent CT9 1EY (01843 583333/583334/ www.tourism.thanet.gov.uk).*
There are plenty of good reasons to visit Margate – and they don't come much better than Main Sands bay, a near flawless strip of the golden stuff, punctuated by kids' amenities from donkey rides to puppet shows. For older children there are games arcades aplenty, but a more thought-provoking afternoon can be spent pondering the obscure paintings of undetermined age and origin in the subterranean Shell Grotto (01843 220008), or head to Margate Caves (01843 220139), a legendary hangout for smugglers and other assorted rogues.

Southend

Getting there *By train* Southend Central or Southend Victoria rail. *By car* J30 off M25. **Tourist information** *Southend Pier, Southend-on-Sea, Essex SS1 1EE (01702 215120/www.southend.gov.uk).*
A notable absence of sand hasn't stopped Southend becoming one of the most popular coastal resorts in the UK: instead, tonnes of the stuff are regularly shipped in to soften up the otherwise inappropriate estuary mud banks. Southend's coastal charms are distinctive. The resort is home to both the world's largest rock factory and its longest pier, the latter clocking in at an impressive 1.33 miles or just over 2km. A pleasure tram runs from end to end if you can't face the walk, and the pier is enlivened by the usual cocktail of arcades, shops and stalls. The Pier Museum (01702 614553) gives a potted history of the construction, but shorter attention spans will favour Adventure Island (01702 468023), a fairly standard theme park. There's tenpin bowling at the Kursaal (01702 322322) and a soft-play emporium called Kids Kingdom (01702 462747). A Sea Life Centre (01702 442200) offers close encounters of a piscatorial kind.

Whitstable

Getting there *By train* Whitstable rail. *By car* J7 off M2. **Tourist information** *7 Oxford Street, Whitstable, Kent CT5 1DB (01227 275482/ www.canterbury.co.uk/www.visitwhitstable.co.uk).*
Picturesque old Whitstable is renowned for both its excellent local oyster harvest and the extensive acting career (spanning almost seven decades) of its most famous local resident, the late Peter Cushing. Both are immortalised in displays at the Whitstable Museum and Gallery (01227 276998; admission free), although for a real taste of the former you can knock a few back at the Whitstable Oyster Fishery Company (01227 276856). Less-developed palates will no doubt prefer fish and chips from one of several fryers in town. The beaches are uniformly pebble affairs, not great for swimming, but there's plenty of scope for bracing outdoor activities all the same. These include clambering on the wooden groynes or flying kites on the grassy Tankerton Slopes, while enthusiastic ramblers follow coastal paths all the way to Margate (*see above*).

Specialist museums

Bentley Wildfowl & Motor Museum

Halland, nr Lewes, East Sussex BN8 5AF (01825 840573/www.bentley.org.uk). By train Uckfield or Lewes rail, then taxi. *By car* A22, then follow signs.
Open *Mid Mar-Sept* 10.30am-4.30pm daily. *Oct, Nov, Feb, early Mar* 10.30am-4pm Sat, Sun. Closed Dec, Jan.
Admission £6; £5 concessions; £4 4-15s; £19 family (2+4); free under-4s. **Credit** MC, V.
The gardens of Bentley House contain a wildfowl reserve and motor museum, so grease monkeys, the green-fingered and twitchers are all happy. Art workshops, a miniature steam railway and an adventure playground provide the action.

The animal collection was started in the 1960s by the late Gerald Askew, and these days breeds and safeguards around 125 species of swan, goose and duck (alongside various flamingos and cranes). A tour of the reserve can include a walk through the formal gardens, as well as a picnic in neighbouring Glyndebourne Wood. The Motor Museum houses Veteran, Edwardian and Vintage cars, and regular rallies and conventions take place throughout the year (check the website). *Buggy access. Café. Car park (free). Disabled access: toilet. Nappy-changing facilities. Nearest picnic place: grounds. Shop.*

The future's white

London's mountains are notoriously thin on the ground. Until recently, 'Alpine' experiences in England have been limited to sliding awkwardly down a shredded plastic mesh, incurring bruises, broken fingers and constant ridicule from our European brethren. But no more.

The ridicule aspect remains: the rash of indoor snow slopes popping up across the UK may provide punters with a sort of winter wonderland, but the machine-generated soft stuff is watery and hard-packed, the 'ambient' whitewash lighting sterile and the echo of kids' voices from the high ceilings more akin to a public swimming pool than an untracked piste or powder field. As an arena for learning the ropes, however, they're perfect: that there has also been a flurry of UK skiers and snowboarders holding their own in professional competitions across the world is no coincidence. Indoor slopes have revolutionised the national ski scene, fostered a number of Olympic hopefuls (including 16-year-old snowboard prodigy Laura Berry) and – most important of all – kids love 'em.

Nearest to London is **Snozone** in Milton Keynes, a great wedge of silver that also houses an indoor climbing wall, a 16-screen cinema, a bowling alley, bars and restaurants. Two 170-metre (549-foot) slopes sit beside a 135-metre (443 foot) nursery run; all kit can be hired (bring gloves, hats and a change of socks). One-hour group classes cost from £27. Recreational riding costs from £15.

The action isn't limited to simply skiing and snowboarding. **Tamworth Snowdome** – the original indoor slope, and still the most popular with snowboarders – has a whole bunch of lighthearted activities perfectly suited to little ones, including descents on a rubber ring or 'tubing' (ages three and up; from £4.50 for 30mins), sledging (ages three and up; £4.50 for 30mins) and tobogganing (ages five and up; £5 for 30mins)

Xscapes are springing up across the UK, with one in Leeds, one under construction in Glasgow and chief executive PY Gerbeau (of Millennium Dome fame) casually mentioning Bath, Brighton and Cardiff as other potential 'resorts'. Closer to home, Tamworth Snowdome is planning a similar arena at Wycombe Summit dry slope, and the development of an indoor slope at the Beckton

Alp in east London appears to be back on track – although it's unlikely to open before spring 2007.

Until then, there's always the small **Snow Park** at Diggerland in Strood (*see p292*), which opened last year (it's closed now until December 2004). It has a 100-metre (328-foot) tubing run, a 50-metre (164-foot) main slope and – best of all – a large play area for building snowmen and throwing snowballs. Again, it's not exactly an Alaskan wilderness, but in the absence of a white Christmas it's one present to make them smile.

For a list of local dry slopes, *see p264*; and visit www.theboarder.co.uk for regularly updated news on indoor slopes across the country.

Snozone
Xscape, 602 Marlborough Gate, Milton Keynes, Bucks MK9 3XS (01908 200020/www.xscape. co.uk). **Getting there** *By train* Milton Keynes rail. *By car* J14 off M1, then A509. **Open** *May-Sept* 9am-10pm Mon-Thur, Sun; 9am-11pm Fri, Sat. *Oct-Apr* 9am-11pm daily. **Admission** *Peak* (after 5pm Mon-Fri; Sat, Sun) £20 1hr, £30 2hrs; £17 1hr, £25 2hrs under-16s. *Off-peak* (9am-5pm Mon-Fri) £16 1hr, £25 2hrs; £13 1hr, £20 2hrs under-16s. Prices include equipment.

Tamworth Snowdome
Leisure Island, River Drive, Tamworth, Staffs B79 7ND (0870 500 0011/www.snowdome.co.uk). **Getting there** *By train* Tamworth rail. *By car* J10 off the M42. **Open** 9am-11pm daily. **Admission** *Skiing & snowboarding: peak* (from 8pm Mon-Fri; Sat, Sun, bank hols, school hols) £22, £16 under-16s; *off-peak* (9am-6.15pm Mon-Fri) £15; £10 under-16s. *Ice skating* £6 1hr, £7 2hrs. *Tobogganing* (30mins) £7, £5 5-16s. *Tubing* (30mins) £5 7-12s; *adrenaline tubing* (30mins) £8 over-12s.

The Snow Park
Diggerland, Medway Valley Leisure Park, Roman Way, Strood, Kent ME2 2NU (0870 034 4437/www.the snowpark.co.uk). **Getting there** *By train* Strood rail. *By car* J2 off M2 on to A228, then follow signs towards Strood. **Open** *Dec-Easter* 10am-6pm daily. **Admission** £2.50; £1.25 concessions; free under-2s. Plus all-day ski/board pass £24.

Chatham Historic Dockyard
The Historic Dockyard, Chatham, Kent ME4 4TZ (01634 823800/www.chdt.org.uk). **Getting there** *By train* Chatham rail. *By car* J1-4 off M2. **Open** *14 Feb-31Oct* 10am-6pm daily (last entry 4pm). *8-30 Nov* 10am-4pm (last entry 3pm) Sat, Sun. Closed Dec, Jan. **Admission** £10; £7.50 concessions; £6.50 5-15s; £26.50 family (2+2; £3.25 per additional child). **Credit** AmEx, MC, V. Shipbuilding activities, which took place here over the centuries, came to an end in 1984. Since then, Chatham Historic Dockyard Trust has been running the 80-acre (32ha) site anchorage as a tourist attraction. There are tours around

both a 40-year-old submarine, HMS *Ocelot*, and World War II destroyer, HMS *Cavalier*. Wooden Walls is a walk-through 18th-century dockyard experience. Lifeboat! is the RNLI's national collection, and the Museum of the Royal Dockyard charts the history of Chatham. The interactive displays include a radio-controlled boat and ship-docking exercise a mock ship fight and a soft-play area and 'walk the plank' fun. Check the website for this year's festivals and events, and children's holiday activities.

Buggy access. Café. Car park (free). Disabled access: toilet. Nappy-changing facilities. Shop.

Chuff chuff!

A great source of sensory interest for the young, steam trains score high in the nostalgia stakes with grandparents. A certain little engine called Thomas turning up during school holidays doesn't do any harm either. He chuffs in for high days and holidays on the UK's first preserved standard-gauge passenger railway, the **Bluebell Railway** (19-20, 26-27 June 2004), which runs along the Lewes to East Grinstead line. Each station the line passes through is restored according to a different era: Victorian, the 1930s and the 1950s. Childish delights include a bedtime story service on summer evenings, teatime specials on Saturday afternoons and Santa Specials in December.

Thomas also makes an appearance at the **Kent & East Sussex Railway** (also, interestingly, on 19-20 and 26-27 June). The antique carriages and engines servicing this railway line were scavenged and restored by enthusiasts, which makes this the most a pleasing method of getting from Bodiam (for the castle, see p283) to Tenterden.

The little blue engine also shows his large round face at the **Watercress Line** (7-15 August), based in the market town of Alresford. It's a ten-mile (16-kilometre) journey through Home Counties countryside. Londoners can hop on the train at Alton, which has a mainline station for Waterloo.

Millionaire racing driver Captain Howley wasn't planning any Thomas specials when he built the 'World's Smallest Public Railway' back in 1927. Nowadays, his unique locomotives, one-third of the scale of the real thing, puff along a similarly downsized track (though it still covers 13.5 miles or 22 kilometres) of the the **Romney, Hythe & Dymchurch Railway** between the Cinque Port of Hythe and eerie Dungeness.

You won't cover much ground at **Didcot Railway Centre**, as it's mostly a static collection of antique carriages and engines. Regular steam days involve steam-age activities like 'turning' locomotives, as well as the chance to ride in an original 1930s carriage. Thomas the Tank Engine makes occasional holiday stopovers on his famously hectic schedule (8-10 October).

Steam train timetables change frequently, but most lines run special trains for the half-term hordes. Ticket prices given are for round trips only. Most prices are due to rise in January 2005.

Bluebell Railway
Sheffield Park Station, on A275 between Lewes & East Grinstead, Sussex TN22 3QL (01825 723777/talking timetable 01825 722370/www.bluebell-railway.co.uk). **Getting there** *By train* East Grinstead rail, then 473 bus. *By car* J10 off M23. **Open** *Easter-Sept* 11am-4pm daily. Phone for details of additional Sat, Sun, school & bank hol openings. **Admission** £9; £7.50 OAPs; £4.50 3-15s; £25 family (2+3); free under-3s. **Credit** MC, V.

Buggy access. Café. Car park (free). Disabled access: toilet, trains. Nappy-changing facilities. Nearest picnic place: grounds. Shop.

Didcot Railway Centre
Didcot, Oxon OX11 7NJ (01235 817200/ www.didcotrailwaycentre.org.uk). **Getting there** *By train* Didcot Parkway rail. *By car* J13 off M4. **Open** 10am-4pm Mon-Fri; 10am-5pm Sat, Sun (last entry 30min before closing). **Tours** bank hols (times depend on events; phone for details). **Admission** *Steam days, incl tour* £7; £6 concessions; £5 4-16s; £22 family (2+2); free under-4s. *Non-steam days* £4; £3.50 concessions; £3 4-16s; £12 family; free under-4s. *Special event days* £8; £6.50 concessions, 4-16s; £23 family; free under-4s. **Credit** MC, V.
Buggy access. Café. Car park. Nappy-changing facilities. Shop.

Kent & East Sussex Railway
Tenterden Town Station, Tenterden, Kent TN30 6HE (Tenterden, Northiam & Bodiam stations 01580 765155/www.kesr.org.uk). **Getting there** *By train* Headcorn rail, then bus to Tenterden. *By car* J9 off M20. **Open** *Apr-July, Sept-Oct* 10am-4pm Sat, Sun. *Aug* 10am-4pm daily. *Nov-Mar* times vary; phone for details. **Admission** £10; £9 concessions; £5 3-15s; £25 family (2+3); free under-3s. **Credit** MC, V.
Buggy access. Café (Tenterden & Northiam stations). Car park. Disabled access: carriage (book in advance), toilet. Nappy-changing facilities. Nearby attractions: Bodiam Castle. Shop.

Romney, Hythe & Dymchurch Railway
New Romney Station, Kent TN28 8PL (01797 362353/www.rhdr.org.uk). **Getting there** *By train* Folkestone Central rail, then 711 bus to Hythe. *By car* J11 off M20. **Open** phone or check website for timetable. **Admission** £9.80; £8.35 concessions; £4.90 3-15s. **Credit** MC, V.
Buggy access. Café. Car park. Disabled access: carriages, toilet. Nappy-changing facilities. Shop.

Watercress Line
The Railway Station, Alresford, Hants SO24 9JG (01962 733810/talking timetable 01962 734866/www.watercressline.co.uk). **Getting there** *By train* Alton rail. *By car* A3, then A31. **Open** *May-Sept* Mon-Thur, Sat, Sun. *Oct, Dec, mid Jan-Feb* Sat, Sun. *Easter hols* daily. Phone or check website for timetable. **Admission** £10; £9 concessions; £5 3-16s; £25 family (2+2); free under-3s; call for special event prices. **Credit** MC, V.
Buggy access (footbridge at Alton). Café. Disabled access: carriages, toilet. Shop.

Teeny, steamy **Romney, Hythe & Dymchurch Railway**. See p290.

Duxford Imperial War Museum

Duxford, Cambs CB2 4QR (01223 835000/www.iwm. org.uk). **Getting there** *By train* Cambridge rail, then bus. *By car* J10 off M11. **Open** *Mid Mar-late Oct* 10am-6pm daily. *Late Oct-mid Mar* 10am-4pm daily. Last admission 1hr before closing. Closed 24-26 Dec. **Admission** £10; £6-£8 concessions; free under-16s. **Credit** MC, V.

Duxford has five vast themed hangars of exhibits, as well as the futuristic glass-fronted American Air Museum, designed by Lord Foster, and the Land Warfare Hall, filled up with tanks and military vehicles. The complex is so huge that a convenient, free 'road train' operates all day, dropping off at the major attractions. The air shows are superb (there are about four each year).

Visitors can learn about the Blitz in the Land Warfare Hall. Here, tanks, military vehicles and artillery pieces are on show in battlefield scenes. Children can leap about in two excellent play areas, including an adventure playground. The latest project to take off at Duxford is AirSpace. Work started in April 2004 to redevelop Hangar 1 into a 108,000sq ft (10,000sq m) exhibition area, and its completion date is scheduled for 2006. AirSpace will be one of the world's largest spaces for the interpretation of aviation heritage. Thirty classic British and Commonwealth aircraft be displayed, some suspended in the roof area as if in flight. A new Education Centre for schoolchildren is also planned. Part of the development will involve moving Concorde outside while they work on her hangar in July, so the familiar pointy nosed superstar will be easier to photograph. Check the website for more details.

Buggy access. Cafés. Car park (free). Disabled access: lift, toilet. Nappy-changing facilities. Restaurant. Shops.

Roald Dahl Children's Gallery

Buckinghamshire County Museum, Church Street, Aylesbury, Bucks HP20 2QP (01296 331441/www. buckscc.gov.uk/museum). **Getting there** *By train* Aylesbury rail. *By car* J8 off M25. **Open** 10am-5pm Sat; 2-5pm Sun. *Term-time* 3-5pm Mon-Fri. *School hols* 10am-5pm Mon-Sat. **Admission** £3.50; £2.75 3-16s; free under-3s. **Credit** MC, V.

An extension of the child-friendly County Museum, this gallery is divided into five main areas, decorated with colourful frescoes by Quentin Blake, which introduce different themes based on Roald Dahl's stories. Visitors encounter James and his mini-beast friends inside the Giant Peach and examine the insect world with the aid of a video microscope. The BFG playing on his giant pipe organ is a jolly introduction to the mysteries of sound, or there's a great glass elevator and a

chance to discover Willy Wonka's inventions. In Matilda's Library you can discover more about Dahl's life and work.

The Dahl Gallery only holds 85 people, so it's worth pre-booking in the school holidays. Picnic in the walled garden or snack in the reasonably priced museum café.

Buggy access. Café. Disabled access: lift, toilet. Nappy-changing facilities. Nearest picnic place: grounds. Shop.

Weald & Downland Open Air Museum

Singleton, Chichester, West Sussex PO18 0EU (01243 811348/811363/www.wealddown.co.uk). **Getting there** *By train* Chichester rail, then 60 bus. *By car* A3, turn off at Millford, A286 to Midhurst and follow signs. **Open** *Mar-Oct* 10.30am-6pm daily (last entry 4pm). *Nov-Feb* 10.30am-4pm Sat, Sun. **Admission** £7.50; £6.50 concessions; £4 5-16s; free under-5s; £20 family (2+3). **Credit** MC, V.

This multi-award-winning open-air museum is a collection of historic buildings dating from the 13th to the 19th centuries, all carefully relocated in over 50 acres (20ha) of Sussex countryside. They include a 19th-century smithy, a rare example of a once-common windpump and a 17th-century watermill that still produces its own stoneground flour (used by the café and sold in the gift store). The museum's centrepiece is a 15th-century farmstead, where, in the kitchen, bread, pottage and sweetmeats are prepared.

Children can test out antiquated building techniques at hands-on holiday workshops, and even drive their own carthorses and bricklaying, while other traditional crafts are kept alive by costumed staff offering regular period-specific demonstrations. It's informative stuff, but never dull, and there are plenty of domestic animals standing about in pens and paddocks to keep younger children amused.

Buggy access. Café. Car park (free). Disabled access: toilets. Nappy-changing facilities. Shop.

Theme parks

Bekonscot Model Village

Warwick Road, Beaconsfield, Bucks HP9 2PL (01494 672919/www.bekonscot.com). **Getting there** *By train* Chiltern Railways from Marylebone to Beaconsfield. *By car* J2 off M40 or J16 off M25. **Open** 15 Feb-Oct 10am-5pm daily. **Admission** £5.30; £4 concessions; £3.20 2-15s; £15 family (2+2). **Credit** MC, V.

The theme, if you like, is a miniature world where children can be as Gulliver in Lilliput. The model villages, in their landscape of farms, fields, woodland, churches, castles and lakes, were created as a hobby by Roland Callingham in 1929.

Days Out

Bekonscot may now be a charitable organisation, but it continues to fascinate children with its tiny details. A busy gauge-one model railway stops at seven stations, and at the zoo you can witness a scaled-down chimps' tea party, aviary and elephant rides. More intricate details can be enjoyed at the fairground, with its working mini-rides. Manicured alpine plants, lawns and dwarf conifers provide a green backdrop to the towers and spires. For full-sized action, there's a play-ground and a ride-on steam railway (50p per person, runs at weekends, bank holidays and during local school holidays). *Buggy access. Car park (free). Disabled access: toilets. Kiosk. Nappy-changing facilities. Shop.*

Chessington World of Adventures

Leatherhead Road, Chessington, Surrey KT9 2NE (0870 444 7777/www.chessington.com). **Getting there** *By train* Chessington South rail, then 71 bus. *By car* J9 off M25/M26. **Open** *Apr-Nov* 10am-5pm or 6pm daily. *Late July-early Sept* 10am-7pm daily; times may vary according to special events. Height restrictions vary on rides. **Admission** £26 (accompanying child free), £18 additional under-12s; £18 concessions. Check website for advance bookings for fast-track entry. **Credit** MC, V.
Chessington is now happy to leave most of the white-knuckle stuff to its sister park, Thorpe (*see below*). It has reinvented itself as family-friendly, and to that end 90% of the rides and attractions are suitable for the under-12s. The infamous (and scary) Samurai has been moved to Thorpe to induce more nausea over there, so now the little ones can enjoy harmless fun on the Dragon's Fury (sponsored by Skips), a spinning, turning, but not-too-thrilling roller-coaster that is ideal for seven-year-olds. The dragon theme continues with Land of the Dragons, which has a soft-play area, adventure playground and puppet shows. Old favourites, such as Animal Land, with its gorilla family, big cats and sea lions, are attractive for all ages, and a small, new rollercoaster called Vampire is meek enough for four-year-olds. Children get in free with every paying adult, so Chessington's new-found mildness has been matched by a price cut. Picnic spots are everywhere, but there are fast-food chains aplenty for those who have forgotten their sandwiches in all the excitement.
Buggy access. Café. Car park (free). Disabled access: toilets. Nappy-changing facilities. Restaurant. Shops.

Diggerland

Medway Valley Leisure Park, Roman Way, Strood, Kent ME2 2NU (0870 034 4437/www.diggerland.com). **Getting there** *By train* Strood rail. *By car* J2 off M2 on to A228, then follow signs towards Strood. **Open** 10am-5pm weekends, bank hols, school hols, half-terms; check website for details.
Fans of heavy kit, such as diggers, forklifts and dumper trucks, need look no further than Diggerland, a rather specialist theme-park concept dreamed up by plant hire firm HE Services. Newcomers to the art of controlling a JCB are, of course, closely watched by instructors. Dumper and Land Rover racing is organised for adults, and themed birthday party packages are available for children. New for 2004 is robot racing: you get to pilot one of the highly manoeuvrable JCB 160 loaders, steering by dint of two levers. There's no age limit, though very young children have to be accompanied by an adult before they can drive off into the sunset at the wheel of a dumper truck. Other on-site activities include a bouncy castle, ride-on toys, a vast sand pit and a land train. But it's the diggers that make it special.
Buggy access. Café. Car park (free). Disabled access: toilet. Nappy-changing facilities. Nearest picnic place: grounds. Shop.

Legoland

Winkfield Road, Windsor, Berks SL4 4AY (0870 504 0404/www.legoland.co.uk). **Getting there** *By train* Windsor & Eton Riverside or Windsor Central rail. *By car* J3 off M3 or J6 off M4. **Open** *Mid Mar-early Nov* 10am-5pm or 6pm (during summer hols) or 7pm (Aug) daily. **Admission** *Peak season (school hols)* £23; £20 3-15s; £20 concessions. *Off-peak season* £21; £19 3-15s; £19 concessions. **Credit** MC, V.
The beauty of this park is the creativity that its designers have put into the use of the vastly adaptable plastic bricks. Take Miniland, for example. It contains the greatest concentration of Lego bricks in the park. Some 35 million pieces have been used to create scenes from Europe, includ-ing iconic London landmarks, such as the British Airways London Eye and the Tower of London, all bustling with sounds, traffic, trains and boats. Then there are old favourites like the Driving School, which gives its successful partici-pants a Legoland driver's licence, the Lego Safari, and the two mildly thrilling rides – the Dragon Coaster and Pirate Falls (with quite a sickening drop as a finale). In fact Legoland is getting a bit daring in its middle age, recognising that some people like a bit of a fright now and then. New for 2004 is the Jungle Coaster, which has a 42ft (13m) plunge and a top speed of nearly 40mph (60km/h) – not one for the tinies, as it's the nearest Legoland has to a white-knuckle ride.
As well as the themed rides, there are playgrounds, numerous restaurants, cafés and ice-cream parlours, Duplo Land for toddlers and any number of shows in the four theatre venues around the complex. The latest show stars plasticky hero Johnny Thunder in *Escape from Dragon Tower*. Audience participation is guaranteed, as are the crowds. Legoland is outrageously popular, especially during school holidays, so always expect queues.
Buggy access. Café. Car park (free). Disabled access: toilet. Nappy-changing facilities. Nearest picnic place: grounds. Restaurants. Shops.

Thorpe Park

Staines Road, Chertsey, Surrey KT16 8PN (0870 444 4466/www.thorpepark.com). **Getting there** *By train* Staines rail, then 950 bus. *By car* M25 J11 or J13. **Open** *Apr-late July, early Sept-early Nov* 9.30am-6pm daily. *Late July-early Sept* 9.30am-7pm daily. Height restrictions vary, depending on rides. **Admission** £17-£27; £15.50-£20 4-11s, concessions; £75 family (2+2, 1+3); free under-4s. Check the website or phone for advance bookings; allow 24hrs to process advance ticket purchases. **Credit** MC, V.
Rejoicing in epithets such as 'buttock-clenching' and 'high-octane', Thorpe Park markets itself as white-knuckle central and gives its rides macho names – Samurai (actually a new arrival from tamer sister Chessington, *see above*), say, or Nemesis Inferno. For thrill-seekers, it's the business. Nemesis Inferno is a legs-dangling swoop through more than 2,460ft (750m) of suspended track, turning through 360° loops, plunging from soaring heights to dreadful depths, at speeds of up to 48mph (77km/h), pulling G-forces of up to 4.5. If that doesn't rearrange your insides, Colossus will: it's the world's first ten looping roller coaster, travelling at speeds of 40mph (65km/h). For those who want to get wet as well as disorientated, there's Tidal Wave, one of the highest water-drop rides in Europe. Although Thorpe's more gruesome rides aren't suitable for little ones, cuddly experi-ences await younger brothers and sisters across the lake at Thorpe Farm's petting zoo, with its goats, pigs and poultry; you can travel to this agricultural haven by boat or land train.
Buggy access. Café. Car park. Disabled access: toilets. Nappy-changing facilities. Restaurants. Shops.

Directory

Directory

GETTING AROUND

The prices listed for transport and services were correct at the time of going to press, but bear in mind that some prices (especially those of tube tickets) are subject to a price hike each January.

For London's domestic rail and coach stations, *see p277*.

Public transport information

All the information below can be accessed online at both www.tfl.gov.uk and www.thetube.com, or by phoning 7222 1234.
Transport for London (TfL) also runs Travel Information Centres that provide maps and general information about the tube, buses, Tramlink, riverboats, Docklands Light Railway (DLR) and national rail services within the London area. You can find them in Heathrow Airport, as well as in Liverpool Street and Victoria stations. The TfL website has a journey planner to help you find the quickest route.

London Transport Users' Committee
6 Middle Street, EC1A 7JA (7505 9000/www.ltuc.org.uk).
Open *Phone enquiries* 9am-5pm Mon-Fri.
This is the official, campaigning watchdog monitoring customer satisfaction with transport in London.

Travelcards

Bus and tube fares are based on a six-zone system that stretches 12 miles (20 kilometres) out from the centre of London. Buying a Travelcard (*see below*) is the cheapest way of getting around, but beware of the on-the-spot £10 penalty fares for anyone caught

without a ticket or outside the zones covered by their Travelcard. Travelcards can be bought at stations, Travel Information Centres or participating newsagents.

One-Day LT Cards
One-Day LT Cards will only be of interest if you intend to travel before 9.30am on weekdays using zones 1-6 and to make several journeys during the day. They're valid for travel throughout Greater London on tube, Tramlink and Docklands Light Railway services, but not on National Rail or on the Bakerloo line between Kenton and Harrow & Wealdstone. They are also valid for travel across the London bus network, but not on special bus services or excursions. A One-Day LT card costs £11.10 and £5.50 for children (5-15s), and is valid from midnight on the date of validity and for any journey that starts before 4.30am the following day.

Day Travelcards
Day Travelcards (peak) can be used from 00.01 Mondays to Fridays (except public holidays). They cost from £5.40 (£2.00 for children) for Zones 1 and 2, with prices rising to £11.10 (£5.50 children) for an all-zones card. If you need a zones 1-5 or 1-6 card and are not using National Rail services, it is cheaper to buy an LT Card. All tickets are valid for journeys before 4.30am the next day.
Most people are happy with the off-peak day Travelcard, which allows you to start travelling after 9.30am. This costs from £4.30 for zones 1 and 2, rising to £5.40 for zones 1-6.

Family Travelcards
Anyone travelling with children can take advantage of this Travelcard. It offers unlimited travel for up to two adults and up to four children. During the week each adult pays £2.80, and each child 80p, in zones 1 and 2, rising to £3.60 per adult and 80p per child for zones 1-6. Each child in the Family Travelcard group travels free in all zones on weekends and bank holidays.

Weekend Travelcards
If you plan to spend a weekend charging around town, you'd do well to buy a Weekend Travelcard. It offers unlimited travel for Saturday and Sunday, at a cost of £6.40 for zones 1 & 2, which rises to £8.10 for zones 1-6.

Oyster card
The Oyster card is a travel smart card, available to adult seven-day, Annual and Monthly Travelcard and Annual Bus Pass customers at ticket offices, on the internet (www.oystercard.com) or by telephone (0845 330 9876). Oyster cards can also be used on buses, Docklands Light Railway, Tramlink and National Rail.

Children
On all buses, tubes and local trains under-5s travel free. Children travelling with adult (seven-day or longer) travelcard holders can have a travelcard for just £1. Children aged 5-10 can travel free on London buses and Tramlink, or at a reduced rate on tubes and trains. A 5-10 photocard is available for travel for periods of seven days, a month or longer periods. Children have to have an 11-15 photocard to prove they are eligible for the child rate. These photocards are available from local travel ticket outlets or Travel Information Centres. Proof of ID and a photograph are required.

London Underground

The tube in rush hour (8-9.30am and 4.30-7pm Mon-Fri), is not pleasant, so if you can travel outside these hours with your children, everyone will be happier.

Using the system
Tube tickets can be purchased from a ticket office or self-service machines. You can buy most tickets, including carnets and One-Day LT Cards, from self-service machines. Ticket offices in some stations close early (around 7.30pm), but it's best to keep change with you at all times: using a ticket machine is quicker than queuing at a ticket office.
There are 12 Underground lines, colour-coded on the tube map for ease of use; we've provided a full map of the London Underground on the back page of this book.

Underground timetable
Tube trains run daily from around 5.30am (except Sunday, when they start an hour or two later, depending on the line). The only exception is Christmas Day, when there is no service. During peak times the service should run every two or three minutes. Times of last trains vary, though they're usually around 11.30pm-1am daily except Sunday, when they finish 30 minutes to an hour earlier. The only all-night public transport is by night bus (*see p295*).

Fares
The single Underground fare for adults within zone 1 is £2. For zones 1 and 2 it's £2.20. An all-zones single fare is £3.80.
The single Underground fare for children in zone 1 is 60p, 80p for zones 1 and 2, rising to £1.50 for an all-zone ticket.

Carnet
If you're planning on making a lot of short-hop journeys within zone 1 over a period of several days, it makes sense to buy a carnet of ten tickets for £15 (£5 for children). Note that if you exit a station outside zone 1 and are caught with only a carnet ticket, you'll be liable to a £10 penalty fare.

Docklands Light Railway (DLR)

7363 9700/www.dlr.co.uk.

The DLR is administered as part of the tube system. Its driverless trains run on a raised track from Bank (Central or Waterloo & City lines) or Tower Gateway, close to Tower Hill tube (Circle and District lines), to Stratford, Beckton and down the Isle of Dogs to Island Gardens, then south of the river to Greenwich, Deptford and Lewisham. Trains run 5.30am-12.30am Monday to Saturday and 7am-11.30pm Sunday.

Fares

Prices vary according to zone. Docklands Shuttle South (Lewisham to Canary Wharf) tickets cost £2; Docklands Shuttle East (valid between Beckton/Stratford and Island Gardens via Westferry) tickets are £2.60; City Flyer South (valid between Bank and Lewisham) tickets are £3.60; and City Flyer East (valid between Beckton/Stratford and Bank) tickets are £4. Child tickets cost from 80p to £2.

The DLR also offers one-day **Rail & River Rover** tickets that combine unlimited DLR travel with a riverboat trip between Greenwich, Tower and Westminster piers (boats run 10am-6pm; call City Cruises on 7740 0400 for exact times). Tickets cost £9 for adults, £4.50 for kids and £25 for a family pass (two adults and up to three kids); under-5s travel free. Family tickets may only be purchased in person from the piers. During the summer, a guided service runs hourly on Saturdays (10am-3pm) from Tower Gateway to Cutty Sark; call 7363 9700 for details.

Buses

Improvements in the London bus network, the provision of more lanes and the introduction of the Congestion Charge (*see p296*) have made the bus a more reliable, if still comparatively slow, option. New, low-floored buses are more buggy friendly. Many buses in London require you to pay before you board, either at a dedicated machine by the bus stop or at Travel Information Centres.

Fares

Single bus fares are £1 (40p children). A one-day bus pass for unlimited bus travel is £2.50 (£1 children). Children aged 5-10 in possession of a valid photocard travel free on buses.

Savers

Bus Saver tickets are the equivalent of the tube's carnet: a book of six tickets costs £4.20 (£2.10 children). Savers can be bought at newsagents displaying the relevant sign and at London Underground ticket offices.

Night buses

Night buses are the only form of public transport that runs all night, operating from 11pm to 6am about once an hour on most routes (more often on Fridays and Saturdays). Many pass through central London and the majority stop around Trafalgar Square, so head there if you're unsure which bus to get. Night buses have the letter 'N' before their number, and are free to holders of One-Day Travelcards, Weekend Travelcards, Family Travelcards and One-Day LT Cards. You'll find free maps and timetables at Travel Information Centres. Fares for night buses are the same as for day buses.

Green Line buses

Green Line buses (0870 608 7261, www.greenline.co.uk) serve the suburbs and towns within a 40 mile (64km) radius of London. Their main departure point is Eccleston Bridge (Colonnades Coach Station, behind Victoria station).

Routes 205 & 705

Bus routes 205 and 705 (7222 1234) connect all the main London rail termini (except Charing Cross) on circular trips. Bus 205 runs from Whitechapel station to Euston Square station via Aldgate, Aldgate East, Liverpool Street, Moorgate, Old Street, Angel, King's Cross, St Pancras and Euston. Starting at around 5am (6am on Sunday) to just after midnight every day, they run every 10-15 minutes, check the timetable. Route 705 starts at Paddington around 7.50am (8.15am from Liverpool Street) and runs about every 30 minutes until 7.50pm (8.15pm from Liverpool Street), stopping at Victoria, Waterloo, London Bridge and Fenchurch Street.

Rail services

Independently run commuter services to suburban London and the shires leave from the city's main rail stations (*see p277*). Travelcards are valid on these services within the right zones. Perhaps the most useful is Silverlink (0845 601 4867/ www.silverlink-trains.com; or National Rail Enquiries on 0845 748 4950), which runs from Richmond in the south-west to North Woolwich in the east, via London City Airport. Trains run about every 20 minutes daily except Sunday, when they run every half an hour.

Tramlink

Trams run between Beckenham, Croydon, Addington and Wimbledon in south London. Travelcards and bus passes taking in zones 3-6 can be used on trams; otherwise, cash single fares cost from £1 (40p children). A weekly Tram Pass costs £9.50 (zone 4) or £12.50 (zones 3 and 4).

Water transport

The times of London's assortment of river services vary, but most operate every 20 minutes to one hour between 10.30am and 5pm. Services may be more frequent and run later in summer. Journey times are longer than by tube, but it's a nicer way to travel. Call the operators listed below for schedules and fares, or see www.tfl.gov.uk. Travelcard holders can expect one-third off scheduled Riverboat fares. Thames Clippers (www.thamesclippers.com) runs a fast, reliable, commuter boat service. Piers to board the Clippers from are: Savoy (near Embankment tube), Blackfriars, Bankside (for the Globe), London Bridge and St Katharine's (Tower Bridge).

The names in bold below are the names of piers.

Embankment–Tower (30mins)–**Greenwich** (30mins); Catamaran Cruises 7087 1185.
Greenland Dock Canary Wharf (8mins)–**St Katharine's** (7mins)–**London Bridge City** (4mins)–**Bankside** (3mins)–**Blackfriars** (3mins)–**Savoy** (4mins); Collins River Enterprises 7977 6892.
Savoy–Cadogan (15-20mins)–**Chelsea** (2mins); Riverside Launches 07831 574 774.
Westminster–(Thames) **Barrier Gardens** (1hr 30mins); Thames Cruises 7930 3373/www.thamescruises.com.
Westminster– Festival (5mins)–London Bridge City (20mins)–**St Katharine's** (5mins); Crown River 7936 2033/www.crownriver.com.
Westminster–Greenwich (1hr); Westminster Passenger Services 7930 4097/www.westminsterpier.co.uk.
Westminster–Kew (1hr 30mins) –**Richmond** (30mins)–**Hampton Court** (1hr 30mins); Westminster Passenger Service Association 7930 2062.
Westminster–Tower (25-30mins); City Cruises 7740 0400/www.citycruises.com.

Taxis

Black cabs

Drivers of black cabs must pass a test called 'the Knowledge' to prove they know every street in central London and the shortest route to it.

If a taxi's yellow 'For Hire' sign is switched on, it can be hailed. If a taxi stops, the cabbie must take you to your destination, provided it's within seven miles. You can also book black cabs in advance. Both Radio Taxis (7272 0272; credit cards only) and Dial-a-Cab (7253 5000) run 24-hour services for black cabs (there'll be a booking fee in addition to the regular fare). Enquiries or complaints about black cabs should be made to the Public Carriage Office.

Public Carriage Office
200 Baker Street, Marylebone, NW1 5RZ (7918 2000). Baker Street tube. **Open** *By phone 9am-4pm Mon-Fri. In person 9am-2pm Mon-Fri.*

Minicabs

Minicabs (saloon cars) are generally cheaper than black cabs, but be sure to use only licensed firms. There are, happily, plenty of trustworthy and licensed local minicab firms. Among the London-wide firms are **Lady Cabs** (7272 3300), which employs only women drivers (great for women travelling alone), and **Addison Lee** (7387 8888). Whoever you use, ask the price when you book and confirm it with the driver.

Driving

Congestion Charge

Every driver driving in central London – an area defined as within King's Cross (N), Old Street roundabout (NE), Aldgate (E), Old Kent Road (SE), Elephant & Castle (S), Vauxhall (SW), Hyde Park Corner (W) and Edgware Road tube (NW) – between 7am

and 6.30pm Monday to Friday has to pay a £5 fee. Expect a fine of £80 if you fail to do so (reduced to £40 if you pay within 14 days). Passes can be bought from newsagents, garages and the like; the scheme is enforced by countless CCTV cameras.

For more information about the Congestion Charge call 0845 900 1234 or go to www.cclondon.com. For a map of central London by area, *see pp310-11*. Plans to increase the range of the Congestion Charge in a westerly direction to include Kensingon & Chelsea remain extremely controversial.

Parking

Central London is scattered with **parking meters**, but finding one that's unoccupied can take ages and, once you're parked, you'll pay up to £1 for every 15 minutes and be limited to two hours.

In the evening (from 6.30pm or 7pm in much of central London) and at various times at weekends, parking on single yellow lines is free. If you find a clear spot on a single yellow, check a nearby sign before you leave your car: this sign should tell you at which times parking is legal; times vary from street to street. Meters also become free after a certain time in the evening and at various times on weekends: always check before paying. Parking on double yellow lines and red routes is illegal at all times.

NCP 24hr **car parks** (0870 606 7050, www.ncp.co.uk) in central London are numerous but expensive. Prices vary, but expect to pay £6-£10 for two hours. Central car parks include Arlington House, Arlington Street, Mayfair, SW1A 1RL; 99 Upper Ground, Southbank, SE1 9PP; and 2 Lexington Street, Soho, W1R 3FD. A word of warning: almost all NCPs in central London are underground, and a few – such as the car park on Adeline Place

behind Tottenham Court Road – are frequented by drug users looking for a quiet place in which to indulge. Take care.

Cycling

London, even inside the Congestion Charge zone, is tough for cyclists, but the dedicated London Cycle Network (7974 2016, www.londoncyclenetwork.org) or the London Cycling Campaign (*see below*) help make it better. A safety helmet, a filter-mask and a determined attitude are advisable. Children should wear a helmet and stick to cycle paths and parks where possible.

London Cycling Campaign
Unit 228, 30 Great Guildford Street, South Bank, SE1 0HS (7928 7220/www.lcc.org.uk). **Open** *Phone enquiries 10am-5pm Mon-Fri.* Individual membership (£27.50 a yr) allows discounts at selected bike shops, advice and information on bike maintenance, insurance deals, route maps and a subscription to *London Cyclist* magazine.

Cycle hire

London Bicycle Tour Company
1A Gabriel's Wharf, 56 Upper Ground, South Bank, SE1 9PP (7928 6838/www.londonbicycle.com). Southwark tube, Blackfriars or Waterloo tube/rail. **Open** *Easter-Oct 10am-6pm daily. Nov-Easter by appointment.* **Hire** £2.50/hr; £14/1st day, £7 each day thereafter. *Deposit* £100 (unless paying by credit card). **Credit** AmEx, DC, MC, V. **Map** p320 N7. Bike hire, rickshaw hire (which costs £12/hr, self-drive) and daily bicycle tours. *See also p35.*

Walking

The best, least stressful way to see London is on foot. Most people rely heavily on their *A-Zs* when they're in an unfamiliar part of town. We've included a selection of street maps covering central London in the back of this book (*see p310-22*), but we recommend that you also buy a separate map of the city: both the standard Geographers' *A–Z* and Collins' *London Street Atlas* versions are very easy to use.

RESOURCES

Councils

Barnet 8359 2000/www.barnet.gov.uk
Brent 8937 1234/www.brent.gov.uk
Camden 7278 4444/www.camden.gov.uk
Corporation of London 7606
3030/www.cityoflondon.gov.uk
Ealing 8825 5000/www.ealing.gov.uk
Greenwich 8854
8888/www.greenwich.gov.uk
Hackney 8356 5000/www.hackney.gov.uk
Hammersmith & Fulham 8748
3020/www.lbhf.gov.uk
Haringey 8489 0000/www.haringey.gov.uk
Hounslow 8583
2000/www.hounslow.gov.uk
Islington 7527 2000/www.islington.gov.uk
Kensington & Chelsea 7937
5464/www.rbkc.gov.uk
Lambeth 7926 1000/www.lambeth.gov.uk
Lewisham 8314
6000/www.lewisham.gov.uk
Merton 8543 2222/www.merton.gov.uk
Newham 8430 2000/www.newham.gov.uk
Richmond-upon-Thames 8891
1411/www.richmond.gov.uk
Southwark 7525
5000/www.southwark.gov.uk
Tower Hamlets 7364
5000/www.towerhamlets.gov.uk
Waltham Forest 8527
5544/www.walthamforest.gov.uk
Wandsworth 8871
6000/www.wandsworth.gov.uk
Westminster 7641
6000/www.westminster.gov.uk

Education

To find out more about the state schools and nurseries in your area, contact your local council.

Advisory Centre on Education (ACE)

0808 800 5793/exclusion advice line 0808 800 0327/www.ace-ed.org.uk. Open Exclusion advice line 2-5pm Mon-Fri. Ring the centre for advice about your child's schooling; the advice line is for parents whose children have been excluded from school.

British Association for Early Childhood Education

136 Cavell Street, E1 2JA (7539 5400/www.early-education.org.uk). Open 9am-5pm Mon-Fri. A charitable organisation that provides information on infant education from birth to eight years. Send an SAE for additional publications.

Gabbitas Educational Consultants

Carrington House, 126-30 Regent Street, W1B 5EE (7734 0161/www.gabbitas.co.uk). Open 9am-5pm Mon-Fri. The consultants at Gabbitas give advice on choosing an independent school.

Home Education Advisory Service

PO Box 98, Welwyn Garden City, Herts AL8 6AN (01707 371 854/www.heas.org.uk). Open 9am-5pm Mon-Fri. Call HEAS for information if you want to educate your child at home. An introductory pack costs £2.50, a year's subscription £12.

ISC Information Service

London & South-east 7798 1560/www.iscis.uk.net. Open 9am-5pm Mon-Fri. The Independent Schools Council information service works to help parents find out about independent schools.

National Association for Gifted Children

Suite 14, Challenge House, Sherwood Drive, Bletchley, Milton Keynes, Bucks MK3 6DP (0870 770 3217/www.nagcbritain.org.uk). Support and advice on education for the parents of gifted children.

Parenting Education & Support Forum

Unit 431, Highgate Studios, 53 79 Highgate Road, NW5 1TL (7284 8389/www.parenting-forum.org.uk). Open 11am-5pm Mon-Thur. Information about parenting classes and support for parents.

Pre-School Learning Alliance

Units 213-16, 30 Great Guildford Street, SE1 0HS (7620 0550/www.pre-school.org.uk). Open 9am-5pm Mon-Fri. The PSLA runs courses and workshops in pre-schools around the country for parents of children under the age of five.

Fun & games

Indoor play

Crechendo

1 George Mills Weir Road, SW12 0NF. (8772 8120/www.crechendo.com). Open Phoneline 9am-1pm Mon-Fri. Active play classes throughout London; phone for your nearest.

Gymboree Play & Music

0800 092 0911/www.gymboreePlayUK.com. A parent-and-child play organisation, based on music and movement, for children aged 16 months to four and a half years. New recruits receive a free trial session.

National Association of Toy & Leisure Libraries (NATLL)

68 Churchway, NW1 1LT (7255 4600/helpline 7255 4616/www.natll.org.uk). Open 9am-5pm Mon-Fri. For information on the more than 1,000 toy libraries, invaluable resources that lend out toys to children across Britain.

TumbleTots

0121 585 7003/www.tumbletots.com. Phone to find out about TumbleTot play centres in your area.

One O'Clock Clubs

These weekday clubs within parks, with indoor and outdoor play facilities, open around lunchtime (12.30-1.30pm) and go on till school's out. They're a useful meeting place for parents and carers of pre-school children.

North London

Barnard Park Copenhagen Street, Islington, N1 (7278 9494). Angel tube.
Clissold Park Stoke Newington Church Street, N16 (8809 6700). Bus 73.
Highbury Fields The Bandstand, Highbury Fields, N5 (7704 9337). Highbury & Islington tube/rail.
Parliament Hill Fields Peggy Jay Centre, NW5 (7485 6907). Gospel Oak rail.

East London

Haggerston Park Queensbridge Road, Hackney, E2 (7729 6662). Bus 26, 48, 55.
Millwall Park Stebondale Street, Poplar, E14 (7515 6807). Mudchute DLR.
Springfield Park Springfield Lane, Clapton, E5 (no phone). Clapton rail/253 bus. The club is just outside the park.
Victoria Park Cadogan Terrace, Mile End, E9 (8986 6150). Bus 277, S2.
Wapping Park opposite St Patrick's Church, off High Street, Wapping, E1 (7481 9321). Wapping tube.

South-east London

Crystal Palace Park Crystal Palace Park Road, SE26 (8659 6554). Crystal Palace, Penge East or Penge West rail.
Geraldine Mary Harmsworth Park St George's Road, Lambeth, SE1 (7820 9724). Lambeth North tube.
Kennington Park Bolton Crescent, Camberwell, SE5 (7735 7186). Oval tube/36, 45, 131, 159 bus.
Leyton Square Peckham Park Road, SE15 (7639 1812). Bus 53, 78, 172, 381.
Myatts Fields Cormont Road, Camberwell, SE5 (7733 3609). Bus P5.
Norwood Park Salters Hill, SE19 (8761 1752). Gipsy Hill rail.
Peckham Rye Peckham Rye Road, SE15 (8693 0481). Bus 12, 312, 343, 363, 484.
Ruskin Park Denmark Hill, Camberwell, SE5 (7733 6659).Denmark Hill rail.
Southwark Park Hawkstone Road, Rotherhithe, SE16 (7231 3755). Canada Water tube/DLR or Surrey Quays DLR.

South-west London

Agnes Riley Gardens corner of Clarence Avenue & Poynders Road, Clapham, SW4 (8673 1277). Clapham South tube.
Bishops Park Rainbow Playhouse, Stevenage Road, Putney, SW6 (7731 4572). Putney tube/14, 74, 220 bus.
Brockwell Park Arlingford Road, Herne Hill, SW9 (8671 4883). Herne Hill rail.

Clapham Common *Windmill Drive, Clapham, SW4 (8673 5736). Clapham Common or Clapham South tube.*
Streatham Vale Park *Abercairn Road, Streatham, SW16 (8764 3688). Streatham Common rail/60, 118 bus.*
Vauxhall Park *Fentiman Road, SW8 (7582 3209). Vauxhall or Oval tube/rail.*
Windmill Gardens *Blenheim Gardens, SW2 (8671 5587). Brixton tube/rail/ 3, 45, 109, 159 bus.*

West London
Meanwhile Gardens *Elkstone Road, W10 (8960 7894). Westbourne Park tube.*
Ravenscourt Park *under-5s centre, Ravenscourt Park, W6 (8748 3180). Ravenscourt Park tube.*

Health

Contact-A-Family
7608 8700/helpline 0808 808 3555/www.cafamily.org.uk.
Open 10am-4pm Mon-Fri.
Support for parents of children with disabilities.

National Asthma Campaign
Helpline 0845 701 0203/www.asthma.org.uk.
Open 9am-5pm Mon-Fri.
Advice and help if you or your child has asthma.

NHS Direct
Helpline 0845 4647/www.nhsdirect.nhs.uk.
Open 24hrs daily.
Staffed by nurses and health information advisors, NHS Direct is a useful service, providing confidential information and health advice. Calls are charged at the local rate and all are recorded.

Help & support

Bestbear
7352 5852/www.bestbear.co.uk. **Open** 9am-6pm Mon-Fri; 24hr answerphone.
Information about childcare agencies and everything you need to know about hiring, or becoming, a child carer.

Childcare Link
(0800 096 0296/www.childcarelink.gov.uk).
Open 8am-8pm Mon-Fri; 9am-noon Sat.
The Link provides information on all manner of childcare options. If possible, callers will be given a list of childcare organisations in their area.

ChildLine
0800 1111/www.childline.org.uk.
ChildLine is a free, completely confidental 24-hour helpline for children and young people in the UK. Children can call about any problem, at any time – day or night. Counsellors are there to help find ways to sort things out.

Childminders
6 Nottingham Street, W1U 5EJ (7935 3000/www.childminders. co.uk). **Open** 8.45am-5.30pm Mon-Thur; 8.45am-5pm Fri; 9am-4.30pm Sat.

Childminders is a long-established and respected babysitting agency. Sitters on its books are locally based nurses, teachers and nannies with impeccable references. Most London areas can be covered.

Daycare Trust
21 St George's Road, SE1 6ES (7840 3350/www.daycaretrust.org.uk).
Open 9.15am-5.15pm Mon-Fri.
A national childcare charity promoting high-quality, affordable childcare. It publishes a range of useful booklets, including *No More Nine to Five: Childcare in a changing world* (£5).

4Children
7512 2112/info line 7512 2100/ www.4children.org.uk. **Open** 9.30am-5.30pm Mon-Fri.
Information on after-school clubs, children's and family services.

Nannytax
PO Box 988, Brighton, East Sussex BN1 3NT (0845 226 2203/www.nanny tax.co.uk). **Open** 9am-5pm Mon-Fri.
For £250 a year Nannytax will register your nanny with the Inland Revenue, issue his or her payslips, organise National Insurance payments and give employment advice.

National Family & Parenting Institute
430 Highgate Studios, 53-79 Highgate Road, NW5 1TL (7424 3460/www.nfpi.org/www.e-parents.org).
Kentish Town tube/rail. **Open** 9.30am-5.30pm Mon-Fri/24hr answerphone.
A resource centre with factsheets on all aspects of parenting.

Night Nannies
7731 6168/www.nightnannies.com.
A useful service for parents whose children are denying them sleep. After the initial phone call, to discuss parents' needs (how many nights the nanny will be needed, for example, and from what time), Night Nannies provides a list of qualified carers, who may be able to provide respite.

Simply Childcare
16 Bushey Hill Road, SE5 8QJ (7701 6111/www.simplychildcare.com).
Open 9am-5.30pm Mon-Fri.
A boon for many working parents in the city. If you are seeking a nanny to work in or near London, you can pay £30 to advertise the job in three issues of this listings magazine, or £40 for five issues. Entry on the list is free for prospective nannies.

Parent courses

Holy Trinity Brompton
Brompton Road, SW7 1JA (7581 8255/www.htb.org.uk). South Kensington tube. **Open** *Office* 9.30am-5.30pm Mon, Wed-Fri; 10.30am-5.30pm Tue.
Runs 'The Parenting Course' for parents with children under the age of 12, with the price of admission £25. 'Parenting Teenagers', for parents of children aged 13-18, costs £30. Both courses are four two-hour sessions; prices include supper and materials.

The Parent Company
6 Jacob's Well Mews, W1U 3DY (7935 9635/www.theparent company.co.uk). **Open** 9am-5pm Mon-Fri.
The Parent Company runs seminars on weekday evenings on diverse subjects, from time-management to discipline issues. Seminars cost £45 per session per person, or £60 for two people. The company has also introduced six-week teleclasses by email and a BT conference line, for those who'd prefer to learn at home.

Parentline Plus
Parentline Plus 0808 800 2222/www.parentlineplus.org.uk.
Open 24hrs.
Organises nationwide courses on how to cope with being a parent. For more details phone the free helpline, Parentline Plus.

Parent Support Group
Helpline 8469 0205/www.psg.co.uk. **Open** 10am-7pm/24hr answerphone.
As well as the helpline, staff run one-to-one support sessions and offer courses on parenting skills to the parents and carers of adolescents who are acting in an antisocial or criminal manner.

Parents for Inclusion
7735 7735/helpline 7582 5008/freephone 0800 652 3145/www.parentsforinclusion. org. **Open** 10am-noon, 1-3pm Tue-Thur.
Organises a series of workshops for parents of disabled children.

Tourist information

Visit London (7932 2000, www.visitlondon.com) is the city's official tourist information company. Other tourist offices are located in Vinopolis, at **Bankside** (*see p36*), in the **Greenwich Gateway Visitor Centre** (*see p125*) and next to **St Paul's Cathedral** in The City (*see p55*).

Britain & London Visitor Centre
1 Lower Regent Street, Piccadilly Circus, SW1Y 4XT (8846 9000/ www.visitbritain.com). Piccadilly Circus tube. **Open** *Oct-May* 9.30am-6.30pm Mon; 9am-6.30pm Tue-Fri; 10am-4pm Sat, Sun. *June-Sept* 9.30am-6.30pm Mon; 9am-6.30pm Tue-Fri; 9am-5pm Sat; 10am-4pm Sun.
Map p319 K7.

London Information Centre
Leicester Square, WC2H 7BP (7437 4370/www.londontown.com). Leicester Square tube. **Open** 8am-midnight Mon-Fri; 10am-6pm Sat, Sun.

London Visitor Centre
Arrivals Hall, Waterloo International Terminal, SE1 7LT. **Open** 8.30am-10.30pm Mon-Sat; 9.30am-10.30pm Sun.
Map p319 M8.

Advertisers' Index

Please refer to relevant sections for
addresses / telephone numbers

Index

Index

and under cookery; dance;
drama; music
Clerkenwell 57-60
  restaurants 60, 160
climbing 112, 127, 148, 238, **254-256**
Clink Prison Museum 42
Clissold Park **100-101**, 269, 297
clothes 190-200
  budget 190-191
  designer 150, **191-195**
  ecological 188
  mail order 204
  mid-range & high street 75, **195-196**
  second-hand 196-197
  sportswear 199-200
  street 200
see also fancy dress; shoes
Clown Town 252
clowns 95, 100, 243, 245, 246
Clowns International Gallery 109, **110**
Cnut (Canute) 11
coffee, history of 14, 15
Coin Street Festival 26
Coliseum theatre 23, 75, **219**
College of Arms 50
Colour House Theatre 221
Columbia Road Market 184
comedy 222
congestion charge 20, **296**
cookery
  parties *234*, 235
  school 152, **229, 232**
Coram, Thomas 17, 64
Coram's Fields 17, 61, *62*, **64**, 252
  café 63
councils, borough 297
country parks 285
County Hall 20, 36, 37, 38, 40, 41
  Travel Inn Capital 210
Courtauld Institute Gallery 57, 213
  Gallery Café 60
Covent Garden 30, **75-77**
  restaurants 75, 166-169
  shops 201
crafts
  parties 233-234
  workshops 47, 77, 86, 93, 96, 104,
    109, 110, 113, 117, 125, 135, 138,
    139, 142, 143, 144
Crechendo 297
crèches 104, 140, 182
Creekside Centre 123
cricket
  AMP Oval **128**, 273
  clubs & coaching 101, 128, **256**
  Lord's Ground & MCC Museum 94
  matches 272-273
Cromwell, Oliver 14
Crouch End 100
Crown Jewels 49, 56
Croydon 55, 224
  tramlink 295
Croydon Clocktower 135
cruises *see* boat trips
Crystal Palace **133**, 134, *178*
  National Sports Centre 26, 133, 266
Crystal Palace Museum 133
Crystal Palace Park *133*, *134*, 297
Cutty Sark 122, 123
cycling 256-257, **296**
  bike hire 132, 137-138, 142, 296
  bike repairs 200
  bike shops 199, **200, 202**
  organised rides 35, 123
  parks, commons & trails 100, 138,
    140, 142
  as sport 256
  training 256-257

d

Daisy & Tom 183, 185
Dali Universe 37
Dalston 100
  restaurants 173, 176

Rio Cinema **217**, 235
dance
  classes 148-149, 221, 223, 228, 229,
    230, 231
  parties 246
  schools 257
  workshops 64, 84, 125, 126, 127,
    213, 215, 227
Danson Park 133-134
Deen City Farm 140
Denmark Street 76
Dennis Severs' House 105, **106**
department stores 17, **183-184**
Deptford 123
  Laban *226*, 228
Derby Day 29
Design Museum 36, **47**
  restaurant 41
Diana, Princess of Wales *20*, 20
Diana, Princess of Wales Memorial
  Playground *84*, **85**, 86
Dickens, Charles 12, 17, 47, 59, 60,
  126, 288
  museums 61, **63-64**, 288
Diggerland 292
disabled & special needs resources
  Contact-A-Family 298
  cookery school 229
  dance 230
  gardens 151, 287
  horse riding 136, 140
  music 232
  playgrounds 85, 97, 139
  sport 257
  wildlife 232
discos 243, 245, 247
Discover 111, *112*, 112
Discover Dogs 30
Discovery Planet 252
Diwali 140
Docklands 20, **114-116**, 176
  watersports 120, **271-272**
Docklands Light Railway **114**, 123,
  126, **295**
Dr Johnson's House 50
Dollis Valley Green Walk 103
Downing Street (No.10) 14
drama
  classes 40, 99, 120, 219, 223, **227-231**
  parties 235-237, 246, 247
  workshops 47, 77, 126, 127, 130,
    135, 143, 151, 152, 154, 213,
    215, 218, 219, 221, 223, 224,
    227-231
see also theatre
Dramarama **227**, 235
Drusillas Park 279-280
Duck Tours, London 35
Duke's Meadows 152
Dulwich *130*, **131-132**, 221
Dulwich Park 131, 132
  Pavilion Café 162, 178
Dulwich Picture Gallery 131, 132

e

Ealing **154**, 297
Earl's Court 16, **149 151**
East Ham Nature Reserve 117
East London 105-119
  restaurants 175-177
  shops 201
East Sheen Common 142
Eastbourne 288
Easter
  egg hunts 96, 100, 113, 135, 137,
    144, 209, 279, 283
  egg-making 132
  horse parade 32
ecology centres & parks 100, 112, 120,
  149
  Greenwich Peninsula 27, 123, **124**
  see also nature reserves
education 297
  history of 12

Edward the Confessor 11
Edward VII 17
Edward Alleyn Theatre 221
Electric Cinema 147, **216**
Elephant & Castle 128
'Elephant Man' 106
Elizabeth I 14
Eltham Palace 135
Emslie Horniman Pleasance Gardens
  148
entertainers 243-245, 246, 248
entertainment 64, 95-96, 97, **215-231**
Epping Forest 119
executions 16, 47, 78, 114, 128, 134, 146

f

face-painting parties 237, 246, 247
fairground, indoor 245
Fan Museum 123
fancy dress 206, 241, 243, 249, 250
fantasy parties 247
Faraday Museum 73
farms
  Coram's Fields 64
  country 278-279
  Deen 140
  Freightliners 99-100
  Hackney 109, **110**, 176
  Hounslow 156
  Kentish Town 96
  Lee Valley 119
  Mudchute 116
  Newham 117
  Spitalfields 106
  Stepping Stones 110, 113
  Surrey Docks 122
  Vauxhall 136, *137*
  Woodlands 135
Fashion & Textile Museum 47
Fawkes, Guy 14
see also Bonfire Night
fencing 257-258
Fenton House 95
Festival of Britain 19, 23
festivals & events **25-32**, 60, 79, 86
  north London 95, 99, 100, 103, 104
  outside London 278, 288
  south-east London 120, 126, 131,
    132, 134, 135
  south-west London 140, 144
  west London 146, 151, 154
Finchley **103-104**, 266
  artsdepot 219
  Cross Keys camps 282
  London International Gallery of
    Children's Art **213**, 234
  Phoenix cinema 235
Finsbury Park **99**, 100, 172, 270
  Michael Sobell Leisure Centre 99,
    238, 260
Fire of London, Great *11*, 14
  tours 35
Firepower 126, 127
fireworks
  suppliers 249, 250
  see also Bonfire Night
fishing 96, 114, 119, 134, 138, 285, 287
fitness centres 130, 137, 139, **268**
Fitzrovia 61-65
  restaurants 63, 160, 163
Fleet, river 92, 95
Florence Nightingale Museum 37-38
food, history of 15
football 258-259
  clubs 99, 104, 114, 150, 151, **273**
  coaching 259
  Hackney Marsh events 110
  parties 237
  pitches 64, 70, 114, 139, 140, 146,
    148
  supplies 199
Fortis Green 183
Fortnum & Mason 164, 174
Foundling Museum 61, **64**
Fountain Leisure Centre 152, 267

Frank Banfield Park 151
Freightliners City Farm 99-100
French language workshops 232
Freud Museum 94
Frost Fair 31
Fulham **150-151**, 179, 227, 297
Fulham FC 150, 273
Fulham Palace 150-151

g

Gabriel's Wharf 26, 38
games
  history of 16
  shops 123, **206**
gardens 40, 55, 75-76, 78
  Chelsea Physic Garden **84**, 85
  east London 108
  for disabled & visually impaired
    151, 287
  Kew 143
  north London 95, 96, 99
  outside London 285-287
  south-east London 123, 126, 130-131, 132, 134, 135
  south-west London 136, 143, 144
  west London 149, 152
  wildlife 64, 89, 122, 127, 132
Gasworks 128
Gate Cinema 147
Gatti, Carlo 93
Geffrye Museum 108
General Strike 17
Georgian era 14, 17
'gherkin' *see* Swiss Re building
ghosts 104, 125, 144, 156
  tours 35
Gilbert Collection 57
Globe *see* Shakespeare's Globe
Golden Hinde **42**, 250
Golden Jubilee Bridge 36
Golders Hill Park 95
  Refreshment House 162, 172
Goldfinger, Ernö 94
golf 152, 154, **259**
Great River Race 29
Green Chain Walk 128, 134
Greenman, Leon 102
Greenwich 122, **123-126**, 297
  foot tunnel 116
  restaurants 177, 178
  tourist information 123
Greenwich & Docklands
  International Festival 11, 26-27
Greenwich Heritage Centre 127
Greenwich Market 123, **187**
Greenwich Park *121*, 123, 124
Greenwich Peninsula Ecology Park
  27, 123, **124**
greyhound racing 273-274
Groombridge Place Gardens 287
Guards' Museum 78, 80, *80*
Guildhall 11, **50-51**
Guildhall Art Gallery 51
Gunnersbury Park 152
Gunnersbury Triangle Nature
  Reserve 152
Gymboree Play & Music 146, **297**
gymnastics 259-260

h

Hackney **109-110**, 184, 297
  Clissold Centre 24
  Ocean 232
Hackney City Farm 109, 110
  Frizzante café 176
Hackney Downs 110
Hackney Empire 109, **221**
Hackney Marsh 110
Hackney Museum 109, 110
Haggerston Park **109**, 297
Half Moon Young People's Theatre
  223, *225*
Hall Place 134, 135
Hallowe'en events 223, 279, 287

Index

fine & decorative arts: Gilbert Collection 57; Ranger's House 125; V&A Museum 90
historic houses: Apsley House 73; Charlton House 128; Dennis Severs' House 105, **106**; Marble Hill House 144; Osterley House 154, 156; Prince Henry's Room 57, 59; Sutton House 110
Jewish culture: Jewish Museum, Camden 91; Jewish Museum, Finchley 102, 103-104
literature: British Library **61**, 63; Charles Dickens Museum 61, **63-64**; Dickens House Museum 288; Dr Johnson's House 50; Keats House 94, 96, *97*; Roald Dahl Children's Gallery 291; Sherlock Holmes Museum 70
local history: Age Exchange Reminiscence Centre 126; Bruce Castle Museum 101, **104**; Burgh House 94-95; Croydon Clocktower 135; Crystal Palace Museum 133; East Ham Nature Reserve museum 117; Hackney Museum 109, 110; Hop Story Museum 285; Islington Museum 100; Museum in Docklands 115, 116; Museum of Kent Life 284; Museum of London 48, **50**, **53**, 56; Museum of Richmond 142; Old Royal Naval College 123, *124-125*, 125; Vestry House Museum 118; Wandsworth Museum 139-140; Weald & Downland Open Air Museum 291
maritime: Chatham Historic Dockyard 289; HMS *Belfast* **42-43**, 250; National Maritime Museum 123, 124-125; Old Royal Naval College 123, *124-125*, 125
medical: Alexander Fleming Laboratory Museum 146; Florence Nightingale Museum 37-38; Hunterian Museum 57; Museum of the Order of St John 57, 58-59; Old Operating Theatre Museum 43-45; Royal London Hospital Museum 106; St Bartholomew's Hospital Museum 53
music: Fenton House 95; Handel House Museum **73**, **74**, 219; Horniman Museum **127**, 131, **132**, *133*; Musical Museum 152
natural history: Horniman Museum **127**, 131, **132**, *133*; Natural History Museum 85, *87*, **87-89**
science & technology: Brunel Engine House & Tunnel Exhibition 120; Faraday Museum 73; Kew Bridge Steam Museum 152-154; Royal Observatory 125-126; *see also* Science Museum
social history: Linley Sambourne House 149, 150; No.19 Princelet Street 105, **106**, **107**
specialist: Avenue House (Ink Museum) 103; Bank of England Museum 48; Bramah Museum of Tea & Coffee 42; Cartoon Art Trust Museum 61, **62-63**; Clockmakers Company Museum 51; Freud Museum 94; London Canal Museum 93; London Fire Brigade Museum 38-40, *40*; Museum of Garden History 37, 40; Museum of Methodism 53; Theatre Museum 75, **76**, 77; Windmill Museum 140
sport: MCC Museum 94; Museum of Rugby 144; Wimbledon Lawn Tennis Museum 141, 143

transport: Bentley Motor Museum 288; Didcot Railway Centre 290; London's Transport Museum 75, **76**, **77**; North Woolwich Old Station Museum *105*, 117
war & militaria: Britain at War Experience 46; Cabinet War Rooms 78, **79-80**, **81**; Firepower 126, 127; Guards' Museum 78, 80, *80*; Imperial War Museum 128, *129*, 291; National Army Museum 85, **86**, 87; Royal Air Force Museum 104
Museums & Galleries Month 32
music
  church recitals 57, 83, 126, 128
  concerts 47, 73, 76, 78, 95, 97, 212, 213, **217**, 284
  courses 64, 148-149, 221, 228, 229 for disabled 232
  opera 76, 212, **219**
  Promenade Concerts 26
  shops (instruments) 189-190
  workshops 73, 126, 127, 149, 213, 217, 223, **232**
Music House for Children 232
Musical Museum 152
Muswell Hill 101
  restaurants 172, 175

n

Namco Station 40
nannies 298
nappies 188
National Archives 143
National Army Museum 85, 87
  events 86, 87
National Film Theatre
  Movie Magic 216-217
National Gallery 11, 22-23, **81**
  Gallery Café 82
  workshops 79
National Maritime Museum 123, 124-125
National Portrait Gallery 81
National Theatre *see* Royal National Theatre
National Youth Music Theatre 228
Natural History Museum *87*, 87-89
  Globe Café 85
nature reserves 92, 93, 100, 104, 117, 119, 120, 124, 152, 156 *see also* wildlife parks
Nature Study Centre 139
nature trails 140, 142, 147, 151, 283
Neal's Yard 75, 168
Nellie's Art Parties 242
Nettlefold Theatre 223
New Peckham Varieties 130, **229**
Newham City Farm 117
NHS Direct 298
Nightingale, Florence 37-38, 80, 87, 106
Normans 11, 284
North London 91-104
  restaurants 171-175
  shops 201
North Woolwich Old Station Museum *105*, 117
Northcote Road 138, 183, 184
Notting Hill **147-149**, 182
  Electric Cinema 147, **216**
Notting Hill Carnival **27**, 147, 149
Nunhead Cemetery 130, 131

o

Ocean 232
Oily Cart 218
Old Operating Theatre Museum & Herb Garret 43-45
Old Royal Naval College 123, *124-125*, 125
Olympic Games
  bid 24, 109, **258**
  history 19

One O'Clock Clubs 297-298
Open House 29
opera 76, 212, **219**
Oriental City 104
Orienteering 253
Orleans House Gallery 144, **213-215**
Osterley House 154, 156
Oval, AMP 128, 273
Oxford Circus 71
Oxford Street 30, 183
Oxleas Wood 134

p

Paddington 146
Paddington Recreation Ground 146
Painshill Landscape Garden 282, **285**
paintball 127, 251, 252
Pancake Day Race 32, *32*
parenting advice & courses 298
parking 296
parks cafés 162
see also specific parks
parties 233-252
  activities 229, 231, **233-238**, **242**
  best teas 237
  cakes 238, 241, 249
  costumes 241, 243
  entertainers **243-245**, 246, 248
  equipment hire 245
  makeovers 237, 246
  mobile 243
  organisers 188, **246-247**
  pop & dance 246, 247
  shops & suppliers 94, 202, 206, **249-250**
  top five 233
  venues 103, 127, 206, **250-252**, 279, 292
pâtisseries 177
pavement art 29
Pearly Kings & Queens Harvest Festival 30
Peckham 130-131
Peckham Library 130, 131
Peckham Pulse health club 130
Peckham Rye Common **130**, 297
pedicabs 35
Pepys, Samuel 57, 59, 77
Perform **229**, 237
Peter Jones 171, 174
Peter Pan 55, 85, 86
Petrie Museum of Egyptian Archaeology 64
Petticoat Lane Market 105
Phoenix cinema 235
Phoenix Garden 76
photography exhibitions 89, 90
Piccadilly Circus 71, 74
pie & mash 109, 118
Pineapple Performing Arts School 230
pirates 47, 85, 114, 123, 285
Pitshanger Manor & Gallery 154, 156
Place, The 230, 230
plague 11-12, 14, 117
Planetarium, Greenwich 125-126
Planetarium, Marylebone 69
play centres 40, 74, 111, 139, 140, 148, 152, 297
playgrounds
  adventure 95, 101, 126, 130, 136, 138, 149, 151, 152, 154
  Diana Memorial 84, **85**, 86
  as party venues 251-252
  with special features 95, 97, 100, 140
  suitable for disabled & special needs 85, 97, 139
  see also individual parks & commons
Playscape Pro Racing 238, *239*, 260
PlayStation Skate Park 148, 264, *265*
police, history of 17
Polka Theatre for Children 140, *141*, **224**
poll taxes 12, 20
Pollock's Toy Museum 61

pollution, history of 11, 17, 19
pond dipping 93, 140, 149, 232
Pop-Up Theatre 218
Port Lympne Wild Animal Park 280
Portobello Road Market 147, 187
Postman's Park 53
Potter, Harry 93
pottery *see* ceramic art
Primrose Hill 93
Prince Charles Cinema 71, 235
Prince Henry's Room 57, 59
Princelet Street (No.19) 105, **106**, **107**
Priory Park 101
Prom in the Park, CBBC 29
Promenade Concerts 26
Prospect of Whitby 114
Public Records Office *see* National Archives
pubs 41, 96, 110, 114, 118, 120, 152, 176, 178
puppet shows & theatre
  at Jackson's Lane 223
  Little Angel Theatre 99, **218**
  May Fayre & Puppet Festival 32
  party entertainers 243, 245
  Punch & Judy 30, 32, 114
  Puppet Theatre Barge 91, **218**
  shop events 185
  summer events 26, 60, 95, 114, 124
  workshops 149
Putney 141

q

Queen Elizabeth's Hunting Lodge 119
Queen's Gallery 79
Queen's House 125
Queen's Park 146 147, *148 149*
Queen's Park Rangers FC 151
Queen's Wood 97
Queensway 146
Questors Theatre 154
Quicksilver Theatre 218

r

race riots 19
Ragged School Museum 110, 113
ragged schools 12
Rail & River Rover 114
railways 295
  day trips 277
  history 17, 92
  miniature 288
  stations 277
  steam 290
Ranger's House 125
Ravenscourt Park **151**, 298
  Teahouse 162, 182
Red House 130
Regent Street Festival 29
Regent's Canal 32, 91, 112, 146
  London Canal Museum 93
Regent's Park 66, *66*, **69-70**, 93, 270
  cafés 69
  Golf & Tennis School 259
  Open-Air Theatre 70, **224**
Remembrance Sunday 30
restaurants 158-182
  by area see individual boroughs and areas
  best birthday teas 237
  best burgers 173
  chains 163
  cheap food 179
  diabetic food 164
  park cafés 162
  by cuisine: Afghan 171; American/burgers 163, 164, 167, 168, 169, 171, 172, 173, 174, 175, 180, 182; fish 103, 158, 160, 164, 168, 175, 176, 177, 178; French 159, 163; Greek 172; Indian 106, 140, 164, 173; Italian 158, 159, 160, 163, 165, 166, 176, 178; Mexican 167; Middle Eastern 163; Moroccan 182;

Index

Place of interest and/or entertainment	....	▮
Railway station	....	▮
Park	....	▦
Hospital	....	▮
Neighbourhood	....	SOHO
Pedestrian street	....	▬
Tube station	....	⊖
Church	....	✚
Synagogue	....	✡
Casualty unit	....	✚
Toilet	....	WL
Congestion Zone	....	Ⓒ

Maps

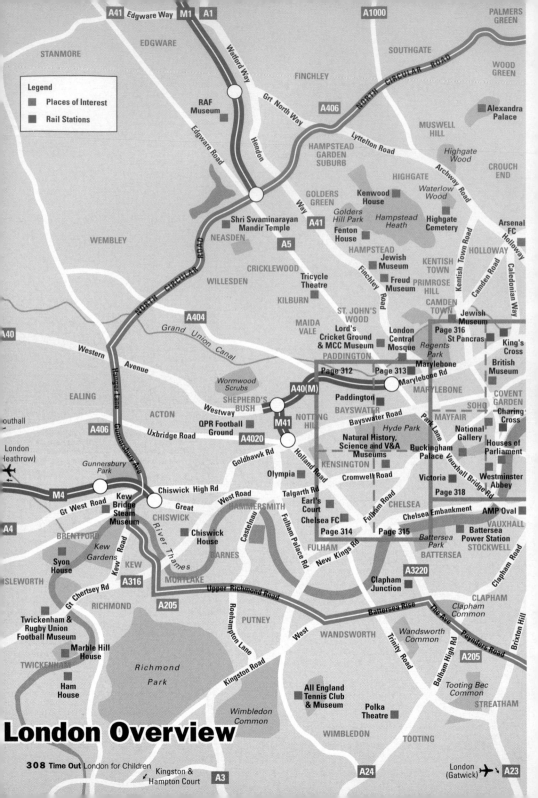

London Overview

Legend
- Places of Interest
- Rail Stations

A41 Edgware Way   M1   A1   A1000   PALMERS GREEN

STANMORE   EDGWARE   Watford Way   SOUTHGATE   WOOD GREEN

FINCHLEY   NORTH CIRCULAR ROAD

RAF Museum   Grt North Way   A406   MUSWELL HILL   Alexandra Palace

Hendon   Lyttelton Road   Highgate Wood   CROUCH END

HAMPSTEAD GARDEN SUBURB   HIGHGATE   Archway Road

Edgware Road   GOLDERS GREEN   Kenwood House   Waterlow Wood   Arsenal FC

WEMBLEY   A41   Golders Hill Park   Hampstead Heath   Highgate Cemetery   HOLLOWAY   Holloway

Shri Swaminarayan Mandir Temple   Fenton House   HAMPSTEAD   Kentish Town Road   Caledonian Way

NEASDEN   A5   Jewish Museum   KENTISH TOWN   Camden Road

CRICKLEWOOD   Freud Museum   PRIMROSE HILL   Jewish Museum

WILLESDEN   Tricycle Theatre   CAMDEN TOWN   St Pancras   King's Cross

NORTH CIRCULAR   KILBURN   MAIDA VALE   ST. JOHN'S WOOD   Lord's Cricket Ground & MCC Museum   London Central Mosque   Regents Park   Page 316   British Museum

A404   Grand Union Canal   PADDINGTON   Page 312   Page 313   Marylebone   MARYLEBONE   COVENT GARDEN

Western   Avenue   Wormwood Scrubs   SHEPHERD'S BUSH   A40(M)   Paddington   BAYSWATER   Marylebone Rd   SOHO   MAYFAIR   Charing Cross

EALING   Hanger Lane   Westway   QPR Football Ground   Bayswater Road   Hyde Park   Park Lane   National Gallery   Houses of Parliament

ACTON   Uxbridge Road   A4020   M41   NOTTING HILL   Buckingham Palace   Vauxhall Bridge Rd   Westminster Abbey

London (Heathrow)   Gunnersbury Ave   Goldshawk Rd   Holland Road   Natural History, Science and V&A Museums   KENSINGTON   Cromwell Road   Victoria   Page 318

A406   Gunnersbury Park   Olympia   CHELSEA   AMP Oval

M4   Gt West Road   Chiswick High Rd   West Road   Talgarth Rd   Earl's Court   Page 314   Page 315   Chelsea Embankment   Battersea Power Station   VAUXHALL   STOCKWELL

Kew Bridge Steam Museum   Great   HAMMERSMITH   Chelsea FC   Fulham Palace Rd   Fulham Rd   Battersea Park   BATTERSEA   Clapham Road

A4   BRENTFORD   CHISWICK   Chiswick House   Castelnau   FULHAM   New Kings Rd   A3220   CLAPHAM

Syon House   Kew Gardens   Kew Road   BARNES   Clapham Junction   Clapham Common

ISLEWORTH   KEW   River Thames   MORTLAKE   Upper Richmond Road   A205   Battersea Rise   The Ave   Paynders Road   Brixton Hill

A316   A205   RICHMOND   PUTNEY   West   WANDSWORTH   Wandsworth Common   Trinity Road   Balham High Rd   A205

Twickenham & Rugby Union Football Museum   Gt Chertsey Rd   Roehampton Lane   Kingston Road   Tooting Bec Common   STREATHAM

Marble Hill House   Richmond Park   All England Tennis Club & Museum   WIMBLEDON   TOOTING

TWICKENHAM   Ham House   Wimbledon Common   Polka Theatre

Kingston & Hampton Court   A3   A24   London (Gatwick)   A23

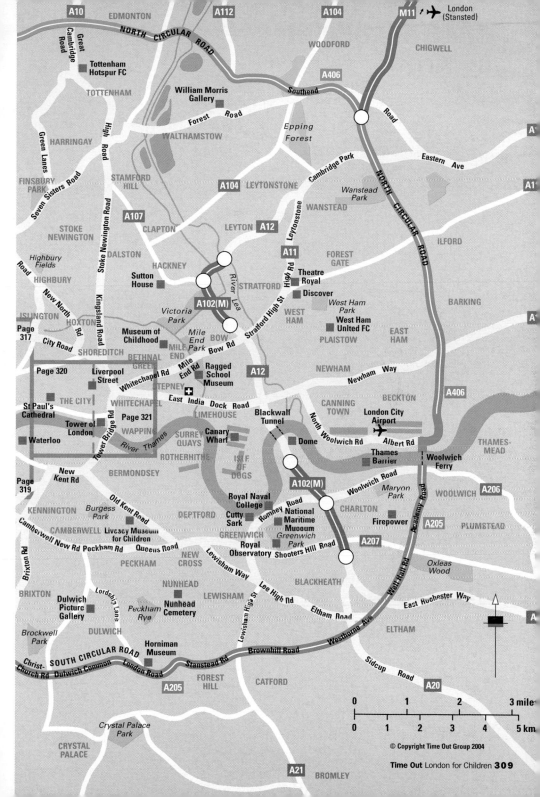

A10
EDMONTON
A112
A104
M11 ✈ London (Stansted)

NORTH CIRCULAR ROAD
Great Cambridge Road
Tottenham Hotspur FC
TOTTENHAM
WOODFORD
CHIGWELL

A406
Southend
Road
Eastern Ave

William Morris Gallery
Forest Road
WALTHAMSTOW
Epping Forest

HARRINGAY
High Road
STAMFORD HILL
A104
LEYTONSTONE
Cambridge Park
Wanstead Park
WANSTEAD
NORTH CIRCULAR ROAD
ILFORD
A1

FINSBURY PARK
Seven Sisters Road
STOKE NEWINGTON
A107
CLAPTON
LEYTON
A12
A11
FOREST GATE
Leytonstone
High Rd
BARKING
A406

Green Lanes
Highbury Fields
HIGHBURY
Stoke Newington Road
DALSTON
HACKNEY
Sutton House
River Lea
STRATFORD
Theatre Royal
Discover
WEST HAM
West Ham Park
West Ham United FC
PLAISTOW
EAST HAM
A

New North Road
HOXTON
ISLINGTON
Page 317
City Road
Kingsland Road
SHOREDITCH
BETHNAL GREEN
Victoria Park
A102(M)
Museum of Childhood
MILE END
Mile End Park
BOW
Bow Rd
Stratford High St
NEWHAM
Newham Way
BECKTON
A406

St Paul's Cathedral
THE CITY
Liverpool Street
Page 320
Whitechapel Rd
WHITECHAPEL
STEPNEY
Ragged School Museum
Mile End Rd
A12
CANNING TOWN
London City Airport ✈

Waterloo
Tower of London
WAPPING
Tower Bridge Rd
Page 321
East India Dock Road
LIMEHOUSE
Blackwall Tunnel
North Woolwich Rd
Dome
Albert Rd
Thames Barrier
Woolwich Ferry
THAMESMEAD

Page 319
New Kent Rd
River Thames
SURREY QUAYS
Canary Wharf
ISLE OF DOGS
A102(M)
Woolwich Road
Maryon Park
WOOLWICH
A206

BERMONDSEY
ROTHERHITHE
Royal Naval College
Cutty Sark
National Maritime Museum
Romney Road
CHARLTON
Firepower
A205
PLUMSTEAD

Old Kent Road
Burgess Park
KENNINGTON
DEPTFORD
GREENWICH
Greenwich Park
Royal Observatory
Shooters Hill Road
A207
Academy Road
Oxleas Wood

Camberwell New Rd
CAMBERWELL
Livesey Museum for Children
Peckham Rd
Queens Road
NEW CROSS
Lewisham Way
Lee High Rd
BLACKHEATH
Westhorne Ave
Well Hall Rd
East Rochester Way
A

Brixton Rd
PECKHAM
NUNHEAD
LEWISHAM
Eltham Road
ELTHAM

BRIXTON
Dulwich Picture Gallery
Lordship Lane
Nunhead Cemetery
Peckham Rye
Lewisham High St
Brockwell Park
DULWICH
Horniman Museum
SOUTH CIRCULAR ROAD
Brownhill Road
Sidcup Road
A20

Christ-Church Rd
Dulwich Common
London Road
A205
Stansead Rd
FOREST HILL
CATFORD

Crystal Palace Park
CRYSTAL PALACE
A21
BROMLEY

0   1   2   3 mile
0   1   2   3   4   5 km

© Copyright Time Out Group 2004

Time Out London for Children **309**

Central London by Area

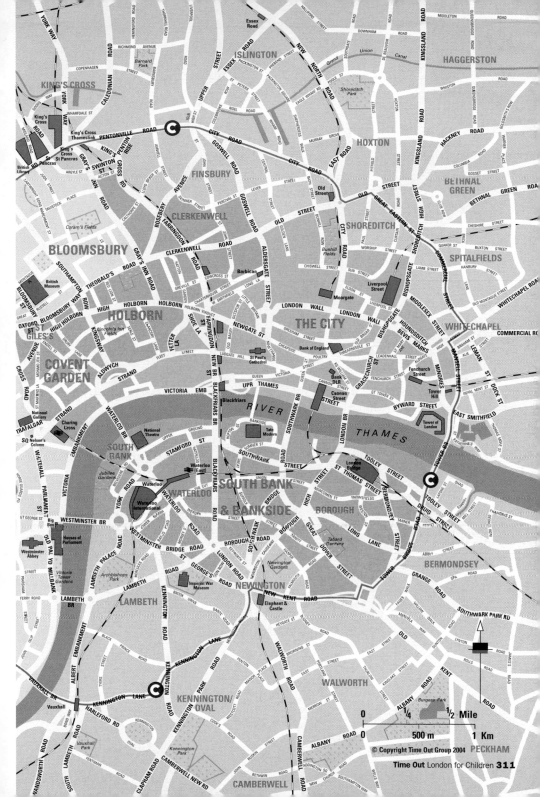

© Copyright Time Out Group 2004

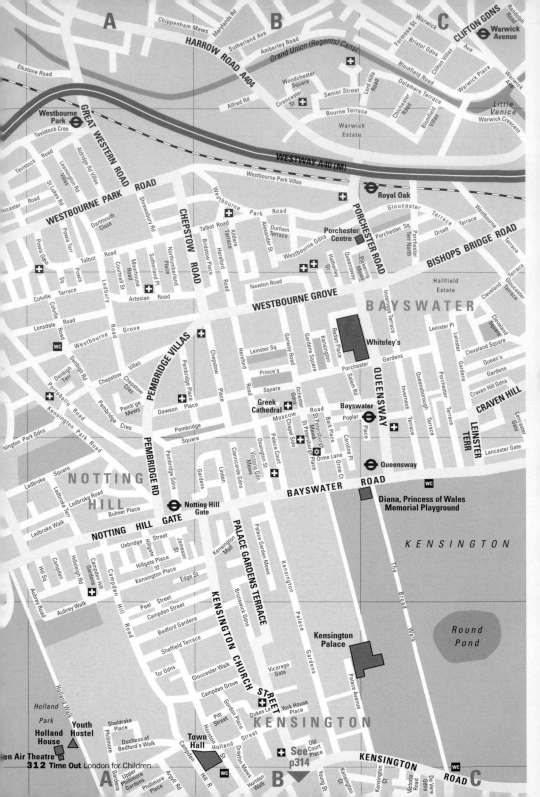

A

B

C

CLIFTON GDNS

Warwick Avenue

Little Venice

HARROW ROAD A404

Grand Union (Regents) Canal

Chippenham Mews

Maryland Rd

Sutherland Ave

Amberley Road

Elkstone Road

Woodchester Square

Senior Street

Lord Hills Road

Delamere Terrace

Warwick Place

Warwick Ave

Alfred Rd

Cirencester St

Bourne Terrace

Blomfield Road

Clifton Villas

Formosa St

Bristol Gdns

Warwick Estate

Warwick Crescent

WESTWAY A40 (M)

Great Western Park

Tavistock Cres

Tavistock Road

Aldridge Rd Villas

Leamington Rd Villas

St Lukes Rd

Lancaster Road

Westbourne Park Villas

Royal Oak

Gloucester Terrace

Westbourne Terrace

WESTBOURNE PARK ROAD

CHEPSTOW ROAD

Talbot Road

Westbourne Park Road

PORCHESTER ROAD

BISHOPS BRIDGE ROAD

Porchester Centre

Porchester Terr North

Orsett Terrace

Cleveland Square

Dartmouth Close

Powis Terr

Colville Road

Colville Terrace

Talbot Road

Courtnell St

Moorhouse Road

Powis Sq

Powis Gdns

Ledbury Road

Artesian Road

Westbourne Gdns

Durham Terrace

Alexander St

Hereford Road

Kildare Terrace

Kildare Gardens

Newton Road

Hatherley Grove

Pickering Mews

Queensway

WESTBOURNE GROVE

BAYSWATER

Hallfield Estate

Cleveland Terrace

Gloucester Terrace

Lonsdale Road

Westbourne Grove

Chepstow

PEMBRIDGE VILLAS

Leinster Sq

Prince's Square

Garway Road

Gardens Square

Porchester Gardens

Redan Place

Whiteley's

Leinster Pl

Cleveland Square

Queen's Gardens

Craven Hill Gdns

Denbigh Terr

Denbigh Rd

Chepstow Villas

Chenston Cres

Pemb'ge Mews

Pembridge Place

Dawson Place

Hereford Road

Square

Ilchester Gdns

Moscow Road

Greek Cathedral

St Petersburgh Mews

Bark Place

Bayswater

Inverness Terrace

Queensborough Terrace

Porchester Terrace

Queen's Gardens

CRAVEN HILL

Lancaster Gate

Kensington Park Gdns

Portobello Road

Kensington Park Road

Pembridge Cres

PEMBRIDGE RD

Pembridge Square

Pembridge Gdns

Chepstow Place

Ossington St

Victoria Gdn Mews

Clanricarde Gdns

Linden Gardens

Palace Court

St Petersburgh Place

Chapel Side

Orme Lane

Orme Ct

QUEENSWAY

Poplar Place

Queensway

Inverness Terrace

Leinster Terr

Lancaster Gate

Ladbroke Square

Ladbroke Terr

Ladbroke Walk

Ladbroke Road

Bulmer Place

NOTTING HILL

Notting Hill Gate

NOTTING HILL GATE

Uxbridge Street

Hillgate Place

Hillgate St

Kensington Place

Jameson St

Edge St

Caroline Pl

BAYSWATER ROAD

WC

Diana, Princess of Wales Memorial Playground

KENSINGTON

The Broad Walk

Campden Hill Gardens

Hillsleigh Rd

Peel Street

Campden Street

Bedford Gardens

Hill Sq

Campden Hill Road

Sheffield Terrace

Tor Gdns

Campden Grove

Gloucester Walk

PALACE GARDENS TERRACE

Palace Gardens Mews

Palace Mall

Kensington Mall

Brunswick Gdns

KENSINGTON CHURCH STREET

Kensington Palace Gardens

Kensington Palace

Round Pond

Palace Avenue

Hill Sq

Campden Hill

Aubrey Road

Aubrey Walk

Campden Grove

Vicarage Gate

York House Place

Dukes Lane

Holland Park

Holland House

Youth Hostel

Holland Walk

Sheldrake Place

Duchess of Bedford's Walk

Phillimore Gardens

Upper Phillimore Gardens

Argyll Road

Pitt Street

Gordon Place

Camden Hill R

Town Hall

Horton Street

Drayton Mews

See p314

Old Court Place

KENSINGTON

De Vere Gardens

Kensington Ct

Victoria Rd

WC

KENSINGTON ROAD

Holland Street

Open Air Theatre

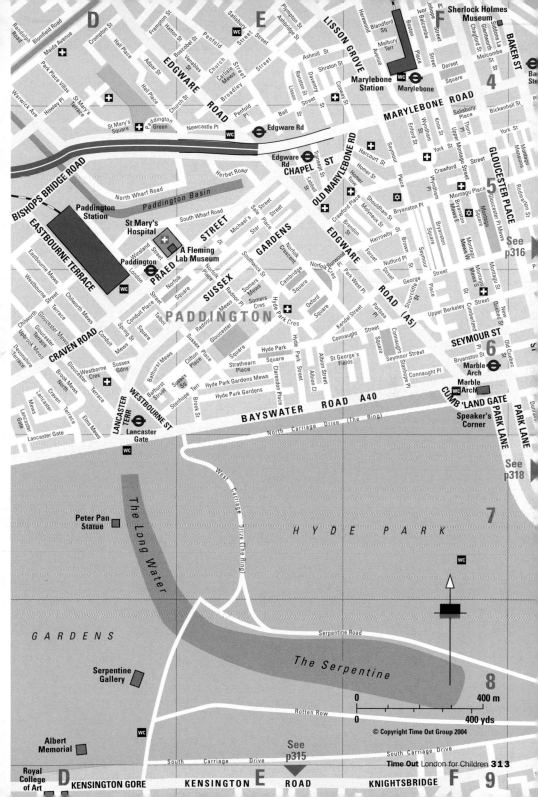

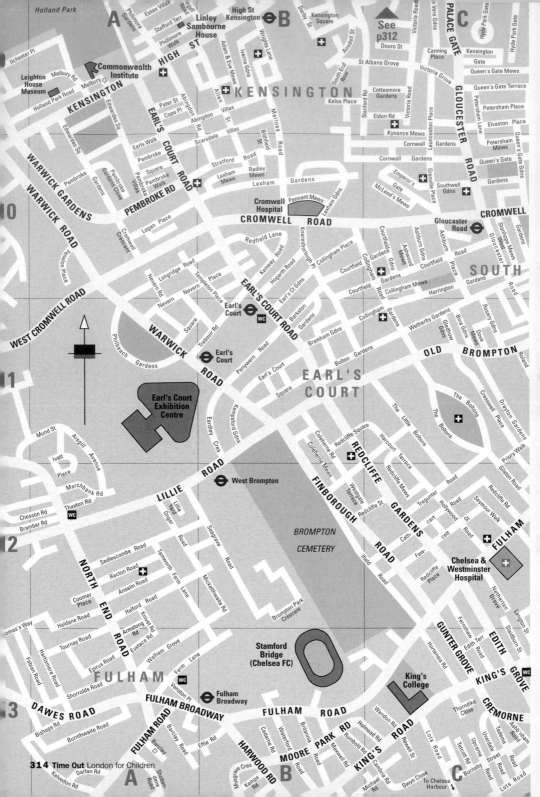

Holland Park

A

Essex Villas

Phillimore Gdns
Stafford Terr

Linley
Sambourne
House

High St
Kensington

B

Derby St

Kensington
Square

C

PALACE GATE

See
p312

Douro St

Hyde Park Gate

Victoria Rd

Hyde Park Gate

Phillimore
Gardens

HIGH

ST

Adam & Eve Mews

Wrights Lane

Ansdell St

St Albans Grove

Kensington
Gate

Queen's Gate Mews

Leighton
House Museum

Melbury Rd

Commonwealth
Institute

Iverna Gdns

Canning
Place

KENSINGTON

Allen

Victoria Grove

Queen's Gate Terrace

Melbury

Edwardes Sq

Abingdon

St

Villas

KENSINGTON

Marloes

South End
Row

Cottesmore
Gardens

Kelso Place

Stanford Rd

Eldon Rd

Petersham Place

Elvaston Place

Holland Park Road

Pater St

Cope Pl

Abingdon

Villas

Stratford

Blithfield
St

Road

Kynance Mews

Cornwall

GLOUCESTER

Gardens

Petersham
Mews

Warwick Gardens

Edwardes Sq

EARL'S

Pembroke

Square

Scarsdale

Lexham
Mews

Radley
Mews

Cornwall

Gardens

Emperor's
Gate

Granville Place

Southwell
Gdns

Queen's Gate

ROAD

Warwick Gardens

Pembroke
Gardens

COURT

Villas

Gardens

Cromwell Hospital

Pennant Mews

Lexham Gdns

McLeod's Mews

Gardens

10

WARWICK GARDENS

Pembroke
Gardens Close

Pembroke
Villas

ROAD

Lexham

Gardens

CROMWELL

Gloucester
Road

CROMWELL

PEMBROKE RD

Logan Place

ROAD

ROAD

SOUTH

WARWICK ROAD

Cromwell
Crescent

Redfield Lane

Kenway

Road

Knaresborough Pl

Collingham Place

Ashworth
Mews

Ashburn Gdns

Ashburn

Stanhope Mews West

Kenway Place

Longridge

Road

Templeton
Place

Nevern Rd

Nevern Place

Hogarth Road

Courtfield
Gardens

Collingham

Gardens

Courtfield

Place

Gloucester

Harrington

Road

Rosary Gdns

WEST CROMWELL ROAD

Philbeach

Nevern

Square

EARL'S

Earl's Ct Gdns

Barkston

Collingham

Courtfield

Collingham Mews

Wetherby Gardens

Bina Gdns

Gledhow
Gdns

Dove
Mews

11

WARWICK

Gardens

Trebovir Rd

COURT

Earl's
Court

Gardens

Gardens

Bramham Gdns

Collingham

OLD

BROMPTON

Roland

Penywern

Road

Bolton

Gardens

Wetherby Gardens

Creswell Place

Drayton Gardens

Priory Walk

Gliston Road

Earl's

Court

Earl's Court Exhibition Centre

Kempsford Gdns

Square

The
Little
Boltons

The
Boltons

The Boltons

Trequnter

Hollywood

EARL'S

COURT

Eardley Cres

LILLIE

Mund St

Ivatt
Place

Alsopp

Avenue

Marchbank Rd

Thaxton Rd

Chesson Rd

Bramber Rd

WC

ROAD

West Brompton

FINBOROUGH

Coleherne Rd

Redcliffe Square

Coleherne Mews

REDCLIFFE

Harcourt
Terrace

Westgate
Terrace

Redcliffe Mews

Redcliffe St

GARDENS

Ifield

Road

Redcliffe Rd

Seymour Walk

FULHAM

Chelsea & Westminster Hospital

Netherton Grove

Langton St

12

NORTH

Sedlescombe

Racton

Road

Road

Anselm Road

Halford

Road

Coomer
Place

Haldane Road

Tournay Road

Fabian Road

Harbinger Road

Bishops Rd

Burnthwaite Road

FULHAM

DAWES ROAD

13

END

ROAD

Tamworth

Street

Mickelthwaite Rd

BROMPTON
CEMETERY

Brompton Park
Crescent

Stamford Bridge
(Chelsea FC)

King's College

FULHAM

Seagrave

Road

Lillie
Yard

Ongar

Armstrong
Rd

Knivet Rd

Eustace Rd

Walham Grove

Farm
Lane

Vanston Pl

WC

Fulham
Broadway

FULHAM BROADWAY

FULHAM ROAD

Barclay

Effie Rd

FULHAM

ROAD

HARWOOD RD

MOORE

PARK RD

Britannia

Cedarne Rd

Waterford Rd

Maxwell Rd

KING'S

Holmead Rd

Rumbold Rd

Wandon Rd

Reveil St

Hortensia Rd

Edith Terr

GUNTER GROVE

Fenelena Rd

Ashburnham
Road

Uverdale

Tetcott Rd

Thorndike
Close

EDITH GROVE

KING'S GROVE

CREMORNE

WC

To Chelsea
Harbour

Lots Rd

Burnaby

Lots Rd

A

B

C

314 Time Out London for Children

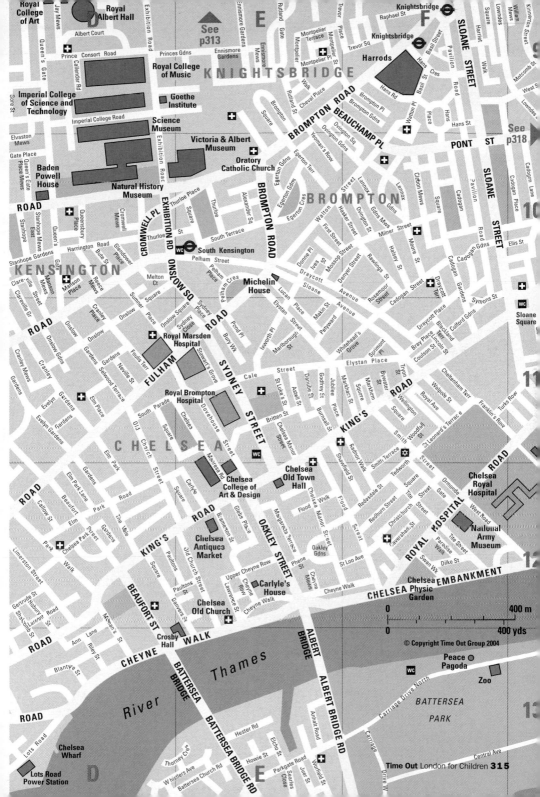

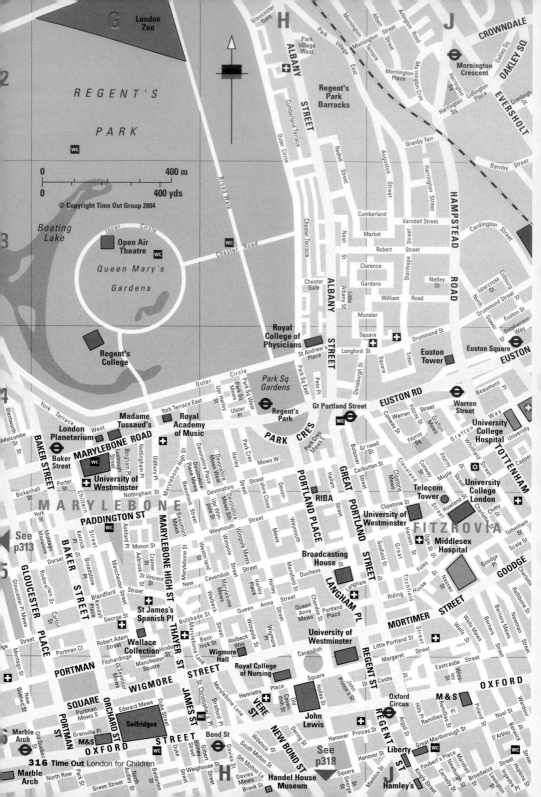

G
London Zoo

R E G E N T ' S

P A R K

H

ALBANY

STREET

Park Village West
Gloucester Gate
Park Village East

Albert
Mornington Terrace

Arlington Road

Mornington Street

J

CROWNDALE

Regent's Park Barracks

Mornington Place

Mornington Cres

Mornington Crescent

Oakley Sq

OAKLEY SQ

EVERSHOLT

wc

Inner Circle

Boating Lake

Open Air Theatre

Queen Mary's Gardens

wc

Regent's College

Broad Walk

Cumberland Terrace

Outer Circle

Chester Road

wc

Chester Terrace

Redhill Street

Augustus Street

Granby Terr

Cumberland

Market

Varndell Street

Nash St

Robert Street

Clarence Gardens

Stanhope Street

Cardington Street

Harrington Square

Lidington Place

HAMPSTEAD ROAD

Barnby Street

Istarcross Street

North Gower

Coburg St

Drummond Street

Euston St

Stephenson Way

© Copyright Time Out Group 2004

0   400 m
0   400 yds

Chester Gate

ALBANY STREET

Little Albany St

Munster Square

William Road

Clarence

Triton Square

Drummond St

Euston Tower

Euston Square

EUSTON

Royal College of Physicians

St Andrew's Place

St Andrew's Place

Park Sq East

Peto Pl

Longford St

Osnaburgh St

EUSTON RD

Warren Street

Beaumont Pl

University College Hospital

University

Park Sq Gardens

Park Sq West

Upr Harley St

Ulster Pl

Regent's Park

PARK CRES

Gt Portland Street

wc

Conway St

Warren St

Fitzroy Sq

Grafton Way

Way

Grafton

Whitfield Street

York Terrace

York Terrace East

Madame Tussaud's

Royal Academy of Music

Harley St

Devonshire Place Mews

Park Cres Mews W

Park Cres Mews E

Gr'nwell St

Bolsover Street

Carburton Street

Cleveland Street

Clipstone Mews

Conway St

Fitzroy St

Maple St

Capper

MARYLEBONE ROAD

London Planetarium

West

Baker Street

BAKER STREET

wc

University of Westminster

Glenworth St

Melcombe St

Bickenhall St

Porter St

Chiltern Street

Luxborough St

Bingham Place

Nottingham Place

Oldbury Pl

Marylebone High St

Devonshire Street

Devonshire Place Mews

Beaumont Street

Beaumont Mews

Devonshire Close

Devon- shire Mews Sth

Upr Wim- pole St

Hallam St

Portland Place

RIBA

GREAT PORTLAND STREET

Clipstone St

Howland St

Telecom Tower

Maple St

Charlotte Street

Chitty St

Tottenham

TOTTENHAM

University College London

University of Westminster

Middlesex Hospital

FITZROVIA

GOODGE STREET

Goodge St

Scala St

Rathbone St

Bernard Mews

Charlotte

MARYLEBONE

York St

Kendrick Pl

Dorset St

Broadstone Pl

PADDINGTON ST

wc

Moxon St

Cramer St

St Vincent St

New

Cavendish St

Weymouth St

Devonshire St

Weymouth Mews

Mansfield St

Duchess St

Hallam St

Langham St

University of Westminster

Hanson St

Foley St

Riding House St

Ogle St

Tottenham

Nassau St

Goodge St

Rathbone Pl

See p313

Baker Street

BAKER STREET

Montagu Mansions

Kenrick Pl

George St

Blandford St

Manchester Street

St James's Spanish Pl

Wallace Collection

Approx St

Bulstrode St

Marylebone Lane

Wimpole St

Harley St

Wimpole Mews

Queen Anne St

Harley Pl

Wigmore Hall

Cavendish Square

Portland Place

Mortimer St

MORTIMER STREET

REGENT ST

Little Portland St

Margaret St

Eastcastle St

Wells St

Wells St

Berners Mews

Newman St

Berners St

GLOUCESTER PLACE

Rodmarton St

Crawford St

Kendall Pl

Fitzhardinge St

Seymour St

Bentinck St

Welbeck Way

Welbeck St

Wimpole St

Henrietta Place

Old Cavendish St

Holles St

John Lewis

Princes St

Oxford Circus

Castle St

Argyll Pl

M&S

Foubert's Place

Ramillies Pl

Poland St

Noel St

D'Arblay

Berwick

Wardour

Great Marlborough St

Kingly St

PORTMAN

PORTMAN SQUARE

ORCHARD STREET

Selfridges

M&S

Portman Mews S

Edward Mews

Granville Pl

Robert Adam Street

Manchester Square

WIGMORE STREET

THAYER ST

JAMES ST

St Christopher's Pl

Stratford Pl

VERE STREET

NEW BOND ST

Royal College of Nursing

Marylebone Lane

Binney St

Gilbert St

Weighouse St

Bourdon St

Brook St

Davies Mews

South Molton La

Woodstock St

Dering St

Hanover St

Hanover Square

St George St

Maddox St

Regent St

REGENT ST

Liberty

wc

Kingly St

Conduit

Broadwick

Marshall

Hopkins St

Lexington

wc

316 Time Out London for Children

Marble Arch

North Row

Green Street

Wood's Mews

Upper Brook Street

OXFORD STREET

Duke St

wc

Bond St

Balderton St

Davies Mews

Brook St

Handel House Museum

South Molton St

Hamley's

H

J

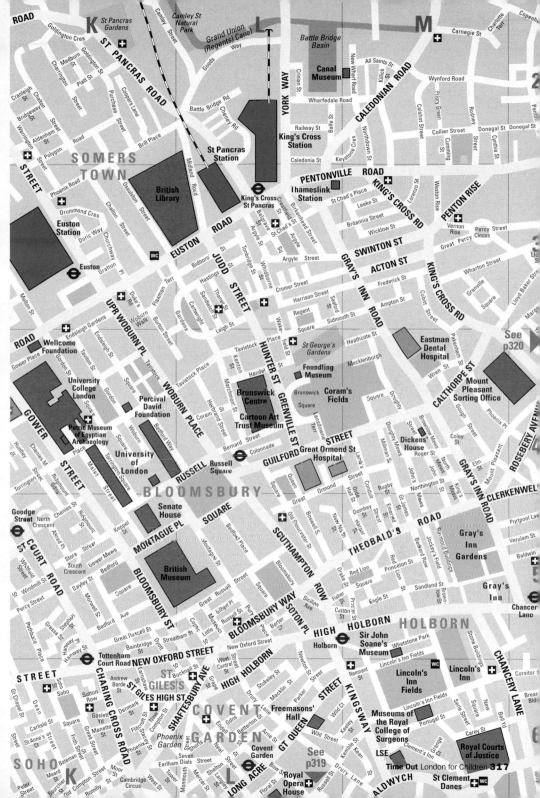

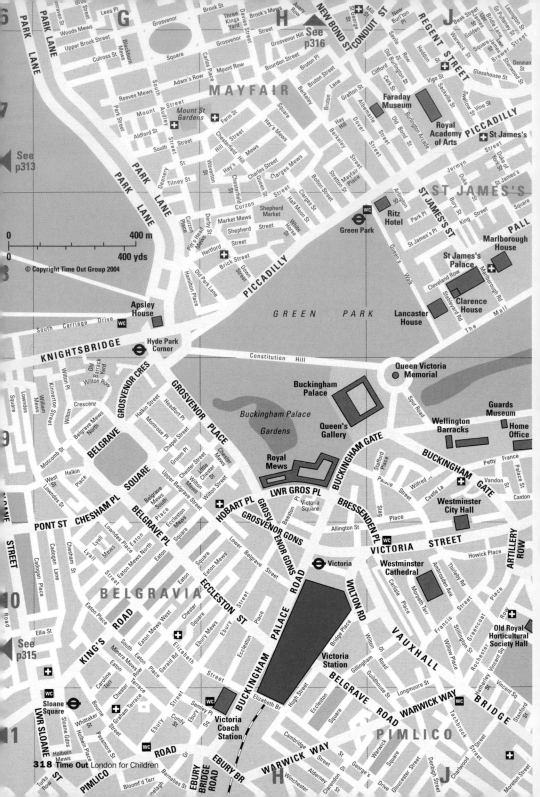

PARK LANE

Lees Pl

Woods Mews

Upper Brook Street

Culross St

G

Grosvenor

Square

Carlos Place

Adam's Row

Mount Row

South

Street

Mount

Street

Reeves Mews

Park Street

Upper

Aldford St

MAYFAIR

Mount St
Gardens

Farm St

Chesterfield Hill

Hill Street

Charles Street

Hay's Mews

Clarges Mews

Three Kings Yard

Brook's Mews

Davies
Street

Grosvenor Hill

Bourdon Street

Bruton Place

Berkeley

Square

Bruton St

Brook St

Avery
Row

Grosvenor Street

NEW BOND ST

CONDUIT ST

Hay Hill

Dover Street

Albemarle Street

Old Bond St

Clifford St

Cork St

Old Burlington St

Savile Row

New
Burlton Pl

Mill
St

St George
St

Haddon

Vigo St

Sackville St

Burlington Arcade

Faraday
Museum

Royal
Academy
of Arts

REGENT STREET

Beak Street

Warwick St

Glasshouse St

Brewer

Denman
St

PICCADILLY

St James's

St James's
Street

PARK LANE

Deanery

Tilney St

Curzon

Derby St

Curzon Street

Market Mews

Shepherd

Shepherd Market

Brick Street

Down Street

Old Park Lane

Hamilton Place

Hertford

White Horse Street

Half Moon St

Clarges St

Bolton Street

Stratton Street

Berkeley Street

Mayfair
Place

Jermyn

ST JAMES'S ST

Arlington
Street

Park Pl

St James's Pl

**St James's
Palace**

Cleveland Row

Stableyard Rd

**Clarence
House**

Queen's
Walk

ST JAMES'S

Duke St

Bury St

King
St

PALL

**Marlborough
House**

Marlborough Rd

The
Mall

WC

**Ritz
Hotel**

Green Park

PICCADILLY

**Lancaster
House**

G R E E N   P A R K

**See
p313**

0   400 m

0   400 yds

© Copyright Time Out Group 2004

**Apsley
House**

South   Carriage   Drive

WC

KNIGHTSBRIDGE

**Hyde Park
Corner**

Constitution   Hill

**Queen Victoria
Memorial**

Spur Road

Wilton Pl

Old
Barrack Yard

Wilton Row

GROSVENOR CRES

Halkin Street

Headfort Pl

Montrose Pl

Chapel Pl

Groom Pl

Chester Street

Little
Chester

Wilton
Mews

Wilton
Street

Chester
Mews

GROSVENOR   PLACE

**Buckingham
Palace**

*Buckingham Palace
Gardens*

**Queen's
Gallery**

**Royal
Mews**

LWR GROS PL

BUCKINGHAM GATE

Stafford
Place

Palace Street

Buckingham

BUCKINGHAM

GATE

Petty
France

Vandon

Palace St

Caxton

**Wellington
Barracks**

**Guards
Museum**

**Home
Office**

**Westminster
City Hall**

Lowndes
Square

William
Mews

Kinnerton Street

Motcomb St

West
St

Halkin
Place

Lowndes St

BELGRAVE

SQUARE

Belgrave Mews
North

Belgrave Mews
South

Upper Belgrave
Street

CHESHAM PL

PONT ST

BELGRAVE PL

Eccleston
Mews

Eaton
Square

Lyall
Mews

Lowndes Place

Eaton

Lyall
Street

HOBART PL

GROSVENOR GDNS

GROSVENOR GDNS

Lower
Belgrave
Street

Beeston
Place

Victoria
Square

Allington St

BRESSENDEN PL

VICTORIA

Stag
Place

Wilfred St

Castle La

Howick Place

Thirleby Rd

STREET

ARTILLERY

ROW

PALACE

ROAD

WILTON RD

**Victoria
Station**

Victoria

**Westminster
Cathedral**

WC

Carlisle
Place

Ambrosden Ave

Morpeth Terr

Francis

Stillington St

Willow Place

Greencoat

VAUXHALL

Rochester
Row

**Old Royal
Horticultural
Society Hall**

Vincent Sq

BELGRAVIA

ECCLESTON ST

Eaton
Place

Eaton Mews West

Chester
Square

Ebury Mews

Eccleston
Place

Gillingham

Street

Guildhouse St

Longmoore St

KING'S

ROAD

Minera Mews

Gerald Rd

Elizabeth

Street

Ebury

Street

Eccleston

Bridge

Bridge Place

Hugh Street

Wilton
Road

BELGRAVE

ROAD

WARWICK WAY

Francis

Willow Place

Warwick

Charlwood Street

**SLOANE
STREET**

Cadogan
Place

Chesham
Place

Chesham
Street

Ellis St

Cadogan
Lane

Lyall
Street

Eaton
Terr

Caroline
Terr

Chester
Terrace

Bourne
Street

Graham Terrace

Semley Pl

**Victoria
Coach Station**

Cundy
St

WC

Elizabeth Br

Cambridge

Street

Denbigh St

Moreton St

Tachbrook

PIMLICO

WC

**Sloane
Square**

**See
p315**

LWR SLOANE

Turks
Row

ST

Holbein Pl

Holbein
Mews

Passmore Street

Whittaker Street

Sloane Gdns

PIMLICO

Bloomf'd Terr

Barnabas St

**EBURY
BRIDGE
ROAD**

EBURY BR

WARWICK WAY

H

Winchester

George's

Drive

Gloucester Street

Clarendon

Alderney St

J

Charlwood

Sutherland

Moreton Ter

Stafford

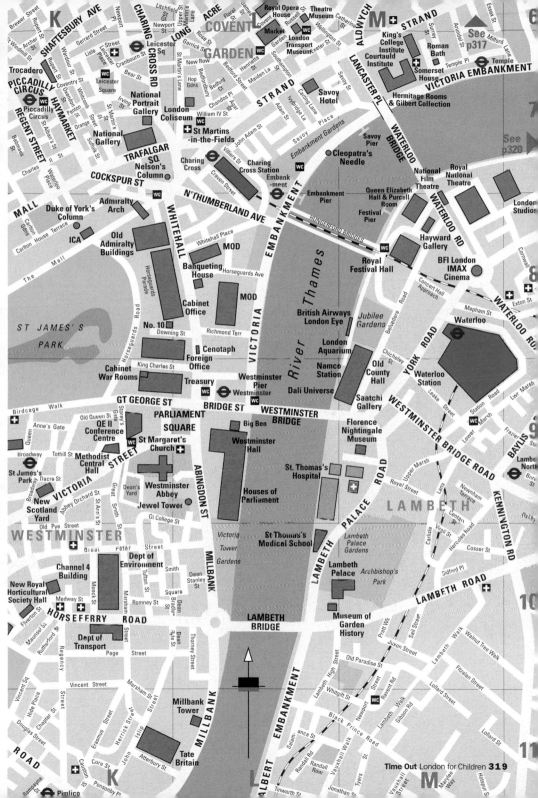

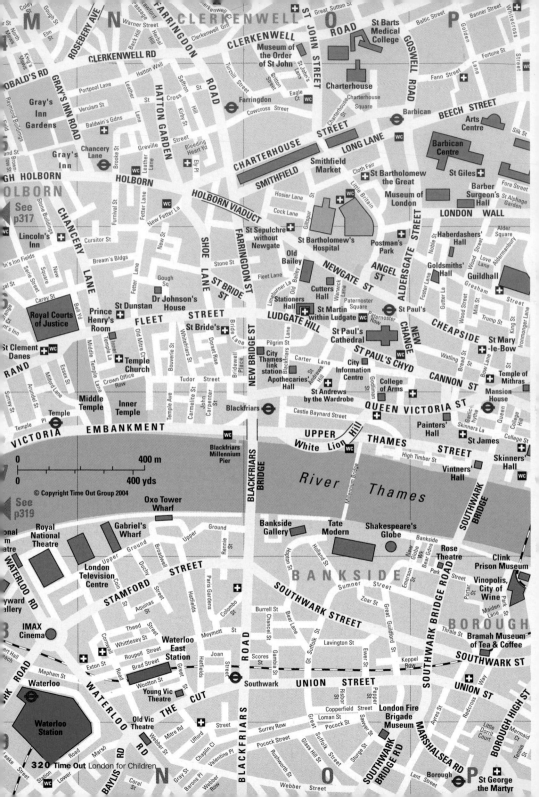

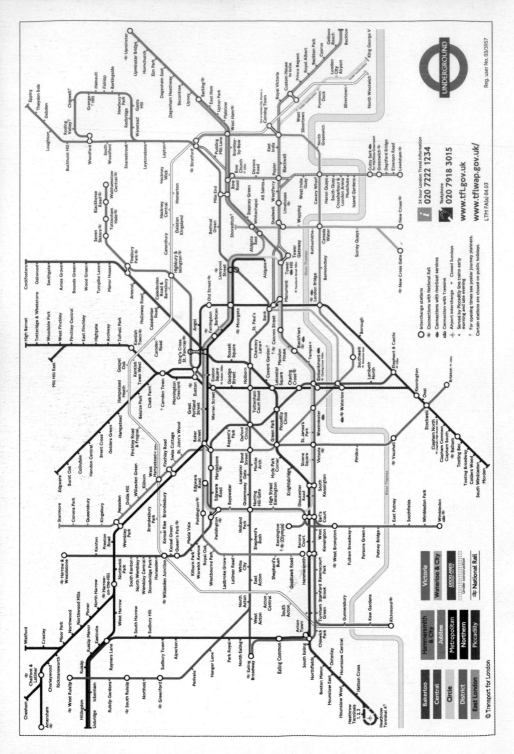